# THE OXFORD HANDBOOK OF

# ECONOMIC INEQUALITY

# THE OXFORD HANDBOOK OF

# ECONOMIC INEQUALITY

*Edited by*

WIEMER SALVERDA
BRIAN NOLAN
*and*
TIMOTHY M. SMEEDING

OXFORD

UNIVERSITY PRESS

# OXFORD

### UNIVERSITY PRESS

Great Clarendon Street, Oxford OX2 6DP

Oxford University Press is a department of the University of Oxford.
It furthers the University's objective of excellence in research, scholarship,
and education by publishing worldwide in

Oxford  New York

Auckland  Cape Town  Dar es Salaam  Hong Kong  Karachi
Kuala Lumpur  Madrid  Melbourne  Mexico City  Nairobi
New Delhi  Shanghai  Taipei  Toronto

With offices in

Argentina  Austria  Brazil  Chile  Czech Republic  France  Greece
Guatemala  Hungary  Italy  Japan  Poland  Portugal  Singapore
South Korea  Switzerland  Thailand  Turkey  Ukraine  Vietnam

Oxford is a registered trade mark of Oxford University Press
in the UK and in certain other countries

Published in the United States
by Oxford University Press Inc., New York

© Oxford University Press, 2009

The moral rights of the authors have been asserted
Database right Oxford University Press (maker)

First published 2009

British Library Cataloguing in Publication Data

Data available

Library of Congress Cataloging in Publication Data

Data available

Typeset by SPI Publisher Services, Pondicherry, India
Printed in Great Britain
on acid-free paper by
CPI Antony Rowe, Chippenham, Wiltshire

ISBN  978–0–19–923137–9

3  5  7  9  10  8  6  4  2

# PREFACE

........................

This Handbook provides an excellent illustration of the value of networking in scientific research. First, although many of the authors had never met before, they enthusiastically agreed to work together, and accepted the discipline of producing and linking their results according to the agreed division of labor. The editors are very grateful indeed to the authors for their excellent cooperation, for the spirit in which they engaged in the enterprise, and for their hard work. We are confident our readers will agree.

Second, the volume is the culmination of twelve and a half years of activity by the European Low-Wage Employment Research network, LoWER and reflects the co-operation of the EQUALSOC Network of Excellence for this purpose. Since 1996 the LoWER network has profited from the financial support of the European Union's research programs (4th, 5th and 6th Framework Programmes) while EQUALSOC was established in 2005, also with EU support. Without this support it would not have been possible to bring the authors together for an extremely stimulating week-long conference where the draft chapters could be discussed and the division of labor and papers refined. The editors are grateful to the European Commission for its stimulus and support. They are also grateful to the members of both networks who were willing to contribute time, money and graduate students!

We also thank the Luxembourg Income Study and the Russell Sage Foundation (RSF), each of whom provided facilities where we could productively meet as an editorial team. Also at RSF, Eric Wanner made it possible for us all to benefit from a special one-day seminar on four of the chapters for the book.

Third, drawing on these and other networks, four leading scholars in the field, Tony Atkinson, Susan Mayer, Stephen Nickell, and Eugene Smolensky, were willing to comment on the draft chapters and give their views on the project as a whole. The editors are very grateful for their participation in the conference and the help they provided so generously, enthusiastically, and without hesitation. This produced some wonderfully heated discussions and a much better understanding of views on inequality research on both sides of the Atlantic.

Last and certainly not least, the 'technical' partners in the project deserve recognition and the editors' thanks. Oxford University Press, particularly its economics publisher, Sarah Caro, were supportive of the project from the very start—thus helping to establish the virtuous circle needed for its success—and OUP willingly contributed to the funding of the above-mentioned conference. Chris Champion at the Press helped with the website, which was very helpful for communication between the authors. Angelique Lieberton, office manager of the Amsterdam Institute for Advanced Labour Studies, provided important organizational support and good cheer.

Before handing it over to the reader, we would like to dedicate the Handbook to the memory of Andrew Glyn of Oxford University. Andrew was a very good and extremely kind friend and active member of the LoWER network. Sadly, the first symptoms of the illness that was to take away his life manifested themselves during the above conference. More importantly, Andrew, who happened to be born at the high end of the income distribution, himself, was exemplary to many in his dedication to reducing inequality and his own honest and straightforward lifestyle fully matched that ideal. We consider ourselves lucky indeed to have benefited from his contribution.

All in all, it took us three years to get here, but the product of outstanding cooperation is, we trust, a book of which all those involved can be proud.

Wiemer Salverda, Brian Nolan, and Tim Smeeding

# Contents

## PART I   INEQUALITY: OVERVIEW, CONCEPTS, AND MEASUREMENT

## PART II   THE EXTENT OF INEQUALITY

---

[1]  Sadly Andrew died in December 2007; the chapter was finished by Wendy Carlin (UCL) and Bob Rowthorn (Cambridge).

# PART III   EARNINGS INEQUALITY

# PART IV   DIMENSIONS OF INEQUALITY

# PART V   THE DYNAMICS OF INEQUALITY

# LIST OF FIGURES

# LIST OF TABLES

# LIST OF CONTRIBUTORS

**Anders Björklund** is Professor of Economics at the Swedish Institute for Social Research (SOFI), Stockholm University. He is an empirically oriented labor economist with a strong focus on his own country, Sweden, but often in a comparative perspective. His research has focused on topics such as the consequences of unemployment and labor-market programs, income and earnings inequality, and intergenerational mobility.

**Francine D. Blau** is the Frances Perkins Professor of Industrial and Labor Relations and Labor Economics at Cornell University. She is a Research Associate of the National Bureau of Economic Research, a Research Fellow of CESifo and IZA, and a Fellow of the Society of Labor Economists and the American Academy of Political and Social Science. She has served as President of the Society of Labor Economists and of the Labor and Employment Relations Association (formerly the Industrial Relations Research Association), and as Vice President of the American Economic Association.

**Andrea Brandolini** is the Head of the Economic Structure and Labor Market Division at the Department for Structural Economic Analysis of the Bank of Italy.

**Richard V. Burkhauser** is the Sarah Gibson Blanding Professor of Policy Analysis, Department of Policy Analysis and Management, Cornell University and a Research Professor of the German Institute for Economic Research (DIW-Berlin).

**Gary Burtless** holds the Whitehead Chair in Economic Studies at the Brookings Institution in Washington, DC, USA. After obtaining a Ph.D. in Economics from the Massachusetts Institute of Technology in 1977, he worked as an economist in the US government before coming to Brookings in 1981.

**Daniele Checchi** is currently Professor of Labor Economics at the University of Milan (Italy). He studies the role of institutions in the labor market. He also has an interest in the economics of education.

**Kenneth A. Couch** is Director of the Center for Population Research and an Associate Professor in the Department of Economics at the University of Connecticut.

**James Davies** is a Professor of Economics at the University of Western Ontario, where he served as Chair of his department from 1992 to 2001. Currently the Editor of *Canadian Public Policy*, he has published and consulted widely on issues of both taxation and the distribution of income and wealth.

**Gøsta Esping-Andersen** is Professor of Sociology at Universitat Pompeu Fabra, Barcelona.

**Francisco H. G. Ferreira** is a Lead Economist with the World Bank's Research Department, and a co-editor of the *Journal of Economic Inequality*. He holds a Ph.D. from the London School of Economics, and has taught at PUC-Rio de Janeiro.

**Ada Ferrer-i-Carbonell** holds a Ph.D. in Economics from the University of Amsterdam. Her main research interest is the use of subjective well-being questions to understand individuals' preferences. She is an ICREA researcher at the IAE-CSIC (Barcelona).

**Nancy Folbre** is Professor of Economics at the University of Massachusetts Amherst. Her most recent book is *Valuing Children: Rethinking the Economics of the Family* (Harvard, 2008).

**Richard Freeman** is Ascherman Professor of Economics at Harvard University, Co-Director of the Labor and Worklife Program, Harvard Law School, Director of Labor Studies, National Bureau of Economic Research, and senior researcher at Centre for Economic Performance, London School of Economics. His most recent book is *America Works* (Russell Sage, 2007).

**Andrew Glyn** taught economics at Oxford University from 1969 until his death in 2007. He published widely on inequality, unemployment, and post-war capitalist economic development. His last book was *Capitalism Unleashed* (Oxford University Press, 2006).

**Mary Gregory** is attached to the Department of Economics, Oxford University, and is Fellow and Tutor at St Hilda's College. She is a founder member of the European Low-Wage Employment Research network (LoWER).

**Markus Jäntti** is Professor of Economics at Åbo Akademi University and Research Director at the Luxembourg Income Study. His research interests center on international comparisons of and methods for the study of income inequality, income mobility and poverty, and issues in applied labor economics.

**Christopher Jencks** is the Malcolm Wiener Professor of Social Policy at Harvard University's John F. Kennedy School of Government. His current research focuses on claims about the costs and benefits of letting economic inequality rise.

**Stephen Jenkins** is a professor at the University of Essex, and Director of the Institute for Social and Economic Research. He is Chair of the Council of the International Association for Research in Income and Wealth, 2006–8. Stephen's current research mostly addresses methodological and substantive issues in analysis of income distribution trends and dynamics.

**Martin Kahanec** is a Senior Research Associate and the Deputy Program Director of the Migration Program Area at the Institute for the Study of Labor (IZA Bonn). His main research interests are labor and population economics, migration, and ethnicity.

**Lawrence M. Kahn** is a Professor of Labor Economics and Collective Bargaining at Cornell University. He is a Research Fellow of CESifo and IZA, Associate Editor of the *Industrial & Labor Relations Review*, Co-editor of *Economic Inquiry*, and a Fellow of the Society of Labor Economists.

**Julia Lane** is Program Director, Science of Science and Innovation Policy at the National Science Foundation. She was previously Senior Vice President and Director of the Economics, Labor and Population Department at the National Opinion Research Center, University of Chicago. She, together with John Abowd and John Haltiwanger, founded the first large-scale linked employer–employee data set in the United States: the Longitudinal Employer Household Dynamics program at the U.S. Census Bureau.

**Andrew Leigh** is an Associate Professor in the Economics Program of the Research School of Social Sciences at the Australian National University. His academic website is http://econrss.anu.edu.au/~aleigh/.

**Claudio Lucifora** is Professor of Economics at the Università Cattolica in Milan and IZA research fellow. He has published books on low pay employment, the economics of education, and the shadow economy, as well as articles in refereed journals on earnings mobility, wage determination, unemployment, and labor market institutions. He has been the treasurer and an elected member of the Executive Committee of the European Association of Labour Economics.

**Stephen Machin** is currently Professor of Economics at University College London, Research Director of the Centre for Economic Performance at the London School of Economics and Director of the Centre for the Economics of Education. He is one of the Editors of the *Economic Journal*. Previously he has been visiting Professor at Harvard University (1993/4) and at the Massachusetts Institute of Technology (2001/2). He is an elected fellow of the British Academy (since 2006), is the incoming President of the European Association of Labour Economists (from 2008) and is an independent member of the Low Pay Commission (since 2007).

**Ive Marx** is a research fellow at the Centre for Social Policy at the University of Antwerp, Belgium. The main focus of his research is poverty and minimum income protection, especially in relation to labor market change and migration.

**Nolan McCarty** is the Susan Dod Brown Professor of Politics and Public Affairs and Associate Dean at the Princeton University's Woodrow Wilson School. His research interests include US politics, democratic political institutions, and political game theory. He has recently published *Political Game Theory* (Cambridge

University Press, 2006, with Adam Meirowitz) and *Polarized America: The Dance of Ideology and Unequal Riches* (MIT Press, 2006, with Keith Poole and Howard Rosenthal).

**John Myles** is Canada Research Chair and Professor of Sociology at the University of Toronto and Senior Visiting Research Scholar at Statistics Canada. He has written widely on topics related to the politics of the welfare state, classes in contemporary capitalism, income inequality, and child and old-age poverty.

**Brian Nolan** is Professor of Public Policy in the School of Applied Social Science, University College Dublin. He is an economist, with a Ph.D. from the London School of Economics. He has published widely on income inequality, poverty, public economics, social policy, and health economics.

**Jonas Pontusson** is Professor of Politics at Princeton University. His most recent book is *Inequality and Prosperity: Social Europe versus Liberal America* (Cornell University Press, 2005). His current research focuses on the consequences of rising inequality for political participation, policy preference, and vote choice.

**Martin Ravallion** is the Director of the World Bank's Research Department. He sits on a number of editorial boards, and has published three books and some two hundred journal articles on poverty and income distribution in developing countries, and other topics.

**John E. Roemer** is Elizabeth S. and A. Varick Stout Professor of Political Science and Economics at Yale University. He is a fellow of the Econometric Society, the American Academy of Arts and Sciences and the British Academy. He works currently on issues of democratic political competition, theories of distributive justice, and in particular, inter-generational justice in the presence of a fragile global biospheric commons.

**Wiemer Salverda** is Director of the Amsterdam Institute for Advanced Labour Studies (AIAS) at the University of Amsterdam. He also coordinates the activities of the European Low-Wage Employment Research network (LoWER), which was established in 1996 with the support of the European Commission. He contributes expert advice to the OECD, EU, and ILO. His research focuses on the low-wage labor market and earnings inequality from an international comparative perspective, in particular the role of labor and product demand and the interaction with labor supply. His work also targets comparative employment performance, top incomes, ageing, and the evolution of youth labor.

**Timothy M. Smeeding** is Distinguished Professor of Economics and Public Administration at the Maxwell School of Syracuse University where he is also the founding director of the Center for Policy Research. In fall 2008 he will take up the position of Arts and Sciences Distinguished Professor of Public Affairs at

University of Wisconsin-Madison's Robert M. Lafollette School of Public Affairs, and Directorship of the Institute for Research on Poverty at the same institution. Smeeding is also the Founder and Director Emeritus of the Luxembourg Income Study Project, which he began in 1983. His research focuses on national and cross-national comparisons of income and wealth inequality, poverty, social policy and social mobility.

**Philippe Van Kerm** is a researcher at CEPS/INSTEAD (Luxembourg). His research interests are in applied micro-econometrics and labor and welfare economics with particular reference to the measurement of income mobility and income distribution dynamics.

**Bernard Van Praag** is Emeritus University Professor of the University of Amsterdam. Since 1971 he has written numerous articles on subjective well-being, poverty and inequality, labor, pensions, and econometric methodology. Van Praag and Ferrer-i-Carbonell are the authors of the monograph *Happiness Quantified* (Oxford University Press, 2004, 2008).

**Jelle Visser** is Professor of Sociology of Labour and Organisation at the University of Amsterdam, where he is Scientific Director of the Amsterdam Institute for Advanced Labour Studies. He has written widely on trade unionism, labour relations, employment policy and comparative welfare state, and has been the chief editor of various *Industrial Relations in Europe* reports for the European Commission.

**Sarah Voitchovsky** is a researcher at the School of Applied Social Sciences, University College Dublin, Ireland. Her interests include the causes and consequences of income and wealth inequality, household allocation of resources, and economic growth.

**Klaus F. Zimmermann** is a Professor of Economics at Bonn University, the Director of the Institute for the Study of Labor (IZA Bonn), the President of the German Institute for Economic Research (DIW Berlin), and Honorary Professor at the Free University Berlin and the Renmin University Peking. His current research interests cover labor and population economics, migration, and ethnicity.

# PART I

## INEQUALITY: OVERVIEW, CONCEPTS, AND MEASUREMENT

CHAPTER 1

.......................................................

# INTRODUCTION

.......................................................

WIEMER SALVERDA

BRIAN NOLAN

TIMOTHY M. SMEEDING[1]

DRAWING on the expertise of some of the most capable scholars in the field of economic inequality, this Handbook aims to fulfill several ambitions and objectives. First the book hopes to provide the reader with an overview and evaluation of the current state of international research on economic inequality in a precise fashion. The second objective is to add new insights and open up novel perspectives for future research. In so doing it hopes to both stimulate further interest in the field and highlight directions and priorities for future development. Along the way, we also seek to convey both how this burgeoning research arena has been evolving, and then how it connects to research in economics more generally.

The book concentrates for the most part on research related to high-income countries, since the developing world differs in fundamental ways and merits separate treatment. None the less, the book does place inequality in the rich countries in its worldwide context of growth and trade and their distributive effects. It also concentrates primarily, but not exclusively, on research that comes from the disciplinary perspectives of economics and public policy—again because it would be impossible also to do justice to the substantial body of research on inequality from other social sciences. The focus on economic inequality may justify this disciplinary concentration. However, a number of contributions to the book take

[1] Our thanks to Anders Björklund and Andrew Leigh for comments on an earlier version of this chapter.

on selected perspectives from sociology, demography, politics, as well as philosophy and law. This will hopefully convey the extent to which one can address 'economic inequality' from a number of disciplinary perspectives.

In this introductory chapter we begin by discussing why economic inequality is of such profound interest, particularly in the light of recent changes in national and global economies. We go on to consider the concept of economic inequality and the breadth of topics it encompasses. The distinctive nature of this field of research is discussed, followed by a description of a framework within which the various elements or aspects can be viewed and organized. The aim of the book and its intended audience are then set out in more detail. Finally, the structure of the book itself is outlined, to help the reader navigate through the very broad range of topics and issues covered and also to indicate what the book could not embrace.

# 1. WHY IS ECONOMIC INEQUALITY SO IMPORTANT?

Economic inequality has long been one of the major themes of socio-political debate and conflict, but interest in this topic from the point of view of economic research has waxed and waned over time. Having been rather neglected during the period of sustained economic growth in Western Europe and North America that followed the Second World War, the 1960s and 1970s saw a resurgence in interest that has been further accentuated by recent trends. In the USA the federal government's War on Poverty from the mid-1960s was accompanied by a substantial body of research, while a similar 'rediscovery' of poverty occurred in Britain, Sweden, and a number of other European countries. Increasing interest in inequality more broadly was reflected in landmark academic publications such as Atkinson's *The Economics of Inequality* (1975) and Sen's *On Economic Inequality* (1973), at about the time Britain established an official Royal Commission on the Distribution of Income and Wealth. Since then, a very substantial body of research on inequality has been accumulated, building on the potential of improved data and focused on clarifying concepts and measures, capturing trends, and understanding the causal processes at work back and forth to the economy.

As Jenkins and Micklewright (2007) highlight in their discussion of the up-surge in academic interest in inequality, this can be linked to changes in both the context—in terms of factual inequality levels and trends—and the policy environment in which research is carried out. For some years, levels of inequality were sufficiently stable for one analyst to describe tracking them as about as exciting as 'watching the grass grow' (Aaron, 1978), but this changed as the post-Second World

War boom petered out. The 1980s, for example, saw a dramatic widening in the dispersion of wages in both the UK and the USA, and this gave rise to a sustained and wide-ranging investigation into why this was happening and whether it was confined to those two countries or pervasive throughout the industrialized world (e.g. Gottschalk and Smeeding, 1997, 2000).

Awareness was also growing that inequality in the distribution of income among households, a key aspect of overall economic inequality, was increasing in those countries at the same time. Most recently, there has been a great deal of interest in what has been happening to the remuneration of top executives and the dramatic increase in the gap between their pay and that of the median wage-earner, as well as in the sharply increasing share of overall household income going to the very top of the distribution—the top 1%, for example—that can be observed in many rich countries (e.g. Atkinson and Piketty, 2007). At the other end of the scale, poverty and the related concept of social exclusion have become a significant focus of attention in the European Union (Atkinson et al., 2002). And while the official poverty rate in the USA has remained stubbornly high in spite of the poverty measure lagging behind the general evolution of incomes, interest in better measures of poverty to reflect the reality of low-income life in the USA has taken on new life (Blank, 2008).

Setting the broader context for these developments, globalization has become an important influence on economic and political conditions in the developed countries, as well as raising new concerns about the gap between developed and developing countries. In that situation the share of profits in national income has risen in rich nations, mobile capital threatens to make workers in these countries more insecure, and a 'race to the bottom' in terms of social provision is one possible response. The enormous increase in the size of the labor force engaged in the global economy with the opening up of China and India to greater levels of trade in goods and services over the past decade has potentially dramatic implications for workers in OECD countries, not least for labor's bargaining power vis-à-vis mobile capital. On the other hand, Welfare States in many countries, although challenged by these global trends, have proved more resilient to date than some had expected or feared. None the less, a growing concern about economic, social, and even political polarization and the possible consequences of a step-change to higher levels of economic inequality can be detected in many rich and poor countries alike.

In this setting, interest in the topic of economic inequality among researchers reflects the concerns of policy-makers and the broader public as well as economists. However, research may approach this complex and politically charged topic from different perspectives, and unpacking these issues helps to answer the important question 'why should economists "care" about inequality'?

The first motivating factor is simply scientific interest—the desire to know and understand the world around us that underpins the social sciences as it does the physical sciences. For the discipline of economics in particular, the distribution of economic resources and the factors that influence that distribution were among the central concerns of market economics at the outset, as evidenced by the writings of such key early figures as Adam Smith and David Ricardo. They are now coming to the forefront of the field once again.

The second reason is normative in origin: inequality is something about which people often feel strongly. A concern with social justice on the part of the researcher may of course play a role, but the fact that others—including economic agents and those engaged in the political process—have strong views about inequality and equity (fairness) is more than enough to motivate scientific research on the topic.

Finally, for many analysts concern with inequality may be primarily instrumental. It has been remarked that if one tells an economist that inequality has increased, the doctrinaire response is 'so what?' That is, even if inequality *per se* was not of significant concern, economists and others will want to know what real world consequences may be associated with rising inequality. These 'so what's' encompass a variety of other phenomena ranging from health status and life expectancy, crime and community breakdown, political power, and temporal patterns of income and poverty mobility, to intergenerational immobility and the transmission of poverty from one generation to the next, all of which are of societal concern. If inequality influences such outcomes or finds itself reinforced by them, understanding the linkages and their significance is an important task for research (Neckerman and Torche, 2007; Burtless and Jencks, 2003).

From the perspective of economics in particular, another key motivating factor is the linkage between inequality and economic efficiency. Economics is concerned with the use of scarce resources and how they can be employed to meet competing ends. Because improving efficiency can make some people better off without reducing anyone else's access to resources, this proposition is on the face of it very attractive. However, the notion that there may be a trade-off between equality and efficiency has played an important part in the way economists (certainly from a standard neoclassical perspective) have approached the topic. If seeking to redistribute income and other economic resources reduces efficiency and economic growth and thus the size of the 'pie', how do we evaluate the costs and benefits? Whether and in what circumstances such a trade-off operates is clearly a key issue, and theoretical and empirical analysis of this question has been an important theme in research and policy debates on economic inequality for many years. In particular, the concern that provision of welfare support to the poor or the unemployed creates dependency and undermines work effort goes back to the British Poor Laws and beyond. Conversely, aspects of the conditionality associated with such support in some countries may give rise to concerns about undue interference with basic individual rights. Even more important is the realization that policies might improve both equity and efficiency simultaneously and avoid the trade-off altogether.

The notion that some degree of inequality is not only inevitable but also functional from an economic perspective is a deep-seated one (Welch, 1999). It should be pointed out, however, that different industrialized countries have achieved sustained economic growth while maintaining rather different levels of income inequality and Welfare State support, so there is scope for societal choices to be made (Lindert, 2004). More recently, considerable attention has also been paid to the ways in which higher inequality could act as a barrier to growth, with inequality in capabilities, for instance, serving to reduce the size of pie. Here social protection and the Welfare State more broadly (e.g. via education and health care) can potentially serve to provide an environment that supports rather than undermines economic growth. Indeed, the need to understand the complex interactions between inequality and efficiency would suffice to bring economic inequality high up the research agenda of economics, and is clearly one of the areas where the economic perspective should have most to offer to the broader social science study of inequality.

It is clearly the case that these different sources of concern have different weight for individual researchers, and it may well be that some are more important than others in different countries and in different time periods. To speculate, it might be the case in recent years that the dominant sources of concern underpinning research on economic inequality in North America have derived from instrumental and efficiency perspectives, whereas in Europe the notion that inequality is itself of normative concern may have played a more important role. Such divergences may influence the directions in which inequality research itself develops, illustrating the impact of the broader socio-economic, political, and cultural setting in which it is carried out. The core point to be emphasized is that in both instances the scientific imperative to understand the sources and consequences of economic inequality emerges as a top research concern. In seeking to do so, there is a related disciplinary perspective: to bring the study of income distribution 'in from the cold' as far as economics is concerned, as Atkinson (1997) has written, re-integrating it with the core concerns of that discipline. This Handbook is intended to contribute towards all of these objectives and to broadening the view to inequalities in dimensions of key social goods beyond incomes, such as education and health.

## 2. THE CONCEPT AND COVERAGE OF ECONOMIC INEQUALITY

As Amartya Sen (1973) put it, the idea of inequality is both very simple and very complex. It is simple and intuitively appealing enough to move people in very different settings and societies throughout history and across the globe, while being at the same time so complex as to engage some of the most gifted philosophers, political theorists, sociologists, and—not least—economists in teasing out its meanings and implications. The focus of this volume is on economic inequality, which serves to narrow the scope somewhat but still leaves a very broad field to be covered. Economic inequalities can be conceived of as inequalities with an economic effect or an economic origin, being as much an outcome of the underlying economic process as an input into these processes. Individual differences, and therefore distributions, are an unmistakable element of economic theorizing, even if only to provide behavioral incentives to work, save, or take an entrepreneurial risk (Welch, 1999). But in another sense, inequalities start where incentive effects end. They tend to be self-enforcing and self-sustaining, be it on their own or in conjunction with other inequalities. Also, inequality in one respect or for one group may hang together with equality in another respect or for other groups. Thus they can be part and parcel of the economy itself, supporting or weakening its dynamics and aggregate outcomes. Linkages and effects amongst and between inequalities are not necessarily obvious and their unraveling requires analytical effort. The contributions to this Handbook bear witness to that reality.

The distribution of income (or earnings), the key variable of economics, would certainly be seen as at the core of economic inequality, and has been the focus of much of the economic research on the topic, as has low income as an indicator of poverty. However, the flow of income is only part of the story. The accumulated stock of wealth also constitutes a key economic resource, be it for its major role in economic 'power' towards the top of the distribution on the one hand or its provision of coverage for financial risks, for example, in old age, on the other hand. Towards the bottom of the income and wealth distribution poverty may also be a matter of exclusion not just from income or wealth but from various aspects of the life of society, reflecting a broader lack of economic power or strength. This brings out that the economic perspective on inequality has at its core a concern with opportunities and constraints. Life-chances, the opportunities, obstacles, and misfortunes that different people face in striving for the sort of life they want to lead, are the fundamental arena where economic inequalities operate, however difficult they may be to capture when it comes to measurement. Economic inequalities can be found in many areas other than income or wealth as illustrated by the (non-exhaustive) range of topics covered in this book. And so, economic inequality remains a concept of challenging breadth and complexity.

It is clear still that inequality in access to economic resources, in endowments, and in opportunities, and the way these affect economic outcomes for individuals and families are crucial. Sen's notion of capabilities, for example, highlights the role of such resources as education and health care in allowing people to function and flourish in the society in which they live. These inequalities are inextricably tied up with institutional structures, including the market and concomitant private and social property rights, and they may both affect, and be affected by, aggregate economic performance. Understanding these relationships is the primary aim of research on economic inequality.

# 3. Research on Economic Inequality

As already outlined, a very substantial body of research on economic inequality has been accumulated over the past 40–50 years, building on such pioneering empirical studies as those of Kuznets (1955) and Mincer (1958). While inequality research has to be set and understood within the broader development of economics as a discipline, some distinctive features of this area of research may be identified. These include a particular focus on clarifying concepts and developing satisfactory measures and a concern with data and a reliance on its availability, but also a tendency for theory and empirical investigation to become somewhat detached from each other, and to downplay causality. There is the risk that the income distribution field itself can become somewhat separated from the broader field of economics, especially when focusing on non-monetary dimensions. Conversely, given the level of general interest in the topic of inequality, research outcomes and observations are often closely linked to political and social debates.

By their nature the core concept of inequality itself, as well as related ones such as poverty, exclusion, or mobility, have been open to a variety of conceptual interpretations, and considerable effort in the literature has gone into scrutinizing the distinctions and, if not arriving at a consensus, at least ensuring that there is greater clarity surrounding how the terms are being employed. This has proceeded in parallel with the development of measures which can be employed to empirically apply these concepts, and the exploration of their properties and the advantages and disadvantages of alternative measures. Atkinson's (1970) paper "On the Measurement of Inequality" and Sen's (1976) paper on summary poverty measures opened up a rich vein that represents a substantial sub-field in the subsequent literature as well as fundamentally affecting empirical research.

Much of the emphasis in that empirical literature has been on accurately capturing levels and trends in inequality, notably in terms of earnings or income. As Jenkins and Micklewright (2007) emphasize, developments in the type and quality of the data available have underpinned this research. Much wider availability of micro data, as opposed to reliance on grouped data in published reports, has been central. There have also been substantial returns on effort put into harmonizing definitions and measures so that data can be used more reliably for cross-country comparisons—as exemplified by the Luxembourg Income Study (LIS) and Wealth Study (LWS) databases covering many OECD countries and the work of

Eurostat in relation to the European Union. The increasing number of longitudinal datasets available for a variety of countries has also made possible the studies of income and labor market dynamics that have played such an important part in the recent literature. Comparative data—notably Cornell's Cross-National Equivalent File (CNEF) and the European Community Household Panel (ECHP)—have paid significant dividends.[2] Finally matched employer–employee data from firm registers in many nations have opened a new arena for estimating employer demand for labor (Abowd *et al.*, 2004). These data, properly utilized, create an increasingly reliable picture of inequality levels and trends and therefore allow researchers to concentrate on the 'why's' and 'so what's' of their emergent patterns, rather than on the factual accuracy of the measures themselves.

The literature has naturally also invested a great deal of effort in seeking to understand the causal processes at work in producing and sustaining economic inequality. However, the linkage between theory and empirics has sometimes been looser than in some other areas of economics, with a tendency for empirical research to prioritize careful treatment of the available data. More fundamentally, the study of economic inequality can seem on occasion—at least to economists working on other topics—to have become rather detached from the broader field of economics. This explains, for example, Atkinson's (1997) plea to bring the study of income distribution 'in from the cold'. On the other hand, economists working in the area can benefit from interaction with other disciplines such as sociology and social policy that share the focus on inequality and its causes and consequences. One may be optimistic that current socio-economic trends such as the generally increasing intertwining of the household and the labor market, through growing female participation (Chapter 12) as well as household worklessness (Gregg *et al.*, 2004), or the rapidly deepening interconnections of incomes and labor worldwide (Chapters 23 and 24), can only help give the study of inequality a place among the central concerns of the economic discipline.

# 4. ANALYTICAL FRAMEWORK

Atkinson and Bourguignon (2000), in reviewing the components of a theory of income distribution, emphasize that no unified theory exists as yet; income distribution is only one element of broader inequality, so an encompassing theory of economic inequality is even further away. However, we can try to sketch out some

---

[2]  Covering Australia, Canada, Germany, the UK and the US, and the 15 older EU member states respectively.

starting points for a framework within which the various aspects of inequality—and thus the range of topics covered in this book—can be set.

This framework would start with the distribution of income among households, which is at the core of economic inequality, and the way it is produced. That distribution is influenced most importantly by the earnings from work accruing to different household members. Understanding these patterns requires one to focus on the one hand on individuals in the labor market, their skills and opportunities and the returns they receive, and on the other on patterns of family formation and how earners cluster together with others in households. Labor market institutions, with employers and unions as key actors and the role of the State in regulating minimum wages in particular, are an important influence on the distribution of earnings, as are structured differences between groups of workers by gender, ethnicity or other factors, whether malleable (e.g. education) or not.

Another important component of household income, though less important than earnings at an aggregate level, is income derived as a return on capital—interest, dividends, and rent, as well as capital gains and profits. To understand this capital element, one must turn to the distribution of wealth, and to the relationship between that distribution and other elements of household income. Once again, this requires an understanding of asset holdings and their accumulation at the individual level, including through inheritance, as well as how individuals with different levels of wealth group together in households, and how different forms of wealth produce income streams via the financial and property markets, including pensions.

The third most significant element in household income, which may be the main or only source of income for a substantial proportion of households, is social protection received by its members from the State in the form of cash transfers. These are structured in different ways in different countries, and such institutional differences—including the way they feed back to the labor market and the distribution of earnings—are very important to the lower part of the distribution in particular. Private pensions, paid from occupational schemes or as a result of personal investment rather than from the social security system, again bring the financial markets directly into the picture but for a more advantaged part of the distribution.

Cash transfers and other aspects of State spending have to be financed, of course, and the income tax and social insurance contributions levied on individuals and families make a substantial contribution towards doing so. However, the way the income tax and social insurance systems are structured is also an important influence on the shape of the income distribution, in terms of the proportion of total income involved and the degree of progressivity with which it is raised as well as any structure of refundable tax credits (negative taxes) such as child allowances or in-work tax credits such as the Earned Income Tax Credit in the USA.

Institutional structures, and the political economy considerations they reflect, are also a major force when considering the broader impact of the Welfare State on economic inequality. This includes most obviously the provision of human services, notably health care and education, where approaches differ across countries (in particular the extent to which funding is collectively or privately determined) and can have a major influence on the living standards associated with a given level of household income. Health and education also are key influences on human capital, earnings, and therefore income in themselves, and the relationship between these social goods and economic inequality at individual and aggregate level is an increasingly important part of the picture.

Income is not static over time for individuals and households, and one of the major advances in the research literature has been to recognize the importance of adopting a dynamic perspective. This relates to both individual earnings and to household income, from month to month and year to year, but also to intertemporal trajectories over the work career and life-span and to mobility in income and wealth from one generation to the next. Changes in household structure and migration can each play an important role in generating changes in household income, so demography and migration must also be incorporated into the analysis of economic inequality.

The global context is also critical to understanding the structure and evolution of economic inequality in high-income countries, as amply illustrated by the expansion of global trade and capital flows and the concerns to which this has given rise in rich countries. The impact this may have on the distribution of earnings and returns to different levels of education and skills has been the subject of much research, but the potential effects on the overall distribution of income and on the ability of individual welfare states to influence inequality in income and life-chances also need to be incorporated into the framework.

The extent and nature of economic inequality is a core characteristic of and concern for the society as a whole. This means finally that the scope for policy and politics to affect inequality, the choices that this involves, and how they are made, has to be incorporated into the framework of this book.

# 5. THE AIM AND COVERAGE OF THIS HANDBOOK

As made clear at the outset, the aim of this Handbook is to provide the reader with an overview and evaluation of the current state of research on economic inequality and a forward-looking perspective of future research. It seeks to convey what the basic accomplishments of this very broad area of research are and how it has been evolving, and in so doing, to both stimulate further interest in the field and highlight fruitful directions and priorities for its future development.

One primary audience for which it is written is a student at a master's degree or advanced undergraduate level, of course including those studying economics but not confined to those for whom economics is the principal subject being studied. It can indirectly serve to assist their primary studies, and it may also help them think about future research they may decide to contribute to themselves.

The other audience is professionals, either governmental or non-governmental, engaged in the policy arena as well as the interested 'layperson' with a keen interest in the subject of inequality.[3] They will find in a single volume a synopsis of the best knowledge on most of the policy-relevant aspects of inequality. The style of presentation is thus designed to be non-technical (except in a very limited number of instances where it could not be avoided). This means that the content should also appeal to researchers on inequality coming from other disciplines seeking an overview of what economics has to offer. It is a defining characteristic of the field that it is focused on issues that are of very broad societal concern, and the volume seeks to reflect that in its mode of presentation insofar as this can be done without compromising the material.

The comparative perspective is also central to our endeavor. There is much to be learned from direct international comparison that is difficult to uncover at the national level. Quite naturally countries differ with respect to inequalities—something that is amply borne out in the contributions to this book. But also if direct comparability is lacking, usually because data are unavailable, studies in one country might well inspire other countries. The stress on the USA in some chapters should be interpreted in that way.

In terms of coverage, the volume includes a broad range of the topics where economic research on inequality over the past 40 or 50 years has focused and is blossoming today. As already noted, it concentrates for the most part on research related to high-income countries, since the developing world differs in fundamental ways and merits separate treatment. However, inequality in the rich countries is placed in its global context, with the chapters of Part VI devoted to inequality and growth, world income inequality and poverty, and the impact of global economic forces on what is happening in high-income countries. The book also concentrates primarily—but not exclusively—on research from the disciplinary perspective of economics. It would be impossible to represent this research at all adequately in a single volume, while at the same time doing justice to the substantial literature on inequality from for example sociology, politics, philosophy, and law. Still, several

---

[3]  In contrast, the very valuable recent surveys on income distribution edited by Silber (1999) and Atkinson and Bourguignon (2000), for example, are aimed at a more advanced level, the economics Ph.D. student alone.

of the chapters in this book convey the perspectives of sociology, demography, and political science, as well as philosophy and law.

# 6. STRUCTURE AND CONTENT OF THE HANDBOOK

The volume comprises 27 chapters, which are grouped into seven sections covering the following areas of discourse:

1) Overview, Concepts, and Measurement—providing the basic epistemological and methodological starting points;
2) Extent of Inequality—laying the empirical foundations and setting out extant stylized facts of inequality for household incomes, labor and capital incomes, wealth and top incomes;
3) Earnings Inequality—treating the role of the economy's core arena: the labor market and its institutional, personal, and gender-based components;
4) Dimensions of Inequality—highlighting the importance of particular elements or dimensions of distributional study, namely poverty, and household consumption and time use, and the relationship between inequality and happiness, health, and education respectively;
5) Dynamics of Inequality—focusing on the time perspective of demographic change, migratory movements of people and jobs, and lifetime (intertemporal and intragenerational) mobility as well as intergenerational mobility;
6) Global Perspectives on Inequality—discussing economic growth and inequality, the effects of globalization on labor and capital incomes, and the study of global poverty and inequality;
7) Changing Inequalities—considering ways of addressing inequality as practiced by the Welfare State, by policy-making more generally and, finally, the limits to the degree of equality that can be achieved by market economies.

The 26 chapters that make up this framework share a common broad structure. After explaining the relevance of the chapter's subject to the study of inequality, they review the state-of-the-art theory, followed—after an overview of data and sources—by a discussion of the empirical state-of-the-art. Many chapters also add new insights based on original work. Then they provide an evaluation of both theory and evidence, and end with suggestions for future research and, where relevant, possible implications for policy-making.

The volume begins with an overview of the philosophical and normative approaches to inequality in Chapter 2. It summarizes the important advances made by political philosophy and shows how these ideas have filtered into economic thinking. It concludes by stressing the fundamental importance of certain questions that this raises. This contrasts with the empirical and positivist approaches to methods and techniques for actually measuring inequalities in Chapter 3. An extensive state-of-the-art overview is given of the instruments of inequality studies. The methods and technical terms outlined in this chapter are deployed throughout the remainder of the book.

The second part, on the extent of inequality, begins with Chapter 4 and the evidence on how the distribution of income among persons varies across developed countries, and how it has been changing in recent years. Inequalities in market incomes (from work and capital), in disposable incomes (after public transfers are added and income taxes and social contributions subtracted), and the role of cash and non-cash redistribution are all discussed. The aim is to provide a picture of key 'stylized facts' and recent trends, various specific aspects of which are also taken up in subsequent chapters. This is followed by Chapter 5 on the more traditional economics of functional distribution and the shares accruing to both labor and capital sectors. Indeed as seen in later chapters on high incomes and globalization, functional share research is just beginning a new resurgence. Wealth (net worth, debt) and the transfer of wealth (*inter vivos* and at death) in rich societies are increasingly key elements of economic well-being and inequality. Chapter 6 explores the level and trend of wealth inequality while suggesting the lacunae in the field, especially our very inexact measures of retirement wealth. The final chapter (7) of Part II deals in depth with the issue of how high incomes have been changing over long time periods for many rich countries, noting especially the increases in top shares within most nations over the past two decades.

The third part of the book is about earnings and labor market inequality and begins in Chapter 8 with a review of the distribution of individuals' earnings and how that reflects differences in both wages and work effort, and how in turn these feed into the more aggregate measure of income inequalities. This individual focus is in contrast to the relationship of employer behavior to labor market inequalities, the subject of Chapter 9. Matched employer–employee data are casting an important new light on how variation in wage-setting practices across firms can affect the structure of earnings and earnings mobility. The chapter finds that very different wages are paid to equivalent labor across and within firms. The chapter also argues in tantalizing fashion that policies targeting firm selection of workers may affect inequality as much as policies of training and education which played the key role in the previous chapter. Institutions are first addressed head on in Chapter 10, which focuses on the role of unions, a core feature of labor market institutions, and their influence on economic inequality. While the union wage gap has generated an enormous body of empirical research, particularly for the USA and the UK, there has been much less research into the impact of unions on wage dispersion and wage inequality. The chapter considers the separate contributions of union power, membership composition, bargaining coordination, and wage policy, the combination of which determines the impact on inequality. It then summarizes new estimates of how the presence of trade unions has influenced the extent and dynamics of earnings inequality across advanced economies during the 1980s and 1990s. Next, Chapter 11 is also concerned with earnings, but deals with the bottom of the distribution, low pay. It discusses theoretical frameworks within which low pay may be analyzed, and how it is generally defined and measured. The varying patterns across countries in terms of the extent of low pay and the profile of those affected are presented. The policy issues to which low pay gives rise—notably the much-debated issue of the role and impact of minimum wage regulation—are also discussed. The unequal treatment of women in the labor market goes back to the first written sources on gender bias even if major changes have been occurring over the last 50 years. However, the transformation remains seriously incomplete as detailed in Chapter 12. Deficiencies in employment levels, occupational structure, and earnings are scrutinized. These massive changes are linked back to the educational attainment of women, technological change, and employment shifts toward the service sector. Effects on household incomes and fertility are discussed. Due attention is paid to the important role and the nature of policies for gender equality. Gaps in the proper understanding of the processes of the transformation of women to paid labor as well as their implications are identified as issues for further research, with a careful consideration of the use and justification of policy interventions.

Part IV of the book opens with Chapter 13, where a central policy-relevant facet of economic inequality, poverty and social exclusion, is treated. The chapter discusses the nature of the concept of poverty and how it is generally measured. It then reviews the evidence about the extent and nature of poverty in developed countries, thought of and measured in different ways, absolute and relative. It also focuses on what is known about the key influences on poverty, at the individual and societal levels. It discusses how poverty is related to income inequality and to social exclusion as well as multidimensional approaches to thinking about and capturing poverty in rich societies. Inequalities in what people do with their money and their time are the next dimensions of inequality that we address. The subjects of time use and the explicit and implicit consumption of households are covered in Chapter 14. Non-market time-use patterns are well laid out and the importance of radical changes over time and cross-country differences for the study of inequality is argued to lie in their implications for relative well-being. Though there still is a paucity of cross-national comparative studies of either expenditure or consumption inequality, the time seems ripe to strengthen the focus on the conceptual framework (see also Chapter 4 on the topic of consumption inequality).

The last three chapters in this part deal with three dimensions which are both precedents and antecedents of inequality: happiness, health, and education. In recent years an interesting new literature has grown up on subjective well-being (or happiness). Chapter 15 defends the use of the modern approach against mainstream skepticism, working its way back to the origins of the new development in the 1970s. It explains the concepts and discusses their different dimensions, with an extensive treatment of the debate on the measurability of happiness. The chapter concludes by highlighting the potential importance of the study of inequality for happiness researchers. Next, Chapter 16 deals with the relationship between economic inequality and health. It first reviews the most common hypotheses about how inequality might affect health and vice versa. It then turns to an assessment of the empirical evidence for a link between health and inequality. It emphasizes that the cross-sectional relationship between inequality and health is quite likely to provide biased estimates so use of panel data and appropriate techniques represents a significant advance in the literature to date. The evidence for a relationship between inequality and health (in either direction) is found to be weak, and the field is characterized as one with too many theories for the number of available data points at this time. Educational attainment is a key influence on economic inequality, through both the inequalities of education acquisition itself and the unequal effects of educational outcomes on economic and social outcomes—in employment as well as earnings. Chapter 17 therefore reflects on the very big literatures that have grown on each of these aspects, making important methodological progress regarding the causality of linkages. Those with low levels of educational attainment are heavily penalized in present-day labor markets. Policy-making in education seems to lag behind these new market insights and therefore education provides an important area for future research activity related to inequalities of both schooling and its outcomes.

Dynamic aspects of inequality are the focus of the fifth part of this volume. Indeed the way that we measure income inequality is often affected by demography—changes in the age and gender composition of workers and households more generally. Chapter 18 shows the effects of changes in the size and composition of the population itself on measures of economic inequality. Population ageing and retirement patterns, increased labor force participation, and the growth of female-headed families have all had major 'demographic' effects on the composition, level, and the trend in inequality. Similarly falling fertility rates and increasing migration from poor to rich countries will have a still different impact on future patterns of inequality. Chapter 19 focuses on migration and its implications for the level and structuring of economic inequality. The theoretical framework within which this can be examined is first set out, focusing on the potential labor market impacts and the wage and employment consequences of in-migration. A picture of native-immigrant differences in labor force participation, unemployment, and occupational and educational attainment in OECD countries is then presented. The empirical evidence on economic absorption (or assimilation) over time and across generations, the role that self-selection and selection through admission rules can play, and the impact of cultural or ethnic identity on economic performance, and hence inequality, are all discussed in some detail.

The final two chapters in this section are about the nature of dynamics *per se* as they are measured by datasets which follow the same people or generations of the same families over time. Chapter 20 deals with an issue of abiding interest, the transmission of economic inequality from one generation to the next. It begins with a theoretical discussion of various mechanisms that might lie behind the associations between income and family background, and what can be learnt from an economic model of parental investments in their children. The income concepts and measures used to describe intergenerational associations in income in the research literature are then described. An overview of what is known from recent research about cross-national patterns in intergenerational income mobility is provided. The question of whether parental income has a causal impact on the economic success of offspring, and results from a variety of approaches about what lies behind the association between income and family background, are also discussed. Chapter 21 is then concerned with economic mobility within, rather than across, generations. It begins with a detailed explanation of the most common methods used to calculate intragenerational mobility and the empirical problems of implementing these measures across countries, using panel data. It goes on to describe the relationship between the data used in studies of mobility and the conceptual content of the research. It then reviews the major findings of empirical studies of intragenerational income mobility, pointing out for example that most studies find no clear relationship between greater cross-sectional inequality and greater intragenerational mobility, as is often casually assumed. The field is judged to be relatively underdeveloped in comparison to the cross-sectional inequality literature, due partly to the scarcity of the type of data required to study such mobility.

Part VI of the book develops the perspective of worldwide inequality, globalization, and economic development. Chapter 22 investigates how inequality and its corollaries may affect a country's economic growth or undermine its institutions. It reveals complex and multidimensional effects of inequality on growth. The chapter advocates replacing the common, overall approach to the effects of inequality on economic growth with a finer methodology relating these effects to the different parts of the distribution: poverty at the bottom, wealth and incomes at the top, and the middle class in between. In addition, it argues for the role of institutions in place (or not) as a determinant of the size of these effects. The contentious relationship between globalization and inequality is the subject of Chapter 23. It takes stock of (existing) knowledge about this as well as how we know it, spelling out the uncertainties of this knowledge and the ways to study these. A detailed treatment of the channels of transmission leaves no doubt that globalization is for real and is rapidly advancing, doubling the global labor force. Globalization is also shown to reduce between-country inequalities and potentially increase within-country inequalities. The upbeat conclusion is that policy should and can 'lean against the wind of rising inequality' assuring a wider distribution of the benefits.

The global context of economic inequality in developed countries is examined in Chapter 24 which summarizes the recent evidence on global poverty and inequality, including both developed and developing countries. The issues involved in aggregating inequality indices across countries to construct a meaningful measure of global inequality are discussed, and the main results from research that has sought to measure global income inequality are summarized. The empirical relationship between economic growth, poverty, and inequality dynamics is discussed, bringing out the key stylized facts to emerge from these data. The likely economic determinants of poverty and inequality changes are also discussed.

Finally, the extent and nature of intervention by the state and its critical influence on and by economic inequality is addressed in Part VII of the book. Chapter 25 focuses on the Welfare State, which includes social protection, health, education and training, housing, and social services, but can also be conceived more broadly to include policies that affect earnings capacity and the structure of the labor market. It discusses the difficulties of capturing the impact of the Welfare State on income inequality, given that one does not observe what the distribution would be in the absence of the Welfare State or specific aspects of it. Theories of Welfare State redistribution are reviewed, and the conventional categorization into welfare 'regimes' discussed. The empirical evidence about the extent and nature of redistribution by the Welfare State is described, including non-cash services as well as cash transfers, and the impact on poverty in particular is discussed. Economic inequality is also strongly affected by the political process, and vice versa. In Chapter 26, the intricacies of politics and policies which affect inequality are reviewed. The idea that inequality is self-correcting in democratic societies cannot explain persistent inequalities or recent governmental responses to rising inequality. The perceptions and realities of social risk, different beliefs about the link between individual effort and economic outcomes and mobility, and the formation and change of cultural issues and identities all have important effects. While more definitive research has to be undertaken, it appears that access to political power by the wealthy has been found to counteract median voter theorems and lead to a less than egalitarian outcome in most Welfare States. The possibility of attaining equality in principle concludes the book in Chapter 27. It considers different ways (socialist, social-democratic) in which, conditional on democracy and market processes, more egalitarian outcomes might be brought about. It is argued that the spread of egalitarian ideas through argument and persuasion has an important role to play in introducing or reinforcing the institutions needed to bring about more solidaristic societies. The results, while not optimistic, offer at least one way in which a more egalitarian society might be realized in market economies.

# 7. SOME FURTHER ISSUES

Even a substantial volume such as this cannot hope to be comprehensive, and in concluding this introductory chapter it is useful to highlight some topics that merit particular attention in future research over and above the issues brought to the fore in the individual chapters. These may be divided into two groups: other topics to which the research literature has paid some attention and those which have been neglected to date.

In the first category one could include the purely theoretical investigation of issues related to inequality, notably the investigation of theoretical models of for example wealth accumulation and intergenerational transmission—a distinct strand of the literature to which a chapter could well have been devoted. Other topics related to inequality to which considerable attention has been paid by researchers include discrimination, pensions and the economic circumstances of older people, the relationship between macroeconomic fluctuations or 'economic conditions' and inequality, and the range of issues arising when one tries to open up the 'black box' of the household and explicitly consider within-household inequality. These are touched on in various chapters in the volume, but could undoubtedly have merited more attention that we had either time or space to give to them.

In the second category are issues which have not been adequately treated in the literature, and this is reflected in their treatment in this Handbook. One can start in this case with the tendency for the field to ignore or neglect its own history, rediscovering issues and relationships that have in fact been the focus of concern and analysis for many years. Another major gap is the failure to analytically link the personal and functional distributions of income comprehensively and robustly—a pressing concern for the future given what have often been dramatic shifts in both these distributions in recent years. Chapter 5 serves to highlight its importance but could not fill the gap. Consumption inequality itself is not often studied in a cross-national context due to severe conceptual measurement and data limitations. A variety of issues relating to the impact of the globalizing international economy have emerged so recently that they have not yet been adequately researched—with outsourcing from the rich countries and its potential extent and impact one of the most obvious.

Another important issue in analyzing global inequality relates to the construction and use of Purchasing Power Parities (PPPs) to allow national household and aggregate income data to be converted into a common currency.[4] In using PPPs with household income micro data both the quality of the income data (relative to

---

[4] The best-known efforts come from the International Comparison Project (ICP) of the United Nations (<http://unstats.un.org/unsd/methods/icp/index.htm>), and especially the OECD and World Bank's efforts. See <http://siteresources.worldbank.org/ICPINT/Resources/ICPreportprelim.pdf>, and the Penn World Tables (PWT) at <http://pwt.econ.upenn.edu/php_site/pwt_index.php>.

the aggregates on which the PPP are based) and the types of goods and services purchased in each nation can introduce biases,[5] and further research into their construction and use for inequality and poverty comparisons is a priority. This is illustrated by the fact that the scale of the measured contribution of China to reducing world income poverty depends on a set of PPPs just recently calculated.[6]

In introducing this Handbook on economic inequality, we conclude by emphasizing that the relationship between inequality and economic performance, although it has been the subject of considerable research, remains poorly understood and hotly debated. Each of the subsequent chapters highlights a variety of topics on which research is often urgently needed, and our hope is that this Handbook will act as a stimulus to this intellectually exciting and substantively indispensable enterprise.

## REFERENCES

AABERGE, R., BJÖRKLUND, A., JÄNTTI, M., PALME, M., PEDERSEN, P., SMITH, N., and WENNEMO, T. 2002. 'Income Inequality and Income Mobility in the Scandinavian Countries Compared to the United States'. *Review of Income and Wealth*, 48(4): 443–69.

AARON, H. 1978. *Politics and the Professors*. Washington: Brookings.

ABOWD, J., HALTIWANGER, J., and LANE, J. 2004. 'Integrated Longitudinal Employee–Employer Data for the United States'. *American Economic Review*, 94: 224–9.

ATKINSON, A. B. 1970. 'On the Measurement of Inequality'. *Journal of Economic Theory*, 2: 244–63.

—— 1975. *The Economics of Inequality*. Oxford: Clarendon Press.

—— 1997. 'Bringing Income Distribution in from the Cold'. *The Economic Journal*, 107(44): 297–321.

—— and BOURGUIGNON, F. (eds.). 2000. *Handbook of Income Distribution*, vol. 1. Amsterdam: Elsevier.

—— CANTILLON, B., MARLIER, E., and NOLAN, B. 2002. *Social Indicators: The EU and Social Inclusion*. Oxford: Oxford University Press.

—— and PIKETTY, T. (eds.) 2007. *Top Incomes Over the Twentieth Century: A Contrast between Continental European and English-Speaking Countries*. Oxford: Oxford University Press.

BLANK, R. M. 2008. 'How to Improve Poverty Measurement in the United States'. *Journal of Public Analysis and Management*, 27(2), Spring: 1–34

---

[5] For instance, countries that use tax systems to purchase health care and education will find that the PPPs undervalue their disposable incomes compared to ones where they are left to the market. Moreover, increasing world trade which drives down prices of tradeable goods and services is not often accounted for in national price surveys.

[6] See Elekdag and Lall (2008) at <http://www.imf.org/external/pubs/ft/survey/so/2008/RES018A.htm>.

BURTLESS, G., and JENCKS, C. 2003. 'American Inequality and its Consequences', in H. Aaron, J. Lindsay, and P. Nivola (eds.), *Agenda for the Nation*. Washington: Brookings Institution, 61–108.

GOTTSCHALK, P., and SMEEDING, T. 1997. 'Cross-National Comparisons of Earnings and Income Inequality'. *Journal of Economic Literature*, 35: 633–87.

—— —— 2000. 'Empirical Evidence on Income Inequality in Industrialized Countries', in Atkinson and Bourguignon (2000), 261–307.

GREGG, P., SCUTELLA, R., and WADSWORTH, J. 2004. 'Reconciling Workless Measures at the Individual and Household Level: Theory and Evidence from the United States, Britain, Germany, Spain and Australia'. LSE, Centre for Economic Performance, Discussion Paper 635.

JÄNTTI M., BRATSBERG, B., ROED, K., RAAUM, O., NAYLOR, R., ÖSTERBACKA, E., BJÖRKLUND, A. 2006. 'American Exceptionalism in a New Light: A Comparison of Intergenerational Earnings Mobility in the Nordic Countries'. IZA Discussion Paper No. 1938. Bonn: IZA.

JENKINS, S., and MICKLEWRIGHT, J. 2007. *Inequality and Poverty Re-examined*. Oxford: Oxford University Press.

KUZNETS, S. 1955. 'Economic Growth and Income Inequality'. *American Economic Review*, 45: 1–28.

LINDERT, P. H. 2004. *Growing Public: Social Spending and Economic Growth since the Eighteenth Century*, 2 volumes. Cambridge: Cambridge University Press.

MINCER, J. 1958. 'Investment In Human Capital and the Personal Income Distribution'. *Journal of Political Economy*, 66: 281–302.

NECKERMAN, K. M., and TORCHE, F. 2007. 'Inequality: Causes and Consequences'. *Annual Review of Sociology*, 33: 335–7

SEN, A. 1973. *On Economic Inequality*. Oxford: Clarendon Press.

—— 1976. 'Poverty: An Ordinal Approach to Measurement'. *Econometrica*, 44: 219–31.

SILBER, J. (ed.) 1999. *Handbook of Income Inequality Measurement*. New York: Springer.

WELCH, F. 1999. 'In Defense of Inequality'. *American Economic Review*, 89(2): 1–17.

CHAPTER 2

...............................................

# EQUALITY: ITS JUSTIFICATION, NATURE, AND DOMAIN

...............................................

## JOHN E. ROEMER

## 1. INTRODUCTION

...............................................

DURING the last 40 years, political philosophers have made important advances in our understanding of why equality is valuable, and what kind of equality is important. In this chapter, we summarize the development of these ideas, in particular, the contributions of John Rawls, Amartya Sen, Ronald Dworkin, Robert Nozick, Richard Arneson, and G. A. Cohen, and we show how these ideas have filtered into economic thinking in the conceptualization of equality of opportunity. We conclude with a brief discussion of how these ideas might be extended to evaluate intergenerational and global distributions of income or welfare.

# 2. IS EQUALITY DESIRABLE, AND IF SO, WHAT KIND OF EQUALITY?

There are three principal reasons put forth for the desirability of economic equality. The first is grounded in justice, and has its modern statement in the work of John Rawls (1971). Rawls argues that the features of persons that determine the economic outcomes that they will enjoy are arbitrary from the moral viewpoint: talents, birth-families, and environments. Consequently, economic inequalities cannot be deserved. The second reason is that equality is the fairest way to share scarcity. As long as there is insufficient wealth for everyone to have enough to develop a reasonable plan of life, equality is the fairest way to ration. The third argument is that inequality (as opposed to poverty) has deleterious effects on human welfare (see Chapters 17 and 18).

Each of these arguments can be challenged. Even though one's genetic constitution, and one's family, are not chosen, it may still be claimed that one has a moral property right in these assets, and thereby has a right to benefit from them. The most careful statement of this anti-Rawlsian view is Nozick (1974). Even though these assets are not chosen, the individual may still be rightly held responsible for what he or she does with them, and so, as long as requirements of non-discrimination and equality of opportunity are met, unequal outcomes are morally acceptable. Furthermore, even if equality is deemed desirable, implementing it might impoverish everyone, because of deleterious incentive effects. Redistribution should be limited, because if too extreme, those who are very productive and innovative may cease to perform their socially valuable activities. Rawls, in particular, recognizes this, and does not call for total equality, but rather, to maximize the bundle of goods which the worst-off group receives. That 'maxi-min' formula might permit considerable inequality, if the elasticity of supply of highly talented labor is high.

Equality as the best way to ration scarce resources can be challenged by pointing out that an equal distribution may not be the one which maximizes the number of people who have satisfactory lives. If a lifeboat can only support three people, and five are occupying it, better that two jump overboard than that all suffer almost certain death.

If one believes that equality is desirable, or at least, that more equality than currently exists is desirable, what is the right *currency* of equality—wealth, income, welfare, opportunity, or resources? And what is the *domain* of persons over which equality is desirable—members of a nation, of a state, the world population, or individuals over many generations in one of these entities? In this chapter, I will summarize recent contributions by philosophers and economists to the first question, and will offer some comments on the second.

Economists have always viewed income or wealth as instrumental for producing welfare, and hence the natural assumption was, until around 1970, that if equality was desirable, then it must be human welfare (or well-being or utility) that should be equalized. Indeed, the nineteenth-century utilitarians (such as J. S. Mill) tacitly assumed that all persons possessed the same utility function of money, which exhibited decreasing returns to scale (i.e. concavity), and so if one desired to distribute a given sum of money to maximize total welfare, then the optimal solution was to distribute it equally (i.e. to equalize across persons the marginal utility of money, which implied the equalization of money endowments). Thus, at least some nineteenth-century utilitarians were also egalitarians.

With the twentieth-century ordinal revolution, however, the utility function began to be viewed only as a representation of an individual's preference order over commodities, rather than as an absolute measure of interpersonally comparable welfare. Indeed, general equilibrium theory requires only, as data, individual preference orders (as well as endowments and technology); the Walrasian or competitive equilibrium of a market economy is independent of any interpersonal comparisons of utility that one might wish to append to these data. Utilitarianism, on the other hand, requires as data what is called unit comparability of welfare across persons. For a discussion of the kinds of information that can be assumed about interpersonal comparability, see Roemer (1996, chapter 1).

Because the Walrasian or competitive equilibrium is well-defined absent any information on interpersonal comparisons of welfare, many economists concluded, mistakenly, that such comparisons were meaningless. The error in this inference is clear if one contemplates inferring that, because we do not need to know the color of an object to compute how fast it falls from the tower of Pisa, therefore color is a meaningless attribute of objects. Rather, and conversely, the insensitivity of Walrasian equilibrium to interpersonal comparability of welfare implies that *if* one thinks interpersonal comparisons are essential in a theory of distributive justice, as many believe, then a market economy cannot by itself deliver justice, impervious as markets are to interpersonal welfare comparisons. Of course one might be able to redistribute endowments or income flows, through taxation, in such a way that the market will produce an outcome conforming with some view of justice in which interpersonal comparisons are salient, but the market's achievement of justice, in this case, would be only incidental.

# 3. Rawls's Primary Goods, and Sen's Functionings

In 1971, John Rawls revolutionized discussions of distributive justice, and of egalitarian political philosophy in particular, by publishing *A Theory of Justice* (1971). Rawls attacked utilitarianism, the predominant view of justice among philosophers and economists at that time, in two ways: first, he said that utility or well-being should not be the currency of justice, but rather 'primary goods' should be, and second, justice is not achieved by maximizing the *sum* of well-being (or even primary goods) but rather by *equalizing* the distribution of primary goods across persons. As Rawls understood that an equal distribution might not be efficient, he replaced 'equality' with 'maximizing the minimum bundle of primary goods' across persons, a distribution that might Pareto-dominate the highest achievable equal distribution of such goods, because of failures of incentive, as pointed out above. Rawls called his proposal, of maxi-minning the distribution of primary goods, the 'difference principle'.

What are primary goods? They are, according to Rawls, those goods which all need to achieve their own life-plans—in modern society, an education, sufficient food, and housing, and those things which people must have to engender self-respect. In some places, Rawls says that money is the main primary good. The question immediately arises: How can one 'equalize' or 'maxi-min' a *vector* of goods across persons? Rawls gestured towards having an 'index' of primary goods to make equalization coherent, but he never solved the problem of what that index should be, and many writers say there can be no such universal index. It is the individual's utility function which gives the right index, they say, and that is not universal; and if the utility index were adopted, one would be back to welfare equalization.

Why did Rawls not argue for maxi-minning utility or welfare across persons? Because he argued for *neutrality*, the view that the state should not be in the business of equalizing welfare, but rather of providing persons with the inputs that everyone needs for achieving his own idiosyncratic concept of welfare. Rawls wrote that persons should be responsible for their own conception of welfare, and so the state should not be held accountable for providing the resource bundles that some might need to achieve a reasonable level of a hard-to-achieve kind of welfare (like climbing Mount Everest without help). This issue of *responsibility for tastes*, which Rawls only mentioned in a peripheral way, will become central in the years to follow.

In 1974, shortly after Rawls's book was published, Robert Nozick published *Anarchy, State, and Utopia*, his anti-egalitarian manifesto, in which he argued that any outcome resulting from voluntary exchanges, from initially just endowments, was just. Nozick argued that only a minimal state, to protect property rights, was justified, and that compulsory redistribution through taxation was an incursion against just property rights. He took issue with Rawls's view of the moral arbitrariness of personal endowments, and argued for the correctness of the *thesis of self-ownership*, that a person has a right to use his or her powers for personal benefit. Even though outcomes in the present world were surely not established with a morally clean history (replete as history is with major episodes of slavery, theft, and pillage), one could imagine very unequal outcomes evolving with a clean history in which all exchanges were voluntary.

Besides voluntary exchange, a second premise is needed to start the Nozickian engine, his principle which governs the privatization of resources that are unowned in the external world. Nozick proposed that an individual has the right to claim any such resource, as long as, consequently, others are not rendered worse off than they were when the resource was unowned. Thus, if Abraham knows how to make sand into a medicine that can cure fatal diseases, he may fence off the beach, use the sand to make medicine, and sell it to the villagers, who, let us assume, are thereby better off than had the medicine not existed. Abraham may become much wealthier than the others by this maneuver, and the resulting inequality is Nozick-just. Thus Abraham's ingenuity (self-ownership) allows him to extend his ownership over resources in the external world. Although there may be no more beaches to claim for members of generations born too late, they will arguably be better off than if the beaches had not been privatized in the past, and so they, too, gain by the early privatizations.

Several philosophers (Cohen, 1986; Gibbard, 1976; and Grunebaum, 1987) pointed out that Nozick's principle of acquisition of unowned resources is arbitrary. Why should one not view resources that are *legally* unowned as being jointly owned by the community, from the *moral* viewpoint? Were this the arrangement, then Abraham would have to bargain with the community over the distribution of profits from the medicine he would manufacture from the sand. This would lead to a more equal distribution of the benefits of innovation.

Thus, Nozick's theory of distributive justice combines the thesis of self-ownership with a particularly inegalitarian rule for privatization of the external world. Although Nozick argued for this rule as a generalization of John Locke's principle, that it was morally permissible to take pieces of the external world so long as one left 'enough and as good for others', in fact that Lockean proviso can be generalized in many ways. When the resource is scarce, so it is not possible to take some of it and leave enough and as good for others, Nozick's move was to substitute 'so long as nobody is made worse off than when the resource was in its unowned state'. The alternative of joint ownership of those resources might lead to a generalization of Locke's proviso which says that the resource should be employed in a Pareto-efficient manner and its benefits distributed to the community in a way that they decide.

The import of this discussion is that one need not challenge Nozick's thesis of self-ownership in order to nullify the morality of the unequal distribution of income that his theory sanctifies: it suffices to challenge his thesis of appropriation. This comprises an approach which is not as egalitarian as that of Rawls (who denied the thesis of self-ownership) but surely more egalitarian than that of Nozick. Those who endorse this view today are known as 'left-libertarians' (see Vallentyne and Steiner, 2000).

Several years after Nozick's book, but within the egalitarian camp, Amartya Sen (1980) criticized Rawls for being too concerned with equalizing goods, rather than in equalizing what goods *do* for people. He called Rawls a commodity fetishist at one point, borrowing a Marxist term. One might think, then, that Sen would call for equalizing welfare; however, he did not, but said that what should be equalized across persons were their abilities to *function*. Functionings, for Sen, are abilities to perform certain kinds of tasks necessary for a normal life—being healthy, literate, able to move around, and so on. Thus Sen located, as ethically important, a human state *between* possessing goods and enjoying welfare—Cohen (1990) later credited Sen with the invention of 'midfare', that thing which is achieved by the ability to function in various ways, but is short of welfare.

Sen initially proposed an objective list of functionings. Clearly, his proposal would run into the same problem as Rawls faced, with regard to equalizing a vector of functionings across persons, but rather than proposing an index (of functionings), Sen defined a person's *capability* as the set of possible functionings that she could achieve, and argued that justice requires only *equalizing capabilities* across persons. To be able to speak coherently of such equality, one needs a way of comparing sets, and deciding when they are equal or equivalent: that is, a preference relation on sets (capabilities) is required. There arose a literature in social-choice theory in which writers proposed axiomatic characterizations of preference relations on sets, but it is fair to say there is no universal agreement on what the right answer is. Sen himself has never said that his theory requires a complete ordering of capabilities: partial orderings are probably enough to decide when one person is better off than another (the Mumbai beggar and the Princeton professor).

Sen initially limited functionings to objectively observable aspects of behavior, such as health, mobility, and literacy. Later, however, he added 'happiness' to the list (Sen, 1992), compromising the objective nature of the proposal, for the degree of a person's happiness is subjective and may be difficult to observe. Sen also argued for his capability proposal by invoking the value of individual choice: what matters is that people have sets of options which are equivalent, not that they indeed choose the same option. Thus, there is a great difference between a person who starves for lack of an ability to purchase food, and one who starves in a hunger strike, voluntarily undertaken. Both may have the same level of nutrition-functioning, although their capabilities are very different.

Sen's approach inspired the United Nations Development Program (UNDP) to create its Human Development Index (HDI), which is computed for a set of 180 countries annually and published in its *Human Development Report*. The ranking of countries according to HDI is by no means the same as their ranking by GDP per capita.

## 4. RONALD DWORKIN AND RESPONSIBILITY

In 1981, Ronald Dworkin published two papers (1981a, 1981b) that were to have a major impact on egalitarian theory. He argued in the first of these papers that equality of welfare is incoherent, because of the incommensurability across persons of conceptions of well-being, and that, second, even if comparisons were possible, it would be ethically undesirable to equalize welfare because of the phenomenon of expensive tastes. Does society owe the person who only can be happy with champagne more money than it owes to her who is content with beer? Dworkin said no, and hence welfare could not be the right currency of an egalitarian theory. Rather, Dworkin said, the right egalitarian currency is *resources.* Resources, however, comprise not just wealth and commodities, but internal traits of persons that determine or limit what they can accomplish, and also, importantly, the environments and families into which they are born. To this extent, Dworkin was in Rawls's company. But he departed from Rawls in arguing that individuals are responsible for their preferences, if, indeed, they identify with them. The question for Dworkin became: What distribution of transferable resources (chiefly wealth) would engender an *overall* distribution of resources (including the inalienable ones like talents and early environments) that comprised an *equal* distribution?

For Dworkin, the natural distribution of resources is unjust, because it is unequal, but once equality of initial resources has been implemented, inequalities in outcomes which emerge from the exercise of choices emanating from preferences are morally acceptable. Although Rawls had spoken peripherally about holding persons responsible for their choice of life-plan, his discussion was sketchy and not clearly consistent with his difference principle. (If money is a primary good, and if one's income is the consequence at least in part of one's life-plan choice, and if one is responsible for one's life-plan, why should the difference principle apply to the distribution of income?) Dworkin focused upon the responsibility of individuals for their choices.

There is, Dworkin said, an important distinction between the results of what he called option and brute luck. Option luck is the consequence of events whose occurrence the individual can insure against; brute luck is uninsurable. The results of brute luck are unjust, while the results of option luck are just, because in the latter case, a person can choose to insure. Inequality of the distribution of resources allocated through the 'birth lottery' is brute luck, and hence unjust.

Dworkin proposed to rectify the brute luck of the birth lottery through an ingenious scheme, a hypothetical insurance market, in which it would be ascertained how much persons would have insured against the outcome of the birth lottery, had they had an opportunity to do so. Thus, his hypothetical insurance scheme would convert the brute luck of the birth lottery into an episode of option luck. Although the hypothetical insurance market never operates, equality of resources could be achieved by taxing individuals to mimic the results of what the insurance market would have produced.

Dworkin was not familiar with the theory of contingent claims and how economists model equilibrium in the market for insurance; he attempted to deduce what the outcome of insurance would be in an ad hoc manner. Roemer (1985) presented a general equilibrium model of Dworkin's proposal. We present a version of this model here to show that the insurance market behind Dworkin's veil of ignorance can produce outcomes quite different from what Dworkin imagined would occur. The following example is taken from Moreno-Ternero and Roemer (forthcoming).

Suppose there are two individuals, Andrea and Bob. Andrea is lucky: she has a fine constitution, and can transform resources (wealth) into welfare at a high rate. Bob is handicapped; his constitution transforms wealth into welfare at exactly one-half of Andrea's rate. In this simple example, we assume that Andrea and Bob have interpersonally comparable welfare. The internal resource which Andrea possesses and Bob lacks is a fine biological constitution.

We assume that Bob and Andrea have the same risk preferences over wealth: they are each risk averse and have the von Neumann–Morgenstern utility function $u(W) = \sqrt{W}$. Suppose that the distribution of (material) wealth in the world is $(W^A, W^B)$.

We construct Dworkin's hypothetical insurance market as follows. Behind the veil of ignorance, there is a soul Alpha who represents Andrea, and a soul Beta who represents Bob. These souls know the risk preferences of their principals, and the constitutions of Andrea and Bob, but they do not know which person they will become in the birth lottery. Thus, from their viewpoint, there are two possible states of the world, summarized in the table:

| | | |
|---|---|---|
| State 1 | Alpha becomes Andrea | Beta becomes Bob |
| State 2 | Alpha becomes Bob | Beta becomes Andrea |

Each state occurs with probability one-half. *We* know that state 1 will indeed occur, but the souls face a birth lottery with even chances, in which they can take out insurance against bad luck (i.e. becoming Bob).

There are two commodities in the insurance market: a commodity $x_1$, which pays to the owner $1 if state 1 occurs, and a commodity $x_2$ which pays $1 if state 2 occurs. Each soul can either purchase or sell these commodities: selling one unit of the first commodity entails a promise to deliver $1 to the owner, if state 1 occurs. Each soul possesses, initially, zero income with which to purchase these commodities.

It is not difficult to show that the equilibrium in this insurance market involves contracts in which, if state 1 occurs, Andrea will end up with two-thirds of the total wealth, and Bob will have one-third. Indeed, as noted, state 1 does occur. Thus Dworkin's insurance market tilts the distribution of wealth toward the able person and away from the disabled one! It does not compensate Bob for his disability, as intended.

Why does this happen? Because, even though the souls are risk averse, they are not sufficiently risk averse to induce them to shift wealth into the bad state (of turning out to be Bob); it is more worthwhile (in terms of expected utility) to use wealth in the state when it can produce a lot of welfare (when one turns out to be Andrea). If the agents were *sufficiently* risk averse, this would not occur. (If the utility function is $u(W) = W^c/c$, and $c < 0$, then Bob ends up with more wealth than Andrea.) But the example shows that in general the hypothetical insurance market does not implement the kind of compensation that Dworkin desires: for Bob is the one who suffers from a deficit in an internal resource.

Despite the problem exhibited with Dworkin's proposal, it was revolutionary in that, in the words of G. A. Cohen, it transported into egalitarian theory the most powerful tool of the anti-egalitarian Right, personal responsibility. One might argue, after seeing the above demonstration, that Dworkin's insurance market is an appealing thought experiment, and one should give up on equality. Moreno-Ternero and Roemer (forthcoming) consider this, and argue instead that the veil of ignorance is an inappropriate thought experiment for ascertaining what justice requires.

A second critique of Dworkin's contribution soon appeared. Richard Arneson (1989) argued that Dworkin was right, because of the expensive-taste argument, to say that equality of welfare was not ethically desirable, but he was wrong to propose equality of resources as the amendment: rather, one should equalize *opportunities for welfare*. Cohen (1989) argued that the introduction of responsibility into egalitarian theory was undeniably important, but that Dworkin made the wrong 'cut' between those things for which one should be held responsible and those for which one should not be. For example, if one's preferences for champagne were engendered by an aristocratic adolescence, for which one was not responsible, it did not follow that one should be held responsible for them. More saliently, perhaps, is that individuals who, because of an indigent childhood, grow up with preferences that are insufficiently ambitious should not be held responsible for those preferences. Sen (1987) had called this the 'tamed housewife' problem: one should not decree that justice had been achieved if the housewife with modest preferences was satisfied with her lot: think of illiterate Indian women with heavy burdens who report themselves happy. Indeed, Sen's point is to challenge the notion that 'happiness' (see Chapter 17) is the right currency for equality.

Where should that cut be? Cohen did not profess to solve the problem of responsibility. All one can say, in general, and tautologically, is that individuals should be indemnified against the consequences of effects for which they are not rightly held responsible, but not against the consequences of effects for which they are responsible. Conceivably, nobody is responsible for anything, and in this case, the theory would reduce to equality of condition (welfare, functioning, or whatever complex currency one decided was right). But the *facts* of responsibility are a separate question from the *principle* of compensation.

# 5. EQUALITY OF OPPORTUNITY

As mentioned, Arneson (1989) argued that the obvious alternative to equalizing welfare was not to equalize resources: it was to equalize the *opportunities* people have to acquire welfare. Here, we are reminded of Sen's capability approach. Arneson suggested that each person faces a complex decision tree of possibilities; equalizing opportunities for welfare, he proposed, meant to distribute wealth so that these trees would be isomorphic across individuals, in the sense that there would be a mapping of the paths on any tree onto the paths of any other tree in which expected welfare is preserved. The problem, however, is that there may exist no distribution of wealth for which such a set of interpersonal isomorphisms exists. Indeed, this will almost surely be the case.

Roemer (1993, 1998) proposed an algorithm to implement the equality of opportunity for welfare that Arneson had proposed. The language of Roemer's proposal comprises five words: circumstance, type, effort, objective, and policy. Circumstances are the aspects of persons for which they are not to be held responsible. Effort comprises the actions they take for which they are responsible. The set of individuals is partitioned into types, where an element of the partition consists of all those with the same circumstances. The objective is the condition for which the acquisition of opportunities is to be equalized: Roemer proposed this could be something quite concrete, such as life expectancy, or income. The policy is the intervention of the (presumably state) agency that is employed to equalize opportunities for acquisition of the objective.

What policy equalizes opportunities for acquisition of the objective? Denote the set of types for a given problem by $T$. Let us measure the degree of the acquisition of the objective by an individual of type $t$ in $T$ by a function $u^t(e, \varphi)$, where $e$ is effort and $\varphi$ is the policy. Thus, we take a statistical approach, and assume that circumstances, effort, and policy completely determine the outcome, or that $u^t(e, \varphi)$ is the average outcome for individuals of type $t$ who expend effort $e$ when the policy is $\varphi$. We assume that $u^t$ is an increasing function of $e$—thus, it is not the traditional utility function of economic theory, in which effort is often assumed to be costly to the individual. For example, the objective might be life expectancy, effort might be the degree to which one leads a healthy lifestyle, and type might be defined by socio-economic traits (class, race). Facing a given policy $\varphi$, there will ensue a distribution of effort among the individuals of type $t$: denote this distribution function by $F_\varphi^t$. The effort decision for an individual presumably is made by the maximization of some preference order, but we do not need to know the details of that process here. All that is relevant is that the individuals within a type are to be held responsible for these differences in effort, as we have decided that the circumstances (type) summarize everything for which we are *not* holding people responsible.

A key point is that the distribution function $F_\varphi^t$ is a *characteristic of the type*, not of any individual: and so, if we wish to indemnify persons against the consequences of their circumstances, we must indemnify them against the bad luck of being in a type with a poor *distribution* of effort. We thus require a measure of effort that sterilizes away the particular absolute levels of effort characteristic of the distribution $F_\varphi^t$. Roemer proposed that a suitable measure of a person's effort was the *rank* he or she occupied in the distribution of effort of her type. Thus, we would consider two persons of different types, who were at the same rank of their respective type-distributions of effort, to have behaved equally responsibly.

It follows that equality of opportunity would hold if, for any rank $\pi \in [0, 1]$, all those at rank $\pi$ in the different types acquire the objective to an equal degree. In this way, individuals would be compensated for their circumstances, but not for their effort. If we denote by $v^t(\pi, \varphi)$ the average value of the objective for all those of type $t$ who lie at the $\pi^{th}$ quantile of the effort distribution $F_\varphi^t$, then a policy $\varphi$ equalizes opportunities if:

$$\text{for all } \pi \in [0, 1] \quad \text{for all } t_1, t_2 \in T \quad v^{t_1}(\pi, \varphi) = v^{t_2}(\pi, \varphi).$$

However, such a policy will in general not exist: it would require equalizing numbers in each of an infinite number of sets simultaneously. Some second-best compromise is required. One possibility would be to choose the policy that equalized the value of the objective across types for those, say, at the medians of their type distributions of effort, that is: choose $\varphi$ so that

$$\text{for all } t_1, t_2 \quad v^{t_1}(0.5, \varphi) = v^{t_2}(0.5, \varphi).$$

Roemer proposed choosing the policy $\varphi$ to maximize the area under the lower envelope of the functions $v^t$, that is

$$\max_\varphi \int_0^1 \min_t v^t(\pi, \varphi) d\pi.$$

The conception of equal opportunity discussed here takes as data the delineation of circumstances and the space of policies. Effort is the residual which explains outcomes, once circumstances and policy are held fixed. The proposal is simply an algorithm that computes a policy that equalizes opportunities in a way consonant with these choices. In particular, if one chooses a sequence of typologies (i.e. partitions of the space of circumstances into types) which becomes increasingly fine, then the equal-opportunity policy will approach the Rawlsian policy, which maximizes the minimum value of the objective across individuals. In the other direction, viewing all individuals as members of a single type, the policy becomes utilitarian: that policy which maximizes the average value of the objective. The conception of responsibility, and hence circumstances, will fix a policy somewhere on this continuum.

Recently, Fleurbaey and Maniquet (2007, forthcoming) have extended the equal opportunity approach further, applying it to tax policy in a novel way. Indeed, they show that even without making interpersonal comparisons of the objective, as we have above, much can be said about tax policies that equalize opportunities, in the sense of not holding persons responsible for circumstances but holding them responsible for effort.

Some writers (Anderson, 1999; Scheffler, 2003; Hurley, 2003) have referred critically to the Dworkin–Arneson–Cohen–Roemer line of thought as 'luck egalitarianism'. They have written that too much attention is paid by these authors to material goods, and the allocation thereof, and that equality is more saliently conceived of as 'democratic equality', a kind of equality in human relationships in which people interact as free and equal. An excellent discussion of these critiques and rebuttals to them is found in Arneson (2004).

There have been a number of empirical applications of the equal-opportunity approach. Roemer *et al.* (2001) ask to what extent income taxation in a set of 11 advanced democracies equalizes opportunities for income acquisition, where types are defined with respect to the educational achievement or occupation of parents. Betts and Roemer (2007) compute how educational finance would be allocated in the United States, were the goal to equalize opportunities for the acquisition of wage-earning capacity among male workers. Lefranc and Trannoy (2005) compare inequality of opportunity in France and the United States. The most extended application of equal-opportunity logic is found in the World Bank's (2006) *Equity and Development*, which argues for conceptualizing development as improvement in equality of opportunity. See as well Roemer (2006a) for a comment and critique. Bourguignon, Ferreira, and Menéndez (2007) have analyzed inequality of opportunity in Brazil.

# 6. INTERGENERATIONAL AND GLOBAL EQUALITY

Thus far, the discussion has been of equality in a group of people who are citizens of a state, and exist contemporaneously. Most of the philosophical literature on equality has assumed these conditions. Nevertheless, the issues of intergenerational distribution and international distribution are extremely important.

Do the arguments for static equality imply that equality should hold across generations? This is not a settled question. Suppose one thinks that inequality is bad because of its effects on people: inequality breeds lack of self-esteem and stress. If this is the main reason to oppose inequality, then one cannot argue that intergenerational inequality is bad, for, *ex hypothesi*, members of different generations do not interact in the relevant way. On the other hand, if one endorses inequality as the fairest way of sharing scarcity, then intergenerational equality is also desirable. The earth's resources are scarce: is it not fairest to share them so as to produce equal outcomes across generations?

This view is reflected in the call for *sustainability*, a word which has two meanings in this context. One meaning is green: use the earth's resources in that way which diminishes them as little as possible. The second meaning is more human-species oriented: use the earth's resources in such a way as to engender a path of equal welfare for all future generations.

How can we state this goal in a precise way? Think of a dynamic world populated by a representative agent at each date of an infinite number of dates going indefinitely into the future. Suppose that the welfare of the generation (agent) alive at date $t$ is $u(x_t, R_t)$, a function of consumption $x_t$ and the stock of earth's resources at date $t$, $R_t$ (such as clean air, green forests, and a temperate climate). Consumption includes not only private commodities, but also public goods, the state of human knowledge, leisure, and education. At any date there is a technology $F^t$ which produces consumption vectors from commodities inherited from the past (capital), $K_{t-1}$, and newly harvested earthly resources, $r_t$. Thus a *feasible path* of consumption given an initial condition $(K_0, F^1, R_1)$ is a sequence of commodity–resource pairs $\{(x_1, R_1), (x_2, R_2), \ldots\}$ each of which is a feasible outcome given the capital stock, technology, and resource endowment of the previous period.

The intergenerational egalitarian problem is to choose that feasible path which maximizes the level of welfare that can be enjoyed by *every* generation, that is, the level that can be sustained forever.

One justification for the desirability of this kind of equality is equality of opportunity. The date at which an individual is born is a circumstance, in the sense of that theory. Hence welfare should be, so far as possible, independent of that date.

Against the desirability of the egalitarian solution, one can argue that parents want their children to be better off than they are. One can, alternatively, compute the solution to the following problem: Find the feasible path that maximizes the level of welfare of the first generation subject to permitting a growth of welfare at rate $g$ per generation forever. This might be justified on the grounds that parents want their children to be better off than they are. Clearly, the path which solves the growth program for positive $g$ will involve a sacrifice by the early generations, compared to what they receive in the solution to the sustainable program. Is this ethically acceptable?

Neither of the above approaches is, however, common in the economic literature on growth. The usual practice is to propose the 'discounted utilitarian' objective, which is to maximize the discounted sum of utilities over all future generations. The best justification of discounted utilitarianism is as follows. Suppose that there is a probability $1 - \delta$ that the human species will disappear at each date, due to global catastrophe. Suppose a planner is utilitarian, in the sense that, *if* the world were to last for precisely $T$ dates, she would want to maximize $\sum_{t=1}^{T} u(x_t, R_t)$. She faces, however, the following lottery: with probability $\delta^{T-1}(1 - \delta)$ the human species will last exactly $T$ generations (it survives the first $T - 1$ dates and implodes at date $T$). Then, if the planner's von Neumann–Morgenstern utility function is utilitarian, one can deduce that her expected utility is given by $\sum_{t=1}^{\infty} \delta^{t-1} u(x_t, R_t)$.

Despite this justification of discounted utilitarianism, the discount rates usually used by applied growth theorists are around 0.96 or 0.98. This corresponds to a probability of human-species implosion of 2 to 4% at each date, which is too high. A more appropriate discount rate would be above 0.99. But even with a more defensible discount rate, one must ask whether the underlying ethics are as cogent as the ethics behind the programs of sustainability or sustained growth.

For an attempt to calibrate the sustainability model, see Llavador, Roemer, and Silvestre (2007). For an important contribution to the debate on climate change which uses a relatively high discount factor, see Stern (2006). For critiques of the Stern report which take it to task for using too high a discount rate, see Weitzman (2007), whose critique is implicitly based upon a discounted-utilitarian ethic.

We turn finally to global equality. An analysis of global inequality is presented in Chapter 27. Here, we comment on the philosophical literature. The position of *cosmopolitanism* is that inequality between individuals of different nationalities is morally arbitrary, and hence it is desirable to annihilate global inequality, ignoring national boundaries as morally arbitrary. See Pogge (2001) for a recent discussion. Even among those who are otherwise egalitarian, there are some who do not advocate cosmopolitanism. Nagel (2005), for example, argues that the demand for equality among individuals is only ethically persuasive if they are members of a single state. Because there is no global state, there is no moral presumption of global equality. Replies to Nagel's parochial egalitarianism are found in Cohen and Sable (2006) and Julius (2006).

The issue of global equality is in the background in policy discussions of immigration, agricultural subsidies in the developed countries, and international aid. Many participants in these discussions believe that reducing global inequality is desirable. The effects of these policies on global equality are, however, highly contentious.[1]

---

[1]  Some (e.g. Easterly, 2006) argue that foreign aid does more harm than good. Rodrik (2004) maintains that agricultural subsidies to farmers in developed countries have uncertain and heterogeneous effects on income of farmers in developing countries. Roemer (2006b) argues that a global maxi-minner might well want to limit immigration into the developed North below what the 'free access' level would be.

# 7. CONCLUSION

Political philosophers have thought deeply about equality, and economists interested in inequality should pay heed to their work. Economists, generally speaking, uncritically endorse utilitarianism (in cost–benefit analysis, in taking GNP per capita as the best measure of national welfare, in growth theory, and in the influential view held by some practitioners of law and economics that laws should maximize total wealth). It is probably fair to say that a plurality of philosophers are egalitarians of some kind, and in this sense, economists are behind the times.

The currency in which equality should be measured, moreover, is not one with which economists are familiar—wealth or welfare—but something more subtle, such as opportunity or capability or advantage. Lest one think that these points are too refined or of second-order importance, consider the evaluations of ordinary people in advanced democracies today. There is much evidence that they endorse substantial inequalities because they view these as deserved, the consequence of differential effort. Or, if they view inequalities as unjust, it is because they are due to circumstances that bestow upon some people advantages for which they did not work. Thus, the philosophical ideas of self-ownership, moral arbitrariness, and equality of opportunity are present in daily discourse, if not articulated in so many words.

Philosophical sensitivity will help economists avoid mistakes. Given preference endogeneity and cognitive dissonance, what sense does it make to take happiness as the currency of equality? Just because market equilibrium is insensitive to interpersonal welfare comparisons, are such comparisons meaningless? Is a policy 'inefficient' because it does not maximize total welfare? Is meritocracy the *summum bonum* if it rewards individuals for traits they acquired by the luck of the birth lottery? Many more such questions can be posed.

## REFERENCES

ANDERSON, E. 1999. 'What is the Point of Equality?' *Ethics*, 109: 287–337.

ARNESON, R. 1989. 'Equality and Equality of Opportunity for Welfare'. *Philosophical Studies*, 56: 77–93.

——2004. 'Luck Egalitarianism Interpreted and Defended'. *Philosophical Topics*, 32(1–2): 1–20.

BETTS, J., and ROEMER, J. E. 2007. 'Equalizing Opportunity for Racial and Socioeconomic Groups in the United States through Educational Finance Reform', in P. Peterson (ed.), *Schools and the Equal Opportunity Problem*. Cambridge, Mass.: MIT Press.

BOURGUIGNON, F., FERREIRA, F., and MENÉNDEZ, M. 2007. 'Inequality of Opportunity in Brazil'. *Review of Income and Wealth*, 53: 585–618.

COHEN, G. A. 1986. 'Self-Ownership, World Ownership, and Equality', in F. Lucash (ed.), *Justice and Equality Here and Now*. Ithaca, NY: Cornell University Press.

—— 1989. 'On the Currency of Egalitarian Justice'. *Ethics*, 99: 906–44.

—— 1990. 'Equality of What? On Welfare, Goods, and Capabilities'. *Recherches Economiques*, 56(3–4).

COHEN, J., and SABLE, C. 2006. 'Extra rempublicam nullia justitia'. *Philosophy & Public Affairs*, 34: 147–75.

DWORKIN, R. 1981a. 'What is Equality? Part 1: Equality of Welfare'. *Philosophy & Public Affairs*, 10: 185–246.

—— 1981b. 'What is Equality? Part 2: Equality of Resources'. *Philosophy & Public Affairs*, 10: 283–345.

EASTERLY, W. 2006. *The White Man's Burden*. Harmondsworth: Penguin Press.

FLEURBAEY, M., and MANIQUET, F. 2007. 'Help the Low-Skilled or Let the Hardworking Thrive? A Study of Fairness in Optimal Income Taxation'. *Journal of Public Economic Theory*, 9: 467–500.

—— —— forthcoming. 'Compensation and Responsibility', in K. J. Arrow, A. K. Sen, and K. Suzumura (eds.), *Handbook of Social Choice and Welfare*, vol. 2. Amsterdam: North-Holland.

GIBBARD, A. 1976. 'Natural Property Rights'. *NOUS*, 10: 77–86.

GRUNEBAUM, J. O. 1987. *Private Ownership*. London: Routledge & Kegan Paul.

HURLEY, S. 2003. *Justice, Luck, and Knowledge*. Cambridge, Mass.: Harvard University Press.

JULIUS, A. J. 2006. 'Nagel's Atlas'. *Philosophy & Public Affairs*, 34: 176–92.

LEFRANC, A., and TRANNOY, A. 2005. 'Intergenerational Earnings Mobility in France: Is France more Mobile than the US?' *Annales d'Economie et de Statistique*, 79–80.

LLAVADOR, H., ROEMER, J. E., and SILVESTRE, J. 'A Dynamic Approach to Human Welfare'. Unpublished paper. Available at <http://pantheon.yale.edu/~jer39/>.

MORENO-TERNERO, J., and ROEMER, J., forthcoming. 'The Veil of Ignorance Violates Priority'. *Economics & Philosophy*.

NAGEL, T. 2005. 'The Problem of Global Justice', *Philosophy & Public Affairs*, 33: 114–47.

NOZICK, R. 1974. *Anarchy, State, and Utopia*. New York: Basic Books.

POGGE, T. W. (ed.) 2001. *Global Justice*. Oxford: Blackwell.

RAWLS, J. 1971. *A Theory of Justice*. Cambridge, Mass.: Harvard University Press.

RODRIK, D. 2004. 'How to Make the Trade Regime Work for Development', <http://ksghome.harvard.edu/~drodrik/How%20to%20Make%20Trade%20Work.pdf>.

ROEMER, J. E. 1985. 'Equality of Talent'. *Economics and Philosophy*, 1: 151–81.

—— 1993. 'A Pragmatic Theory of Responsibility for the Egalitarian Planner'. *Philosophy & Public Affairs*, 22: 146–66.

—— 1996. *Theories of Distributive Justice*. Cambridge, Mass.: Harvard University Press.

—— 1998. *Equality of Opportunity*. Cambridge, Mass.: Harvard University Press.

—— 2006a. 'Review Essay: The 2006 World Development Report, "Equity and Development"'. *Journal of Economic Inequality*, 4: 233–44.

—— 2006b. 'The Global Welfare Economics of Immigration'. *Social Choice and Welfare*, 27: 311–25.

—— AABERGE, R., COLOMBINO, U., FRITZELL, J., JENKINS, S., LEFRANC, A., MARX, I., PAGE, M., POMMER, E., RUIZ-CASTILLO, J., SAN SEGUNDO, M., TRANAES, T., TRANNOY, A., WAGNER, G., and ZUBIRI, I. 2003. 'To what Extent do Fiscal Systems Equalize Opportunities for Income Acquisition among Citizens?' *Journal of Public Economics*, 87: 539–65.

SCHEFFLER, S. 2003. 'What is Egalitarianism?' *Philosophy & Public Affairs*, 31: 5–39.

SEN, A. 1980. 'Equality of What?' in S. McMurrin (ed.), *The Tanner Lectures on Human Values*. Salt Lake City: University of Utah Press.

—— 1987. *The Standard of Living*. Cambridge: Cambridge University Press.

—— 1992. *Inequality Re-examined*. New York: Russell Sage Foundation.

STERN, N. 2006. *The Economics of Climate Change: The Stern Review*. Cambridge: Cambridge University Press.

VALLENTYNE, P., and STEINER, H. (eds.) 2000. *Left Libertarianism and its Critics: The Contemporary Debate*. London: Palgrave Publishers.

WEITZMAN, M. 2007. 'A Review of the Stern Review on the Economics of Climate Change'. *Journal of Economic Literature*, 45: 703–24.

WORLD BANK 2006. *World Development Report 2006: Equity and Development*. New York: Oxford University Press.

C H A P T E R  3

............................................................................................................

# THE MEASUREMENT OF ECONOMIC INEQUALITY*

............................................................................................................

## STEPHEN P. JENKINS

## PHILIPPE VAN KERM

## 1. INTRODUCTION

............................................................................................................

THIS chapter provides an introduction to methods for the measurement of economic inequality. We provide a reference point for the other chapters of the book, and a self-contained review for applied researchers more generally.[1] The focus on inequality measurement and space constraints mean that much is omitted from our

* This work was supported by core funding for the Research Centre on Micro-Social Change from the Economic and Social Research Council and the University of Essex. It is also part of the MeDIM project (Advances in the Measurement of Discrimination, Inequality and Mobility) supported by the Luxembourg Fonds National de la Recherche (contract FNR/06/15/08) and by core funding for CEPS/INSTEAD by the Ministry of Culture, Higher Education and Research of Luxembourg. We thank the editors, Tony Atkinson and other Handbook contributors for their comments and suggestions. The Stata code used to draw the figures is available from the Handbook website.

[1] For a technical review of inequality measurement, see Cowell (2000). Jenkins and Jäntti (2005) discuss special issues arising in the measurement of wealth inequality (the subject of Chapter 6). For software, see Duclos and Araar (2006) and Jenkins (2006).

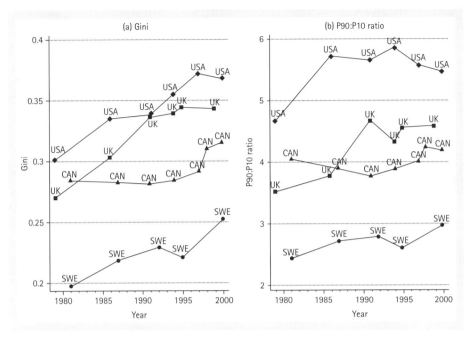

**Fig. 3.1. Inequality in Canada, Sweden, the USA, and the UK, by year**

*Source:* LIS Key Figures, accessed from <http://www.lisproject.org/figures.htm> on 6 December 2007.

review. For example, methods for the measurement of poverty are not considered.[2] Also not considered are multidimensional inequality measurement,[3] or issues of statistical inference,[4] measurement error, and robustness.[5]

To set the scene, consider Figure 3.1, which shows for four OECD countries inequality trends over 20 years according to two inequality indices. Clearly, the pattern of inequality across countries, and inequality trends within countries, depend on the index chosen. But is the Gini coefficient a better index than the P90:P10 ratio? Are there other indices which might tell a different story, and which are better in some sense? This chapter provides a review of the inequality measures that economists have developed, and explains how one might choose between indices or check whether conclusions about inequality difference can be derived without choosing any specific index. Diagrams like Figure 3.1 provide snapshots of the income distribution at particular points in time for a country, but they do not tell us whether those individuals who were poor in one year were also poor in the next year, or whether the rich stay rich. This is the subject of mobility measurement, and

---

[2]  Poverty measurement methods are surveyed by Zheng (1997). See also Chapters 11 and 13.

[3]  See Maasoumi (1986).

[4]  See *inter alia* Biewen (2002), Biewen and Jenkins (2006), Binder and Kovačević (1995), Davidson and Duclos (2000), Davidson and Flachaire (2007).

[5]  See Cowell and Flachaire (2007), Cowell and Victoria-Feser (1996, 2002), Van Praag *et al.* (1983), Van Kerm (2007).

we review this too. Figure 3.1 also raises more fundamental questions about how the distributions of economic interest are defined. We begin with this topic.

# 2. Essential Preliminaries

There are three aspects to consider: the economic variable of interest for the inequality assessment, and the demographic unit and time period to which the variable refers. The methods discussed in subsequent sections are compromised if these definitions are not right. We summarize the key issues.[6] Aspects of these topics are taken up in more detail in Chapters 4, 14, 18, and 24.

## The Variable of Interest

The two variables most commonly studied are household income and household consumption expenditure ('consumption' for short). Gross household income in a given year is the sum, across all household members, of labor market earnings from employment or self-employment, income from savings and investments, incoming private transfers such as receipts of gifts or alimony, and public transfers such as social insurance or social assistance benefits. Deducting from this total outgoing private transfers (e.g. gifts to private individuals or child support payments), and income taxes and social insurance contributions yields net (or disposable) household income. Consumption is net income minus accrued savings.

The conventional welfarist approach to measuring economic well-being suggests that consumption is a more appropriate measure for distributional analysis than income because it is consumption that enters an individual's utility function. The welfarist view is not universally accepted, however. Economic inequality is often considered to be about differences in access to or control over economic resources rather the actual exercise of that power, in which case income is the measure preferred to consumption: a miserly millionaire is considered rich rather than poor.

The definitions of income and consumption given above leave many issues of practical application unresolved, and there are conflicting principles to take into account. On the one hand, one wants as comprehensive a measure as possible for, if one neglects to take into account particular types of income or expenditure, then one will get biased measures of economic inequality, with the magnitude of

---

[6]  For longer reviews, see Expert Group on Household Income Statistics (2001) and Atkinson *et al.* (2002, especially chapter 5). On the measurement of consumption expenditure using household surveys, see Browning *et al.* (2003).

the problem depending on the importance of the source on average and how its inequality compares and correlates with other sources. On the other hand, there are issues of data quality, availability, and comparability over time or countries and regions. The more comprehensive a measure is, the greater the risk of incorporating components that are potentially measured with error, or for which valuation methods are difficult or controversial, or that are inordinately costly to collect data about.

The treatment of non-monetary (non-cash) sources of income illustrates some of these problems. These can be major sources of economic resources and substitute for money income; without them, households could have maintained consumption levels only by spending money income. Examples include subsistence agriculture and home production, publicly provided access to education and health care, and non-cash fringe benefits in employee remuneration. The importance of such sources differs across countries. For example, much effort has been given to measurement and valuation of subsistence agriculture in low-income countries but not in high-income countries. However, the issue is increasingly pertinent in the expanded EU, which now includes a large number of middle-income countries where home production plays a substantial role. Construction of the new EU Statistics on Living Conditions (EU-SILC) needs to address this issue in order to ensure cross-national comparability (see Eurostat, 2006, and the Council and European Parliament regulation 1177/2003).

Derivation of accurate measures of income from self-employment and income from financial assets such as bank deposits, bonds, stocks and shares, etc. is also a tricky issue. So, too, is the measurement of income taxes and social insurance contributions. Concerns regarding accuracy of respondent recall, respondent burden, and constraints on questionnaire length mean that many surveys do not attempt to collect this information directly from respondents, and simulation models are used to impute income tax and social insurance contributions to households. Similar issues constrain the collection of comprehensive household consumption expenditure data. Detailed diary methods are commonly used in specialist expenditure surveys but, in general purpose surveys, information about only a small number of expenditure components is typically collected; for example, food, utilities, housing, and total household expenditure may need to be imputed (see Browning *et al.*, 2003).

## The Time Period

The choice of the time period over which income is measured matters because, other things equal, lengthening the reference period will reduce measured inequality. Transitory fluctuations are smoothed out, arguably producing a more representative picture of household circumstances. In practice, however, a person's ability to smooth income over time depends on her income or assets. For example, if poor people are less able to borrow or save than rich people, then variations in their income on a week to week or month to month basis may provide a more accurate reflection of their access to resources than an annual income measure would.

Another consideration, less commonly cited, arises from the common requirement to analyze income or consumption expenditure with reference to the characteristics of the individuals or household to which the measure refers. With a short-period measure, the reference period and the members of the income or spending unit are closely matched. The longer the reference period prior to the interview, the more likely it is that the household itself may have changed composition. It is difficult to collect information about individuals who were present at some time during the reference period but who had left by the date of data collection.

The Expert Group on Household Income Statistics (2001) recommended that a year be used as the reference period on the basis that this was the natural accounting period for a number of income sources, for example, profit and loss accounts for self-employed people, or employment earnings derived from administrative sources. However the Group were also careful to note that different periods may be relevant in different contexts, especially when data are collected using household surveys. For example, if sources such as wages and salary income, or social security benefits, are paid on a regular weekly or fortnightly basis, then the respondent burden may be lower and reporting accuracy higher if a shorter reference period is used.

Many of the same issues also arise in the measurement of consumption. For example, spending over a shorter period may not measure consumption, because consumption may also be based on accumulated stocks. Spending may also reflect purchase of consumer durables that do not directly contribute to consumption.

## The Income Unit and Related Issues

In principle, income or consumption might refer to a household, a family or an individual. However, it is widely accepted that it is the income or consumption of a population of individuals that is of key interest. The analytical issue is how to measure this distribution given the data typically available.

For employment earnings, there is a one-to-one link between the income earner and the income recipient. However this is no longer true when one moves to the household level. Some individuals may not receive any income at all in their own name, and yet they benefit from income and consumption sharing within the household. The problem is that the final within-household distribution is unobserved.

The standard practice is to assume that income and consumption within households are equally shared among each household member; equivalently, each individual within the same household has the same amount, which is almost certainly wrong in most cases. Some useful progress has been initiated on this issue using economic models of family decision-making (see e.g. Bourguignon and Chiappori, 1992), but no allocation method has yet been widely acknowledged to be sufficiently accurate and reliable to implement routinely.

There are also issues of how to compare incomes (or expenditures) across recipient units of different household composition in different time periods, and located in different geographical regions within countries or between countries. Equivalence scales adjust for differences in household size and composition: $5,000 per month is of greater benefit to a single person than a family of four. Comparisons based on income per capita ignore the fact that adults and children have different needs, and that larger-sized units can benefit from economies of scale. Equivalence scales deflate household income (or expenditure) by a household-specific factor that is less than one for each extra household member, and often differentiate between adults and children.

There is a large literature concerning the appropriate relativities. Derivation methods are surveyed by Coulter et al. (1992a) who emphasize the essentially normative content of equivalence scales: a 'correct' scale cannot be determined from observational data alone. This has led to a stream of theoretical and empirical research investigating the sensitivity of distributional analyses to the choice of equivalence scale (see inter alia Buhmann et al., 1988; Coulter et al., 1992b; Jenkins and Cowell, 1994b).

For comparisons of income or expenditure for households at different dates, one requires a suitable index of inflation so that the purchasing powers of nominal amounts at different times are equivalized. The most commonly used approach is simply to deflate incomes or expenditures by an inflation index that is common to all households, that is, ignoring the fact that different inflation rates may be relevant to households of different types.

The choice of price deflators for comparisons of households across geographical regions within a country or across countries has received greater emphasis. For example, in low-income countries, there are often substantial differences in prices between urban and rural areas (see e.g. Deaton, 1997). For cross-national comparisons of income and expenditure distributions, exchange rates can provide a misleading picture of the true relative purchasing power of different currencies and be unduly influenced by foreign exchange market dealing. More appropriate are Purchasing Power Parities (PPPs). For further discussion of the issues, see, for example, Gottschalk and Smeeding (2000) and Chapters 4 and 24.

## Summary

The best measure of household income or consumption expenditure is likely to be a compromise between desired principles and necessary pragmatism, and to vary with the purpose for which the statistics are to be employed, and the context.

However, substantial progress has been made in the last decade in producing harmonized data incorporating a high degree of comparability.

An example of high quality data for studying income distribution trends over time within a given country is Britain's official income distribution statistics, the so-called Households Below Average Income series (Department for Work and Pensions, 2006). The ability to make reliable cross-national comparisons of income has been substantially advanced by the Luxembourg Income Study (<http://www.lisproject.org>). LIS produces harmonized data for a large number of countries. Atkinson *et al.* (1995) is an influential study based on it. For developing countries, the World Bank has sponsored Living Standards Measurement Surveys (LSMS) in over 40 countries since 1980, promoting a high quality research-orientated methodology (see Deaton, 1997, chapter 1). There have also been initiatives providing cross-nationally harmonized panel data such as the Cross National Equivalent File (Frick *et al.*, 2007).

# 3. CHARTING DISTRIBUTIONS

In this section, we review the main ways to summarize distributions graphically, noting that there is no obvious best way of representing income distributions graphically; each uses the same data but provides a different perspective.

We assume that all essential preliminaries have received their due attention and, for convenience, the variable of interest will be referred to as 'income', the reference period as the 'year', and the economic unit as the 'individual'. We conceptualize income as a random variable $Y$ with a distribution from which the income of each individual in a given society is drawn. The cumulative probability distribution function (CDF), $F(y) = \Pr[Y \leq y]$, shows the probability that $Y$ is smaller or equal to some value $y$. The probability density function (PDF), $f(y)$, summarizes the concentration of individual incomes at exactly $y$, with $f(y) = dF(y)/dy$. The mean is denoted $\mu_Y$. The quantile function is the inverse of the CDF, $Q(p) = F^{-1}(p)$, and shows the income value below which a fraction $0 \leq p \leq 1$ of individuals is found. The median is the income splitting the population ranked in income order into two equal-sized groups, $Q(0.5)$; the $x$th percentile is $Q(x/100)$.

## Histograms and Kernel Density Estimates

A histogram typically shows, for each of a series of income ranges ('bins'), the fraction of the population with an income in that range. This device is related

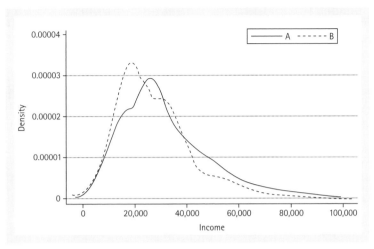

**Fig. 3.2. Probability density functions for countries A and B (kernel density estimates)**

to the CDF since the population proportion with income in some range $[a, b]$ is $(F(b) - F(a))$. If we were to make $[a, b]$ so small, so that $b$ was only infinitesimally larger than $a$, then the height of the histogram between $a$ and $b$ (divided by $b - a$) would equal the density function at $b$, $f(b)$. This suggests that the PDF might be estimated using a histogram with very narrow bin widths. This is problematic, however, because the number of sample observations is finite and so, if histogram bin widths are narrowed, then in practice, they either contain no or very few observations. Kernel density estimation avoids this problem by smoothing the histogram values over a number of overlapping income intervals (see e.g. Silverman, 1986). The idea is to take a 'window' of some chosen width, and to slide this along the income range, smoothing the histogram values as one goes, allocating a relatively high weight to observations close to the middle of the window ($y$) and a low (possibly zero) value to observations further away from $y$. The weighting function is known as a 'kernel', and there is a substantial literature about its functional form, and the appropriate width of the window.

PDFs are useful for identifying the income ranges with high concentration of incomes, the mode(s), and the overall location and spread of the distribution. Income PDFs are typically skewed to the right, with the mean above the median. This is illustrated in Figure 3.2 using data from two hypothetical countries A and B.[7] In A, the mean income is 33,897 and the median is 28,675; in B, the mean and median are 29,905 and 26,100. The 'bumps' in the PDFs may represent the aggregation of different-shaped distributions among subgroups of the population: see below.

---

[7]  For this and all subsequent graphs, we use the test data for the 'USA' (A) and 'Italy' (B), downloadable from <http://www.lisproject.org/dataaccess/stata_samplefiles.htm>.

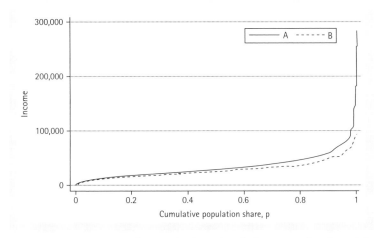

**Fig. 3.3. Pen's Parades (quantile functions) for countries A and B**

## Pen's Parade—The Quantile Function

The quantile function highlights the presence of very large incomes, and can be interpreted as follows. Suppose each individual in the population is represented by someone who has a height proportional to the individual's income. Now line these representatives up in order of height with the shortest at the front and have them all march past a certain spot in an hour. Heights increase slowly for a very long time: the person with median size walks by after half an hour, it is well over half an hour before the representative with mean income passes the finishing post, and the one with twice mean income only arrives in the last five minutes. And there is a dramatic increase in heights at the very end of the parade as the representatives of the very rich pass by. Hence Jan Pen's evocative reference to a Parade of Dwarfs and and a few Giants (Pen, 1971).[8]

Figure 3.3 illustrates the shapes of the income parades for countries A and B. There are no millionaires in these countries; if there were, the graphs would be well off the top of the page. Incomes are higher in A than in B at each point in the parade, a result that can be interpreted in terms of differences in social welfare in A and B (see below).

## Lorenz Curves

Call upon the representatives in Pen's Parade again. This time we ask each individual to put her income into a communal pot as she passes by. The Lorenz curve summarizes the cumulative amount of income in the pot as people walk by, normalized by the total amount of income in the pot at the end of the parade. By contrast, the

---

[8]  See also Jenkins and Cowell (1994a).

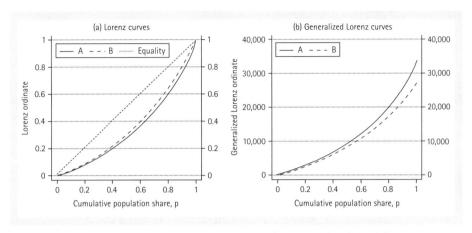

**Fig. 3.4. Lorenz and generalized Lorenz curves for countries A and B**

generalized Lorenz curve also summarizes cumulative incomes, but the normalization is instead by the total population size. Put another way, the Lorenz curve is the graph of cumulative income shares against cumulative population shares, and the generalized Lorenz curve is the Lorenz curve scaled up by mean income.

The curvature of the Lorenz curve summarizes inequality: if everyone had the same income (the perfect equality case), the Lorenz curve would lie along a 45° ray from the origin and, if all income were held by just one person (complete inequality), the curve would lie along the horizontal axis. The generalized Lorenz curve has the same general shape, but ranges from 0 to $\mu_Y$ rather than from 0 to 1. Whereas a Lorenz curve conveys information about inequality—how income shares are distributed—the generalized Lorenz curve also shows information about income levels: distributions with higher mean will finish higher on the right axis than distributions with lower mean, regardless of inequality.

Figure 3.4(a) shows the Lorenz curves for countries A and B. Although the Lorenz curve for A lies everywhere on or below that for B, A's generalized Lorenz curve is everywhere above that for B—it is pulled upwards by a mean that is larger than B's: see Figure 3.4(b). We interpret these results further below.

# 4. INEQUALITY INDICES

Many indices have been used to summarize inequality in terms of a single number. We first describe the most commonly used ones and then discuss their properties in order to identify differences in the concept of inequality encapsulated in them. We also introduce the Lorenz ordering, a concept that refers to whole classes of indices.

## Commonly Used Indices of Inequality

In statistics, the variance (or its square root, the standard deviation) is often used to summarize dispersion. One problem with the variance for inequality measurement is that, if every income is increased equiproportionately, inequality increases: the variance is not 'scale invariant'. Scale invariance is usually considered desirable: inequality should be the same for a given country regardless of whether income is expressed in euros, dollars, or yen.[9] A scale-invariant counterpart to the variance is the coefficient of variation (CV), which is the standard deviation divided by the mean. A different way of imposing scale invariance would be to take a logarithmic transformation of every income before computing the variance, thus generating the 'variance of the logs' inequality index.

Other commonly used scale-invariant indices include those based on percentile ratios, such as the ratio of the 90th percentile to the 10th percentile ('P90:P10 ratio') or, to compare dispersion at the top of the distribution with dispersion at the bottom, the P90:P50 and P50:P10 ratios. One oft-cited advantage of the P90:P10 ratio is that it avoids problems of 'top-coding' in survey data.[10] However, by their very nature, percentile ratio measures ignore information about incomes other than the percentiles selected.

Inequality indices can also be derived directly from the Lorenz curve. Because the Lorenz curve plots income shares, it is scale invariant, and so measures derived from the Lorenz curve inherit this property. One index is the Pietra ratio, also known as the Ricci-Schutz index, the Robin Hood index, or half the relative mean deviation. It is defined as the largest difference between the Lorenz curve and the perfect equality line, and is also equal to the proportion of total income that would have to be redistributed from those above the mean to those below the mean in order to achieve perfect equality.

Perhaps the most commonly used inequality index is the Gini coefficient, which ranges from 0 (perfect equality) to 1 (perfect inequality). It is the ratio of the area enclosed by the Lorenz curve and the perfect equality line to the total area below that line:[11]

$$G(Y) = 1 - 2 \int_0^1 L(p; Y) dp$$

---

[9] The variance is unchanged by equal absolute additions to each income ('translation invariant'). See Cowell (2000) and references therein for discussion of this property and absolute, intermediate, and relative inequality indices.

[10] Top-coding arises when data producers, to maximize confidentiality and minimize disclosure risk, replace all incomes above a particular value with that value (the 'top code'). See Burkhauser *et al.* (2007) and Chapters 4, 6, and 7.

[11] There are many alternative formulae: see Yitzhaki (1998).

A generalization of the Gini coefficient is the Generalized Gini (or S-Gini) class of indices (Donaldson and Weymark, 1980; Yitzhaki, 1983):

$$S_v(Y) = 1 - \int_0^1 W(p; v)L(p; Y)dp$$

where $v > 1$ and weighting function $W(p; v) = v(v - 1)(1 - p)^{v-2}$. The standard Gini coefficient arises if $v = 2$. Higher values of $v$ mean that a given income difference among bottom-ranked individuals counts more towards overall inequality than the same difference among top-ranked ones.

A family of inequality indices originating from quite different considerations (Cowell and Kuga, 1981), is the Generalized Entropy class, $E_a$, of which prominent members are the Theil index,

$$E_1(Y) = \int \frac{y}{\mu_Y} \log\left(\frac{y}{\mu_Y}\right) f(y)dy,$$

the Mean Logarithmic Deviation,

$$E_0(Y) = E_0(Y) = \int \log\left(\frac{\mu_Y}{y}\right) f(y)dy,$$

and half the squared coefficient of variation,

$$E_2(Y) = CV^2/2.$$

The general formula for Generalized Entropy indices is

$$E_a(Y) = \frac{1}{a^2 - a} \int \left(\left(\frac{y}{\mu_Y}\right)^a - 1\right) f(y)dy$$

for $a \neq 0, 1$. Different values of $a$ correspond to differences in the sensitivity of the inequality index to differences in income shares in different parts of the income distribution. The more negative that $a$ is, the more sensitive is the index to differences in income shares among the poorest incomes; the more positive that $a$ is, the more sensitive is the index to differences in income shares among the rich. A useful feature of the Generalized Entropy class is that every member is additively decomposable by population subgroup: see Section 6.

Finally, there is the Atkinson family of inequality measures (Atkinson, 1970):

$$A_\varepsilon(Y) = 1 - \left(\int \left(\frac{y}{\mu_Y}\right)^{1-\varepsilon} f(y)dy\right)^{\frac{1}{1-\varepsilon}}$$

where $\varepsilon > 0$, and $\varepsilon \neq 1$, and

$$A_1(Y) = 1 - \exp\left(\int \ln\left(\frac{y}{\mu_Y}\right) f(y)dy\right).$$

$\varepsilon > 0$ is an inequality-aversion parameter that we discuss later. The Atkinson and Generalized Entropy measures are closely related. For each value of $\varepsilon$, there is a Generalized Entropy index $E_a$ with $a = 1 - \varepsilon$ that ranks a pair of distributions in the same way as $A_\varepsilon$.

## Properties of Inequality Measures

One way to choose between the large number of inequality indices available is to evaluate them in terms of their properties. We have already encountered the scale invariance property. Another property is 'replication invariance': it holds if a simple replication of the population of individuals and their incomes does not change aggregate inequality. The symmetry (or anonymity) axiom says that the index depends only on the income values used to construct it and not additional information such as who the person is with a particular income. This property underlines the importance of equivalization: if incomes were not adjusted to take account of differences in household size and composition, then these characteristics would be relevant for inequality assessments.

A fourth and fundamental property is the Principle of Transfers. Consider some distribution $A$ from which a person (labeled $i$) is arbitrarily chosen. Now form a new distribution $B$ by transferring a small amount of income from person $i$ to a poorer person $j$, though keeping $i$ richer overall. This is a Pigou-Dalton transfer, also called a progressive transfer. Most people would agree that inequality falls in going from $A$ to $B$, though they may disagree about how much. An inequality measure $I$ satisfying $I(A) > I(B)$ is said to satisfy the Principle of Transfers.

For infinitesimal transfers of the type described, the Principle of Transfers reduces to the condition $dI < 0$, where

$$dI = \left(\frac{\partial I}{\partial y_j}\right) dy_j + \left(\frac{\partial I}{\partial y_i}\right) dy_i = dy \left[\frac{\partial I}{\partial y_j} - \frac{\partial I}{\partial y_i}\right],$$

and the change in inequality, $dI$, is the total differential of $I$ and, by construction, the transfer $dy_i = -dy_j$.[12] Views about the precise size of the inequality reduction from the transfer $dy$ are likely to depend on the income level of the recipient. Taking two pairs of individuals the same income distance apart, where one pair is relatively rich and the other relatively poor, many would argue that a given transfer from richer to poorer should reduce inequality more for the second pair than the first. Inequality measures satisfying this property are known as 'transfer sensitive' (Shorrocks and Foster, 1987).

It can be shown that the Principle of Transfers is satisfied by the Gini, Generalized Entropy, and Atkinson indices, but not by percentile ratio indices, the variance of

---

[12] Jenkins (1991) evaluates the expressions for various indices and provides more extensive discussion.

logs, or the Pietra ratio. All Atkinson indices are transfer-sensitive but the CV, for instance, is not. Nor are Generalized Gini indices because of their dependence on ranks rather than income.

## The Lorenz Ordering

Lorenz curves have a useful role to play other than as descriptive devices. A key result is that if the Lorenz curves of two distributions do not cross, that is, $L(p; A) \leq L(p; B)$ for any cumulative population share $p$ (and the two Lorenz curves are not identical), then one can conclude unambiguously that inequality is higher in distribution $A$ than in distribution $B$ according to any inequality index that respects the properties of scale invariance, replication invariance, symmetry, and the Principle of Transfers (Foster, 1985). Distribution $B$ is said to Lorenz-dominate distribution $A$. With non-intersecting Lorenz curves, it does not matter whether one chooses Generalized Entropy measures, Atkinson indices, or Generalized Gini coefficients to compare inequality in $A$ and $B$: in every case, inequality would be higher for distribution $A$. This is what we saw in Figure 3.4(a).

The Lorenz curve ordering is only partial. Unambiguous conclusions cannot be drawn when Lorenz curves intersect unless further restrictions are placed on the inequality measure. For example, if two Lorenz curves cross only once, and if (i) the Lorenz curve for $A$ crosses the Lorenz curve for $B$ from above and (ii) CV($A$) $\leq$ CV($B$), then inequality is lower in $A$ for any transfer-sensitive inequality measure (Dardanoni and Lambert, 1988; Davies and Hoy, 1995; Shorrocks and Foster, 1987). Thus comparisons of CVs may result in unambiguous inequality orderings according to a broad class of inequality indices.

## 5. SOCIAL WELFARE AND INEQUALITY

It is standard practice to evaluate policy outcomes with reference to their effects on social welfare where this is evaluated using a social welfare function (SWF) that aggregates information about the income distribution into a single number. Inequality indices aggregate incomes and so are a form of SWF. This suggests that another systematic approach to inequality measurement could be to start with a SWF known to incorporate specific ethical principles, and then to derive an inequality index from this, knowing that it must reflect these same properties.

## Properties of Social Welfare Functions

The following properties are commonly imposed on the SWF. First, the SWF is individualistic and satisfies the Pareto principle, that is, if the income of one person increases and the income of no other person decreases, then the SWF must record an improvement in social welfare or at least leave it unchanged. Second, the SWF satisfies symmetry, as for inequality indices. Third, the SWF is usually assumed to be additive in individual utilities, where utility for person $i$ is a function of her income only, $U(y_i)$. Social welfare is then the average of the individual utilities:

$$W(Y) = \int U(y)f(y)dy.$$

Fourth, it is typically assumed that $U$ is concave. In other words, the social marginal utility of income for each income not only increases with income but increases at a decreasing rate $(\partial U^2(y)/\partial y^2 \leq 0)$. This is fundamental because it implies social preference for equality, guaranteeing that a Pigou-Dalton transfer increases aggregate social welfare.

Two routes can be taken from here. First, as for the Lorenz ordering, one may look for criteria that lead to unambiguous orderings of distributions using only these properties. Clear-cut conclusions derived using this approach are robust in the sense that they rely on relatively few assumptions. However, there is no guarantee that one will be able to order any two distributions. A second route is to select a particular functional form for the SWF, and to compare scalar values for estimated SWFs. We discuss these two strategies next.

## Stochastic Dominance and the SWF Ordering

A powerful result links social welfare orderings with configurations of generalized Lorenz curves: if the generalized Lorenz curve for distribution $A$ lies nowhere below that for distribution $B$, then social welfare is higher in distribution $A$ than in $B$ according to any individualistic, symmetric, increasing, and concave SWF (Shorrocks, 1983). This was the configuration shown in Figure 3.4(b) and, for countries A and B, the social welfare ordering is the reverse of the inequality ordering.

It is also possible to compare distributions without using the concavity assumption. If the quantile function for $A$ lies above that for $B$, then social welfare is higher in society $A$ according to any individualistic, symmetric, and increasing SWF (cf. Figure 3.3). Quantile function dominance implies generalized Lorenz dominance.

An equivalent set of conditions is stochastic dominance (Hadar and Russell, 1969; Saposnik, 1981). First-order stochastic dominance involves comparisons of CDFs. If the CDF of distribution $A$ lies below the CDF of $B$ then social welfare is higher in

$A$ according to any individualistic, anonymous, and increasing SWF. This result is unsurprising because comparisons of CDFs are equivalent to comparisons of quantile functions. Second-order stochastic dominance involves comparisons of cumulations of CDFs. Dominance of $A$ over $B$ at the second order is equivalent to generalized Lorenz dominance—social welfare is higher in $A$ for any individualistic, symmetric, increasing, and concave SWF. Higher-order dominance can be checked by continuing the sequence and comparing cumulations of the curves obtained at the lower order. Increasing the order imposes stricter restrictions on higher-order derivatives of the $U(\cdot)$ function. For example, third-order dominance corresponds to an ordering of distributions according to SWFs that are transfer sensitive.

## SWF-based Inequality Indices

Dominance checks may not yield clear-cut orderings and, in any case, one may wish to estimate the magnitude of a difference in social welfare. For this purpose, one needs to specify a particular functional form for the SWF. The standard assumption made, in addition to the four properties stated above, is that individual utility functions have constant elasticity. Equiproportionate changes in each individual's income change total social welfare by the same proportion. The constant elasticity assumption leads to a specification for $U_\varepsilon(y)$ of the form

$$U_\varepsilon(y) = y^{1-\varepsilon} / (1 - \varepsilon), \quad \varepsilon \neq 1,$$

with $\varepsilon > 0$ to ensure concavity, and with $U_1(y) = \ln(y)$ as the limiting case when $\varepsilon = 1$.

This can also serve as a basis for developing SWF-based inequality measures. Consider the income that, if it were received by every individual in a hypothetical, inequality-free society, would generate the same social welfare as observed in $Y$. This income is the equally distributed equivalent income, $\xi$, satisfying $W(\xi(Y; W)) = W(Y)$, and with a social preference for equality, $\xi \leq \mu_Y$. The welfare loss from inequality is an inequality index:

$$I(Y) = 1 - (\xi / \mu_Y).$$

In the constant elasticity case, this formula characterizes the Atkinson class of inequality indices with $\varepsilon$ being the constant elasticity parameter. Larger values of $\varepsilon$ correspond to a greater concern for inequality differences towards the bottom of the distribution (greater 'inequality aversion').[13]

---

[13] Generalized Gini inequality indices can be similarly motivated: set $U(y) = v(1 - F(y))^{v-1}y$, $v > 1$.

# 6. Explaining Inequality: Decomposition and Regression Methods

Having summarized inequality, one might now ask how income differences within particular groups of a society combine to shape the overall level of inequality, or how overall inequality is related to the different types of income comprising an individual's total income. Breaking down inequality into its components helps one to explain the aggregate. Two main types of decomposition approach can be distinguished: non-regression-based approaches and multivariate regression-based approaches.

## Decompositions by Factor Components and by Population Subgroups

Household income is the sum of income from different sources, for example, labor income, capital income, transfers, etc.: $y_i = \sum_{k=1}^{K} y_i^k$. Decompositions by factor components identify the contribution of each factor source, $k$, to total inequality. Shorrocks (1982) proved that, given a set of 'reasonable' assumptions, the share of total inequality that is accounted for by factor $k$ is:

$$s_k = \frac{\text{Cov}(Y^k, Y)}{\sigma^2(Y)} = \rho(Y^k, Y) \times \frac{\mu_Y^k}{\mu_Y} \times \frac{\text{CV}(Y^k)}{\text{CV}(Y)}$$

for all standard inequality indices. Observe that $s_k$ does not depend on which inequality index is decomposed: the decomposition rule is independent of the inequality measure. The equation shows that the factor inequality shares depend on the correlation between the factor and total income ($\rho(Y^k, Y)$), the share of the factor in total income, and inequality of the source relative to the inequality of total income, where inequality is summarized using the CV. Factors may have equalizing effects on inequality of total incomes, when $\rho(Y^k, Y)$ and therefore $s_k$ is negative, whereas other factors may be disequalizing as when $\rho(Y^k, Y)$ and $s_k$ are positive. For example, we expect social security transfers to be inequality reducing while labor and capital income tend to be inequality increasing.[14]

   Decompositions by population subgroups begin with a partition of the population into $M$ distinct non-overlapping groups of individuals, defined by characteristics such as, for example, age, sex, workforce attachment, etc. Decompositions by population subgroup allow the disaggregation of overall inequality into the contribution arising from the inequality within each of the groups and the contribution

---

[14]   For non-axiomatic approaches, see e.g. Fei *et al.* (1978) and Lerman and Yitzhaki (1985).

from inequality between the groups.[15] For example, does overall wage inequality largely reflect wage differences within skill groups, or wage differences between skill groups?

Generalized Entropy inequality indices have played a special role because they are decomposable by population subgroup.[16] In particular, we can write total inequality as the sum of the inequality between groups and the inequality within groups, where the latter is the weighted sum of the inequalities within each subgroup:

$$E_a(Y) = E_a^B(Y) + E_a^W(Y)$$

with

$$E_a^W(Y) = \sum_{m=1}^{M} v_m^a \omega_m^{1-a} E_a(Y^{(m)})$$

where $v_m$ is subgroup $m$'s share of total income, $\omega_m$ is $m$'s population share, and $E_a(Y^{(m)})$ is the inequality within $m$. Between-group inequality, $E_a^B$, is the inequality obtained by imputing to each person the mean income of the subgroup to which she belongs. Other inequality measures cannot be so conveniently expressed.[17]

Graphical tools can also be used to undertake decompositions by population subgroup because a PDF for a population can be expressed as the population share-weighted sum of the PDFs for each subgroup. If the number of groups is small, it is easy to visualize changes in subgroup relative incomes (between-group inequality), the shapes of each subgroup distribution, and the relative sizes of the groups (Jenkins and Van Kerm, 2005). A development of this idea is discussed further below.

## Regression-Based Methods

Decomposition methods are useful for describing the structure of income distributions, but differ in nature from the multivariate regression tools that economists instinctively use to explain incomes and their distribution. We now consider some regression-based approaches to explaining distributions. See Lemieux (2002) for a detailed discussion of alternative approaches.

Suppose that each individual's income depends on her observed characteristics, the 'returns' to those characteristics, and unobserved characteristics. If the relationship is assumed to take the standard linear regression form—income is the

[15] See Shorrocks (1984) for a formal characterization of subgroup-decomposable inequality indices.

[16] For an application combining decompositions by population subgroup and factor components, see Jenkins (1995).

[17] Decomposition of the Gini requires a third term if the subgroup income ranges overlap. The three-term decomposition has useful interpretations in particular contexts: see e.g. Aronson and Lambert (1994). On Atkinson index decomposition, see Blackorby et al. (1981).

sum of each characteristic times its return (regression coefficient) plus an 'error' term summarizing unobservable factors—then, it is straightforward to show that the difference in means of two distributions $A$ and $B$ can be expressed as an exact linear function of a term representing differences in observed characteristics plus a term representing differences in returns to those. This is the celebrated Oaxaca-Blinder method for decomposing differences between the means of two distributions (Blinder, 1973; Oaxaca, 1973).

This framework has two limitations: it only considers differences in mean outcomes, although distributions may vary in other important respects, such as their dispersion, and the decomposition relies heavily on the linear regression functional form. These issues have been addressed in a number of ways. Whereas the classic linear regression approach links the mean of a distribution to observed characteristics, the quantile regression approach expresses each of a number of quantiles (e.g. the median, upper, and lower quartiles) to observed characteristics, and provides a more comprehensive picture of the whole conditional distribution and of the effect of covariates on the location and shape of the distribution.[18]

Other approaches include modeling the conditional distribution itself, rather than the quantiles. For example, one can assume that the income distribution is described by a parametric functional form and express each of the parameters as a regression function of observed characteristics. Thus, Biewen and Jenkins (2005), for example, employ the Singh-Maddala functional form and relate cross-national differences in income distribution to differences in characteristics and differences in returns to those characteristics. Semi-parametric approaches to modeling the whole distribution have also been proposed, of which a leading example is Donald *et al.* (2000).

Another strand of literature, initiated by DiNardo *et al.* (1996), has modeled the whole distribution (PDF) non-parametrically using a clever variation on the kernel density estimation methods reviewed earlier. Suppose we wish to relate changes in the distribution of income between Year 1 and Year 2 to changes in the income distribution for particular groups and to changes in the relative sizes of these groups. The difference in PDFs between the two years is:

$$\Delta f^{(1,2)}(y) \equiv f^{(2)}(y) - f^{(1)}(y).$$

Since the PDF is additively decomposable, it may be written as the weighted sum (integral) of the PDF for each subgroup of individuals that is implicitly defined by a particular combination of observed characteristics:

$$f^{(m)}(y) = \int f^{(m)}(y|X)g^{(m)}(X)dX.$$

---

[18]  Koenker and Hallock (2001) review quantile regression methods. The methods are applied to wage inequality by Buchinsky (1994), Gosling *et al.* (2000), and Mata and Machado (2005).

The goal is to decompose the overall PDF change $\Delta f^{(1,2)}(y)$ into differences attributable to changes in the conditional distributions $f^{(m)}(y|X)$ and changes in group sizes as defined by changes in the configuration of covariates $g^{(m)}(X)$. The decomposition is unproblematic if the number of covariate combinations is small but, if it is large (the typical case), accurate estimation is difficult.

DiNardo *et al.* (1996) saw that this problem could be circumvented by using reweighting methods. A reweighting function is defined, and expressed using Bayes Rule, as

$$\psi^{(1,2)}(X) = \frac{g^{(1)}(X)}{g^{(2)}(X)} = \frac{\Pr[m=1|X]}{\Pr[m=2|X]} \times \frac{\Pr[m=2]}{\Pr[m=1]}.$$

$\Pr[m=i|X]$ is the probability that a randomly selected individual with characteristics $X$ belongs to group $i$ if individuals from both groups are pooled in a common population. $\Pr[m=i]$ is the probability that any randomly selected individual belongs to group $i$ after pooling the groups. Whereas $g^{(m)}(X)$ is a multidimensional function difficult to estimate, the four probabilities in the expression above are relatively easy to compute from probit regression estimates, and can be used to derive weights. Thus explanation of overall distributional change is accomplished by a sophisticated 'what if' exercise. This simulates the effects of compositional changes using weighted kernel density estimation (with weights derived as discussed), and infers the effect of subgroup distributional change from the difference that remains after taking account of the effects of composition differences.[19]

# 7. INCOME MOBILITY AND INEQUALITY

All the methods considered so far summarize an income distribution at a point in time or consider differences between distributions across time or space or groups. But this snapshot information does not tell us how income changes over time for each individual within the population. Income mobility analysis provides tools for summarizing this. Information about income mobility enables us to link inequality at a point in time to inequality over the longer term. High point-in-time inequality combined with high mobility can result in low long-term inequality. It is this instrumental role of mobility as an equalizer of long-term attainments that leads some to argue that more of it is desirable.

Assessments of mobility involve additional considerations, however (Gottschalk and Spolaore, 2002). First, high mobility involves considerable income fluctuation over time. Because individuals typically prefer income stability, other things being

---

[19] See Daly and Valletta (2006) and Hyslop and Maré (2005) for recent applications.

equal, fluctuations provide a potentially offsetting force to the welfare gains of lowering long-term inequality. Second, the unpredictability of fluctuations *per se* is a second potentially offsetting force. Greater uncertainty about future outcomes reduces the utility of risk-averse individuals. These multiple considerations mean that mobility analysis is inherently complex.[20]

## Representing Mobility

Graphical representation of mobility patterns is complicated because of the multiple dimensions. When comparing mobility between two periods, two methods are a scatter plot of the (Year 1, Year 2) pairs of income for each individual, or a three-dimensional density plot of the two-period joint distribution (see Chapter 20). Unfortunately, both density plots and the related contour plots are hard to interpret and compare. Trede (1998) suggests plotting smoothed estimates of the distribution of $Y_2$ at each $Y_1 = y$ value using smoothed quantile regressions. Van Kerm (2006) proposes a visualization in which the conditional expectation of a summary measure of individual-level income change is plotted against individuals' ranks in the initial income distribution. This 'mobility profile' is straightforward to interpret and is directly related to a number of mobility indices. As soon as one considers mobility over more years than two, the representation problem becomes even more complex. Virtually all mobility indices have been developed for the two-period case.

Dominance criteria for unambiguous mobility comparisons are few, and rarely applied. The most well-known criterion is based on checks for bivariate stochastic dominance (Atkinson, 1983; see also Dardanoni, 1993).

## Properties of Mobility Indices

There is no consensus about the properties that mobility indices should respect. For example, although scale invariance is widely accepted as an axiom for inequality indices, invariance properties for mobility indices are not. So, there are many different indices, and they encapsulate different mobility concepts (Fields, 2000).[21] See the reviews by Maasoumi (1998) and Fields and Ok (1999a) and Chapter 21.

To assess the numerous measures, it is useful to compare them under four headings. First, measures differ about the pattern of mobility that is associated with the maximum possible. Some measures attain their maximum when there is

---

[20]  Income mobility, within and across generations, is itself the subject of two chapters (see Chapters 20 and 21).

[21]  This is a matter of empirical relevance too, as different approaches have led to different conclusions (Cecchi and Dardanoni, 2003; Van Kerm, 2004).

a complete reversal of individuals' fortunes. By contrast, some mobility measures attain their maximum when Year 2 circumstances are independent of Year 1 circumstances. Independence from origin links mobility with concerns about equality of opportunity. And some measures do not have any maximum mobility reference.

Second, there is the question of whether a mobility index is sensitive to changes in the marginal distribution or only to churning of individuals within the distribution. Structural mobility is mobility due to changes in the distribution of income, which may be contrasted with exchange mobility which is due to changes in the relative ranks of individuals in the distribution (Markandya, 1984). Exchange mobility measures record zero mobility if everyone maintains the same rank in the income parade between any two time periods, and its value is unaffected by any monotonic transformation of incomes at any time period. By contrast, structural measures may register mobility even in the absence of reranking provided nominal incomes attached to ranks are changing. Exchange mobility measures are often seen as pure mobility indicators that are immune to undue influence of changes in marginal distributions. However, considerations of economic growth or redistribution of resources are discarded.

Third, there are scale-invariance and translation-invariance issues. Measures are strongly relative (intertemporal scale invariant) if equiproportionate income growth does not affect the mobility assessment. Measures are said to be weakly relative (or scale invariant) if the units in which income are measured are irrelevant but, by contrast with strongly relative measures, equiproportionate income growth may count as mobility. There are also translation-invariance counterparts of these properties. Exchange mobility indices satisfy both intertemporal translation and scale invariance.

Fourth, there is the issue of directionality, which refers to the roles played by the base year and current year in mobility assessments. An index is directional if it matters whether a particular income change refers to a change from a base year to a current year or vice versa. This is relevant if one wishes to take the temporal ordering of changes into account.

## A Selection of Mobility Indices

We now indicate the variety of mobility indices and their different properties. First we consider two-period distance-based mobility measures. These are all population averages of some function $\delta(y_1, y_2; H)$ that captures the degree of individual-level mobility associated with any income pair $(y_1, y_2)$:

$$M(Y_1, Y_2) = \int \delta(y_1, y_2; H) dH(y_1, y_2),$$

where $H$ is the bivariate CDF.

Fields and Ok's (1996) index arises when $\delta(y_1, y_2; H) = |y_1 - y_2|$. It captures the magnitude of income movements non-directionally, placing no specific value on reranking or inequality, but directly assesses the magnitude of income change. There is no upper limit to mobility and the measure is only translation invariant. Fields and Ok's (1999b) index has $\delta(y_1, y_2; H) = |\log(y_1) - \log(y_2)|$, and so has similar properties except that it is scale invariant.

Hart's index is equal to $1 - r(\log(y_1), \log(y_2))$, where $r(\cdot)$ is Pearson's correlation coefficient (Hart, 1976).[22] The index is symmetric, scale invariant and translation invariant, and also intertemporally scale and translation invariant. Maximum mobility is achieved with a perfect negative correlation of incomes.

The average rank-jump index has $\delta(y_1, y_2; H) = |F_1(y_1) - F_2(y_2)|$. It focuses entirely on income ranks rather than income levels and is therefore a pure exchange mobility index. It is non-directional, and intertemporally scale and translation invariant. Maximum mobility is attained if income ranks are completely reversed.

Jenkins and Van Kerm (2006) proposed a distance-based mobility index based on changes in income ranks. Suppose we let

$$\delta(y_1, y_2; H) = [w\ (F_1(y_1); v) - w\ (F_2(y_2); v)]\ y_2 / \mu(Y_2)$$

where $w(p; v) = v(1 - p)^{v-1}$, $v > 1$, is a function that attaches greater weight to people with low rank in $F_t$ the greater that $v$ is. This index provides a neat way to link changes in cross-sectional inequality over time with income mobility. Jenkins and Van Kerm (2006) show that change in the Generalized Gini coefficient over time is equal to this reranking index minus a measure of the progressivity of income growth (the extent to which income growth is experienced by the poor rather than the rich, itself a type of income-movement mobility index). One implication of this identity is that, even if income growth is pro-poor, inequality may rise over time if reranking more than offsets pro-poor income growth.

A second group of measures includes those that summarize mobility in terms of the extent to which it reduces inequality over time. Shorrocks' index (Shorrocks, 1978) is the most popular index of this group. The idea is that, if one were to longitudinally average each person's income over a number of years, the inequality in these averaged incomes would be less than average annual inequality because each individual's income fluctuations would be smoothed out and no longer contribute to overall dispersion. Mobility is then defined as the proportionate reduction in inequality of aggregated incomes compared to the average of inequality in the marginal distributions. The index is non-directional and scale invariant, but not intertemporal scale invariant. One feature of the Shorrocks mobility index which distinguishes it from all the others cited earlier is that it is well-defined for any number of time periods, not just two. See Chapter 21 for more extensive discussion and empirical illustrations.

---

[22] Cecchi and Dardanoni (2003) give the expression for $\delta(y_1, y_2; H)$ in this case.

# 8. Conclusions and Further Research

What are the priorities for future research on the measurement of economic inequality? Perhaps heretically in the context of a chapter like ours, we suggest that substantial progress on analytical measurement methods has been made and that other developments should receive greater priority, with the exception of further work on mobility measurement as that subject is much less mature. We would give higher priority to the following topics instead.

First, we have emphasized the importance of getting the essential preliminaries right. Choosing the correct PPP exchange rate for cross-national comparisons and global assessments is one example of this, as emphasized in Chapters 4, 23, and 24. Second, we suggest that work should also continue to be devoted to improvements in data quality broadly interpreted. This could include a range of activities, including, for example, improving survey population coverage and response rates, methods of imputation, or collecting more comprehensive but comparable measures of income or consumption expenditure. It is also likely to be valuable to explore further the role of administrative data *vis-à-vis* social surveys, whether used alone or linked. The former are typically much larger and measurement error may be less, but there are issues about coverage, the variables available, and access by researchers. Third, alongside these improvements in data, we would support further development of methods to handle many of the issues that routinely arise with data, including sampling variation, measurement error, outliers, and their implications for non-robustness.

Development of explanatory models of the income distribution, theoretical and empirical, is a fourth priority area. As one of us has said elsewhere, 'Perhaps the greatest challenge is to develop more comprehensive models of the household income distribution, incorporating not only models of labour market earnings but also reflecting income from other sources including social benefits and investment income, and the demographic factors affecting who lives with whom' (Jenkins and Micklewright, 2007: 19).

## References

Aronson, J. R., and Lambert, P. J. 1994. 'Decomposing the Gini Coefficient to Reveal Vertical, Horizontal and Reranking Effects of Income Taxation'. *National Tax Journal*, 47: 273–94.

Atkinson, A. B. 1970. 'On the Measurement of Inequality'. *Journal of Economic Theory*, 2: 244–63.

——— 1983. 'The Measurement of Economic Mobility', in A. B. Atkinson (ed.), *Social Justice and Public Policy*. Harvester Wheatsheaf: Hemel Hempstead, UK, 61–75.

ATKINSON, A. B., CANTILLON, B., MARLIER, E., and NOLAN, B. 2002. *Social Indicators: The EU and Social Inclusion*. Oxford: Oxford University Press.

—— RAINWATER, L., and SMEEDING, T. M. 1995. *Income Distribution in OECD Countries: Evidence from the Luxembourg Income Study (LIS)*, Social Policy Studies, No. 18. Paris: Organisation for Economic Co-operation and Development.

BIEWEN, M. 2002. 'Bootstrap Inference for Inequality, Mobility and Poverty Measurement'. *Journal of Econometrics*, 108: 317–42.

—— and JENKINS, S. P. 2005. 'Accounting for Differences in Poverty between the USA, Britain and Germany'. *Empirical Economics*, 30: 331–58.

—— —— 2006. 'Variance Estimation for Generalized Entropy and Atkinson Inequality Indices: The Complex Survey Data Case'. *Oxford Bulletin of Economics and Statistics*, 68: 371–83.

BINDER, D. A., and KOVAČEVIĆ, M. S. 1995. 'Estimating some Measures of Income Inequality from Survey Data: An Application of the Estimating Equations Approach'. *Survey Methodology*, 21: 137–45.

BLACKORBY, C., DONALDSON, D., and AUERSPERG, M. 1981. 'A New Procedure for the Measurement of Inequality within and among Population Subgroups'. *Canadian Journal of Economics*, 14: 665–85.

BLINDER, A. 1973. 'Wage Discrimination: Reduced Form and Structural Estimates'. *Journal of Human Resources*, 8: 436–55.

BOURGUIGNON, F., and CHIAPPORI, P.-A. 1992. 'Collective Models of Household Behaviour: An Introduction'. *European Economic Review*, 36: 355–65.

BROWNING, M., CROSSLEY, T. F., and WEBER, G. 2003. 'Asking Consumption Questions in General Purpose Surveys'. *Economic Journal*, 113: F540–67.

BUCHINSKY, M. 1994. 'Changes in U.S. Wage Structure 1963–1987: An Application of Quantile Regression'. *Econometrica*, 62: 405–58.

BUHMANN, B., RAINWATER, L., SCHMAUS, G., and SMEEDING, T. M. 1988. 'Equivalence Scales, Well-being, Inequality and Poverty: Sensitivity Estimates across Ten Countries using the Luxembourg Income Study (LIS) Database'. *Review of Income and Wealth*, 43: 319–34.

BURKHAUSER, R. V., FENG, S., and JENKINS, S. P. 2007. 'Using the P90/P10 Index to Measure US Inequality Trends with Current Population Survey Data: A View from Inside the Census Bureau Vaults'. ISER Working Paper 2007-14, Institute for Social and Economic Research, University of Essex, Colchester, UK, <http://www.iser.essex.ac.uk/pubs/workpaps/pdf/2007-14.pdf>.

CECCHI, D., and DARDANONI, V. 2003. 'Mobility Comparisons: Does Using Different Measures Matter?' *Research on Economic Inequality*, 9: 113–45.

COULTER, F., COWELL, F. A., and JENKINS, S. P. 1992a. 'Differences in Needs and Assessment of Income Distributions'. *Bulletin of Economic Research*, 44: 77–124.

—— —— —— 1992b. 'Equivalence Scale Relativities and the Extent of Inequality and Poverty'. *Economic Journal*, 102: 1067–82.

COWELL, F. A. 2000. 'Measurement of Inequality', in A. B. Atkinson and F. Bourguignon (eds.), *Handbook of Income Distribution*. Amsterdam: North-Holland, 87–166.

—— and FLACHAIRE, E. 2007. 'Income Distribution and Inequality Measurement: The Problem of Extreme Values'. *Journal of Econometrics*, 105: 1044–72.

—— and KUGA, K. 1981. 'Inequality Measurement: An Axiomatic Approach'. *European Economic Review*, 15: 287–305.

——and VICTORIA-FESER, M.-P. 1996. 'Robustness Properties of Inequality Measures'. *Econometrica*, 64: 77–101.

————2002. 'Welfare Rankings in the Presence of Contaminated Data'. *Econometrica*, 70: 1221–33.

DALY, M. C., and VALLETTA, R. G. 2006. 'Inequality and Poverty in the United States: The Effects of Rising Dispersion of Men's Earnings and Changing Family Behaviour'. *Economica*, 73: 75–98.

DARDANONI, V. 1993. 'Measuring Social Mobility'. *Journal of Economic Theory*, 61: 372–94.

——and LAMBERT, P. J. 1988. 'Welfare Rankings of Income Distributions: A Role for the Variance and some Insights for Tax Reform'. *Social Choice and Welfare*, 5: 1–17.

DAVIDSON, R., and DUCLOS, J.-Y. 2000. 'Statistical Inference for Stochastic Dominance and for the Measurement of Poverty and Inequality'. *Econometrica*, 68: 1435–64.

——and FLACHAIRE, E. 2007. 'Asymptotic and Bootstrap Inference for Inequality and Poverty Measures'. *Journal of Econometrics*, 141: 141–66.

DAVIES, J. B., and HOY, M. 1995. 'Making Inequality Comparisons when Lorenz Curves Intersect'. *American Economic Review*, 85: 980–6.

DEATON, A. 1997. *The Analysis of Household Surveys*. Baltimore: The Johns Hopkins University Press for the World Bank.

Department for Work and Pensions. 2006. *Households Below Average Income: An Analysis of the Income Distribution 1994/5–2004/5*. Leeds: Corporate Document Services.

DINARDO, J., FORTIN, N. M., and LEMIEUX, T. 1996. 'Labor Market Institutions and the Distribution of Wages, 1973–1992: A Semiparametric Approach'. *Econometrica*, 64: 1001–44.

DONALD, S. G., GREEN, D. A., and PAARSCH, H. J. 2000. 'Differences in Wage Distributions between Canada and the United States: An Application of a Flexible Estimator of Distribution Functions in the Presence of Covariates'. *Review of Economic Studies*, 67: 609–33.

DONALDSON, D., and WEYMARK, J. A. 1980. 'A Single-Parameter Generalization of the Gini Indices of Inequality'. *Journal of Economic Theory*, 22: 67–86.

DUCLOS, J.-Y., and ARAAR, A. 2006. *Poverty and Equity: Measurement, Policy, and Estimation with DAD*. Economic Studies in Inequality, Social Exclusion and Well-being. New York: Springer-Verlag, <http://www.idrc.ca/openebooks/229-5/>.

Eurostat 2006. EU-SILC User Database Description. European Commission, Eurostat.

Expert Group on Household Income Statistics 2001. *Final Report and Recommendations*. Ottawa: Statistics Canada, <http://www.lisproject.org/links/canberra/finalreport.pdf>.

FEI, J. C. H., RANIS, G., and KUO, S. W. Y. 1978. 'Growth and the Family Distribution of Income by Factor Components'. *Quarterly Journal of Economics*, 92: 17–53.

FIELDS, G. S. 2000. 'Income Mobility: Concepts and Measures', in N. Birdsall and C. Graham (eds.), *New Markets, New Opportunities? Economic and Social Mobility in a Changing World*. Washington: The Brookings Institution Press, 101–32.

——and OK, E. A. 1996. 'The Meaning and Measurement of Income Mobility'. *Journal of Economic Theory*, 71: 349–77.

————1999a. 'The Measurement of Income Mobility: An Introduction to the Literature', in J. Silber (ed.), *Handbook of Income Inequality Measurement*. Deventer: Kluwer, 557–96.

————1999b. 'Measuring Movement of Incomes'. *Economica*, 66: 455–71.

FOSTER, J. E. 1985. 'Inequality measurement', in H. P. Young (ed.), *Fair Allocation, Proceedings of Symposia in Applied Mathematics*, 33. Providence, RI: American Mathematical Society.

FRICK, J., JENKINS, S. P., LILLARD, D., LIPPS, O., and WOODEN, M. 2007. 'The Cross-National Equivalent File (CNEF) and its Member Country Household Panel Studies'. *Schmollers Jahrbuch—Journal of Applied Social Science Studies*, 127: 627–54.

GOSLING, A., MACHIN, S., and MEGHIR, C. 2000. 'The Changing Distribution of Male Wages in the U.K.' *Review of Economic Studies*, 67: 635–66.

GOTTSCHALK, P., and SMEEDING, T. M. 2000. 'Empirical Evidence on Income Inequality in Industrialized Countries', in A. B. Atkinson and F. Bourguignon (eds.), *Handbook of Income Distribution*. Amsterdam: North-Holland, 261–307.

—— and SPOLAORE, E. 2002. 'On the Evaluation of Economic Mobility'. *Review of Economic Studies*, 69: 191–208.

HADAR, J., and RUSSELL, W. R. 1969. 'Rules for Ordering Uncertain Prospects'. *American Economic Review*, 59: 97–122.

HART, P. E. 1976. 'The Comparative Statics and Dynamics of Income Distributions'. *Journal of the Royal Statistical Society (Series A)*, 139: 108–25.

HYSLOP, D., and MARÉ, D. 2005. 'Understanding New Zealand's Changing Income Distribution, 1983–1998: A Semi-parametric Analysis'. *Economica*, 72: 469–95.

JENKINS, S. P. 1991. 'The Measurement of Income Inequality', in L. Osberg (ed.), *Economic Inequality and Poverty: International Perspectives*. Armonk, NY: M. E. Sharpe, 3–38.

—— 1995. 'Accounting for Inequality Trends: Decomposition Analyses for the UK, 1971–86'. *Economica*, 62: 29–63.

—— 2006. 'Estimation and Interpretation of Measures of Inequality, Poverty, and Social Welfare using Stata'. Presentation at North American Stata Users' Group Meeting, Boston, Mass. <http://econpapers.repec.org/paper/bocasug06/16.htm>.

—— and COWELL, F. A. 1994a. 'Dwarfs and Giants in the 1980s: Trends in the UK Income Distribution'. *Fiscal Studies*, 15: 99–118.

—— —— 1994b. 'Parametric Equivalence Scales and Scale Relativities'. *Economic Journal*, 104: 891–900.

—— and JÄNTTI, M. 2005. 'Methods for Summarizing and Comparing Wealth Distributions'. ISER Working Paper 2005-05. Institute for Social and Economic Research, University of Essex, Colchester, UK, <http://www.iser.essex.ac.uk/pubs/workpaps/pdf/2005-05.pdf>, forthcoming in *Construction and Usage of Comparable Microdata on Household Wealth: The Luxembourg Wealth Study*. Roma: Banca d'Italia.

—— and MICKLEWRIGHT, J. 2007. 'New Directions in the Analysis of Inequality and Poverty', in S. P. Jenkins and J. Micklewright (eds.), *Inequality and Poverty Re-examined*. Oxford: Oxford University Press, 3–33.

—— and VAN KERM, P. 2005. 'Accounting for Income Distribution Trends: A Density Function Decomposition Approach'. *Journal of Economic Inequality*, 3: 43–61.

—— —— 2006. 'Trends in Income Inequality, Pro-Poor Income Growth and Income Mobility'. *Oxford Economic Papers*, 58: 531–48.

KOENKER, R., and HALLOCK, K. F. 2001. 'Quantile Regression'. *Journal of Economic Perspectives*, 15: 143–56.

LEMIEUX, T. 2002. 'Decomposing Changes in Wage Distributions: A Unified Approach'. *Canadian Journal of Economics*, 35: 646–88.

LERMAN, R., and YITZHAKI, S. 1985. 'Income Inequality Effects by Income Source: A New Approach and Applications to the United States'. *Review of Economics and Statistics*, 67: 151–6.

MAASOUMI, E. 1986. 'The Measurement and Decomposition of Multi-dimensional Inequality'. *Econometrica*, 54: 991–7.

—— 1998. 'On Mobility', in A. Ullah and D. E. A. Giles (eds.), *Handbook of Applied Economic Statistics*. New York: Marcel Dekker, Inc., 119–75.

MARKANDYA, A. 1984. 'The Welfare Measurement of Changes in Economic Mobility'. *Economica*, 51: 457–71.

MATA, J., and MACHADO, J. A. F. 2005. 'Counterfactual Decomposition of Changes in Wage Distributions using Quantile Regression'. *Journal of Applied Econometrics*, 20: 445–65.

OAXACA, R. L. 1973. 'Male–Female Wage Differentials in Urban Labor Markets'. *International Economic Review*, 14: 673–709.

PEN, J. 1971. *Income Distribution*. Harmondsworth: Penguin Books.

SAPOSNIK, R. 1981. 'Rank-Dominance in Income Distributions'. *Public Choice*, 36: 147–51.

SHORROCKS, A. F. 1978. 'Income Inequality and Income Mobility'. *Journal of Economic Theory*, 19: 376–93.

—— 1982. 'Inequality Decomposition by Factor Components'. *Econometrica*, 50: 193–211.

—— 1983. 'Ranking Income Distributions'. *Economica*, 50: 3–17.

—— 1984. 'Inequality Decomposition by Population Subgroups'. *Econometrica*, 52: 1369–85.

—— and FOSTER, J. E. 1987. 'Transfer Sensitive Inequality Measures'. *Review of Economic Studies*, 54: 485–97.

SILVERMAN, B. W. 1986. *Density Estimation for Statistics and Data Analysis*, Monographs on Statistics and Applied Probability. London: Chapman and Hall.

TREDE, M. 1998. 'Making Mobility Visible: A Graphical Device'. *Economics Letters*, 59: 77–82.

VAN KERM, P. 2004. 'What Lies behind Income Mobility? Reranking and Distributional Change in Belgium, Western Germany and the USA'. *Economica*, 71: 223–39.

—— 2006. 'Comparisons of Mobility Profiles'. IRISS Working Paper 2006-03. Differdange, Luxembourg: CEPS/INSTEAD.

—— 2007. 'Extreme Incomes and the Estimation of Poverty and Inequality Indicators from EU-SILC'. IRISS Working Paper 2007-01. Differdange, Luxembourg: CEPS/INSTEAD.

VAN PRAAG, B., HAGENAARS, A., and VAN ECK, W. 1983. 'The Influence of Classification and Observation Errors on the Measurement of Income Inequality'. *Econometrica*, 51: 1093–108.

YITZHAKI, S. 1983. 'On an Extension of the Gini Inequality Index'. *International Economic Review*, 24: 617–28.

—— 1998. 'More than a Dozen Alternative Ways of Spelling Gini', in D. J. Slottje (ed.), *Research on Economic Inequality*. Stamford, Conn.: JAI Press, 13–30.

ZHENG, B. 1997. 'Aggregate Poverty Measures'. *Journal of Economic Surveys*, 11: 123–63.

# PART II

## THE EXTENT OF INEQUALITY

# CHAPTER 4

# INCOME INEQUALITY IN RICHER AND OECD COUNTRIES

ANDREA BRANDOLINI
TIMOTHY M. SMEEDING[1]

## 1. INTRODUCTION

MANY different variables can be used to evaluate the distribution of living standards in a society. These *focal variables*, as labeled by Sen (1992: 20), include monetary indicators, such as expenditure, income, and wealth, as well as non-monetary indicators like multidimensional measures of material standard of living, happiness and life satisfaction, functionings, and capabilities. In this chapter, income is taken as the focal variable, leaving earnings, consumption, wealth, happiness, and other dimensions of social and economic well-being to later chapters.

[1] We thank Tony Atkinson, Brian Nolan, Wiemer Salverda, and attendees at the Seville meeting of the OHEI working group for suggestions, and Federico Giorgi for excellent research assistance. The views expressed here are solely those of the authors; in particular, they do not necessarily reflect those of the Bank of Italy, Syracuse University, or any of our sponsors.

The distribution of income among persons, or households, has attracted the attention of social scientists at least since Pareto's analysis of the revenue curve in 1897. Income is still the most common indicator of economic resources in rich countries, although consumption expenditure is often used in developing countries. Section 2 outlines the conceptual difference between consumption, current income, and permanent income, and then moves on to examine the nuances of the definition of income and the further methodological decisions that need to be taken to study income inequality. Some of these issues are discussed in greater detail in Chapter 3 on measurement and Chapter 14 on consumption and time use. Section 3 deals with the empirics of income distribution in richer countries, leaving to Chapter 24 the discussion of low and middle-income countries. The section covers both the evidence at the turn of the century and the evolution over the last thirty years of the inequality of market and disposable incomes, and the role of cash and non-cash redistribution. Section 4 concludes with suggestions for future research.

## 2. Measuring Inequality in Living Standards: Income as the Focal Variable

### Consumption, Permanent Income, and Current Income

The nearest alternative to income is consumption or consumption expenditure, a variable which is often preferred in less developed countries since it is smoothed over time and is less volatile and less reliant on seasonal variation than is income, especially in agricultural societies (Deaton and Grosh, 2000; see also Chapters 14 and 24).[2] Apart from this practical reason, many economists view consumption as a better proxy of well-being than income. A first argument is that well-being (utility) is a function of the goods and services actually consumed (Slesnick, 1994). However, focusing on the *means available* to purchase commodities (income) rather than the

---

[2] Income-based Gini indices are reported by the World Bank (2005: 280–1, table A2) for 22 of the 27 high-income economies for which the statistics are available, 20 of the 60 middle-income economies, and only one of the 39 low-income economies. As observed by the World Bank (2005: 38, box 2.5), income tends to be more unequally distributed than expenditure to a degree that varies across countries. Mixing income-based and consumption-based statistics confounds international comparisons, and is not to be advised. See Chapter 24 for more on attempts to harmonize measures of inequality when data are missing or quality is suspect.

commodities actually purchased (expenditure) makes the assessment of well-being independent of the purchase choice. Sen offers the example '... of the person with means who *fasts* out of choice, as opposed to another who *has to* starve because of lack of means' (1992: 111–12, emphasis in the original), while Hagenaars *et al.* (1994: 8) argue that using income helps us avoid the trap of identifying voluntary low levels of consumption with deprivation.

A second argument in favor of consumption is that it is more closely related to permanent income or lifetime resources than current income. As described by Friedman (1957: 209), the distributions of current income '... reflect the influence of differences among individual units both in ... the permanent component of income and ... the transitory component. Yet these two types of differences do not have the same significance; the one is an indication of deep-seated long-run inequality, the other, of dynamic variation and mobility.' If one is interested in 'deep-seated long-run inequality', permanent income, and hence consumption, is what matters. However, the simple proportionality between consumption and permanent income in the baseline inter-temporal consumer's optimization problem does not hold if some of its basic hypotheses are relaxed and simple forms of personal heterogeneity are introduced (in life-span, accumulated or inherited wealth, degree of inter-generational altruism, variability of uncertain labor incomes, and capacity to borrow, to name just a few). Therefore, current consumption may not be a very good, and not even the best available, proxy of permanent income. Moreover, it is far from obvious that 'deep-seated long-run inequality' should be our concern. The concept has some natural appeal: an undergraduate may have current income below that of a manual worker of the same age, but he is likely to be better off within a few years, and for most of his lifetime. But 'the promise of resources in the future may do little to pay the bills today' (Deaton and Grosh, 2000: 93). In the real world, capital markets are imperfect and persons face borrowing constraints that render the actual standard of living dependent on current available resources. Conversely, '... the fact that an old person had a high income 30 years ago does not make up for his having a pension that is below his needs today' (Atkinson, 1983: 44).

More generally, the problem is that of defining the reference time period for the analysis of inequality (Atkinson 1983; Atkinson *et al.*, 1995). Typically, the longer the accounting framework, the lower is the degree of measured inequality. At intra-annual frequencies, income may fluctuate owing to seasonal factors (e.g. in agriculture), the movement of workers into or out of jobs, or the timing of payments (e.g. interest on financial assets or liabilities, dividends on stocks): aggregating over the year implies averaging out these differences, although the overall impact on measured inequality may be small (Böheim and Jenkins, 2006). By the same token, lengthening the reference period beyond the year reduces measured inequality by smoothing the variability due to the business cycle or the life-cycle (e.g.

Björklund 1993; Björklund and Palme 2002). But the ex-ante assessment of total lifecycle wealth presents several difficulties and is highly sensitive to measurement assumptions.[3]

Finally, there is the problem ≡ of measurement of 'true' consumption in rich societies. Consumption expenditure data are collected mainly to provide weights and prices for measuring the consumer price index, not for measuring consumption. Very few surveys actually try to measure actual consumption, because purchases of durables such as major appliances, automobiles, and especially housing must all be spread out over the useful life of the good which is bought in one period but consumed in another. Indeed measures of consumption may differ greatly from consumer expenditures for such persons as older units living in an owned but mortgage-free house (Johnson et al., 2005).

In brief, there is a priori no cogent or practical reason to prefer consumption to income, or permanent income to current income. Indeed Haig (1921) and Simons (1938) recognized that income represents the *possibility* to consume, and therefore established their famous identity that income equals consumption plus or minus changes in net worth. Most often, the choice is driven by the available information and there is a clear preference amongst rich nations to rely on income and not consumption. Current income, as measured over a span of a year, appears to be a satisfactory measure of the (material) living standard of people.

## Income Definition

Definitional problems do not cease with the choice of current (yearly) income as the focal variable. There are many different items that concur to form the income of a person, or a household, in a year (Smeeding and Weinberg, 2001). The basic distinction is between the *market* or *original* income and the *disposable* income. On the basis of the recommendations of the final report of the Expert Group on Household Income Statistics—The Canberra Group (2001), market income should include all types of earnings gross of employees' social insurance contributions, self-employment income, all types of capital income including interest, rent, or dividends received and subtracting interest paid, plus private pensions. Disposable

---

[3] Assuming that a person $i$ lives $T$ years, starts working at age $T_1$ and retires at age $T_2$, his lifetime wealth can be defined as $Y_i \equiv \sum_{t=0}^{T-1} (1 + r_t)^{-t}(h_{it}/p_t) + \sum_{t=T_1}^{T_2-1} (1 + r_t)^{-t}(y_{it}/p_t) + \sum_{t=T_2}^{T-1} (1 + r_t)^{-t}(x_{it}/p_t)$, where $h_{it}$ is any capital or money transfer received by the person at time $t$ (other than pension), $y_{it}$ and $x_{it}$ denote his labor earnings and pension, and $p_t$ is a price deflator. In order to measure permanent income, we need to know: (i) person's life-span as well as the ages of entry into the job market and of retirement; (ii) the amount and timing of any transfer a person receives from relatives, friends, private or public institutions; (iii) the path of labor income; (iv) the flow of pension payments; (v) the appropriate discount rates $r_t$ and price deflators $p_t$ (both possibly indexed to $i$). Further complications arise when households rather than individuals are the object of the analysis, as births, divorces, re-marriages, and the like need to be accounted for.

income takes market income and subtracts direct taxes (including employee's contributions to social insurance), but ignores other 'indirect' taxes (property, wealth, and value added taxes); then it adds back in regular inter-household cash transfers received net of those made, and all forms of cash and near-cash public income transfers including social insurance benefits (for social retirement, disability, and unemployment), universal social assistance benefits, and targeted income transfer programs like social maintenance. Near-cash benefits in the form of housing allowances or food stamps are included as are negative taxes (for instance, in-work benefits now popular in many rich nations). In practice, many surveys exclude various elements of market incomes, such as interest paid, or private transfers made to other households.

However broad these definitions may be, they exclude imputed rents, capital gains and losses and other unrealized types of capital income, home production, and in-kind transfer benefits such as education and health insurance. Because these items may account for an important share of the economic resources at the household's disposal, their inclusion in the income definition may affect measured inequality. Indeed, recent research on the United States suggests that uncounted realized and unrealized income from capital raises measured incomes by over 40 percent at the mean and more than 20 percent at the median (Smeeding and Thompson, 2007).

Imputed rents for owner-occupied dwellings tend to benefit a wide range of low to high income units, especially the elderly, but their overall effect may vary across countries, depending on the level of housing prices and the diffusion of home-ownership (Frick and Grabka, 2003). Unrealized appreciation and untaxed income from capital, as well as capital gains, mainly benefit higher income units. Indirect taxes have a relatively larger impact on the budget of lower income units. The same happens, with opposite sign, with the imputation of in-kind public benefits for health care, housing, and education valued at their cost of provision (see also below). As the value of these benefits is spread more or less evenly among beneficiaries ('potential' beneficiaries in the case of health insurance), the result is to augment income by a fixed amount, which accounts for a larger fraction of income at lower income levels. In general, elder households and households with children are net gainers from the imputation, through health insurance and education benefits, respectively, while middle-age childless units are net losers. These results are very sensitive to the imputation assumptions: both valuing benefits according to willingness to pay and accounting for the quality of services provided would lower benefits to the poor (Smeeding, 1982).

As stressed by the Expert Group on Household Income Statistics—The Canberra Group (2001: 62–7), the under-coverage of property and self-employment income, own account production, imputed rent for owner-occupied dwellings, social transfers in-kind, capital gains, and other unrealized income from wealth are major issues to be addressed in expanding internationally comparable income measures.

But the analysis of these augmented notions of income is also scarce at the national level.[4]

## Further Empirical Choices and Data Sources

So far only the focal variable, income, and its definition have been examined. But other basic methodological choices may affect comparisons of income inequality across countries or over time (Chapter 3; Atkinson and Brandolini, 2001). First, the reference unit may be the household, the inner family, the tax unit, or the individual income earner. The broader the definition of household, the more measured inequality tends to decrease, since the dispersion of individual incomes is abated by their aggregation and supposedly egalitarian distribution among all members of the unit (Redmond, 1998). Second, observations may be adjusted for the size ($s$) and the composition of the reference unit in order to take into consideration the economies of scale generated by cohabitation by using an equivalence scale. Eurostat recommends the use of the modified OECD scale which assigns value 1 to the first adult, 0.5 to any other person aged 14 or older, and 0.3 to each child younger than 14. Atkinson et al. (1995) define equivalent income as household income divided by the number of equivalent persons $s^{0.5}$, where 0.5 is a value that captures economies of scale. The choice of the equivalence scale considerably affects inequality comparisons (Buhmann et al., 1988; Coulter et al., 1992). Third, the welfare weighting of the single observations may vary: each observation may receive a weight of one (household-weight) or may be weighted according to its size (person-weight) or its size and composition (equivalent adult-weight) (Danziger and Taussig, 1979; Ebert, 1997).

There are other factors that impinge on data comparability. People who are present for only part of the year, on account of entering or leaving the population, may be excluded, or treated differently from other units. Data may be bottom- and top-coded, either in the course of the collection of the data as in the US Current Population Survey (Ryscavage, 1995), or as a decision of the researcher to reduce the noise that is typically concentrated in the tails of the distribution (Cowell and Victoria-Feser, 1996; Burkhauser et al., 2007). The estimated Gini index may be understated where it is computed on observations that are ranked on a different basis from the variable of concern.

The last cause of limited comparability may be attributable to differences in the source of data. Income data are available both from national household surveys, and from administrative archives. Of these, the most important are income tax records, which have historically provided long runs of continuous data, recently

---

[4]  According to preliminary calculations by Garfinkel et al. (2007, chapter 5), combining the pro-poor effects of non-cash benefits with the pro-rich effect of income from capital would more or less net out in the United States in 2004.

exploited in the literature on top incomes (Chapter 7; Atkinson and Piketty, 2007). Income tax records suffer from potentially serious problems, among them the incomplete coverage of those with incomes below the tax threshold and the tendency to under-report certain types of income. Household surveys are also subject to problems, including the sampling error, which depends on the size and structure of the sample, and the non-sampling errors, caused by non-response and under-reporting (Atkinson *et al.*, 1995, chapter 2). For these reasons, the upper tail of the income distribution tends to be unsatisfactorily covered in sample surveys, unless the rich are over-sampled; in a sense, the survey-based evidence discussed later in this chapter may be seen as being about the incomes of, say, the bottom 99 percent of the population, and it is thus complementary to the results on high incomes based on tax records reported in Chapter 7.[5]

All these factors need to be kept in mind in the analysis of the national trends in income inequality or in cross-national comparisons. While the data include a great deal of 'noise' or possibly unknown errors, the important assumption is that the signal derived from the analysis exceeds the noise for most careful analyses which also include a sensitivity test of assumptions (Atkinson *et al.*, 1995; Gottschalk and Smeeding, 2000).

In some major sense full comparability is an impossible goal. Surveys within countries as well as across countries are subject to changes in methods, and are characterized by differences in sampling and non-sampling errors. Comparability is vastly increased when the researcher can access the individual observations on household incomes available in a national archive, or in international databases where the original databases are harmonized such as the Luxembourg Income Study (LIS) and the European Union Statistics on Income and Living Conditions (EU–SILC).[6] The degree of comparability is lessened substantially, but the major characteristics of underlying data are often available in published material either from an original national source, or from secondary sources like that assembled at the World Bank by Deininger and Squire (1996) or the World Income Inequality

---

[5] Indeed, in the United States the most comprehensive source on the distribution of household incomes is most likely the series estimated by the US Congressional Budget Office (2007) by combining income tax records and household survey data; however, information is available only in highly aggregated published form.

[6] The LIS project began in 1983 with the objective of creating a micro-database containing social and economic data collected in household surveys from different countries (Smeeding, 2004). The database currently contains information for 30 countries for one or more years over the period 1967–2004 (see <http://www.lisproject.org>). EU–SILC has succeeded the European Community Household Panel (ECHP) in providing comparative statistics on income distribution and social exclusion at the European level (Clemenceau and Museux, 2007). In 2005 it covered the 25 EU member states plus Norway and Iceland; it is being extended to Bulgaria, Romania, Switzerland, and Turkey (see <http://epp.eurostat.ec.europa.eu/portal/page?_pageid=1913,47567825,1913_58814988&_dad=portal&_schema=PORTAL>). New comparable longitudinal household income panel datasets provide the opportunity to observe individual household income dynamics, though for a much smaller number of countries (see Chapter 21).

Database (WIID-2b) compiled at the United Nations University—World Institute for Development Economics Research (2007). Chapter 24 makes use of these and other secondary data sources.

# 3. EMPIRICS OF INCOME DISTRIBUTION

## Cross-National Comparisons of Market Income

Market income is the total revenue from labor and investments, and constitutes the primary source of household income. The inequality of its distribution reflects the dispersion of wages and salaries among employees, which is extensively discussed in Chapters 8 to 12, as well as the unequal distribution of wealth, as measured by the annual flow of return, which is examined in Chapter 6. But market income inequality is also influenced by the way earnings from self-employment or job positions are spread across the population. In order to gauge how these different distributions combine to produce the overall degree of inequality of market incomes, it is useful to decompose the Gini index by income source (Pyatt *et al.*, 1980).[7] The Gini index $G$ can be factorized as $G = \Sigma_k(\mu_k/\mu)G_k R_k$, where $\mu$ is mean income, $\mu_k$ and $G_k$ are the mean and the Gini index of income component $k$, with $\mu = \Sigma_k\mu_k$, and $R_k = \text{cov}[y_k, r(y)]/\text{cov}[y_k, r(y_k)]$ is the 'rank correlation ratio', with $r(y)$ being the rank of households according to market income $y$ (subscript $k$ denotes the income component). The rank correlation ratio is equal to unity only if $r(y_k) = r(y)$, that is, if households have the same ranking with respect to $y_k$ and $y$. The Gini index for income component $y_k$ can, in turn, be written as $G_k = (1 - q_k) + q_k G_k^+$, where $q_k$ is the share of households with a positive value of $y_k$ and $G_k^+$ is the Gini index for the distribution of $y_k$ among its earners rather than across the entire population as for $G_k$. The results of the decomposition of the Gini index for the distribution of market incomes among persons are reported in Table 4.1 for seven countries in 1999–2000, selected from the LIS database. These countries represent different welfare regimes according to the classification of Chapter 25. In order to facilitate the comparison with the figures for disposable incomes discussed later, all incomes are equivalized.[8]

---

[7]  Note, however, Shorrocks' (1983) observation that this decomposition is somewhat arbitrary being only one of an infinite variety of potential rules.

[8]  All LIS estimates in this chapter use the square root of the household size as equivalence scale (e.g. the equivalent income of a household of four is obtained by dividing total household income by two). This value is then attributed to each person in the household to derive the distribution among persons. To minimize the impact of outliers, all records with zero disposable income are dropped, and observations are bottom-coded at 1 percent of the mean of equivalent disposable income and top-coded at 10 times the median of unadjusted disposable income. Changes in disposable income due to bottom- and top-coding are entirely attributed to market income.

Table 4.1. Decomposition of the Gini index of market income by income source in seven countries

| Income source | Share of market income (%) [1] | Rank correlation ratio [2] | Gini index [3] | Population share with positive value (%) [4] | Gini index for population with positive value [5] | Absolute contribution [6] | Relative contribution (%) [7] |
|---|---|---|---|---|---|---|---|
| Finland 2000 | | | | | | | |
| Wages and salaries | 83.1 | 0.910 | 0.501 | 79.2 | 0.370 | 0.379 | 80.7 |
| Self-employment income | 9.2 | 0.513 | 0.934 | 18.3 | 0.638 | 0.044 | 9.3 |
| Property income (a) | 7.8 | 0.645 | 0.929 | 50.7 | 0.860 | 0.047 | 9.9 |
| Market income | 100.0 | 1.000 | 0.469 | 90.9 | 0.416 | 0.469 | 100.0 |
| Germany 2000 | | | | | | | |
| Wages and salaries | 80.2 | 0.874 | 0.531 | 73.8 | 0.364 | 0.372 | 77.3 |
| Self-employment income | 11.6 | 0.674 | 0.942 | 11.3 | 0.482 | 0.074 | 15.3 |
| Property income (a) | 8.2 | 0.501 | 0.858 | 83.9 | 0.830 | 0.035 | 7.3 |
| Market income | 100.0 | 1.000 | 0.481 | 95.1 | 0.454 | 0.481 | 100.0 |
| Poland 1999 | | | | | | | |
| Wages and salaries | 86.5 | 0.914 | 0.565 | 68.0 | 0.360 | 0.447 | 84.3 |
| Self-employment income | 12.9 | 0.679 | 0.937 | 11.1 | 0.432 | 0.082 | 15.4 |
| Property income (a) | 0.7 | 0.223 | 0.990 | 2.1 | 0.529 | 0.001 | 0.3 |
| Market income | 100.0 | 1.000 | 0.530 | 74.9 | 0.373 | 0.530 | 100.0 |
| Sweden 2000 | | | | | | | |
| Wages and salaries | 87.7 | 0.946 | 0.505 | 79.7 | 0.379 | 0.419 | 91.2 |
| Self-employment income | 3.0 | 0.345 | 1.303 | 11.8 | 3.578 | 0.014 | 2.9 |
| Property income (a) | 9.3 | 0.336 | 0.856 | 81.1 | 0.823 | 0.027 | 5.8 |
| Market income | 100.0 | 1.000 | 0.459 | 95.8 | 0.436 | 0.459 | 100.0 |

(cont.)

Table 4.1. (Continued)

| Income source | Share of market income (%) [1] | Rank correlation ratio [2] | Gini index [3] | Population share with positive value (%) [4] | Gini index for population with positive value [5] | Absolute contribution [6] | Relative contribution (%) [7] |
|---|---|---|---|---|---|---|---|
| Taiwan 2000 | | | | | | | |
| Wages and salaries | 69.0 | 0.736 | 0.464 | 79.7 | 0.327 | 0.235 | 72.5 |
| Self-employment income | 21.1 | 0.298 | 0.783 | 37.4 | 0.419 | 0.049 | 15.1 |
| Property income (a) | 9.9 | 0.554 | 0.732 | 98.2 | 0.727 | 0.040 | 12.4 |
| Market income | 100.0 | 1.000 | 0.325 | 99.5 | 0.322 | 0.325 | 100.0 |
| United Kingdom 1999 | | | | | | | |
| Wages and salaries | 78.1 | 0.895 | 0.582 | 68.5 | 0.389 | 0.406 | 79.9 |
| Self-employment income | 10.8 | 0.637 | 0.966 | 13.9 | 0.757 | 0.066 | 13.0 |
| Property income (a) | 11.2 | 0.374 | 0.868 | 72.2 | 0.817 | 0.036 | 7.1 |
| Market income | 100.0 | 1.000 | 0.509 | 89.3 | 0.450 | 0.509 | 100.0 |
| United States 2000 | | | | | | | |
| Wages and salaries | 85.7 | 0.925 | 0.512 | 85.6 | 0.429 | 0.405 | 84.5 |
| Self-employment income | 6.3 | 0.610 | 0.983 | 12.0 | 0.862 | 0.038 | 7.9 |
| Property income (a) | 8.0 | 0.507 | 0.891 | 62.0 | 0.824 | 0.036 | 7.6 |
| Market income | 100.0 | 1.000 | 0.479 | 95.5 | 0.455 | 0.479 | 100.0 |

Notes: Observations for disposable income are bottom-coded at 1 percent of the mean of equivalent disposable income and top-coded at 10 times the median of unadjusted disposable income. Changes in disposable incomes due to bottom- and top-coding are entirely attributed to market incomes, proportionally for each income component. All income values are adjusted for household size by the square-root equivalence scale. (a) Includes private pensions.

Source: Authors' calculations from the Luxembourg Income Study database, as of 20 February 2008.

In all countries wages and salaries account for by far the greatest fraction of market income (column 1). Except in Sweden, the share of income from self-employment is not negligible; it exceeds a fifth of the total in Taiwan. Property incomes, which do not include imputed rents for owner-occupied houses, account for about a tenth of market income, but are insignificant in Poland. The rank correlation ratios are all positive and close to one for wages and salaries, suggesting that the ordering of households in terms of this income component is very similar to that in terms of market income (column 2). The Gini index for wages and salaries is higher in Germany, Poland, and the United Kingdom than in Finland, Sweden, and, somewhat surprisingly, the United States (column 3). This ranking reflects the lower share of persons living in households with wage-and-salary earners exhibited by the first three countries (column 4): when the Gini index is calculated among these persons only, the highest inequality is found in the United States (column 5).[9] Between 73 percent (Taiwan) and 91 percent (Sweden) of the overall inequality of market incomes is explained by wages and salaries.

Figure 4.1 compares the inequality of market incomes across persons in 16 nations in 2000, or the closest available year. Poland, Israel, and the United Kingdom exhibit the highest concentration of market incomes, with values of the Gini index above 50 percent; at the other end, Taiwan, the Netherlands, and Romania show values below 40 percent. There appears to be no clear geographical pattern, in contrast to the case of disposable income, as shown below. Using the decomposition described earlier, $G = (1-q) + qG^+$, the inequality of market incomes $G$ rises both with the exclusion of people from the labor or asset markets (a lower value of $q$) and with the concentration of market incomes among those who receive them (a higher value of $G^+$). Figure 4.1 confirms that the overall market income inequality tends to be higher where the share of persons with positive market income, shown by the horizontal lines, is lower.

Figure 4.2 considers the national trends in six countries for which data are available: Canada, Finland, Sweden, West Germany,[10] the United Kingdom, and the United States. Reported series are internally consistent, but their levels are not comparable across nations, as the exact definition of market income may differ. For instance, the series for the United States and Sweden, in the more recent period, include realized capital gains, while the others do not. In five of the six countries, the inequality of market income inequality increased during the 1980s and early 1990s and remained substantially stable afterwards; in West Germany inequality increased only in the 1970s.

[9] This measure of inequality differs from the measures of annual earnings dispersion across employees discussed in Chapter 8 because it aggregates all wages and salaries earned in a year by a household, expresses them in equivalized terms, and then attributes the result to all household members.

[10] Throughout the chapter Germany refers to the Federal Republic of Germany after re-unification in 1991, while West Germany refers to the Federal Republic of Germany until 1990 and to the Western Länder thereafter.

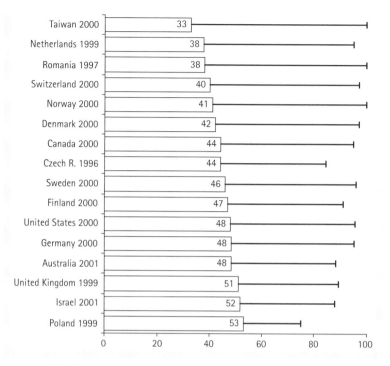

**Fig. 4.1. Gini indices of market income in 16 countries (percent)**

*Note*: Observations for disposable income are bottom-coded at 1 percent of the mean of equivalent disposable income and top-coded at 10 times the median of unadjusted disposable income. Changes in disposable incomes due to bottom- and top-coding are entirely attributed to market incomes. Market incomes are adjusted for household size by the square-root equivalence scale. Horizontal lines indicate the share of households with positive market income.

*Source*: Authors' calculations from the Luxembourg Income Study database, as of 20 February 2008.

## Cross-National Comparisons of Disposable Income

Money disposable income is obtained from market income by adding inter-household cash transfers and public transfers, and by subtracting taxes and employees' social insurance contributions. Figure 4.3 compares the distribution of equivalent disposable income across persons in the 16 nations examined before plus 16 other nations. These figures are calculated from the LIS database except for Portugal, which is estimated from the ECHP database (Waves 1–8, December 2003), and Japan, which was computed according to the same methodology as all other figures by Ishikawa (1996) (see Gottschalk and Smeeding 2000). Following World Bank (2005) categorization, countries are separated into high-income and middle-income economies according to their per capita gross national income in 2004.

There is a wide range of income inequality among the nations of Figure 4.3. The United States is an outlier among rich nations, and only Russia and Mexico,

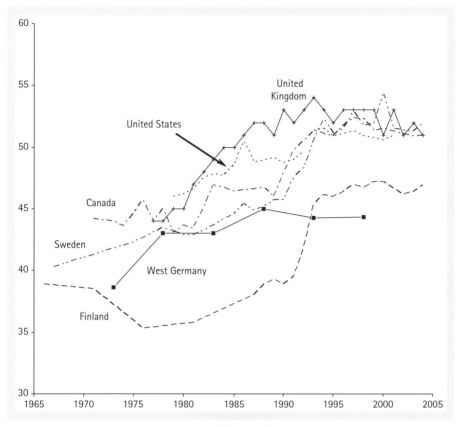

**Fig. 4.2. Gini index of market income (percent)**

*Note*: To facilitate reading, a break in each of the series for Canada, Sweden, and the United Kingdom is eliminated by scaling up or down the figures before the discontinuity by the difference in the first overlapping year.

*Source*: Brandolini and Smeeding (forthcoming).

two middle-income economies, have higher levels of inequality. A low-income American at the 10th percentile has an income that is only 39 percent of the median income (P10). By contrast, in most countries of central, northern, and eastern Europe the income of the poor exceeds 50 percent of the income of a middle-income person; in the other English-speaking nations and in the southern European countries, plus Israel, it is 42 to 47 percent. Only in Russia and Mexico do the poor fare relatively worse than in the United States. In Greece, Portugal, Spain, Israel, as well as the United States and the United Kingdom, the rich persons—those at the 90th percentile—earn more than twice the national median income (P90). In poorer countries the 90th percentile can also be very high in relative terms: for example, Mexico, Russia, and Estonia.

The countries in Figure 4.3 fall into some distinctive clusters. Inequality, as measured by the decile ratio (the ratio between P90 and P10), is least in Nordic

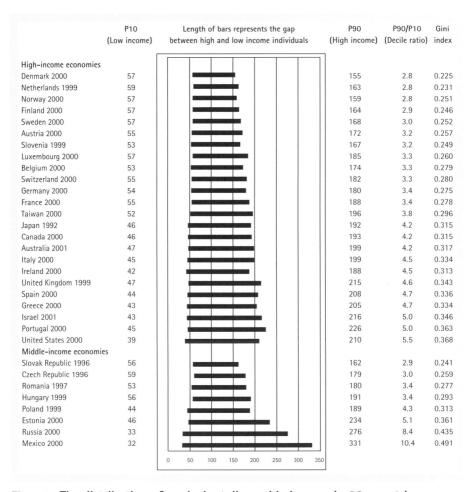

| | P10<br>(Low income) | Length of bars represents the gap<br>between high and low income individuals | P90<br>(High income) | P90/P10<br>(Decile ratio) | Gini<br>index |
|---|---|---|---|---|---|
| **High-income economies** | | | | | |
| Denmark 2000 | 57 | | 155 | 2.8 | 0.225 |
| Netherlands 1999 | 59 | | 163 | 2.8 | 0.231 |
| Norway 2000 | 57 | | 159 | 2.8 | 0.251 |
| Finland 2000 | 57 | | 164 | 2.9 | 0.246 |
| Sweden 2000 | 57 | | 168 | 3.0 | 0.252 |
| Austria 2000 | 55 | | 172 | 3.2 | 0.257 |
| Slovenia 1999 | 53 | | 167 | 3.2 | 0.249 |
| Luxembourg 2000 | 57 | | 185 | 3.3 | 0.260 |
| Belgium 2000 | 53 | | 174 | 3.3 | 0.279 |
| Switzerland 2000 | 55 | | 182 | 3.3 | 0.280 |
| Germany 2000 | 54 | | 180 | 3.4 | 0.275 |
| France 2000 | 55 | | 188 | 3.4 | 0.278 |
| Taiwan 2000 | 52 | | 196 | 3.8 | 0.296 |
| Japan 1992 | 46 | | 192 | 4.2 | 0.315 |
| Canada 2000 | 46 | | 193 | 4.2 | 0.315 |
| Australia 2001 | 47 | | 199 | 4.2 | 0.317 |
| Italy 2000 | 45 | | 199 | 4.5 | 0.334 |
| Ireland 2000 | 42 | | 188 | 4.5 | 0.313 |
| United Kingdom 1999 | 47 | | 215 | 4.6 | 0.343 |
| Spain 2000 | 44 | | 208 | 4.7 | 0.336 |
| Greece 2000 | 43 | | 205 | 4.7 | 0.334 |
| Israel 2001 | 43 | | 216 | 5.0 | 0.346 |
| Portugal 2000 | 45 | | 226 | 5.0 | 0.363 |
| United States 2000 | 39 | | 210 | 5.5 | 0.368 |
| **Middle-income economies** | | | | | |
| Slovak Republic 1996 | 56 | | 162 | 2.9 | 0.241 |
| Czech Republic 1996 | 59 | | 179 | 3.0 | 0.259 |
| Romania 1997 | 53 | | 180 | 3.4 | 0.277 |
| Hungary 1999 | 56 | | 191 | 3.4 | 0.293 |
| Poland 1999 | 44 | | 189 | 4.3 | 0.313 |
| Estonia 2000 | 46 | | 234 | 5.1 | 0.361 |
| Russia 2000 | 33 | | 276 | 8.4 | 0.435 |
| Mexico 2000 | 32 | | 331 | 10.4 | 0.491 |

0    50    100    150    200    250    300    350

**Fig. 4.3. The distribution of equivalent disposable income in 32 countries**

*Sources*: Authors' calculations from the Luxembourg Income Study database, as of 20 February 2008 (figures coincide with those reported in <http://www.lisproject.org/keyfigures/ineqtable.htm>), and for Portugal from the European Community Household Panel database (Waves 1–8, December 2003); statistics for Japan were computed according to the same methodology as all other figures by Ishikawa (1996) for Gottschalk and Smeeding (2000). P10 and P90 are the ratios to the median of the 10th and 90th percentiles, respectively. Observations are bottom-coded at 1 percent of the mean of equivalent disposable income and top-coded at 10 times the median of unadjusted disposable income. Incomes are adjusted for household size by the square-root equivalence scale. Economies are classified by the World Bank (2005) according to 2004 per capita gross national income in the following income groups: low-income economies (LIC), $825 or less; lower-middle-income economies (LMC), $826–3,255; upper-middle income economies (UMC), $3,256–10,065; and high-income economies (HIC), $10,066 or more.

countries, the Netherlands, and the Czech and Slovak Republics with values of 3 or less. The other Benelux countries (Belgium and Luxembourg), those from central Europe (France, Switzerland, Germany, Austria, Slovenia), and two from eastern Europe (Hungary, Romania) come next at 3.2–3.4. These precede the four English-speaking nations (Canada, Australia, Ireland, and the United Kingdom), which have decile ratios between 4.2 and 4.6, and the southern European countries (Italy, Spain, Greece, and Portugal) and Israel, whose ratios fall between 4.5 and 5. Only the United States, Estonia, Mexico, and Russia have values in excess of 5. With decile ratios around 4, the two Asian countries, Taiwan and Japan, are in an intermediate position.

Inequality differs much more across middle-income than high-income economies. While Estonia, Russia, and Mexico show a very unequal distribution of income, the other five countries, all from eastern Europe, exhibit moderate or low levels of inequality. The shape of the income distribution was already noticeably different across these formerly planned economies in the mid-1980s, before they turned into market economies, with Czechoslovakia showing the least inequality and the Soviet Union the highest (Atkinson and Micklewright, 1992).

In Figure 4.3 countries are arranged, within the two categories of high-income and middle-income, by the decile ratio, from lowest to highest. This country rank order does not coincide with that based on the other statistics reported in the same figure: P10, P90, and the Gini index. While these differences may be small and are likely to be within the bounds of sampling error, one should still be aware that the exact ranking of countries in international comparisons may well depend on which part of the distribution is analyzed: different summary measures may lead to different orderings, as they weight differently the top and the bottom of the distribution (see Chapter 3; Burkhauser *et al.*, 2007). In the same vein, the results of empirical tests also are sensitive to the choice of the inequality index, as shown by Voitchovsky (2005) for the relationship between inequality and growth (see also Chapter 22), and by Schwabish *et al.* (2006) for the relationship between inequality and social spending.

A more robust, if partial, ranking is provided by comparing the entire income distribution through the analysis of Lorenz dominance as developed by Atkinson (1970) (see Chapter 3). By summarizing by means of a Hasse diagram the complex pattern of bilateral comparisons which arise for the same 32 countries considered here, Brandolini and Smeeding (forthcoming) show that many of such comparisons are indeed ambiguous, unless a specific inequality index is chosen. At the same time, they confirm the basic pattern sketched above using the decile ratio: Mexico and Russia are at the top of the inequality ranking, followed by the English-speaking countries intertwined with the southern European countries, then by the other continental European nations, with the Nordic countries at the bottom of the scale; eastern European countries are spread throughout the entire tree.

The analysis has been conducted so far in relative terms; that is each citizen's income has been compared to the incomes of his or her national compatriots. However, average income differs across countries. The United States resident is, 'on average', better off than are residents of Italy, because the US real Gross Domestic

Product (GDP) per capita in 2000 is $34,100 international dollars, compared to $25,800 international dollars in Italy (International Monetary Fund, 2007). Does this higher average US standard of living extend to all levels of the income distribution? In order to answer this question, one must compare *real incomes*, that is, incomes deflated by a Purchasing Power Parity (PPP) index. This is a standard, but crude, way of measuring the amount of goods and services that a certain income can purchase. On the one hand, it is questionable that the same conversion factor should be applied across the entire distribution, although the same concern could be raised for within-country differences in the cost of living. On the other hand, real disposable income does not account for goods and services such as education and health care that are provided at different prices and under different financing schemes in different nations. As low-income citizens in some countries need to spend more out of pocket for these goods than do low-income citizens in other countries, their living standard is relatively lower than that measured by PPP-adjusted income (Smeeding and Rainwater, 2004). Further complications arise because the PPP indices are available for various aggregates and from different sources,[11] and are computed for national accounts, which are intrinsically different from survey data (Deaton, 2005).[12]

The statistics for real equivalized incomes in 2000 international dollars are reported in Figure 4.4. Original incomes are adjusted by the national consumer price indices in the case of non-base year observations, and are converted by means of PPP indices for GDP drawn from the International Monetary Fund (2007). In each country, the real P10, P90, and median are recomputed as a fraction of the US median real income.

Even if mostly rich nations are considered here, differences in average real living standards are extremely large. The median person in middle-income economies earns less than a third of the median American income, and about a tenth as much in Russia. But the variation is considerable, even among 'high-income economies'. Portugal, Slovenia, and Greece have median real income which is half or less of the US value; only in Luxembourg is the median higher than in the United States. However, these differences do not necessarily carry forward to the rest of the income distribution. If the living standard of the median Swede or Finn appears to be

[11]   PPP indices are routinely estimated by various international agencies, such as the Organisation for Economic Co-operation and Development or the World Bank, or international research projects like the Penn World Table (Summers and Heston, 1991); moreover, they are computed for various national accounts aggregates, like GDP or household final consumption expenditure (Bradbury and Jäntti, 1999). Methods to estimate PPP indices also differ, as discussed for instance by Dowrick and Akmal (2005).

[12]   This difference shows up in sizeable shortfalls of total survey incomes from GDP aggregates (Brandolini, 2007). As these shortfalls vary across countries, comparisons of living standards based on survey means may differ from those based on national accounts, although the correlation between per capita GDP and survey disposable income per person is positive, if less than one. The comparisons of real incomes discussed below would be affected should household-level data be aligned to aggregate statistics.

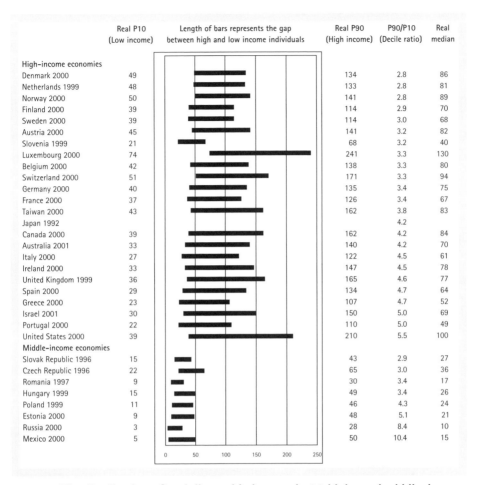

**Fig. 4.4. The distribution of real disposable income in 32 high- and middle-income economies**

*Sources*: Authors' calculations from the Luxembourg Income Study database, as of 20 February 2008, and for Portugal from the European Community Household Panel database (Waves 1–8, December 2003); statistics for Japan were computed according to the same methodology as all other figures by Ishikawa (1996) for Gottschalk and Smeeding (2000). Real P10 and P90 are the percentage ratios to the US median of the 10th and 90th percentiles, respectively; real median is expressed as a percentage ratio of the US median. Observations are bottom-coded at 1 percent of the mean of equivalent disposable income and top-coded at 10 times the median of unadjusted disposable income. Incomes are adjusted for household size by the square-root equivalence scale. Consumer price indices and purchasing power parity conversion factors from local currency units to international dollars are from the International Monetary Fund (2007).

about 70 percent of that of the median American, the living standard of the poor in Sweden and Finland is roughly the same as in the United States, around 39 percent of the US median. Low-income people in Denmark, Norway, the Netherlands, Switzerland, and, especially, Luxembourg are much better off than elsewhere. In all southern European countries, but also, to a lesser extent, in Australia, Ireland, and the United Kingdom, the living standards of low-income households are lower than in the United States. Of course, they are a great deal lower in all middle-income

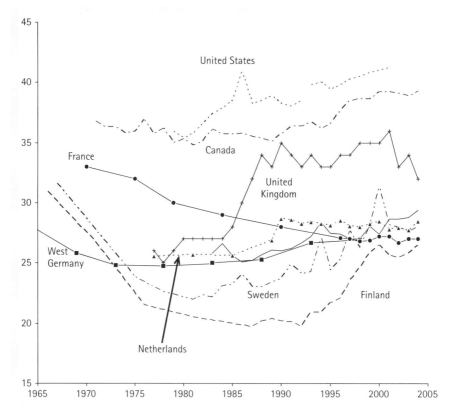

**Fig. 4.5. Gini index of disposable income (percent)**

*Note*: To facilitate reading, a break in each of the series for Canada, the Netherlands, Sweden, and the United Kingdom is eliminated by scaling up or down the figures before the discontinuity by the difference in the first overlapping year.
*Source*: Brandolini and Smeeding (forthcoming).

economies. At the other extreme, the rich Americans far surpass the rich in any other nation observed, save for the Luxembourgers. For instance, the rich American is almost 50 percentage points above the rich Canadian and the rich Briton. The horizontal bars in Figure 4.4 are proportional to the absolute distance between top and bottom incomes. The absolute gap in the United States is 1.5–1.7 times those in Switzerland, Taiwan, Canada, and the United Kingdom, and is much higher than in any of the remaining countries except Luxembourg. The United States enjoys the world's highest living standard as well as the greatest absolute inequality between the rich and the poor among developed countries.

   Figures 4.3 and 4.4 offer a snapshot of income inequality around the turn of the century. However, as is well-known, inequality has increased considerably in recent decades in several countries, prominently in the United States and the United Kingdom (Gottschalk and Smeeding, 1997, 2000; Brandolini and Smeeding, forthcoming). Thus, Figure 4.5 summarizes the evidence at our disposal on long-run patterns in eight rich countries: three Anglo-Saxon nations (Canada, the United States, and the United Kingdom), two Nordic nations (Finland and Sweden), and three continental European countries (the Netherlands, West Germany, and France). As noted before, reported series are a selection of those internally consistent for a sufficiently long span of time, and they are not necessarily comparable across nations. In order to make the picture more readable, some broken series are joined by simply adding to the initial piece of the time series the difference in the overlapping year.

The main conclusion from Figure 4.5 is that national experiences varied during the last four decades and there is no one overarching common story. There was some tendency for the disposable income distribution to narrow until the mid-1970s. Then, income inequality rose sharply in the United Kingdom in the 1980s and in the United States in the 1980s and 1990s, continuing more slowly through the 2000s. But inequality rose more moderately in Canada, Sweden, Finland, and West Germany in the 1990s. Moreover, the timing and magnitude of the increase differed widely across nations. Inequality did not show any persistent tendency to rise in the Netherlands (bowl-shaped trend), and may even have decreased in France.

Changes in inequality do not exhibit clear trajectories, but rather irregular movements, with more substantial changes often concentrated in rather short lapses of time. Together with the lack of a common international pattern, this suggests looking at explanations based on the joint working of multiple factors which sometimes balance out, sometimes reinforce each other, rather than focusing on explanations centered on a single cause like de-industrialization, skill-biased technological progress, or globalization. Identifying and characterizing episodes and turning points in the dynamics of inequality may be more fruitful than searching for overarching general tendencies.

## Cash and Non-Cash Redistribution

Even a cursory comparison of the inequality indices for market and disposable income reveals a large equalizing impact of public redistribution. But the size of the impact and the way in which it is achieved vary from country to country. For the same seven countries included in Table 4.1, Table 4.2 shows how the distribution of market incomes is turned into the distribution of disposable incomes by subtracting taxes and social contribution and adding social insurance and assistance benefits, and private inter-household transfers. Both public transfers and taxes are much higher in Sweden, Finland, and Germany than in the United Kingdom and the United States (column 1), an indication of the different welfare regimes emphasized in Chapter 25. In all five countries, however, the rank correlation ratio is close to one for taxes and contributions, as a consequence of their strict relationship

Table 4.2. Decomposition of the Gini index of disposable income by income source in seven countries

| Income source | Share of disposable income (%) [1] | Rank correlation ratio [2] | Gini index [3] | Population share with positive value (%) [4] | Gini index for population with positive value [5] | Absolute contribution [6] | Relative contribution (%) [7] |
|---|---|---|---|---|---|---|---|
| Finland 2000 | | | | | | | |
| Market income | 105.3 | 0.877 | 0.469 | 90.9 | 0.416 | 0.433 | 175.9 |
| Private transfers | 1.1 | 0.096 | 0.905 | 25.9 | 0.635 | 0.001 | 0.4 |
| Public social transfers | 32.3 | −0.188 | 0.550 | 88.1 | 0.489 | −0.033 | −13.6 |
| Taxes, social contributions | −38.7 | 0.888 | 0.450 | 98.1 | 0.439 | −0.154 | −62.7 |
| Disposable income | 100.0 | 1.000 | 0.246 | 100.0 | 0.246 | 0.246 | 100.0 |
| Germany 2000 | | | | | | | |
| Market income | 109.0 | 0.834 | 0.481 | 95.1 | 0.454 | 0.437 | 159.0 |
| Private transfers | 0.8 | −0.255 | 0.975 | 4.8 | 0.467 | −0.002 | −0.7 |
| Public social transfers | 27.0 | −0.026 | 0.606 | 81.5 | 0.517 | −0.004 | −1.5 |
| Taxes, social contributions | −36.7 | 0.798 | 0.532 | 93.3 | 0.499 | −0.156 | −56.7 |
| Disposable income | 100.0 | 1.000 | 0.275 | 100.0 | 0.275 | 0.275 | 100.0 |
| Poland 1999 | | | | | | | |
| Market income | 74.6 | 0.760 | 0.530 | 74.9 | 0.373 | 0.301 | 96.2 |
| Private transfers | 3.0 | 0.257 | 0.925 | 14.7 | 0.492 | 0.007 | 2.3 |
| Public social transfers | 36.5 | 0.200 | 0.610 | 73.2 | 0.467 | 0.044 | 14.2 |
| Taxes, social contributions | −14.1 | 0.526 | 0.534 | 79.9 | 0.416 | −0.040 | −12.7 |
| Disposable income | 100.0 | 1.000 | 0.313 | 100.0 | 0.313 | 0.313 | 100.1 |
| Sweden 2000 | | | | | | | |
| Market income | 109.0 | 0.906 | 0.459 | 95.8 | 0.436 | 0.453 | 180.2 |
| Private transfers | 0.8 | −0.327 | 0.912 | 12.4 | 0.286 | −0.002 | −1.0 |
| Public social transfers | 33.6 | −0.195 | 0.529 | 88.2 | 0.466 | −0.035 | −13.7 |
| Taxes, social contributions | −43.4 | 0.958 | 0.396 | 97.9 | 0.383 | −0.165 | −65.5 |
| Disposable income | 100.0 | 1.000 | 0.252 | 100.0 | 0.252 | 0.252 | 100.0 |

| | | | | | | |
|---|---|---|---|---|---|---|
| **Taiwan 2000** | | | | | | |
| Market income | 101.1 | 0.971 | 99.5 | 0.322 | 0.319 | 107.7 |
| Private transfers | 4.9 | −0.029 | 79.1 | 0.674 | −0.001 | −0.4 |
| Public social transfers | 4.3 | 0.139 | 98.6 | 0.535 | 0.003 | 1.1 |
| Taxes, social contributions | −10.3 | 0.724 | 97.8 | 0.318 | −0.025 | −8.4 |
| Disposable income | 100.0 | 1.000 | 100.0 | 0.296 | 0.296 | 100.0 |
| **United Kingdom 1999** | | | | | | |
| Market income | 107.3 | 0.923 | 89.3 | 0.450 | 0.504 | 146.9 |
| Private transfers | 1.2 | 0.189 | 6.4 | 0.577 | 0.002 | 0.6 |
| Public social transfers | 18.0 | −0.442 | 76.8 | 0.469 | −0.047 | −13.7 |
| Taxes, social contributions | −26.4 | 0.782 | 90.3 | 0.514 | −0.116 | −33.8 |
| Disposable income | 100.0 | 1.000 | 100.0 | 0.343 | 0.343 | 100.0 |
| **United States 2000** | | | | | | |
| Market income | 117.2 | 0.947 | 95.5 | 0.455 | 0.532 | 144.4 |
| Private transfers | 1.1 | 0.138 | 10.5 | 0.588 | 0.001 | 0.4 |
| Public social transfers | 10.5 | −0.007 | 49.4 | 0.550 | −0.001 | −0.1 |
| Taxes, social contributions | −28.8 | 0.924 | 91.7 | 0.584 | −0.165 | −44.7 |
| Disposable income | 100.0 | 1.000 | 100.0 | 0.368 | 0.368 | 100.0 |

*Notes:* Observations for disposable income are bottom-coded at 1 percent of the mean of equivalent disposable income and top-coded at 10 times the median of unadjusted disposable income. Changes in disposable incomes due to bottom- and top-coding are entirely attributed to market incomes, proportionally for each income component. All income values are adjusted for household size by the square-root equivalence scale.

*Source:* Authors' calculations from the Luxembourg Income Study database, as of 20 February 2008.

with income, and negative for public transfers, signaling some targeting to lower-income households (column 2). Targeting appears to be especially pronounced in the United Kingdom, and limited in the United States. Poland exhibits the largest proportion of public transfers in disposable income, despite the low tax incidence, while Taiwan has the least redistributive public intervention; in both countries, there is no evidence of targeting in social protection, and the share of private inter-household transfers is considerably larger than in the other five nations. In all seven countries taxes and social contributions appear to be the main factor behind the reduction of income inequality, but transfers also play a role in Finland, Sweden, and the United Kingdom (columns 6 and 7).

A common synthetic 'output' measure of the level of redistribution is consti-tuted by the difference between the Gini index for market incomes and the Gini index for disposable incomes. This difference provides only a crude estimate of the actual degree of public redistribution. First, the implicit assumption that market income inequality would remain the same if taxes and benefits did not exist is clearly unrealistic, since it ignores how taxes and benefits encourage, or discourage, earnings or savings. Second, this measure disregards the different impact of pro-grams designed to achieve redistribution: universal benefits, targeted means-tested assistance, or social insurance schemes (see also Mahler and Jesuit, 2006; Smeeding, 2006). Third, it only accounts for cash and near-cash programs, paying no attention to redistribution carried out via non-cash programs. Ideally, one would like to know how people would behave in a different environment with no taxes and benefits, or different assistance schemes, but this would require bold assumptions and a rather complex data-based behavioral micro-simulation model, or a more abstract computable general equilibrium model (Boadway and Keen, 2000). On the contrary, the difference in the Gini indices for market and disposable incomes is an intelligible, if imperfect, way to gauge the level of income redistribution in a country.

As shown by LIS data, in all 16 nations reported in Figure 4.6 disposable incomes are more equally distributed than market incomes, confirming that the direct tax and cash benefit system narrows the overall distribution. On average, inequality falls by about a third, from a Gini index of 45 to one of 29 percent. Cross-country variation in original inequality is wider than after redistribution: the Gini index ranges from 33 to 53 percent for market incomes, and from 23 to 37 percent for disposable incomes. The United States has the highest inequality of disposable incomes, although the dispersion of market incomes is on the high side but not far from most other countries; it is as high as in Germany and Australia and below the values recorded for the United Kingdom, Poland, and Israel. The fact is that in the United States the percentage reduction in inequality brought about by taxes and benefits is a mere 23 percent, the lowest value in the figure, excluding Taiwan where redistribution has a tiny impact.

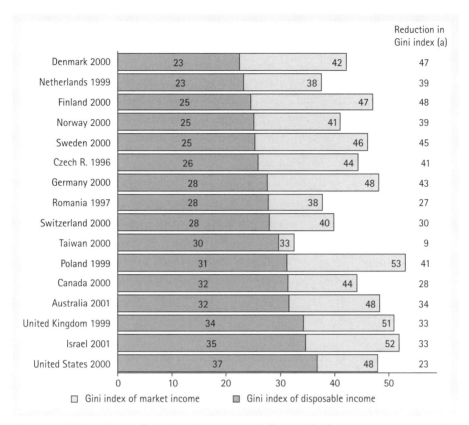

**Fig. 4.6. Gini indices of market income and disposable income in 16 countries (percent)**

*Notes*: Observations for disposable income are bottom-coded at 1 percent of the mean of equivalent disposable income and top-coded at 10 times the median of unadjusted disposable income. Changes in disposable incomes due to bottom- and top-coding are entirely attributed to market incomes. Both market and disposable incomes are adjusted for household size by the square-root equivalence scale. (a) Difference between the Gini index for market income and the Gini index for disposable income, expressed as a percentage of the former.

*Source*: Authors' calculations from the Luxembourg Income Study database, as of 20 February 2008.

These percentage reductions are very consistent with patterns of aggregate public expenditure (see Smeeding, 2005, about non-elderly spending). High-spending northern and central European nations have the highest degree of inequality reduction, from 39 to 48 percent; the Anglo-Saxon (excluding the United States) nations and Israel are next with 28 to 34 percent reductions; Switzerland and Romania follow at 30 percent or less, and the United States and Taiwan are, as just seen, at the bottom of the scale. The degree of redistribution in southern Europe is lower than in Ireland and the United Kingdom, especially if public pensions are not included among transfers, according to the EUROMOD estimates based on micro-simulations rather than the records of the original micro-data sources (Immervoll

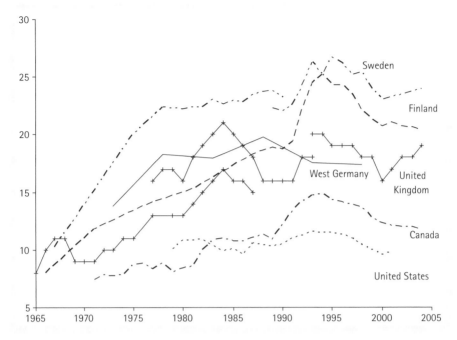

**Fig. 4.7. Equalizing effect of taxes and transfers: absolute difference between the Gini index of market income and the Gini index of disposable income (percent)**

*Notes*: Unadjusted incomes for Canada, the United Kingdom (1961–87), and the United States; equivalent incomes for Finland, Sweden, West Germany, and the United Kingdom (1977–2004).

*Source*: Brandolini and Smeeding (forthcoming).

*et al.*, 2006). The nations that redistribute the most are not necessarily those with the greatest degree of market income inequality: before-tax-and-benefit incomes in Denmark and Norway are far more equally distributed than in the United States. In fact, Schwabish *et al.* (2006) find almost no correlation between the P10 value for market income and the level of social spending. Lindert (2004) provides historical evidence that higher social spending is positively correlated with longer-term economic growth trends.

When time trends are considered, the redistributive impact of tax-and-transfer systems appears to have evolved differently across nations. Time patterns for six countries are shown in Figure 4.7, again by looking at the absolute difference between the Gini index for market income and that for disposable income. Note that these time series also reflect national practices and so the level of redistribution is not completely comparable across nations. What emerges is that the redistributive impact of taxes and transfers initially increased and then stabilized or dropped in all countries except for the United States, where it remained quite stable over time (but the series starts only in 1979). The United Kingdom stands out for having the most dramatic switch of regime, as in the early 1980s it apparently shifted from a situation not too different from the two Nordic countries to a model closer to that of the two North American countries. It is not possible to infer from this simple measure whether changes in redistribution are the automatic response of a progressive tax-and-benefit system to changes in the distribution of market incomes, or are instead the product of explicit policy choices (Atkinson, 2004). Nevertheless, they confirm that a widening of the market income distribution need not result in a drastic increase in the inequality of disposable incomes. Rising levels of redistribution in Finland, Sweden, and to a lesser extent Canada—where policies have been increasingly targeted at the poor—have been more effective in muting increasing market income inequality than have stable but low levels of redistribution in the United States, though periods do matter.

As already said, none of these estimates includes benefits in-kind or indirect taxes. How much difference do they make? In their study of the distribution in seven rich countries in the early 1980s, Smeeding *et al.* (1993) found that including the value of non-cash benefits in household income reinforced the redistributive impact of cash tax-and-transfer mechanisms in all countries, but did not affect markedly the pattern of national differences in income inequality compared with that which emerged from the analysis of cash income alone. More recent analysis for ten rich countries in the late 1990s by Garfinkel *et al.* (2006) confirms the egalitarian impact of non-cash redistribution. After augmenting income to include the value of non-cash benefits for health care and education net of both direct and indirect taxes, the income of the poor turns out to be much closer to the median and the distance between the rich and the poor falls in all countries, except Belgium and Finland. Changes are largest among the English-speaking nations, with the United States showing the greatest drop in the decile ratio. Differences across countries appear to shrink considerably.

Two reasons can account for these results. First, compared to other advanced nations, the English-speaking nations tend to be short on cash and long on in-kind benefits. Thus relatively equal non-cash benefits can go a long way toward equalizing command over total resources, including more unequally distributed cash benefits and other incomes. Second, these countries rely less heavily than the big spending national welfare states on indirect taxes and taxation of cash benefits. Together, these two factors explain the big shift when moving from cash disposable income to augmented income.

These results are to be taken with caution, because they depend crucially on the assumptions made to evaluate and impute non-cash benefits. While this caveat has to be borne in mind, it is clear conceptually that these benefits are worth some non-trivial amount to both rich and poor alike. Empirically, health and education transfers are as large as or a much larger part of what the welfare state does for families than the provision of cash benefits in all nations. This fact must be taken into consideration in studying the relative effectiveness and generosity of all welfare states, and their effect on inequality.

Finally, the after tax and transfer disposable income figures presented above often implicitly include the benefits of 'tax expenditures' (deductions from the income tax base for some actions such as payment of mortgage interest on owned homes, or deferring income on contributions to pensions) or differentially lower tax rates on certain types of incomes such as income from capital. In many countries such benefits rise with tax rates and primarily benefit the well-to-do in the highest tax brackets, even though these benefits cannot be shown as redistribution in the analyses above.

# 4. CONCLUSIONS AND FURTHER RESEARCH

The measurement of the distribution of living standards among households or persons is a demanding task that poses both conceptual and practical problems, from the choice of the focal variable to its precise definition, from the decision about the reference unit or the equivalence scale to the understanding of the impact of sampling and non-sampling errors. The emphasis on the importance of these problems in the first part of this chapter is not meant to discourage research in this field, but it is rather a strong recommendation to take them seriously before drawing conclusions from empirical analysis.

The evidence presented in the chapter shows that around the beginning of this century, the United States had the highest level of disposable income inequality among high-income economies, while central and, especially, northern European countries had the lowest levels. Only in Russia and Mexico, two middle-income economies, was disposable income more unequally distributed than in the United States. The US result is due less to the high concentration in the distribution of market incomes than to the effects of taxes and benefits in reducing market income inequality. The redistributive impact of the government, as captured by the difference between the Gini indices for market and disposable income, is substantially larger in continental and northern European countries. Lastly, no common trend in disposable income inequality is observed since the 1970s across rich nations. However, the overall tendency in the last 20 years has been for an increase in both disposable and market income inequality in the large majority of rich nations.

While some major patterns are clear across and within nations, a great deal of work remains. Amongst the challenges facing researchers are improved measures of income from capital and wealth, more robust trend data for a wider range of rich nations. More comparable data in the LIS style for the fast-growing middle-income countries—including China and India, for instance—would greatly widen the scope of inquiry and add to our basis for assessing the impacts of trade and global economic change on inequality in a comparable format. Finally, attempts to model and understand causal factors and explanations for differences in level and trend in income inequality across nations is the ultimate challenge to which researchers on inequality should all aspire.

# References

Atkinson, A. B. 1970. 'On the Measurement of Inequality'. *Journal of Economic Theory*, 2: 244–63.

——1983. *The Economics of Inequality*, 2nd edn. Oxford: Clarendon Press.

——2004. 'Increased Income Inequality in OECD Countries and the Redistributive Impact of the Government Budget', in G. A. Cornia (ed.), *Inequality, Growth, and Poverty in an Era of Liberalization and Globalization*. Oxford: Oxford University Press, 220–48.

——and Brandolini, A. 2001. 'Promises and Pitfalls in the Use of Secondary Data-Sets: Income Inequality in OECD Countries as a Case Study'. *Journal of Economic Literature*, 39: 771–800.

——and Micklewright, J. 1992. *Economic Transformation in Eastern Europe and the Distribution of Income*. Cambridge: Cambridge University Press.

——and Piketty, T. (eds.) 2007. *Top Incomes over the 20th Century: A Contrast between Continental European and English-Speaking Countries*. Oxford: Oxford University Press.

——Rainwater, L., and Smeeding, T. M. 1995. *Income Distribution in OECD Countries: The Evidence from the Luxembourg Income Study (LIS)*. Paris: Organisation for Economic Co-operation and Development.

Boadway, R., and Keen, M. 2000. 'Redistribution', in A. B. Atkinson and F. Bourguignon (eds.), *Handbook of Income Distribution*, vol. 1. Amsterdam: North-Holland, 677–789.

Björklund, A. 1993. 'A Comparison between Actual Distributions of Annual and Lifetime Income: Sweden 1951–89'. *Review of Income and Wealth*, 39: 377–86.

——and Palme, M. 2002. 'Income Redistribution within the Life Cycle versus between Individuals: Empirical Evidence Using Swedish Panel Data', in D. Cohen, T. Piketty, and G. Saint-Paul (eds.), *The Economics of Rising Inequalities*. Oxford: Oxford University Press, 205–23.

Böheim, R., and Jenkins, S. P. 2006. 'A Comparison of Current and Annual Measures of Income in the British Household Panel Survey'. *Journal of Official Statistics*, 22: 733–58.

Bradbury, B., and Jäntti, M. 1999. 'Child Poverty across Industrialized Nations'. UNICEF International Child Development Centre, Innocenti Occasional Papers, Economic and Social Policy Series no. 71, Sept.

Brandolini, A. 2007. 'Measurement of Income Distribution in Supranational Entities: The Case of the European Union', in S. P. Jenkins and J. Micklewright (eds.), *Inequality and Poverty Re-examined*. Oxford: Oxford University Press, 62–83.

BRANDOLINI, A., and SMEEDING, T. M. Forthcoming. 'Inequality Patterns in Western-Type Democracies: Cross-Country Differences and Time Changes', in P. Beramendi and C. J. Anderson (eds.), *Democracy, Inequality and Representation*. New York: Russell Sage Foundation.

BUHMANN, B., RAINWATER, L., SCHMAUS, G., and SMEEDING, T. M. 1988. 'Equivalence Scales, Well-Being, Inequality, and Poverty: Sensitivity Estimates across Ten Countries Using the Luxembourg Income Study (LIS) Database'. *Review of Income and Wealth*, 34: 115–42.

BURKHAUSER, R. V., FENG, S., and JENKINS, S. P. 2007. 'Using the P90/P10 Index to Measure US Inequality Trends with Current Population Survey Data: A View from Inside the Census Bureau Vaults'. University of Essex, ISER Working Paper no. 2007-14, June.

CLEMENCEAU, A., and MUSEUX, J.-M. 2007. 'EU-SILC (Community Statistics on Income and Living Conditions: General Presentation of the Instrument)', in *Comparative EU Statistics on Income and Living Conditions: Issues and Challenges—Proceedings of the EU-SILC Conference (Helsinki, 6–8 November 2006)*. Luxembourg: Office for Official Publications of the European Communities, 13–36.

COULTER, F. A. E., COWELL, F. A., and JENKINS, S. P. 1992. 'Equivalence Scale Relativities and the Extent of Inequality and Poverty'. *Economic Journal*, 102: 1067–82.

COWELL, F. A., and VICTORIA-FESER, M.-P. 1996. 'Robustness Properties of Inequality Measures'. *Econometrica*, 64: 77–101.

DANZIGER, S., and TAUSSIG, M. K. 1979. 'The Income Unit and the Anatomy of Income Distribution'. *Review of Income and Wealth*, 25: 365–75.

DEATON, A. 2005. 'Measuring Poverty in a Growing World (Or Measuring Growth in a Poor World)'. *Review of Economics and Statistics*, 87: 1–19.

——and GROSH, M. 2000. 'Consumption', in M. Grosh and P. Glewwe (eds.), *Designing Household Survey Questionnaires for Developing Countries. Lessons from 15 Years of the Living Standards Measurement Study*, vol. 1. Washington: World Bank, 91–133.

DEININGER, K., and SQUIRE, L. 1996. 'A New Data Set Measuring Income Inequality'. *World Bank Economic Review*, 10: 565–91. Data available at: <http://econ.worldbank.org/WBSITE/EXTERNAL/EXTDEC/EXTRESEARCH/0„contentMDK:20699070~pagePK:64214825~piPK:64214943~theSitePK:469382,00.html>.

DOWRICK, S., and AKMAL, M. 2005. 'Contradictory Trends in Global Income Inequality: A Tale of Two Biases'. *Review of Income and Wealth*, 51: 201–29.

EBERT, U. 1997. 'Social Welfare When Needs Differ: An Axiomatic Approach'. *Economica*, 64: 233–44.

EXPERT GROUP ON HOUSEHOLD INCOME STATISTICS—THE CANBERRA GROUP 2001. *Final Report and Recommendations*. Ottawa: The Canberra Group.

FRICK, J. R., and GRABKA, M. M. 2003. 'Imputed Rent and Income Inequality: A Decomposition Analysis for Great Britain, West Germany and the U.S.'. *Review of Income and Wealth*, 49: 513–37.

FRIEDMAN, M. 1957. *A Theory of the Consumption Function*. Princeton: Princeton University Press.

GARFINKEL, I., RAINWATER, L., and SMEEDING, T. M. 2006. 'A Reexamination of Welfare State and Inequality in Rich Nations: How In-Kind Transfers and Indirect Taxes Change the Story'. *Journal of Policy Analysis and Management*, 25: 855–919.

——————2007. 'The American Welfare State: Laggard or Leader', Unpublished manuscript, January.

GOTTSCHALK, P., and SMEEDING, T. M. 1997. 'Cross-National Comparisons of Earnings and Income Inequality'. *Journal of Economic Literature*, 35: 633–87.

————2000. 'Empirical Evidence on Income Inequality in Industrialized Countries', in A. B. Atkinson and F. Bourguignon (eds.), *Handbook of Income Distribution*, vol. 1. Amsterdam: North-Holland, 261–308.

HAGENAARS, A. J. M., DE VOS, K., and ZAIDI, M. A. 1994. *Poverty Statistics in the Late 1980s: Research Based on Micro-Data*. Luxembourg: Eurostat.

HAIG, R. M. 1921. 'The Concept of Income: Economic and Legal Aspects', in R. M. Haig (ed.), *The Federal Income Tax*. New York: Columbia University Press, 1–28.

IMMERVOLL, H., LEVY, H., LIETZ, C., MANTOVANI, D., O'DONOGHUE, C., SUTHERLAND, H., and VERBIST, G. 2006. 'Household Incomes and Redistribution in the European Union: Quantifying the Equalising Properties of Taxes and Benefits', in D. B. Papadimitriou (ed.), *The Distributional Effects of Government Spending and Taxation*. Basingstoke: Palgrave Macmillan, 135–65.

INTERNATIONAL MONETARY FUND 2007. *World Economic Outlook*. Washington: International Monetary Fund. Data available at: <http://www.imf.org/external/pubs/ft/weo/2007/02/weodata/index.aspx>.

ISHIKAWA, T. 1996. Data runs conducted by Ministry of Welfare, 26 Nov.

JOHNSON, D. S., SMEEDING, T. M., and TORREY, B. B. 2005. 'Economic Inequality through the Prisms of Income and Consumption'. *Monthly Labor Review*, 128(4): 11–24.

LINDERT, P. 2004. *Growing Public*. Cambridge: Cambridge University Press.

MAHLER, V. A., and JESUIT, D. K. 2006. 'Fiscal Redistribution in the Developed Countries: New Insights from the Luxembourg Income Study'. *Socio-Economic Review*, 4: 483–511.

PARETO, V. 1897. *Cours d'économie politique*. Lausanne and Paris: Rouge and Pichon. Reprinted in *Oeuvres Complètes*, ed. by G.-H. Bousquet and G. Busino. Geneva: Librairie Droz, 1964.

PYATT, G., CHEN, C.-N., and FEI, J. 1980. 'The Distribution of Income by Factor Components'. *Quarterly Journal of Economics*, 95: 451–73.

REDMOND, G. 1998. 'Households, Families and the Distribution of Income'. *Social Policy Research Centre Newsletter*, no. 71: 1, 4–5.

RYSCAVAGE, P. 1995. 'A Surge in Growing Income Inequality?' *Monthly Labor Review*, 118(8): 51–61.

SCHWABISH, J., SMEEDING, T. M., and OSBERG, L. 2006. 'Income Distribution and Social Expenditures', in D. B. Papadimitriou (ed.), *The Distributional Effects of Government Spending and Taxation*. Basingstoke: Palgrave Macmillan, 247–88.

SEN, A. K. 1992. *Inequality Re-examined*. Oxford: Clarendon Press.

SHORROCKS, A. F. 1983. 'The Impact of Income Components on the Distribution of Family Incomes'. *Quarterly Journal of Economics*, 98: 311–26.

SIMONS, H. C. 1938. *Personal Income Taxation: The Definition of Income as a Problem of Fiscal Policy*. Chicago: University of Chicago Press.

SLESNICK, D. T. 1994. 'Consumption, Needs and Inequality'. *International Economic Review*, 35: 677–703.

SMEEDING, T. M. 1982. *Alternative Methods for Valuing Selected In-Kind Transfer Benefits and Measuring their Effect on Poverty*. US Bureau of Census Technical Paper no. 50. Washington: US Government Printing Office.

SMEEDING, T. M. 2004. 'Twenty Years of Research on Income Inequality, Poverty, and Redistribution in the Developed World: Introduction and Overview'. *Socio-Economic Review*, 2: 149–63.

—— 2005. 'Public Policy, Economic Inequality, and Poverty: The United States in Comparative Perspective'. *Social Science Quarterly*, 86 (suppl.): 955–83.

—— 2006. 'Poor People in Rich Nations: The United States in Comparative Perspective'. *Journal of Economic Perspectives*, 20: 69–90.

SMEEDING, T. M., and RAINWATER, L. 2004. 'Comparing Living Standards across Nations: Real Incomes at the Top, the Bottom, and the Middle', in E. N. Wolff (ed.), *What Has Happened to the Quality of Life in the Advanced Industrialized Nations?* Northampton, MA: Edward Elgar, 153–83.

—— SAUNDERS, P., CODER, J., JENKINS, J., FRITZELL, J., HAGENAARS, A. J. M., HAUSER, R., and WOLFSON, M. 1993. 'Poverty, Inequality, and Family Living Standards Impacts across Seven Nations: The Effect of Noncash Subsidies for Health, Education, and Housing'. *Review of Income and Wealth*, 39: 229–56.

—— and THOMPSON, J. 2007. 'Income from Wealth and Income from Labor: Stocks, Flows and More Complete Measures of Well Being', unpublished manuscript, June.

—— and WEINBERG, D. H. 2001. 'Toward a Uniform Definition of Household Income'. *Review of Income and Wealth*, 47: 1–24.

SUMMERS, R., and HESTON, A. 1991. 'The Penn World Table (Mark 5): An Expanded Set of International Comparisons, 1950–1988'. *Quarterly Journal of Economics*, 106: 327–68.

UNITED NATIONS UNIVERSITY—WORLD INSTITUTE FOR DEVELOPMENT ECONOMICS RESEARCH 2007. *World Income Inequality Database V 2.0b May 2007*, available at: <http://www.wider.unu. edu/wiid/wiid.htm>.

US CONGRESSIONAL BUDGET OFFICE 2007. *Historical Effective Federal Tax Rates: 1979 to 2005*, December, available at: <http://www.cbo.gov/ftpdocs/88xx/doc8885/12-11-HistoricalTaxRates.pdf>.

VOITCHOVSKY, S. 2005. 'Does the Profile of Income Inequality Matter for Economic Growth?' *Journal of Economic Growth*, 10: 273–96.

WORLD BANK 2005. *World Development Report 2006: Equity and Development*. New York and Oxford: Oxford University Press.

..................................................................................................

# CHAPTER 5

# FUNCTIONAL DISTRIBUTION AND INEQUALITY

..................................................................................................

## ANDREW GLYN[1,2]

## 1. INTRODUCTION—DOES THE FUNCTIONAL DISTRIBUTION MATTER?

..................................................................................................

MOST chapters in this Handbook are concerned with economic inequality between individuals and the inclusion of a chapter on functional distribution requires an answer to the puzzled comment by Mark Blaug: 'The great mystery of the modern theory of distribution is why anyone regards the *share* of wages and profits as an interesting problem' (Blaug, 1996: 467, emphasis in the original).

Factor shares can clearly be important for the macroeconomic functioning of economies, as was shown in the discussion of 'profits squeeze' alias 'excessive real wages' in relation to the 1960s and 1970s (Glyn and Sutcliffe, 1972; Bruno and Sachs,

[1] Andrew Glyn was unable to revise this chapter and the final version was prepared by Bob Rowthorn and Wendy Carlin. The editors of the Handbook are extremely grateful to them for undertaking this task.

[2] I am most grateful to many people who provided help in several ways. Bob Allen, Steve Broadberry, Casten Burhop, Makoto Itoh, Peter Lindert, Roger Middleton, Pascal Petit, Thomas Piketty, Albrecht Ritschl, Wiemer Salverda, Gianni Toniolo, and Jan-Luiten Van Zanden generously advised on sources or directly provided data used in Section 4. Mary Robertson gave valuable research assistance and comments, and Wendy Carlin and the editors made many helpful suggestions. The financial support of the Nuffield Foundation is gratefully acknowledged.

1985; Eichengreen, 2007). The functional distribution of national income between wages, profits, and rents was central to discussions of distribution by the classical economists, being described by David Ricardo (1817: 5) as 'the principal problem in Political Economy'. As late as the mid-1960s at a high-powered conference on income distribution, five out of the six empirical papers discussing the industrialized countries and six out of seven theoretical papers were concerned with functional distribution (Marchal and Ducros, 1968).

The shift of interest amongst economists away from functional distribution seems to have reflected a number of influences (Goldfarb and Leonard, 2005). Within economics there was a determination to use the powerful tools of orthodox economics to understand personal distribution, described by Stigler as 'a problem of all economies in all times' (Stigler, 1965: 22). Becker's human capital theory constituted part of the response. The empirical study of personal distribution was facilitated by microeconomic data collected in part to monitor the impact of the welfare state on household poverty and inequality.

Moreover an ideological shift away from a class-based view of the economy was being mirrored on the ground by the spread of capital-funded occupational pensions and home ownership. If an economy is divided into workers receiving only wages and capitalists/landlords receiving only profits/rents, then the split of national income between wages and profits must have a major influence on personal income distribution.[3] However as soon as the old slogan 'Everyman a capitalist' (the title of a Conservative Party pamphlet in the 1950s) starts having some reflection in reality, then the profits/wages split diminishes in importance as a direct determinant of personal income distribution.

Despite this shift in focus amongst economic researchers, functional distribution still retains an important public resonance. Flagship publications from both the International Monetary Fund (IMF, 2007) and OECD (2007) have devoted considerable attention to the recent decline in labor's share in national income in advanced economies as reflecting the impact on workers of globalization (see Section 4). The issue has also brought striking comments from policy makers. Ben Bernanke, Chairman of the US Federal Reserve, appearing before a Senate Committee, expressed the hope that 'corporations would use some of those profit margins to meet demands from workers for higher wages' (reported by *New York Times*, July 20, 2006). Germany's finance minister recently called on European companies to 'give workers a fairer share of their soaring profits' or risk igniting a 'crisis in legitimacy' in the continent's economic model (*Financial Times*, February 28, 2007).

---

[3]  If all workers received identical wages and all receivers of property income received identical incomes then the Gini coefficient for personal income inequality would be equal to the difference between the percentages of total income received by workers and their proportion of the population (Atkinson and Bourguignon, 2000: 7). There would be a one-to-one relation between labor's share and income inequality. Of course wage and wealth inequality complicate the picture, even before the fact that households receive income from both sources is taken into account.

Such remarks were surely prompted by an understanding that functional distribution *does* matter to people. Two reasons for this may be suggested. First, despite the spread of 'popular capitalism', wealth and especially high-yielding wealth is still extremely unevenly distributed. Even in the USA where the importance of employee compensation in top incomes has grown spectacularly, the share of total income (including property income and capital gains) of the top 5% is much higher (37%) than their share of wage income (less than one quarter). This indicates a far higher concentration of income from property than of income from labor (Piketty and Saez, 2007, tables 5A.3, 5B.2). Thus redistribution from labor to property still has a significant effect in raising income inequality. This is consistent with a recent study covering 39 countries, both OECD and developing countries (Daudey and Garcia-Peñalosa, 2007), which found that a higher labor share (in manufacturing) is associated with a significantly lower Gini coefficient for income inequality and in particular a lower share for the incomes of the top fifth of the population. A previous economy-wide study, using a panel of OECD countries for the period 1970–96, found 'that the labor share remains a fundamental aspect of overall inequality patterns, with an effect roughly as important as that of relative wages' (Checchi and Garcia-Peñalosa, 2005: 4). The authors concluded that the distribution of wealth still plays a substantial role in income distribution.

Second, as the German finance minister noted, employees' sense of fairness is clearly offended when their employer's profits rise much faster than their wages. The classical notion that the employers' profits derive ultimately from their workers' efforts chimes at least in part with workers' own experience. This leads to the demand for 'fair shares' in any improved prosperity of their firm, and there is no reason to believe that this sentiment evaporates as more workers own financial assets, including corporate equity, through pension funds and the like. A comment from Stephen Roach, a senior economist at Morgan Stanley, when profits were rising especially rapidly in 1996, underlines the point: 'The share of national income going to the owners of capital through corporate profits is surging. The share going to compensation is falling. This is not the way a democracy is supposed to work' (quoted by Harrison, 2002: 2).

Our conclusion is that functional distribution is still important in discussions of economic inequality. The next section reviews theoretical perspectives on functional distribution, albeit rather briefly since Atkinson (1983, chapter 9) provides an excellent discussion. Measurement issues, which are often treated cursorily, are discussed in Section 3. The USA is used as a case study to show how levels and trends in factor shares may be affected by measurement choices. The preferred measure of labor's share shows a very shallow inverted U-shaped pattern, peaking in the late 1970s. In Section 4, the more pronounced rise and decline of labor's share in the post-war period observed in the OECD outside the USA is noted, and the influences behind the recent decline in labor's share are surveyed. Longer-term trends in labor's share from early in the 20th century calculated from national sources are reported in Section 5. The chapter concludes by drawing attention to the need for more research to uncover the causes of swings in factor shares and to establish the links between the functional and personal distribution of income.

# 2. THEORETICAL PERSPECTIVES

Most discussion of factor shares collapses the traditional wages–profits–rent split into the simpler wages–property income breakdown (see Kuznets, 1959 for example). Rents are very hard to distinguish empirically from the return on investment and agricultural rents have also declined radically in importance with the decline of the sector.[4]

Armed with this simplification the share of labor in aggregate income (LS) is the ratio of income from employment (W) to total income (Y). On a per worker basis (with L workers) this can be understood as the ratio of wages per head to average value added per head (W/L)/(Y/L). Dividing top and bottom by the price index for total value added gives labor's share as the ratio of the real wage (w) to real labor productivity (p), LS = w/p. Thus the change in labor's share over time can be seen as dependent on the comparative growth rates of real wages and productivity. When average real wages rise faster than average labor productivity the share of labor rises—there is a 'profits squeeze'. A slower growth of real wages than labor productivity conversely implies a decline in labor's share. The concept of the real wage used here must be the 'real product wage'—that is, wages deflated by the price index for total value added rather than by the index of consumer prices, which reflects the specific bundle of goods and services consumed by workers. This introduces a wedge between changes in the real wage deflated by consumer prices, as is relevant for the personal distribution of income, and labor's share whenever there is a gap between consumer price inflation and GDP inflation (for example, when import prices rise rapidly).

This formulation provides a useful way of summarizing the various theoretical approaches to the determination of labor's share. In the classical approach, the real wage was seen as reflecting socially determined subsistence levels, evolving only slowly. The key point is that the trend in real wages was not closely linked to the trend in labor productivity. Thus Ricardo's pessimistic vision of declining productivity in agriculture, the primary supplier of subsistence goods, implied a declining share for property income and in particular profits. This was because real wages decline more slowly than average productivity, if at all. On Marx's account,

---

[4]  In 1856 farm rents (which include a return on farm buildings etc. as well as pure rents) were 7.5% of UK national income; by 1913 they were 1.9% (Feinstein, 1972, tables 1 and 23).

by contrast, capitalism would systematically increase labor productivity through the substitution of machinery for labor, whilst any long-term rise in real wages would be kept below the growth of productivity by the reserve army of labor. Accordingly labor's share would decline. These ideas of Ricardo and Marx find contemporary echoes in (respectively) fears about sharply rising real costs of fuel and of environmental damage and on the other hand concerns about the impact on workers of the incorporation into the world economy of the enormous labor reserves in China and India (see Chapter 23).

Subsequent theories of distributive shares have tended to propose a tighter link between real wages and average productivity, without precluding changes in factor shares over time. The dominant neoclassical theory sees relative factor prices (w/r) as reflecting factor supplies (K/L), the capital/labor ratio, and the nature of the production function, which combine to determine relative marginal productivities. What happens over time as the capital/labor ratio rises depends on the impact on factor prices as can be seen by noting that

$$\text{Total Profits/Total Wages} = (r/w) \times (K/L).$$

If r/w falls in proportion as K/L rises, then the shares of wages and profits are unaffected, implying an elasticity of substitution between capital and labor equal to one (the Cobb-Douglas case). In effect this establishes a one-to-one link between real wages and productivity since capital accumulation drags up the marginal productivity of labor (and thus wages) in line with average productivity. Cobb-Douglas is both simple and consistent with the widely held, though as we shall see inaccurate, view that factor shares are relatively constant. If the elasticity of substitution is less than one, as econometric evidence suggests (Rowthorn, 1999), then a rising capital/labor ratio will tend to raise labor's share unless this is offset by biased technical progress. This is what Checchi and Garcia-Peñalosa (2005) find in their econometric study of OECD countries. A more complex picture is presented in a recent study by the European Commission (2008). This study finds that the degree of substitutability between capital and labor depends on the kind of labor concerned. Capital and low-skilled labor tend to be close substitutes, whereas capital and medium- or high-skilled labor are on average complements. An increase in the capital/labor ratio will therefore reduce the share of low-skilled labor and increase the share of other types of labor. The latter effect predominates, so an increase in K/L will tend to increase the overall labor share.

Despite the many criticisms leveled at the conceptual basis of the aggregate neoclassical theory of distribution (as reviewed in Atkinson, 1983 or Blaug, 1996), it has remained the dominant approach, being widely used for example in empirical analysis of the contributions of labor, capital, and technology to economic growth.

The assumption of perfect competition in factor pricing is one obvious, though remediable, weakness in the simplest neoclassical story. Kalecki's theory of distribution (Kalecki, 1971) put the focus on to the product market arguing that the greater the degree of monopoly the higher the mark-up of prices and profits over wage costs. A rising degree of monopoly over time would lead to real wages growing more slowly than productivity and to a rising share of profits; increased competition in product markets, deriving from the opening up of product markets to international competition for example, would have the reverse effect.

Increasing strength of trade unions is often posed as a counterweight to increased monopolization. The simplest models of mark-up pricing only allow wage bargaining to affect money wage increases and inflation but in reality there are a variety of routes whereby the trend of real wages and/or productivity may be affected, with direct implications for labor's share.[5] Cost of living escalators, limits on price increases posed by international competition, and fixed exchange rates are examples. A number of recent papers have formulated simple models where union bargaining power affects labor's share (see for example: Giammarioli *et al.*, 2002; Bentolila and Saint-Paul, 2003; Blanchard and Giavazzi, 2003; Checchi and Garcia-Peñalosa, 2005; Azmat *et al.*, 2007).

The classical economists saw a crucial role for the share of profits in determining capital accumulation and thus economic development. Kaldor (1955) turned this relationship on its head by proposing that the profit share was determined by investment levels, in that a rise in the investment share would cause an inflationary redistribution from wages to profits sufficient to finance the investment. This was regarded as a long-term Keynesian theory in the sense that real wages were supposed to respond passively to the level of demand, but with the slack taken up by the profit share in Kaldor's theory rather than employment as in Keynes's theory.[6]

It can be seen that there is no shortage of candidates to influence factor shares, though there is no agreed theoretical framework for combining them and for testing their quantitative importance. Before discussing what has happened to factor shares, the next section turns to the issue of how they should be measured.

# 3. MEASURING FACTOR SHARES

Measuring functional distribution is fraught with practical and conceptual difficulties which have been rather neglected since the classic discussions of the late

---

[5] The danger in assuming that wage militancy on its own must radically squeeze profits was brought out in Kalecki's remarkable analysis of the impact of the huge pay increases instituted under the French Popular Front in 1936–7. He concluded that after taking account of the associated devaluation, inflation, and the relative stickiness of fixed incomes such as pensions, rent, and interest receipts, the biggest gainers were not workers but the industrial entrepreneurs (Kalecki, 1938: 36).

[6] Kaldor is probably best remembered in this context for popularizing the 'stylized fact' with his claim that (inverting Ricardo) 'in different stages of (capitalist) society the proportions of national income allotted to wages, profits etc, are *essentially similar*' (1955: 83).

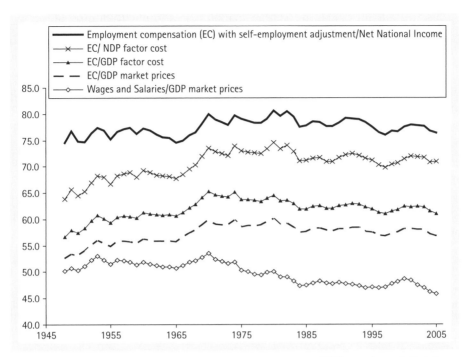

**Fig. 5.1. Labor's % share of total income, 1948–2005, USA: various definitions**

*Source*: National Income and Product Accounts (NIPA) 1.1.10, 1.13, 6.5, 6.8, 7.3.5.

1950s (see Kravis, 1959, on the USA and Kuznets, 1959, for estimates for a range of countries). This section follows the example of Krueger (1999) in taking the case of the USA in the post-World War II period to illustrate the measurement issues. Not only was the USA the most important industrialized country but its Bureau of Economic Analysis provides an exemplary set of downloadable national accounts, the national income and product account (NIPA), covering the whole period, which greatly facilitates comparison of alternative measures. We deal with these in three consecutive steps, focusing on the types of incomes, the coverage of the economy, and its composition.

Figure 5.1 shows the simplest measure of labor's share—wages and salaries as a percentage of Gross Domestic Product (GDP) at market prices—in the lowest series in the chart. After a gentle increase in the first two post-war decades the US share of wages and salaries slid down over the subsequent four decades. Whilst wages and salaries still comprise the major part of the national accounts measure of employee compensation, the latter also includes employers' contributions to pensions and social security and these clearly constitute part of the return from working. These additional employment costs show a strong upward trend in relation to GDP, making the initial rise in labor's share more pronounced, and eliminating the subsequent decline.

Measuring labor's share of GDP at market prices implicitly lumps all indirect taxes in with non-labor incomes. But indirect taxes do not represent a return to property ownership and thus it is preferable to measure labor's share of GDP at factor cost, so that its complement can be identified with (pre-tax) income from property.[7] With indirect taxes having taken a pretty steady share of GDP, the move from market price to factor cost measurement (the black triangles) makes little difference to the trend, whilst boosting labor's share by several percentage points.

When value added is measured by GDP, it is gross of capital consumption, and factor shares are frequently reported in this way.[8] However, the standard definition of property income or profits is to measure them net of depreciation (capital consumption). This is clearly the appropriate measure where the focus is on 'who gets what' and the use of such 'net income' measures is taken for granted by Kuznets (1959). Subtracting capital consumption, thus measuring labor's share of Net Domestic Product (NDP), is shown by the line of crosses in Figure 5.1. Deducting capital consumption pushes labor's share up by some 10 percentage points on average, with a slightly bigger effect in the second half of the period as the weight of capital consumption rose.

The final adjustment to these aggregate series adds to employee income an allowance for an imputed wage component of self-employment income. A substantial part of self-employment incomes represents a return to work, and failure to make such an adjustment means that the longer-term trend away from self-employment automatically pushes up the trend in labor's share. This does reflect an important phenomenon—the spread of wage labor—but would give a misleading impression as to how the underlying division between employment and property incomes was evolving. The opposite approach of including all self-employment income alongside employee compensation would be equally unsatisfactory given the large amounts of capital (not to mention farmland) used by some of the self-employed and the concomitant income from capital and consumption of capital.

The solution is to divide up self-employment income between a labor and property component. The many ways of doing this were thoroughly explored by Kuznets (1959, 1966) and Kravis (1959), and none of them is wholly unproblematic. The most common approach, followed here, is to attribute a wage to the self-employed. The self-employed tended historically to be concentrated heavily in agriculture, where average incomes (and wages) have been well below the national average. If an economy-wide average wage is attributed to peasant farmers, labor's share in agricultural net value added can easily exceed 100%, leaving a negative contribution

---

[7] Indirect taxes may have different incidence on labor and property income, but measuring 'post-tax' shares, dependent also on government redistributive policies, is not the issue here.

[8] Factor shares are often calculated simply in order to weight inputs for Total Factor Productivity (TFP) calculations which are typically applied to GDP.

from agriculture to property income. A preferable approach, data permitting, is to attribute the average agricultural wage to represent the labor income of farmers. The margin of value added per head in agriculture over the agricultural wage is then regarded as accruing to the farmer/landlord as property income flowing from the capital and land employed.[9]

The top solid black line in Figure 5.1 adds this estimate of labor income of the self-employed to employee compensation. The effect is to push up labor's share by some 10 percentage points in the 1950s. However the declining importance of self-employment, especially falling numbers of farmers in the 1950s, delays the rise in labor's share on this measure until the late 1960s/early 1970s and the decline since the early 1980s is fairly small—some 5 percentage points. A final small adjustment produces the preferred measure of labor's share at the aggregate level shown by the black line in Figure 5.1: this includes Net Property Income (NPI) from abroad, to give the share as a percentage of national income rather than net domestic income. Since US NPI was always pretty small (a maximum 2% of GDP), this makes little difference to the level, though the decline in NPI to nearly zero now does help slow the decline in labor's share over the past two decades.

The second issue relates to the coverage of the economy. National income includes not only the business sector, where labor and capital are deployed to generate profits, but also 'non-market' sectors where wages or attributed surpluses do not represent the proceeds of market sales. Three types of employment fall into this category—government employment, employment by not-for-profit institutions, and direct employment by households (for example, wage workers like cleaners not classified as self-employed). None of these generates profits for their employers; by the same token the share of labor in their (net) value added is 100%. An increasing proportion of labor employed in these activities will automatically boost the share of labor in national income. However, the non-market sector, surprisingly, also includes one activity where the 'imputed' share of labor is nearly zero—that is, owner-occupied housing where imputed rent (net of capital consumption) contributes property 'income' to national income (worth nearly 4% of net national income

---

[9]  In 1956 labor's share in US farm incomes was 56% when self-employed farmers are attributed an agricultural wage for their labor, but 126% if they are attributed an economy-wide average wage. Surprisingly, Gollin (2002) neglects this issue in a widely cited article relating labor's shares to the level of development. The use of sector wages could be extended to all the self-employed (as in Feinstein, 1968); here sector wages are applied only to farmers where it makes a major difference. A further very tricky issue concerns how to treat unpaid family workers, especially important in agriculture in many countries in the 20th century (notably Japan). Attributing a wage, particularly an average wage, to these workers would often boost labor's share to over 100%, not just in agriculture but in the whole economy. Unpaid family workers are left out of the calculations for Japan and some other countries in the next section. One major advantage of measures of labor's share which exclude agriculture is that the problem of how to divide up self-employment incomes is much less acute though it retains some relevance for countries with a high concentration of self-employment in low-wage sectors such as retailing or hotels.

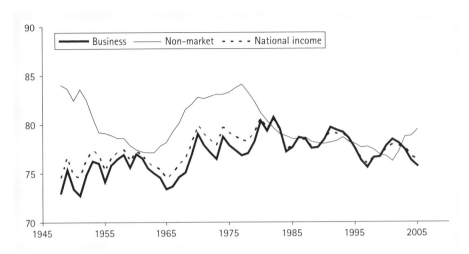

**Fig. 5.2. Labor's shares: US national income, 1948–2005, % of net value added**

*Source*: As Figure 5.1.

(NNI) in 2005.[10] We can combine these activities into a 'non-market' aggregate which contributed 22% of NNI in 2005, up from 13% in 1948. In this sector the share of labor in value added simply reflects the size of non-market wage bills as compared to the estimate of imputed rent. Quite unexpectedly, Figure 5.2 shows that the share of labor in the non-market sector in the USA has recently been very close to labor's share in business (corporations plus unincorporated enterprises). This is entirely coincidental.[11] In countries where government sector employment grew much faster, or where the imputed rents from owner occupied housing rose less rapidly, the rise of the non-market sector would push up labor's share in NNI to a greater extent.

Labor's share in business is the primary determinant of labor's share overall and this is where the proceeds of market sector activity are distributed between labor and property, free from 'non-market' complications. The business sector itself comprises unincorporated enterprises (already discussed above) and the corporate sector, both non-financial (NFCs) and financial. Labor's share for NFCs is un-problematic, but the attribution of value added and net operating surplus to the financial sector by the national accountants involves many subtleties. Financial corporations make much of their profit from the margin between interest received and interest paid, but in standard national accounting conventions net interest received

[10]  Much of imputed rental income on owner occupied housing is 'redistributed' by house owners who pay interest out of their other income to mortgage suppliers (see NIPA, tables 1.13, 7.4.5). Significant international differences exist in the treatment of imputed rent (Kalwij and Machin, 2007: 124) and percentages of NNI may deviate substantially.

[11]  During the period up to the mid-1970s, the rise in labor's share in NNI reflected the rise in labor's share within business combined with the rising share of the non-market sector, which tended to have a higher share of labor.

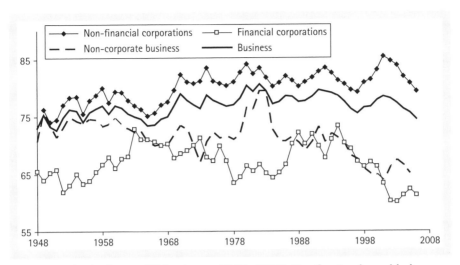

**Fig. 5.3. Labor's shares: US business, 1948–2006, % of net value added**

*Source*: As Figure 5.1 plus NIPA, table 1.14.

represents a transfer of value added rather than constituting part of profits and value added, which would leave finance with negative operating surplus. The US national accounts avoid this by regarding much of the interest margin as payment for implicit services to depositors and borrowers (worth in total more than 5% of NNI in 2005).[12] Figure 5.3 shows labor's share for the business sector as a whole and for the three components.

Labor's share in NFC value added is somewhat higher than for the business sector as a whole, and the difference has risen so that for NFCs there really has not been a clear downward trend in labor's share over the past 30 years despite the sharp fall since the end of the 1990s. By contrast labor's share in the finance sector—lower throughout than in NFCs—shows a very distinct decline since the mid-1990s and with the weight of finance also rising, this drags down labor's share in business.[13] For the non-corporate sector there has been a downward trend in labor's share. Thus the recent decline in labor's share in US business reflects declines in labor shares in finance and in non-corporate enterprises (together with a modest effect from the rising weight of finance), with no contribution from a declining labor share in the value added of non-financial corporations.

Figure 5.4 provides further evidence on the possible influence of compositional changes on labor's share. This diagram refers to employee compensation in private non-agricultural industries; and national income is measured without an

---

[12]  See Fixler *et al.* (2003) for a detailed discussion. The national accounts of other countries approach this question in a variety of ways, which complicates international comparisons (see Askenazy, 2003).

[13]  Financial corporations paid out 10–11% of employee compensation by all companies over the past few years whilst receiving 25–30% of operating surpluses.

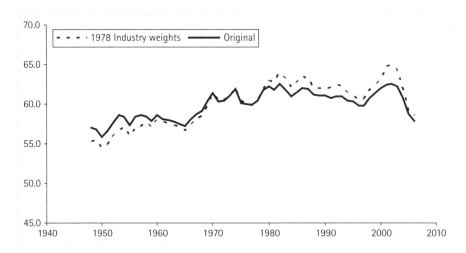

**Fig. 5.4. Employee compensation as % of US national income, 1948–2006**

*Note*: National income without capital consumption adjustment.
*Source*: NIPA, tables 6.1, 6.2.

adjustment for capital consumption. There is evidence of a mild inverted U-shaped pattern with a long rise up to the end of the 1970s followed by an irregular decline thereafter. When the share is recalculated using 1978 industry weights the pattern is similar, although more unstable in recent years.

Employee compensation in the national accounts includes the pay of everybody classified as an employee, from office cleaner to CEO. However, many of those at the top of the pay distribution are more akin to entrepreneurs, employed by share-holders and rewarded with stock options which are literally an entitlement based on future profits and which reduce the future returns to the other shareholders. Alan Krueger puts it thus: 'Because corporate officers control the firm's capital and in many cases include the owners of the firm, one could argue that much of their compensation should be classified as capital income' (Krueger, 1999: 46). Indeed the US tax code reflects the same idea when it stipulates that executive pay in excess of $1 million is not usually allowable as an expense against corporation tax (Coffee, 2006: 96 n. 31).

What proportion of those with top pay fall into this category is anybody's guess, but the sterling work of Piketty and Saez allows an estimate of the top 1% of employment incomes and Figure 5.5 shows the impact of subtracting their incomes to leave labor's share measuring the incomes of the other 99%.[14] The striking result is that the share of the 'bottom 99%' of US labor has fallen much more sharply over the past couple of decades than labor's share as a whole.

[14] Piketty and Saez's (2007) estimates for the share of wages and salaries of the top 1% are applied to employee compensation including employers' contributions etc. Such top rewards may not always be captured in national accounts statistics, e.g. capital gains from stock options.

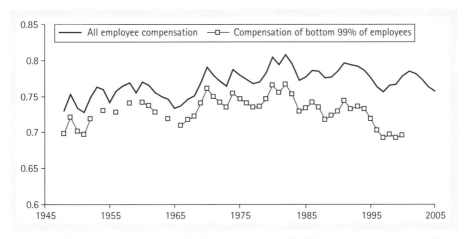

**Fig. 5.5. Ninety-nine percent labor's share as % of US business net value added, 1948–2005**

*Source*: As Figure 5.1 plus Piketty and Saez (2007, table 5B.2).

# 4. THE GREAT REVERSAL FROM THE 1960S TO THE 2000S—IS THE USA A SPECIAL CASE?

The revival of interest in labor's share has been sparked off by data suggesting a decline in the relative fortunes of labor in many countries in recent decades, in striking contrast to the apparently inexorable 'onward march' of labor's share in the 1960s and 1970s. Depending on the measure used, there is some evidence of such a pattern in the USA, but it is more pronounced in Europe and Japan. Figure 5.6 shows what has happened to the average share of labor in gross domestic product for a sample of 14 European OECD countries together with Japan. After rising steeply in the preceding years, the series peaks in 1976 and then falls almost continuously up to the present. The equivalent US series also declines for much of the period but at a slower pace. In principle, as explained in Section 3, such long-term movements in labor's share could be a statistical artifact resulting from shifts in the composition of economic activity or in the importance of self-employment in the economy. For example, the share of labor is much lower in finance than it is in manufacturing (see Figure 5.3 above for the USA). One might expect, therefore, that de-industrialization and the consequent shift from manufacturing to finance will lead to a lower share of labor in GDP as a whole, even without any change in labor's share within individual industries. Likewise, one might expect the decline in self-employment to affect the share of labor in GDP. The evidence suggests that the importance of such compositional effects varies from country to country and

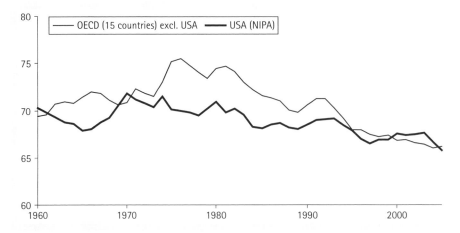

**Fig. 5.6. Labor's share adjusted for self-employment as a percentage of GDP, OECD countries and the USA, 1960–2005**

*Source*: OECD National Accounts; NIPA as in Figure 5.1.

also through time. Compositional differences between countries may also have an effect.

Evidence presented above for the USA suggested that shifts in the pattern of economic activity had little sustained effect on labor's share within the private non-agricultural sector (Figure 5.4). According to De Serres *et al.* (2002), the same is also true for the US economy as a whole since 1980, although prior to then changes in industrial composition were more important. Their study also examines what happened to the wage share in a sample of five European countries, including France, Germany, and Italy. They conclude that, in general, compositional changes have had only a minor long-term effect on the wage share, and where a prolonged decline has occurred this is mostly due to changes within individual industries. The one exception is Germany where changing industrial composition has had a large effect on the labor share. However, the data they present for Germany terminate some years ago and more recent data point to a decline in the labor share which is not of structural origin. In German manufacturing, for example, the share of profits has risen strongly since 2000 (Carlin and Soskice, 2007).

The above discussion refers to a small sample of countries. Figure 5.7 plots the un-weighted average for labor's share across a much larger number of countries (measured because of data limitations as a proportion of gross income). Series are shown both for GDP and for the narrower manufacturing sector, which delivers a similar pattern but with stronger increases up to the end of the 1970s and then a somewhat sharper decline. This is interesting because labor's share in the manufacturing sector would be expected to reflect most strongly the twin influences of a weaker labor movement and globalization, which are often supposed to account

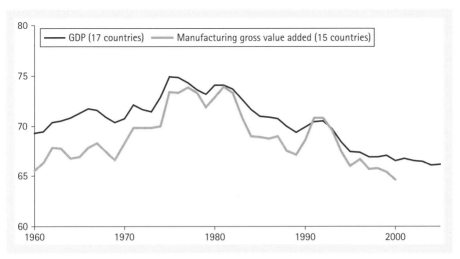

**Fig. 5.7. Labor's share: percentage of gross income, OECD countries, 1960–2005**

*Source:* Glyn (2006).

for the great reversal in the trend evident in the picture. The relatively small differences on average in labor's share in manufacturing and GDP show that de-industrialization cannot have been the major influence on the inverted U-shaped course of labor's share over recent decades.

Before turning to studies which try to account for the most recent developments, it is worth surveying briefly explanations for the rise in labor's share in the 1960s and 1970s. OECD authors have summarized the conventional wisdom as follows: 'it is now widely accepted that the rise observed in the wage share in Europe in the 1970s can be largely related to aggressive wage bidding and/or strong resistance by workers to adjust their wages so as to bear the brunt of high oil prices, tax wedges and lower productivity growth' (De Serres *et al.*, 2002: 7). Matthews *et al.* in their review of the UK experience write:

the importance of *increasing* union strength or militancy is doubtful, at least until the late 1960s, but the high absolute level of union strength limited employers' room for maneuver in the face of foreign competition. The very rapid rise in money wages after 1969 may well have tended to reduce capital's share, not only because price increases were inhibited by foreign competition … but because of lags in price adjustment, partly due to government restrictions and partly to historic cost conventions. On the other side, the post-war rise in the capital/output ratio at constant prices is consistent, in neoclassical terms, with the fall in the profit rate and also (assuming less-than-unit elasticity of substitution) with the fall in capital's share.    (Matthews *et al.*, 1982: 197)

Eichengreen summarizes the European pattern thus:

each element that had contributed to the earlier climate of wage restraint weakened in the 1960s before breaking down in the 1970s. Wage increases won by strikers in 1968–9 were about twice those of the preceding three years ... Real wages also rose faster. And coincident with the wage explosion, productivity growth slowed.... By the early 1970s the share of profits in European national incomes was one fifth lower than it had been fifteen years earlier.    (Eichengreen, 2007: 220–1, footnotes omitted)

The subsequent decline in labor's share over the past 25 to 30 years has begun to receive attention in the academic literature. The various research studies on this subject differ greatly in terms of country coverage (OECD and others), data sources, specification and econometric methods. Some interesting and some surprising results have emerged, as described below, but it is important to remember that this literature is in the early stages of development and really robust results have not yet emerged. The prime suspects for the decline in labor's share are factors that have weakened the bargaining position of labor—globalization, deregulation (labor, product, and capital markets)—and technological shifts that have reduced the demand for unskilled labor.

An IMF Working Paper summarized the various routes by which globalization may put downward pressure on labor's share thus:

According to the Hecksher-Ohlin model trade allows countries to specialize in areas of comparative advantage ... with increasing openness, capital-rich (industrial) countries would specialise in the production of capital-intensive goods. Returns to labor, the relatively scarce factor, would gradually decline, and labor's share would fall as specialization progresses ... Greater factor mobility that also characterizes globalization would only make the effect stronger ... In addition, by making capital more mobile, globalization may have decreased the bargaining position of the less mobile factor. Unionization and employment-protection policies still push income towards labor, but their effect may have been weakened. Finally, globalization pressures might have pushed industrial countries to adopt labor-saving technologies, further squeezing labor's share.    (Guscina, 2006: 5)

There is already support in the literature for effects on labor's share through several of these channels. Negative effects from the higher overall levels of international trade have been picked up in several studies (Harrison, 2002; Guscina, 2006; Jayadev, 2007), and from greater 'offshoring', purchases of intermediate inputs from overseas (IMF, 2007). Negative impacts have also been found from larger flows of FDI (Harrison, 2002; Guscina, 2006) and from the degree of capital account openness (Jayadev, 2007; Harrison, 2002). In addition the IMF (2007) found that higher levels of immigration reduced labor's share. The decline in real oil prices until recently should have reduced labor's share by reducing the pressure on real wages, according to the study of Baghli *et al.* (2005).

The reported negative impact from greater foreign trade is interesting. Greater competition in product markets, by eroding monopolistic positions, should, according to Kalecki's arguments, squeeze profits and *increase* labor's share, as appeared to be the case in the late 1960s. It appears, however, that the impact of this greater competition in eroding labor's bargaining position has outweighed such an effect in recent years. Similar effects have been found in Azmat *et al.*'s (2007) study of privatization and the reduction of barriers to entry in the network industries—prices and profits may be initially squeezed but the pressure appears then to be shifted on to workers (reflected in cuts in manning levels and so forth) so that the net impact is a decline in labor's share.

Most of the studies already mentioned above include a productivity variable. Bentolila and Saint-Paul (2003) interpret a negative effect of TFP growth on labor's share as capturing the effect of capital-augmenting technical progress and the IMF (2007) find a negative effect on labor's share from the accumulation of ICT capital. Blanchard (1997) stressed the probable importance of labor-saving technology in putting downward pressure in recent decades on labor's share.

The impact of labor market institutions has also been examined. Mixed results have been reported for the impact of trade union membership and the degree of industrial conflict. More surprising is the IMF's finding (IMF, 2007) that high unemployment benefits and the tax wedge faced by workers *reduced* labor's share. This allows them to wheel out their old standby, labor market deregulation, as the way to prevent labor's share declining. The mechanisms involved are hard to accept. Labor market deregulation (cutting benefits and the tax wedge for example) no doubt has *some* effect in reducing wages and raising employment (see Howell *et al.*, 2007 for a skeptical review of the quantitative evidence however). But for labor's share to rise as a result, the positive impact on employment would have to be disproportionately greater than the negative impact on wages. This requires an elasticity of substitution of more than one, which seems to fly in the face of the empirical evidence noted above. Indeed Blanchard and Giavazzi (2003: 905) argue that the *decline* in labor's share shows that the effects of 'labor market regulation, at least in the sense of a decrease in the bargaining power of workers, must have dominated the effects of product market deregulation'.

# 5. LONG-TERM TRENDS IN FUNCTIONAL DISTRIBUTION

The contribution of this section is to add to the empirical knowledge needed for further comparative research by bringing together long time series—for about one hundred years—for labor's share for eight advanced economies. The data presented illustrate how difficult it is to generalize about trends in factor shares over the very long run. For many countries, there seems to have been a permanent upward shift in labor's share during World War II but this is not universally the case. The series shown in this section, which are based on national data sources and for the preferred definitions of labor's share, confirm the post-1960 hump-shaped pattern shown in Figures 5.6 and 5.7 for most of these countries.

Figure 5.8 reports on the trends in labor's share in eight of the biggest industrialized economies over the past century. Where available, two series are reported, labor's share in net national income and additionally its share in the net value added of the business or of the narrower corporate sector (leaving out government employment and owner occupation in both cases). Adjustments are made by attributing either a sector or economy-wide wage to the self-employed. Data for the post-1950 period are usually taken directly from the National Accounts as published by National Statistical Offices (supplemented by OECD compilations from the national sources); data for the earlier periods are taken from published

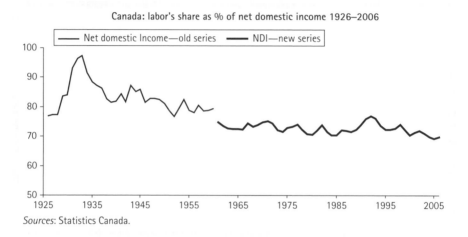

Canada: labor's share as % of net domestic income 1926–2006

*Sources*: Statistics Canada.

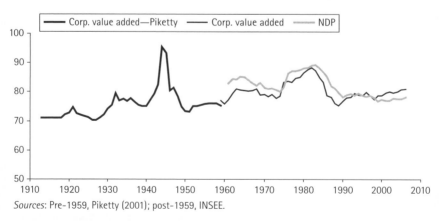

France: Labor's share as % of net incomes 1913–2006

*Sources*: Pre-1959, Piketty (2001); post-1959, INSEE.

## Fig. 5.8. Long-term series for labor's share

Detailed sources and methods are provided in the Data Appendix on the Handbook website.

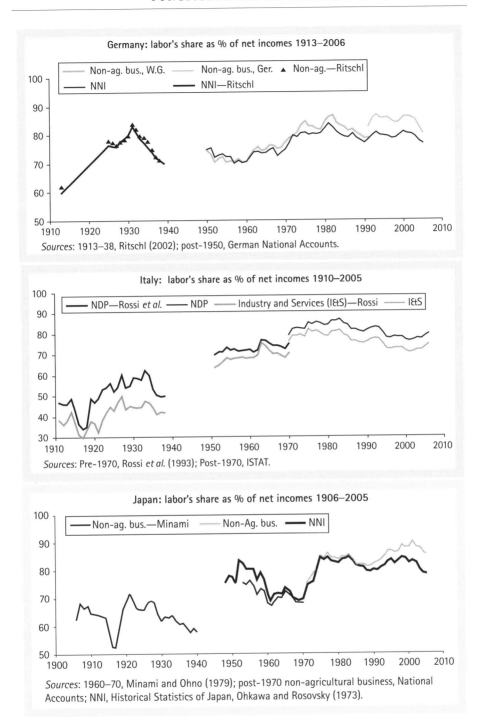

Germany: labor's share as % of net incomes 1913–2006

*Sources*: 1913–38, Ritschl (2002); post-1950, German National Accounts.

Italy: labor's share as % of net incomes 1910–2005

*Sources*: Pre-1970, Rossi *et al.* (1993); Post-1970, ISTAT.

Japan: labor's share as % of net incomes 1906–2005

*Sources*: 1960–70, Minami and Ohno (1979); post-1970 non-agricultural business, National Accounts; NNI, Historical Statistics of Japan, Ohkawa and Rosovsky (1973).

**Fig. 5.8. continued**

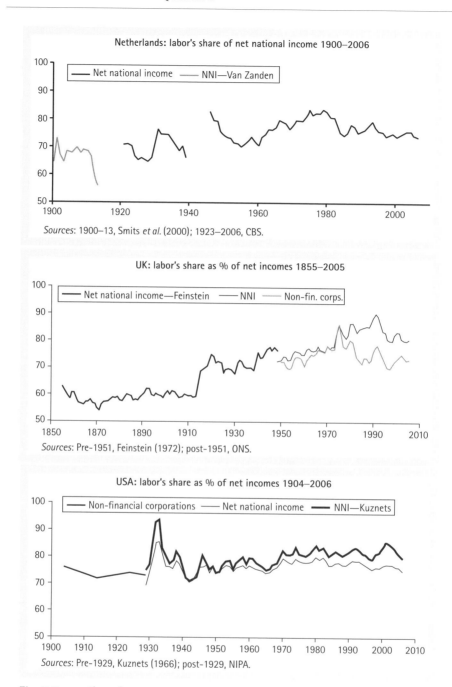

**Netherlands: labor's share of net national income 1900–2006**

Sources: 1900–13, Smits et al. (2000); 1923–2006, CBS.

**UK: labor's share as % of net incomes 1855–2005**

Sources: Pre-1951, Feinstein (1972); post-1951, ONS.

**USA: labor's share as % of net incomes 1904–2006**

Sources: Pre-1929, Kuznets (1966); post-1929, NIPA.

**Fig. 5.8. continued**

national studies.[15] More information about the various series is given in the Data Appendix, which is available from the Handbook website.

What overall conclusions can be drawn from the experience of these eight countries?

1. In the seven or eight decades up to the end of the 1970s all the European countries and Japan showed upward trends in labor's share whilst in North America the trend appears to have been flat (USA) or slightly downwards (Canada). Upward slopes vary from the comparatively slight in France to very sharp in Italy. These results do not depend on whether a broad (NNI) or narrow (business or corporate sector) measure is used. They confirm Kuznets' finding that: 'if any general conclusion is justified, it is that the share of returns on capital declined in almost all countries—in some from almost one half to about a fifth or a quarter; and the share of "labor" must correspondingly have risen' (Kuznets, 1966: 180). His data ended in 1960, but his conclusion was reinforced by further rises in labor's share over the next two decades as the 'golden age' boiled over and then collapsed. The myth of long-term constancy in labor's share (see Atkinson, 1983) lingered on despite Kuznets' evidence.

2. There were major upward shifts in labor's share during the world wars in a number of countries—the UK and Germany during World War I, Italy and Japan during World War II. Even German fascism, though reversing the Weimar period's increases in labor's share, did not push it back down to the pre-1914 level. Such cross-war shifts contrast with the sharp upward spikes in labor's share associated with major recessions (USA in the 1930s) and economic and political collapse (France 1944/5), which proved temporary when economic recovery took place.

3. Since 1980 there has been a general reversal of some of the gains in labor's share of the previous decades. Recent UK experience is unusual in that narrow and broad measures of labor's share tell contrasting stories.[16]

4. The generally declining trend in the most recent period is not unprecedented. As well as falls in the 1930s in a number of countries, reflecting some combination of economic recovery and authoritarian government, there were declines in Germany in the 1950s and Japan from the mid-1950s during periods of very rapid 'catch-up'.

[15]  In most cases the data in the studies cited have been adjusted by me to allow for self-employment, capital consumption, and so forth. The authors of the original series are of course not responsible for these adjustments. Two presentational points to note are that data are missing for many countries for the world war periods and that where sources change for a broadly comparable series, a gap is shown between the two series for the common year in question rather the series being grafted on to each other.

[16]  The 1980s saw a near-doubling in the share of UK self-employment as many workers, in construction in particular, became self-employed, often for tax reasons. This reduced corporate value added because payments to the self-employed are regarded as intermediate inputs not value added. In addition there was a major expansion of the financial sector which, in the UK national accounts, raises labor's share in NNI substantially as financial companies' operating surplus is more than offset by the adjustment made to national income to subtract net interest received by the sector.

Table 5.1. The share of property income: average 2001–5

| Percentage of net incomes | Net national income | Corporate net. value added | Business net value added |
|---|---|---|---|
| France | 22.6 | 20.0 | |
| Italy | 22.7 | | 28.1[2] |
| Germany | 21.2 | | 16.1[2] |
| Japan | 19.1 | | 12.0[2] |
| UK | 19.3 | 26.2[1] | 16.8 |
| USA | 23.2 | 16.7[1] | 22.8 |
| Netherlands | 24.6 | | |
| Canada | 29.3 | | |

*Notes:* [1] Non-financial.
[2] Non-agricultural.
*Source:* As for Figure 5.8.

Intriguingly labor's share in the UK appears to decline for a couple of decades after Feinstein's data begin in the mid-1850s and calculations by Allen (2005) suggest that the decline may have begun well before.

5. Despite their very different long-term evolutions, most countries appear to have a share of labor in net national income that lies in the range 70–80% and with the exception of Japan the share of labor in the net value added of the private sector is in a broadly similar range. However, such apparent similarities in labor shares may conceal large proportional differences in the share of property income. For example, the share of labor in business net value added is equal to 73.8% in the UK and 83.3% in the USA. As can be seen from Table 5.1, the implied share of property income is more than half as high again in the UK (26.2%) as in the USA (16.7%). Differences in the share of property income in non-agricultural business in Japan and Italy appear even larger still. Such international differences may be partly due to the fact that countries use different measurement conventions (treatment of the financial sector, treatment of the incomes of the self-employed, calculation of capital consumption, and so forth) and have different economic structures (share of government employment, share of agriculture, etc). To the extent that these differences in profit shares are genuine, their persistence is difficult to explain in an era of international capital mobility. One factor may be different capital-output ratios; another may be differences in the composition of economic activity. For example, Canada has a large mining sector, which may help to explain the low share of labor, and high share of property, in national income. This issue requires further investigation.

6. The shift from a generally rising to a generally declining labor share over the past five decades or so represents a parallel movement to, and has contributed to, rising personal income inequality (see Chapter 4).

# 6. Conclusions

This chapter has argued that trends in factor shares are still relevant for both normative and positive analysis of how capitalist economies function. Much remains to be done in producing satisfactory series for factor shares, understanding their behavior, and evaluating their impact on household income distribution, patterns of accumulation, and macroeconomic stability. Many tricky measurement issues are involved in estimating labor's share, including whether to measure profits gross or net, how to deal with the finance and non-market sectors, as well as the major issue of dividing the incomes of the self-employed between property and labor. As highlighted by the analysis of the USA, trends in the salaries of the top 1% of incomes can have a marked effect on labor's share, which raises the question of how compensation of this kind is and should be treated. This relates to the broader issue of how changes in factor shares influence the personal distribution of income, where new research points to the importance of the complementarity between capital and medium- and high-skilled labor as compared with low-skilled labor, which tends to be a close substitute for capital. This may directly affect inequality.

A review of the long-term evidence for a number of countries confirms earlier (but often forgotten) findings that labor's share has not been constant over time, with many countries showing pronounced upward trends until the end of the 1970s. The period since 1980 has seen a sharp reversal of the upward tendency, with falling labor shares in most countries. The muted trends in the USA are notable. A number of studies have suggested this reversal has been influenced by globalization and product market deregulation, whilst contradictory conclusions have been drawn for the impact of policies and institutions that support the bargaining position of workers.

Important issues for future research include, first, an improved collection of data and, second, a deeper analysis of trends and country differences. This chapter has provided long time series for a limited number of countries. Extension to other countries, even if only for the post-war period, is highly desirable. Taking the USA as an example, the chapter has illustrated the need to use uniform methods for measuring the labor share when making international or intertemporal comparisons. This is important because the elements that are left out or included may differ substantially over time and across countries. Data on the labor share can also be combined with other new collections of long-run statistics, such as those on top incomes (see Chapter 7), to produce a deeper understanding of how the labor share has evolved. Calculating the impact of changes in the earnings of the top 1% on the share of labor for other countries would reveal the extent to which the USA is a special case.

The analysis can be deepened in two directions: understanding the dynamics of the labor share itself on the one hand, and its relation to the personal distribution of incomes on the other. Long-run trends in labor shares can be related to structural change and political shifts. An obvious example is the great reversal in trend from around 1980 onwards. Institutional changes and differences such as union bargaining power, product market and capital market deregulation come to mind most readily in this context. However, the effects of cross-country differences and trends in industrial composition may also be relevant for the aggregate labor share, for example, the high share of financial services in the UK and USA, of manufacturing in Germany, and of tourist services in certain other countries. It may also be useful to go beyond the aggregate labor share and consider the trends and differences within individual industries or sectors. However, as emphasized in this chapter, the impact of the dynamics of labor shares on the personal distribution of income and its implications for macroeconomic stability are mediated by the wedge between real consumption and real product wages. This relationship may be overlooked in industry-level studies of labor's share.

## References

ALLEN, R. 2005. 'Capital Accumulation, Technological Change and the Distribution of Income during the British Industrial Revolution'. Mimeo, Nuffield College, Oxford.

ASKENAZY, P. 2003. 'Partage de la valeur ajoutée et rentabilité du Capital en France et aux Étas-Unis: une réévaluation'. *Économie et Statistique*, 363–5:, 167–85.

ATKINSON, A. B. 1983. *The Economics of Inequality*, 2nd edn. Oxford: Clarendon Press.

——and BOURGUIGNON, F. 2000. 'Introduction: Income Distribution and Economics', in A. B. Atkinson and F. Bourgignon (eds.), *Handbook on Income Distribution*, vol. 1. Amsterdam: Elsevier.

AZMAT, G, MANNING, A., and VAN REENEN, J. 2007. 'Privatization, Entry Regulation and Labor's Share of GDP: A Cross-Country Analysis of the Network Industries'. Centre for Economic Performance Discussion Paper no. 806.

BAGHLI, M., CETTE, G., and SYLVAIN, A. 2005. 'Les déterminants du taux de marge en France et quelques autres grands pays industrialisés: Analyse empirique sur la période 1970–2000'. Mimeo, Banque de France.

BENTOLILA, S., and SAINT-PAUL, G. 2003. 'Explaining Movements in Labor's Share'. *Contributions to Macroeconomics*, 3(1): 1–31.

BLANCHARD, O. 1997. 'The Medium Run'. *Brookings Papers on Economic Activity*, 2: 89–158.

——and GIAVAZZI, F. 2003. 'Macroeconomic Effects of Regulation and Deregulation in Goods and Labor Markets'. *Quarterly Journal of Economics*, 879–907.

BLAUG, M. 1996. *Economic Theory in Retrospect*, 5th edn. Cambridge: Cambridge University Press.

BRUNO, M., and SACHS, J. 1985. *The Economics of Worldwide Stagflation*. Oxford: Blackwell.

CARLIN, W., and SOSKICE, D. 2007. 'Reforms, Macroeconomic Policy and Economic Performance in Germany'. CEPR Discussion Paper 6415, July. <http://www.cepr.org/pubs/dps/DP6415.asp>.

CHECCHI, D., and GARCIA-PEÑALOSA, C. 2005. 'Labor Market Institutions and the Personal Distribution of Income in the OECD'. IZA Working Paper, DP no. 1681.

COFFEE, J. 2006. *Gatekeepers*. Oxford: Oxford University Press.

DAUDEY, E., and GARCIA-PEÑALOSA, C. 2007. 'The Personal and the Factor Distribution of Income in a Cross-section of Countries'. *Journal of Development Studies*, 43(5): 812–29.

DE SERRES, A., SCARPETTA, S., and MAISONNEUVE, C. 2002. 'Sectoral Shifts in Europe and the United States: How they Affect Aggregate Labor Shares and the Properties of Wage Equations'. OECD Economics Departkent Working Papers No. 326.

EICHENGREEN, B. 2007. *The European Economy since 1945*. Princeton: Princeton University Press.

EUROPEAN COMMISSION 2008. *Employment in Europe*. Brussels: European Commission, chapter 5.

FEINSTEIN, C. 1968. 'Changes in the Distribution of the National Income in the UK since 1860', in Marchal and Ducros (1968).

——1972. *National Income, Expenditure and Output of the United Kingdom 1855–1965*. Cambridge: Cambridge University Press.

FIXLER, D., REINSDORF, M., and SMITH, G. 2003. 'Measuring the Services of Commercial Banks in the NIPAs'. *Survey of Current Business*, Sept.: 33–44.

GIAMMARIOLI, N., MESSINA, J., STEINBERGER, T., and STROZZI, C. 2002. 'European Labor Share Dynamics'. EUI Working Paper ECO 2002/13.

GLYN, A. 2006. *Capitalism Unleashed*. Oxford: Oxford University Press.

——and SUTCLIFFE, R. 1972. *British Capitalism, Workers and the Profits Squeeze*. Harmondsworth: Penguin Books.

GOLDFARB, ROBERT S., and LEONARD, THOMAS C. 2005. ' Inequality of What among Whom?: Rival Conceptions of Distribution in the 20th Century'. *Research in The History of Economic Thought and Methodology*, 23a: 75–118.

GOLLIN, D. 2002. 'Getting Income Shares Right'. *Journal of Political Economy*, 110(2): 458–74.

GUSCINA, A. 2006. 'Effects of Globalization on Labor's Share in National Income'. IMF Working Paper WP/06/294.

HARRISON, A. 2002. 'Has Globalization Eroded Labor's Share: Some Cross-Country Evidence'. Mimeo, University of California at Berkeley.

HOWELL, D., BAKER, D., GLYN, A., and SCHMITT, J. 2007. 'Are Protective Labor Market Institutions at the Root of Unemployment: A Critical Review of the Literature'. *Capitalism and Society*, 2(1).

IMF 2007. 'The Globalization of Labor'. *World Economic Outlook*, Apr., chapter 5.

JAYADEV, A. 2007. 'Capital Account Openness and the Labor Share of Income'. *Cambridge Journal of Economics*, 31: 423–43.

KALECKI, M. 1938. 'The Lessons of the Blum Experiment'. *Economic Journal*, 48(189): 26–41.

——1971. *Selected Essays on the Dynamics of the Capitalist Economy*. Cambridge: Cambridge University Press.

KALDOR, N. 1955. 'Alternative Theories of Distribution'. *Review of Economic Studies*, 23(2): 83–100.

KALWIJ, A., and MACHIN, S. 2007. 'Comparative Service Consumption in Six Countries', in M. Gregory, W. Salverda, and R. Schettkat (eds.), *Services and Employment: Explaining the U.S.–European Gap*. Princeton: Princeton University Press, 109–40.

KRAVIS, I. 1959. 'Relative Income Shares in Fact and Theory'. *American Economic Review*, 49: 917–49.

KRUEGER, A. 1999. 'Measuring Labor's Share'. *American Economic Review*, 89(2): 45–51.

KUZNETS, S. 1959. 'Quantitative Aspects of the Economic Growth of Nations: IV Distribution of National Income by Factor Shares'. *Economic Development and Cultural Change*, 7(3, part 2): 1–100.

——1966. *Modern Economic Growth*. New Haven: Yale University Press.

MARCHAL, J., and DUCROS, B. 1968. *The Distribution of the National Income*. London: Macmillan.

MATTHEWS, R., FEINSTEIN, C., and ODLING-SMEE, J. 1982. *British Economic Growth, 1856–1973*. Stanford, Calif.: Stanford University Press.

MINAMI, R., and ONO, A. 1979. 'Factor Incomes and Shares', in K. Ohkawa and M. Shinohara (eds.), *Patterns of Japanese Economic Development: A Quantitative Appraisal*. New Haven: Yale University Press.

NATIONAL INCOME and PRODUCT ACCOUNTS. Bureau of Economic Analysis. Washington.

OECD 2007. 'OECD Workers in the Global Economy: Increasingly Vulnerable?' *OECD Employment Outlook*, July, chapter 3.

OHKAWA, K., and ROSOVSKY, H. 1973. *Japanese Economic Growth*. Stanford: Stanford University Press.

PIKETTY, T. 2001. *Les Hauts Revenus en France au XX Siecle*. Paris: Grasset.

——and SAEZ, E. 2007 'Income and Wage Inequality in the USA', in A. Atkinson and T. Piketty (eds.), *Top Incomes over the Twentieth Century*. Oxford: Oxford University Press.

RICARDO, D. 1817. *The Principles of Political Economy and Taxation*. London: John Murray. Reprinted in P. Sraffa (ed.) 1970. *The Works and Correspondence of David Ricardo*, vol. 1. Cambridge: Cambridge University Press.

RITSCHL, A. 2002. *Deutschlands Krise und Konjunktur: Binnenkonjunktur, Auslandsverschuldung und Reparationsproblem zwischen Dawes-Plan und Transfersperre 1924–1934*. Berlin: Akademie-Verlag.

ROSSI, N., SORGATO, A., and TONIOLO, G. 1993. 'I conti economici italiani: una ricostruzione statistica, 1890–1990'. *Rivista Di Storia Economia*, 10(1): 1–49.

ROWTHORN, R. 1999. 'Unemployment, Wage Bargaining and Capital Labor Substitution'. *Cambridge Journal of Economics*, 23: 413–25.

SMITS J.-P., HORLINGS, E., and VAN ZANDEN, J. L. 2000. 'Dutch GNP and its Components, 1800–1913'. Groningen Growth and Development Centre.

STIGLER, G. 1965. 'The Influence of Events and Policies on Economic Theory', in *Essays in the History of Economics*. Chicago: University of Chicago Press.

# CHAPTER 6

.........................................................................................

# WEALTH AND ECONOMIC INEQUALITY

.........................................................................................

## JAMES B. DAVIES

## 1. INTRODUCTION

.........................................................................................

INCOME is far from the only determinant of well-being. A family's welfare depends on its size, health, economic and social environment, and economic resources, as well. Resources include human and non-human capital. In this chapter we examine the latter, which we simply call *wealth*.

Wealth is more unequally distributed than human capital, earnings, or income. While the Gini coefficient for disposable income ranges from about 0.30 to 0.50 in OECD countries, the range for wealth is from around 0.50 to 0.80. The current share of the top 1% of families by wealth in the United States is over 30%, and it has been estimated that the top 2% of adults have 50% of the world's household wealth (Davies *et al.*, 2007). Wealth and income are correlated, so this high concentration exacerbates overall inequality.

For human capital, the income flow is observable but the stock is not. The opposite is true for wealth. The value of most forms of wealth can be observed or estimated whereas the income flows, for example capital gains or imputed rent on owner-occupied housing, often are not readily observable. Thus, while on the human side it makes sense to focus on income, on the non-human side it is essential to study the stock as well as the flow. Wealth has other distinctions. Human capital cannot be bought or sold, and cannot be pledged as collateral. This means it can't be used as a store of value. Faced with job loss, divorce, or unexpected medical bills, people can't spend down their human capital. They also can't save for retirement via human capital. In a capitalist society, non-human wealth, unsurprisingly, plays a special role. You need capital to start a business or reap high investment returns. While it is possible to earn a high income through work, a disproportionate share of the highest incomes comes from capital.

Another reason that wealth is important and interesting is that it brings empowerment. If you want to enforce your rights, or perhaps to intimidate others, it helps to be able to hire the best lawyers. Sponsoring political campaigns, lobbying and influencing politicians all require deep pockets. There are limits to the power of the wealthy in a democratic society, but they are less severe than those on the power of the poor or middle class. On a more positive note, great wealth brings the power to do great good. An impressive succession of the world's wealthiest, from Andrew Carnegie to Bill Gates, have devoted a large fraction of their huge fortunes to philanthropy.

The study of wealth has examined the shape of the distribution and levels of inequality, as well as aggregate wealth and the composition of household portfolios. Research has also tried to identify the importance of different sources of wealth inequality. Work on these topics up to the late 1990s was surveyed in Davies and Shorrocks (2000). Much important work has been done since, and it is this work we focus on here. In recent years the rise in inequality in both earned and total incomes in many OECD countries has received much attention. Other chapters in this volume (e.g. Chapter 4 by Brandolini and Smeeding and Chapter 8 by Blau and Kahn) document this increase and investigate its origins. The last few decades have seen a revolution in financial markets; strongly rising prices of stocks and houses in many countries; a 'risk shift' from governments and corporations to individuals through a decline in the welfare state, changes in health insurance, and the replacement of defined benefit (DB) pensions by defined contribution (DC) plans. There is naturally interest in how wealth inequality has behaved over this period. As we shall see, the evidence indicates that it has increased less than income inequality.

## 2. METHODS

Here 'wealth' means the value of non-human assets minus debts. Standard wealth surveys mainly inquire about *marketable* wealth. The assets covered should ideally include cash and deposits, other liquid assets, stocks and bonds, other financial assets, business equity, owner-occupied housing, other real estate, and consumer durables (including such items as antiques, art, and jewelry). In practice not all assets are covered—consumer durables are often represented only by vehicles for example. 'Other financial assets' often include tax-sheltered retirement savings plans, such as IRAs and Keogh plans in the USA but this is not universal. Generally, private and public pension rights are excluded, as they are not marketable.[1] As in other distributional studies there is a choice between individuals, families, or households as the unit of analysis. Studies of income or consumption often focus on families or households, in view of sharing within those units. For wealth, ownership rather than current enjoyment is important, and interest in the individual is greater. Still, while for example estate-tax-based estimates are provided on an individual basis, surveys largely focus on families or households.

## Data Sources

There are three major sources of wealth data: household surveys, wealth taxes, and estate tax.[2] Each has its advantages and disadvantages. Survey evidence is most common and is now found in at least 14 OECD countries. Some of these also have wealth-tax-based estimates (common in Scandinavia), or 'estate multiplier' figures (e.g. France, UK, USA). Survey data is subject to both sampling and non-sampling errors. When sampling from a highly skewed distribution like that of wealth, most samples will underestimate inequality and the length of the upper tail. This problem can be addressed by oversampling the upper tail, a strategy that is followed most successfully in the US Survey of Consumer Finance (SCF), but which has also been applied in Canada, Germany, and a few other countries.[3]

Non-sampling errors take two forms: differential unit non-response and misreporting of asset or debt amounts. Misreporting commonly takes the form of under-reporting or item non-response. Usually the unit response rate is low for the poor, and very low for the genuinely wealthy. This problem can be corrected partially by weighting respondents carefully to get a sample that is representative in terms of age, sex, region, and other demographic characteristics. A better job can be done if a special high wealth sampling frame has been used, since respondents from the main and special samples can be separately weighted. Still, a perfect fix for differential unit response is not available.

Under-reporting and item non-response vary by asset or debt type. They appear to be most severe for financial assets, particularly for stocks and bonds, which

[1]  There are exceptions. The Survey of Consumer Finance in the US includes e.g. 401(k) plans, which may be viewed as employer-based pension plans, since workers may withdraw their funds or take loans from these plans before retirement. And in Canada, a version of the 1999 Survey of Financial Security results is available that has estimates of the value of respondents' private pension rights.

[2]  A fourth, lesser-used source is 'investment income multiplier' estimates. These capitalize investment income to estimate the value of financial assets. For a methodological discussion of the alternative estimation methods see Davies and Shorrocks (2000).

[3]  See Kennickell (2004) for an explanation of how oversampling is conducted in the SCF.

may be under-reported by up to 70–80%. House values, in contrast, show little bias, and mortgages are on average only moderately under-reported (by about 20% according to US validation studies). It is standard to perform imputations in the case of item non-response. Also, reported amounts are sometimes 'aligned' with totals from outside sources, for example the Flow of Funds data in the USA.

Currently there is some concern that non-sampling errors may be growing more severe because both unit and item response rates to household surveys are in decline. It is not clear how severe a problem this is in the case of wealth. In a few countries unit non-response rates in recent surveys are high—40% in Austria and 50% in Italy for example according to the Luxembourg Wealth Study (LWS).[4] However, this non-response rate remains relatively low in Canada, Norway, Sweden, and the UK. In the SCF main sample in the USA in 2001 and 2004 the unit response rates were about 70% (Bucks *et al.*, 2006), the same as for the 1992 and 1995 surveys. On the other hand, the response rate for the list sample was about 30% in 2001 and 2004, down from 34% in 1992 and 1995. Thus, while non-response is not yet a crisis in most countries, efforts to prevent a further decline in response rates are clearly important, as is research on the effects of response rates and their decline on data quality.

Techniques for oversampling the upper tail, as well as those for dealing with item non-response, have become more sophisticated in recent years (Brandolini *et al.*, 2004; Kennickell, 2004). In countries where these techniques are now highly developed it is likely that the quality of survey-based wealth estimates has been increasing rather than declining. New surveys have been established in recent years, for example in Cyprus, Spain, and the UK. And the European Central Bank has launched an initiative to have harmonized wealth surveys in all its member countries. The aim in these new surveys has been to implement state-of-the-art techniques, often with the help and guidance of experts from countries with the most successful wealth surveys.

# 3. EMPIRICAL EVIDENCE: CURRENT PATTERNS

## Recent Estimates of Wealth Inequality

Table 6.1 shows some of the results from two recent international comparisons of wealth inequality. The first panel is from Davies *et al.* (2007). The authors assembled estimates clustered mostly around the year 2000 for 20 countries. Table 6.1 shows

---

[4]   The website of the Luxembourg Income Study (LIS) gives response rates for wealth surveys from 10 countries used in the LWS. See <http://www.lisproject.org>.

Table 6.1. International comparison of wealth inequality indicators, recent studies

| Country | WIDER/UNU World Wealth Study[1] | | | | | | Luxembourg Wealth Study[2] (preliminary results) | | | |
|---|---|---|---|---|---|---|---|---|---|---|
| | Year | Source | Unit | Share of top 10% | Share of top 1% | Gini | Year | Share of top 10% | Share of top 1% | Gini |
| Australia | 2002 | S | H | 45.0 | | 0.622 | 1999 | 53 | 15 | 0.75 |
| Canada | 1999 | S | F | 53.0 | | 0.688 | | | | |
| Denmark | 1975 | WT | F | 76.4 | 28.8 | 0.808 | | | | |
| Finland | 1998 | S | H | 42.3 | | 0.621 | 1998 | 45 | 13 | 0.68 |
| France | 1994 | EM | I | 61.0 | 21.3 | 0.730 | | | | |
| Germany | 1998 | S | H | 44.4 | | 0.667 | 2002 | 54 | 14 | 0.78 |
| Ireland | 1987 | S | H | 42.3 | 10.4 | 0.581 | | | | |
| Italy | 2000 | S | H | 48.5 | 17.2 | 0.609 | 2002 | 42 | 11 | 0.61 |
| Japan | 1999 | S | H | 39.3 | | 0.547 | | | | |
| Korea | 1988 | S | H | 43.1 | 14.0 | 0.579 | | | | |
| New Zealand | 2001 | S | Tax Unit | 51.7 | | 0.651 | | | | |
| Norway | 2000 | S | H | 50.5 | | 0.633 | | | | |
| Spain | 2002 | S | H | 41.9 | 18.3 | 0.570 | | | | |
| Sweden | 2002 | WT | H | 58.6 | | 0.742 | 2002 | 58 | 18 | 0.89 |
| Switzerland | 1997 | WT | F | 71.3 | 34.8 | 0.803 | | | | |
| UK | 2000 | EM | I | 56.0 | 23.0 | 0.697 | 2000 | 45 | 10 | 0.66 |
| USA | 2001 | S | F | 69.8 | 32.7 | 0.801 | 2001 | 71 | 33 | 0.84 |

Notes: S = household survey; WT = wealth tax records; EM = estate multiplier method; H = household; F = family; I = adult individual.

Sources: [1] WIDER Study–Davies et al. (2007), wealth definitions vary across countries;
[2] Luxembourg Wealth Study–Sierminska et al. (2006), all from household surveys, household units, common but limited wealth definition.

the results for 17 OECD countries, 12 of which are represented by survey data (S), three by wealth tax numbers (WT), and two by estate multiplier (EM) estimates. In most cases the unit is the household, while in four cases it is the family and in the two cases with EM it is the adult individual. Wealth definitions also differ somewhat across the countries, for example with regard to the inclusion of consumer durables and real estate other than owner-occupied housing.

The first panel of Table 6.1 shows some common themes across the countries, despite the variety of methods used. In absolute terms wealth inequality is high in all 17 countries. The share of the top 10% ranges from 39 to 76%, and the Gini coefficient from 0.55 to 0.81. For comparison, in the disposable income data used by Davies *et al.* (2007) for these 17 countries the Gini coefficients lie between 0.30 and 0.50.

Given the range of methods used, it is not clear how much importance to place on cross-country differences in the first panel of Table 6.1. The best data are likely those for the USA, which show a share of the top 10% of 69.8% and a Gini of 0.801. Few other countries using the survey approach come close to these levels. That may be because the USA indeed has higher wealth inequality, but it also may be partly due to less successful efforts to capture the upper tail.[5] Perhaps more accurate numbers are given by the wealth tax and estate multiplier estimates, which show shares of the top 10% ranging from 56.0% (UK) to 71.3% (Switzerland) and Gini coefficients ranging from 0.697 (UK) to 0.803 (Switzerland).

Fortunately, estimates prepared using disparate methods are no longer the only international data available. Ten OECD countries are now cooperating to produce internationally comparable data through the LWS. The second panel of Table 6.1 shows preliminary results. All of these data are based on surveys, use the household unit, and have a common definition of wealth. Unfortunately, to achieve a common definition of wealth some components must be omitted from most countries' data. For example, retirement savings accounts and business equity are excluded. Survey techniques also differ across countries, for example through the oversampling of the upper tail in some countries but not in others, as discussed above. Interestingly, results in the two panels of Table 6.1 are quite highly correlated despite differences in data and methods. In both cases the lowest inequality is found in Italy and the highest in the USA. The ranking of countries according to their Gini coefficient is the same in the UNU-WIDER and LWS data except that the UK is much lower ranked in the LWS. The large change in the UK ranking is due to the use of estate multiplier estimates in the WIDER study versus survey estimates from the British Household Panel Study (BHPS) in the LWS. Where both WIDER and LWS results

[5]  The Federal Reserve Board uses tax data to obtain a special high income 'list sample', and applies a wealth model that has been estimated statistically and honed over the years to get a prior estimate of the wealth of households in this sample. This allows not only the sampling error caused by skewness to be addressed, but also allows weighting to correct for differential unit response. (See Kenickell, 2004.)

are available, we may sort countries into the following categories on the basis of their wealth Ginis:

1. high wealth inequality: Sweden, USA;
2. medium wealth inequality: Canada, Germany, UK;
3. low wealth inequality: Italy, Finland.

Note the apparently implausible result that Sweden is in the same category as the USA. The reason is that, although Sweden has lower shares of the top 1 and 10% than the USA, it also has a large population with very little wealth at all. According to the official statistics the bottom 30% have *negative* wealth. This may partly result from measurement difficulties, but it also reflects the high incidence of debt, a relatively low home-ownership rate, and, it is widely believed, the dampening effect of generous public pensions on savings.[6] Finland, which shares good pensions and a strong welfare state with Sweden, is in the bottom category here. There are likely a range of reasons for this, but part of the explanation is that Finland has a lower incidence of negative net worth, as well as higher home ownership.

## Pension Wealth

Pension wealth is in aggregate the largest category among personal financial assets in most OECD countries. It includes equity in, or the right to future benefits from, both private and public pension plans. In Sweden in 1999, for example, it is estimated that median negotiated group pensions and public pension wealth equaled 19.2% and 56.5% respectively of median augmented wealth[7] for white-collar workers (calculated from Klevmarken, 2006a, table 8.4, reporting results of a 2002 study by Andersson *et al.*, published in Swedish). The corresponding figures for blue-collar workers were 13.2% and 74.6%. For the USA Wolff (2005) estimates mean private and public pension wealth in 2001 of $94,800 and $139,500 per household respectively, or 16.9% and 24.9% of mean augmented wealth, which stood at $561,000. Similar results have been found for other countries. (See e.g. Davies and Shorrocks, 2000, table 2 for UK results.)

Public pensions may be contributory or non-contributory.[8] Contributory schemes in which both contributions and benefits are related to earnings are most salient. It was such a pension plan that was famously introduced by Bismarck in Germany in 1889 and the pensions components of the US social security system is

---

[6] On measurement issues in Sweden, which reduce the apparent wealth of the lower deciles, see Klevmarken (2006a). The overall incidence of debt is high (see Klevmarken, 2006b, table 4) in part due to interest deductibility for tax purposes. Student debt is also important. On the effects of pensions see e.g. Domeij and Klein (2002).

[7] 'Augmented wealth' is a term introduced by Edward N. Wolff to refer to the sum of marketable wealth, pension wealth, and social security wealth.

[8] For details of current public pension plans internationally, and their history, see Clark *et al.* (2006). Another useful reference is Rein and Schmähl (2004).

of this type. This type of pension plan spread widely in Western Europe, and also to other parts of the world, such as Latin America. Systems with flat-rate contributions and benefits are also sometimes seen, for example in Britain, which introduced such a plan in 1908 and then rationalized and expanded it in 1946, as part of the implementation of (a modified version of) the Beveridge Plan. Non-contributory schemes with flat-rate benefits have also been important, for example in Australia, Canada, New Zealand, and the Scandinavian countries, although in some cases these have been modified over time by making them means-tested. Countries that relied on such plans exclusively at one time have also supplemented them by a second tier with a contributory plan.

The different forms of public pension vary in their distributional implications. Most equalizing are non-contributory schemes financed out of general revenue, and among those the presence of means-testing results in greater targeting and a stronger equalizing effect. Pay-go schemes typically have an earnings threshold below which contributions are not made, and then an increasing schedule of contributions up to an earnings ceiling. If the earnings ceiling is low, the contribution side of the scheme may be quite regressive. On the other hand, benefits also are subject to ceilings, and sometimes floors. Where these are relatively close together, as for example in Sweden, the equalizing impact of pension benefits can be very strong. (See Domeij and Klein, 2002.)

On the private side there is an important distinction between employer-based pension plans and tax-sheltered private retirement savings, or 'retirement accounts'. The latter may be used to purchase annuities, but referring to them as pension assets is questionable, since holders can generally make pre-retirement withdrawals (although there may be a penalty for doing so, as with IRAs and Keogh accounts in the USA). There can, however, be a grey area in terms of definitions, as in the USA where employer-based DC pensions are now generally set up as 401(k) plans that allow pre-retirement withdrawals. Such plans are included in retirement accounts in the SCF, along with IRAs, Keogh plans, and other individual- rather than employer-based plans.

Both private and public pension systems have seen much change in recent decades. There has been a trend toward at least partial funding of pay-go public systems, and in some cases, for example that of Superannuation in Australia, they have become similar to DC pension plans in some respects, such as allowing an element of choice of investment direction to participants. On the private side, as noted earlier, there has been a trend in most countries away from DB toward DC schemes, which, although riskier for the individual, on average, it is hoped, should provide better returns.

It has been known for some time that adding estimates of private or public pension wealth makes the distribution of net worth more equal, and that the effect is stronger in the case of public pensions. In the UK, for example, adding private and public pension rights in 1993 (in the Inland Revenue's Series E, not published more recently) led to a fall in the share of the top 1% from 17% to 10% and to a decline in the Gini coefficient from 0.65 to 0.48 (Davies and Shorrocks, 2000, table 2).

Research on the impact of recent pension trends on the distribution of household wealth has just begun. Wolff (2005) finds that adding private and public pension rights, or 'retirement wealth', in 1983 reduced the SCF Gini coefficient from 0.799 to 0.590, a fall of 26%. However in 2001 the reduction was only from 0.826 to 0.663, a drop of only 20%. Wolff traces the declining impact to the replacement of much DB pension wealth by DC schemes, which results in private pensions now having only a mild equalizing effect. Also, social security wealth, which is strongly equalizing, has fallen relative to total wealth and private pension wealth. While in 1983 social security wealth made up 68.2% of total pension wealth, in 2001 its share had fallen to 59.5% (computed from Wolff, 2005, table 11).

## Income, Wealth, and Consumption

The impact of wealth inequality on the distribution of economic welfare at a point in time depends partly on how highly correlated wealth is with income. This will in turn affect the relationship between wealth and consumption. Since the early surveys of wealth and income were conducted in the 1950s it has been known that while income and wealth are positively correlated, the correlation is imperfect. The correlation coefficient between income and wealth is typically in the neighborhood of 0.5. (See e.g. Keister, 2000: 10). One reason that income and wealth are not perfectly correlated is due to age. Both variables display a hump shape when charted against age, but the hump in income occurs earlier than that in wealth. Retirees have relatively low incomes but high wealth, and the young may have high incomes but little wealth. Further, many of the self-employed in any given year have fairly high business equity, but (perhaps temporarily) low incomes.

For the most part portfolio composition varies similarly with income and wealth. The share of risky financial assets rises with both income and wealth, for example. However, there are significant differences for business equity and home ownership. In the bottom quintile of the income distribution 40.3% of US families were home owners in 2004 according to the SCF. In contrast, only 15.2% of families in the bottom quarter of the wealth distribution owned a home. For business equity the contrast comes at the high end. While 45.8% of those in the top wealth decile own a business, only 34.7% in the top income decile have this status. This reminds us, for example, that business taxes may have a somewhat mixed redistributive impact.

There has been considerable empirical work on the effects of income and wealth on consumption. This literature goes back to early work on the consumption function, which established a positive impact of wealth. There is broad empirical support for the consumption-smoothing hypothesis embodied in the life-cycle model of saving (Deaton, 1992; Browning and Lusardi, 1996). In this model, and under the related permanent income hypothesis, a temporary positive income shock should mostly be saved, and a temporary negative shock mostly offset through dissaving. Permanent income shocks, however, result in large changes in consumption. A 'helicopter-drop' of wealth, for example via a lottery win, should have a large positive effect on consumption. This effect does not always come through clearly in empirical work since wealth is an endogenous variable, and will be higher for people with lower time preference. One must find a good instrumental variable for wealth in order to test adequately whether it affects consumption. Efforts to do so, for example using the food consumption data in the PSID, confirm a positive effect.

Also of interest in recent years has been the impact of stock and house price gains on consumption. Significant positive effects on consumption are found (Muellbauer, 2007). This has fed concern that a market fall may lead to a significant drop in consumer spending and the risk of recession.

## Composition

Tables 6.2 and 6.3 provide information on portfolio composition. In Table 6.2, which is based on national economic statistics rather than survey evidence, we see a wide range of household asset/debt structures across countries. On average across the 12 countries shown, non-financial assets make up 53% of total assets. Half or more of these non-financial assets are in the form of housing. (Other real estate and business equity are the most important other non-financial elements.) There

Table 6.2. Composition of household wealth in household balance sheets, 2000

| Country | % of Total assets | | | % of Financial assets | | |
|---|---|---|---|---|---|---|
| | Financial assets | Non-fin. assets | Debts | Liquid assets | Stocks | Other |
| Australia | 41 | 59 | 17 | 22 | 20 | 58 |
| Canada | 57 | 43 | 18 | 25 | 32 | 43 |
| Denmark | 55 | 45 | 30 | 21 | 54 | 25 |
| France | 40 | 60 | 11 | 33 | 32 | 35 |
| Germany | 40 | 60 | 16 | 34 | 37 | 29 |
| Italy | 42 | 58 | 3 | 23 | 55 | 21 |
| Japan | 50 | 50 | 14 | 53 | 16 | 31 |
| Netherlands | 54 | 46 | 16 | 19 | 24 | 57 |
| New Zealand | 32 | 68 | 20 | 35 | 40 | 25 |
| Spain | 31 | 69 | 10 | 40 | 43 | 17 |
| UK | 53 | 47 | 13 | 21 | 25 | 57 |
| USA | 67 | 33 | 15 | 13 | 51 | 36 |

Source: Davies et al. (2007, table 3).

Table 6.3. Household investment in risky financial assets

| Country | Total asset group | | | | | |
|---|---|---|---|---|---|---|
| | Quartile I | Quartile II | Quartile III | Quartile IV | Top 5% | Average |
| *I. Participation Rates (%)* | | | | | | |
| Germany | 8.9 | 24.1 | 29.2 | 38.2 | 51.4 | 25.1 |
| Italy | 4.4 | 13.5 | 24.1 | 44.2 | 57.7 | 22.1 |
| Netherlands | 0.8 | 8.0 | 26.0 | 64.4 | 87.5 | 24.8 |
| UK | 4.9 | 12.0 | 38.5 | 74.0 | 86.9 | 32.4 |
| USA | 4.4 | 38.6 | 66.4 | 87.2 | 93.8 | 49.2 |
| *II. Share of total financial assets, participants only (%)* | | | | | | |
| Germany | 28.9 | 25.0 | 24.8 | 27.2 | 30.2 | 26.3 |
| Italy | 51.4 | 54.2 | 53.1 | 56.4 | 77.1 | 65.4 |
| Netherlands | na | 31.0 | 36.4 | 50.6 | 61.7 | 49.7 |
| UK | na | na | na | na | na | na |
| USA | 40.7 | 44.9 | 49.0 | 61.3 | 65.2 | 60.5 |

*Source*: Guiso *et al.* (2002, tables I.5 and I.7).

is considerable variation in the relative importance of non-financial assets across countries—from a low of 33% in the USA to a high of 69% in Spain.

Financial assets vary considerably in composition. Again the USA is at one extreme, with just 13% of household financial assets in the form of liquid assets like bank accounts and 51% in the form of stocks.[9] Canada is more typical, with 25% of financial assets in liquid form and 32% in stocks. France and Germany each have approximately one-third of financial assets in liquid form and one-third in stocks. Japan is an outlier, with 53% in liquid form and only 16% in stocks.

Variation in the composition of household wealth across countries is interesting for a number of reasons. For example, one might expect to see a relationship between the risk/return characteristics of household portfolios and wealth inequality. Also, the degree of risk to which households are exposed may affect their behavior and consequently macroeconomic performance. A relationship to bankruptcy and mortgage foreclosure rates can also be expected.

Table 6.3 shows some results from the international comparison of risky financial asset-holding by households in Guiso *et al.* (2002). As in Table 6.2 we see that there is considerable variation across countries, but Table 6.3 also shows patterns across wealth groups. In all countries the majority of those in the top 5% invest in risky financial assets, while only a minority of those below the median do so. However, participation rates vary from 51.4% for the top 5% in Germany to 93.8% for this

---

[9] Stock ownership here includes not only direct, but indirect holdings via e.g. mutual funds and retirement accounts. Stock-holding by institutional pension funds is included in 'other' financial assets.

group in the USA. Among those who participate, the share of financial wealth in risky form rises with wealth, to a high of 77.1% for the top 5% in Italy. Italy and the USA have the highest shares of financial assets in risky form among participants, the Netherlands is at a medium level, and the fraction of assets in risky form is low in Germany.

# 4. TRENDS OVER TIME

Estate and wealth tax data have been available in a number of countries now for a century or more. Ohlsson *et al.* (2006) have assembled long (although inter-rupted) time series for seven countries, going back to the 18th century in five cases. Reasonably continuous time series are available from the early 20th century for Denmark, France, Norway, Sweden, Switzerland, the UK, and the USA. Figure 6.1 shows the share of the top 1% for France, Sweden, the UK, and the USA from 1904 to 2004.

Figure 6.1 reveals a large decline in wealth concentration in the 20th century in each of the countries depicted. The size of the decline, and the timing, differ but the decrease in inequality is large in each case. A similar decline was seen in Denmark and Norway. (Switzerland, interestingly, showed no such decrease.[10]) These declines were preceded by a long period of rising wealth inequality during the earlier industrialization phase in most of these countries. Thus the Kuznets curve seems to be alive and well in the case of wealth inequality!

A few authors have studied carefully the causes for the decline in wealth inequal-ity in the 20th century in the UK and USA. (See Davies and Shorrocks, 2000.) In both countries the decline is associated with the spread of 'popular assets'—owner-occupied housing and consumer durables, which occurred rapidly in the USA and more gradually in the UK and other countries. For the UK, Atkinson and Harrison (1982) find some evidence of a negative effect of the rate of estate taxation on wealth concentration, but the effect cannot be distinguished statistically from a simple time trend. More robust is the impact of asset prices. Rising share prices increase inequality since shares are owned disproportionately by the rich. Higher house prices reduce top shares, since housing is relatively more important for the middle class, but the impact on overall inequality is ambiguous since housing is also more important for the middle class than the poor.

---

[10]  Ohlsson *et al.* (2006) point out that Switzerland escaped both world wars and also did not impose highly progressive taxation during the time when it was in force in the other countries. These factors may help to explain the lack of decline in wealth inequality there.

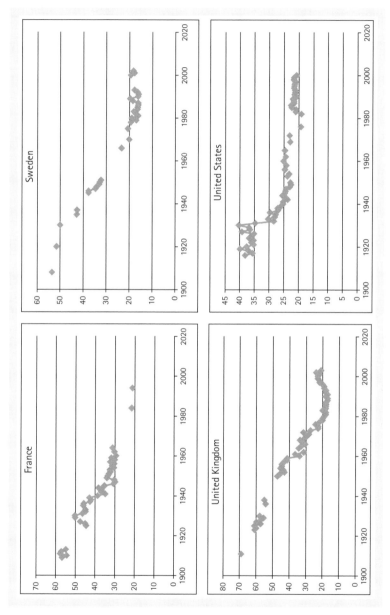

**Fig. 6.1. Wealth shares of top 1%, time series for France, Sweden, the UK, and USA**

*Source:* Constructed using data from Ohlsson *et al.* (2006, table 1). Note that US is the 'USA adults' series in this source.

Figure 6.1 calls attention to a puzzle mentioned earlier: in the last few decades measured wealth inequality has not risen sharply in countries like the UK and USA where income inequality has been on a strong upward trend.[11] Part of the explanation may lie in the depressing effect on top shares of rising house prices. And one would expect the effect of higher income inequality on wealth to be delayed, since wealth is more a mirror of past than present income inequality. Also, wealth has been rising throughout the distribution, preventing measured wealth inequality from rising much despite the growing riches at the top. Finally, Wolff (2005) finds that when pension wealth is added there has indeed been a sharp upward trend in wealth inequality in the USA. Thus the 'puzzle' of why wealth inequality has not risen much may have been largely illusory.

While inequality in private marketable wealth has not been rising much, it has been found recently that concentration *among the rich* has been increasing.[12] Atkinson (2006) classifies the wealthy as rich, 'super-rich', or 'mega-rich', with wealth cutoffs equal to 30, 30 × 30, or 30 × 30 × 30 times mean income. Using historical data for France, Germany, the UK, and USA, he shows that the number exceeding these thresholds has been rising, especially in recent decades. Atkinson reports a range of measures that indicate rising concentration among the rich. *Forbes* magazine, for example, publishes an annual list of the net worth of the top 400 Americans, among whom concentration has been rising strongly.[13] Thus while the share of the top 100 in the total wealth of the 400 was about 50% in the early 1980s it had risen to 65% by 2002 (Atkinson, 2006, figure 3). This trend may partly be due to strengthening of the 'winner take all' aspect of modern business resulting from globalization and technological change.

Changes seen in household portfolios over the last two decades are also interesting. (See e.g. Kennickell, 2006.) The decline in the stock market and recession after 2001 introduce a discontinuity in some trends, but over the period as a whole there has been an increase in the relative importance of financial assets, a rise in debt, and a large shift within the financial asset category towards risky assets. The rise of mutual funds (the most important component of 'pooled investment funds') and retirement accounts is particularly noteworthy. Strongly reinforcing these trends has been a parallel shift toward more risky pensions, with the replacement of DB by DC plans in the USA. A shift towards higher participation in risky assets over the

---

[11]  A reflection of this is that, as Piketty and Saez (2003) pointed out, the highest income groups in the USA now get a larger share of their income from salaries and related compensation than from capital.

[12]  Since pension and social security wealth are relatively unimportant for the truly wealthy, it is not unreasonable to believe that this observation would hold up if we examined the augmented rather than just the marketable wealth of the rich.

[13]  Kennickell (2006: 21) estimates that the total wealth of the Forbes 400 group in 2001 was 2.2% of aggregate household wealth in the USA. There had been a rising trend since 1989, when the share was just 1.5%.

period 1983–98 was also found in the UK, the Netherlands, Germany, and Italy in Guiso *et al.* (2002, table I.4).

# 5. EXPLANATIONS

Wealth can either result from accumulation over the lifetime or from inheritance. A prime motive for life-cycle accumulation is saving for retirement, but people also save for their education or as a precaution against income shocks, bad health, and so on. The need for life-cycle saving is affected by some key institutions and policies in any country, for example in housing, pensions, and health. We will deal with each in turn.

Countries differ in how easy they make it to buy a house. Supply-side controls affect the stocks of housing available for owner occupation versus rental, and mortgage regulations and practices affect demand. Broadly speaking, OECD countries can be divided into those that make it easy to get a mortgage and buy a house, and those that make it difficult. The former include most English-speaking and Scandinavian countries. The latter include, for example, Germany, Italy, and Japan.

Where there are high down-payment requirements young people who want to own a house eventually need to save hard, unless they expect to inherit. Both their wealth and portfolio composition will be affected. On the other hand, where down-payment requirements are less stringent, people will become home owners earlier. This means their portfolios will be dominated by housing rather than financial assets, but it is not clear how wealth *levels* will be affected. Home equity may rise fairly rapidly due to capital gains or repayment of mortgages.

Both public and private pension plans may affect wealth levels, age profiles, and inequality. There are two aspects. First, as pensions are introduced or expanded they will tend to substitute for own saving and if pension rights are not included measured wealth will be lower. Top shares, and perhaps overall inequality, may also be higher since pensions are more important for the middle class than the wealthy. These are illusory effects that may be corrected through better measurement. But there can also be a true effect on household wealth if pensions result in higher effective saving, or either higher or lower rates of return than people would obtain on their own. Employer-based DB pensions or pay-as-you-go public pension schemes like the Social Security system in the US may increase wealth for low earners by boosting their effective saving but at the same time reduce accumulation for high earners via low rates of return. Concern about the latter effect underpins the sea-change in public pensions seen in the last two decades around the world with DC pensions crowding out DB schemes and many pay-go public systems being at least partly converted to funded schemes. While these changes may boost rates of return on average, they also expose households to greater risk and may increase wealth inequality since different people and different cohorts may have varying luck with pension investments (Wolff, 2005). Where greater individual choice regarding contribution rates or early withdrawals is allowed than in the past, for example as 401(k) schemes have replaced DB pensions in the USA, low earners or bad planners may save less than formerly and approach retirement with insufficient assets.[14]

The tax treatment of retirement savings can have major effects on household wealth too. Tax-sheltered retirement saving plans are becoming increasingly important. For example, they accounted for 32% of household financial assets in the 2004 US SCF. Since these plans are generally most important for higher income and wealth groups, overall their rise has likely disequalized the distribution of household wealth. However, the effect on the upper tail is more complex. Annual contribution limits are sufficiently small to make retirement savings plans unimportant for the rich in most countries. While home ownership is generally eased through regulations and policy in English-speaking countries, making an extended period of anticipatory saving unnecessary, the situation with regard to college and health-care costs is less uniform. In Australia, Canada, New Zealand, and the UK the latter costs are still quite heavily subsidized. Putting your children through college, and getting satisfactory health care can be extremely expensive in the USA and in some other OECD countries, which would seem to make anticipatory saving advisable. The need for institutional long-term care in old age has also been increasing in many countries, and again this care can be very expensive, creating another motive for saving.[15]

While saving to put children through college, or as a precaution against medical or long-term care expenses, might seem natural, effects can be more complex. For example, private universities in the USA do not charge uniform fees, but price discriminate on the basis of parental wealth and income. This can discourage, rather than encourage, saving. Similarly, Medicare for working-age people and various other social benefits are means-tested in the USA. If a low income person without private health insurance falls ill, he/she will first be expected to exhaust savings before Medicare will begin paying the bills. The only effect of saving in anticipation of health-care costs for people in this situation may be to lower consumption, since the health care ultimately received will not depend on their assets. Such effects may be partly responsible for the low financial assets of many low and middle income US households, and therefore for the country's high level of wealth inequality (Hubbard *et al.*, 1995).

---

[14]  For a popular discussion of these drawbacks from pension reforms see Hacker (2006).
[15]  There is an emerging market for long-term care insurance in the USA and some other countries. However, most people still enter old age without such insurance.

Tax and transfer systems also affect accumulation, and some of those effects have already been mentioned. The lower marginal tax rates on top incomes, and lower capital gains taxes seen in many countries since 'supply-side' reforms began in the Reagan/Thatcher years, have apparently made accumulation easier for the rich. The spread and development of tax-sheltered retirement saving vehicles have done something similar for middle and upper-middle income groups. On the other hand, there has been increased targeting of benefits to low income groups through tax and transfer systems. In the UK and Canada, for example, there was formerly heavy emphasis on *universal* transfer programs, with generous old age pensions and family allowances paid irrespective of income. Today benefits are generally targeted at the poor and are 'clawed back' by tax systems as income rises above relatively low thresholds. Like means-testing, such clawbacks discourage saving.

Taking all the above into account, one may well ask whether institutions and policy in OECD countries are contributing to wealth inequality by separating the population into high income *savers* and low income *non-savers*. The 'bottom half' receive education, health care, and pensions that are better than they could achieve through private saving. This seems to make it unnecessary for them to save much. The effect is reinforced by means-tests and clawbacks. In contrast, with increased targeting of transfer payments, higher tuition fees, and increased needs for example for long-term care, the 'top half' have an increased need to save. The result may be significantly more wealth inequality than would otherwise be observed.

## Inheritance

The distribution of inherited wealth is highly unequal. It might therefore seem clear that inheritance must be an important part of the explanation for the high level of wealth inequality. However, on average inheritance is a relatively small fraction of lifetime income—about 8% according to a recent estimate using SCF data in the US (Wolff, 2003).[16] The impact on wealth inequality is further reduced by the imperfect correlation between inherited wealth and earnings, as well as by the crowding-out of life-cycle savings. The net effect is that while the high inequality of inheritance may push up the shares of the top 1 and 5% significantly, it appears to have little effect on wealth inequality among the bottom 95%.[17]

[16]   Another way to judge the quantitative importance of inheritance is to ask what fraction of current wealth 'was inherited'. There has been much debate on this issue, with answers ranging from about 20% to 80%. For the USA, Davies and Shorrocks (2000) conclude that the best answer is about 35–40%.

[17]   Empirically, the ratio of inherited assets to current wealth tends to decline with wealth (see e.g. Wolff, 2003), at least up to net worth of $1 million. This does not necessarily imply that inheritance has an equalizing effect for the bottom 95% of the distribution, however, since behavioral response is ignored in this calculation.

Of course, concentration in the upper tail is one of the most interesting aspects of wealth distribution and a large fraction of household wealth is held by the top 1%. Thus inheritance is very far from being unimportant. A stylized fact is that about one-third of the rich owe their wealth to inheritance, another third benefited from inheritance but are partly 'self-made', and a final third are wholly self-made. Atkinson (2006) adds to that picture by showing that the incidence of being self-made currently rises as one looks at higher and higher tranches of the extreme upper tail.

An important question concerns the effects of gift and estate taxes on inheritance and wealth accumulation. Such taxes have been a common feature in OECD countries for many years. These taxes have been credited by some with helping to cause the large decrease in wealth inequality observed over the 20th century, despite avoidance. Part of the reason for an impact on wealth inequality in fact lies in avoidance strategies. Tax can generally be reduced by splitting the estate more. Gifts *inter vivos* are also employed, moving wealth into the hands of following generations more quickly.[18] While it might appear that these impacts are spurious, since wealth is still held within the same extended families, there is a great difference between concentrated patterns of inheritance and more equal and/or accelerated division. The latter patterns can lead to much lower wealth inequality in the long run, as shown e.g. in simulations (Davies and Shorrocks, 2000).

In recent years there has been a move away from estate and gift taxation. For example, federal estate or inheritance taxes were abolished in both Australia and Canada in the 1970s. And for a time, under President Bush's tax cuts, federal estate tax was slated to gradually disappear by the year 2010. There remains a vociferous anti-estate tax movement in the USA. If one believes that a significant part of the reduction in wealth inequality in the last century was due to estate and gift taxes, then the removal of these taxes should be expected to have the opposite effect.

## Demographic Change

It has long been understood that demographic factors may have a significant impact on aggregate wealth, wealth inequality, and wealth trends over time. Wealth levels and inequality vary for example by age, family composition, gender, race and ethnicity, region, and immigration status.[19] The overall wealth picture depends, in

---

[18] Another important avoidance tool has been the use of trusts, whose provisions have tended to become more complex over time in order to counter the efforts of tax authorities to combat the revenue losses they create.

[19] Demographics are interesting not only because demographic changes can affect observed overall trends, but also because patterns of wealth-holding vary across groups. The latter variation is rich and

part, on the relative population shares of the different demographic groups, and can change as these shares vary over time. Effects are analogous to those studied extensively for income, and surveyed by Burtless (this volume, Chapter 18). But the possible effects may be different than for income, and may be larger since between-group differences are often greater for wealth.[20] For example, many young people have low or even negative wealth, so that the ratio of the wealth of those aged, say, 55–64 to those aged 25–34 is much higher than for income. Similarly, the discrepancy between the wealth of blacks and whites in the USA dwarfs the difference in income. In the 2001 SCF we find, for example, that while black households' mean income was 48% of whites', the corresponding figure for wealth was just 14% (Wolff, 2006: 125).[21]

The analysis of life-cycle saving suggests that the population growth rate could have a large impact on saving and wealth levels. High population growth means a young population and few retired people, leading to high saving but perhaps to lower mean wealth in an older society (since the young on average have lower wealth than the old). As is well known, most OECD countries saw high fertility during the 'baby boom' period after World War II, which did not end until the early or mid-1960s. Subsequently, fertility rates fell and have been below replacement in most OECD countries now for many years. Eventually this lower fertility should reduce aggregate saving according to the LSM but until recently the great majority of baby-boomers were still of working age, which is widely believed to have contributed to the high wealth accumulation and general buoyancy in assets markets that we have seen in the last two decades. Increased life expectancy is another important demographic factor that has likely increased accumulation rates.

Demographic trends may also affect wealth composition, which may in turn have various effects, for example on asset prices. There is a sequencing of demand, first for housing and durables, and then for financial assets, as households progress through young adulthood and middle age. The effect of the baby-boomers moving up the age ranges should, then, have been an expansion in the demand for housing starting around the late 1960s, and a later expansion in the demand for financial assets beginning when the first baby-boomers hit their mid-30s, in the

---

complex, and of course changes over time. Surveying these aspects is beyond the scope of this chapter. See e.g. Oliver and Shapiro (1995), Kennickell (2006), and Wolff (2006) for work in this area,

[20]  This is not invariably the case. For example, while income inequality tends to rise fairly continuously with age, wealth inequality tends to decline with age up to around 40–45 and only then begins to increase (Davies and Shorrocks, 2000). Hence while in an ageing population income inequality will tend to rise, that result will not always hold for wealth and the impact may tend to be weaker.

[21]  Keister (2000) reports an interesting simulation experiment assessing the effects of race on wealth accumulation. The effects of race are removed from a micro-simulation whose base case generates an overall wealth distribution similar to actual in the USA. The effects of race considerably reduce the wealth shares of lower groups.

early 1980s. When one looks at the data, for example for the USA, one does see that housing construction and house prices have been strong since the early 1970s. Most impressively, there has been a continuing boom in financial assets since the mid-1980s. While this boom owes much to financial deregulation and innovation, the latter trends may in part be a response to pressures created by the baby-boomers themselves.

Booms in housing and in financial assets have different implications for observed distributional variables. A rise in financial assets, which are quite highly concentrated, tends to give a rise in wealth inequality, whereas a rise in housing wealth has the opposite impact.[22] The asymmetry between housing and financial assets in terms of their impact on income and consumption is even greater, since the return to housing is a form of income in kind and is not included in most measures of household income or consumption. So the disequalizing impact of higher financial assets comes through in the income data, but the equalizing effect of higher housing wealth does not. This may be one reason why measured income inequality has risen faster than wealth inequality in the USA and some other countries in the last few decades.

The effect of population composition and changes in that composition have not been studied as extensively for wealth as for income. In the USA it is found that a relatively small fraction of the large increase in income inequality in recent years can be attributed in an accounting sense to changing demographic composition of the population. Burtless reports the results of studies that examined the long-term impact over the 1970s, 1980s, and 1990s. Changes in family living arrangements and other demographic characteristics appear to have accounted for one-quarter or less of the upward trend in income inequality as measured by the Gini coefficient. The impacts of demographic changes for *wealth* may not, however, be similarly restricted. The effects have been studied carefully for Canada by Morisette *et al.* (2006), using 1984 and 1999 wealth survey data. They find that changes in family structure had little effect, but that the ageing of the population that took place between 1984 and 1999 *reduced* the wealth Gini in 1999 from 0.750 to 0.727 in an accounting sense, which is quite significant.[23] Additional studies of this type for other countries would be valuable.

---

[22]  The increased demand for financial assets in recent years has gone along with higher participation rates by a larger group of households, which might tend to reduce the concentration of these assets. While such a mechanism may be at work, the concentration of financial assets has not shown a downward trend. This may be explained partly by the fact that an increase in the demand for financial assets by ordinary people raises not only their financial wealth but that of the rich as well, through a rise in security prices.

[23]  This is a doubly interesting result because it illustrates the ambiguous, and potentially negative, effect of population ageing on wealth inequality, commented on in an earlier footnote.

# 6. Conclusions and Further Research

This chapter has surveyed the distribution of wealth and its relationship to economic inequality more broadly. We have seen that wealth inequality is high and contributes significantly to inequality in income and consumption, although higher wealth inequality is not always an indicator of greater inequality in well-being. In particular, welfare state policies can improve the well-being of low income groups while at the same time reducing their incentive to save. This may lead to high observed wealth inequality in places where it would otherwise not be expected, such as some of the Scandinavian countries. More research is needed to better illuminate such connections between public policy and wealth inequality.

We have also seen that there are significant differences in household asset portfolios and the importance of debt across countries. The USA is a leader in the riskiness of the average household portfolio and participation in risky assets. Some investors in risky financial assets are found at all wealth and income levels in the USA, and risk is increased in many cases by high levels of indebtedness. This high level of risk may partly be responsible for the fact that the USA shows one of the highest levels of wealth inequality overall, and the longest upper tail of any country. In countries like Germany, Italy, and Japan there is lower participation in risky financial assets, and generally lower debt. These countries have significantly less concentrated wealth distributions than the USA.

While income inequality has been rising strongly for three decades in the USA, and has also gone up in the UK and many other OECD countries, we have seen there is only a small upward trend in inequality of marketable wealth. More research is needed to establish the reasons for this contrast, but possible explanations include the omission of pension wealth, the effects of house price increases, and increased incentives for middle and low groups to save due to the withdrawal of social safety nets and DB pensions. In addition, as Atkinson (2006) has documented, the rich in major OECD countries really have been getting richer, both in absolute terms and relative to mean incomes. This does not show up strongly in overall measures of wealth concentration or inequality, however, since the wealth of the rest of the population has also been rising, so relative shares of wealth have not changed dramatically. Within the rich and super-rich, however, there is good evidence of rising concentration, perhaps reflecting the growing 'winner take all' tendency in the globalizing modern business world.

Wealth allows consumption-smoothing and also self-insurance. In a world where households are exposed to increasing levels of risk, partly through choice but also through a broad and widespread policy shift, success in building personal assets is becoming increasingly important. Increased life expectancy and the ageing of the population reinforce the importance of household assets. Not only do we have more people in late middle age, but they are looking forward to longer periods of retirement and the need to save harder than earlier cohorts, for example in anticipation of long-term care expenses. These aspects suggest that greater attention should be paid in more countries to obtaining good data on wealth, including importantly pension wealth, and to analyzing the role of personal assets and debt in the determination of welfare.

# References

ATKINSON, A. B. 2006. 'Concentration among the Rich'. UNU-WIDER Research Paper no. 2006/151.

——and HARRISON, A. 1982. 'The Analysis of Trends over Time in the Distribution of Personal Wealth in Britain', in D. Kessler, A. Masson, and D. Strauss-Kahn (eds.), *Accumulation et Répartititon des Patrimoines*. Paris: CNRS and Economica, 557–74.

BRANDOLINI, A., CANNARI, L., D'ALESSION, G., and FAIELLA, I. 2004. 'Household Wealth Distribution in Italy in the 1990s'. Termi di discussione no. 530. Rome: Bank of Italy.

BROWNING, M., and LUSARDI, A. 1996. 'Household Saving: Micro Theories and Micro Facts'. *Journal of Economic Literature*, 34: 1797–855.

BUCKS, B. K., KENNICKELL, A. B., and MOORE, K. B. 2006. 'Recent Changes in U.S. Family Finances: Evidence from the 2001 and 2004 Survey of Consumer Finances'. *Federal Reserve Bulletin*, 92, Feb.: A1–38.

CLARK, G. L., MUNNELL, A., and ORSZAG, J. M. (eds.) 2006. *Oxford Handbook of Pensions and Retirement Income*. Oxford: Oxford University Press.

DAVIES, J. B., SANDSTROM, S., SHORROCKS, A., and WOLFF, E. 2007. 'Estimating the Level and Distribution of Global Household Wealth'. UNU-WIDER Research Paper no. 2007/77, Nov.

——and SHORROCKS, A. F. 2000. 'The Distribution of Wealth', in A. B. Atkinson and F. Bourguignon, *Handbook of Income Distribution*, vol. 1. Amsterdam: North-Holland, 605–75.

DEATON, A. 1992.*Understanding Consumption*. Oxford: Clarendon Press.

DOMEIJ, D., and KLEIN, P. 2002. 'Public Pensions: To What Extent Do They Account for Swedish Wealth Inequality?' *Review of Economic Dynamics*. 5: 503–34.

GUISO, L., HALIASSOS, M., and JAPPELLI, T. 2002. *Household Portfolios*. Cambridge, Mass. and London: MIT Press.

HACKER, J. S. 2006. *The Great Risk Shift*. Oxford and New York: Oxford University Press.

HUBBARD, R. G., SKINNER, J., and ZELDES, S. P. 1995. 'Precautionary Saving and Social Insurance'. *Journal of Political Economy*, 103(2): 360–400.

KEISTER, L. 2000. *Wealth in America: Trends in Wealth Inequality*. Cambridge: Cambridge University Press.

KENICKELL, A. B. 2004. 'The Good Shepherd: Sample Design and Control for Wealth Measurement in the Survey of Consumer Finances'. Presented at the Perugia meeting of the Luxembourg Wealth Study, Jan. 2005.

——2006. 'A Rolling Tide: Changes in the Distribution of Wealth in the US, 1989–2001', in Wolff (2006), 19–88.

KLEVMARKEN, N. A. 2006a. 'On Household Wealth Trends in Sweden over the 1990s', in Wolff (2006), 276–94.

—— 2006b. 'The Distribution of Wealth in Sweden: Trends and Driving Factors'. Department of Economics Working Paper 2006: 4. Uppsala University.

MORISETTE, R., ZHANG, X., and DROLET, M. 2006. 'The Evolution of Wealth Inequality in Canada, 1984–99', in Wolff (2006), 151–94.

MUELLBAUER, J. 2007. 'Housing and Personal Wealth in a Global Context'. UNU-WIDER Research Paper no. 2007/27.

OHLSSON, H., ROINE, J., and WALDENSTROM, D. 2006.'Long-Run Changes in the Concentration of Wealth'. UNU-WIDER Research Paper no. 2006/103.

OLIVER, M. L., and SHAPIRO, T. M. 2006. *Black Wealth/White Wealth: A New Perspective on Racial Inequality*, 10th anniversary edn. New York: Routledge.

PIKETTY, T., and SAEZ, E. 2003. 'Income Inequality in the United States, 1913–1998'. *Quarterly Journal of Economics*, 118(1), Feb: 1–39.

REIN, M., and SCHMÄHL, W. (eds.) 2004. *Rethinking the Welfare State: The Political Economy of Pension Reform*. Cheltenham, UK and Northampton, Mass.: Edward Elgar.

SIERMINSKA, E., BRANDOLINI, A., and SMEEDING, T. M. 2006. 'Comparing Wealth Distribution across Rich Countries: First Results from The Luxembourg Wealth Study'. Luxembourg Wealth Study Working Paper no. 1, Aug. 9.

WOLFF, E. N. 2003. 'The Impact of Gifts and Bequests on the Distribution of Wealth', in Alicia H. Munnell and Annika Sundén, *Death and Dollars: The Role of Gifts and Bequests in America*. Washington: Brookings Institution Press, 345–88.

—— 2005. 'Is the Equalizing Effect of Retirement Wealth Wearing Off?' Levy Economics Institute Working Paper no. 420, Mar.

—— 2006. *International Perspectives on Household Wealth*. Cheltenham, UK and Northampton, Mass.: Edward Elgar.

# CHAPTER 7

................................................................

# TOP INCOMES*

................................................................

## ANDREW LEIGH

## 1. INTRODUCTION

................................................................

MUCH research into inequality is concerned with the bottom of the distribution. However, changes in top income shares may have important implications in their own right. A concentration of income at the top of the distribution may have significant consequences for economic and political power. If a small elite receives a large share of the income in a society, it may wield disproportionate influence in certain industries, and may have the ability to influence political outcomes through campaign contributions. The proliferation of 'rich lists' in business magazines over recent decades testifies to the strong interest among the general public in knowing who the richest people are, how much money they have, and how they made their money.

Frank (2007) argues that increased expenditures by top earners can affect the middle class because it leads to an 'expenditure cascade'. He gives the example of

* This chapter builds on the work of Facundo Alvaredo, Tony Atkinson, Fabien Dell, Chiaki Moriguchi, Brian Nolan, Thomas Picketty, Jesper Roine, Emmanuel Saez, Wiemer Salverda, Michael Veall, and Daniel Waldenström, who have painstakingly used taxation studies and other historical data to estimate top income shares for the countries analyzed herein. Parts of this chapter draw upon Leigh (2007). Elena Varganova provided outstanding research assistance. Dalton Conley, Nicholas Gruen, Ian Irvine, Thomas Piketty, Kenneth Scheve, David Stasavage, Daniel Waldenström, seminar participants at the Handbook conference in Seville, and the editors provided feedback on earlier drafts. I owe a particular debt to Tony Atkinson, who taught me a great deal through our collaborative work, and provided especially valuable comments on this chapter. All remaining errors are mine.

housing, in which higher incomes cause those at the top of the distribution to build mansions, which in turn leads the next tier to build larger houses, which in turn means that the middle class must spend more on housing or face the prospect of sending their children to below-average schools. Frank argues that the same cascade process operates in the cases of motor vehicles, professional wardrobes for job applicants, and gifts given to co-workers. In each instance, expenditure on positional goods by the most affluent individuals in society changes what is considered 'adequate' by people of median income.

Beyond this, understanding the concentration of incomes at the top of the distribution can tell us something about the bottom of the distribution. As Tawney (1913) noted: 'what thoughtful rich people call the problem of poverty, thoughtful poor people call with equal justice a problem of riches'. Mechanically, of course, it must be true that if those at the top have a larger share of national income, then the rest of the population must have a smaller share. But it also turns out to be the case that income concentration at the top of the distribution is highly correlated with relative poverty.

This suggests that top income shares are not only important for understanding the rich; they may also help us better understand the poor. As we shall see, estimates of top income shares (e.g. the income share of the top 10 percent, 1 percent, 0.1 percent, etc.) are available on an annual basis for many years prior to the advent of national income surveys, during eras when little else is known about the distribution of income. In these cases, top income shares may serve as a useful proxy for inequality across the entire distribution.

The remainder of this chapter is structured as follows. In Section 2, I discuss the basic methodology used for creating recent top incomes estimates, and issues that arise about comparability across countries. One of the most important of these is tax underreporting, but there are also methodological differences that exist between the studies, and it is useful to see the extent to which these are likely to affect comparability. In Section 3, I present time trends for both Anglo-Saxon and non-Anglo-Saxon countries. A distinct feature of this exercise is the similarity across Anglo-Saxon countries, where top incomes have followed a U-shaped path over the course of the twentieth century.

Another set of issues concerns the degree to which top incomes can be compared with other measures of inequality. In Section 4, I assess top income shares against the standard axioms of inequality, and present empirical evidence on the relationship between top income shares and other commonly used measures of inequality, such as the Gini coefficient.

Two sections of the chapter then summarize research on the causes and consequences of changing top income shares. In Section 5, I consider possible drivers of top incomes, including major events (such as world wars and depressions), superstar labor markets, changes in taxation, and political partisanship. In Section 6, I discuss research on outcomes that may be affected by top incomes, including health, economic growth, and national savings. The chapter concludes with a discussion of the many fruitful directions for research that remain in this rapidly growing field.

## 2. METHODOLOGY AND COMPARABILITY

The use of tax data to estimate income inequality has a long history (e.g. Bowley, 1914; Kuznets, 1953). Here, I draw upon a series of recent papers that have combined tax data with external population and income control totals to estimate the changing share of income going to families and individuals above the 90th percentile of the distribution. The studies in this 'new top incomes literature' follow Piketty (2001) in using all available taxation data (rather than just selected years). In these respects, such studies provide a more complete picture of the top of the income distribution than has previously been available.[1]

Top incomes series have now been produced for at least 14 developed countries. These include Australia (Atkinson and Leigh, 2007a), Canada (Saez and Veall, 2005), Finland (Riihelä *et al.*, 2005), France (Piketty, 2001, 2003, 2007; Landais, 2007), Germany (Dell, 2005, 2007), Ireland (Nolan, 2007), Japan (Moriguchi and Saez, forthcoming), the Netherlands (Atkinson and Salverda, 2005; Salverda and Atkinson, 2007), New Zealand (Atkinson and Leigh, 2005), Spain (Alvaredo and Saez, 2006), Sweden (Gustafsson and Jansson, 2007; Roine and Waldenström, 2008), Switzerland (Dell, 2005; Dell *et al.*, 2007), the United Kingdom (Atkinson, 2005, 2007b), and the United States (Piketty and Saez, 2001, 2003, 2006b).[2] Although I do not address them in this chapter, it is worth noting that estimates are also available for at least four developing nations, including Argentina (Alvaredo, 2007), China (Piketty and Qian, 2006), India (Banerjee and Piketty, 2005), and Indonesia (Leigh and van der Eng, 2006).[3]

---

[1]   Feenberg and Poterba (1993) used taxation data to estimate the income share of the richest 0.5 percent in the United States from 1951 onwards. Their methodology used external population controls, but not external income controls.

[2]   The analysis that follows is restricted to the countries and years covered in the comparable dataset in Leigh (2007). It therefore excludes the work of Landais (2007) on French top incomes after 1998, and the work of Riihelä *et al.* (2005) on Finland. For Sweden, I use data from Roine and Waldenström (2008) on the basis that it covers more years than the series in Gustafsson and Jansson (2007). Other researchers are presently preparing series on Denmark and Norway.

[3]   The series for China are based exclusively on survey estimates, and do not make use of taxation statistics.

In each case, the series have been produced using a similar methodology. Using published tabulations of total income into income bands, statistics on the adult population, and data on total personal income, researchers estimate the share of income held by the top $x$ percent of the population. Although it is possible to extrapolate slightly beyond the available data, it is reasonably accurate to say that estimates of the top 10 percent share are only available for periods in which 10 percent or more of the adult population file an income tax return. Thus while top incomes series for many countries start around World War I, the top 10 percent share is typically unavailable until the 1920s or 1930s, when the personal income tax is expanded to cover more than one-tenth of the population.

In what follows, I focus on three factors that affect the accuracy of any single estimate of top income shares, and six factors that affect comparability across countries. What appears here is only an overview; more detailed treatments may be found in Atkinson (2007a), Atkinson and Leigh (2007b), and Leigh (2007).[4]

## (a) Tax Avoidance and Evasion

Perhaps the most troubling aspect about using taxation data to estimate inequality is that individuals have a strong incentive to underreport income to the tax authorities. If the extent of underreporting varies systematically over time or between nations, this may affect the validity of temporal or international comparisons. The underreporting of income to tax authorities is an issue that has been taken seriously by top incomes researchers. In some cases, this has involved omitting years when the data are of dubious accuracy. For example, Alvaredo and Saez (2006) only present estimates of the top 1 percent share in Spain from 1981 onwards. In other cases, it has involved testing the hypothesis that the rich are keeping their money in 'safe haven' countries. In their paper on top income shares in Switzerland, Dell et al. (2007) show that attributing all foreign income in Switzerland to French taxpayers would have only a small effect on French top income shares.

Although data on tax underreporting is limited, it is nonetheless possible to say something about the plausible magnitude of these factors. Some of the best data on underreporting comes from random audits in the United States, conducted under the Taxpayer Compliance Measurement Program (TCMP), and its successor, the National Research Program (NRP). One way that these data can be used is to compare changes in underreporting in the United States over time. Estimates from the Internal Revenue Service (1996, 2006) put the gross underreporting gap on individual income taxes (i.e. the share of income not reported) at 17–18 percent in 1985, 1988, and 1992, and 16 percent in 2001. Although Slemrod (2007)

---

[4]  Regarding US top income shares, Reynolds (2006) has argued that Piketty and Saez's estimates are biased upwards by tax evasion, and do not accord with Census Bureau estimates on the share of the richest 5 percent. See Piketty and Saez (2006c) for a detailed response to this critique.

points out that these estimates are inexact, they do not point to any significant changes in underreporting. Similarly, in their study of top incomes in Sweden, Roine and Waldenström (2008) discuss four studies on the size of the tax gap, and conclude that the gap has not changed significantly from the 1930s to the 1990s (they speculate that while the incentives to underreport may have grown over time, the administrative machinery for monitoring compliance may have also improved).

Across countries, comparisons are also inexact, yet the evidence that exists does not point to major differences in underreporting. Results from random audit studies in Sweden (Swedish Tax Agency, 2004) and the United Kingdom (O'Donnell, 2004) have found that the tax gap in those countries is of a similar magnitude to the United States tax gap. Another approach (suggested by Slemrod, 2007) is to compare attitudes to compliance. In the 1999–2001 World Values Survey, respondents are asked whether cheating on taxes is ever justifiable. On a scale where 'never justifiable' is 1, and 'always justifiable' is 10, there is surprisingly little cross-national variation. In the 13 developed countries discussed below, the mean is between 2.1 and 2.7 for all except two nations (Japan is 1.5, France is 3.1).[5] The close similarity in attitudes suggests that—given the same taxation regime—underreporting is likely to be similar across developed nations.

Finally, results from random audit studies can be used to look at how underreporting varies across income groups and income types. Using data from the United States TCMP, Christian (1994) finds that taxpayers with (auditor-adjusted) earnings above $100,000 reported 97 percent of their true incomes to the IRS, compared with an 86 percent reporting rate for those with incomes under $25,000. Slemrod and Yitzhaki (2002) also suggest that non-compliance is much lower for wage incomes, as there is a greater chance that understatement of wage incomes will be detected. In most countries, the wage share in top incomes has risen since World War II: if overall underreporting remained constant, one might therefore expect this to have had a small positive effect on top income shares.

## (b) Tabulated Income Distributions

The raw data used to produce top incomes series are typically drawn from tabulations of income in income ranges that are published annually in hard copy by taxation authorities. Estimating top income shares from these data therefore involves making some assumptions about the distribution of income within bands.

---

[5]  The precise question is 'Please tell me for each of the following statements whether you think it can always be justified, never be justified, or something in between . . . Cheating on taxes if you have a chance'. The means for each country are Australia 2.2, Canada 2.1, France 3.1, Germany 2.4, Ireland 2.3, Japan 1.5, Netherlands 2.7, New Zealand 2.3, Spain 2.3, Sweden 2.4, Switzerland 2.6, United Kingdom 2.4, United States 2.3.

The standard approach to this problem is to assume that the data follow a Pareto distribution. The different methods by which this can be done are discussed in some detail by Atkinson (2005, 2007a). For present purposes, it is sufficient to note that in instances where researchers have estimated upper and lower bounds for the interpolation, or compared results using microdata with those derived from grouped data, the results have been very similar. In principle, it should be possible to estimate standard errors to take account of the problems that arise from using grouped data, though I am not aware of any researchers having done so.

## (c) Part-Year Incomes

There are various ways in which part-year units can arise. Emigrants may choose to file a return when they leave the country. Individuals who die part-way through the year may nonetheless have a return filed on their behalf. Immigrants or young persons entering the labor market may file a return based only on a few months' earnings. In countries where married couples file jointly, a person who divorces midway through the year may file both as a couple and an individual. Although these are all theoretical problems in estimating the distribution of top incomes, their practical importance seems to be minimal. For example, the United Kingdom Royal Commission on the Distribution of Income and Wealth (1979, cited in Atkinson 2005) found that excluding part-year units would only reduce the share of the top 1 percent by 0.1 percentage point.[6]

Issues affecting comparability include the following.

## (d) The Tax Year

In Canada, France, Japan, the Netherlands, Spain, Sweden, Switzerland, and the United States, the tax year and calendar year are one and the same. However, this is not true of all countries. The tax year commences on July 1 in Australia, April 1 in New Zealand, and April 6 in Ireland and the United Kingdom. Since many other data sources are collected on a calendar year basis, Leigh (2007) averages across tax years for these four countries, creating a comparable calendar year top incomes dataset. While this dataset allows a more direct comparison with countries where the tax and calendar year are the same, the price of the exercise is that it tends to over-smooth the top incomes series for Australia, Ireland, New Zealand, and the United Kingdom.

---

[6]  The population restriction affects numbers, and therefore incomes, more strongly for the top 1 percent.

## (e) The Appropriate Age Cut-Off for the Adult Population

The estimates for Australia, the Netherlands, New Zealand, and the United Kingdom use persons aged 15 and over, the estimates for Sweden use persons aged 16 and over, the estimates for Ireland use persons aged 18 and over, while those for Canada, France, Japan, Spain, Switzerland, and the United States use persons aged 20 and over.[7] To give some sense of the magnitude of the effect, Atkinson and Leigh (2005, 2007a) find for Australia and New Zealand that shifting from a population control total of 15 and over to persons aged 20 and over reduces the top 1 percent share by approximately 0.5 percentage points, and the top 10 percent share by approximately 2 percentage points.[8] They do not discern any substantial change in this effect over time (see also Roine and Waldenström, 2008, who show a similar robustness check for Sweden).

## (f) The Income Unit

In Australia, Canada, and Spain, the tax unit is the individual. In France, Ireland, the Netherlands, Switzerland, and the United States, the tax unit is a married couple or single individuals, and the population control total is therefore the adult population minus the number of married females. Germany has a hybrid system, with most taxpayers filing as tax units, and the very rich filing as individuals.

In 1948, the United States changed the incentives for married women to file separately, so Piketty and Saez adjust the estimated income shares for the period 1913–47 (Piketty and Saez, 2001). A more significant shift occurred in Japan (1950), New Zealand (1953), Sweden (1971), and the United Kingdom (1990), when the tax unit switched from the household to the individual. In the case of Japan, Moriguchi and Saez (forthcoming) are able to subtract dependent income from head-of-household income for earlier years. For Sweden, Roine and Waldenström (2008) find little impact of this shift, so do not adjust their series. Atkinson and Leigh (2005) adjust the New Zealand series, assuming that the whole of the increase in the top shares from 1952 to 1953 represented the effect of the move from a tax unit to an individual basis, and apply this constant adjustment to 1952 and all previous years. Leigh (2007) suggests a similar correction to the United Kingdom change in 1990, noting that since United Kingdom top income shares were steadily rising in the 1980s and 1990s, attributing all of the change from 1989 to 1990 to the shift in the tax unit probably underestimates the true increase in top income shares.

This issue is also relevant to the comparability of top income shares with other measures of inequality. Top income shares from countries with individual filing are

---

[7] Two changes over time have affected the appropriate age cut-off (in opposite directions): a fall in the average age at which individuals form independent income units, and a rise in the average age at which individuals enter the labor market.

[8] See n. 6.

conceptually more comparable with measures of earnings inequality across individuals; while top income shares from countries with joint filing are conceptually more comparable with measures of household income inequality. In principle, one could use taxation statistics on singles and couples to derive more comparable measures, but I am not aware of this having yet been done.

## (g) The Personal Income Total

The appropriate income control total used to derive the top income shares in each country is the sum that would have been reported if all adults filed an income tax return.[9] This figure is typically derived by starting with the national accounts and subtracting the income of the government sector, corporate sector, and non-profit sector, as well as making other adjustments to account for the differences in tax reporting regimes.[10] While the accuracy of the personal income control total will doubtless vary from country to country (depending largely on the quality of the national accounts), there do not appear to be systematic differences between nations. On average, the personal income control total is about two-thirds of GDP, and this ratio appears quite similar across countries, and shows no systematic trends, either upwards or downwards.

## (h) Income Definition—Taxable and Total Income

In the earlier years, taxation statistics for several countries were tabulated by assessable income (income less deductions). In later years, this shifted to total income. In the case of Australia, New Zealand, and the United Kingdom, this change has been accounted for in the production of the top incomes series. Another issue is that certain types of income are not included in taxation statistics. In the case of the United States, Piketty and Saez (2001) note that non-taxable (and partially taxable) social security benefits grew as a share of personal income during the post-war decades, but find that these changes had only a trivial impact on top income shares. However, differences in the definition of taxable income may have a greater impact when comparing top income shares across countries.

---

[9] As Atkinson (2007a) points out, this does not necessarily correspond to the definition of income put forward by the Canberra Group established by the Expert Group on Household Income Statistics (The Canberra Group), nor to the Haig-Simons comprehensive definition of income. Atkinson gives the example of social security benefits, whose tax treatment differs across countries, and even within the same country over time.

[10] Personal income in the national accounts is typically constructed from a variety of sources, including surveys and data on wage bills. However, as Nolan (2007) points out, in some instances total taxable income may itself be used in the construction of the national accounts personal income figure.

# (i) Income Definition—Treatment of Capital Gains

Published series differ on their treatment of realized capital gains. For Canada, Germany, Spain, Sweden, Switzerland, and the United States, researchers have compiled separate top incomes series including capital gains and excluding capital gains. For France, Japan, the Netherlands, and the United Kingdom, researchers have excluded capital gains. The top incomes estimates for Australia, Ireland, and New Zealand include realized capital gains, to the extent that such gains were taxable.

Leigh (2007) makes some adjustments to top incomes series for 13 developed countries (Australia, Canada, France, Germany, Japan, the Netherlands, New Zealand, Spain, Sweden, Switzerland, the United Kingdom, and the United States) in order to make them more comparable. The main adjustments are: (a) using series that exclude capital gains where possible; (b) taking account of the shift from joint to individual filing in New Zealand and the United Kingdom; (c) linearly interpolating missing years in cases where the gap is four years or less; and (d) shifting to a calendar year basis for those countries where the tax year and calendar year differ.[11]

This adjusted series covers just 13 countries, with a comparatively large number of country-year observations. There are a total of 761 observations for the share of the top 10 percent, and 937 observations for the share of the top 1 percent. This is more than five times as many observations as in the Luxembourg Income Study (LIS), and exceeds the number of high-quality country-year observations in both the Deininger and Squire database and the World Income Inequality Database (WIID).[12] These data are used in the analysis that follows.

In sum, while top income series have their imperfections, these are by no means insurmountable.[13] Nor are they necessarily more problematic than the comparability problems that afflict other cross-national inequality datasets (with the possible exception of the LIS). Given the extensive coverage of top income series, these data compare well with other sources for studying trends, determinants, and effects of inequality across countries and over time.

---

[11]   In Leigh (2007), the interpolation is carried out as follows. Where the gap is four years or less, the missing years are linearly interpolated. In the case of Switzerland, taxpayers are only required to file returns every two years, so the same figure is assigned to both years. During the period 1887–98, Japanese tax returns were for overlapping three-year periods, so the top income estimate is assigned to the middle year. For France, top income shares for 1900–10 are based on average data for the period, so this estimate is assigned to 1905.

[12]   Deininger and Squire (1996) identify 693 observations that they label 'accept'. Version 2a of the WIID contains 1,223 observations classified as Quality = 1, but many of these are repeated observations for the same country-year, so there are only 540 high-quality country-year observations in the WIID.

[13]   One way of circumventing the problem of measurement error in population and income control totals is to focus on shares-within-shares (e.g. the share of the top 1 percent within the top 10 percent), which are not affected by control totals. Empirically, the concentration of income within the top 10 percent is positively related to the share of the top 10 percent (where S1 and S10 are the shares of the top 1 percent and top 10 percent respectively, the mean within-country correlation between [S1/S10] and S10 is 0.6).

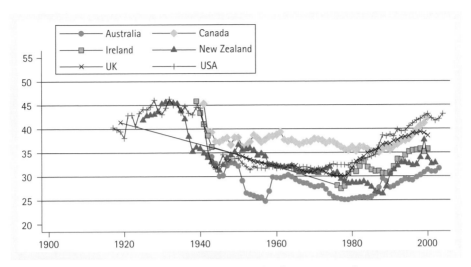

Fig. 7.1. Income share of richest 10% in Anglo–Saxon countries

# 3. TRENDS IN TOP INCOMES

Figures 7.1 and 7.2 depict the top 10 percent share for Anglo-Saxon and non Anglo-Saxon countries; while Figures 7.3 and 7.4 show the top 1 percent share for these two sets of countries (note that the top 10 percent share is unavailable for Japan).[14] In all countries except Switzerland, top income shares tended to fall from the 1920s to the 1970s (data for Spain are unavailable over this period). Since the 1970s, top income shares in the Anglo-Saxon countries (Australia, Canada, Ireland, New Zealand, the United Kingdom, and the United States) have risen sharply, while shares in Japan and in the continental European countries (France, the Netherlands, Spain, Sweden, and Switzerland) remained relatively stable.

When did top incomes peak? For almost all countries in the sample, top income shares were at their highest at some point between the start of World War I and the end of World War II. For example, the highest level of the top 1 percent was reached in Canada in 1938, France in 1916, Germany in 1938, Ireland in 1939, Japan in 1938, the Netherlands in 1916, New Zealand in 1928, Sweden in 1916, Switzerland in 1939–40, and the United Kingdom in 1919. For Ireland and the United Kingdom, the peak year is also the first year in the series. The only exceptions to the rule that top incomes tended to peak in the inter-war era are Australia (where the 1950 wool

---

[14]  As can readily be observed from the charts, the top 1 percent and top 10 percent series track one another quite closely. For the countries and years shown in Figures 7.1–7.4, the mean within-country correlation between these two measures is 0.8.

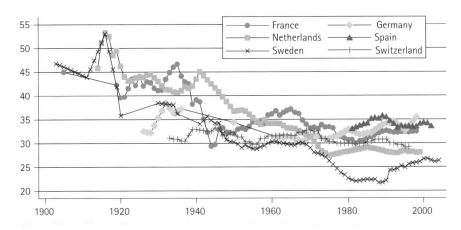

Fig. 7.2. Income share of richest 10% in non-Anglo-Saxon countries

boom caused the top 1 percent share to peak in that year), and Spain (for which top incomes data have only been available since 1981).

A similar pattern emerges when looking at the year when top incomes were at their lowest level. The income share of the top 1 percent bottomed out during the 1970s in four countries (Canada 1978, Ireland 1977, United Kingdom 1978, United States 1973), in the 1980s in four countries (Australia 1982, France 1983, New Zealand 1986, Sweden 1988), and in the 1990s in four countries (Germany 1995, Netherlands 1993, Switzerland 1995–6). The only exception to this pattern is Japan, where the top 1 percent share was at its lowest level in 1945. (Again, I do not take Spain into account for the purposes of this analysis.)

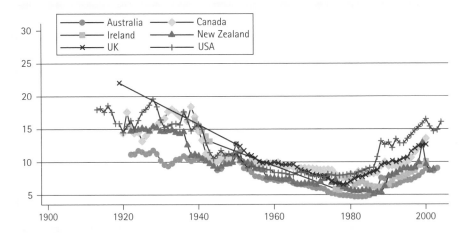

Fig. 7.3. Income share of richest 1% in Anglo-Saxon countries

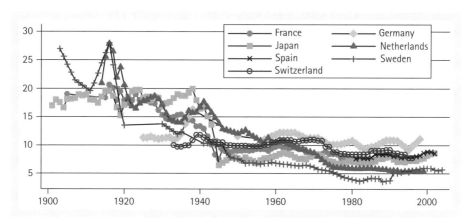

Fig. 7.4. Income share of richest 1% in non-Anglo-Saxon countries

A more formal way of analyzing the time series path of top income shares is to use time series econometric techniques to test for regime switches. With this approach, Roine *et al.* (2007b) identify three 'formative periods' in the past century: World War II, the mid-1970s and the mid/late-1980s. The authors also note that the regime switches found for the top 1 percent (percentile 99–100) are often different from those found for the next 9 percent (percentiles 90–9); suggesting some heterogeneity in the experiences of top income groups.

Across countries, the differential impact of world wars can be observed. The highest concentration of top income shares in the sample may be observed in 1916, when the top 1 percent in Sweden held 28 percent of the national income, and the top 10 percent in the Netherlands held 53 percent of national income. But in all European countries, a large drop in top income shares can be observed during both World War I and World War II. Below, I discuss some of the channels through which wars affected top incomes.

Another important trend has been the rising share of wage incomes in many countries over time. For example, Atkinson and Leigh (2007b) discuss the share of top 1 percent income that comes from wages in Australia, Canada, the United Kingdom, and the United States. In each of these countries, the series start with the top percentile group drawing a minority of their income from wages, and end around 2000 with the top percentile group in all four countries drawing a majority of their income from wages. In Chapter 5, Andrew Glyn points out that in the United States, the rising share of wage income among the top 1 percent has coincided with a steady decline in labor's share of national income.

# 4. COMPARISON WITH OTHER INEQUALITY MEASURES

Are top incomes a useful measure of inequality? As the introduction to this chapter noted, there may be instances in which researchers are particularly concerned with the top of the distribution. For this purpose, series derived from taxation data are most likely preferable to survey data, since surveys are known to under-sample high earners (Moore *et al.*, 2000), and because taxation data allow one to study the income share of very small groups (e.g. the top 1/10,000th of the distribution) which would be represented by only a handful of individuals in a typical survey.

However, for many purposes, researchers may use top income shares as a *proxy* for inequality across the distribution, providing insights into the distribution of income for countries and years about which we do not have reliable data on the distribution of incomes. One way to judge how well top incomes shares can serve this purpose is to turn to theory, and see how well top incomes measures satisfy the standard axioms of inequality. Another approach is to answer the question empirically, by observing how closely top income shares track other measures of inequality.

Cowell (1995) sets out five desirable properties ('axioms') of inequality measures. Income scale independence requires that the inequality measure be unaffected by proportional changes in income (e.g. expressing income in pence rather than pounds should not change inequality). The principle of population requires that the inequality measure be unaffected by replications of the population (e.g. merging two identical distributions should not change inequality). Anonymity requires that the inequality measure be unaffected by characteristics apart from income. The Pigou-Dalton transfer principle requires that an income transfer from a richer person to a poorer person should decrease (or at least not increase) inequality. And decomposability requires that a rise in inequality among some sub-group of the population should increase overall inequality.

Top income shares satisfy the first three of these axioms: income scale independence, principle of population, and anonymity. However, top income shares only weakly satisfy the Pigou-Dalton transfer principle: a transfer from rich to poor will never increase the top income shares, but if the transfer is between two individuals who are both within the top group or both outside the top group, then the share measure will remain unchanged. Top income shares are also not decomposable into within-group inequality and between-group inequality.

Another theoretical issue is that top income shares are based on pre-tax incomes, and are not adjusted for household size. To the extent that household size or the redistributive effect of taxation differs across countries and over time, top income shares may be a poor proxy for the differences in true economic resources across a given society.

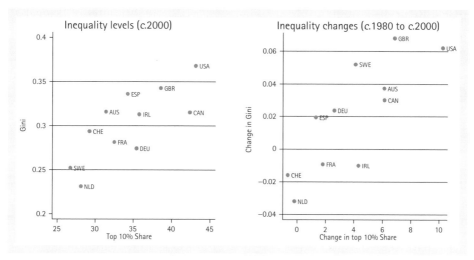

**Fig. 7.5. Top income shares and LIS Gini coefficients**

*Notes*: 1. New Zealand is not shown, since it is not in the LIS.
2. Gini Coefficients are based on equivalized post-tax income.
3. Top income shares are unequivalized and based on pre-tax income.

Since theory is somewhat ambiguous on the usefulness of top income shares, it is useful to the empirical correlation between top incomes and other measures of inequality, over a period where both are available. Using data from the WIID and the LIS, Leigh (2007) shows that top income shares are strongly correlated with estimates of the Gini coefficient, in both pooled ordinary least squares (OLS) specifications, and with country and year fixed effects.[15] Using various inequality measures available in the LIS (all of which are based on post-tax, size-equivalized household incomes), the Gini, Atkinson index, and the 90/50 ratio are each positively and significantly associated with the share of the top 10 percent. This remains true when country and year fixed effects are included in the regression.

To see this pattern visually, Figure 7.5 plots the relationship between a country's LIS Gini coefficient and the income share of the top 10 percent (at around 2000); and the relationship between the *change* in the Gini and the *change* in the top 10 percent share (from about 1980 to about 2000). Both levels and changes are strongly correlated with one another, suggesting that the same factors which affect inequality at the top of the distribution also affect the Gini coefficient.[16]

This close correspondence between top incomes and relative poverty reflects the fact that, from a theoretical standpoint, many of the hypotheses about inequality have the same predictions for inequality at the top of the distribution as for

[15]  On the limitations of the Deininger–Squire database and the WIID, see Atkinson and Brandolini (2001).
[16]  Indeed, one can see the same pattern even within the LIS. The correlation between the 90/50 ratio and the 50/10 ratio is 0.9, indicating that when the 90th percentile is further above the median, the 10th percentile also tends to be further below the median.

inequality at the bottom of the distribution. Theories about causes of inequality that have similar predictions for both ends of the distribution include trade, immigration, union membership, skill-biased technological change, and assortative mating. Similarly, theories about effects of inequality that have similar predictions for both ends of the distribution include growth, saving, and public expenditure. This suggests that for periods where other inequality measures are unavailable, top income shares may help fill in the gaps.

# 5. FACTORS AFFECTING TOP INCOME SHARES

What have been the chief drivers of changes in top income shares? In their discussion of United States top income shares, Piketty and Saez (2003) argue that top capital incomes were reduced by several major events, including the Depression, the two world wars, and periods of high inflation. In the case of top labor incomes, they argue that social norms mattered, via their effect on executive compensation, which rose rapidly during the 1980s and 1990s. For both capital and labor incomes, Piketty and Saez argue that top tax rates played an important role, with high taxes on capital lowering the rate of capital accumulation, and high taxes on labor income reducing work incentives.

One possible explanation for the fact that top incomes in Anglo-Saxon countries rose more rapidly in the 1980s and 1990s than in continental Europe and Japan is that the international market for English-speaking 'superstars' grew more globalized during this period. For example, in the 1970s, a top Australian CEO might have benchmarked his wage against other Australian CEOs. By the early 2000s, such a CEO would have more likely asked his remuneration committee to benchmark his salary against CEOs in Canada, the United Kingdom, and the United States.

One piece of evidence in favor of this theory is presented by Saez and Veall (2005), who separate top wage shares for the Canadian province of Quebec into English-speakers and French-speakers. Over the period 1982–2000, they find that those in the top 1 percent who spoke English doubled their income share from 7 to 14 percent; while the income share of the French-speaking top 1 percent only rose from 4.5 to 6.5 percent. This is consistent with the English-speaking rich in Canada having a more powerful 'brain drain threat' than their French-speaking countryfolk rich.

Another strategy is that pursued by Kaplan and Rauh (2007), who match the tax-derived estimates of Piketty and Saez (2003) on the share of the top 0.1 percent with publicly available information on the earnings of financial and non-financial executives, lawyers, professional athletes, and celebrities. They observe a larger rise in the incomes of financial executives than non-financial executives. Kaplan and Rauh conclude that this evidence is most consistent with theories of superstars, skill-biased technological change, and greater scale (though since the publicly available data only allows them to account for between one-sixth and one-quarter of the individuals in the top 0.1 percent, these conclusions must be regarded as merely suggestive).

Several studies have estimated the relationship between marginal tax rates and top income shares. These include Saez (2004) for the United States; Saez and Veall (2005) for Canada; Moriguchi and Saez (2007) for Japan; Roine and Waldenström (2008) for Sweden; and Atkinson and Leigh (2007b) for five Anglo-Saxon countries (Australia, Canada, New Zealand, the United Kingdom, and the United States). Not surprisingly, the methodology used in these studies differs somewhat, but three general conclusions can be drawn about the relationship between marginal tax rates and pre-tax top income shares. First, tax rates seem to be an important determinant of top income shares across a range of developed countries. In Anglo-Saxon countries, Atkinson and Leigh (2007b) conclude that cuts in top tax rates can explain one-third to one-half of the rise in top income shares since 1970. Second, taxes appear to affect top income shares through two channels: an immediate work disincentive effect, and a lagged effect via capital accumulation. Third, the further one goes up the distribution, the more responsive top income groups appear to be to tax rates. For example, top tax rates are a more powerful explanator of the top 1 percent share than the next 9 percent share.

While models that take account only of personal income taxes have the advantage of parsimony, they may not fully capture the changing tax burden on high income individuals. For example, Piketty and Saez (2007) show that in the United States in 2004, the average total federal tax rate for taxpayers in the top 1 percent was around 32 percent. Yet only two-thirds of this was individual income taxes, with the rest being payroll taxes, corporate taxes, estate, gift, and wealth taxes. Another problem is the fact that income taxes as a share of the tax burden have not held steady over time, nor constant across countries. For example, individual income taxes constituted half of all federal taxes for the top 1 percent of United States taxpayers in 1960. In the most recent year, individual income taxes comprised only about one-third of total taxes for the top 1 percent of French taxpayers; but three-quarters of the total tax burden for the United Kingdom top 1 percent. Developing more precise estimates of the taxes faced by the very rich should facilitate better modeling of the effect of taxes on their behavior.

Interestingly, while taxes appear to have a large effect on top income shares, there is much less evidence that some of the other political explanations for changes in inequality can successfully explain variation in top incomes (for a more detailed discussion of politics and inequality, see Chapter 26). Scheve and Stasavage (2007) combine data on top income shares for 13 advanced democracies with measures of government partisanship (an indicator variable denoting whether the country had a Prime Minister and/or President from a left party in a given year), centralized wage bargaining (i.e. at the national level), decentralized wage bargaining (i.e. at the firm level), and union density. They find no evidence that partisanship or centralized wage bargaining are significant drivers of top income shares; a surprising finding in the case of centralized wage bargaining, given that a large political science literature has argued that it is a significant driver of earnings inequality. Scheve and Stasavage also find that decentralized wage bargaining and higher union density both affect top income shares in the expected direction, but the magnitude of the effects suggests that these factors can explain only a small share of the variation in top income shares over the twentieth century.

To illustrate this, Table 7.1 shows changes in top income shares under left-wing and right-wing governments in 13 countries. Since top incomes in the first half of the twentieth century were largely driven by the world wars, I focus on the period from 1960 onwards. Across these countries, no systematic pattern emerges. In the nine countries that had both left-wing and right-wing governments over this period, the increase in the top 10 percent share was larger under left-wing governments in five countries, and larger under right-wing governments in four countries. Similarly, the increase in the top 1 percent share was larger under left-wing governments in four countries, and larger under right-wing governments in five countries. For Ireland, New Zealand, the United Kingdom, and the United States, the partisan difference is in the expected direction for both inequality measures, but even in these cases it is not statistically significant.

In a wide-ranging analysis of factors correlated with top income shares in 16 developed and developing countries, Roine *et al.* (2007a) analyze the relationship between top income shares and financial market capitalization, stock market capitalization, trade openness, government expenditure, growth, population, and income taxes. To account for the possibility that the control totals may differ systematically across countries, they focus primarily on the share of the top 1 percent within the top 10 percent, a figure that is unaffected by each country's population and personal income control totals. They find that higher growth, lower income taxes, financial development, and international trade (for the Anglo-Saxon countries only) are associated with higher top income shares. As they point out, since their analysis is based on contemporaneous changes, it is difficult in some cases to know whether their macroeconomic variables are causes or consequences of changes in top income shares.

# 6. EFFECTS OF CHANGING TOP INCOME SHARES

Until now, this chapter has focused on explaining changes in top income shares. But might fluctuations in the income share of the super-rich affect other outcomes?

Table 7.1. Top income shares and partisanship since 1960

| Country | ΔTop 10% Share | | | | ΔTop 1% Share | | | | Total years | |
|---|---|---|---|---|---|---|---|---|---|---|
| | Right-wing govt. | Left-wing govt. | Diff (R−L) | p-value on diff. | Right-wing govt. | Left-wing govt. | Diff (R−L) | p-value on diff. | Right-wing govt. | Left-wing govt. |
| Australia | 0.70 | 1.26 | −0.56 | 0.88 | 0.00 | 1.74 | −1.74 | 0.97 | 27 | 16 |
| Canada | −1.02 | 4.58 | −5.60 | 0.53 | −0.44 | 4.23 | −4.67 | 0.43 | 29 | 11 |
| France | −3.83 | 0.22 | −4.05 | 0.46 | −1.38 | −0.61 | −0.77 | 0.31 | 24 | 14 |
| Germany | | 4.00 | | | | −1.10 | | | 0 | 37 |
| Ireland | 4.95 | 3.38 | 1.57 | 0.66 | 2.48 | 1.92 | 0.55 | 0.51 | 21 | 19 |
| Japan | | | | | 0.48 | | | | 42 | 0 |
| Netherlands | −3.28 | −2.80 | −0.48 | – | −1.78 | −3.32 | 1.54 | – | 5 | 34 |
| New Zealand | 3.91 | −3.35 | 7.26 | 0.88 | 3.32 | −1.97 | 5.29 | 0.94 | 30 | 12 |
| Spain | | 0.52 | | | | 0.98 | | | 0 | 21 |
| Sweden | −2.58 | −1.43 | −1.15 | 0.53 | −0.81 | −0.30 | −0.51 | 0.75 | 9 | 35 |
| Switzerland | | −2.25 | | | | −2.78 | | | 0 | 36 |
| United Kingdom | 7.95 | −1.60 | 9.56 | 0.88 | 4.46 | −1.78 | 6.23 | 0.81 | 26 | 14 |
| United States | 7.39 | 4.06 | 3.33 | 0.68 | 4.43 | 3.29 | 1.14 | 0.79 | 24 | 20 |
| Mean | 1.58 | 0.55 | 1.06 | 0.45 | 1.08 | 0.03 | 0.81 | 0.79 | 18.23 | 20.69 |

*Notes*: Top income shares from Leigh (2007) and partisan coding from Armingeon (2006). The party coding refers to whether right-wing or left-wing parties hold the largest share of cabinet posts. For simplicity, we include center parties with left-wing parties. The mean difference refers to the mean of the column (i.e. the mean difference for countries that have data on changes in top income shares under both right-wing and left-wing parties). The p-value is from a t-test of equality between right-wing and left-wing governments, with each run of right-wing or left-wing governments treated as a separate observation (e.g. in the United Kingdom case, the period of Conservative rule from 1979–97 would be treated as a single observation for the purpose of this t-test). For the Netherlands, there is only one run of right-wing governments during this period, so the p-value cannot be estimated. In the last row, the p-value is from a t-test that combines data from all countries.

And given that top income shares track other inequality measures (such as the Gini coefficient), might it be possible to use top incomes series to look at some of the 'inequality and' questions?

Using top income shares from a panel of developed countries, in a specification with country-specific and time-specific fixed effects, three studies address different possible consequences of inequality. I briefly outline each in turn.

Testing the hypothesis of a negative relationship between inequality and health, Leigh and Jencks (2007) regress four different mortality measures—life expectancy, infant mortality, homicide, and suicide—on the income share of the top 10 percent. In each case, they find no evidence of a significant negative relationship between health and inequality, with standard errors sufficiently tight as to rule out economically large negative effects. This finding is consistent with much of the empirical literature in this field (see Chapter 16).

Estimating the relationship between inequality and savings, Leigh and Posso (2007) find no consistent evidence that lagged top income shares (measured as either the top 10 percent share or the top 1 percent share) have any significant impact on future savings rates. This remains true even holding constant per-capita incomes and interest rates.

As Piketty and Saez (2006a) note, top incomes data provide an opportunity to 'renew the analysis of the interplay between inequality and growth' (this issue is discussed in more detail in Chapter 22). In a panel of 12 developed countries, Andrews et al. (2007) find no systematic relationship over the period 1920–99. However, in the years 1960–99, they find that top income inequality appears to be positively correlated with faster economic growth, a relationship that is robust to the inclusion of country and period fixed effects, and controls for educational attainment, investment, and even tax rates. The effect of top income shares on growth is quite large: a 10 point increase in the top 10 percent share (equivalent to the increase in inequality in the United States between 1980 and 2000) is associated with a 1 percentage point increase in the annual rate of per-capita economic growth.

Naturally, the issue of reverse causality looms large in such analyses. In the case of top incomes and health, the authors address the issue by saying that since they do not find any negative relationship between within-country changes in inequality and within-country changes in health, they do not pursue further the direction of causality. In the case of top incomes and savings, and top incomes and growth, the authors use lagged specifications, regressing current macroeconomic variables on past top income shares. An alternative would be to use two-stage least squares, instrumenting changes in top income shares with some exogenous variable. However, for most outcomes, it is difficult to imagine an instrument that would satisfy the exclusion restriction.

# 7. Conclusions and Future Directions

The careful creation of top incomes series over recent years provides a window into the long-run distribution of incomes in an (increasing) number of nations. But using these data as a long panel requires careful attention to the various differences between them. This chapter discusses those various differences, and considers what adjustments might be made to account for them. For recent decades, the adjusted series show a strong correlation with other measures of inequality, such as the Gini coefficient. This remains true even if one looks at within-country changes in inequality. This suggests that where other data sources on inequality are limited, they may help to fill in some of the gaps.

Future research in this area will doubtless involve estimating top income shares for other countries. The path to creating top incomes series is now becoming well-worn, and the methodological differences catalogued above should help researchers decide whether they wish to—for example—use a population control total of 15+ or 20+; include or exclude capital gains; and so on. While the current series have focused on advanced democracies, there are several Southern European nations for which top income shares have yet to be estimated. In addition, it is natural to ask whether the taxation data for any Eastern European countries are appropriate for estimating top income shares. In the case of developing countries, the estimates may involve combining two sources: taxation data and survey data.

In the countries for which we already have top incomes estimates, a variety of intriguing questions remain. The age and gender composition of top incomes has been analyzed for the United States (Kopczuk et al., 2007) and Canada (Finnie and Irvine, 2006) but not—so far as I am aware—for other nations. The results of Kaplan and Rauh (2007) also suggest that occupational breakdowns may provide insights.[17] And understanding the returns to education at the very top of the distribution would also be potentially instructive.

Another question is whether changes in top incomes represent differences in transitory or permanent income. With few exceptions (e.g. Switzerland, nineteenth century Japan), tax authorities require taxpayers to file returns on an annual basis, so most of the data presented in this chapter are based on the distribution of single-year incomes. One way to test the sensitivity of the results to this approach is to use panel data, which allow the researcher to estimate top income shares based on

---

[17]  A closely related literature looks at the composition of national 'rich lists', and specifically at the question of whether the super-rich tended to have made their fortunes in industries that were uncompetitive at the time. See Siegfried and Roberts (1991); Blitz and Siegfried (1992); Siegfried and Round (1994); Hazledine and Siegfried (1997).

incomes averaged over a number of years (see e.g. Saez and Veall, 2005; Kopczuk *et al.*, 2007). Another is to estimate top wealth shares, as has been done for several countries (e.g. Kopczuk and Saez, 2004 for the United States; Alvaredo and Saez, 2006 for Spain; Roine and Waldenström, 2007 for Sweden; Dell *et al.*, 2007 for Switzerland). A more detailed discussion of the literature on top wealth shares can be found in Chapter 6. Important work remains to be done on explaining the relationship between top income shares and top wealth shares. Lastly, an interesting line of research concerns intergenerational patterns. Using Canadian data, Finnie and Irvine (2006) find that a majority of individuals in the top 0.1 percent grew up in a top 10 percent household. It would be fascinating to know whether similar patterns hold in other countries.

Another possibility is that top incomes series may be created using sub-national data. In a few specific cases, this has already been done. In the case of Canada, Saez and Veall (2005) estimate top income shares for the province of Quebec in order to see whether speaking English had an impact on top income shares. In their study of Australia, Atkinson and Leigh (2007) estimate top income shares for the state of Victoria for a period before taxation data were tabulated at a federal level. Unlike survey analysis, which is often imprecise at a state level, top incomes data are based on the universe of taxpayers, and should therefore be accurate even in small states or regions.

Datasets of sub-national top income shares may help answer many of the questions that have interested researchers. For example, comparing across states in the United States, it might be reasonable to think that more of the unobservables were held constant than when comparing across countries. There are drawbacks in such an approach (interstate migration is more common than international migration), but better data on sub-national top incomes would be valuable nonetheless.

Finally, we may hope to see more work on the causes and consequences of changes in top income shares. Among the plausible drivers of inequality, it would be interesting to see whether variables such as immigration, inflation, product market competition, social norms, or the demographic structure of the labor force have significant effects on top income shares. As to the consequences of inequality, top incomes data are particularly well-suited to analyzing elite-driven outcomes, such as campaign contributions or industrial innovation. However, it may also be worth considering how top incomes affect factors such as trust, happiness, average working hours, residential segregation, and political polarization.

## REFERENCES

ALVAREDO, F. 2007. 'The Rich in Argentina over the Twentieth Century: From the Conservative Republic to the Peronist Experience and beyond 1932–2004'. Paris School of Economics Working Paper 2007-02.

ALVAREDO, F., and SAEZ, E. 2006. 'Income and Wealth Concentration in Spain in a Historical and Fiscal Perspective'. CEPR Discussion Paper 5836. London: Centre for Economic Policy Research.

ANDREWS, D., JENCKS, C., and LEIGH, A. 2007. 'Do Rising Top Incomes Lift All Boats?' Mimeo, Australian National University.

ARMINGEON, K., LEIMGRUBER, P., BEYELER, M., and MENEGALE, S. 2006. 'Comparative Political Data Set 1960–2004'. Institute of Political Science, University of Berne.

ATKINSON, A. B. 2005. 'Top Incomes in the UK over The Twentieth Century'. *Journal of the Royal Statistical Society, Series A*, 168, Feb.: 325–43.

—— 2007a. 'Measuring Top Incomes: Methodological Issues', in Atkinson and Piketty (2007), 18–42.

—— 2007b. 'Top Incomes in the United Kingdom over the Twentieth Century', in Atkinson and Piketty (2007), 82–140.

—— and BRANDOLINI, A. 2001. 'Promise and Pitfalls in the Use of "Secondary" Data-Sets: Income Inequality in OECD Countries as a Case Study'. *Journal of Economic Literature*, 39, Sept.: 771–99.

—— and LEIGH, A. 2005. 'The Distribution of Top Incomes in New Zealand'. CEPR Discussion Paper 503, Australian National University.

—— —— 2007a. 'The Distribution of Top Incomes in Australia'. *Economic Record*, 83(262): 247–61.

—— —— 2007b. 'The Distribution of Top Incomes in Five Anglo-Saxon Countries over the Twentieth Century'. Mimeo, Australian National University.

—— and PIKETTY, T. 2007. *Top Incomes over the Twentieth Century: A Contrast between Continental European and English Speaking Countries*. Oxford: Oxford University Press.

—— and SALVERDA, W. 2005. 'Top Incomes in the Netherlands and the United Kingdom over the 20th Century'. *Journal of the European Economic Association*, 3(4): 883–913.

BANERJEE, A., and PIKETTY, T. 2005. 'Top Indian Incomes, 1922–2000'. *The World Bank Economic Review*, 19, Dec.: 1–20.

BLITZ, R., and SIEGFRIED, J. J. 1992. 'How did the Wealthiest Americans Get So Rich?' *Quarterly Review of Economics and Finance*, 32(1): 5–26.

BOWLEY, A. L. 1914. 'The British Super-Tax and the Distribution of Income'. *Quarterly Journal of Economics*, 28: 255–68.

CHRISTIAN, C. 1994. 'Voluntary Compliance with the Individual Income Tax: Results from the 1988 TCMP Study'. IRS Research Bulletin, 1993/1994, Publication 1500 (Rev 9–94), Internal Revenue Service, Washington.

COWELL, F. A. 1995. *Measuring Inequality*, 2nd edn. Hemel Hempstead: Harvester Wheatsheaf.

DEININGER, K., and SQUIRE, L. 1996. 'A New Data Set Measuring Income Inequality'. *World Bank Economic Review*, 10, Sept.: 565–91.

DELL, F. 2005. 'Top Incomes in Germany and Switzerland over the Twentieth Century'. *Journal of the European Economic Association*, 3(2–3), Apr.–May: 412–21.

—— 2007. 'Top Incomes in Germany throughout the Twentieth Century: 1891–1998', in Atkinson and Piketty (2007), 365–425.

—— PIKETTY, T., and SAEZ, E. 2007. 'Income and Wealth Concentration in Switzerland over the Twentieth Century', in Atkinson and Piketty (2007), 472–500.

EXPERT GROUP ON HOUSEHOLD INCOME STATISTICS (THE CANBERRA GROUP). 2001. *Final Report and Recommendations*. Ottawa. Available at http://www.lisproject.org/links/canberra/finalreport.pdf.

FEENBERG, D., and POTERBA, J. 1993. 'Income Inequality and the Incomes of Very High Income Taxpayers: Evidence from Tax Returns', in J. Poterba (ed.), *Tax Policy and the Economy*, vol. 7. Cambridge, Mass.: MIT Press, 145–77.

FINNIE, R., and IRVINE, I. 2006. 'Mobility and Gender at the Top Tail of the Earnings Distribution'. *Economic and Social Review*, 37(2): 1–25.

FRANK, R. 2007. *Falling Behind: How Rising Inequality Harms the Middle Class*. Berkeley: University of California Press.

GUSTAFSSON, B., and JANSSON, B. 2007. 'Top Incomes in Sweden during Three-Quarters of a Century: A Micro Data Approach'. IZA Discussion Paper 2672. Institute for the Study of Labor, Bonn.

HAZLEDINE, T., and SIEGFRIED, J. J. 1997. 'How Did the Wealthiest New Zealanders Get So Rich?' *New Zealand Economic Papers*, 31(1): 35–47.

KAPLAN, S. N., and RAUH, J. 2007. 'Wall Street and Main Street: What Contributes to the Rise in the Highest Incomes?' NBER Working Paper no. 13270.

KOPCZUK, W., and SAEZ, E. 2004. 'Top Wealth Shares in the United States, 1916–2000: Evidence from Estate Tax Returns'. *National Tax Journal*, 57(2), part 2: 445–87.

—— —— and SONG, J. 2007. 'Uncovering the American Dream: Inequality and Mobility in Social Security Earnings Data since 1937'. NBER Working Paper no. 13345.

KUZNETS, S. 1953. *Shares of Upper Income Groups in Income and Savings*. New York: National Bureau of Economic Research.

LANDAIS, C. 2007. 'Les Hauts Revenus en France 1998–2006: Une Explosion des Inégalités?' Paris School of Economics Working Paper.

LEIGH, A. 2007. 'How Closely Do Top Income Shares Track Other Measures of Inequality?' *Economic Journal*, 117(524): F619–F633.

—— and JENCKS, C. 2007. 'Inequality and Mortality: Long-Run Evidence from a Panel of Countries'. *Journal of Health Economics*, 26(1): 1–24.

—— and POSSO, A. 2007. 'Top Incomes and Savings'. Mimeo, Australian National University.

—— and VAN DER ENG, P. 2007. 'Top Incomes in Indonesia, 1920–2004'. Australian National University CEPR Discussion Paper 549.

MOORE, J. C., STINSON, L. L., and WELNIAK, E. J. 2000. 'Income Measurement Error in Surveys: A Review'. *Journal of Official Statistics*, 16(4): 331–62.

MORIGUCHI, C., and SAEZ, E. 2007. 'The Evolution of Top Wage Incomes in Japan, 1951–2005'. Mimeo, Northwestern University.

—— —— Forthcoming. 'The Evolution of Income Concentration in Japan, 1885–2002: Evidence From Income Tax Statistics'. *Review of Economics and Statistics*.

NOLAN, B. 2007. 'Long-Term Trends in Top Income Shares in Ireland', in Atkinson and Piketty (2007), 501–30.

O'DONNELL, G. 2004. 'Financing Britain's Future: Review of the Revenue Departments'. London: HM Treasury. Mar. 17. CM 6163.

PIKETTY, T. 2001. *Les Hauts Revenus en France au 20$^{ème}$ siècle*. Paris: Grasset.

—— 2003. 'Income Inequality in France, 1901–1998'. *Journal of Political Economy*, 111(5), Oct.: 1004–42.

——— 2007. 'Income, Wage and Wealth Inequality in France, 1901–1998', in Atkinson and Piketty (2007), 43–81.

——— and QIAN, N. 2006. 'Income Inequality and Progressive Income Taxation in China and India, 1986–2015'. CEPR Discussion Paper 5703. London: Centre for Economic Policy Research.

——— and SAEZ, E. 2001. 'Income Inequality in the United States, 1913–1998'. NBER Working Paper 8467.

——— ——— 2003. 'Income Inequality in the United States, 1913–1998'. *Quarterly Journal of Economics*, 118(1), Feb.: 1–39.

——— ——— 2006a. 'The Evolution of Top Incomes: A Historical and International Perspective'. *American Economic Review*, 96(2): 200–5.

——— ——— 2006b. 'Income Inequality in the United States'. Tables and Figures updated to 2004 in Excel format, <http://emlab.berkeley.edu/users/saez/> (downloaded Dec. 6, 2006).

——— ——— 2006c. 'Response to Alan Reynolds'. Mimeo, Dec. 20, <http://emlab.berkeley.edu/users/saez/> (downloaded Oct. 4, 2007).

——— ——— 2007. 'How Progressive is the U.S. Federal Tax System? A Historical and International Perspective'. *Journal of Economic Perspectives*, 21(1): 3–24.

REYNOLDS, A. 2006. 'The Top 1% . . . of What?' *Wall Street Journal*, Dec. 14, A20.

RIIHELÄ, M., SULLSTRÖM, R., and TUOMALA, M. 2005. 'Trends in Top Income Shares in Finland', VATT Discussion Papers 371.

ROINE, J., VLACHOS, J., and WALDENSTRÖM, D. 2007a. 'What Determines Top Income Shares? Evidence from the Twentieth Century'. IFN Working Paper, Stockholm, Sweden.

——— ——— ——— 2007b. 'Trend Breaks in Income Inequality over the Twentieth Century: Evidence from Top Incomes'. IFN Working Paper, Stockholm, Sweden.

——— and WALDENSTRÖM, D. 2007. 'Wealth Concentration over the Path of Development: Sweden, 1873–2005'. IFN Working Paper.

——— ——— 2008. 'The Evolution of Top Incomes in an Egalitarian Society: Sweden, 1903–2004'. *Journal of Public Economics*, 92: 366–87.

SAEZ, E. 2004. 'Reported Incomes and Marginal Tax Rates, 1960–2000: Evidence and Policy Implications', in J. Poterba (ed.), *Tax Policy and the Economy*, vol. 18. Cambridge, Mass.: MIT Press, 117–73.

——— and VEALL, M. 2005. 'The Evolution of High Incomes in Northern America: Lessons from Canadian Evidence'. *American Economic Review*, 95(3), June: 831–49.

SALVERDA, W., and ATKINSON, A. B. 2007. 'Top Incomes in the Netherlands over the Twentieth Century', in Atkinson and Piketty (2007), 426–72.

SCHEVE, K., and STASAVAGE, D. 2007. 'Institutions, Partisanship, and Inequality in the Long Run'. Mimeo, New York University.

SIEGFRIED, J. J., and ROBERTS, A. 1991. 'How Did the Wealthiest Britons Get So Rich?' *Review of Industrial Organization*, 6:19–32.

——— and ROUND, D. K. 1994. 'How Did the Wealthiest Australians Get So Rich?', *Review of Income and Wealth*, 40(2): 191–204.

SLEMROD, J. 2007. 'Cheating Ourselves: The Economics of Tax Evasion'. *Journal of Economic Perspectives*, 21(1): 25–48.

——— and YITZHAKI, S. 2002. 'Tax Avoidance, Evasion, and Administration', in A. Auerbach and M. Feldstein (eds.), *Handbook of Public Economics*, vol. 3. Amsterdam: North-Holland, 1423–70.

SWEDISH TAX AGENCY. 2004. *Taxes in Sweden*. Solna, Sweden.

TAWNEY, R. 1913. 'Poverty as an Industrial Problem'. Inaugural lecture, reproduced in *Memoranda on the Problems of Poverty*. London: William Morris Press.

US DEPARTMENT OF THE TREASURY: INTERNAL REVENUE SERVICE 1996. *Federal Tax Compliance Research: Individual Income Tax Gap Estimates for 1985, 1988, and 1992*. Pub. no. 1415 (rev. 4-96), Apr. Washington.

—— 2006. *Updated Estimates of the TY 2001 Individual Income Tax Underreporting Gap. Overview*. Feb. 22. Washington: Office of Research, Analysis, and Statistics.

# PART III

## EARNINGS INEQUALITY

CHAPTER 8

........................................................................

# INEQUALITY AND EARNINGS DISTRIBUTION*

........................................................................

## FRANCINE D. BLAU

## LAWRENCE M. KAHN

## 1. INTRODUCTION

........................................................................

THE level of wage inequality generated by a country's labor market is of fundamental importance for those interested in understanding poverty and social stratification, as well as the economic incentives facing workers and employers. Labor
earnings are by far the most important component of national income, comprising
for example about 67% of personal income in the USA in 2003 (Ehrenberg and
Smith, 2006: 1). Hence, in the absence of any compensatory government policies,
low living standards in market economies will be associated with low labor incomes.
This in turn means that wage rates are a central determinant of individual and
family incomes. For example, in the 1980s, rising wage inequality in the USA was
sufficient to counteract the effects of economic expansion in reducing poverty
(Blank, 1993). More generally, labor market inequality is a major determinant of
disparities in living standards and may also affect social solidarity.

* The authors thank Tony Atkinson, Steve Nickell, Brian Nolan, Wiemer Salverda, Tim Smeeding,
and participants at the Oxford Handbook on Economic Inequality Conference, Seville, Spain,
September 24–8, 2007, for helpful comments and suggestions.

To the extent that labor market inequality reflects economic returns to skills or rents associated with jobs in higher-paying sectors, international differences in inequality imply differences in economic incentives. Countries with high rewards to skills have a wage structure that encourages skill acquisition by workers, while the compression of wage premia for skills may dampen workers' incentives to acquire training. Moreover, centralized wage-setting mechanisms which reduce wage variation tend to limit firms' flexibility in responding to differences in market conditions across industries or geographical areas.[1] Also of concern is that the imposition of relatively high wage floors for low-skill groups may reduce their relative employment (Bertola *et al.*, 2007) or relegate them to temporary jobs when they are employed (Kahn, 2007).

On the other hand, high rewards to labor market skills or employment in high-paying sectors penalize demographic groups that have below average levels of skills or a lower representation in higher-paying sectors, even in the absence of explicit discrimination against them. So, for example, rising returns to skill or sector in the USA in the 1980s reduced the relative wages of black workers (Juhn *et al.*, 1991) and immigrants (LaLonde and Topel, 1992); and slowed the economic progress of women (Blau and Kahn, 1997). Similarly, Blau and Kahn (1996b) found that the higher rewards to skills and economic rents in the USA compared to other industrialized countries were the most important reason for the relatively large US gender pay gap in the 1980s. In addition to reducing demographic wage differentials, countries with low levels of wage inequality implicitly provide income insurance, at least to those with jobs (Agell and Lommerud, 1992).

This chapter will document and provide explanations for levels of and trends in earnings inequality, with a central focus on international differences in these outcomes. We restrict ourselves to the OECD countries, which are largely advanced industrialized nations, and typically have similar levels of labor productivity but often very different labor market institutions and changes in the supply of or demand for labor of various skill levels (Nickell and Layard, 1999; Freeman and Katz, 1995). As a result, one can use international differences to test hypotheses about the role of supply and demand and institutions in influencing levels and trends in earnings inequality. We first provide an analytical framework for understanding earnings inequality in which we distinguish labor earnings from wage rates. We then place inequality of wage rates in a supply and demand framework, augmented by consideration of labor market institutions. Next, after providing some data on the extent of earnings and wage inequality across countries and over time, we discuss evidence on the determinants of differences and changes in earnings inequality.

---

[1] Employers voiced both these complaints about Sweden's 'solidarity' wage policy of 1968–83. Indeed, it has been argued that Sweden's generous student stipends and subsidized loans for higher education may be viewed in part as a means of offsetting the distortions caused by wage compression (Edin and Holmlund, 1995; see also Edin and Topel, 1997).

Individual earnings inequality is a central component of inequality in family incomes, and ultimately in economic wellbeing, as discussed in Chapter 4. Family income is the sum of the incomes of family members, including labor and non-labor incomes. Overall inequality in family income can be affected by inequality in its components for individuals in different families as well as the correlation between income levels across individuals within families. For example, there may be high levels of inequality in family incomes because of inequality in income across people, or because high income people tend to live with other high income people, or both. To fully understand family income inequality, one needs to understand labor supply decisions and family formation decisions, as well as the determinants of inequality of income across people. To make our review manageable, we have focused on overall inequality of individual earnings, which, as we mentioned earlier, is the main source of income for most individuals and therefore central to the issue of family well-being.[2] In what follows, we focus on individuals with earnings, that is, on those with positive work hours. The fact that some individuals have zero hours and hence no earnings is undoubtedly a factor in earnings inequality broadly defined. However, the determinants of employment, unemployment, and labor force participation are outside the scope of this chapter. A focus on employed individuals in an examination of earnings inequality raises the question of selection bias. While this is a valid concern, an examination of this issue is also outside the bounds of this chapter. We note, however, that when the issue of selection has been considered, the broad conclusions that we emphasize here are not affected (see, e.g., Blau and Kahn, 2005).

## 2. A Framework for Understanding Earnings Inequality

In this section, we conceptually break down earnings inequality among the employed into its component parts, which will then become the subjects of further analysis. The following identity will be useful in this regard:

$$E = w \times h, \tag{1}$$

where E is an individual's annual earnings, w is the wage rate (average hourly earnings), and h is annual work hours.

---

[2] More detailed discussion of particular segments of the earnings distribution can be found in Chapter 7 on top incomes and Chapter 11 on low pay.

Taking logs and computing the variance of both sides of the equation, we have:

$$\text{var}(\log E) = \text{var}(\log w) + \text{var}(\log h) + 2\text{cov}(\log w, \log h). \tag{2}$$

According to equation (2), we can decompose the variance of log earnings into the variance of log wages, the variance of log work hours, and the covariance of log wages and log work hours. The first term on the right-hand side of equation (2), var(log w), can be affected by heterogeneity in individuals' productivity and demographic characteristics as well as in their location in the labor market (e.g. union membership, industry, or occupation). It can also be affected by the returns to these characteristics, as well as the distribution of unmeasured characteristics and the returns to these. The second term, var(log h), may reflect differences in individuals' labor supply decisions or constraints on finding jobs at their preferred work hours. The third term, 2cov(log w, log h), is influenced by the average labor supply elasticity, the impact of wages on employer hiring decisions, any part-time wage penalty or overtime premium, etc.

As will become clear below, almost all empirical research on earnings inequality has in fact focused on inequality in wage rates, which is of course only one of the components in equation (2). This focus may be due to the importance of wage rates in providing market signals to employers and workers that affect their demand and supply decisions. To understand inequality in wage rates, consider the following wage regression:

$$\log w_{ijt} = B'_{jt} X_{ijt} + u_{ijt}, \tag{3}$$

where for individual i in country j at time t, X is a vector of factors that influence wages, such as education, experience, union coverage, industry, and occupation, B is a vector of coefficients, and u is a disturbance term summarizing unmeasured influences on wages. First, focusing on measured characteristics X, country j may have a high level of wage inequality because its workers have a diverse distribution of the measured Xs and/or because the return to these measured Xs (included in B) is higher in country j than elsewhere. So, for example, inequality may be high in a country because its workers have a relatively diverse distribution of education or because it has an especially high wage return to education. Second, the residual includes information on unmeasured skills or aspects of location in the labor market and the returns to these characteristics. For example, the residual may include motivation, which we cannot measure, as well as the labor market returns to motivation.

The prices (B) and to some extent the residual (u) can in turn be affected by supply and demand in the labor market, as well as by labor market institutions. For example, consider the wage gap between workers with a college degree and workers with a high school degree, controlling for other demographic factors such as experience, race, gender, etc. We can interpret this gap as a labor market price, in this case the price of the skills associated with a college degree relative to a high school degree. Assume first that the labor market is perfectly competitive and that high school and college educated workers are imperfect substitutes. Then changes or differences in relative demand or supply will affect relative wages of these groups. An intuitive result from supply and demand analysis is that, controlling for factors that influence the location of the demand curve, there will be an inverse relationship between relative wages and relative employment: all else equal, employers have downward-sloping labor demand curves.[3] As explained in detail in the Technical Appendix, if we know how substitutable college- and high school-educated workers are for each other, we can infer from data on wages and employment the impact of supply or demand changes on the relative wage rates of college graduates. For example, as discussed by Katz and Murphy (1992), in the 1980s in the USA, the relative wages and relative employment of college-educated workers both rose, implying that the relative demand for their labor must have risen.

If we now relax the assumption of perfectly competitive labor markets, a natural framework to use is that of union–management bargaining. Suppose, for example, that wages are set in union contracts, but firms are allowed to set the employment level. Then the inverse relationship between relative wages and relative employment discussed above[4] will still hold, since firms will choose employment to maximize profits given the union wage bargain. In this case, unions will face a tradeoff between raising some groups' relative wages and lowering their relative employment. Analyses of trade union behavior using this framework predict that unions will negotiate higher wage increases for workers facing lower demand elasticities, since when demand elasticity is lower, a given union wage increase causes a smaller loss in employment.[5] Moreover, such models also predict a larger union wage effect when labor supply elasticity is higher, since unemployed workers have better alternative uses of their time when supply is more elastic (Bertola *et al.*, 2007). Thus, the net effect of unions on wage inequality depends at least in part on which groups have higher demand and supply elasticities. An additional consideration is that concerns about union solidarity and income insurance are likely to lead to wage compression (Agell and Lommerud, 1992; Bertola *et al.*, 2007). Moreover, the more centralized union wage-setting is, the more likely the resulting contract is to feature industry-wide or even economy-wide wage floors, also implying a compression of wages at the bottom of the distribution (Blau and Kahn, 1996a). In what follows, we will briefly refer to empirical findings on the impact of unions and direct the reader to the more detailed presentation in Chapter 10 on unions and earnings inequality.

---

[3] This result of course may not hold under employer monopsony. The potential role of monopsony is explored further in Chapter 11 on low pay. As we will see, however, many of the predictions from the analysis of the labor market assuming competition are very useful in understanding wage inequality.

[4] See also Technical Appendix Equation (A3).

[5] We should point out if unions bargain over *both* wages and employment, then, at the micro-level, unions could raise both the wages and employment of their members (Farber, 1986).

Table 8.1. Decomposition of the variance of log annual earnings (1994–1998)

| Country | Variance of log annual earnings | Variance of log hourly wages | Variance of log annual hours | 2*Covariance of log hourly earnings and log annual hours | Survey year(s) |
|---|---|---|---|---|---|
| A. Men | | | | | |
| Canada | 0.517 | 0.315 | 0.189 | 0.013 | 1994 |
| Denmark | 0.363 | 0.200 | 0.118 | 0.045 | 1998 |
| Finland | 0.486 | 0.282 | 0.244 | −0.040 | 1998 |
| Italy | 0.317 | 0.283 | 0.122 | −0.088 | 1998 |
| Netherlands | 0.325 | 0.250 | 0.132 | −0.057 | 1994 |
| Norway | 0.324 | 0.251 | 0.121 | −0.048 | 1998 |
| Switzerland | 0.430 | 0.427 | 0.114 | −0.111 | 1994 and 1998 |
| USA | 0.595 | 0.414 | 0.132 | 0.049 | 1994 |
| Average | 0.420 | 0.303 | 0.147 | −0.030 | |
| B. Women | | | | | |
| Canada | 0.497 | 0.398 | 0.226 | −0.127 | 1994 |
| Denmark | 0.272 | 0.177 | 0.168 | −0.073 | 1998 |
| Finland | 0.439 | 0.213 | 0.225 | 0.001 | 1998 |
| Italy | 0.346 | 0.246 | 0.231 | −0.131 | 1998 |
| Netherlands | 0.374 | 0.317 | 0.225 | −0.168 | 1994 |
| Norway | 0.310 | 0.253 | 0.217 | −0.160 | 1998 |
| Switzerland | 0.462 | 0.336 | 0.230 | −0.104 | 1994 and 1998 |
| USA | 0.509 | 0.347 | 0.145 | 0.017 | 1994 |
| Average | 0.401 | 0.286 | 0.208 | −0.093 | |

*Notes*: See Data Appendix for variable definitions and sample inclusion rules. Swiss French- and German-speaking regions were surveyed in 1994 and the Swiss Italian-speaking region was surveyed in 1998.

*Source*: International Adult Literacy Survey.

# 3. DECOMPOSITION OF EARNINGS INEQUALITY: HOURS VERSUS WAGE RATES

Tables 8.1 and 8.2 show the decomposition of the variance of the log of annual earnings into the components in equation (2) for eight countries based on the International Adult Literacy Survey (IALS) which was collected over the 1994–8 period.[6] These tables indicate a strong positive relationship across the included countries

[6] For details on the sample and variable construction, see the Data Appendix. For further description of the IALS, see Blau and Kahn (2005). The particular countries shown in Table 8.1 are those Western countries with available data in the IALS. Earnings are measured gross of deductions for all countries except the Netherlands and Switzerland.

Table 8.2. Fraction of variance of log annual earnings accounted for by components (1994–1998)

| Country | Variance of log annual earnings | Variance of log hourly wages | Variance of log annual hours | 2*Covariance of log hourly earnings and log annual hours | Survey year(s) |
|---|---|---|---|---|---|
| **A. Men** | | | | | |
| Canada | 1.000 | 0.609 | 0.366 | 0.025 | 1994 |
| Denmark | 1.000 | 0.551 | 0.325 | 0.124 | 1998 |
| Finland | 1.000 | 0.580 | 0.502 | −0.082 | 1998 |
| Italy | 1.000 | 0.893 | 0.385 | −0.278 | 1998 |
| Netherlands | 1.000 | 0.769 | 0.406 | −0.175 | 1994 |
| Norway | 1.000 | 0.775 | 0.373 | −0.148 | 1998 |
| Switzerland | 1.000 | 0.993 | 0.265 | −0.258 | 1994 and 1998 |
| USA | 1.000 | 0.696 | 0.222 | 0.082 | 1994 |
| Average | 1.000 | 0.733 | 0.356 | −0.089 | |
| **B. Women** | | | | | |
| Canada | 1.000 | 0.801 | 0.455 | −0.256 | 1994 |
| Denmark | 1.000 | 0.651 | 0.618 | −0.268 | 1998 |
| Finland | 1.000 | 0.485 | 0.513 | 0.002 | 1998 |
| Italy | 1.000 | 0.711 | 0.668 | −0.379 | 1998 |
| Netherlands | 1.000 | 0.848 | 0.602 | −0.449 | 1994 |
| Norway | 1.000 | 0.816 | 0.700 | −0.516 | 1998 |
| Switzerland | 1.000 | 0.727 | 0.498 | −0.225 | 1994 and 1998 |
| USA | 1.000 | 0.682 | 0.285 | 0.033 | 1994 |
| Average | 1.000 | 0.715 | 0.542 | −0.257 | |

*Notes*: See Data Appendix for variable definitions and sample inclusion rules. Swiss French- and German-speaking regions were surveyed in 1994 and the Swiss Italian-speaking region was surveyed in 1998.
*Source*: International Adult Literacy Survey.

between the extent of earnings and wage inequality. As may be seen in Table 8.1, there is a strong, statistically significant positive correlation between the variance of log earnings and the variance of wage rates for both men (0.66, significant at the 8% level) and women (0.77, significant at the 3% level). For example, the table shows that the USA, Canada, and Switzerland have relatively high levels of both earnings and wage inequality, while Denmark and Norway have low levels of both. Moreover, Table 8.2 indicates that, with only one exception,[7] the variance in log hourly wages 'explains' the largest portion of the variance in log earnings: ranging from 55% (Denmark) to 99% (Switzerland) for men, and from 49% (Finland) to 85% (the Netherlands) for women. Taking an unweighted average across the eight countries, wage rate variation accounts for 73% of male and 72% of female earnings variation. Table 8.1 also shows that hours are more variable for women than for men, and

[7] The exception is Finnish women for whom the variance of work hours is especially high.

Table 8.2 shows that hours variation explains 36% of earnings variation for men and 54% for women. Female hours variation is especially high in Scandinavia and the Netherlands, with these countries' high incidence of part-time employment, and also in Italy.[8]

A positive correlation between inequality in annual earnings and wage rates can also be inferred from Luxembourg Income Study data for the 1984–92 period. Specifically, Gottschalk and Smeeding (1997) use these data to compute measures of inequality in annual earnings for all workers and annual earnings for full-time, year-round workers. The latter is an approximate measure of the wage rate, since it roughly controls for work hours (although these may vary among full-time workers). Using the authors' reported figures, we find that across seven OECD countries (Australia, Canada, Germany, the Netherlands, Sweden, the UK, and the USA) the 90-10 ratio in annual earnings had a 0.98 (significant) correlation with the 90-10 ratio in full-time year-round earnings for men; for women, the correlation was 0.43 but it was insignificant. In the IALS, we found qualitatively similar corresponding correlations (between annual and hourly earnings) for the log 90-10 ratio of 0.75 for men (significant) and 0.51 for women (insignificant).[9]

These data suggest that earnings inequality is greater than wage rate inequality. Some of the difference between these two concepts likely results from voluntary labor supply decisions and some may be due to constraints on finding work, or incentives to work part-time, or work norms. For example, in the USA, weekly work hours are strongly positively correlated with income, while in countries such as Italy and Switzerland the opposite is true (Alesina et al., 2001). Consistent with this result is Table 8.1's finding that hours and hourly earnings are more positively correlated in the USA than for the other countries, although as mentioned, measurement error may be affecting this correlation. And work hours are generally much longer in the USA than in other countries, possibly due to pro-work norms or to less influence there by unions and government (Alesina et al., 2001 and 2005; Blau and Kahn, 2002).[10] In this regard, Alesina et al. (2005) emphasize that international differences in weeks worked (themselves importantly affected by differences in mandated

---

[8] Hours and hourly earnings have a negative correlation on average, especially for women, possibly reflecting the fact that the hours variable appears in both elements of the correlation, and its appearance in the denominator of hourly earnings may be inducing the negative correlation.

[9] Note that for women in the IALS, there is a strong, significantly positive correlation between the variance of log earnings and the variance of log wage rates, although the correlation, while still reasonably high, is not significant for 90-10 gaps. It is possible that idiosyncratic factors affect wages or hours at the extremes for women that are averaged out in the variances.

[10] Norms can affect other dimensions of work-time inequality such as the gender gap. For example, Burda et al. (2007) find evidence suggesting that women's total (market and non-market) work time is relatively greater in countries where people believe that scarce jobs should be offered to men first. On the other hand, women's market-work participation has been growing relative to men's in most Western countries since 1980, with considerable convergence across countries in the gender gap in labor force participation (Blau and Kahn, forthcoming).

vacation duration) account for more of these differences in annual work hours than does variation in usual hours worked per week.

An additional implication of the correlation between wages and hours concerns growing earnings inequality over time. For example, Coleman and Pencavel (1993a and 1993b) report that, in the 1980s, among both men and women, annual work hours rose for the college-educated relative to those with a high school degree or less. This development of course occurred at the same time that the college wage premium was rising sharply, implying that labor income inequality was growing even faster than wage inequality across education groups.

The foregoing suggests that variation in hours can play a role in both differences and changes in the extent of earnings inequality. Nonetheless, as we have seen, differences in earnings inequality across countries are mostly explained by wage rate inequality. Therefore in what follows we focus our attention on international differences in wage inequality.

## 4. INTERNATIONAL DIFFERENCES IN WAGE INEQUALITY: DESCRIPTIVE PATTERNS

Tables 8.3 and 8.4 provide data from the OECD on levels of and changes in wage inequality over roughly the 1980 to 2000 period for twelve countries. In addition to overall inequality (90-10 ratios), the tables show wage inequality at the bottom (50-10 ratios) and the top (90-50 ratios) separately because different factors may influence different portions of the wage distribution.[11] For example, binding wage floors are most likely to affect the 50-10 gap, while norms for executive pay are most relevant for the 90-50 gap. For both men and women, Table 8.3 shows that the USA and Canada had the highest levels of overall wage inequality throughout the period, as indicated by the 90-10 gap. In contrast, Denmark, Italy, Japan, and Sweden consistently had the lowest levels of overall inequality for both men and

---

[11] The Data Appendix and Table 8.3 show that the earnings concept and sample covered are not the same across the OECD datasets, and Atkinson and Brandolini (2001) raise important concerns about making international comparisons of income inequality based on such data. We should point out, however, that the analysis of the changes, shown in Table 8.4, in effect controls for the earnings definition and may thus suffer less from comparability problems than analyzing the inequality levels in Table 8.3. Further, despite these potential difficulties, the overall inequality differences and changes shown in Tables 8.3 and 8.4 are broadly consistent with studies that use microdata that are collected under comparable conditions. For example, wage inequality is found to be higher in and to have risen faster in the USA and the UK than in countries such as Germany or those in Scandinavia in these studies. For a review of this literature, see Blau and Kahn (2002).

Table 8.3. Levels of wage inequality, 1980, 1990, 2000

| Country | Earnings concept | 50–10 ratio | | | 90–50 ratio | | | 90–10 ratio | | |
|---|---|---|---|---|---|---|---|---|---|---|
| | | 1980 | 1990 | 2000 | 1980 | 1990 | 2000 | 1980 | 1990 | 2000 |
| A. Men | | | | | | | | | | |
| Australia | Gross weekly full-time | 1.60 | 1.68 | 1.70 | 1.70 | 1.62 | 1.84 | 2.72 | 2.71 | 3.13 |
| Canada | Gross annual FTYR | 2.07 | 2.28 | 2.18 | 1.67 | 1.75 | 1.73 | 3.47 | 3.98 | 3.76 |
| Finland | Gross annual FTYR | 1.46 | 1.49 | 1.46 | 1.67 | 1.72 | 1.73 | 2.44 | 2.57 | 2.53 |
| France | Net annual FTYR | 1.66 | 1.62 | 1.59 | 2.03 | 2.13 | 2.06 | 3.38 | 3.46 | 3.28 |
| Germany | Gross monthly full-time | 1.49 | 1.43 | 1.58 | 1.70 | 1.70 | 1.82 | 2.53 | 2.44 | 2.86 |
| Italy | Gross monthly full-time | 1.39 | 1.41 | 1.40 | 1.50 | 1.68 | 1.74 | 2.09 | 2.38 | 2.44 |
| Japan | Gross monthly full-time | 1.60 | 1.64 | 1.59 | 1.63 | 1.73 | 1.73 | 2.60 | 2.84 | 2.74 |
| Netherlands | Gross annual FTYR | 1.43 | 1.51 | 1.62 | 1.62 | 1.65 | 1.75 | 2.32 | 2.49 | 2.83 |
| New Zealand | Gross weekly full-time | 1.64 | 1.75 | 1.82 | 1.66 | 1.76 | 1.95 | 2.72 | 3.08 | 3.55 |
| Sweden | Gross annual FTYR | 1.31 | 1.33 | 1.40 | 1.61 | 1.56 | 1.74 | 2.11 | 2.07 | 2.44 |
| UK | Gross weekly full-time | 1.62 | 1.78 | 1.80 | 1.63 | 1.83 | 1.88 | 2.65 | 3.25 | 3.39 |
| USA | Gross weekly full-time | 1.97 | 2.13 | 2.15 | 1.82 | 2.07 | 2.21 | 3.57 | 4.40 | 4.76 |
| Average | | 1.60 | 1.67 | 1.69 | 1.69 | 1.77 | 1.85 | 2.72 | 2.97 | 3.14 |
| B. Women | | | | | | | | | | |
| Australia | Gross weekly full-time | 1.66 | 1.65 | 1.56 | 1.54 | 1.59 | 1.64 | 2.55 | 2.62 | 2.56 |
| Canada | Gross annual FTYR | 2.12 | 2.28 | 2.25 | 1.76 | 1.75 | 1.78 | 3.73 | 3.97 | 4.00 |
| Finland | Gross annual FTYR | 1.40 | 1.37 | 1.31 | 1.47 | 1.54 | 1.53 | 2.06 | 2.11 | 2.00 |
| France | Net annual FTYR | 1.61 | 1.66 | 1.55 | 1.69 | 1.72 | 1.72 | 2.73 | 2.86 | 2.66 |
| Germany | Gross monthly full-time | 1.75 | 1.69 | 1.71 | 1.64 | 1.55 | 1.63 | 2.86 | 2.62 | 2.78 |
| Italy | Gross monthly full-time | 1.58 | 1.32 | 1.30 | 1.44 | 1.58 | 1.64 | 2.27 | 2.08 | 2.14 |
| Japan | Gross monthly full-time | 1.40 | 1.41 | 1.43 | 1.55 | 1.63 | 1.58 | 2.18 | 2.30 | 2.26 |
| Netherlands | Gross annual FTYR | 1.65 | 1.67 | 1.63 | 1.49 | 1.53 | 1.61 | 2.46 | 2.55 | 2.62 |
| New Zealand | Gross weekly full-time | 1.57 | 1.74 | 1.67 | 1.54 | 1.56 | 1.68 | 2.43 | 2.71 | 2.82 |
| Sweden | Gross annual FTYR | 1.25 | 1.22 | 1.35 | 1.32 | 1.40 | 1.47 | 1.64 | 1.72 | 1.98 |
| UK | Gross weekly full-time | 1.51 | 1.62 | 1.67 | 1.63 | 1.81 | 1.83 | 2.46 | 2.93 | 3.06 |
| USA | Gross weekly full-time | 1.72 | 1.83 | 1.92 | 1.77 | 2.02 | 2.12 | 3.03 | 3.69 | 4.06 |
| Average | | 1.60 | 1.62 | 1.61 | 1.57 | 1.64 | 1.69 | 2.53 | 2.68 | 2.74 |

Note: FTYR–full-time year-round workers.

Source: OECD Earnings Database. Years are 1980, 1990 and 2000, except as follows: Canada (81, 90, 94), France (80, 90, 98), Germany (84, 90, 98), Italy (86, 90, 96), Japan (80, 90, 99), Netherlands (85, 90, 99), New Zealand (84, 90, 97).

women by this measure. Moreover, on average, men had higher levels of wage inequality than women.

Table 8.3 also reveals interesting patterns in the level of inequality at different portions of the wage distribution. For example, among men, across all years, the USA and Canada have especially large 50-10 gaps. While Canada's 50-10 gap is much higher than the average for all countries, its 90-50 gap is roughly the same as the average. For US men, both the 50-10 and 90-50 gaps are much larger than the all-country average, but the difference between the USA and the all-country average is larger for the 50-10 gap. In contrast, again among men, Finland, Germany, Italy,

## Table 8.4. Changes in wage inequality

| Country | Earnings concept | Log 50–10 ratio | | | Log 90–50 ratio | | | Log 90–10 ratio | | |
|---|---|---|---|---|---|---|---|---|---|---|
| | | 1980–90 | 1990–2000 | 1980–2000 | 1980–90 | 1990–2000 | 1980–2000 | 1980–90 | 1990–2000 | 1980–2000 |
| **A. Men** | | | | | | | | | | |
| Australia | Gross weekly full-time | 0.021 | 0.006 | 0.027 | −0.023 | 0.057 | 0.034 | −0.002 | 0.063 | 0.061 |
| Canada | Gross annual FTYR | 0.040 | −0.019 | 0.021 | 0.019 | −0.005 | 0.014 | 0.059 | −0.024 | 0.035 |
| Finland | Gross annual FTYR | 0.009 | −0.010 | −0.001 | 0.015 | 0.002 | 0.017 | 0.023 | −0.008 | 0.016 |
| France | Net annual FTYR | −0.011 | −0.009 | −0.021 | 0.021 | −0.015 | 0.007 | 0.010 | −0.024 | −0.014 |
| Germany | Gross monthly full-time | −0.016 | 0.041 | 0.026 | 0.001 | 0.028 | 0.028 | −0.015 | 0.069 | 0.054 |
| Italy | Gross monthly full-time | 0.007 | −0.003 | 0.004 | 0.050 | 0.015 | 0.065 | 0.057 | 0.011 | 0.068 |
| Japan | Gross monthly full-time | 0.012 | −0.015 | −0.003 | 0.026 | 0.000 | 0.026 | 0.038 | −0.015 | 0.023 |
| Netherlands | Gross annual FTYR | 0.021 | 0.031 | 0.052 | 0.008 | 0.025 | 0.033 | 0.029 | 0.056 | 0.086 |
| New Zealand | Gross weekly full-time | 0.030 | 0.017 | 0.047 | 0.024 | 0.045 | 0.069 | 0.054 | 0.062 | 0.116 |
| Sweden | Gross annual FTYR | 0.006 | 0.024 | 0.030 | −0.013 | 0.047 | 0.034 | −0.007 | 0.071 | 0.064 |
| UK | Gross weekly full-time | 0.040 | 0.005 | 0.045 | 0.048 | 0.014 | 0.062 | 0.088 | 0.019 | 0.108 |
| USA | Gross weekly full-time | 0.035 | 0.004 | 0.039 | 0.055 | 0.030 | 0.086 | 0.090 | 0.034 | 0.125 |
| Average | | 0.018 | 0.005 | 0.023 | 0.020 | 0.020 | 0.040 | 0.039 | 0.024 | 0.063 |
| **B. Women** | | | | | | | | | | |
| Australia | Gross weekly full-time | −0.002 | −0.024 | −0.026 | 0.015 | 0.014 | 0.029 | 0.013 | −0.010 | 0.003 |
| Canada | Gross annual FTYR | 0.032 | −0.005 | 0.027 | −0.004 | 0.008 | 0.004 | 0.027 | 0.003 | 0.030 |
| Finland | Gross annual FTYR | −0.008 | −0.022 | −0.030 | 0.020 | −0.002 | 0.018 | 0.012 | −0.023 | −0.011 |
| France | Net annual FTYR | 0.011 | −0.030 | −0.018 | 0.008 | −0.002 | 0.006 | 0.019 | −0.031 | −0.012 |
| Germany | Gross monthly full-time | −0.016 | 0.005 | −0.011 | −0.023 | 0.021 | −0.002 | −0.039 | 0.026 | −0.013 |
| Italy | Gross monthly full-time | −0.077 | −0.005 | −0.082 | 0.038 | 0.019 | 0.057 | −0.038 | 0.013 | −0.025 |
| Japan | Gross monthly full-time | 0.003 | 0.004 | 0.006 | 0.022 | −0.013 | 0.009 | 0.025 | −0.009 | 0.016 |
| Netherlands | Gross annual FTYR | 0.004 | −0.010 | −0.006 | 0.012 | 0.022 | 0.033 | 0.016 | 0.012 | 0.027 |
| New Zealand | Gross weekly full-time | 0.043 | −0.017 | 0.027 | 0.004 | 0.034 | 0.038 | 0.047 | 0.017 | 0.064 |
| Sweden | Gross annual FTYR | −0.008 | 0.041 | 0.033 | 0.027 | 0.020 | 0.047 | 0.019 | 0.061 | 0.080 |
| UK | Gross weekly full-time | 0.031 | 0.014 | 0.045 | 0.045 | 0.005 | 0.050 | 0.076 | 0.019 | 0.095 |
| USA | Gross weekly full-time | 0.028 | 0.020 | 0.048 | 0.057 | 0.022 | 0.079 | 0.085 | 0.042 | 0.127 |
| Average | | 0.005 | −0.003 | 0.003 | 0.019 | 0.012 | 0.031 | 0.024 | 0.010 | 0.035 |

*Note:* FTYR—full-time year-round workers.

*Source:* OECD Earnings Database. Years are 1980, 1990 and 2000, except as follows: Canada (81, 90, 94), France (80, 90, 98), Germany (84, 90, 98), Italy (86, 90, 96), Japan (80, 90, 99), Netherlands (85, 90, 99), New Zealand (84, 90, 97).

the Netherlands, and Sweden all have especially small 50-10 gaps, both compared to the all-country average and relative to their 90-50 gaps. Among women, Canada has especially large 50-10 gaps, while the 50-10 gaps in Finland, Japan, and Sweden are especially small. These findings for the 50-10 gap suggest the importance of wage floors, since, as Table 8.5 shows, all of the countries with low 50-10 gaps except Japan have extensive coverage by collective bargaining agreements; in contrast, the USA and Canada, the countries with the highest 50-10 gaps, have a much lower incidence of collective bargaining coverage. Finally, US women have an especially high 90-50 gap, perhaps reflecting a lower level of occupational segregation there than in most other Western countries (Blau and Kahn, 1996b).

Table 8.4 shows how wage inequality has been changing for these countries. First, regarding overall wage inequality, for both men and women, the 90-10 ratio has risen on average, with a larger increase in the 1980s than the 1990s and larger increases for men than women in each subperiod. Among men, the USA, the UK, and New Zealand stand out as having experienced the largest increases in inequality, while among women, again the USA and the UK have the largest growth in overall wage inequality. In contrast, Finland and France were notable for their relatively stable overall wage inequality among both men and women. Second, at the bottom of the distribution, there were especially large increases in inequality for the Netherlands, New Zealand, the USA, and the UK among men and for the USA and the UK among women. At the top, the 90-50 gap grew fastest among men in Italy, New Zealand, the UK, and the USA and among women in Italy, the UK, and the USA.

The data in Tables 8.3 and 8.4, and indeed almost all research on earnings inequality, examine the earnings distribution at a point in time or changes in this overall distribution. Yet it is possible for inequality to be high at a point in time but for lifetime incomes to be much more equally distributed, due to mobility. If so, concerns about rising inequality over time or large international differences in inequality may be overblown. However, studies of individuals followed over time suggest that the basic conclusions we have reached from Tables 8.3 and 8.4—that wage inequality is rising at least in the USA and that it is higher in the USA than most other countries—also hold for inequality in individuals' permanent earnings. These issues are treated in some detail in the portion of Chapter 21 on intragenerational income mobility, but this research suggests that the qualitative conclusions we have reached in Tables 8.3 and 8.4 may hold for lifetime earnings as well.

Overall, Tables 8.3 and 8.4 show relatively high and fast-growing wage inequality in the USA. In addition, Canada has historically had high levels of wage inequality, while inequality grew very quickly in the UK. These patterns will form the background for examining evidence on the causes of levels of and changes in wage inequality. In particular, as shown in Table 8.5, New Zealand, the UK, and the USA had relatively large declines in collective bargaining coverage over this period,

Table 8.5. Collective bargaining coverage (% of employees), selected countries

| Country | 1980 | 1990 | 2000 | Changes 1980 to 2000 | |
|---|---|---|---|---|---|
| | | | | Percentage points | Percent |
| Australia | 80+ | 80+ | 80+ | 0.0 | 0.0 |
| Canada | 37 | 38 | 32 | −5.0 | −13.5 |
| Finland | 90+ | 90+ | 90+ | 0.0 | 0.0 |
| France | 80+ | 90+ | 90+ | 10.0 | 12.1 |
| Germany | 80+ | 80+ | 68 | −14.5 | −17.6 |
| Italy | 80+ | 80+ | 80+ | 0.0 | 0.0 |
| Japan | 25+ | 20+ | 15+ | −10.0 | −36.4 |
| Netherlands | 70+ | 70+ | 80+ | 10.0 | 13.8 |
| New Zealand | 60+ | 60+ | 25+ | −35.0 | −56.0 |
| Sweden | 80+ | 80+ | 90+ | 10.0 | 12.1 |
| UK | 70+ | 40+ | 30+ | −40.0 | −55.2 |
| USA | 26 | 18 | 14 | −12.0 | −46.2 |
| Average | 66.9 | 64.3 | 59.7 | −7.2 | −10.8 |

Note: A plus sign means that the estimate is considered by the OECD to be a lower bound. In computing averages, we have followed OECD convention and added 2.5 percentage points to each lower-bound estimate.
Source: OECD (2004: 145).

and the USA has always had the lowest level of coverage. The pattern of levels and changes in wage inequality in Tables 8.3 and 8.4, together with the data on collective bargaining coverage shown in Table 8.5, thus suggests the importance of wage-setting institutions in driving these outcomes. Of course, there may also be other factors responsible for differences and changes in wage inequality, and we now turn to an assessment of research in this area.

# 5. DETERMINANTS OF DIFFERENCES AND CHANGES IN WAGE INEQUALITY

## Quantities versus Prices

Table 8.6 shows results of an analysis decomposing overall differences in wage inequality between the USA and eight other countries during the 1994–8 period into portions due to heterogeneity in measured characteristics (Measured Characteristics Effect), prices of these characteristics (Wage Coefficients Effect), and

Table 8.6. Decomposition of US–other countries differences in wage inequality (weekly earnings of full-time workers), 1994–1998

| | US differential – Country j differential | Measured characteristics effect | Wage coefficients effect | Wage equation residual effect |
|---|---|---|---|---|
| **Men** | | | | |
| *50-10 Log wage differential* | | | | |
| Canada (1994) | 0.134 | 0.029 | 0.024 | 0.081 |
| Denmark (1998) | 0.421 | 0.073 | 0.209 | 0.139 |
| Finland (1998) | 0.203 | 0.063 | 0.130 | 0.010 |
| Italy (1998) | 0.421 | 0.097 | 0.194 | 0.130 |
| Netherlands (1994) | 0.347 | 0.182 | 0.036 | 0.129 |
| Norway (1994) | 0.380 | 0.164 | 0.118 | 0.098 |
| Sweden (1994) | 0.327 | 0.084 | 0.164 | 0.079 |
| Switzerland (1994 and 1998) | 0.236 | 0.237 | 0.098 | −0.099 |
| Non-US average | 0.309 | 0.116 | 0.122 | 0.071 |
| Share of total | 1.000 | 0.376 | 0.394 | 0.229 |
| *90-50 Log wage differential* | | | | |
| Canada (1994) | 0.246 | 0.021 | 0.098 | 0.127 |
| Denmark (1998) | 0.272 | 0.009 | 0.095 | 0.168 |
| Finland (1998) | 0.286 | 0.049 | 0.088 | 0.150 |
| Italy (1998) | 0.090 | −0.120 | 0.129 | 0.081 |
| Netherlands (1994) | 0.067 | −0.144 | 0.083 | 0.129 |
| Norway (1994) | 0.313 | 0.032 | 0.141 | 0.140 |
| Sweden (1994) | 0.371 | 0.064 | 0.118 | 0.188 |
| Switzerland (1994 and 1998) | 0.068 | −0.145 | 0.082 | 0.131 |
| Non-US average | 0.214 | −0.029 | 0.104 | 0.139 |
| Share of total | 1.000 | −0.137 | 0.487 | 0.650 |
| **Women** | | | | |
| *50-10 Log wage differential* | | | | |
| Canada (1994) | −0.049 | −0.122 | −0.003 | 0.076 |
| Denmark (1998) | 0.533 | 0.187 | 0.089 | 0.257 |
| Finland (1998) | 0.506 | 0.148 | 0.115 | 0.244 |
| Italy (1998) | 0.301 | −0.050 | 0.118 | 0.234 |
| Netherlands (1994) | 0.378 | 0.098 | 0.092 | 0.188 |
| Norway (1994) | 0.312 | 0.068 | 0.096 | 0.147 |
| Sweden (1994) | 0.601 | 0.115 | 0.194 | 0.293 |
| Switzerland (1994 and 1998) | 0.343 | 0.110 | 0.119 | 0.113 |
| Non-US average | 0.366 | 0.069 | 0.102 | 0.194 |
| Share of total | 1.000 | 0.189 | 0.280 | 0.531 |
| *90-50 Log wage differential* | | | | |
| Canada (1994) | −0.071 | −0.088 | 0.049 | −0.032 |
| Denmark (1998) | 0.247 | 0.001 | 0.131 | 0.116 |
| Finland (1998) | 0.303 | 0.063 | 0.128 | 0.112 |
| Italy (1998) | 0.259 | 0.066 | 0.125 | 0.069 |
| Netherlands (1994) | 0.186 | 0.066 | 0.053 | 0.067 |

Table 8.6. (*Continued*)

|  | US differential – Country j differential | Measured characteristics effect | Wage coefficients effect | Wage equation residual effect |
|---|---|---|---|---|
| Norway (1994) | 0.296 | 0.065 | 0.162 | 0.069 |
| Sweden (1994) | 0.272 | −0.045 | 0.175 | 0.142 |
| Switzerland (1994 and 1998) | 0.163 | 0.006 | 0.078 | 0.079 |
| Non-US average | 0.207 | 0.017 | 0.113 | 0.078 |
| Share of total | 1.000 | 0.080 | 0.544 | 0.376 |

*Notes*: Dependent variable is the log of weekly earnings for full-time workers. Measured characteristics include age dummies for 26–35, 36–45, 46–55 and 56–65 years (the omitted category is 16–25 years), years of schooling, and average of quantitative, document, and prose cognitive scores on common tests administered by the IALS. The base for the comparisons is US measured characteristics and other country coefficients and residuals.

*Source*: IALS data used in Blau and Kahn (2005).

residual effects (Wage Equation Residual Effect).[12] The components were computed using a full-distributional accounting method developed by Juhn *et al.* (1993).[13] The residual effect potentially reflects the impact of unmeasured prices but may also be due to differences in the distribution of unmeasured productivity characteristics (i.e. unobserved worker heterogeneity) and measurement errors. We take the wage coefficients effect and perhaps some portion of the residual effect as measures of the importance of labor market prices in explaining international differences in wage inequality.

The data used in Table 8.6 were taken from the IALS, and the results come from regressions reported in Blau and Kahn (2005). The measured characteristics include a series of age dummy variables, years of schooling, and the average of the respondent's quantitative, document, and prose cognitive test scores on common tests administered by the IALS. The inclusion of these test scores makes the IALS a unique dataset that allows one to compare outcomes for workers of similar cognitive skill in different countries.

Table 8.6 shows that, with the exception of the Canada–US comparisons for women, the raw 50-10 and 90-50 pay gaps (shown in column 1) are much higher in the USA than in the other countries. For example, for men, the 50-10 gap is 0.309 log points higher, and the 90-50 gap is 0.214 log points higher in the USA than the average of the other countries; the corresponding figures for women are

---

[12]  See the Data Appendix for a description of the sample selection rules and details on the wage concept used, which is weekly earnings of full-time workers.

[13]  See Juhn *et al.* (1993) and Blau and Kahn (1996a) for details of this decomposition. In the decompositions reported here, pair-wise comparisons between the USA and each of the other countries were implemented using the USA as the base for the personal characteristics distribution and the other country as the base for coefficients and residuals. However, results were similar when we used the opposite weighting scheme.

0.366 (50-10) and 0.207 (90-50). These are large international differences in wage inequality, and are quite consistent with the OECD data in Table 8.3. For both the male and female 50-10 gaps, an important portion of US–other country differences in wage inequality is accounted for by the greater heterogeneity in US characteristics, with measured characteristics explaining 38% of the US–other country differences in the 50-10 gap for males and 19% for females. In other words, part of the reason for higher US wage inequality at the bottom of the distribution is that US workers at the bottom have a less favorable distribution of age, schooling, and test scores relative to the median than is the case for other countries. Test scores at the bottom of the distribution in the USA are especially low relative to the middle in comparison to other countries (Blau and Kahn, 2005). Nonetheless, a more important part of the explanation of higher US wage inequality at the bottom comes from wage coefficients and wage residuals suggesting that prices, both measured and unmeasured, play a role.

Table 8.6 shows that measured characteristics do not help to explain much of the higher 90-50 gap for women (accounting for only 8% of US–other country differences) and actually go in the wrong direction for explaining the 90-50 gap differences for men. That is, the measured characteristics effect averages $-14\%$ for men, implying that the gap between male skills at the top and the middle of distribution is actually smaller in the USA than in other countries, although the wage gap is larger. Again, labor market prices and residuals are important for explaining US–other country differences in the 90-50 gap as well. In fact measured prices are roughly equally important at both ends of the distribution for both men and women. In earlier work based on the 1980s (Blau and Kahn, 1996a), we found stronger price effects at the bottom than the top in explaining higher US wage inequality among men. Table 8.6's findings of similar price effects at the bottom and the top for the 1990s may reflect the growing wage inequality at the top of the distribution in the USA in the 1990s (Autor et al., 2008) or the superior measure of skills in the IALS which was not available in the 1980s.[14]

In addition to the studies already mentioned, other empirical studies find an important role for labor market prices in explaining the growth of wage inequality over time or differences in wage inequality across countries at a point in time. For example, Devroye and Freeman (2002) show that wage inequality is much higher in the USA than in several other IALS countries even among those who have virtually identical scores on the survey's cognitive tests. And both Leuven et al. (2004) and

---

[14]  It is possible that the higher returns to skills in the USA are an artifact of its larger size and in fact reflect cost of living differences rather than true returns. However, when we analyzed wages using 2000 US Census of Population microdata, we found that for both men and women, the returns to education and age, as well as residual wage inequality, were virtually unaffected when we added a series of dummy variables for each state. Thus, the high returns to skills and residual inequality in the USA that are the basis of Table 8.6 occur within detailed regions (i.e. states) and thus are not an artifact of the large size of the country.

Blau and Kahn (2005) find higher wage returns to education and IALS test scores in the USA than in other Western countries. And as discussed further below and in more detail in Chapter 10 on unions and Chapter 11 on low pay, a variety of research finds that union wage-setting institutions cause international differences in the returns to skills.

As noted, Table 8.4 shows that wage inequality has grown over time in several countries, and a variety of research finds that an important part of this growth has come from rising returns to labor market skills such as education. For example, studies of the USA, Sweden, and Britain in the 1980s all find that rising returns to schooling were an important feature helping to explain rising wage inequality in these countries (Katz and Murphy, 1992; Juhn *et al.*, 1993; DiNardo *et al.*, 1996; Edin and Holmlund, 1995; Schmitt, 1995; Katz *et al.*, 1995). In addition, several authors (Katz and Murphy, 1992; Juhn *et al.*, 1993; Lemieux, 2006; Autor *et al.*, 2005) have found rising residual inequality in the USA (i.e. inequality of the disturbance term in equation (3) above), potentially suggesting rising prices of unobserved skills (Juhn *et al.*, 1993). Although, as Lemieux (2006) points out, residual inequality can itself be affected by compositional changes such as an ageing labor force, Autor *et al.* (2005) find evidence suggesting the importance of unmeasured prices in causing rising residual inequality, controlling for work force composition.

Additional evidence of the importance of skill prices comes from studies of Scandinavian wage inequality. First, the reduction of wage inequality in Sweden in the 1968–83 period was partly accounted for by a sharp decline in the returns to schooling (Edin and Holmlund, 1995). And, second, the fall in Norwegian wage inequality during the 1987–91 period was also mostly accounted for by falling returns to skills (Kahn, 1998a).

## Causes of Changes or Differences in Labor Market Prices: The Role of Supply of and Demand for Labor Market Skills

In this subsection, we review evidence on supply and demand factors, and in the next, we discuss the impact of wage-setting institutions in causing the changes and differences in labor market prices discussed above. On the demand side, we have seen that Katz and Murphy (1992) noted that in the USA in the 1980s, both the returns to a college degree and the relative quantity of college-educated workers rose, implying an outward shift in the relative demand for college-educated labor during this period. Goldin and Katz (2007) come to a similar conclusion about rising demand for skilled labor over a longer time period (1890–2005). Two factors have been proposed for explaining rising relative demands for skilled labor, particularly since 1980: skill-biased technological change and growing exposure to international trade have both potentially lowered the relative demand for unskilled labor. Indirect evidence for technological change as an important factor comes from within-industry data linking the increased use of computers, an indicator of technological change, to increased use of college-educated workers in the 1980s and 1990s (Autor *et al.*, 1998). Moreover, Berman *et al.* (1998) found consistent skill upgrading within industries across many OECD countries during the 1980s at the same time that skill differentials in wages were rising in most countries.[15] And the authors found that across countries, the same industries experienced the most skill upgrading, implying the spread of technological change across the advanced countries.[16]

An additional demand factor concerns the technology of compensation methods themselves. Lemieux *et al.* (2007) suggest that with improved information technology, it is now possible to better monitor individual workers' performance. The authors show that the share of workers whose pay is directly affected by their performance (e.g. through bonuses or commissions) has risen in the USA and inequality of pay is higher among those with pay-for-performance than among those whose pay is not directly tied to their performance. They find that the growth in the incidence of pay-for-performance in the USA can account for nearly all of the increase in wage dispersion at the top of distribution between the late 1970s and the early 1990s. Of course, as suggested by the authors, technological change could be the driving force behind the growing use of contingent pay; however, it is also possible that changing norms could have had an independent effect on inequality if they facilitate the use of contingent pay methods.

Evidence on the impact of international trade has been found for the USA by computing the factor content of imports and exports over the post-1980 period. Specifically, Borjas *et al.* (1997) find that the volume of unskilled labor directly replaced by trade with less-developed countries during the 1980–90 period was too small to have a major impact on raising wage inequality in the US.[17] The authors note, however, that the threat of trade can lower unskilled workers' wages even if trade does not take place (as argued in Wood, 1998), so globalization could have had a larger wage effect than its impact on factor content would imply. In addition, Borjas and Ramey (1995) find evidence that trade reduces workers' rents in heavily unionized industries, lowering the relative wages of less-skilled workers, again suggesting a role for trade beyond its effects on the demand for unskilled

---

[15]  These countries included the USA, Norway, Luxembourg, Sweden, Australia, Japan, Denmark, Finland, West Germany, Austria, the UK, and Belgium.

[16]  Card and DiNardo (2002) cast some doubt on the importance of technological change in explaining rising US wage inequality, since the increase in wage inequality occurred disproportionately over a short period (1979–83), while technological change occurred gradually over a long period. The authors suggest instead that institutional change was important, and we turn to that explanation below.

[17]  Borjas *et al.* (1997) treat the low-skill factor content of imports as an effective increase in the supply of less skilled labor, which is analytically similar to characterizing the factor content as a fall in the domestic demand for less skilled labor.

labor. Moreover, Blinder (2007) emphasizes the importance of offshoring of both manufacturing jobs and service jobs (e.g. editing books or reading x-rays) in reducing the demand for some kinds of labor, both skilled and unskilled. In some cases, offshoring is facilitated by technological progress through the internet, and in others it represents a kind of international trade. In either case, it can result in the displacement of many workers who then compete downward the wages of similarly skilled workers. In addition to these direct effects on wage inequality, it is likely that trade and technology have contributed to deunionization in the USA and the UK by lowering the relative demand for blue-collar workers.

On the supply side, Katz and Murphy (1992) noted that the supply of college graduates grew more slowly in the USA in the 1980s than in the 1970s. The authors argue that the switch from falling returns to a college degree in the 1970s to rising returns in the 1980s was likely caused at least in part by this change in supply. Again, more generally, Goldin and Katz (2007) find that over the whole 1915–2005 period, rising demand for highly skilled labor roughly balanced its rising supply; however, since 1980 the demand effect outran supply, leading to a sharply rising return to a college degree.

An additional source of supply changes is immigration. On the one hand, Borjas (2003) finds that the large volume of immigration of workers with less than a high school education and also college graduates to the USA between 1980 and 2000 lowered the relative wages of both native high school dropouts and native college graduates (compared to high school graduates). On the other hand, Card (2005) disputes this conclusion by noting that at the local labor market level, immigration raises the supply of unskilled workers without affecting their relative wages. Thus, there is a lack of consensus on the impact of immigration on the native wage structure.

International comparative research on the effect of supply on labor market prices finds some important effects. First, Card and Lemieux (2001) find that the return to education rose by more during the 1980s and 1990s for younger men than older men in the USA, the UK, and Canada. The authors note that in each of these countries, the growth in the supply of college graduates slowed for young men relative to older men over this period, helping to explain the especially rapid growth of the education premium for young men. Second, Gottschalk and Joyce's (1998) study of changes in the wage structure for male household heads in eight countries during the 1979–92 period[18] found that changes in the return to education and in age premiums were each negatively correlated with the growth in relative supply of the target group, suggesting the importance of supply shifts. Third, Abraham and Houseman (1995) note that in the 1980s, the return to education rose in the USA, while it was stable in Germany. The authors attribute some of this difference to a more rapidly increasing supply of skilled labor in Germany than in the USA, although

---

[18]  The countries were Australia, Canada, Finland, Israel, the Netherlands, Sweden, the UK, and the USA.

they note that Germany's centralized wage-setting regime may also have played a role. Finally, Leuven *et al.*(2004) constructed indexes of demand for and supply of skill for men in 15 countries and found that across countries, the wage return to skill was negatively correlated with the net supply (supply minus demand) of skill.[19]

## Causes of Changes or Differences in Labor Market Prices: The Role of Wage-Setting Institutions

There is abundant evidence that centralized wage-setting institutions lead to wage compression. We briefly describe these findings here and refer the reader to the more detailed discussions in Chapter 10 on unions and Chapter 11 on low pay.

Several studies compare a variety of countries and obtain results consistent with wage-setting institutions reducing wage inequality, including Blanchflower and Freeman (1992), Edin and Zetterberg (1992), Kahn (1998b), Wallerstein (1999), Kahn (2000), and Blau and Kahn (2003 and 2005). Moreover, some of the most striking evidence on the impact of institutions on wage inequality comes from dramatic interventions within particular countries, where episodic change in labor market institutions can be tied to corresponding changes in the wage distribution. These country-specific studies have found that increased centralization or conscious union wage policies have caused wage compression in Sweden (Edin and Topel, 1997; Davis and Henrekson, 2005) and Norway (Kahn, 1998a). Deunionization resulting from government policies in the 1980s has been found to raise wage inequality in Britain (Freeman and Pelletier, 1990; Schmitt, 1995), with some suggestive, although weaker, evidence of similar effects in New Zealand (Dixon, 1998; Crawford *et al.*, 1999).

It is interesting to note that Card (1996) and DiNardo *et al.* (1996) also found an important role for deunionization in the USA in accounting for an increase in wage inequality in the 1980s, although our earlier discussion implies that this effect may itself have been partly due to technology and trade.

The discussion of institutions has so far centered around collective bargaining. Additional institutions that have been found to compress wage differentials include minimum wage laws and wage indexation schemes. Many studies of minimum wages in several countries find robust evidence that they compress the bottom of the wage distribution and especially raise the relative wages of young people.[20] And Italy's system of wage indexation, the *scala mobile*, which was in place from 1975 to 1992 and gave low-paid workers the largest increases, has been found to cause considerable wage compression (Erickson and Ichino, 1995).

---

[19]   The countries were Canada, Chile, Czech Republic, Denmark, Finland, Germany, Hungary, Italy, the Netherlands, Norway, Poland, Slovenia, Sweden, Switzerland, and the USA.

[20]   For evidence on the impact of minimum wages, see Chapter 11 on low pay.

# 6. CONCLUSIONS AND FURTHER RESEARCH

There are large international differences in wage inequality and also important changes in wage inequality over time. We have presented evidence that these changes and differences reflect both diversity of the working population as well as the impact of changes and differences in prices in the labor market—the returns to skills and location in favorable sectors. These prices in turn have been affected by both supply and demand forces and wage-setting institutions. Institutional interventions such as large-scale collective bargaining contracts or minimum wages can in particular bring up the bottom of the wage distribution, and our review does indeed suggest that they have a strong effect on wage inequality. However, it is important to point out that there is also evidence that these interventions in the labor market have, in many cases, led to employment losses either in low-wage industries (Davis and Henrekson, 2005; Edin and Topel, 1997), among low-skill workers (Kahn, 1998a), or among women and young people generally (Bertola et al., 2007). Moreover, wage floors appear to interact with systems of employment protection to relegate employed women, youth, and immigrants disproportionately into temporary jobs (Kahn, 2007). These studies illustrate the potential tradeoffs between raising wages and fostering high employment levels in permanent, protected jobs. We should also point out that some international studies do not find that high wage floors lower less-skilled workers' relative employment (e.g. Card et al., 1999 and Krueger and Pischke, 1998). But there is enough evidence in the studies previously cited to make one concerned that high wage floors could lead to employment problems for some low-wage groups.

We conclude with a brief discussion of recent developments in earnings inequality and some gaps in our understanding. First, as discussed by Blinder (2007), offshoring is likely to put increasing pressure on the earnings of those whose jobs can be done elsewhere. As he emphasizes, these are not only unskilled but also some skilled jobs, such as computer programming and, possibly, radiology. Thus, this kind of technological advance has the potential to actually narrow wage differentials in advanced economies. Second, while we have emphasized collective bargaining in our discussion of institutions, there are other interventions whose impacts on the wage structure are not yet well understood. These include employment protection mandates as well as product market regulation (on the latter, see, for example, the recent work of Guadalupe, 2007, who finds that increased product market competition raises the return to skill). And finally, labor economists are increasingly studying the role of norms in explaining wage inequality and other labor market outcomes such as work time. While norms can affect these phenomena, it is likely that labor market outcomes also affect norms. Disentangling these effects is an important area for future research.

# DATA APPENDIX

## IALS Data

The data in Table 8.1 come from the IALS. There were no excluded sectors, and with the exceptions of the Netherlands and Switzerland, earnings are measured gross of deductions (Leuven *et al.*, 2004: 484). We only included those with at least 200 annual work hours, 10 hours worked per week, and 10 weeks worked per year, in order to focus on those who had at least some noticeable connection to the labor market. These hours restrictions led to the exclusion of a very small number of people with very low annual work hours, ranging from: 2–6% of men and 4–10% of women. Hourly earnings were computed by dividing annual wage and salary earnings by annual work hours. We excluded anyone with hourly wages less than the equivalent of US$2 or greater than US$200 (using exchange rates). Deletion of these extreme values led to the exclusion of a very small number of observations, ranging from 0.2% to 1.0% of the sample.

For two countries, earnings were topcoded: Switzerland (French- and German-speaking samples), and the Netherlands. For Switzerland, earnings data were collected in 1994 (1993 earnings) for the French- and German-speaking subsamples with a 100,000 franc top code (about US$66,000) and in 1998 (1997 earnings) for the Italian-speaking subsample with no topcode. To produce a single Swiss sample, we first used the Swiss consumer price index, as reported on the BLS web site, to inflate the 1993 earnings figures to 1997. The topcoded value became 104,930 francs. We then took the average 1997 earnings in the Italian-speaking Swiss sample for those who earned at least 104,930 francs and assigned this value (132,903.1 francs) to everyone in the French and German subsamples who was at the top code. For the Netherlands, the topcoded value of 200,000 guilders (about US$105,000 in 1993) was multiplied by 1.2.

The data used in Table 8.6 also come from the IALS. Wages are defined as weekly earnings for full-time workers (this definition enables us to include one more country than using hourly earnings). Further, in order to produce a homogeneous sample of those with strong labor force commitment, we included only those who were employed at least 26 weeks in the previous year. Finally, we excluded those with measured weekly earnings less than the equivalent of US$80 using exchange rates (or for full-time workers, less than about $2.00 per hour at a time when the US minimum wage was $4.25) or more than US$10,000. These exclusions reduced the sample by 0.2–3.0%, with an average reduction of 1.5%.

## The OECD Earnings Database

The data in Tables 8.3 and 8.4 come from the OECD Earnings Database. The samples for each country include all adult workers except for the following exclusions: France (agricultural and general government workers); Germany (apprentices); Italy (agricultural and general government workers); Japan (employees in establishments with fewer than 10 regular workers and employees in agriculture, forestry, fishing, public administration, public education, the army, or the police); Sweden (employees less than 20 or over 64 years old, as well as those with self-employment earnings); USA (workers less than 16 years old). In addition, for Australia, data before 1988 include only earnings on one's main job.

# TECHNICAL APPENDIX: SUPPLY, DEMAND, AND THE RELATIVE WAGES OF COLLEGE GRADUATES

Following Katz and Autor (1999), to analyze supply, demand, and the relative wages of college graduates, assume an aggregate production relationship between these groups for a given country at time t:

$$Q_t = \left[ a(a_t N_{ct})^p + (1-a)(b_t N_{ht})^p \right]^{1/p}, \tag{A1}$$

where, suppressing the time subscript t, Q is the value of output (i.e. assume a constant output price of 1), $a$ is a share parameter, $N_c$ and $N_h$ are, respectively, employment of college-educated and high school-educated workers, a and b are demand shifters, and p is a parameter related to the elasticity of substitution between college-educated and high school-educated workers ($\sigma$) as follows:

$$\sigma = 1/(1-p). \tag{A2}$$

Assuming that firms are on their labor demand curves, wages will equal marginal revenue products, implying:

$$\log(W_{ct}/W_{ht}) = p\log(a_t/b_t) + \log(a/(1-a)) + (1-p)\log(N_{ht}/N_{ct}) \tag{A3}$$

$$= \log(a/(1-a)) + (1/\sigma)(\sigma-1)\log(a_t/b_t) - (1/\sigma)\log(N_{ct}/N_{ht}))$$

$$= \log(a/(1-a)) + (1/\sigma)(\sigma-1)\log(a_t/b_t)$$

$$- (1/\sigma)(\log(EPOP_{ct}/EPOP_{ht}) - (1/\sigma)(POP_{ct}/POP_{ht}),$$

where $W_c$ and $W_h$ are respectively wage rates for college-educated and high school-educated workers, $EPOP_c$ and $EPOP_h$ are their respective employment-to-population ratios, and $POP_c$ and $POP_h$ are their respective population levels. If we have good estimates of $\sigma$, we can infer the impact of population changes, for example, on relative wages.

## REFERENCES

ABRAHAM, K. G., and HOUSEMAN, S. N. 1995. 'Earnings Inequality in Germany', in Freeman and Katz (1995), 371–403.

AGELL, J., and LOMMERUD, K. E. 1992. 'Union Egalitarianism as Income Insurance'. *Economica*, 59(235): 295–310.

ALESINA, A., GLAESER, E., and SACERDOTE, B. 2001. 'Why Doesn't the United States Have a European-Style Welfare State?' *Brookings Papers on Economic Activity*, 2: 187–254.

———— 2005. 'Work and Leisure in the U.S. and Europe: Why so Different?' Harvard Institute of Economic Research Discussion Paper no. 2068, Apr.

ATKINSON, A. B., and BRANDOLINI, A. 2001. 'Promise and Pitfalls in the Use of "Secondary" Data-Sets: Income Inequality in OECD Countries as a Case Study'. *Journal of Economic Literature*, 39(3): 771–99.

AUTOR, D. H., KATZ, L. F., and KEARNEY, M. S. 2005. 'Rising Wage Inequality: The Role of Composition and Prices'. Working Paper, Massachusetts Institute of Technology, Aug.

—— —— —— 2008. 'Trends in U.S. Wage Inequality: Revising the Revisionists'. *The Review of Economics and Statistics*, 90(2): 300–23.

—— —— and KRUEGER, A. B. 1998. 'Computing Inequality: Have Computers Changed the Labor Market?' *Quarterly Journal of Economics*, 113(4): 1169–213.

BERMAN, E., BOUND, J., and MACHIN, S. 1998. 'Implications of Skill-Biased Technological Change: International Evidence'. *Quarterly Journal of Economics*, 113(4): 1245–79.

BERTOLA, G., BLAU, F. D., and KAHN, L. M. 2007. 'Labor Market Institutions and Demographic Employment Patterns'. *Journal of Population Economics*, 20(4): 833–67.

BLANCHFLOWER, D., and FREEMAN, R. 1992. 'Unionism in the U.S. and Other Advanced O.E.C.D. Countries'. *Industrial Relations*, 31(1): 56–79.

BLANK, R. 1993. 'Why Were Poverty Rates So High in the 1980s?' in D. Papadimitriou and E. Wolff (eds.), *Poverty and Prosperity in the USA in the Late Twentieth Century*. London: Macmillan, 21–55.

BLAU, F. D., and KAHN, L. M. 1996a. 'International Differences in Male Wage Inequality: Institutions Versus Market Forces'. *Journal of Political Economy*, 104(4): 791–837.

—— —— 1996b. 'Wage Structure and Gender Earnings Differentials: An International Comparison'. *Economica*, 63(250(S)): S29–S62.

—— —— 1997. 'Swimming Upstream: Trends in the Gender Wage Differential in the 1980s'. *Journal of Labor Economics*, 15(1), part 1: 1–42.

—— —— 2002. *At Home and Abroad: U.S. Labor Market Performance in International Perspective*. New York: Russell Sage Foundation.

—— —— 2003. 'Understanding International Differences in the Gender Pay Gap'. *Journal of Labor Economics*, 21(1): 106–44.

—— —— 2005. 'Do Cognitive Test Scores Explain Higher U.S. Wage Inequality?' *The Review of Economics and Statistics*, 87(1): 184–93.

—— —— Forthcoming. 'Women's Work and Wages', in S. Durlauf and L. Blume (eds.), *The New Palgrave Dictionary of Economics*, 2nd edn. London: Palgrave Macmillan.

BLINDER, A. S. 2007. 'Offshoring: Big Deal, or Business as Usual?' Center for Economic Policy Studies, Princeton University, Working Paper no. 149, June.

BORJAS, G. J. 2003. 'The Labor Demand Curve is Downward Sloping: Reexamining the Impact of Immigration on the Labor Market'. *Quarterly Journal of Economics*, 118(4): 1335–74.

—— FREEMAN, R. B., and KATZ, L. F. 1997. 'How Much Do Immigration and Trade Affect Labor Market Outcomes?' *Brookings Papers on Economic Activity*, 1: 1–90.

—— and RAMEY, V. A. 1995. 'Foreign Competition, Market Power, and Wage Inequality'. *Quarterly Journal of Economics*, 110(4): 1075–110.

BURDA, M., HAMERMESH, D. S., and WEIL, P. 2007. 'Total Work, Gender and Social Norms'. National Bureau of Economic Research Working Paper no. 13000, Mar.

CARD, D. 1996. 'The Effect of Unions on the Structure of Wages: A Longitudinal Analysis'. *Econometrica*, 64(4): 957–79.

—— 2005. 'Is the New Immigration Really so Bad?' *The Economic Journal*, 115(507): F300–F323.

—— and DiNARDO, J. E. 2002. 'Skill-Biased Technological Change and Rising Wage Inequality: Some Problems and Puzzles'. *Journal of Labor Economics*, 20(4): 733–83.

—— KRAMARZ, F., and LEMIEUX, T. 1999. 'Changes in the Relative Structure of Wages and Employment: A Comparison of the United States, Canada, and France'. *Canadian Journal of Economics*, 32(4): 843–77.

—— and LEMIEUX, T. 2001. 'Can Falling Supply Explain the Rising Return to College for Younger Men? A Cohort-Based Analysis'. *Quarterly Journal of Economics*, 116(2): 705–46.

COLEMAN, M. T., and PENCAVEL, J. 1993a. 'Changes in Work Hours of Male Employees, 1940–1988'. *Industrial & Labor Relations Review*, 46(2): 262–83.

—— —— 1993b. 'Changes in Market Work Behavior of Women Since 1940'. *Industrial & Labor Relations Review*, 46(4): 653–76.

CRAWFORD, A., HARBRIDGE, R., and WALSH, P. 1999. 'Unions and Union Membership in New Zealand: Annual Review for 1998'. *New Zealand Journal of Industrial Relations*, 24(3): 383–95.

DAVIS, S. J., and HENREKSON, M. 2005. 'Wage-Setting Institutions as Industrial Policy'. *Labour Economics*, 12(3): 345–77.

DEVROYE, D., and FREEMAN, R. B. 2002. 'Does Inequality in Skills Explain Inequality of Earnings Across Advanced Countries?' Centre for Economic Performance Discussion Paper no. 552, Nov.

DiNARDO, J., FORTIN, N. M., and LEMIEUX, T. 1996. 'Labor Market Institutions and the Distribution of Wages, 1973–1992: A Semiparametric Approach'. *Econometrica*, 64(5): 1001–44.

DIXON, S. 1998. 'The Growth of Earnings Inequality 1984–1997: Trends and Sources of Change'. Paper Presented at the Eighth Conference on Labour, Employment, and Work, Victoria University of Wellington, Nov.

EDIN, P.-A., and HOLMLUND, B. 1995. 'The Swedish Wage Structure: The Rise and Fall of Solidarity Wage Policy', in Freeman and Katz (1995), 307–43.

—— and TOPEL, R. 1997. 'Wage Policy and Restructuring: The Swedish Labor Market since 1960', in R. B. Freeman, R. Topel, and B. Swedenborg (eds.), *The Welfare State in Transition: Reforming the Swedish Model*. Chicago: University of Chicago Press, 155–201.

—— and ZETTERBERG. J. 1992. 'Interindustry Wage Differentials: Evidence from Sweden and a Comparison with the United States'. *American Economic Review*, 82(5): 1341–9.

EHRENBERG, R. G., and SMITH, R. S. 2006. *Modern Labor Economics*, 9th edn. Boston: Pearson Addison Wesley.

ERICKSON, C. L., and ICHINO, A. 1995. 'Wage Differentials in Italy: Market Forces and Institutions', in Freeman and Katz (1995), 265–305.

FARBER, H. S. 1986. 'The Analysis of Union Behavior', in O. Ashenfelter and R. Layard (eds.), *Handbook of Labor Economics*, vol. II. Amsterdam: North-Holland, 1039–89.

FREEMAN, R. B., and KATZ, L. F. (eds.). 1995. *Differences and Changes in Wage Structures*. Chicago: University of Chicago Press.

—— and PELLETIER, J. 1990. 'The Impact of Industrial Relations Legislation on British Union Density'. *British Journal of Industrial Relations*, 28(2): 141–64.

GOLDIN, C., and KATZ, L. F. 2007. 'The Race between Education and Technology: The Evolution of U.S. Educational Wage Differentials, 1890–2005'. National Bureau of Economic Research Working Paper no. 12984, Mar.

GOTTSCHALK, P., and JOYCE, M. 1998. 'Cross-National Differences in the Rise in Earnings Inequality: Market and Institutional Factors'. *The Review of Economics and Statistics*, 80(4): 489–502.

—— and SMEEDING, T. M. 1997. 'Cross-National Comparisons of Earnings and Income Inequality'. *Journal of Economic Literature*, 35(2): 633–87.

GUADALUPE, M. 2007. 'Product Market Competition, Returns to Skill, and Wage Inequality'. *Journal of Labor Economics,* 25(3): 439–74.

JUHN, C., MURPHY, K., and PIERCE, B. 1991. 'Accounting for the Slowdown in Black–White Wage Convergence', in M. H. Kosters (ed.), *Workers and their Wages*. Washington: AEI Press, 107–43.

—— —— 1993. 'Wage Inequality and the Rise in Returns to Skill'. *Journal of Political Economy*, 101(3): 410–42.

KAHN, L. M. 1998a. 'Against the Wind: Bargaining Recentralisation and Wage Inequality in Norway, 1987–1991'. *The Economic Journal*, 108(448): 603–45.

—— 1998b. 'Collective Bargaining and the Interindustry Wage Structure: International Evidence'. *Economica*, 65(260): 507–34.

—— 2000. 'Wage Inequality, Collective Bargaining and Relative Employment 1985–94: Evidence from Fifteen OECD Countries'. *The Review of Economics and Statistics*, 82(4): 564–79.

—— 2007. 'The Impact of Employment Protection Mandates on Demographic Temporary Employment Patterns: International Microeconomic Evidence'. *The Economic Journal*, 117(521): F333–F356

KATZ, L. F., and AUTOR, D. H. 1999. 'Changes in the Wage Structure and Earnings Inequality', in O. Ashenfelter and D. Card (eds.), *Handbook of Labor Economics*, vol. IIIA. Amsterdam: North-Holland, 1463–555.

—— LOVEMAN, G. W., and BLANCHFLOWER, D. G. 1995. 'A Comparison of Changes in the Structure of Wages in Four OECD Countries', in Freeman and Katz (1995), 25–65.

—— and MURPHY, K. M. 1992. 'Changes in Relative Wages, 1963–87: Supply and Demand Factors'. *Quarterly Journal of Economics*, 107(1): 35–78.

KRUEGER, A. B., and PISCHKE, J.-S. 1998. 'Observations and Conjectures on the U.S. Employment Miracle', in German-American Academic Council (ed.), *Third Public German-American Academic Council Symposium: Labor Markets in the USA and Germany*. Bonn: German-American Academic Council, 99–126.

LALONDE, R. J., and TOPEL, R. H. 1992. 'The Assimilation of Immigrants in the U.S. Labor Market', in G. Borjas and R. Freeman (eds.), *Immigration and the Work Force*. Chicago: University of Chicago Press, 67–92.

LEMIEUX, T. 2006. 'Increasing Residual Wage Inequality: Composition Effects, Noisy Data, or Rising Demand for Skill?' *American Economic Review*, 96(3): 461–98.

—— MACLEOD, W. B., and PARENT, D. 2007. 'Performance Pay and Wage Inequality'. National Bureau of Economic Research Working Paper no. 13128, May.

LEUVEN, E., OOSTERBEEK, H., and VAN OPHEM, H. 2004. 'Explaining International Differences in Male Skill Wage Differentials by Differences in Demand and Supply of Skill'. *The Economic Journal*, 114(495): 466–86.

NICKELL, S., and LAYARD R. 1999. 'Labor Market Institutions and Economic Performance', in O. Ashenfelter and D. Card (eds.), *Handbook of Labor Economics*, vol. IIIC. Amsterdam: North-Holland, 3029–84.

SCHMITT, J. 1995. 'The Changing Structure of Male Earnings in Britain, 1974–1988', in Freeman and Katz (1995), 177–204.

WALLERSTEIN, M. 1999. 'Wage-Setting Institutions and Pay Inequality in Advanced Industrial Societies'. *American Journal of Political Science*, 43(3): 649–80.

WOOD, A. 1998. 'Globalisation and the Rise in Labour Market Inequalities'. *The Economic Journal*, 108(450): 1463–82.

CHAPTER 9

·······································································

# INEQUALITY AND THE LABOR MARKET: EMPLOYERS

·······································································

## JULIA LANE

## 1. INTRODUCTION

·······································································

THE central role of earnings dispersion in contributing to income inequality has long been recognized.[1] Yet disentangling the sources of changes in earnings dispersion has been difficult.[2] Although the theoretical literature has provided both demand (employer) and supply (worker) side explanations, most analytical work has been based on the examination of the individual characteristics of workers, explaining at most 30 percent of variation in earnings.[3] The new availability of matched employer–employee data is providing new sets of facts that can inform our understanding of the impact of employers on earnings dispersion. First, it has been established that different firms pay observationally equivalent workers

Thanks to Eugene Smolensky, Brian Nolan, Tim Smeeding, Wiemer Salverda, and participants in the Seville workshop for their very helpful comments.

[1] Indeed, Gottschalk and Smeeding (1997) noted more than a decade ago that increased earnings dispersion was the driving force behind increased family income inequality in the United States.

[2] Atkinson and Brandolini (2006).     [3] As Mortensen (2005) points out.

different wages. Thus variation in wage-setting practices across firms can affect the earnings distribution.[4] Second, cross-country analysis shows that very different wages are paid within each firm: the variation in earnings within firms is nearly as high as the variation in the overall earnings distribution. Thus changes in wage-setting practices within firms, particularly at the top end of wages, can change the earnings distribution.[5] Finally, there is a burgeoning literature that suggests that the way in which workers are matched to different types of firms is non-random: high-wage workers tend to be matched with high-wage firms, low-wage workers with low-wage firms, and changes in that allocation can change earnings distributions over time.[6]

Understanding the impact of employers on the earnings distribution is important for at least two reasons. One is that the structure of employment constantly changes because of the enormous amount of turbulence that characterizes economic activity. In any given quarter, about one in *four* job matches in the United States either begins or ends, one in *thirteen* jobs is created or destroyed, and one in *twenty* establishments closes or is born. Thus understanding the impact of the entry and exit, as well as the expansion and contraction of firms and the sorting of workers and firms based on underlying worker 'skills', will be critical to understanding changes in the earnings distribution. The second is the role of public policy. If the driving force of economic change is the entry and exit of firms, which in turn affects the selection of new technologies, and the associated workforce, public policy that is targeted at affecting that selection may affect the earnings distribution as much as interventions in education and training.

This chapter begins by providing a simple conceptual framework. Because the issue is essentially an empirical one, this is then followed by an in-depth discussion of the data necessary to address the topic. This is followed by an overview of a selected subset of recent work. The chapter concludes by discussing the current gaps in knowledge.

# 2. CONCEPTUAL FRAMEWORK AND LITERATURE REVIEW

The most basic framework linking employers and wage dispersion is derived from standard competitive theory. Here the demand for labor is derived from the demand for the product that is produced, together with the relative prices of the factors of production. In this framework, changes in wage differentials come about

---

[4] Abowd *et al.* (1999).     [5] See Lazear and Shaw (2008).     [6] See Brown *et al.* (2006).

either because of changes in the demand for the product that is produced or because of changes in production technologies. If competitive assumptions are relaxed, and firms can be monopsonistically competitive in the labor market, different firms may well pay observationally identical workers different amounts. Finally, wage dispersion can also be generated by differentially successful matches between firms and workers. Changes in inequality that are driven by employers can then be generated by changes in each of these factors: changing product markets or technologies, changing firm premia, or changes in the match between workers and firms. Each of these is discussed in turn below.

## Different Product Markets or Technologies

An important strand of the literature has teased out the impact of changing product markets or technologies using only worker-based data (see e.g. Katz and Murphy, 1992 and Autor *et al.*, 2008). This approach uses a simple demand and supply framework to describe how changes in the relative wages of different types of labor can be affected by changes in demand for the product that a firm produces, or a change in the technology used in that production.[7] Briefly, if output is produced by skilled and unskilled workers ($N_s$ and $N_u$ in Figure 9.1), changes in technology or product demand affect the relative demand for the different types of workers, and hence relative wages. The key empirical focus of an analysis of the impact of changing demand is to examine the relative ratio of skilled to unskilled employment $N_s/N_u$ and then relative ratio of skilled to unskilled wages $w_s/w_u$. Skill-biased technological change should lead to an increase in the relative demand for skilled labor, increasing relative wages. The increase in relative wages should also be matched by an increase in the relative employment of skilled versus unskilled workers.

A conceptually similar approach to examining the impact of relative demand shifts, but based on firm data, was first developed by Davis and Haltiwanger (1991).[8] They examine between- and within-firm difference in earnings, reasoning that changes in demand and supply conditions derived from technological change or changes in product demand affect both the overall wage distribution for skill types as well as the distribution of skill types between and within plants. Their quantity metric is then the hours worked and wages earned by workers of different skill type at different plants. Both hours and wages are affected by plant-level demand shifters (such as technology and product demand) and supply shifters for different skill types, so the differentials of interest are wages and hours across plants. It is worth noting, however, that this formulation can also be used to describe other

---

[7]  Machin and Van Reenen (2007) provide a very straightforward summary of the approach, which is reproduced in the appendix.

[8]  A technical summary is provided in the appendix.

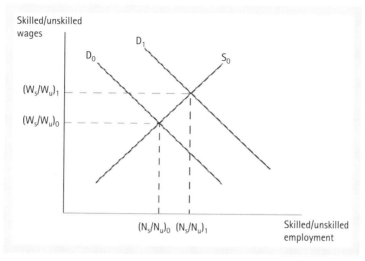

**Fig. 9.1. The structure of the longitudinal employer–household dynamics program**

*Source:* Machin and Van Reenen (2007, figure 3).

employer-driven changes in wages, such as rent sharing, unionization, and, over time, job reallocation across firms.

In sum, then, the implication of this kind of model is that employer-driven earnings inequality arises as a natural resource reallocation response to product and technology shocks, such as globalization and technological change. Wage differences should reflect arbitrage costs and are of concern if individuals are either unable to change skill levels in response to shifting demand conditions, or face unreasonably high costs associated with that change.

## Firm Differences in Pay

The notion that observationally equivalent workers could receive different wages depending on where they worked was famously highlighted by John Dunlop (1957), who found that the hourly wages of unionized short-haul male truck drivers in Boston varied dramatically depending on whether they delivered wholesale laundry or magazines. An early and much-cited synthesis of the subsequent literature on wage differentials is provided by Groshen (1991), who suggests a number of reasons other than differences in worker quality for wages to differ across workers. Two fairly straightforward reasons include compensation for the type of work performed as well as simple random variation. The other reasons result in there being 'good' jobs, and hence job rationing. The first of these is that firms pay 'efficiency wages' in order to minimize shirking, reduce turnover, improve the pool of applicants, or to create a high-morale, high-productivity work environment. The second reason, extensively discussed by Mortensen (2005), is that rents arise as a result of market frictions, and that firms share rents with their workers.

The best-known empirical estimation of the size of the firm effect is that of Abowd et al. (1999) who decomposed individual log wages for individuals into four separate components: a time-invariant person effect, a time-invariant firm effect, the component due to time-varying observable individual characteristics, and finally the statistical residual, orthogonal to all other effects in the model.[9] This approach permits the decomposition of earnings into the amount that is paid for 'who you are' (the individual and worker characteristics effect) and 'where you work' (the firm effect). A major assumption of the early Abowd et al. approach, however, is that mobility is exogenous, which is not true if, as Gibbons and Katz (1991) and subsequent papers suggest, observed mobility originates from a process that sorts heterogeneous workers into heterogeneous firms. Indeed, this assumption is relaxed in later work (Abowd et al., 2006).

## The Match between Workers and Firms

The match between firms and workers is the third way in which firms can affect wages. This term 'match effect' refers to the additional production value that is added by a particular worker working for a particular firm and can be thought of as the value of production complementarities between the worker and firm. Seminal recent work has been contributed by Mortensen, using Danish-linked employer–employee data (Mortensen, 2005) and Postel-Vinay and Robin, using French linked employer–employee data (Postel-Vinay and Robin, 2002). They both argue that wage differentials are due to job search frictions when workers do not know the wages offered by all employers, and to cross-firm differences in wage policy and productivity. Mortensen uses Danish data to demonstrate the importance of search. Postel-Vinay and Robin construct and estimate a model using French data which attributes firm effects to search frictions, and heterogeneous matches between workers and firms. The essential notion is that more efficient firms extract higher rents and hence the key to firm differences in wage premia is the matching process. On the one hand more productive firms devote less effort to hiring, so they are less productive in hiring new employees, but on the other, they generate greater match surpluses so are more likely to hire the ones they do match with.

This view ties into a plethora of research that contributes to our understanding of the sources of the firm effect. The sharing of economic rents between firms and workers, as a result of temporary frictions, for efficiency wage reasons, or because

---

[9] When estimating the wage decomposition in equation (9), we use only dominant employer earnings, defined as the job (person firm match) in a given year with the highest earnings. This restriction results in only one employer per person per year.

of union power, has often been offered as a reason (see Guertzgen, 2006, for a recent review). Indeed, Guadalupe (2005) shows that as product market competition increases, even in competitive labor markets, firms will be willing to pay more to attract good workers and increase the amount of profits they share. In a related thread of the literature, Andersson, Freedman *et al.* (forthcoming) argue that product-market differences drive differences in both the level and distribution of wages: software firms that operate in product markets with high potential upside gains to innovation (as in video games or Internet firms) have a greater return to hiring 'stars' than do other firms that operate in stable markets (like mainframe software).

The match premium can also be tied into the way in which the firm organizes itself in terms of its human resource practices and wage differentials. Although the literature on this is too vast to summarize, one interesting thread is exemplified by the work of Garicano and Ross-Hansberg (2006). They argue that the very existence of a knowledge economy means that production requires that agents must acquire knowledge, and, given that workers differ in their cognitive abilities, a universe of 'knowledge-based hierarchies' develops. Wage differentials then occur in direct proportion to the span of managerial control: greater layers of management leverage knowledge more. Some empirical evidence for this view is found in Smeets and Warzynski (forthcoming). Another example is the work of Bandiera *et al.* (2007), who found empirical evidence that differential incentives for managers resulted in very different productivity levels and wages for workers.

Finally, it is important to note that firm wage policies may not simply affect individual wage differentials at one point in time, but may be dynamic in nature. As a consequence, the initial match or job assignment can affect subsequent effort, learning, task-specific human capital and training with clear implication for an individual's future earnings. The tournament models originating with Lazear and Rosen (1981) argue that pay differentials act as an incentive to increase effort. Gibbons and Waldman (1999) develop a model of wage and promotion dynamics that features three elements that can vary across firms: job assignment, on-the-job human-capital acquisition, and learning. Their subsequent addition of task-specific human capital (Gibbons and Waldman, 2006) adds to the theoretical basis whereby the initial worker–firm match can have long-term implications for the overall earnings distribution. This notion is reinforced by the research of, among others, Von Wachter and Bender (2006) who note that the initial assignment of young workers to firms can affect the subsequent training investments and their earnings.

## Firm and Worker Dynamics

The final set of issues has to do with the potential of firm dynamics to change the earnings distribution. The fact that every country's labor market is characterized by enormous amounts of job creation and destruction is by now well documented: annual rates of job creation and destruction range between 10 and 15 percent. The amount of worker reallocation is substantial as well, both that induced by job reallocation and the excess, known as churning (Burgess *et al.*, 2000). Most recently, substantial attention has been paid to changes in the structure of the product market through deregulation (see Wozniak, 2006, and Guadalupe, 2005, for good reviews) and globalization (see Muendler, 2008).

Whatever the reason, the impact of job creation and job destruction and firm entry and exit on the earnings distribution is likely to be complex. One way is through net entry: new firms, with different ways of doing business, and with different firm fixed effects, can replace old. Another way is through changing composition: if one set of firms, with one way of doing business, grows at a different rate than does another set. A third way is through changing workforce practices: if firms change the way in which they organize themselves. Finally, the earnings distribution can change if there are changes in the way in which workers are assigned to firms.[10] Again, since there is a substantial literature in this area, I only reference an illustrative subset.

The role of firm entry and exit, as well as job creation and destruction, in changing the composition of production is well known. Basic economic principles help explain the complex relationship between firm performance, entry, and exit. Businesses enter an industry and if they are successful they survive and grow; if not successful, they contract and exit. Accordingly, the economy is constantly replenishing itself with low-productivity exiting businesses being replaced by more productive entering and expanding businesses. Recent work by Brown *et al.* (2006) found that, across five industries, there were very large within-industry differences in productivity. The data suggest that poor performers by and large do not survive and this is important for understanding both firm dynamics and aggregate industry dynamics. However, it takes time for firms to learn whether their poor performance warrants changing how they are doing business or exiting (see Haltiwanger *et al.*, 2007).

Changes in the way in which firms organize themselves can occur if firms adopt new technologies. Klump and Grandville (2000) theorized that differences in the elasticity of substitution across firms may be the reason that there are differences in capital intensity and workforce composition across firms. Work by Dupuy and DeGrip (2002) extends this work to first theoretically show that firms will have higher labor productivity the greater the elasticity of substitution between skilled and unskilled labor and then empirically demonstrate that large firms have greater elasticities of substitution between skilled workers in skilled jobs with all other labor inputs and capital. The implication, then, is that large firms are more able to adjust

---

[10]   A detailed decomposition, derived from Andersson, Davis *et al.* (2007) is provided in an appendix shown on the Handbook website.

their input mix than are small firms. Conversely, however, research by Haltiwanger *et al.* (2007, 1999) and Brown *et al.* (2006) suggests that firms' choice of workforce composition is remarkably persistent over time.

Changes in the way in which firms and workers are assigned to firms can also affect the earnings distribution. A good review of this is found in Burgess *et al.* (forthcoming). The core notion developed by Acemoglu (1997) is that more efficient matching (in terms of a greater degree of assortative assignment) can lead to higher wage inequality. The same paper illustrates the co-movement of within-group and between-group inequality and suggests that assortative matching may have increased in the United States. Burgess *et al.* do find evidence supporting the potential for changes in sorting to affect earnings inequality, and there is similar evidence of worker sorting by Hellerstein and Neumark (2008) and Hellerstein *et al.* (2008, 1999).

Of course, it is a major computational challenge to capture the impact of firm and worker entry and exit, as well as the changing match between workers and firms on the earnings distribution, as will be seen in the subsequent sections.

# 3. DATA AND MEASUREMENT ISSUES

## Data Sources

The analysis of the interactions of firms and employees has followed two distinct paths. One path has focused on large-scale, often nationally representative, datasets on firms and employees, typically housed at federal statistical agencies. In some cases, this path has intensively used administrative data, alone or integrated with survey data, and in other cases has involved the use of surveys designed to collect information about both firms and workers. The other path has been the development of specialized surveys and gathering of personnel records of a small number of firms (or even one firm) and/or intensive observation (essentially collection of qualitative data) from case studies based on site visits to firms by researchers; data typically housed at universities or think-tanks.

The challenges faced in collecting data on businesses are very different from those faced in collecting data on individuals. One is the skewed nature of the size distribution. Even though most workers are employed by big firms, most firms are very small. Thus they can be difficult to find without access to administrative records. Another is that the complex structure of firms means that it can be very difficult to find the right informant to respond to surveys. And yet another is that it is often difficult to define the appropriate unit of analysis over time due to changes in firm structure, outsourcing, mergers, acquisitions, and spinoffs. Yet, three things are striking when surveying the current state of data collection. The first is the imaginative set of methods whereby data can be collected from individual firms; the second is how many more datasets have become available since the seminal review by Abowd and Kramarz in 1999; and the third is the number of innovative approaches taken to enhance the breadth and depth of information derived from linked data.

### Worker surveys with industry information matched in

It is not surprising that much of the work examining the effects of technological change and product market changes has been derived from the analysis of worker-based surveys, such as the Current Population Survey in the United States (e.g. Katz and Murphy, 1992, or Autor *et al.*, 2008) or the New Earnings Survey in the UK (e.g. Guadalupe, 2005). This approach has the obvious advantage of providing detailed information on worker characteristics, particularly skill levels. Detailed information is also provided on the different components of earnings, such as hours and weeks worked, as well as hourly wage rates, thus enabling researchers to abstract from quantity effects. This permits a calculation of the relative wages of skilled and unskilled workers, as well as the relative quantities of each. In addition, the data have been collected for long periods of time in a consistent fashion, which permits researchers to study the evolution of earnings over time.

However, there are some clear drawbacks. First, as with any survey data, the information relies on self-report, and there is ample documentation (see Roemer, 2000) of the errors associated with such self-reports. In addition, the rate of imputation of earnings has increased substantially over time. A recent paper by Hirsch and Schumacher (2004) points out that as many as 30 percent of respondents to the Current Population Survey—the major source of information on earnings inequality in the literature—do not respond to income questions, and are consequently imputed. There are other concerns as well. No information is available on the characteristics of the employer, other than the employer size and industry (which appear to be substantially mis-reported). And there is limited information on technology adoption. Indeed, as Snower (1998) points out, there is a real danger of posing a tautological claim, since 'technological change hypothesis is unfalsifiable, and thus is not a proper scientific hypothesis at all. In fact, when we say that the rising U.S. inequality is due to "technological change," we come quite close to saying that we don't have a clue about why U.S. inequality has increased' (p. 17).

### Case studies

The importance of case studies is becoming increasingly apparent in economics, although it has long been apparent in related fields and interest areas, such as the Sloan Industry Centres. Lazear (1992) examined one large firm and found striking results on the relationship between wages and productivity. Baker *et al.* (1994) also studied an entire firm to understand its wage determination structure and promotion policies. More recently, Bandiera *et al.* (2007) examined a large fruit-processing firm to understand the relationship between managerial incentives and inequality. Indeed, as Snower (1998) notes, with a phenomenon as complex as the relationship between employers and wage inequality, it would be better to generate an entire raft of case study analyses—what Bartel *et al.* (2004) refer to as 'insider econometrics'.

A recent book (Bender *et al.*, 2008) on the analysis of firms and employees[11] provides some sense of the variety of new approaches to understanding the interaction of firms and employees. Of the three case studies in the book, two are based on administrative records of the firm. The third is a statistical case study of a single trucker firm and its employees which matches proprietary personnel and operational data. They combine traditional survey instruments with behavioral economics experiments.

Of course, a major drawback to case studies is that it is extremely difficult to generalize the results. In addition, the data are typically extremely confidential and proprietary, so replication, which is the essence of science, is not possible.

## Longitudinal data on firms and workers

The new attention to the interaction on firms and workers has largely come about because of the new availability of linked employer–employee data in many countries. Important advances can be made in understanding the relationship between firms and workers, when universe longitudinal data on firms, workers, and the match between the two is available. In many of these datasets there is detailed information on firms—particularly trade, technology, and ownership structure; and detailed information on workers—particularly measures of their skill.

A prototypical example is the Longitudinal Employer Household Dynamics (LEHD) program at the US Census Bureau. It brings the household and business data together at the micro level using state-level wage record data to create a comprehensive and unique resource for new data products and analysis (Abowd *et al.*, 2004).

Figure 9.2 provides a graphical illustration of the program. Briefly, the records that integrate the worker and firm information at the Census Bureau are derived from state unemployment insurance wage records from (currently) 18 partner states covering some 70 percent of US employment. Each covered employer in each state files quarterly records for each individual in their employment, covering about 98 percent of employment in each state.

---

[11]  Conference on the Analysis of Firms and Employees (CAFÉ) 2006 in Nuremberg, Germany.

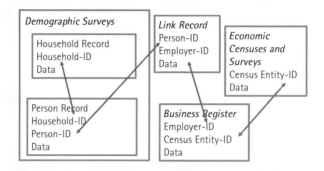

Fig. 9.2. The longitudinal employer–household dynamics
program

These data have a number of key characteristics. They are both universal and longitudinal for firm and worker information, resulting in very large sample sizes. The data are extensive and current. For most states the data series begins in the early 1990s and are updated on a quarterly basis (six months after the transaction date). The rich state data are complemented by the extensive micro-level data at the Census Bureau: data on firms, such as technology, capital investment, and ownership, and data on workers, such as date of birth, place of birth, race, and sex. There are also a number of drawbacks outlined in Vilhuber (2008), including coding errors, incorrect identifiers, and linkage units, entities that are administrative rather than economic in scope, and sample selection problems.

Other approaches are of course possible. The basic approach is to use a single data source for building up a linked employer–employee dataset based on a unique firm identifier. An alternative approach (e.g Hellerstein *et al.*, 2008; Vilhuber, 2008) use alphanumerical matching algorithms, such as Automatch, based on the name and addresses of the firms. In yet a third approach, if neither identifiers nor addresses are available as a basis for linking one dataset, subsets of common variables are used, to get unique firms per cell for matching.

## Data Access

Despite the importance of the analysis of firm data, researchers have limited access to high quality data that can be used to examine firm behavior. Access to data on businesses is limited because of both legal and ethical protections. The challenge that this creates for the study of businesses is obvious. Too little research is conducted, and junior researchers and graduate students are not trained in empirical firm analysis.

Several approaches have been used by national statistical institutes, but many of them are unsatisfactory. Probably the most well-known approach is provide access via Research Data Centers, but the cost in time and money for researchers to access the data has led to serious underutilization (Dunne, 2001). Remote buffered access, like the Luxembourg Income Study, has the advantage of providing access to many users, but is not particularly applicable to business data, given the skewed nature of most interesting outcomes associated with businesses.

It should be a major concern that so many researchers have turned to commercial datasets, like Compustat and CRSP. The availability of these files, which provide financial and accounting information on publicly traded companies, has had a major influence on financial and accounting research. Similarly, datasets like Dunn and Bradstreet/NETS and ABI/Inform are often used as sample frames for academic surveys. However, getting representative research data from such commercial sources is difficult since both Compustat and CRSP are aimed at serving institutional investors, and Dunn and Bradstreet/NETS or ABI/INFORM are primarily for marketing purposes. As a result, there are substantial quality problems if these data are used in the context of academic research.

The new movement to online remote access systems must be encouraged. This approach uses modern computer science technology, together with researcher certification and screening, to replace the burdensome, costly, and slow human intervention associated with buffered remote access.

## Measurement Issues

### Technology and skill

Measuring technology and skill is a substantial technical challenge. Berman *et al.* (1994) used four-digit data from the Annual Survey of Manufactures for 1959 to 1989, which were augmented to include measures of the capital stock and price indices for the inputs, to examine the changing demand for skills in response to changes in technology. Their measure of skill was the ratio of non-production to production workers.[12] They found that the increased use of non-production workers within manufacturing industries was directly related to the increased investment in computers and research and development. Very little of the increase was associated with increased demand for goods produced by non-production worker-intensive manufacturing industries.[13]

---

[12]  These data are now known as the NBER-CES Manufacturing Industry Database (Bartelsman *et al.*, 2000).

[13]  Dunne, Haltiwanger and Troske (1997), using establishment-level micro-data, were also forced to use the same crude measure of skill.

Micro-data on individuals have also been used extensively to create industry and industry-occupation time series to study the impact of technology on the demand for skilled workers. While such data inherently miss important features of the relationship that can only be captured using enterprise or establishment micro-data, it is important to note the major contributions from this source. Autor *et al.* (1998) studied the period from 1940 to 1996, measuring skill with educational attainment as reported in the decennial Censuses of Population and Housing Public-Use Micro Samples and the Current Population Surveys (CPS), aggregated to the industry level. They added computer-use data from the October CPS, and three other sources, as a technology measure. They found that the rate of skill upgrading was greatest in industries that were more computer intensive, which they interpreted as supporting the complementarity of education and information technology.

Integrated employer–employee micro-data are still relatively rare but have already been used to study problems like the ones we pose here. Although the focus of their study was the relation between human resource management (HRM) practices and productivity, Ichniowski *et al.* (1997) provided direct evidence on skill-technology trade-offs for the single type of steel finishing process they studied. They used extensive production-line longitudinal data, collected on site, for the specific technologies adopted and the HRM practices used. Their employee skill variables included directly measured recruitment and training components of the HRM system. They concluded that a particular combination of 'high-performance' HRM practices, which included selection and training of skilled workers, was highly complementary with the successful adoption and integration of information-technology-intensive capital investments.

Bresnahan *et al.* (2002) directly studied the complementarities between employee skill and information technology capital for the period from 1987 to 1994. Their employee skill measures included education, occupation, and an employer-assessed 'skill level of work' variable data that came from a single cross-sectional survey of organizational practices and labor force characteristics conducted in 1995 and 1996. They merged longitudinal data on information technology capital, measured for the same organizations as completed the cross-sectional organization survey, with enterprise-level financial data from Compustat to construct their other measures of inputs and output. Their study comprised about 300 large, publicly traded firms. They found that increased use of information technology capital was directly related to increased demand for skilled employees.

Hellerstein *et al.* (1999) used a cross-section of integrated employer–employee data based on matching the 1990 Census of Population and Housing long-form data with data from the 1989 Annual Survey of Manufactures. Their worker skill measures included education, occupation, and age. Their technology measure was the capital stock that has been developed for the ASM establishments, which is the same capital stock measure we use here. Although the focus of their study was on estimating the difference between pay and marginal productivity, they do provide some mixed evidence about the complementarity of capital and skilled labor, which is positive in their main analysis, but negative in other specifications.

Another empirical challenge is developing direct measures of technology, particularly ones that are comparable across sectors. Clearly, physical capital intensity is a natural candidate, as are direct measures of the use of information technology such as computers or computer software. In addition, changes in other observable dimensions of a firm's activity may prove useful. For example, since information technology has been associated with a variety of changes in the manner of doing business, variation in the relation between inventory and sales might prove a useful indicator of changes in supply-chain management technology.

Several quite interesting direct measures of technology are available, and are described in what follows. However, in common with the rest of the literature, much is left unmeasured, especially with regard to the intangible capital components of technology. An indirect way of capturing some firm heterogeneity is to use the firm-effects wage decompositions. These reflect the component of the wage rate that is due to unmeasured firm heterogeneity. Such firm effects presumably reflect many factors, one of which is rent sharing—that is, firms may share rents from high levels of profitability/productivity, which may in turn be related to the type of technology (broadly defined) that has been implemented at a business. Including the firm effect in a regression, then, permits an indirect assessment of difficult-to-measure components of the technology of a business, for which the firm effects serve as a potential control. This was done by Abowd *et al.* (2007) who found a strong positive empirical relationship between advanced technology and skill in a cross-sectional analysis of businesses in both services and manufacturing.

## Defining employers

Defining an individual's employer is a major challenge. As Golan *et al.* (2007) note, about 26 percent of workers who had previously exhibited a substantial degree of attachment to their employer reallocate in a given year. About two-thirds of this reallocation is within the economy, roughly evenly split within and across broadly defined industries. Identifying the 'dominant' employer is an often used strategy.

Another challenge is the changing nature of the firm. The transformation of the US economy from manufacturing to services over the last several decades is a primary factor underlying these changes. The ubiquitous use of the computer and, of late, the Internet in the workplace has also transformed both the way businesses do business and the way workers within and between businesses interact. These changes, and others, increasingly imply that the key input into the activity of a business is the skill and knowledge of its total workforce. At a conceptual level, consideration of these issues requires re-thinking about the theory of the firm at its most fundamental level. What constitutes a business? Why are businesses organized in the way that they are? What constitutes the value created by a business activity? Although these issues may seem to be abstract and theoretical, they profoundly impact the way we collect and process data on businesses and workers.

Data collected by the federal statistical system on US businesses is slowly changing to reflect the changes in the economy. Historically, the most comprehensive data on businesses have been collected on manufacturing businesses. The collection of this data has focused on a traditional view of a manufacturing establishment in terms of a physical location at which materials, physical capital, and labor are combined to produce some specific good. However, the growing tendency for firms to reorganize how they carry out work themselves, and increasingly in collaboration with other firms, means that the boundary of businesses appears to be changing. The physical location of businesses is less important in an environment in which the workforce is increasingly interacting through advanced communication mechanisms such as the Internet and video conferencing. Put differently, since the wealth creation process is increasingly dominated by human rather than physical capital, it is the connections between the workers that matter the most rather than the physical location of a business.

There are large related theoretical and empirical literatures to draw upon for this analysis. For example, on the theory side, Milgrom and Roberts (1992) devote an entire chapter to the boundaries and structures of the firm while Kremer (1993) provides insights into thinking about the factors determining how workers of different type/s are grouped.

# 4. BASIC FINDINGS

## Differential Product Markets or Technologies

As Acemoglu (2002), Autor *et al.* (2008), and Machin and Van Reenen (2007) note, there is substantial consensus, using basic demand and supply analysis, that skill-biased technological change has had an impact on the earnings distribution.

There is intriguing evidence of differences between and within plants, however. A forthcoming book by Lazear and Shaw (2008) that compares wage differences within and across firms across a number of countries with linked employer–employee data uncovered the following. The general structure of wages is remarkably similar across all countries. The wage dispersion within firms is nearly as high as the wage dispersion overall. The variance in wage growth rates across individuals within the firm is very high. Wage levels and raises vary considerably across workers within the firm. Firms, while not identical, are more similar than they are dissimilar. Skill segregation appears to be prevalent, which is consistent with the Kremer and Maskin (1996) view of the impact of skill-biased technical change.

This thread has recently been added to by Faggio *et al.* (2007), who use combined individual and firm data to show that the increase in individual wage inequality in the UK is due to increases in inequality between firms rather than within firms. They find that this increase is driven by a rise in between-firm productivity dispersion, with little role for within-firm inequality. Indeed, their findings are consistent with the theoretical work of Caselli (1999), suggesting that there has been a differential adoption of a new technology across firms, although it is certainly possible that these observed outcomes represent changing firm structures, rather than changing firm policies. Interestingly, however, this result is consistent with work by Nordström-Skans *et al.* (2008) who note that a trend rise in Sweden in between-plant wage inequality accounts for the entire increase in wage dispersion during the period.

## Firm Differences in Pay

Just how much the firm effect differs across industries is evident from a perusal of Table 9.1. In some of the highest paying industries, such as security brokers, the

**Table 9.1. Sources of industry earnings differentials**

| SIC | Name | Industry wage premium | Premium attributable to workforce human capital | Premium attributable to firm wage setting policy |
|-----|------|------|------|------|
| Highest Paying Industries | | | | |
| 62 | Security, commodity, brokers and services | 82% | 34% | 37% |
| 67 | Holding and other investments | 70% | 34% | 27% |
| 48 | Communication | 63% | 7% | 52% |
| 49 | Electric, gas and sanitary services | 54% | 0% | 55% |
| 81 | Legal services | 54% | 18% | 31% |
| Lowest Paying Industries | | | | |
| 58 | Eating and drinking places | −45% | −12% | −38% |
| 01 | Agriculture-crops | −35% | −10% | −31% |
| 72 | Personal services | −33% | −12% | −24% |
| 79 | Amusement and recreation services | −32% | −8% | −28% |
| 70 | Hotel and lodging services | −32% | −17% | −19% |
| 54 | Food stores | −30% | 1% | −30% |

*Source:* Abowd (2002).

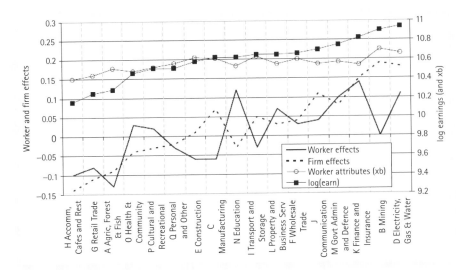

**Fig. 9.3.** Industry earnings differentials—attributes, worker effects, and firm effects

*Source*: Hyslop and Mare (2006).

industry wage premium is roughly equally due to differential individual characteristics and differential firm characteristics. In others, such as the transportation
equipment industry, the firm effect explains almost all the difference in wage premia
in the industry. Indeed, the regulated industries have much higher firm effect
than do the unregulated industries in this analysis, consistent with rent-sharing
theories. By contrast, the very competitive service industries, such as food, hotel,
and amusement industries, have workers that are very similar to the economy-wide
average; the industry wage differential is due to a very low fixed effect.

Hyslop and Mare (2006) use very similar techniques to demonstrate the relative
importance of worker and firm effects across industries in a small, open economy
(New Zealand). Despite the fact that the United States and New Zealand are very
different structurally, the same industry patterns are evident: as Hyslop and Mare
point out, the average worker effect varies from a low of about 13 percent below the
overall average in agriculture, forestry, and fishing to a high of 14 percent above the
average in finance and insurance, while the average firm effect ranges from a low of
14 percent below the overall average in accommodation, cafes, and restaurants to a
high of 19 percent above the average in mining.

Including worker and firm fixed effects substantially increases economists' ability
to explain earnings variation. In New Zealand, France, and the United States, the
proportion explained exceeds 85 percent; in Brazil (where the individual fixed effect
was not directly estimated) the proportion is about 50 percent. Table 9.2 provides
an overview of the relative importance of firm fixed effects ($\psi$) in earnings variation

Table 9.2. Importance of firm fixed effects in earnings variation across countries and time

| Correlations | Time | Earnings with | | | | Time-varying individual characteristics | | Individual effect |
|---|---|---|---|---|---|---|---|---|
| | | Time-varying individual characteristics | Individual effect | Firm effect | Error | Individual effect | Firm effect | Firm effect |
| Washington[1] | | 0.304 | 0.511 | 0.518 | 0.306 | −0.530 | 0.143 | −0.025 |
| France[1] | | 0.141 | 0.704 | 0.201 | 0.169 | −0.068 | 0.023 | −0.283 |
| US[2] | | 0.224 | 0.468 | 0.484 | 0.402 | −0.553 | 0.095 | 0.080 |
| Brazil 1990[3] | | 0.667 | | 0.358 | 0.700 | | 0.160 | |
| Brazil 1997[3] | | 0.622 | | 0.435 | 0.705 | | 0.161 | |
| NZ FTE weighted[4] | 0.046 | 0.507 | 0.697 | 0.495 | 0.305 | −0.088 | 0.202 | 0.119 |
| NZ unweighted[5] | 0.053 | 0.538 | 0.645 | 0.487 | 0.400 | −0.087 | 0.214 | 0.175 |
| NZ FTE weighted (highly connected firms)[4] | 0.044 | 0.519 | 0.714 | 0.518 | 0.311 | −0.073 | 0.264 | 0.168 |

Notes: [1] Abowd (2002); [2] Abowd et al. (2003); [3] Menezes-Filho et al. (2006); [4] Hyslop and Mare (2006).

across several countries. Interestingly, although firm and worker effects are roughly equally important in the United States, worker effects are more important in other countries, although firm effects became more important in Brazil after exposure to globalization in the early 1990s. Using a completely different dataset, Lane *et al.* (2007) find that controlling for detailed occupation, establishment dummies account for more than one-fifth of individual wage variation, and that these establishment effects are only partially explained by observable characteristics, such as the location, size, age, and industry of the establishment.

One other point is worth noting about the correlations presented in Table 9.2, and that is the correlation between worker and firm fixed effects. There is clear negative assortative matching in France, no strong relationship in the United States, and a strong positive matching in New Zealand.

New work by Hipolito (2008) reviews a set of studies that used a common dataset, the 2002 European Structure of Earnings Survey, in examining the impact of firm and job characteristics on earnings inequality for a set of representative European countries (Spain, the Netherlands, Norway, the Czech Republic, Latvia, Slovakia, and Portugal). His survey also is consistent with firm and job factors being more important than individual factors in contributing to earnings inequality.

Yet even these estimates of the importance of the firm in explaining wage dispersion may be an understatement. Postel-Vinay and Robin (2002) find not only that the importance of the person effect is much less than that using the Abowd approach but that it decreases substantially as the skill level of the individual decreases. As they point out, the share of the total log-wage variance explained by person effects lies around 40 percent for managers, and quickly drops as the observed skill level decreases, to almost zero for the three (of seven) least-skilled job categories, which include manual workers.

One important consequence of these findings is pointed out by Mortensen (2005): they are consistent with search frictions as the most important explanation of wage dispersion. Another is the likely increased contribution of firms to earnings dispersion as the service sector, and the associated search frictions, expands in economic importance.

Finally, Lazear and Shaw (2008) note in their cross-country study that firm fixed effects are becoming more important over time—suggesting both that firms are becoming more dissimilar over time and that their contribution to the earnings distribution is increasing.

## The Match between Workers and Firms

A review of the tournament and promotion literature provides ample evidence that the match between firms and workers can have an important effect on the wage distribution. Indeed, Lazear and Shaw's (2008) cross-country study finds that there is a high variance of pay levels and pay increases across firms in all countries, which they attribute to firms being more hierarchical than homogeneous, setting up policies that variously reward effort and teamwork within the firm as well as being sensitive to outside options.

However, direct estimates of the match have been hard to come by. In essence what is needed is a model that estimates the firm and the individual fixed effects as well as the joint effect of the worker's employment with the particular firm. The computational challenge is enormous but has been addressed by Woodcock (forthcoming). He estimates that individual fixed effects and personal character-istics account for over 50 percent of earnings variation, the firm effect 25 percent and the match effect 19 percent. This separation of effects makes it clear that the sorting between firms and workers can also be a powerful contributor to earnings differences.

Even more interesting, Woodcock's work overturns the earlier finding, when match effects are not estimated, that workers and firms are negatively sorted: he finds strong (0.6) positive correlation of sorting between firms and workers. If match effects are not taken into consideration, high wages in some industries, such as mining, might be wrongly attributed to low-wage workers working in high-wage firms; the match effect model suggests that it is due to a combination of high-wage workers and high-wage firms. He also finds that a sizeable component of the male/female earnings differential is due to females working in lower-paying industries and in lower-paying firms within those industries, consistent with very early work by Blau (1977).

# Firm and Worker Dynamics

Andersson, Davis *et al.* (2007) and Brown *et al.* (2006) are two of the few studies to directly examine the way in which changes in workforce composition, firm entry and exit, and job reallocation affect industry-specific earnings distributions.

They found that while there were differences across industries in the magnitudes and directions of change in various aspects of the earnings distribution over the 1992 to 2003 time period, most factors had similar qualitative effects across all industries. In particular, even in industries in which there was very little change on the aggregate earnings distribution between 1998 and 2003, there were enormous, albeit offsetting, changes in the factors contributing to earnings change. Similar factors were at work in industries with declining inequality as well as those with increasing inequality. The magnitudes of these effects, however, varied consider-ably. In particular, they found that worker entry and exit had very little impact on changes in the earnings distributions over this time period for the industries examined. In other words, despite the ample opportunities for firms to change their workforce composition, industry workforces remained, by and large, very similar, and earnings gains due to experience tended to be higher at the lower end of the distribution. They argued that this did not lend credence to the notion that individual firms are changing their production technologies in a way that is biased towards skill.

Changes in observable characteristics, which mainly involved the aging of the workforce within each industry, tended to shift the earnings distributions of all industries to the right. The effect of an increasingly experienced workforce on earnings inequality was to decrease it in three of the four industries with declining inequality and in all of the five increasing-inequality industries—in each case primarily by increasing earnings at the bottom of the earnings distribution.

On the other hand, the net impact of firm entry and exit is to reduce the dispersion of earnings for all industries. In almost all industries this effect acted to increase earnings at the bottom end of the distribution more than at the top. Since firm wage premia are likely to primarily reflect rent sharing, unionization, and/or efficiency wage payments, it is difficult to reconcile the fact that these premia are disproportionately being paid to workers at the bottom end of the earnings distribution with a declining importance of wage-setting institutions for low-wage workers. In addition, they did not find the changing sectoral earnings inequality in low-wage and highly unionized industries that would be consistent with hypotheses about the impact of changing unionization and real minimum wages.

Finally, sorting of workers based on the 'human capital' measures over time tended to increase the dispersion of industry earnings distributions between 1992 and 2003. This is consistent with the idea that the driving force of economic change is the entry and exit of firms, and can be linked to the selection of new technologies, and the associated workforce, by new firms.

Their findings suggest that even when earnings distributions seem superficially not to change, or to shift in opposite directions, the extensive amounts of worker and firm reallocation that have been documented in the literature do have large effects on different parts of the earnings distribution. In particular, the entry and exit of firms and sorting of workers and firms based on underlying worker 'skills' are important determinants of changes in industry earnings distributions over time.

# 5. Conclusions and Further Research

This necessarily brief survey has provided ample evidence of the way in which employers influence the level of earnings, and hence the earnings distribution. There is overwhelming evidence that firms in many countries pay observationally equivalent workers different wages. Firms also have different wage-setting practices, particularly at the top end of the distribution. The allocation of workers to firms is also non-random, and can potentially have a substantial effect if the way in which workers are matched to different types of firms is non-random: high-wage workers tend to be matched with high-wage firms, low-wage workers with low-wage firms, and changes in that allocation can change the earnings distributions over time.[14] The link between these changes in earnings dispersion and income inequality has been less well studied,[15] and is certainly an area for future research.

As always, much more needs to be done. Probably the most important is securing new and better data, as well as better data access. Most of the results presented in this chapter have been uncovered because of the new availability of matched employer–employee data. But the data have substantial deficiencies from an academic point of view since they were gathered from administrative records. Without academic investment in data on organizations, the situation is unlikely to change. Getting new information on representative federal surveys can take up to a decade. Capturing high quality information about key measures, like technology and personnel practices, is difficult because of both respondent burden and problems with identifying the right respondent. In addition, data collected by federal statistical agencies are often not well suited to the task, since they are collected for very different purposes, such as producing income and product accounts or unemployment and employment statistics. The profession needs more and better studies of businesses, including better, direct, and more comprehensive measures of technology and skill at the firm level informed by high-quality case study evidence and firm-specific studies.

When these data become available, a broad range of cross-country studies, along the lines of the PIEP[16], could usefully be mounted to further understand the impact of wage-setting policies within and between firms on earnings inequality. The better the understanding of the interaction of firms and workers, the greater the likelihood of understanding changes in the earnings distribution. Better theoretical and empirical understanding should, in turn, lead to better informed public policy.

## REFERENCES

ABOWD, JOHN. 2002. 'Unlocking the Information in Integrated Social Data'. *New Zealand Economic Papers*, 36(1): 9–31.

——HALTIWANGER, JOHN, and LANE, JULIA. 2004. 'Integrated Longitudinal Employee–Employer Data for the United States'. *American Economic Review*, 94: 224–9.

[14]  See Brown *et al.* (2006).
[15]  See Burgess *et al.* (forthcoming) and Andersson, Davis *et al.* (2007) for examples of such links.
[16]  Pay Inequalities and Economic Performance, <http://cep.lse.ac.uk/piep/>.

Abowd, John, Haltiwanger, John, Lane, Julia, McKinney, Kevin, and Sandusky, Kristin. 2007. 'Technology and the Demand for Skill: An Analysis of within and between Firm Differences'. NBER Working Paper 13043.

——and Kramarz, Francis. 1999. 'The Analysis of Labor Markets Using Matched Employer–Employee Data', in O. Ashenfelter and D. Card (eds.), *Handbook of Labor Economics*, vol. 3B. Amsterdam: North Holland, 2629–710.

————and Margolis, David. 1999. 'High Wage Workers and High Wage Firms'. *Econometrica*, 67(2): 251–334.

————and Roux, Sebastian. 2006. 'Wages, Mobility and Firm Performance: Advantages and Insights from Using Matched Worker–Firm Data'. *Economic Journal*, 116: F245–F285.

——Lengerman, Paul, and McKinney, Kevin. 2003. 'The Measurement of Human Capital in the United States'. LEHD Technical Paper 2002-09 (updated Mar. 2003).

Acemoglu, Daron. 1997. 'Matching, Heterogeneity and the Evolution of Income Distribution'. *Journal of Economic Growth*, 2(1): 61–92.

——2002. 'Technical Change, Inequality, and the Labor Market'. *Journal of Economic Literature*, 40: 7–72.

Andersson, Fredrik, Davis, Elizabeth, Lane, Julia I., McCall, Brian, and Sandusky, Kristin. 2007. 'Decomposing the Sources of Earnings Inequality: An Industry Approach'. Available at <SSRN: http://ssrn.com/abstract=905006>.

——Freedman, Matthew, Haltiwanger, John, Lane, Julia I., and Shaw, Kathryn. forthcoming. 'Reaching for the Stars: Who Pays for Talent in Innovative Industries?' Economic Journal.

Atkinson, Anthony, and Brandolini, Andrea. 2006. 'From Earnings Dispersion to Income Inequality', in Francesco Farina and Ernesto Savaglio (eds.), *Inequality and Economic Integration*. London and New York: Routledge.

Autor, David, Katz, Lawrence, and Kearney, Melissa. 2008. 'Trends in US Wage Inequality: Reassessing the Revisionists'. *Review of Economics and Statistics*, 90(2): 300–23.

————and Krueger, Alan. 1998. 'Computing Inequality: Have Computers Changed the Labor Market?' *Quarterly Journal of Economics*, 113: 1169–214.

Baker, George, Gibbs, Michael, and Holmstrom, Bengt. 1994. 'The Internal Economics of the Firm: Evidence from Personnel Data'. *Quarterly Journal of Economics*, 109: 881–919.

Bandiera, Oriana, Barankay, Iwan, and Rasul, Imran. 2007. 'Incentives for Managers and Inequality among Workers: Evidence from a Firm-Level Experiment'. *Quarterly Journal of Economics*, 122(2): 729–73.

Bartel, Ann, Ichniowski, Casey, and Shaw, Kathryn. 2004. 'Using "Insider Econometrics" to Study Productivity'. *American Economic Review*, 94: 217–23.

Bartelsman, Eric J., Becker, Randy A., and Gray, Wayne B. 2000. http://www.nber.org/nberces/ NBER-CES Manufacturing Industry Database.

Bender, Stefan, Lane, Julia, Shaw, Kathryn, Andersson, Fredrik, and Von Wachter, Till (eds.) 2008. *The Analysis of Firms and Employees: Quantitative and Qualitative Approaches*. Chicago: University of Chicago Press.

Berman, Eli, Bound, John, and Griliches, Zvi. 1994. 'Changes in the Demand for Skilled Labor within U.S. Manufacturing Industries: Evidence from the Annual Survey of Manufacturing'. *Quarterly Journal of Economics*, 109: 367–98.

Blau, Francine. 1977. *Equal Pay in the Office*. Lexington, Mass. and Toronto: Lexington Books.

BRESNAHAN, TIMOTHY, BRYNJOLFSSON, ERIK, and HITT, LORIN M.. 2002. 'Information Technology, Workplace Organization, and the Demand for Skilled Labor: Firm-Level Evidence'. *Quarterly Journal of Economics*, 117(1): 339–76.

BROWN, CLAIR, HALTIWANGER, JOHN, and LANE, JULIA I. 2006. *Economic Turbulence: Is Volatility Good for America?* Chicago: University of Chicago Press.

BURGESS, SIMON, LANE, JULIA I., and MCKINNEY, KEVIN. forthcoming. 'Jobs, Workers and Changes in Earnings Dispersion'. *Oxford Bulletin of Economics and Statistics*.

———— and STEVENS, DAVID. 2000. 'Job Flows, Worker Flows, and Churning'. *Journal of Labor Economics*, 18: 473–502

CASELLI, FRANCESCO. 1999. 'Technological Revolutions'. *American Economic Review*, 89: 78–102.

DAVIS, STEVEN J., and HALTIWANGER, JOHN. 1991. 'Wage Dispersion within and between Manufacturing Plants'. *Brookings Papers on Economic Activity: Microeconomics*, 115–80.

DUNLOP, JOHN. 1957. 'The Task of Contemporary Wage Theory', in G. W. Taylor and and F. C. Pierson (eds.), *New Concepts in Wage Determination*. New York: McGraw-Hill.

DUNNE, TIMOTHY, HALTIWANGER, JOHN, and TROSKE, KENNETH R. 1997. 'Technology and Jobs: Secular Changes and Cyclical Dynamics'. Carnegie-Rochester Conference Series on Public Policy, Elsevier, vol. 46, pages 107–78

DUNNE, TIMOTHY. 2001. 'Issues in the Establishment and Management of Secure Research Sites', in P. Doyle, J. Lane, J. Theeuwes, and L. Zayatz (eds.), *Confidentiality, Disclosure and Data Access: Theory and Practical Applications for Statistical Agencies*. Amsterdam: North-Holland.

DUPUY, ARNAUD, and DEGRIP, ANDRIES. 2002. 'Do Large Firms Have More Opportunities to Substitute between Skill Categories than Small Firms?' CLS Working Paper. Aarhus, Denmark.

FAGGIO, GIULIA, SALVANES, KJELL G., and VAN REENEN, JOHN. 2007. 'The Evolution of Inequality in Wages and Productivity: International Panel Data Evidence'. National Bureau of Economic Research Working Paper 13351.

GARICANO, LUIS, and ROSS-HANSBERG, ESTEBAN. 2006. 'Inequality and the Organization of Knowledge'. *Quarterly Journal of Economics*, 121(4): 1383–435.

GIBBONS, ROBERT, and KATZ, LAWRENCE F. 1991. 'Layoffs and Lemons'. *Journal of Labor Economics*, 9(4): 351–80.

—— and WALDMAN, MICHAEL. 1999. 'A Theory of Wage and Promotion Dynamics inside Firms'. *The Quarterly Journal of Economics*, 114(4): 1321–58.

———— 2006. 'Enriching a Theory of Wage and Promotion Dynamics inside Firms'. *Journal of Labor Economics*, 24(1): 59–107.

GOLAN, AMOS, LANE, JULIA, and MCENTARFER, ERIKA. 2007. 'The Dynamics of Worker Reallocation within and across Industries'. *Economica*, 74(293): 1–20.

GOTTSCHALK, PETER, and SMEEDING, TIMOTHY M. 1997. 'Cross-National Comparisons of Earnings and Income Inequality'. *Journal of Economic Literature*, 35(2): 633–87.

GROSHEN, ERICA. 1991. 'Sources of Intra-Industry Wage Dispersion: How Much Do Employers Matter?' *Quarterly Journal of Economics*, 106(3): 869–84.

GUADALUPE, MARIA. 2005. 'Product Market Competition, Returns to Skill and Wage Inequality'. IZA Discussion Papers 1556.

GUERTZGEN, NICOLE. 2006. 'Rent-Sharing and Collective Bargaining Coverage: Evidence from Linked Employer–Employee Data'. Paper presented at Conference on the Analysis of Firms and Employees: Qualitative and Quantitative Approaches. Nuremberg, Germany.

HALTIWANGER, JOHN C., LANE, JULIA I., and SPLETZER, JAMES R. 1999. 'Productivity Differences across Employers: The Roles of Employer Size, Age, and Human Capital'. *The American Economic Review*, 89(2): 94–8.

—— —— —— 2007. 'Wage, Productivity and the Dynamic Interaction of Businesses and Workers'. *Labour Economics*, 14(3): 575–602.

HELLERSTEIN, JUDITH, and NEUMARK, DAVID. 2008. 'Workplace Segregation in the United States: Race, Ethnicity, and Skill'. *Review of Economics and Statistics*.

—— —— and MCIRNENY, MELISSA. 2008. 'Changes in Workplace Segregation in the United States between 1990 and 2000: Evidence from Matched Employer–Employee Data', in Bender *et al.* (2008).

—— —— and TROSKE, KENNETH R. 1999. 'Wages, Productivity, and Worker Characteristics: Evidence from Plant-Level Production Functions and Wage Equations'. *Journal of Labor Economics*, 17: 409–46.

HIPOLITO, SIMON. 2008. '*International Differences in Wage Inequality: A New Glance with European Matched Employer–Employee Data*'. MPRA Paper 7932. University Library of Munich, Germany.

HIRSCH, BARRY, and SCHUMACHER, EDWARD. 2004. 'Match Bias in Wage Gap Estimates Due to Earnings Imputation'. *Journal of Labor Economics*, 22: 689–722.

HYSLOP, DEAN, and MARE, DAVID. 2006. 'Worker–Firm Heterogeneity and Matching: An Analysis using Worker and Firm Fixed Effects Estimated from LEED'. Statistics New Zealand.

ICHNIOWSKI, CASEY, SHAW, KATHRYN, and PRENNUSHI, GIOVANNA. 1997. 'The Effects of Human Resource Management Practices on Productivity: A Study of Steel Finishing Lines'. *American Economic Review*, 87: 291–313.

KATZ, LAWRENCE F., and MURPHY, KEVIN M. 1992. 'Changes in Relative Wages, 1963–1987: Supply and Demand Factors'. *The Quarterly Journal of Economics*, 107(1): 43.

KLUMP, RAINER, and DE LA GRANDVILLE, OLIVIER. 2000. 'Economic Growth and the Elasticity of Substitution: Two Theorems and Some Suggestions'. *The American Economic Review*, 90(1): 282–91.

KREMER, MICHAEL. 1993. 'The O-Ring Theory of Economic Development'. *Quarterly Journal of Economics*, 108: 551–75.

—— and MASKIN, ERIC S. 1996 'Wage Inequality and Segregation by Skill'. NBER Working Paper no. W5718.

LANE, JULIA, SALMON, LAURIE, and SPLETZER, JAMES. 2007. 'Establishment Wage Differentials'. *Monthly Labor Review*, 90(5): 130(4): 3–17.

LAZEAR, EDWARD. 1992. 'Performance Pay and Productivity'. *American Economic Review*, 90(5): 1346–61.

—— and ROSEN, SHERWIN. 1981. 'Rank-Order Tournaments as Optimum Labor Contracts'. *The Journal of Political Economy*, 89(5): 841–64.

—— and SHAW, KATHRYN. 2008. *Wage Structure, Raises and Mobility: International Comparisons of the Structure of Wages within and across Firms*. Chicago: University of Chicago Press.

MACHIN, STEPHEN, and VAN REENEN, JOHN. 2007. 'Changes in Wage Inequality'. London: Center for Economic Performance.

MENEZES-FILHO, NAERCIO, MUENDLER, MARC-ANDREAS, and RAMEY, GAREY. 2006. 'The Structure of Worker Compensation in Brazil, with a Comparison to France and the United States'. CESifo Working Paper Series no. 1643.

MILGROM, PAUL, and ROBERTS, JOHN. 1992. *Economics, Organisation and Management.* Englewood Cliffs, NJ: Prentice Hall.

MORTENSEN, DALE. 2005. *Wage Dispersion: Why are Similar Workers Paid Differently?* Cambridge, Mass.: MIT Press.

MUENDLER, MARC. 2008. 'Trade and Workforce Changeover in Brazil', in Bender *et al.* (2008).

NORDSTRÖM-SKANS, OSKAR, EDIN, PER-ANDERS, and HOLMLUND, BERTIL. 2008. 'Wage Dispersion between and within Plants: Sweden 1985–2000', in Lazear and Shaw (2008).

POSTEL-VINAY, FABIEN, and ROBIN, JEAN-MARC. 2002. 'Equilibrium Wage Dispersion with Worker and Employer Heterogeneity'. *Econometrica*, 70(6): 2295–350.

ROEMER, MARC. 2000. 'Assessing the Quality of the March Current Population Survey and the Survey of Income and Program Participation Income Estimates, 1990–1996'. US Census Bureau.

SMEETS, VALÉRIE, and WARZYNSKI, FREDERIC. Forthcoming. 'Too Many Theories, Too Few Facts? What the Data Tell us About the Link Between Span of Control, Compensation and Career Dynamics'. *Labour Economics.*

SNOWER, DENNIS. 1998. 'Income Inequality: Issues and Policy Options'. A Symposium Sponsored by the Federal Reserve Bank of Kansas City; <http://www.kc.frb.org/PUBLICAT/SYMPOS/1998/sym98prg.htm>.

VILHUBER, LARS. 2008. 'Adjusting Imperfect Data: Overview and Case Studies', in Lazear and Shaw (2008).

VON WACHTER, TILL, and BENDER, STEFAN. 2006. 'In the Right Place at the Wrong Time: The Role of Firms and Luck in Young Workers' Careers'. *American Economic Review*, 96(5): 1679–705.

WOODCOCK, SIMON. Forthcoming. 'Wage Differentials in the Presence of Unobserved Worker, Firm, and Match Heterogeneity'. *Labour Economics.*

WOZNIAK, ABIGAIL. 2006. 'Product Markets and Paychecks: Deregulation's Effect on the Compensation Structure in Banking'. IZA Discussion Paper 1957.

CHAPTER 10

# INEQUALITY AND THE LABOR MARKET: UNIONS

## JELLE VISSER

## DANIELE CHECCHI

## 1. INTRODUCTION

THROUGHOUT their existence, trade unions have been an important force tempering inequality. 'Equal pay for equal work' has a strong resonance in unions across the world. In their overviews, Elster (1989) and Hyman and Brough (1975) present thick descriptions of norms of fairness and equality that guide union wage policies. 'A fair day's wages for a fair day's work' was in 1881 cited in the *Manchester Times* by Friedrich Engels as 'the old, time-honored watchword' of British unions. This norm dictated equal hourly pay for like jobs, regardless of the characteristics of the worker. Relativities have played a large role in union wage policy and lay at the root of many conflicts. However, large unions and federations, encompassing different sectors, occupations, and categories of workers, tend to 'expand parochial, myopic bases of comparison that inform workers' perception of injustice' (Svensen, 1989: 24; Olson, 1982).

A large share of wage variation cannot be explained by worker attributes like education, experience, or ability. Much of this residual variation occurs *between* rather than *within* firms and is correlated with the firm's ability to pay (Teulings and Hartog, 1998). From the position of an individual worker and assuming imperfect information, it may be a matter of luck where one ends up. Exchange of information about pay and conditions is one of the oldest union activities, but often 'they have gone beyond this to agitate for equalization of pay' (Clegg, 1970: 265). According to Sydney and Beatrice Webb, 'among trade union regulations there is one which stands out as practically universal, namely, the insistence on payment according to some standard, uniform in application' (Webb and Webb, 1920 [1987]: 279). Wages are usually not exactly related to all observable characteristics of workers, especially not under collective bargaining, which typically provides for wages 'determined by some procedure for a reference worker or a reference job' (Pencavel, 1991: 24). By setting standard rates across firms, unions provide a form of insurance (Agell, 1999). Tying pay to job descriptions or seniority rather than performance diminishes the possibilities for managerial favoritism and discrimination; extending standard rates across firms in the industry helps to suspend competition between workers. Together, these principles are at the root of unionism, allowing workers to act in solidarity (Streeck, 2005).

In Section 2 we will first review the literature regarding the union effect on wages and wage inequality. Examining the differential between union and non-union wages is typically a first step in studies of the union effect on wage dispersion (Freeman, 1980; Card *et al.*, 2003) and is often taken as a measure of union power to influence wages. Alison Booth (1995: 157) observes that the union wage gap has generated 'an enormous body of empirical research', with most studies relating to the USA, the UK, and Canada; she adds, 'there has been surprisingly little research into the impact of unions on wage dispersion and wage inequality' (p. 179).

We shall consider in Section 3 the separate contributions of union power, membership composition, bargaining coordination, and wage policy. It is the combination that determines the impact on inequality. It matters greatly whether union members start from a position of advantage or disadvantage and whether union contracts extend 'beyond the walls of membership' (Visser, 1990). Where the union differential comes from is also relevant. Section 4 introduces the distinction between membership and coverage, while the following two sections discuss the impact of union power on earnings inequality when coverage is either exclusive or inclusive. We do not assume that markets perform to perfection before trade unions arrive on the scene. To the contrary, an argument can be made that, given labor market uncertainty and the absence of a full set of insurance markets, institutions like trade unions make these markets sustainable by providing stability and insurance (Agell, 1999; Streeck, 2005). Other aspects of inequality, like access to jobs, overtime, working hours, pensions, or health plans, as well as leave rights, have received much less attention in the empirical literature and will also receive much less attention here.

In the final part of this chapter we discuss the rationale for unions aiming for wage compression (Section 7) and we engage in an estimation of how the presence of trade unions has influenced the extent and dynamics of earnings inequality across advanced economies during the 1980s and 1990s (Section 8). For this purpose we have developed indicators for trends in equality and union presence from different sources. Section 9 concludes.

# 2. WHAT DO UNIONS DO?

In answer to that question Richard Freeman and James Medoff conclude that despite the small size of the union sector, the unions' net effect on the whole US labor market has been an equalizing one. They attribute this to the equalizing effect of union wage policies *within* the union sector, which offsets any disequalizing effect of unions causing wage differentials *between* the union and non-union sector (Freeman and Medoff, 1984: 78–9). With that conclusion, the authors went against the orthodox view that unions increase inequality. In his landmark study of relative union wage effects, Lewis (1963) had found that mean union wage *differentials* correlated with sectoral wage *levels*. This led him to conclude that US unions increased the inequality of average wages across sectors by 2 to 3 percentage points. US union membership in the 1950s was probably concentrated among workers in the upper half of the earnings distribution (Rees, 1962). Noting that unions of skilled workers tend to be most successful in raising the wages of their members, Milton Friedman (1956) concluded that this must have an employment-reducing effect and increase competition for less-skilled jobs, hence increasing the inequality between skilled and unskilled workers. He generalized this to the view that in addition to distorting job allocation, '(unions) have also made the incomes of the working class more unequal by reducing the opportunities available to the most disadvantaged workers' (Friedman, 1962: 127).

Against the orthodox view there were studies of industrial relations scholars and institutional economics showing that union-negotiated pay scales tended to compress wages (Reynolds and Taft, 1956). Turner (1952) found that in wartime and post-war Britain the craft unions, representing the elite of skilled workers, had supported wage-leveling policies in an attempt to expand downwards and recruit semi-skilled workers. Skilled workers may support such leveling policies not just for solidaristic reasons, but because it lowers the incentive for employers to replace them with cheaper hands. Maybe reflecting a change in membership composition, studies of US labor markets in the 1960s documented with micro-data that in unionized firms and sectors the unskilled–skilled (Rosen, 1970) and black–white pay gap (Ashenfelter, 1972) was narrower. Metcalf *et al.* (2001) report that UK unions narrow the pay differentials between women and men, blacks and whites, manual and non-manual workers, and people with and without health problems.

Freeman (1980) was the first to introduce a dual model, distinguishing between the effect of union wage policies *within* the union sector and the effect on the differences *between* the union and non-union sector. This dual approach was crucial for disentangling the effects of unions on earnings inequality in the USA and other economies where unions negotiate only or mainly for a minority of union members. However, this approach is less fruitful in countries (like the European ones) where union-negotiated contracts cover most or all workers and union-covered firms or workers cannot be neatly distinguished from non-union firms or workers. Ceteris paribus, under such high coverage conditions the equalizing effect of union policies will be greater, as they do not need to offset the disequalizing effect of a distinction between the union and non-union sector.

# 3. WHOM DO UNIONS REPRESENT AND HOW DOES IT AFFECT INEQUALITY?

Historically, workers with the highest skills and best able to communicate with one another were the first to organize and best positioned to obtain wage gains and benefits (Katznelson and Zollberg, 1986). In the craft unions of 19th century Britain, membership boundaries coincided by and large with the 'aristocracy of labor' of skilled workers with regular earnings, prospects of social security, and advancement for their children. They owed that to Britain's imperial rule over world markets, the ability to restrict entry and defend the differential in wages, social status, and security against less skilled workers (Hobsbawm, 1964). In their history, '(unions) have ranged from exclusionary to ambivalent in their attitude to women' (Cook *et al.*, 1984: 12). African-American, Latino, and Asian workers have formally and informally been denied representation in US craft unions until the 1960s and the failure to organize the South is partly a self-inflicted wound on US unions until the present day (Goldfield, 1987) Many trade unions in Western Europe failed to organize and recognize the interests of various 'guest worker' groups who came from Southern Europe and North Africa (Penninx and Roosblad, 2000). In many developing countries, unions limit themselves to the state sector and disregard the interests of large majorities working in the informal sector (ILO, 1997; Visser, 2003).

Exclusion from the union contributes directly to inequality when insurance, protection, and collective worker rights are tied to union membership. For instance, if insurance against unemployment is conditional upon union membership under the so-called Ghent system (Rothstein, 1992), unskilled workers and those with unstable work histories tend to be excluded and denied protection. There are today only a few Ghent systems left (in Sweden, Finland, Denmark, Iceland, partly in Belgium) and in each case, as in most advanced market economies, there is also mandatory unemployment insurance and the link between union membership and insurance has been attenuated or severed (Ebbinghaus and Visser, 2000). In the USA access to health insurance plans and pension schemes tends to be associated with union membership, though the magnitude of union effects appears to have declined over time together with the decline of unions (Buchmueller *et al.*, 2005). In Europe, health insurance is usually provided under a mandatory scheme and coverage of occupational pensions is often extended beyond an already high coverage rate to include non-organized firms. In the USA union members tend to experience less fluctuating working hours (Buchmueller *et al.*, 2005); in Europe workers in highly unionized sectors tend to work shorter hours (Eiro, 2007).

When rights are optional—for instance the right to re-arrange or reduce working hours or take additional leave under the Fairness at Work legislation in Britain since 1998—union presence in the workplace tends to increase the awareness and use of these rights, and improve employer compliance (Dickens and Hall, 2005). Brown *et al.* (2000: 627) find that unions act as 'custodians of individual rights' and report that in the UK union density rates at company level correlate with the provision of written details in contracts. National and sectoral agreements can extend the union rule beyond organized firms. Elected works councils can extend the union rule beyond a unionized minority *within* firms, thus guaranteeing more equal access to rights, as a functional equivalent to the closed shop—though taking away direct incentives to join (Olson, 1965).

Table 10.1 provides some recent data on the composition of trade unions for a selection of countries. The first thing to note is that in Northern Europe and in the Anglo-American world the female–male gap in unionization has disappeared. Second, while more retired workers retain membership and unions are ageing, there are ever fewer young people in unions. Density rates among the young have fallen to historically low levels. Median voter models would predict union wage and pension policies favoring the generation that is preparing for retirement in the next 10 to 20 years to the disadvantage of the young. Unions are also heavily concentrated in the public sector, with density rates that are often twice or more those in the private sector. Data from the European Social Survey (ESS)[1] show that unionization in

---

[1]  Wave of 2002–3, R. Jowell and Central Coordinating Team (2003), *European Social Survey 2002/2003*. Technical Report. London: Centre for Comparative Social Surveys, City University, <http://www.europeansocialsurvey.org>.

## Table 10.1. Density and union presence

| Country | United States | | Canada | | Australia | | United Kingdom | | Ireland | | Netherlands | | Sweden | |
|---|---|---|---|---|---|---|---|---|---|---|---|---|---|---|
| Year | 1985 | 2004 | 1992 | 2004 | 1985 | 2004 | 1985 | 2004 | 1988 | 2004 | 1987 | 2004 | 1994 | 2004 |
| **ISSP data** | | | | | | | | | | | | | | |
| Density rate | 19.6 | 7.8 | 32.1 | 35.6 | 50.8 | 30.1 | 47.6 | 27.4 | 43.2 | 38.2 | 30.8 | 31 | 87.4 | 79.1 |
| Men | 23.2 | 8.4 | 30.3 | 32.3 | 53.2 | 28.4 | 52.8 | 28.9 | 44.2 | 39 | 34.6 | 33.3 | 83.6 | 80.5 |
| Women | 13.1 | 7.2 | 33.9 | 39.7 | 46.9 | 31.8 | 41.4 | 26 | 42 | 37.4 | 23.8 | 27.5 | 90.7 | 77.8 |
| Age < 30 | 15.7 | 5.1 | 18.6 | 25 | 47.9 | 20.4 | 42.6 | 20.5 | 35.8 | 31.5 | 22.4 | 19.6 | 76.7 | 57.6 |
| Age 31–50 | 20.2 | 8.7 | 38.6 | 37.9 | 54.9 | 32.6 | 47.7 | 28.9 | 47.7 | 40.7 | 33.6 | 30.5 | 91.3 | 81.4 |
| Age 51–65 | 23.1 | 8.7 | 46.8 | 33.9 | 44 | 31.4 | 55.4 | 29.3 | 56.8 | 42.4 | 41.2 | 40.4 | 87.6 | 89.2 |
| Full-time | 20.1 | 8.7 | 34.7 | 35.1 | 51.7 | 31.6 | 51.4 | 28.8 | 46.6 | 43.2 | 34.1 | 32.9 | 85.4 | 80.7 |
| Part-time | 16.7 | 3.1 | 22.3 | 38.6 | 47.9 | 26.2 | 38.3 | 22.6 | 17.1 | 23.3 | 20.3 | 26.3 | 93 | 72.7 |
| Private sector | 17.8 | 5.3 | 11.8 | 19.1 | 34.2 | 20.4 | 30.2 | 18 | 30.5 | 23.7 | 26.1 | 23.4 | 78.3 | 69.6 |
| Public sector | 26.3 | 17.9 | 54.6 | 52.4 | 74.5 | 55 | 78.7 | 49.2 | 65.1 | 66 | 40 | 43.4 | 95.4 | 89.6 |
| Secondary education | 24 | 9.4 | 34.1 | 41.3 | 52 | 26.6 | 48.1 | 29.9 | 38.3 | 38.9 | 25.9 | n.a. | 82.4 | 69.2 |
| College degree | 8.1 | 9.7 | 32.9 | 31.9 | 60 | 35.6 | 47.1 | 32.1 | 59.6 | 41.5 | 38.3 | 22.5 | 83 | 78.4 |
| **ICTWSS data** | | | | | | | | | | | | | | |
| Density rates | 18.0 | 12.5 | 35.6 | 29.9 | 46.3 | 22.7 | 46.2 | 28.8 | 56.1 | 38.1 | 24.7 | 22.4 | 87.4 | 78.0 |
| Coverage | 21 | 14 | 37 | 36 | 85 | 80 | 65 | 35 | n.a. | n.a. | 78.85 | 84 | 89 | 92 |
| Barg. coordination | 1 | 1 | 1 | 1 | 4 | 2 | 1 | 1 | 4 | 5 | 4 | 4 | 3 | 3 |
| Union centralization | 0.26 | 0.29 | 0.35 | 0.44 | 0.52 | 0.29 | 0.29 | 0.29 | 0.39 | 0.50 | 0.60 | 0.67 | 0.50 | 0.52 |

| Country | Denmark | | France | | Spain | | Italy | | Germany | | Poland | |
|---|---|---|---|---|---|---|---|---|---|---|---|---|
| Year | 1997 | 2004 | 1996 | 2004 | 1996 | 2004 | 1985 | 1998 | 1985 | 2004 | 1991 | 2004 |
| **ISSP data** | | | | | | | | | | | | |
| Density rate | 87.9 | 85.9 | 20.1 | 17.7 | 16 | 20.2 | 48.4 | 36.2 | 35.2 | 19.3 | 32.8 | 18.2 |
| Men | 87.3 | 82.2 | 21.1 | 19.4 | 16.6 | 21.9 | 51.7 | 36.1 | 42.4 | 22.4 | 34.7 | 13.9 |
| Women | 88.4 | 89.5 | 18.6 | 15.7 | 14.8 | 17.9 | 41.3 | 36.4 | 23.3 | 15.2 | 30.4 | 23.3 |
| Age < 30 | 77.6 | 72.6 | 9.6 | 6.9 | 9.6 | 14.7 | 40.4 | 23.3 | 28.5 | 10.2 | 24.5 | 6.9 |
| Age 31–50 | 91.8 | 87.1 | 21.7 | 18 | 20.6 | 23.4 | 52.7 | 39.7 | 34.7 | 20 | 34.4 | 21.2 |
| Age 51–65 | 89.9 | 90.3 | 37.8 | 26.6 | 15 | 21.5 | 55.3 | 47.6 | 46.6 | 26.1 | 41.7 | 25 |
| Full-time | 89.8 | 87.4 | 20.7 | 18.3 | 16 | 21 | n.a. | 38.6 | 38.3 | 20.4 | 34.1 | 19.3 |
| Part-time | 79.6 | 75.3 | 16.5 | 14.3 | 0 | 15.9 | n.a. | 22.2 | 17.2 | 12.8 | 12 | 9.1 |
| Private sector | 83.9 | 80.4 | 10.5 | 12.8 | 11.9 | 17 | n.a. | 28.3 | 30.3 | 16.3 | 13.2 | 9.6 |
| Public sector | 91.9 | 92.7 | 34.9 | 24.8 | 26 | 34.2 | n.a. | 48 | 46.5 | 27.3 | 36.5 | 26.8 |
| Secondary education | 82.7 | 85.2 | 18.8 | 12.7 | 12.4 | 22.3 | 44.3 | 35.1 | 33.3 | 5.4 | 38.5 | 15.7 |
| College degree | 90.4 | 78.8 | 13.8 | 17 | 12.7 | 16.5 | 57.4 | 26.8 | 21 | 18.5 | 30.2 | 20.6 |
| **ICTWSS data** | | | | | | | | | | | | |
| Density rates | 75.6 | 71.7 | 8.3 | 8.4 | 16.1 | 16.0 | 42.5 | 34.0 | 34.7 | 22.1 | n.a. | 14.1 |
| Coverage | 73 | 80 | 81 | 82 | 79 | 82 | 85 | 82 | 75 | 63 | n.a. | n.a. |
| Barg. coordination | 3 | 3 | 2 | 2 | 3 | 4 | 2 | 4 | 4 | 4 | 2 | 2 |
| Union centralization | 0.47 | 0.46 | 0.24 | 0.22 | 0.35 | 0.40 | 0.33 | 0.37 | 0.38 | 0.44 | n.a. | 0.23 |

*Source*: Density rates computed from ISSP (various surveys)—union presence measures from ICTWSS database.

manufacturing, the historical birthplace and stronghold of union and strike action, is often no higher than in the economy at large. The new stronghold is in the collective sector and in the professions. According to the ESS, managerial and professional employees rival skilled manual workers in unionization levels. Union membership tends to rise with higher level of vocational, not general education. Data on tenure, working hours, and contract status, available for a few countries only, show that unions are relatively underrepresented among those with low tenure, temporary contracts, and part-time hours. Finally, union density increases almost everywhere with firm size.

The overrepresentation of union membership among older workers with long tenure in larger firms is the characteristic most clearly associated with the theory that by using their 'insider power' trade unions retard job growth and make the burden of unemployment fall disproportionately on the less privileged 'outsiders' by prolonging its duration (Lindbeck and Snower, 1988). Unions, in other words, may be a cause of inequality and, hence, a public policy case might exist to reduce union power, for instance by lowering employment protection or placing restrictions on strikes and picketing.

More recently, Nickell *et al.* (2005) have studied the determinants of the unemployment rate for 20 countries over the period 1961–92, including a list of exogenous shocks. They find a positive and significant correlation of the unemployment rate with replacement rates and the rate of change in union density. Bertola *et al.* (2002) have challenged this view and show the existence of *institutional* variations in the trade-off between employment and real wage. In their view unions contain earnings dispersion in continental Europe, but not in Anglo-American countries, at the expense of increased unemployment, especially among the young and among women. However, Bassanini and Duval (2006) did not find any statistically significant *general* association between unemployment and union density in a sample of 21 OECD countries over the period 1982–2003. By contrast, highly centralized and/or coordinated wage bargaining systems are estimated to reduce unemployment. They interpret their finding as supportive of the view that, in centralized/coordinated bargaining systems, unions and employers are able to internalize the adverse employment consequences of their wage claims (Calmfors and Driffill, 1988; Soskice, 1990). In general this type of research is inconclusive and correlations are highly dependent on the countries included and indicators used in the analysis (Flanagan, 1999).

The data in Table 10.1 show huge cross-national variations not only in union density, but also in bargaining coverage, coordination across bargaining units, and union centralization. At this point, the great divide between continental Western Europe and the Anglo-American world emerges. While in Western Europe only a minority of workers—including a large group of higher earning professionals—is *not* covered by collective bargaining, in the USA, Canada, and the UK only a minority, and a decreasing one, is covered by union-negotiated agreements. In the first, *inclusive* group, coverage exceeds membership by a large margin. In the second, *exclusive* group, membership and coverage are nearly the same thing and affect only a minority of employees. The exclusive model also applies to large parts of Eastern Europe, Japan, South Korea, and other East-Asian countries with enterprise unions and company bargaining (Visser, 2003). This difference between inclusive and exclusive bargaining models has implications for how to estimate and interpret the union wage differential.

# 4. UNION POWER, COVERAGE, AND THE UNION WAGE GAP

There are a number of ways in which a union wage premium or differential can emerge. We have already discussed, in connection with the practice of craft workers, the possibility of a union-induced wage hike in combination with limits on worker entry in the union sector and job cuts that increase unemployment and lower wages in the non-union sector. Unions tend to limit or retard downward wage flexibility in business downturns relative to the non-union sector (Phelps Brown, 1962). Working in the other direction, non-union employers may raise wages in response to union organizing or strike threats in the non-organized sector (Rosen, 1969; Farber, 2003; Mosher, 2006). The union effect on wages may operate via worker voice and job tenure, altering the incentives of workers and employers to invest in training.

In empirical work, it is difficult to disentangle these mechanisms. To complicate matters, union status is not randomly assigned and may be endogenous with regard to wages. Union wage policies, in particular standardization of wages through pay scales, may be most attractive for workers with a low underlying earnings capacity. On the other hand, where such jobs are scarce, employers may be able to select more able workers (Abowd and Farber, 1982). Union wage differentials may also compensate for working conditions, for instance a lower degree of control over one's work in the large hierarchical firms where union membership is concentrated (Duncan and Stafford, 1980; Lockwood, 1958). Finally, in order to establish the effect of union status on an individual's wage, we must disentangle the effect of the level of unionization of the sector, occupation, or firm, and the effect of one's own union status (Booth, 1995: 162).

Aggregate data cannot offer these controls, but most analysis based on micro-data also fails to control for establishment effects and other unobserved variables (worker quality, for instance).[2] Estimations techniques, which allow union membership to be simultaneously determined with wages, address the endogeneity issue, but tend to produce unstable estimates. After considering many of these studies, Lewis (1986) concluded that ordinary least squares (OLS) yielded the least-biased estimators of union wage effects, probably with an upward bias. All but a handful of the empirical studies of the union wage differential deal with data from the USA, the UK, or Canada. The simple reason is that identification of the union wage differential in household data is only meaningful when union membership is roughly coterminous with bargaining coverage. If union agreements also cover non-union members, the differential of interest is not whether somebody is unionized, but whether she is covered by a collective contract. Survey data on bargaining coverage is rare and probably only reliable in the case of company contracts.

In spite of the many reservations regarding the *meaning* of a union wage differential in bargaining contexts other than the USA, Canada, and the UK, Blanchflower and Bryson (2003) have nonetheless estimated the differential in a large number of countries with International Social Survey Programme (ISSP) data. Their estimates confirm that outside the Anglo-American context, the union wage gap cannot be related to union power, as conventionally measured by union density or union centralization. In fact, the correlation between union density and the union wage differential for the 21 countries in Figure 10.1 is negative, albeit not significantly different from zero. There is, however, a significant and inverse relationship with union coverage. The larger the coverage rate, or the fraction of workers covered by one or more collective agreements, the lower the union wage differential.[3]

As indicated by the two circles drawn in Figure 10.1, it is possible to identify at least two groups of countries: one group of countries where coverage is high and exceeds half of the workers and another group with much lower coverage. That union wage differentials are not significantly different from zero in France, Germany, Italy, the Netherlands, Norway, and Sweden is, according to Blanchflower and Bryson (2003: 211), 'primarily due to the fact that unions are also able to control wage outcomes in the non-union sector', for instance via administrative extension of agreements and (in Eastern Europe) the application of the minimum wage. These differences also reflect union wage policy. With one of the highest coverage rates, Austrian unions are notoriously unconcerned about wage distribution as they have consistently prioritized the full employment goal as the best distributive union strategy (Guger, 1998). This shows in a relatively high differential as Austrian union members are concentrated in high wage industries. As a consequence of the broad coalitions needed for centralized wage policies, in Sweden and a number of

---

[2] The role of wage policies at firm level, in a demand–supply framework with matching frictions, is discussed in Chapter 9 of the present volume.

[3] Note that ISSP data control for education, age, age squared, sex, public or private employment, but not for sector or establishment.

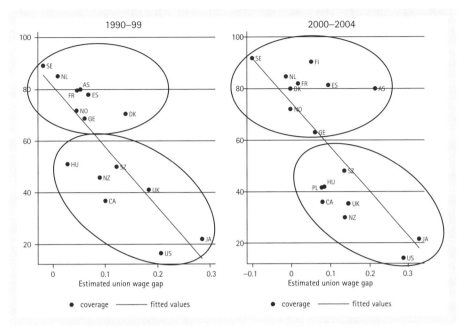

**Fig. 10.1. Union gap and coverage**

*Notes*: The wage gap is the estimated return on union member status, controlling for gender, age, education on ISSP dataset, averaged over the decades. Coverage rates from ICTWSS.
AS–Australia; AU–Austria; BE–Belgium; CA–Canada; CZ–Czech Rep; DK–Denmark; ES–Spain; FI–Finland; FR–France; GE–Germany; HU–Hungary; IE–Ireland; IT–Italy; JA–Japan; NL–Netherlands; NO–Norway; NZ–New Zealand; PL–Poland; PT–Portugal; SE–Sweden; SL–Slovenia; SK–Slovakia; SZ–Switzerland; UK–United Kingdom; US–United States.

other Northern countries, trade unions have consistently tried to compress wages (Iversen, 1999).

Probably as a sign of union weakening and contraction of the union sector, union wage premiums in the US and UK have decreased in recent times. Adjusting for different skill groups, Card *et al.* (2003) report a declining union wage differential for male workers in the US, Canada, and the UK between 1983 and 2001.

## 5. Union Power and Wage Dispersion when Union Coverage is Exclusive

Where there is a sharp distinction between the union and non-union sector of employment, there is evidence that the earnings structure is flatter in the union sector (Bell and Pit, 1998; Card, 2001; Card *et al.*, 2003; DiNardo *et al.*, 1996; Freeman, 1980; Gosling and Machin, 1995; Metcalf, 1982; Metcalf *et al.*, 2001). This compression of wages in the unions is explicitly attributed to union policies that seek to standardize wages within and across firms. Combined with the tendency to reduce the wage gap between blue- and white-collar workers, this offsets the disequalizing 'between' effect of the differential between union and non-union workers. In Britain, age–earnings profiles tend to be less steep among union members than among non-union members, but only for men. The same pattern does not hold for women, possibly because many of the higher-paid female jobs like teachers and nurses are in the highly unionized public sector. Most interesting is the evidence that in firms where unions are recognized and even in firms where they are present but not recognized, the incidence of low pay is lower. This conclusion relates to Britain in 1998, before the introduction of the statutory minimum wage.

The power of unions to contain wage dispersion has waned. Using the 1987–8 Current Population Survey, Freeman (1993) concluded that the decline in unionization accounted for about 20 percent of the increase in the standard deviation of male wages in the USA between 1978 and 1988. Gosling and Machin (1995) reach a similar conclusion for Britain, estimating that the fall in unionization during the 1980s accounted for some 15 percent of the increase in wage inequality among semi-skilled male workers. Metcalf *et al.* (2001: 69) claim that the equalizing effect of union presence after 1998 was only one-third compared to what it had been in an earlier and comparable study with data for 1978, when British unions registered their maximum post-war power (Metcalf, 1982).

Newer studies have introduced variation in union coverage or membership across subgroups (gender, skill level) and differences in union wage gaps for these different subgroups in Freeman's model. If union coverage is higher for less-skilled workers, or if the union wage impact is higher for these workers, the equalizing effect on wage dispersion will be larger. The conclusions remain broadly the same, though they show a different effect for men and women (Bell and Pitt, 1998; Gosling and Lemieux, 2001; DiNardo *et al.*, 1996; Machin, 1999). Membership decline among men was concentrated among average and above average earning workers in manufacturing, whereas membership retention rates were strongest among higher earning professionals and public sector employees. Consequently, both in the USA and in the UK, unions had, and have, a smaller equalizing effect on female earnings than on male earnings.

Controlling for about 25 age-education groups in the UK and Canada and 150 age-occupation-skill groups in the USA, Card *et al.* (2003) report that the mean union wage tends to be much higher for males in skill groups with low average wages, while the union mark-up for groups with high average wages (middle-aged college and university graduates) is small. Within each group, unions also have an equalizing effect on wages, as was reported by Freeman (1980), even after adjusting for the fact that union members tend to be more homogeneous in skill levels than their non-union counterparts. Together these effects imply that unions in all three countries flatten wage differentials across skill groups. However, this effect has decreased over time. Had the variation of male wages in the union sector remained at its 1970s level, overall inequality in male earnings in the USA would have been nearly one-third less in 2001 than it actually was. Effects of somewhat similar magnitude are found in the UK, whereas in Canada overall inequality would have declined had the union impact stayed the same as in 1983–4. Union effects on *female* wage inequality are slight in all three countries and within the overall pattern of rising wage inequality there is no clear trend of a larger or smaller union contribution.

# 6. Union Power and Wage Dispersion when Union Coverage is Inclusive

If nearly everybody is covered by union contracts or if the same mechanism for adjusting wage rates applies to all workers, we cannot infer the effect of unions or union-based institutions from a comparison of union and non-union wages. There are two alternative methods, of which the second is probably more effective (Freeman, 2005).

First, we can compare earnings distributions across countries with different levels of collective bargaining and union coverage. Such comparisons invariably show that countries with the highest coverage have the lowest wage dispersion—as argued before, union policies compressing wages do not have to compensate for the inequality-increasing effect of the union wage differential. Other measures, reinforcing this association, relate to union structure (unions encompassing low and high earning groups) and bargaining centralization (Blau and Kahn, 1996; Iversen, 1999; Wallerstein, 1999). Our data—comparing earnings inequality data, as measured by the P90/P10 ratio available from the OECD, and various indicators of union density and union centralization—show that the association between union centralization—measured by the Iversen index (Iversen, 1999)—and earnings equality has slightly weakened. The correlation between union centralization and inequality for the cross-section of 22 countries shown in Figure 10.2 is $-0.608$ in 2000 compared to $-0.672$ in 1980.

The second method tries to test whether changes in unionization and wage-setting institutions are associated with changes in wage dispersion. Breaking away from sector agreements or from union recognition gives firms more scope for merit- and performance-based pay. According to Brown *et al.* (2000), for many UK firms the advantage of breaking away from the existing structure of collective bargaining was to increase the dispersion of pay and there was a greater tendency

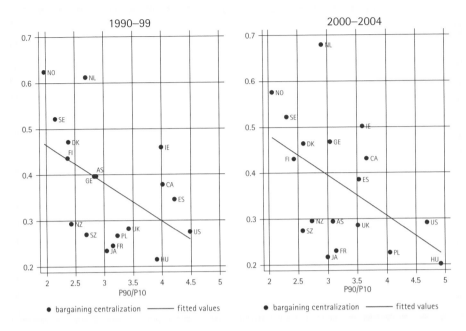

**Fig. 10.2. Bargaining centralization and inequality**

*Note:* For key to country labels, see Fig. 10.1.

towards linking pay rises to individual performance in derecognizing firms. Changing from national to sectoral or from sectoral to company bargaining tends to raise the inter-industry or inter-firm earnings dispersion. Åberg (1994: 80) reports data on wages among manual workers in Swedish manufacturing, showing that the dispersion continued to fall in the 1970s but began to increase again after 1983, when a long period of national bargaining ended (see also Iversen, 1999; Hibbs and Locking, 2000).

Using data from the European Structure of Earnings Survey of 1995, Plasman *et al.* (2007) concentrate on the increased role of supplementary company-level bargaining in Belgium, Spain, and Denmark. They find that in Belgium and Denmark company-level bargaining raises average wages and increases wage dispersion compared to sectoral agreements; in Spain company agreements decrease dispersion, but this must be seen in the context that sectoral agreements in Spain were much less standardizing. Comparing Belgium, Spain, and Italy, and using the same database, Dell'Aringa and Pagani (2007) examine also the effects of different bargaining regimes, which change over time. They do not find that wages are more compressed when workers are covered by sectoral agreements rather than by two-level, sectoral, *and* company agreements. They suggest that increases in wage dispersion arising from an additional layer of enterprise bargaining are mirrored in wage drift under centralized bargaining at the sectoral or national level, a point made by Holden (1987) in his study of centralized bargaining and wage drift in Norway. These results suggest that both the level of bargaining and coordination across levels matters for the capacity of unions to stem the rise of inequality.

In Germany, as in the Netherlands, company bargaining is not a supplement to industry bargaining but an *alternative*, used by a minority of firms, affecting from 6 (Germany) to 14 (Netherlands) percent of workers. Stephan and Gerlach (2005) cannot find a significant differential between the two types of agreements. Gürtzgen (2006) studies firms that switched bargaining regimes in order to identify wage effects, using fixed effects for unobservables that determine selection into different bargaining regimes. She found a small premium of about 2 percent for industry-level as compared to company-level agreements in West Germany and a similar premium for company agreements in East Germany. The explanation may be historical—sectoral bargaining is the rule in West Germany and with some exceptions (Volkswagen, Lufthansa) company bargaining is mainly a phenomenon of smaller firms unable to pay the high sectoral standard; in East Germany sectoral bargaining is less established. The maximum effect on wages found by Hartog *et al.* (2002) was 4 percent in favor of company bargaining, which in the Netherlands applies in particular to multinational firms and privatized firms in the utilities. These small effects cannot explain the increase in wage inequality that we observe. Probably, the fact that unions negotiate minimum rather than standard rates and concede greater variation in actual wages tied to performance is of greater importance.

# 7. WHY UNIONS LIKE OR DISLIKE EARNINGS INEQUALITY

Empirical evidence, based on the ISSP surveys, shows that the likelihood of union membership decreases when the earnings distance to the mean increases (Checchi *et al.*, 2007). Highly skilled workers may believe that they do better by staying outside the union, especially when unions favor wage flattening. In addition, they may have sufficient bargaining power as individuals. Agell (1999) develops an insurance rationale for union membership and egalitarian pay structures based on uncertainty about the future place in the wage distribution and ability to keep up with others. Assuming that risk aversion is inversely correlated with income (or wealth) and assuming that risk aversion motivates people to buy insurance, unions should be more attractive for lower than for higher earning workers. However, lower-paid workers tend be concentrated in sectors, establishments, and occupations that are often most difficult to unionize and they may have more frequent spells of unemployment or inactivity, making it more difficult to retain membership ties. Those that need the union most, from an insurance point of view, may be least able to get it (Crouch, 1982).

There are different reasons why trade unions should compress the wage distribution relative to the productivity distribution. 'Leaving aside the problem of how employers' wage policies are determined by economic conditions, it is certain that trade unions are influenced decisively by other considerations, by their internal and external politics and by the conventions current among their members' (Flanders, 1954: 318). In the opening of this chapter we mentioned the widely cited 'equal pay for equal work' norm. The rationale for equalitarian policies may be less idealistic or principled and be the consequence rather than the cause of centralized policies. Wage compression was the price paid for the support that lower-paid workers gave to centralized incomes policies (Iversen, 1999). Streeck (1994) has described how in the system of interconnected industry-wide wage setting in Germany electoral competition for union office ensures that union leaders have an incentive to follow the trend set by the strongest union, the metalworkers. More generally, Elster (1989: 218) claims that envy or 'preventing others from getting ahead' has played a role in the competition between unions representing lower- and higher-paid workers that preceded the break-up of centralized bargaining in Sweden.

Secondly, trade unions have defended wage-compressing strategies as part of a growth- and productivity-enhancing strategy, seeking to raise standards by squeezing low-paid work and inefficient firms or sectors out of the market (Agell and Lommerud, 1993; Horn and Wolinsky, 1998; Streeck, 1992). Unions may also try to redistribute income as an alternative to progressive taxation (Agell, 1999), though adverse effects on employment temper such attempts.

Thirdly, internal union politics may favor wage policies tending to the vote of the median union member. Since most modern unions organize heterogeneous workers with different skill and pay levels, there must be a political mechanism for aggregating the potential diverse preferences of union members. For instance, when deciding on annual wage increases, lower-paid members are better off with absolute rather than percentage increases. Generally, under the median voter model and given a mean wage higher than the median, union policies will tend towards wage compression (Freeman and Medoff, 1984).

The puzzle of explaining wage patterns as a result of egalitarian union policies is why workers with higher earnings join such unions and how they can be made to stay rather than move to the non-union sector or set up rival unions with less egalitarian preferences. In fact, rival unions did spring up among professionals and academics in the 1970s, for instance in Norway, Denmark, and the Netherlands, and this has been related to the leveling-down policies of the major union confederations at the time (Ebbinghaus and Visser, 2000). One possibility is that industrial unions, covering all grades and skills, have more bargaining power and extra rents which they then can redistribute among members (Horn and Wolinsky, 1998).

# 8. Is Union Decline a Cause of Increased Inequality?

If unions aim at wage compression for ideological or principled reasons as well as to retain and expand their membership, we should observe a negative correlation between earnings inequality and union presence. However, causality can run in both directions, since union decline yields an increase in inequality, but at the same time an exogenous increase in earnings inequality reduces membership support to unions, since workers feel less protected against uncertainty. In the absence of purely exogenous variations (like natural experiments), we can just speak of correlations among these two dimensions. Nonetheless, the strength of this association heavily depends on the institutional framework. Countries characterized by low coverage tend to experience higher levels of inequality, with unions being less important in affecting the wage distribution. On the contrary, other things held constant, countries with high coverage experience more wage compression; in such a case, a decline in union presence may translate into a reduction of coverage and an increase in inequality.

In this section we provide additional new evidence. For this analysis we have collected data on earnings inequality from three different sources (the Luxemburg Income Study or LIS, the International Social Survey Programme or ISSP and the OECD database on earnings). The institutional data are from the ICTWSS (Institutional Characteristics of Trade Unions, Wage Setting, State Intervention and Social Pacts) Database, covering 26 countries between 1960 and 2006 (Visser, 2008). Information on data sources, descriptive statistics, and variables plots, plus additional regression tables, are contained in an Appendix, available from the authors as well as from the following website: <http://www.oup.ac.uk>.

We have resorted to principal component analysis in order to get a summary picture (Table 10.2). Most countries have experienced an increase in earnings inequality in recent years, while they exhibit a diverging trend in the previous decade.[4]

---

[4] A note of caution should be raised here. Data availability does not allow us to control for hours worked, and we therefore depict trends in overall inequality that may be attributable to either differences in hourly wages or hours worked or both. Increased flexibilization of the labor market may have increased earnings inequality by raising the turnover in and out of unemployment (especially in young age cohorts), while potentially leaving the hourly wage unaffected (Bertola *et al.*,

Table 10.2. Summary dynamics of inequality and union presence

| Country | Inequality trends | | Union presence trends | |
|---|---|---|---|---|
| | 80/90 | 90/00 | 80/90 | 90/00 |
| Australia | ↘ | ↗ | ↘ | ↘ |
| Austria | ↘ | ↗ | ↘ | ↘ |
| Belgium | ↘ | n.a. | → | ↘ |
| Can ada | ↘ | ↗ | → | ↘ |
| Czech Rep. | n.a. | ↗ | n.a. | ↘ |
| Denmark | ↗ | → | ↘ | ↗ |
| Finland | → | → | ↗ | ↘ |
| France | → | ↘ | ↘ | ↘ |
| Germany | → | ↗ | ↘ | ↘ |
| Hungary | ↗ | ↗ | n.a. | ↘ |
| Ireland | ↘ | ↗ | ↘ | ↘ |
| Italy | ↗ | ↗ | → | → |
| Japan | → | → | ↘ | ↘ |
| Netherlands | ↗ | ↗ | → | → |
| New Zealand | ↗ | ↗ | ↘ | ↘ |
| Norway | → | → | → | → |
| Poland | ↗ | ↗ | n.a. | ↘ |
| Portugal | ↗ | ↘ | ↘ | ↘ |
| Slovakia | n.a. | ↗ | n.a. | ↘ |
| Slovenia | n.a. | → | n.a. | ↘ |
| Spain | ↗ | ↗ | ↗ | → |
| Sweden | → | → | ↗ | ↘ |
| Switzerland | ↗ | ↗ | ↘ | → |
| United Kingdom | ↗ | ↗ | ↘ | ↘ |
| United States | ↘ | ↗ | ↘ | ↘ |

| Inequality | Union presence | 1980s | 1990s |
|---|---|---|---|
| ↗ | ↘ | 5 | 12 |
| ↗ | ↗ or → | 5 | 4 |
| ↘ or → | ↘ | 7 | 7 |
| ↘ or → | ↗ or → | 5 | 1 |

The trend in union presence is downward, affecting 19 out of 25 countries in the 1990s compared to 12 out of 20 in the 1980s. The combination of rising earnings inequality and declining union presence characterizes the situation in 12 countries compared to five in the previous period. The opposite situation of decreasing or

2002). We partially control for these confounding factors in our estimates by including country and year fixed effects, which also capture unmeasured institutional differences.

Table 10.3. Pair-wise correlations between inequality and union presence

|  | Union density | Bargaining coverage | Wage coordination | Kaitz index (minimum/median) |
|---|---|---|---|---|
| St. dev. log wage ISSP | −0.5005* | −0.6268* | −0.3923* | −0.1248 |
| St. dev. log wage LIS | 0.3318* | −0.3845* | −0.0475 | −0.4622* |
| P90/P50 OECD | −0.6710* | −0.4983* | −0.4907* | −0.2940* |
| P50/P10 OECD | −0.5758* | −0.6512* | −0.5529* | −0.4420* |
| Gini on wages LIS | −0.0699 | −0.6842* | −0.3686* | −0.6383* |

Note: * Significant at 5%.

rather unchanged inequality and rising or equal union presence is limited to the unique case of Denmark, compared to five such cases in the 1980s.

We now move to the analysis of correlation between alternative measures of wage inequality and measures of union presence.[5] When we consider unconditional correlation measures, we find the expected negative association between union presence and inequality, using various measurements of both union presence (density, coverage, and coordination) and inequality (Table 10.3).

However we could be facing spurious correlations, since other labor market institutions (like minimum wage provision) could be responsible for this outcome.[6] In order to partially dispense with these effects, in Table 10.4 we have included country and year fixed effects. We observe that higher union density or more wage coordination do not seem to decrease inequality, but that minimum wage legislation and higher bargaining coverage do.[7] This is rather intuitive, since both variables capture the impact or diffusion of external norms in wage setting. However, when we restrict our analysis to public employment (as we do in the two final columns), we observe that the relative power locally expressed by the unions (thanks to their high membership) is positively associated with wage compression.

If the bulk of the wage distribution does not strongly correlate with union presence, the two tails of the same distribution exhibit more statistically significant correlations. In Table 10.5 we repeat the exercise using decile ratios as dependent variables. We find that union density exhibits a negative correlation with the top tail, and to a lesser extent with the bottom tail, of the earnings distribution. This effect is reinforced in liberal economies, when bargaining coverage is limited. Bargaining coverage is also negatively correlated with earnings dispersion, but this

[5]  While Chapter 8 of this volume analyzes earnings inequality using a supply–demand framework, we consider the alteration of competitive wages due to labor market institutions.

[6]  Koeninger et al. (2007) show that wage inequality is also negatively associated with the employment protection legislation index and argue that unions offer different degrees of protection to high- and low-skilled workers.

[7]  Analogous results are obtained when the dependent variable is replaced with analogous measure from the LIS, or even when the inequality measure is the Gini concentration index.

Table 10.4. Correlations with standard deviation of log-earnings

| | Total economy | | | | | | | | Public admin. | | |
|---|---|---|---|---|---|---|---|---|---|---|---|
| | 1 | 2 | 3 | 4 | 5 | 6 | 7 | 8 | 9 | 10 | 11 |
| Union density ISSP data | −0.0342 [0.56] | | | | | | −0.0821 [1.04] | | −0.1529 [1.61] | −0.1264 [1.60] | −0.1748 [2.11]** |
| Bargaining (or union) coverage, adjusted | | −0.0023 [2.34]** | | −0.0589 [0.90] | −0.0029 [2.80]*** | | | −0.0029 [2.81]*** | −0.0024 [2.29]** | | |
| Coordination of wage bargaining | | | −0.0016 [0.25] | | | −0.0003 [0.05] | −0.0029 [0.46] | −0.0008 [0.09] | −0.0019 [0.21] | | −0.0132 [1.60] |
| Minimum wage to the median OECD | | | | −0.0784 [1.77]* | −0.107 [2.19]** | −0.0838 [1.86]* | −0.0927 [2.00]** | −0.1067 [2.17]** | −0.1213 [2.29]** | −0.1494 [2.88]*** | −0.1557 [2.95]*** |
| Observations | 283 | 240 | 283 | 283 | 240 | 283 | 280 | 240 | 239 | 267 | 264 |
| R² | 0.87 | 0.88 | 0.87 | 0.87 | 0.88 | 0.87 | 0.87 | 0.88 | 0.88 | 0.79 | 0.8 |
| Log likelihood | 423.35 | 355.95 | 422.63 | 424.8 | 357.41 | 424.11 | 421.02 | 357.42 | 357.27 | 375.29 | 374.95 |

Notes: Robust t statistics in brackets—* significant at 10%; ** significant at 5%; *** significant at 1%. Country and year controls included. Minimum wage = 0 when absent.

effect is for obvious reasons more pronounced in the group of countries where coverage is high and union density low. Finally, wage coordination does not display a consistent pattern of correlation with both decile ratios, while minimum wage continues to exhibit a consistent negative association. These results suggest that unions contribute to wage compression by restricting wage decline among low-wage earners and restraining wage hikes among high-wage workers.[8] However, the channels through which this happens vary with the bargaining framework. When coverage is low, local presence or power of unions matters. In contrast, when coverage is high, union membership becomes less relevant, but inequality reduction occurs on a larger scale. For obvious reasons, the combination of high coverage and high density, observed in Northern Europe, is associated with the lowest level of earnings dispersion.

A key element in union wage policies is the negotiation of pay criteria based on job descriptions and seniority rather than performance, thus limiting the discretion of managers. We examine this along three directions. First, if wages are associated with jobs, then individual worker characteristics, including education, should be less relevant. For instance, we expect the return to education to be lower under higher bargaining activity of unions. Secondly, if pay and promotion criteria are related to seniority, we should find that the variance explained by age (and age squared) increases with union bargaining activity. Finally, under high union bargaining activity, wage differentials between male and female workers should be lower.

We have used the various ISSP surveys to estimate the average return to education with a Mincerian function, where gender, age and age squared, and working less than full-time are included as regressors.[9] We neglect information about sector of employment and status, because we are interested in the gross rate of return, which takes into account better employment opportunities associated with formal schooling.[10] Individual membership is also added as regressor in order to capture the possibility that a wage premium is associated with union membership. We find, as expected, that this is indeed the case in the USA, the UK, Ireland, Australia, and, unexpectedly, in Austria (capturing the concentration of union members in high-paying sectors and the absence of union-leveling policies across sectors).

In the final three columns of Table 10.5 we report the result of OLS regressions of estimated returns to education (ranging from $-0.02$ to $0.17$) on the aforementioned

[8]  This is also consistent with the findings that union membership declines with the distance of the individual wage from the median one (Checchi *et al.*, 2007).

[9]  This exercise could not be replicated using LIS samples because for most countries only the maximal educational attainment is reported.

[10]  We are perfectly aware that the estimated coefficients (including the return to education) are quite likely to be biased, due to omitted variables (e.g. ability) and/or measurement errors. In the absence of good instruments available for the entire sample period (e.g. parental education is available in a few surveys only), we cannot correct for this bias. However, if the distortion is consistent across-countries and years, cross-country comparisons still make sense.

Table 10.5. Correlations between union presence (ICTWSS) and other measures of inequality

| | P90/P50 decile ratio | | | P50/P10 decile ratio | | | Return to education | | |
|---|---|---|---|---|---|---|---|---|---|
| | 1 | 2 | 3 | 4 | 5 | 6 | 7 | 8 | 9 |
| Union density × group 1 | -0.0028 [1.93]* | | 0.0052 [2.78]*** | 0.002 [1.02] | | 0.0062 [2.14]** | -0.0241 [0.47] | | -0.0227 [0.40] |
| Union density × group 2 | 0.0025 [1.68]* | | -0.0006 [0.39] | 0.0069 [3.15]*** | | 0.0037 [2.03]** | -0.0246 [0.47] | | 0.0587 [1.11] |
| Union density | -0.0037 [3.14]*** | | -0.0039 [3.49]*** | -0.0064 [3.75]*** | | -0.0079 [5.39]*** | -0.0048 [0.09] | | -0.0316 [0.64] |
| Bargaining (or union) coverage × group 1 | | -0.0054 [5.03]*** | -0.0087 [5.86]*** | | -0.0068 [5.07]*** | -0.0081 [3.76]*** | | 0.0018 [1.64] | 0.0021 [1.87]* |
| Bargaining (or union) coverage × group 2 | | -0.0057 [4.07]*** | -0.006 [4.49]*** | | -0.0055 [2.88]*** | -0.0062 [3.11]*** | | 0.0001 [0.10] | -0.0003 [0.20] |
| Bargaining (or union) coverage, adjusted | | 0.0006 [0.65] | 0.0021 [2.37]** | | 0.0045 [4.65]*** | 0.0059 [6.31]*** | | -0.0018 [1.98]** | -0.0019 [2.00]** |
| Coordination of wage bargaining × group 1 | -0.0014 [0.15] | -0.0034 [0.39] | -0.0051 [0.59] | 0.0326 [2.73]*** | 0.0116 [0.93] | 0.0147 [1.18] | -0.0127 [3.49]*** | -0.0056 [1.57] | -0.0046 [1.23] |
| Coordination of wage bargaining × group 2 | -0.0136 [1.65] | -0.0246 [2.63]*** | -0.0118 [1.40] | 0.012 [0.98] | -0.0088 [0.97] | 0.0078 [0.88] | -0.0019 [0.51] | -0.0033 [0.94] | -0.0013 [0.36] |
| Coordination of wage bargaining | 0.0014 [0.23] | 0.0075 [1.08] | 0.007 [1.01] | -0.0197 [0.98] | 0 [0.00] | -0.0027 [0.46] | 0.0048 [2.16]** | 0.0034 [1.70]* | 0.003 [1.24] |
| Minimum wage to the median OECD | -0.0819 [3.61]*** | -0.0759 [3.22]*** | -0.1156 [5.12]*** | -0.1426 [3.56]*** | -0.0653 [2.12]** | -0.1118 [3.70]*** | -0.0985 [4.71]*** | -0.0933 [3.73]*** | -0.1074 [4.02]*** |
| Observations | 377 | 365 | 353 | 380 | 369 | 356 | 265 | 236 | 234 |
| $R^2$ | 0.94 | 0.95 | 0.96 | 0.9 | 0.93 | 0.94 | 0.7 | 0.74 | 0.75 |
| Log likelihood | 640.46 | 654.52 | 671.76 | 465.91 | 526.81 | 521.63 | 754.84 | 686.18 | 682.79 |

*Notes:* Robust t statistics in brackets—* significant at 10%; ** significant at 5%; *** significant at 1%. Country and year controls included. Minimum wage = 0 when absent. Group 1 of countries includes countries with coverage below 50% (United States, Japan, Canada, Czech Republic, Poland, Hungary, Slovakia, New Zealand, United Kingdom, Switzerland). Group 2 includes countries with coverage above 50% and excess coverage (= coverage – density) above 50% (Slovenia, Australia, Netherlands, Austria, Spain, France, Germany, Portugal). The residual group is composed of Belgium, Denmark, Sweden, Finland, Norway, and Italy.

indicators of union presence, weighting the observations by the (absolute value of the) inverse of their standard errors. We also introduce clustered cross-national variations, in order to account for institutional diversities in bargaining regimes. Rates of return to education exhibit negative correlation with union presence only in Nordic countries, where both membership and coverage are high.[11] On the contrary, in the other regions, all indicators of union presence exhibit no correlation with return to education. We draw attention to the fact that minimum wage legislation, by raising the lowest wages irrespective of educational attainment, negatively correlates with the return on education.

In order to assess the impact of seniority rules in shaping the earnings distribution, we have regressed individual earnings on age (as a proxy for potential work experience) and age squared (to take into account the possibility of entry wages and gradual retirement) using the LIS surveys. By retrieving the variance explained exclusively by these regressors, which ranges from 0.03 to 0.35, we have a proxy for the extent of seniority rules in accounting for (log)wage dispersion. When we regress this variable on measures of union presence, we find evidence of positive correlation of union presence with the variance explained by age: countries where unions are stronger and/or coverage is higher, also witness a larger fraction of wage variability explained by 'objective' criteria like seniority.

Finally, we consider gender differentials. Irrespective of the selected proxy for gender discrimination, we also find some evidence of an association between union presence and a gender gap in earnings—estimated from regressing (log) earnings on gender, age, age squared, years of education, working less than full-time, and union status over various ISSP surveys. When we leave out country fixed effects (while retaining a year fixed effect), we find that all measures of union presence (membership, coverage, and bargaining coordination) are associated with a relative improvement in female earnings, with an additional contribution brought in by a minimum wage.[12] When we allow for country-group variations, we find a negative association with union membership and coverage in liberal economies, the same correlation reverting to positive in the other groups. However almost all correlations become insignificant when we introduce country fixed effects, suggesting that gender discrimination in the labor market is associated with local factors that go beyond union presence (cultural attitudes, labor market segmentation, access to technical education, to name some).

---

[11] Carbonaro (2006) performs a similar analysis, estimating the return to literacy from IALS and correlating it with labor market institutions. He finds that labor market institutions tend to compress the earnings distribution in coordinated market economies.

[12] Recall that the dependent variable (wage differential) is a negative one. A positive correlation with union presence thus implies that its increase is associated with an increase in the relative wage of working women.

# 9. Conclusion and Further Research

In this chapter we have shown how and why unions compress wages, if they do. Emerging historically as craft unions and evolved into mass organization, unions bargain for tying pay to jobs and not to workers. This can be achieved in different ways, depending on whether the degree of workers' coverage is limited (as in liberal economies) or high (as in many European countries). The reduced coverage can be partially offset by other institutional arrangements (like minimum wages), and locally powerful unions (at workplace or at sector level) can compress wages within the union sector, albeit often at the price of increasing the differential between the union and non-union part of the economy.

We have also provided aggregate evidence on union presence being negatively associated with earnings inequality in a sample of developed countries observed in the last two decades. Most of this correlation is accounted for by two variables: bargaining coverage and minimum wage legislation. These two institutional measures are potential substitutes (Checchi and Lucifora, 2002), because both aim to generalize a uniform wage treatment in the population. However, while bargaining coverage potentially extends to the entire earnings distribution, the impact of the minimum wage focuses on the bottom tail.

There are at least two issues which deserve further investigation. One is the appropriate measure of union presence in both workplaces and the society at large. Coverage measures are insufficient to capture the spill-over of union presence, when most union activity takes place in the workplace. The other is the endogeneity of membership, which is reflected in the egalitarian attitude of unions. The existence of a negative association between union presence and earnings inequality has been proved by several articles and books. Whether causality runs in one way or the other (or whether it is bi-directional), is still an open question needing further research.

## References

ÅBERG, R. 1994. 'Wage Control and Cost-Push Inflation in Sweden since 1960', in R. Dore, R. Boyer, and Z. Mars (eds.), *The Return to Incomes Policy*. London: Pinter, 71–93.

ABOWD, J. M., and FARBER, H. S. 1982. 'Job Queues and the Union Status of Workers'. *Industrial and Labor Relations Review*, 35(3): 354–67.

AGELL, J. 1999. 'On the Benefits from Rigid Labor Markets: Norms, Market Failures, and Social Insurance'. *Economic Journal*, 109: 143–64.

——and LOMMERUD, K. E. 1993. 'Egalitarianism and Growth'. *Scandinavian Journal of Economics*, 95: 559–79.

ASHENFELTER, O. 1972. 'Racial Discrimination and Trade Unionism'. *Journal of Political Economy*, 80(3): 434–64.

BASSANINI, A., and DUVAL, R. 2006. 'Employment Patterns in OECD Countries: Reassessing the Role of Policies and Institutions'. OECD Economics Department Working Papers no. 486.

BELL, B. D., and PITT, M. K. 1998. 'Trade Union Decline and the Distribution of Wages in the UK: Evidence from Kernel Density Estimation'. *Oxford Bulletin of Economics and Statistics*, 60(4): 509–28.

BERTOLA, G., BLAU, F., and KAHN, L. 2002. 'Comparative Analysis of Labor Market Outcomes: Lessons for the US from International Long-Run Evidence', in A. Krueger and R. Solow (eds.), *The Roaring Nineties: Can Full Employment be Sustained?* New York: Russell Sage and Century Foundations, 159–218.

BLANCHFLOWER, D. G., and BRYSON, A. A. 2003. 'Changes over Time in Union Relative Wage Effects in the UK and the USA Revisited', in J. T. Addison and A. Bryson (eds.), *International Handbook of Trade Unions*. Cheltenham: Edward Elgar, 197–245.

BLAU, F., and KAHN, L. 1996. 'International Differences in Male Wage Inequality: Institutions versus Market Forces'. *Journal of Political Economy*, 104(4): 791–837.

BOOTH, A. L. 1995. *The Economics of the Trade Union*. Cambridge: Cambridge University Press.

BROWN, W., DEAKIN, S., NASH, D., and OXENBRIDGE, S. 2000. 'The Employment Contract: From Collective Procedures to Individual Rights'. *British Journal of Industrial Relations*, 38(4): 611–29.

BUCHMUELLER, T. C., DiNARDO, J. E., and VALETTA, R. G. 2005. 'A Submerging Labor Market Institution? Unions and the Nonwage Aspects of Work', in R. B. Freeman, J. Hersch, and L. Mishel (eds.), *Emerging Labor Market Institutions for the Twenty-First Century*. Chicago: The University of Chicago Press, 231–64.

CALMFORS, L., and DRIFFILL, J. 1988. 'Bargaining Structure, Corporatism, and Macroeconomic Performance'. *Economic Policy*, 6: 12–61.

CARBONARO, W. 2006. 'Cross-National Differences in the Skills-Earnings Relationship: The Role of Labor Market Institutions'. *Social Forces*, 84(3): 1819–42.

CARD, D. 2001. 'The Effect of Unions on Wage Inequality in the U.S. Labor Market'. *Industrial and Labor Relations Review*, 54(2): 296–315.

—— LEMIEUX, T., and RIDDELL, W. C. 2003. 'Unionization and the Wage Structure', in J. T. Addison and C. Schnabel (eds.), *International Handbook of Trade Unions*. Cheltenham: Edward Elgar, 246–92.

CHECCHI, D., and LUCIFORA, C. 2002. 'Unions and Labor Market Institutions in Europe'. *Economic Policy*, 17(2): 362–401.

—— VISSER, J., and VAN DE WERFHORST, H. G. 2007. 'Inequality and Union Membership: The Impact of Relative Earnings Position and Inequality Attitudes'. IZA Discussion Paper no. 2691

CLEGG, H. A. 1970. *The System of Industrial Relations in Great Britain*. Oxford: Blackwell.

COOK, A. H., LORWIN, V. R., and KAPLAN DANIELS, A. (eds.) 1984. *Women and Trade Unions in Eleven Industrialized Countries*. Philadelphia: Temple University Press, 3–36.

CROUCH, C. J. 1982. *Trade Unions*. Glasgow: Fontana.

DELL'ARINGA, C., and PAGANI, L. 2007. 'Collective Bargaining and Wage Dispersion in Europe'. *British Journal of Industrial Relations*, 45(1): 29–54

DICKENS, L., and HALL, M. 2005. 'The Impact of Employment Legislation: Reviewing the Research'. London: Department of Trade and Industry: Employment Relations Research Series no. 45.

DiNardo, J., Fortin, N. N., and Lemieux, T. 1996. 'Labor Market Institutions and the Distribution of Wages, 1973–1992. A Semi-parametric Approach'. *Econometrica*, 64(5): 1001–44.

——and Lemieux, T. 1997. 'Diverging Male Wage Inequality in the United States and Canada, 1981–1998: Do Institutions Explain the Difference?' *Industrial and Labor Relations Review*, 50(4): 629–51.

Duncan, G. J., and Stafford, F. P. 1980. 'Do Union Members Receive Compensating Wage Differentials?' *American Economic Review*, 70, June: 355–71.

Ebbinghaus, B., and Visser, J. 2000. *Handbook on European Societies: Trade Unions in Western Europe since 1945*. London: Palgrave-Macmillan.

Eiro 2007. 'Working Time Developments 2006'. Doblin: European Foundation for the Improvement of Living and Working Conditions.

Elster, J. 1989. *The Cement of Society. A Study of Social Order*. Cambridge: Cambridge University Press.

Farber, H. S. 2003. 'Nonunion Wage Rates and the Threat of Unionization'. NBER Working Paper no. 9705.

Flanagan, R. J. 1999. 'Macroeconomic Performance and Collective Bargaining: An International Perspective'. *Journal of Economic Literature*, 37(3): 1150–75.

Flanders, A. 1954. 'Collective Bargaining', in A. Flanders and H. A. Clegg (eds.), *Industrial Relations in Great Britain*. Oxford: Blackwell, 252–321.

Freeman, R. B. 1980. 'Unionism and the Dispersion of Wages'. *Industrial and Labor Relations Review*, 34(1): 3–23.

——1993. 'How Much has Deunionization Contributed to the Rise of Male Earnings Inequality', in S. Danziger, and Peter Gottschalk (eds.), *Uneven Tides: Rising Income Inequality in America*. New York: Russell Sage Foundation, 133–63.

——and Medoff, J. L. 1984. *What do Unions Do?* New York: Basic Books.

Friedman, M. 1956. 'Some Comments on the Significance of Labor Unions for Economic Policy', in D. McCord Wright (ed.), *The Impact of the Union*. New York: Kelley and Millman, 204–34.

——1962. *Capitalism and Freedom*. Chicago: University of Chicago Press.

Goldfield M. 1987. The Decline of Organized Labor in the United States. Chicago: University of Chicago Press.

Gosling, A., and Machin, S. 1995. 'Trade Unions and the Dispersion of Wages in UK Establishments 1980–90'. *Oxford Bulletin of Economic and Statistics*, 57(2): 167–84.

——and Lemieux, Th. 2001. 'Labour Market Rejoins and Changes in Wage Inequality in the United Kingdom and the United States'. Cambridge, Mass.: National Bureau of Economic Research.

Guger, A. 1998. 'Economic Policy and Social Democracy: The Austrian Experience'. *Oxford Review of Economic Policy*. 14(1): 87–110.

Gürtzgen, N. 2006. 'The Effects of firm- and Industry-Level Contracts on Wages: Evidence from Longtodinal Linked Employer–Employed Data'. ZEW Discussion Paper 06-082.

Hartog, J., Leuven, E., and Teulings, C. 2002. 'Wages and the Bargaining Regime in a Corporatist Setting: the Netherlands'. *European Journal of Political Economy*, 18: 317–31.

Hibbs, D. A., and Locking, H. 2000. 'Wage Dispersion and Productive Efficiency: Evidence for Sweden'. *Journal of Labor Economics*, 18, Oct.: 755–82.

Hobsbawm, E. J. 1964. *Labouring Men: Studies in the History of Labor*. London: Weidenfeld and Nicolson.

HOLDEN, S. 1987. 'Local and Central Wage Bargaining', *Scandinavian Journal of Economics*, 90: 93–9.

HORN, H., and WOLINSKY, A. 1998. 'Worker Substitutability and Patterns of Unionization', *Economic Journal*, 98: 484–97.

HYMAN, R., and BROUGH, I. 1975. *Social Values and Industrial Relations. A Study of Fairness and Inequality*. Oxford: Blackwell.

ILO 1997. *World Labor Report 1997–98: Industrial Relations, Democracy and Social Stability*. Geneva: International Labor Office.

IVERSEN, T. 1999. *Contested Economic Institutions: The Politics of Macroeconomics and Wage Bargaining in Advanced Democracies*. Cambridge, Mass.: Cambridge University Press.

KATZNELSON, I., and ZOLLBERG, A. R. 1986. *Working-Class Formation: Nineteenth Century Patterns in Western Europe and the United States*. Princeton: Princeton University Press.

KOENINGER, W., LEONARDI, M., and NUNZIATA, L. 2007. 'Labor Market Institutions and Wage Inequality'. *Industrial & Labor Relations Review*, 60(3): 340–56.

LEWIS, H. G. 1963. *Unionism and Relative Wages in the United States*. Chicago: University of Chicago Press.

——1986. *Union Relative Wage Effects. A Survey*. Chicago: University of Chicago Press.

LINDBECK, A., and SNOWER, D. J. 1988. *The Insider-Outsider Theory of Employment and Unemployment*. Cambridge, Mass.: The MIT Press.

LOCKWOOD, D. 1958. *The Blackcoated Worker*. London: Unwin.

MACHIN, S. 1999. 'Pay Inequality in the 1970s, 1980s and 1990s', in P. Cregg and J. Wadsworth (eds.), *The State of Working Britain*. Manchester: Manchester University Press.

METCALF, D. 1982. 'Unions and the Dispersion of Earnings'. *British Journal of Industrial Relations*, 20(2): 163–9.

—— HANSEN, K., and CHARLWOOD, A. 2001. 'Unions and the Sword of Justice: Unions and Pay systems, Pay Inequality, Pay Discrimination and Low Pay'. *National Institute Economic Review*, 176: 61–75

MOSHER, J. 2006. 'U.S. Wage Inequality, Technological Change, and Decline in Union Power'. *Politics & Society*, 35(2): 225–64.

NICKELL, S., NUNZIATA, L., and OCHEL, W. 2005. 'Unemployment in the OECD since the 1960s. What do we Know?' *Economic Journal*, 115: 1–27.

OLSON, M. J. 1965. *The Logic of Collective Action*. Cambridge, Mass.: Harvard University Press.

——1982. *The Rise and Decline of Nations*. New Haven: Yale University Press.

PENCAVEL, J. 1991. *Labor Markets under Trade Unionism*. Oxford: Blackwell.

PENNINX, R., and ROOSBLAD, J. (eds.) 2000. *Trade Unions, Immigration and Immigrants in Europe, 1960–1993*. New York: Berghahn.

PHELPS BROWN, E. H. 1962. *The Economics of Labor*. New Haven: Yale University Press.

PLASMAN, R., RUSINEK, M., and RYCX, F. 2007. 'Wages and Bargaining Regime under Multi-level Bargaining: Belgium, Denmark and Spain'. *European Journal of Industrial Relations*, 13: 16–80.

REES, A. 1962. *The Economics of Trade Unions*. Chicago: University of Chicago Press.

REYNOLDS, L. G., and TAFT, C. H. 1956. *The Evolution of Wage Structure*. New Haven: Yale University Press.

ROSEN, S. 1969. 'Trade Union Power, Threat Effects and the Extent of Organization'. *Review of Economic Studies*, 36(2): 185–96.

ROSEN, S. 1970. 'Unionism and the Occupational Wage Structure in the United States'. *International Economic Review*, 11(2): 269–86.

ROTHSTEIN, B. 1992. 'Labor-Market Institutions and Working-Class Strength', in S. Steinmo, K. Thelen, and F. Longstreth (eds.), *Structuring Politics: Historical Institutionalism in Comparative Analysis*. Cambridge, Mass.: Cambridge University Press, 33–56.

SOSKICE, D. W. 1990. 'Wage Determination: The Changing Role of Institutions in Advanced Industrialised Countries'. *Oxford Review of Economic Policy*, 6(4): 36–61.

STEPHAN, G., and GERLACH, K. 2005. 'Union Wage Differentials in an Era of Declining Unionisation'. *Oxford Bulletin of Economics and Statistics*, 57: 143–66.

STREECK, W. 1992. *Social Institutions and Economic Performance: Studies of Industrial Relations in Advanced Capitalist Economies*. London: Sage.

——1994. 'Pay Restraint without Incomes Policy: Institutionalised Monetarism and Industrial Unionism in Germany', in R. Dore, R. Boyer, and Z. Mars (eds.), *The Return to Incomes Policy*. London: Pinter, 118–40.

——2005. 'The Sociology of Labor Markets and Trade Unions', in N. J. Smelser and R. Swedberg (eds.), *The Handbook of Economic Sociology*. Princeton and New York: Princeton University Press, with Russell Sage Foundations, 254–83.

SVENSEN, P. 1989. *Fair Shares. Unions, Pay, and Politics in Sweden and West Germany*. Ithaca, NY: Cornell University Press.

TEULINGS, C., and HARTOG, J. 1998. *Corporatism or Competition: Labor Contracts, Institutions and Wage Structures in International Comparison*. Cambridge: Cambridge University Press.

TURNER, H. A. 1952. 'Trade Unions, Differentials and the Levelling of Wages'. *The Manchester School*, 20, Sept.: 227–82.

VISSER, J. 1990. 'In Search of Inclusive Unionism'. *Bulletin of Comparative Labor Relations*, 18: 5–278.

——2003. 'Unions and Unionism around the World', in J. T. Addison and C. Schnabel (eds.), *The International Handbook of Trade Unions*. Cheltenham: Edward Elgar, 366–40.

——2008. Institutional Characteristicks of Trade Unions, Wage Setting, State Intervention and Social facts (ICTWSS), NEWGOV project, financed under the EU FP7 research framework, on 'Distributive Politics, Learning and Reform: National Social Facts'.

WALLERSTEIN, M. 1999. 'Wage-Setting Institutions and Pay Inequality in Advanced Industrial Societies'. *American Journal of Political Science*, 43: 649–40.

WEBB, S., and WEBB, B. 1920. *The History of Trade Unionism*, Revised edn. (original: 1894). New York: Longmans, Green and Co.

# CHAPTER 11

# LOW PAY

## CLAUDIO LUCIFORA
## WIEMER SALVERDA

## 1. INTRODUCTION

THE analysis of low pay focuses on a specific part of the earnings distribution, with the aim of understanding which labor market features and institutional constraints make it more likely for individuals to be located further away below the middle of the earnings distribution. Research on earnings inequality (Chapter 8) has highlighted the importance of the tails of the earnings distribution for understanding poverty, social stratification, and economic incentives facing workers and employers. Whilst low pay and inequality are closely linked, they are not identical nor are their economic implications, inequality being concerned also with what happens at the top of the distribution. The same holds for low pay and poverty (Chapter 13), the two being connected through the so-called 'working poor' but often diverging in the economic and social context. Here we explicitly focus on the significance of low pay, investigating: who is low paid and why, and who is low paying and why? This elaborates on two important aspects outside the scope of the other chapters: the determinants of being paid a wage towards the bottom of the earnings distribution, and the individual chances of remaining in the lower part, moving into or out of it, and up or down the distribution. Answering such questions may help us understand international differences better and consider the 'penniless-jobless' dilemma (Krugman, 1994) dominating the economic debate on these issues.

The idea of low pay has a long tradition in economics. The concept can be traced back to the thinking of philosophers and economists from the 1800s. The underlying idea was that of a 'natural' law according to which real wages in the long run would tend to the subsistence level because without this laborers would be unable to work. Starting from Malthus's demographic theory, wages would tend to a level equating labor supply (i.e. population) and labor demand, creating a dynamic convergence towards a 'subsistence wage' equilibrium with constant population (Malthus, 1798). The idea was codified by the German socialist Lassalle as the 'Iron Law of Wages', suggesting that it was the competition among laborers for employment that drives wages down to subsistence level. Later developments brought in the role of labor demand showing that real wages in equilibrium may remain indefinitely above (or below) subsistence level (Ricardo, 1817, chapter 5). In other words, it was not a natural tendency for wages to be set at the subsistence level but the result of the interactions of demand and supply of labor on the market. From a different perspective, Marx believed that the class struggle between capitalists and workers over the means of production, by relegating a share of total labor supply to the 'reserve army' of labor, would drive wages down (Marx, 1859). This idea of a natural tendency towards some minimal level or even below has survived and nowadays the explanations are only marginally different, as the notion of a 'living wage' illustrates.

Indeed, while low pay may be an elusive concept both theoretically and empirically, it has been at the centre of the debate on wage formation, wage inequalities, poverty, and social exclusion for a long time. International Labor Organization (1928) recommendations, the Universal Declaration on Human Rights (1948), European Social Charters all have stipulations for fair pay and adequate living standards. Many European constitutions and various US Local Government Ordinances have similar requirements as does private certification of corporate responsibility. The concerns are reflected in the fact that the great majority of OECD countries have a formal or *de facto* minimum wage.

Definitions of low pay and methodologies for measuring a 'living' or 'fair' wage are numerous, as shown by the lively debate among economists, policy makers, and civil society. The challenge is that of identifying a 'fair' threshold for the wage that can combine economic efficiency with social equity. The debate emphasizes the importance of setting the right price for labor services in the labor market without negatively impacting on productivity or employment rates, and at the same time is concerned about the ability of the 'working poor' to meet their basic needs of food, housing, education, transportation, health care etc. The interest of current low-wage employment for policy is that while historically poverty was often associated with joblessness, and the first policy response was always trying to get the poor to work, nowadays some of the poor are already in work and traditional measures are no longer appropriate. There is also concern that increasing numbers of employees on low pay will generate further economic distress and social exclusion (Lucifora and Salverda, 1998; Wilkinson and Pickett, 2007).

In sum, there are good reasons to care about low pay, for scholars and for policy makers. Low earnings may affect the ability to maintain decent living standards. If wage differentials are perceived as unfair, cohesion and cooperation among workers may be affected to the disadvantage of efficiency. From the perspective of firms, a significant undercutting based on low pay may hinder fair competition, and persistently cheap labor can negatively affect the evolution of productivity and the macroeconomic efficiency of labor supply and human capital investment. Given the objectives of social cohesion, a higher incidence of low pay can have direct implications for public policy, in terms of rising costs of welfare programs.

The structure of the chapter is as follows. Section 2 discusses the economic analysis of low pay. Section 3 presents definitions, measurement, and data issues. In Section 4, some stylized facts on low pay are presented and the main results from the empirical literature are critically reviewed. Section 5 contains a discussion of policy issues and suggestions for future research.[1]

# 2. THE ECONOMICS OF LOW PAY

What is low pay, and how can low-wage employment be identified? Which economic forces can drive wages down to the subsistence level? To address these issues, we first look at the earnings distribution and the implications for low pay, then we review some of the economic explanations for the existence and persistence of low pay.

## The Distribution of Wages

Consider a general framework where (heterogeneous) workers supply labor and are remunerated according to their endowments, and employers post jobs with a given productive capacity.[2] In equilibrium, in the absence of frictions, all workers will be matched to the existing jobs and a distribution of wages will emerge. In this context, low pay identifies all workers who due to either poor endowments (ability, skills, etc.) or low returns to those endowments (low productivity jobs, obsolete technology, segregated occupations, fringe industries, etc.) are likely to be

---

[1]  For additional detail about the literature see the OHEI website.
[2]  Productive capacity $\theta$ indicates the expected productivity of a given job—for a given capital stock and other job attributes—once the vacancy is filled.

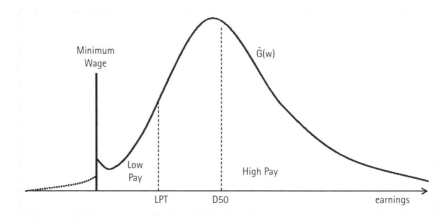

**Fig. 11.1. Wage distribution and low pay**

located in the lower part of the pay distribution. Of course not all 'potential' low-paid workers and low-paid jobs are likely to be observed in the economy: workers whose reservation wage is higher than the market (low) wage will not effectively search for a job, and firms will only post and fill a vacant job if marginal revenue is at least equal to marginal cost. Hence, the actual shape of the wage distribution—and the extent of low-paid employment—is likely to be affected by both *supply side decisions* and *demand side factors*, as it is only for successful worker–job matches that a wage will be observed.[3] If we further assume that there are frictions and that information is not perfect, there will also be some workers who, despite their search efforts, will not find a job and some firms will be unable to fill their vacant jobs such that, in equilibrium, unemployment and vacancies can co-exist (Pissarides, 2000; Blanchard and Diamond, 1994). Additionally, if wage regulations (e.g. statutory minimum wage) or other institutional features (e.g. unemployment benefits, collective bargaining, or mandatory extension of collective contracts) set a minimum threshold for pay levels, the distribution will be truncated from below.

Figure 11.1 provides a convenient framework for the analysis of low pay. First, low pay refers to the shaded area of the earnings distribution, $G(W)$, which falls below the low-pay threshold (LPT) and whose size is related to the shape of the distribution: the wider the dispersion of endowments and the lower the returns to these endowments, the larger the incidence of low pay can be. Also note that—as previously discussed—a significant share of (potentially) low-pay worker-job matches may not be observed. Thus, depending on market conditions, labor market imperfections and the institutional framework, the 'observed' share of low-pay employment can differ substantially over time and across countries.

What happens below the threshold is an interesting question. On the one hand, in countries with generous welfare benefits workers may find it optimal to engage in

---

[3]  Low pay refers to employee jobs and excludes the self-employed.

wait unemployment or not to participate in the labor market instead of accepting a low-paid job (or do so only on a part-time basis); on the other hand, low-paid jobs will not be posted by firms if the implied costs exceed the expected returns.[4] Nevertheless some wages may be observed below the minimum, due to for example specific provisions for young workers or categories excluded from the application of the statutory minima (see dotted line in Fig. 11.1).

While this shape and partition of the wage distribution describe the labor market at one point in time (i.e. a static perspective), there is likely to be substantial change in both the employment/non-employment status of individuals and the low-pay/high-pay position of workers within a given distribution (i.e. a dynamic perspective). Hence, the overall share of low-paid workers can be consistent with a rather different functioning of the labor market. For example, the evidence concerning the increase in inequality and the rise of low-pay incidence, is consistent with an increase in the incidence of low pay or in the transitory fluctuations in earnings (or a combination of both). In two countries with exactly the same aggregate share of low-paid workers over time, workers may be confined to a low-paid job year after year in one and move jobs from year to year and change their low-pay/high-pay position in the other. Thus, there is a substantial difference in the welfare of individual workers, the relationship between the proportion of low-paid workers and the individual fortunes of wage earners being tight or loose. The implications of income mobility for overall income inequality are discussed elsewhere (Chapter 21), this chapter only considers mobility in relation to low pay.

Clearly, high taxation and social-security contributions, by driving a wedge between workers' consumption wage and employers' labor costs, can exacerbate market failures in the low-pay end of the labor market such that fewer matches are observed than the optimal. Also, in those segments of the labor market where mobility is lower, wage regulation is absent (or weak) and thus firms' demand power is stronger, wages (and employment) may well fall below the competitive level. It is possible that a significant number of worker–job matches occur in the irregular economy (firms avoiding social security contributions and workers avoiding income taxes), where matches and related wages are usually not observed. In other words, depending on the overall economic setting, the 'observed' share of low pay may significantly underestimate the economy's extent of potential low-pay employment.

## Some Economic Explanations

An extensive literature has tried to clarify the different causes and economic factors which may explain the changes in earnings inequality (Chapter 8). Here this

---

[4] Wage regulations, by setting a reference wage for those jobs below and immediately above the threshold, often determine a spike in the distribution.

amounts to explaining economic and non-economic forces impacting on the supply and demand schedules altering the wage distribution from below, i.e. inward shifts of demand and/or outward shifts of supply. Among the leading explanations are: demographic changes, migration flows, changes in industry composition (services gaining importance over manufacturing), skill-biased technological change (skilled–unskilled mismatch), increased globalization of trade, and new forms of work organization. On the institutional side, the erosion of trade union power, collective bargaining, and reduced labor market regulation have been considered as complementary explanations. Although there is little controversy among economists over the basic facts and the complex interactions that exist among the above factors, less consensus exists about their relative importance.

However, a more coherent framework to analyze wage setting in the lower part of the distribution of wages is to consider an imperfectly competitive model, in which workers may face high mobility costs and firms may have some market power in setting wages such that, if wage levels were to be cut, workers would not leave the firm instantaneously (Green et al., 1996; Manning, 1996, 2003). Both labor market frictions or monopsony power are expected to be stronger in the lower part of the wage distribution where—in the absence of unions or wage regulation—low-skilled workers generally have low bargaining power and inferior outside opportunities. To illustrate the source of monopsony power in a dynamic context, consider a firm paying a low wage to its workers and experiencing both a significant workers' separation rate—either toward non-employment (due to low opportunity cost) or to other firms (due to workers' continuous on-the-job search)—as well as a significant rate of absenteeism (due to low attachment of workers to the firm). If this firm were to increase wage levels to match competing firms, turnover and absenteeism rates (and associated costs) would drop, increasing labor supply. Thus, monopsony power originates from labor market frictions and mobility costs and through its depressing effect on wages may increase the likelihood of low-paid employment. Alternative explanations for low pay are based either on disequilibrium models (Neumark and Wascher, 2002), or on the idea that the labor market is segmented into a primary sector with 'good' jobs (high-wage) and a secondary sector with 'bad' jobs (low-wage) with little possibility for workers to move from one segment to the other (Doeringer and Piore, 1971; Wilkinson, 1981; Acemoglu, 2001). In the former case, low pay characterizes workers who are off their supply schedule; while in the latter, low pay is likely to identify mainly workers who are in the secondary segment of the labor market.

In these contexts, the presence of institutional mechanisms that set a minimum threshold to the wage distribution (be it statutory or collectively bargained) may reduce the incidence of low-paid employment by bringing wages and employment closer to the competitive level (Card and Krueger, 1995; Nickell and Layard, 1999). The efficacy of such measures clearly depends on both the level of the minimum wage and its effective coverage. However, it should not be ignored that if wage minima are set too high, they can have displacement effects on employment, crowd-ing out some workers from the labor market. These are essentially the terms of the controversy that has generated the heated debate among economists and policy makers on the effects and desirability of minimum-wage legislation. What is of interest here is which economic forces determine the size of low-wage employment and to what extent wage regulations are able to force employers to pay a 'fair' wage. As previously discussed, the main effects will happen around the minimum-wage level, while it is unclear what the likely effects are for the very low-paid jobs (i.e. some job–worker matches will no longer be observed in the (regular) market).

# 3. DEFINITION, MEASUREMENT AND DATA

Conceptually the threshold below which pay is considered to be low is sometimes based on the standard of living that the wage can buy for the worker. This brings into play the worker's household situation, which determines the needs that have to be met, which is outside the scope of the wage contract with the employer. This definition may be adequate for evaluating wages in terms of poverty, but is less suited for analyzing the workings of the low-wage labor market and thus for a full understanding of in-work poverty[5] (see Chapter 13 for an analysis of poverty).

Here, we take low pay as a concept relating to the gross earnings distribution, regardless of the household position of the worker. One can choose between ei-ther taking a fixed quantile, say the bottom 20 or 30 percent, or looking below a threshold. In practice either a relative or an absolute wage level might be chosen. The threshold approach is capable of showing aggregate changes over time which the quantile definition cannot. In particular, the threshold of two-thirds of me-dian[6] earnings adopted by the European Commission and the OECD and most frequently used in empirical studies seems well suited to facilitating cross-country comparisons, though the demand it puts on the data is still considerable. Evidently, this second definition cannot in itself help in evaluating poverty but it may help in analyzing the wage level as one of its determinants. For the rest of this chapter we embrace this second definition.

---

[5]  American research (e.g. Mishel *et al.*, 2007) often speaks about poverty-level wages. The USA has an absolute poverty line based on a bundle of goods and adapted to price changes only, eroding significantly relative to growing welfare. The European approach to poverty is relative, based on 60% of median household income, equivalized for needs. The former puts a much greater demand on internationally comparative data

[6]  Starting from the median reduces the effects of outliers at the tails.

Given the definition, the measurement of the incidence of low pay will be sensitive to the inclusion of part-time workers, the earnings concept used, and the choice of data source. The recent growth and internationally diverging role of part-time employment suggests that measurement cannot be limited to full-time workers only. This is particularly important because in practice part-time work and low pay appear to be strongly connected. It implies the need to use hourly wages to compare across workers regardless of their hours of work, to separate the effects of the choice of working hours from those of the level of pay.[7] The determination of the threshold and of the incidence of low pay can be in terms of persons working (head-count) or of hours worked. It seems best to do both, as the latter reflects economic efforts better while the former links better to hiring and firing behavior in the labor market and to the significance of pay for the receiving worker.

Low pay is usually defined at the level of gross wages to the worker, including income tax and worker contributions but excluding employer contributions and payroll taxes. However, in terms of the labor-market behavior of individual actors, it would be appropriate to (also) know gross labor costs for the employer on the one hand and net wages after tax and social contributions for the worker on the other hand. The growth of part-time jobs lends this distinction additional importance. Unfortunately, the data usually do not allow these distinctions to be made. To filter out the effects of hours worked, earnings are best measured on an hourly basis. This can make a huge difference compared with weekly or even annual earnings.[8]

As no obvious internationally comparative data collection is available, national sources have to be used which, unfortunately, are often of a very different nature across countries, with important advantages and disadvantages concerning coverage, reliability, and accuracy. They can be based on administrative records (e.g. for social security), which enhances the accuracy of information on earnings, or on establishment surveys, which improves information on earnings, hours, industry but come at a cost to the coverage of the economy.[9] Both may also be lacking in individual worker characteristics such as education, for which household surveys are a better source. However, those may be less accurate on earnings, hours, and firm characteristics. Naturally, the scale of the surveys also matters for the precision— here administrative records are usually more encompassing.

---

[7]  This is best done on a consistent basis for earnings and hours—in practice on a weekly basis. Within country when annual holiday entitlements are the same for the low and high paid this does not matter, but it does matter cross-country—an important caveat to keep in mind for a Europe–US comparison. Note also that 'full-time' covers a range that may extend from 35 to 60 hours per week, and on average often means different numbers of hours over time and cross-sectionally.

[8]  In the country with the highest level of part-time employment, the Netherlands, the incidence of low pay in 2005 was 31% on an annual basis and 18% on an hourly basis (authors' estimations on earnings survey of Dutch Statistics). Moreover, earnings may change, from year to year, because of piece-rates or bonuses, short-time or overtime working, or shifting between full-time and part-time work, which again underlines the desirability of focusing on hourly pay.

[9]  Salverda et al. (2001) show that for certain countries the European Structure of Earnings Survey covers only half of the economy, and likely much less of the low-paid part of the economy.

# 4. Stylized Facts and Empirical Analysis

Stylized facts can be explored along two main dimensions: across and within countries. On the difference across countries, popular views attribute high and rising levels of low-pay incidence to Anglo-Saxon countries (USA, UK, Ireland, Australia, Canada), lower and stable ones to Continental Europe, and particularly low levels to Scandinavian countries. Though the latter may be true, the Anglo-Saxon/Continental distinction may be less clear-cut. Data assembled from a wide variety of sources by the OECD, with varying earnings concepts and notably

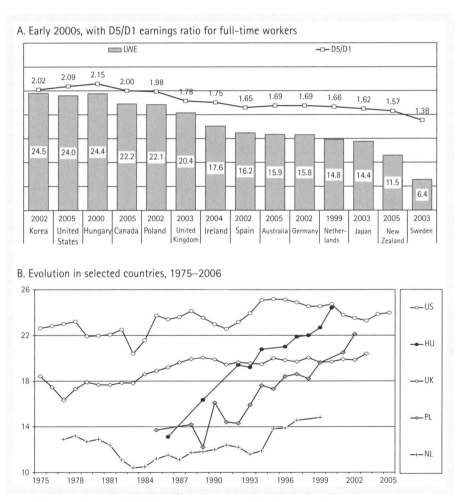

**Fig. 11.2. Incidence (%) of low pay among full-time workers**

*Source*: Authors' calculations using OECD data.

Table 11.1. Low-wage employment among all workers by characteristics (%), 2001

|  |  | Denmark | France | Germany | Netherlands | United Kingdom | United States |
|---|---|---|---|---|---|---|---|
| Total |  | 12 | 15 | 23 | 23 | 22 | 24 |
| Young (15/16–24) | men | 68 | 56 | 71 | 75 | 44 | 51 |
|  | women | 56 | 57 | 68 | 75 | 54 | 61 |
| Prime-age (25–49) | men | 4 | 8 | 11 | 9 | 7 | 12 |
|  | women | 7 | 17 | 24 | 23 | 23 | 23 |
| Older (50–64) | men | 2 | 5 | 9 | 5 | 10 | 12 |
|  | women | 6 | 16 | 30 | 19 | 33 | 22 |
| Primary education |  | 38 | 19 | 48 | 48 | 33 | 60 |
| Secondary education |  | 9 | 20 | 21 | 27 | 26 | 25 |
| Tertiary education |  | 2 | 8 | 10 | 11 | 13 | 6 |
| Small jobs, <15 hours/week |  | 61 | n.a. | 61 | 62 | 51 | 60 |
| Intermediate jobs, 15–<35 hours/week |  | 10 | 20 | 28 | 25 | 38 | 53 |
| Full-time jobs, ≥35 hours/week |  | 10 | 14 | 19 | 14 | 15 | 17 |
| Non-nationals |  | 36 | 23 | 25 | 33 | 19 | 33 |
| Selected occupations |  |  |  |  |  |  |  |
| Personal services workers |  | 19 | 33 | 46 | 41 | 46 | 51 |
| Sales persons, sales, and services |  | 45 | 36 | 47 | 53 | 59 | 37 |
| Building and craft |  | 25 | 24 | 27 | 25 | 19 | 16 |
| Agriculture workers & laborers |  | 15 | 32 | 45 | 43 | 38 | 51 |
| Selected industries |  |  |  |  |  |  |  |
| Agriculture |  | 12 | 37 | 54 | 38 | 38 | 51 |
| Trade |  | 18 | 19 | 36 | 40 | 42 | 36 |
| Hotels and restaurants |  | 42 | 40 | 59 | 54 | 65 | 58 |
| Personal services |  | 23 | 32 | 37 | 38 | 28 | 39 |

*Note*: Head-count based on hourly wages.

*Source*: Schmitt *et al.* (2009). Calculated from European Community Household Panel and Current Population Survey (CEPR extract of ORG).

restricted to full-time workers, show levels for Australia and New Zealand to be more in line with European than with British or American experience (Fig. 11.2A). Also, levels appear to have been increasing in Continental countries such as the Netherlands, Poland, and Hungary, and roughly stable in other countries, including the USA (Fig. 11.2B).

Concerning within-country differences, there is surprising international similarity in terms of low pay incidence as well as composition, at least for simple descriptives (Table 11.1). Usually, the incidence of low pay is much higher among youths, women, immigrants, and the less skilled, and among part-time workers, albeit to varying degrees. (Denmark is an exception where adult women face a below-average chance of being low paid.) Given that wages tend to increase with experience, skill, and tenure, it is not surprising that younger workers are more likely to be in low-paid jobs. For women this is less obvious. Occupations also show a similar pattern, while there seem to be four virtually universal broad industries where low pay is largely concentrated: (retail) trade, hotels and catering, personal services, and agriculture.[10]

## Wage Inequality and Poverty

The variation in the incidence of low pay across countries closely mirrors differences in earnings dispersion in the bottom half of the earnings distribution (Fig. 11.2A). The countries with large inequality also have a higher incidence of low pay. This is not too surprising as a higher D5/D1 ratio implies a wider range of pay below the threshold down to the first decile. However, the incidence of low pay goes down much more quickly than the decile ratio. The within-country evolution of both since the 1970s also runs strikingly parallel for all countries, albeit not for all individual years in every country. The precise significance of inequality for the low-wage incidence may again be somewhat different as in the UK and the USA the incidence seems relatively high compared to the level of inequality in comparison to Australia, Germany, and Netherlands. We come back to the role of minimum wages below.

Another major interest is the significance of low pay for poverty. There is no one-to-one relation as poverty depends on factors beyond the wage such as the scale of unemployment and inactivity, household characteristics, and a country's income taxation and benefit systems. It is important to know though, especially in a cross-country perspective, what low pay is contributing to the poverty rate. Household poverty levels may—for a large household—go together with wages levels well above the low-pay threshold and, the other way around, a worker receiving low pay may be a member of a household that is not poor.

Various studies are available concerning the overlap of poverty with low pay defined by two-thirds of the median wage.[11] Though the two are often linked they are by no means identical—a low-paid worker's household may not be poor and the wage of a poor household's worker may be well above the low-pay threshold. The low-paid job of a second earner may actually lift a household out of poverty. Results point to a large variation in the incidence of poverty in work with Denmark on one end and the UK on the other. In all countries the incidence of low pay exceeds that of in-work poverty. Lohmann (2008) has measured low pay on an hourly basis, as is done here, to enable the contribution of hours worked to poverty to also be explored.

---

[10]  With a more detailed breakdown of industries, parts of manufacturing also show a high incidence, e.g. textiles and clothing. High-wage industries tend to be more diverse internationally: Salverda *et al.* (2001) (high pay defined as more than 1.5 times median earnings).

[11]  For interesting new results for a range of countries see Gregory *et al.* (2000) and Andresz and Lohmann (2008).

## Individual Probability of Low Pay

Descriptive evidence from aggregate data has shown that workers' earnings differ with personal characteristics, such as gender, age, education, training and location, job characteristics and characteristics of the firm where people are employed, such as its industry and size (Table 11.1). Multivariate analysis of individual data largely corroborates this. Given information on wages of $N$ individuals, indexed by $i$, at time $t$, a low-paid individual can be identified using an indicator, $d_{it}$, which takes value 1 depending on whether his/her wage, $w_{it}$, falls above or below the low-pay threshold $\lambda_t$ that is taken as a starting point:

$$d_{it} = 1 \text{ if } w_{it} < \lambda_t;$$

$$d_{it} = 0 \text{ otherwise.}$$

The standard approach in the literature has been to estimate a discrete response model (i.e. linear probability or a probit) linking individual characteristics of the workers and of the jobs with the probability of being low paid,

$$d_{it} = \beta' X_{it} + a_i + u_{it}, \tag{1}$$

where $d_{it}$ is the low pay indicator and $X_{it}$ is the vector of individual, and job and firm-related characteristics, $a_i$ identifies a time-invariant firm fixed-effect, and $\beta$ is a vector of coefficients to be estimated.[12] Individual covariates in equation (1) generally include gender, marital status, and a set of human capital variables, such as: education (measured in terms of the highest level attained), potential experience (measured as age minus age of first entry into the labor market after leaving full-time schooling), and quadratic terms may be added to capture non-linearities in the effect on low pay. Job characteristics often include dummies for occupation, type of contract, full-time/part-time working hours, and tenure with the same firm. Firm characteristics are mostly firm size and industry while studies including other firm attributes or, alternatively, a vector of firms' fixed effects to proxy for time-invariant establishment attributes are scarce (Bazen *et al.*, 1998; Boushey *et al.*, 2007).[13]

Most international studies confirm that the incidence of low pay is higher among young people, women, less skilled persons, manual workers, and in less developed regions after controlling for other characteristics (Fernandez *et al.*, 2004). In the case of women, their higher risk of being low paid relative to men is only partly

---

[12]  The widely used discrete response model has been seriously criticized for the loss of information imposed by the a priori discrete reclassification of the (continuous) wage variable into low and high pay. As an alternative Stewart and Swaffield (1999) consider a monotonic transformation of wages implying the existence of a latent threshold for low pay and allowing the determinants of wages to differ along the distribution.

[13]  Education and potential experience are included in the estimates as proxies for general human capital, while seniority in the firm is intended to proxy for specific human capital.

accounted for by gender differences in average job tenure and experience as well as in the composition of employment by industry and occupation.[14]

Several studies have addressed the issue of whether a wider dispersion of skills among workers can explain higher earnings inequality and incidence of low-paid workers. Results are mixed. Some studies, using appropriate measures of skills (i.e. scores on literacy and numeracy tests) which are considered to be comparable across countries, find that the distribution of skills is the main factor underlying wage inequality (Leuven *et al.*, 2004; Nickell and Bell, 1996). Other studies, using similar cognitive measures, maintain that the largest part of wage inequalities remains unexplained (i.e. due to different returns or to residual inequality) even after controlling for the skill distribution (Freeman and Schettkat, 2001; Blau and Kahn, 2005). In particular, Devroye and Freeman (2000), using both the OECD's International Adult Literacy Survey and the US National Adult Literacy Survey, reject the claim that inequality of skills explains much of the differences in wage inequality between the USA and Europe. They show that: (i) inequality in skills in the USA is overstated due to inclusion of immigrants, (ii) differences in skill dispersion across countries explain only a modest proportion of differences in the dispersion of earnings, (iii) dispersion of pay and the share of low pay is higher for US workers as compared to EU workers even in narrowly defined skill groups. The low-skilled nature and the part-time nature of jobs also contribute to the chances of being low paid. Firm size appears as well with small-sized establishments paying lower wages (Salverda *et al.*, 2001; OECD, 1997; Keese *et al.*, 1998). In other words, the (conditional) probability of low pay is shown to depend on both personal attributes and firm characteristics. The relative importance of individual and job characteristics versus establishment effects, however, seems to vary widely across countries.[15]

## Labor Market Transitions: Low Pay–High Pay and Low Pay–No Pay

Human capital theory and empirical evidence on earnings clearly document the importance of earnings dynamics. An unchanged earnings distribution may conceal a high level of mobility around the low-pay threshold, with considerable portions of workers moving out of low pay and up the wage distribution or moving into and out of employment. The point is that individual labor market behavior will

[14] Blau and Kahn (2004), for example, find that a substantial part of the gender pay gap remains unexplained even after controlling for these and many other factors and that the unexplained part is important for understanding the evolution of the gap.

[15] For example, in four European countries, Belgium, Ireland, Italy, and Spain, covered by Fernandez *et al.* (2004), establishment characteristics explain considerably more of wage variability than personal characteristics, but in Denmark the inverse holds.

vary greatly. The extent to which low-paid employment results in poverty and social exclusion partly depends on the degree to which it is more than a transitory phenomenon. Most workers start off their careers in relatively low-paid jobs but see their earnings grow with experience and career moves. However, some workers may experience little upward mobility or be stuck cycling between poorly paid jobs and unemployment or inactivity. Low pay as a transitory phenomenon may be a stepping stone to more stable and better paid jobs; however, when low pay is more permanent it can lock workers into a trap that is difficult to escape—even across generations (see Chapter 20). Still low-paid employment can be associated with a high individual job turnover that is involuntary and characterized by a low pay–no pay cycle. In other words, in order to understand low pay, we need to know more about the movements up and down the distribution.

The literature on earnings mobility has burgeoned over the last 15 years, developing a focus on low pay. It is typically defined as changing individual positions within the wage distribution over time, which does not necessarily imply changing jobs or firms (Asplund *et al.*, 1998). The analysis requires panel data on individual wage profiles for identification (Atkinson *et al.*, 1992; Gottschalk and Moffitt, 1994; Gottschalk, 1997)[16] and has mostly been in terms of transition probabilities. Given a partition of the cross-sectional wage distribution into low-pay and high-pay classes, empirical models—assuming exogenous initial conditions—estimate the probability that workers belonging to the low-pay wage class at time $t - k$ (i.e. the beginning of a time interval) end up in the high-pay wage class at time $t$ (i.e. the end of that period).[17]

The assumption of exogenous initial conditions in modeling low pay dynamics has been strongly criticized. An alternative approach accounts for both unobserved heterogeneity and initial conditions (i.e. initial low–high pay status is jointly estimated with transition probabilities), allowing the identification of true state dependence. Given persistence in low pay, those in low-wage jobs are also more likely to become unemployed, and the unemployed are more likely to be low waged on re-entry into employment, generating the so-called *low pay–no pay cycle* (Stewart and Swaffield, 1999; Stewart, 2006; Gregory and Jukes, 2001; Cappellari, 2000b, 2002).[18] Results show strong and significant state dependence in unemployment and low-wage employment. Low-wage jobs are the main determinants of repeat

---

[16] Panel data tend to exacerbate the problems of non-response and measurement error. Non-response tends to cumulate over time and the resulting sample attrition can be very high and may be non-random with respect to low pay, giving rise to erroneous conclusions (Westergård-Nielsen, 1989; Cappellari and Jenkins, 2004).

[17] To avoid endogeneity between changes in wages and changes in observed characteristics, covariates are traditionally measured at the start of the transition period (Contini *et al.*, 1998; and Cappellari, 2000b, 2002).

[18] In practice the probability of being low paid is jointly estimated with the initial state equation (also for those starting above the low-pay threshold at the beginning of the period). Note that the specification also allows one to test whether initial conditions and low–high pay transition states are correlated. A different approach, based on a nested probit model, is used in Sloane and Theodossiou (1998).

unemployment: those who get a better job reduce the impact of past unemployment to insignificance. However, the effects differ between countries and seem relatively strong for the UK and the Netherlands (Mason and Salverda, 2009, table A1). Main findings on low pay dynamics suggest that the probability of being low paid is much higher for those who were already low paid in the previous period, while the probability of falling into low pay for previously high-paid workers is rather small. Moreover, while having more human capital reduces the probability of falling into low pay, the impact of human capital on exit rates from low pay is rather modest (Contini *et al.*, 1998, and Cappellari, 2000b, 2002, for Italy; Sloane and Theodossiou, 1996, for the UK; Andersson *et al.*, 2005, for the USA). Transition probabilities for a number of OECD countries indicate that there is considerable movement out of low-paid jobs, but also considerable variation in the job prospects of workers across countries. While earnings mobility and the probability of moving out of low pay increase with length of period studied, a considerable share is still low paid or experiences downward earnings mobility after a five-year span in most countries. The share of low-paid workers still low paid five years later is large (from 6% in Denmark up to 40% in the USA; Deding, 2002). In countries with a more egalitarian earnings distribution, the fewer workers below the low-pay threshold in any single year also have a relatively lower risk of remaining below this over time. The exit rate from employment into non-employment is substantially higher for low-paid workers. A large proportion of entries into low-paid jobs is accounted for by shifts from outside full-time employment (i.e. young people from part-time work or non-employment—Podgursky and Swaim, 1987; Ruhm, 1991). The probability of moving out of low pay is highest for young people, because at early ages workers are more likely to receive training or to be shopping around for the right jobs (Mincer and Jovanovic, 1982). However, there is some controversy on the robustness of this result (compare Gustafsson, 1994, for Sweden, Gittleman and Joyce, 1995, for the USA). Last but not least, the probability of moving out of low pay is higher for males than for females (Atkinson *et al.*, 1992; Gregory and Elias, 1994; and Gittleman and Joyce, 1995).

## The Low-Pay Trap and Lifetime Effects

Long-term, life-cycle studies of pay dynamics across countries are scarce, since data requirements are quite demanding. Available studies cover a modest number of years (e.g. OECD, 1996) and international comparison is mostly rather limited and restricted to aggregate patterns, paying little attention to the determinants of mobility (e.g. Gregory and Elias, 1994; Gottschalk and Moffit, 1994; Eriksson, 1998; McKnight, 1998; Buchinsky *et al.*, 2003; Lucifora *et al.*, 2005).[19]

---

[19] European Commission (2004), chapter 4, compares one-year transition rates only, averaged over seven pooled waves of ECHP (1994–2001), and lumps all available EU countries together for analyzing the determinants of mobility.

The main results do not support the existence of a long-run trade-off between low-wage employment and unemployment. Common to most countries is that, over the last 25 years, women's position in employment improved while at the same time their low-pay employment share declined (OECD, 1997; Lucifora *et al.*, 2005). Some studies have investigated the long-run relationship between low pay and occupations. Greenhalgh and Stewart (1985) and Elias and Blanchflower (1989) find significant heterogeneity in wage mobility and wage profiles by occupation and family background.[20] McKnight (1998, 2000), in an analysis of age–earnings profiles by occupation for Great Britain, shows that the long-run increase in inequality was mainly driven by an increase in the dispersion of these profiles by social class, with big gains for managerial and professional employees but continuing flat age–wage curves for employees in low-skilled occupations. Without significant upward occupational mobility, employees in low-skilled (low-paid) occupations face little prospect of wage progression. A comparison of earnings mobility across a number of OECD countries shows that the most unequal economies do not show higher mobility. Although mobility does reduce long-run measures of inequality, its impact is fairly small, and in Britain earnings inequality rose rapidly over the last quarter of the 20th century while earnings mobility actually fell.

An alternative approach to low-pay persistence is provided by analyzing the different components of wage variation, decomposing the total variance into 'permanent' and 'temporary' effects. Results show that the probability of low pay virtually coincides with total (permanent) probability for older cohorts, while it is very small for young cohorts (with very high transitory probability), supporting the view that low pay is largely a 'stepping stone' for the young and often a 'trap' for the old (Dickens, 2000; Cappellari, 2000a, 2004, 2006).

## Employer Behavior

Firm characteristics play a central role as there is enormous heterogeneity in firm behavior with respect to wage formation also within the lower part of the earnings distribution (Abowd and Kramarz, 1999; Abowd *et al.*, 1999, 2006; Cardoso, 2006; Scott and Neumark, 2005; Bingley and Lanot, 2003; Bazen *et al.*, 2005). Firm effects on low pay have been addressed in various ways, by simply augmenting the individual human capital specification with firm attributes, by adding firm fixed effects to the wage equation or, in more recent contributions, by modeling firm behavior more explicitly. An important issue is whether the distinction between low-wage employment and the rest of the economy is due to the level of pay simply being lower than elsewhere or a different functioning of the labor market. The

---

[20] Greenhalgh and Stewart (1985) use event history, Elias and Blanchflower (1989) work history.

international evidence shows a high concentration of low pay in specific industries that mainly depend on consumer demand. Combined with the high levels of worker turnover and the important roles of small firms and of job characteristics such as flexible contracts and working part-time, this may provide support to the structural view. However, it is difficult to find strong evidence on this as we still know very little about the role of the firm in (low) wage setting (Holzer, 2005). Matched employer–employee data show the importance of accounting for the firm when linking the likelihood of escaping low pay to the sector of the firm employing the low-paid person (Bolvig, 2005). Lam et al. (2006) examine the way the UK minimum wage affects the pay structure of relevant companies, by wage compression or a broader uplifting of wages above the minimum wage. Other analyses focus on the role of a firm's wage bill and the significant effects on this of the pay of employees leaving and joining the firm (Duhautois and Kramarz, 2006). The role of the economy and the diverging structure of (consumer) demand in explaining low-paid service employment is developed in Gregory et al. (2007). Several contributions use legislative changes in institutions as natural experiments to assess the degree of firms' monopsony power in wage setting. Manning (1996) exploits the UK Equal Pay Act of 1970 to investigate the effects on female employment and concludes that wage setting in the female labor market is, in part, monopsonistic. Card and Krueger (1994, 1995) exploit the 1992 increase in the New Jersey minimum wage to evaluate the impact on the fast-food industry in comparison with adjacent Pennsylvania. They find no evidence of reduced employment, to the contrary, thus supporting the view that the low-wage labor market is often monopsonistic. Other contributions (Dickens et al., 1999; Machin and Manning, 1994) use data on Wages Council coverage from the UK to examine the impact of mandated minimum wages on wage dispersion and employment and find evidence consistent with dynamic monopsony. Finally, some contributions focusing more broadly on the low-wage segment find evidence of non-competitive behavior consistent with monopsony power (Machin et al., 1993; Manning, 2000; Machin et al., 2003; Green et al., 1996).

More recent research has focused on the effect of skill-biased labor demand on wage inequality and low pay (Autor et al., 2006; Autor and Dorn, 2007; Spitz-Oener, 2006; and Goos and Manning, 2007). Their main findings suggest that the growth of employment and earnings in the service sector—both for high-skilled services (financial services) and low-skilled jobs (personal and household services)—has resulted in a progressive polarization of the occupational distribution between 'good jobs' and 'bad jobs' and of the wage distribution between high-wage jobs and lower-paying ones,[21] while routine jobs in the middle (clerical, decision-making, and production tasks) are displaced by automation.

---

[21] Also Burtless (1990) for US evidence.

## Institutions and Labor Market Regulation

One highly relevant issue for analyzing low-wage employment is the relationship with labor-market institutions. These can affect the extent of low pay through a variety of channels, some of which are more direct than others. The literature shows that certain institutions significantly affect the characteristics and the evolution of the wage structure. The establishment of wage floors, formally through statutory minimum wages or bargained minima and materially through social-security benefits, is an important feature. When the compressing effect of wage floors is concentrated on the bottom end of the wage distribution, its impact on low-wage employment may be substantial (Dell'Aringa and Lucifora, 1994; Lucifora, 2000; Robson et al., 1999; Koeniger et al., 2007). Indeed, in the empirical literature, part of the substantial international variation in the incidence of low pay results from differences in institutional settings.[22] Blau and Kahn (1996) find that institutional features, such as high rates of unionization and collective-bargaining coverage, appear to create wage floors and reduce earnings dispersion, particularly in the bottom half of the distribution. Other empirical evidence (Lucifora et al., 2005) shows that where unionization is low a larger pool of low-wage workers is observed. In the USA only 14 percent of workers are members of a trade union and the proportion of low-paid workers is over 25 percent, whilst in Sweden union density is over 80 percent and less than 6 percent of workers are below the low-pay threshold. However, unionization has been traditionally low in some countries, such as France, which have at the same time experienced a fairly low incidence in low-wage employment. Here the provisions for mandatory extension of collective bargaining can make the degree of bargaining coverage a more appropriate indicator of the effective 'strength' of unions in protecting against low wages. Accounting for the extension of collective agreements confirms the negative correlation between union power and low-wage employment. However, the Netherlands seems to provide an example of high and unchanged coverage of collective agreements going together with a surge in low-wage employment (Salverda et al., 2008).

The presence of a statutory minimum wage and the generosity of unemployment benefits may impact on the bottom end of the wage distribution and on the propensity of individuals to enter the labor market and take up low-paid jobs. In general, a high (low) minimum wage relative to the average wage (as measured by the Kaitz index) tends to be associated with lower (higher) levels of low-wage employment.[23] Mishel and Bernstein (1994) and Dinardo et al. (1996) suggest that the decline in the value of the Federal minimum wage relative to average wages was

---

[22]  Keese et al. (1998), Lucifora (2000), and Lucifora et al. (2005) summarize the role of institutions in comparative analysis of low-wage employment and earnings inequality in general.

[23]  Recent OECD data suggest a decline of the Kaitz index in many countries in recent years. See Immervoll (2007) for a review of minimum wages, labor costs, and tax treatment of low-wage employment. The Low Pay Commission (1998) reviews the coverage and dynamics of the UK minimum wage.

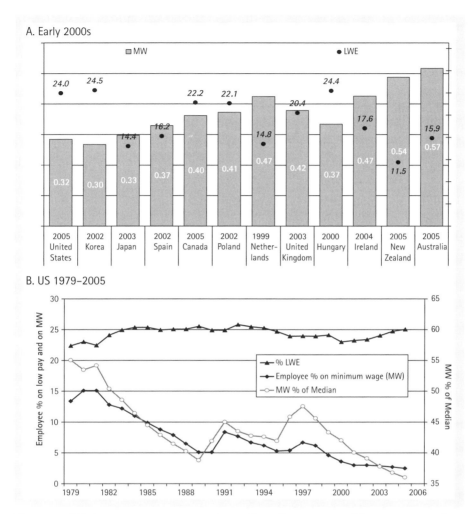

Fig. 11.3. **Minimum wage as percentage of median wage and low-wage employment as percentage of employees (full-time)**

*Notes*: Panel A: Upper end of graph corresponds with low-pay threshold of two-thirds of median wage. Note that earnings definitions and the nature of national sources differ significantly. Panel B: on hourly basis, incidence of minimum-wage (MW) earners among employees paid by the hour.
*Sources*: Authors' calculations from OECD (Panel A) and EPI, *State of Working America 2006/2007* and BLS, *Characteristics of Minimum-Wage Workers 2005* (Panel B).

an important factor behind the rise in US earnings inequality during the 1980s. In the UK, minimum wages in a number of low-pay sectors prior to 1993 were established by Wages Councils, which have subsequently been abolished. Machin and Manning (1994) estimated that, in these sectors, the decline in the minimum relative to the average wage over the 1980s accounted for between 9 to 20 percent of the rise in the dispersion of earnings. In cross-section (Fig. 11.3A) similar levels of the minimum wage correspond to different levels of low-wage employment and vice versa. The long-run evolution, for the USA (Fig. 11.3B), indicates that lowering the minimum wage does not automatically raise the incidence of low pay as the incidence of the minimum wage also declines. In 1979 when the relative minimum wage was at a much higher level (55%), comparable to other countries, the incidence of low pay differed little from that of today.

Other institutional settings beyond wage determination and social benefits may influence the incidence of low pay indirectly. Labor-market deregulation has been suggested as another important determinant of the increase in wage inequality and in the share of low pay (Peoples, 1998). The increasing numbers of flexible employment contracts and working-time arrangements, the less stringent controls on employers' hiring and firing practices and the associated reduction in the degree of job protection, the growing decentralization of bargaining, and the weakening of trade unions throughout Europe, are some of the facets of the deregulation process that have affected labor markets and contributed to the increase in low-wage employment. In particular, the diffusion of non-standard forms of employment (examples are: the Italian 'Co.Co.Co.', the French Contrat Première Embauche, or the German 'Mini-jobs') have had important implications for the incidence of low-paid jobs: over one-third of all employment relationships in Europe belong to some form of non-standard employment and are at risk of low pay (Booth *et al.*, 2002).[24]

# 5. Conclusion and Further Research

Despite the considerable evidence accumulated in the literature surveyed here, the corpus of results is still rather heterogeneous and fragmented and a number of important issues are still uncertain or unknown and merit further attention.

First, to address most of the issues it would be very useful to establish an international, systematic database of low-pay incidence and dynamics adopting strictly comparable definitions of (low) pay and a uniform measurement across the economy, and covering as much of the economy, as many countries, and as many years as possible. This could generate a superior set of stylized facts and would enable the links between micro-level outcomes and the macroeconomic context to be explored in an international comparison. Are the incidence of low pay and mobility out of it sensitive to the stage in the business cycle? What is the significance

---

[24] Typical examples of non-standard jobs are: insurance company representatives, truck drivers in the transport trade, construction workers, shop assistants, freelancers who work in the media, but also white-collar workers whose contracts of employment have been replaced by consultancy agreements. From the employer's point of view there are several advantages in offering non-standard jobs: labor costs and social security contributions are significantly reduced (usually no collective agreement or industrial and social laws apply).

of low pay for the economy? Also the question whether countries face a trade-off between 'allowing' earnings inequality to rise and worsening the employment prospects of low-skilled workers is far from being resolved. Earnings inequality has risen slightly or remained stable in a number of countries, but there is little evidence that the relatively low incidence of low-paid jobs is associated with lower employment rates for low-skilled and inexperienced workers.

A second aspiration may be developing comparable research on high pay, say above 1.5 times the median wage. The contrast may sharpen the understanding of low-wage employment and the attraction of moving upward, including the hurdle a declining middle may pose.

Third, in spite of the many microeconometric studies the individual explanation of low pay is not well established. For example, is the high incidence of low pay among women a sign of discrimination or does it reflect a trade-off against other uses of time in life, given the modest overlap of low pay and household poverty and the often part-time nature of participation? Also, such a trade-off may involve net after-tax wages while virtually all studies of low pay focus on gross wages. Fourth, the modest overlap of low pay and poverty is based on cross-section analysis, a 'snapshot' perspective that ignores issues of income distribution within households and masks the dynamics of social exclusion over a lifetime. Poverty transitions in conjunction with earnings mobility warrant more attention. Adequacy of income in retirement is for most based on labor incomes over their working lives and low earnings may lead to poverty in later life due to inadequate pensions (Hughes and Nolan, 2000). The relationship between trends in earnings inequality at any point in time and lifetime inequality of earnings needs to be investigated further. Fifth, low-paid workers in any one year tend to have very diverse career and earnings prospects, with many moving up the earnings ladder, but also with many remaining in low-paid jobs or leaving (full-time) employment altogether. The factors determining why some workers move into better jobs, but others do not, are not well understood.

Employer behavior is another dimension where more useful internationally comparative work can be carried out. More work on the labor-cost aspect of earnings will help in understanding the workings of the low-wage labor market from the point of view of the firms demanding labor. A direct analysis of firms operating low pay and minimum wages among their workforce seems an important avenue for research. Only a minority of firms operate here and it will be important to consider their characteristics within and across countries, and also their individual evolution—how many manage to develop and move away from low pay over their lifetime? How do they react to the state of the economy?

Last but not least, what are the implications of the above for policy making and future research? It is outside the scope of this contribution to consider the literature on policy measures bearing some relation to low pay, for example minimum wages, income support for low-earning families, social benefits, or active labor market policies (see e.g. Salverda *et al.*, 2000). Instead we briefly consider the implications of the above for policy making and research thereon. This is all the more important as international integration and globalization may increasingly limit the national room for maneuver. It is clear, first, that there is good reason for policy to be focused on these issues, not only for social reasons (poverty) but also for reasons of economic efficiency—both in the long run if the price of labor may be non-accidentally distorted and negatively affect productivity growth, and in the short run if pay differentials are considered unfair among the workforce. Second, the possibility of low-wage and high-wage equilibria implies that there will be much more at stake than just the level of pay. For example, education and training inside or outside the labor market and firm behavior in this and other respects will have to be addressed as well. This implies that policies that simply focus on increasing the amount of low-wage employment—quite popular in various European countries in recent years—risk ignoring potential effects in a range of other fields and in the long run. Finally, the lack of well-established and longer-run stylized facts on low pay and the consequent inadequacy of the economic analysis of low pay imply that a proper policy analysis should cover low-wage incidence and dynamics. In the absence of that an 'optimal' scale for low pay cannot be determined.

## References

ABOWD, J. M., and KRAMARZ, F. 1999. 'The Analysis of Labor Markets Using Matched Employer–Employee Data', in O. Ashenfelter and D. Card (eds.), *Handbook of Labor Economics*. Amsterdam: Elsevier, 2629–710.

———— and MARGOLIS, D. 1999. 'High Wage Workers and High Wage Firms'. *Econometrica*, 67: 251–333.

—— KRAMARZ, F., and ROUX, S. 2006. 'Wages, Mobility, and Firm Performance: An Analysis Using Matched Employee and Employer Data from France'. *Economic Journal*, 116: F245–F285.

ACEMOGLU, D. 2001. 'Good Jobs versus Bad Jobs', *Journal of Labor Economics*, 19: 1–21.

ANDERSSON, F., HOLZER, H., and LANE, J. 2005. *Moving Up or Moving On: Who Advances in the Low-Wage Labor Market?* New York: Russell Sage.

ANDRESZ, H.-J., and LOHMANN, H. (eds.) 2008. *The Working Poor in Europe*. Cheltenham: Edward Elgar.

ASPLUND, R., SLOANE, P., and THEODOSSIOU, I. (eds.) 1998. *Low Pay and Earnings Mobility in Europe*. Cheltenham: Edward Elgar.

ATKINSON, T., BOURGUIGNON, F., and MORRISSON, C. 1992. *Empirical Studies of Earnings Mobility*. Newark, NJ: Harwood Academic Publishers.

AUTOR, D., and DORN, D. 2007. 'Inequality and Specialization: The Growth of Low-Skill Service Jobs in the United States'. Mimeo.

—— KATZ, L. F., and SCHETTINI KEARNEY, M. 2006. 'The Polarization of the U.S. Labor Market'. *American Economic Review*, 96(2): 189–94.

BAZEN, S., GREGORY, M., and SALVERDA, W. (eds.) 1998. *Low-Wage Employment in Europe*. Cheltenham: Edward Elgar.

—— LUCIFORA, C., and SALVERDA, W. (eds.) 2005. *Job Quality and Employer Behaviour*. Basingstoke: Palgrave Macmillan.

BINGLEY, P., and LANOT, G. 2003. 'The Incidence of Income Tax on Wages and Labour Supply'. *Journal of Public Economics*, 83(2); 173–94.

BLANCHARD, O. J., and DIAMOND, P. A. 1994. 'Ranking, Unemployment Duration, and Wages'. *Review of Economic Studies*, 61: 417–34.

BLAU, F., and KAHN, L. 1996. 'International Differences in Male Wage Inequality: Institutions versus Market Forces'. *Journal of Political Economy*, 104(4): 791–836.

—— —— 2004. 'The US Gender Pay Gap in the 1990s: Slowing Convergence'. NBER Working Paper 10853.

—— —— 2005. 'Do Cognitive Test Scores Explain Higher U.S. Wage Inequality?' *Review of Economics and Statistics*, 87(1): 184–93.

BOLVIG, I. 2005. 'Within- and Between-Firm Mobility in the Low-Wage Labor Market', in Bazen *et al.* (2005), 132–56.

BOOTH, A., FRANCESCONI, M., and FRANK, J. 2002. 'Temporary Jobs: Stepping Stones or Dead Ends?' *Economic Journal*, 112: 189–213.

BOUSHEY, H., FREMSTAD, S., GRAGG, R., and WALLER, M. 2007. *Understanding Low-Wage Work in the United States*. Washington: CEPR.

BUCHINSKY, M., FIELDS, G. S., FOUGERE, D., and KRAMARZ, F. 2003. 'Francs or Ranks? Earnings Mobility in France, 1967–1999'. CEPR Discussion Papers no. 3937.

BURTLESS, G. (ed.) 1990. *A Future of Lousy Jobs? The Changing Structure of U.S. Wages*. Washington: Brookings Institute.

CAPPELLARI, L. 2000a. 'The Covariance Structure of Italian Male Wages'. *The Manchester School*, 68(6): 659–84.

—— 2000b. 'Low-Wage Mobility in the Italian Labour Market'. *International Journal of Manpower*, 21(3–4): 264–90.

—— 2002. 'Do the "Working Poor" Stay Poor? An Analysis of Low Pay Transitions in Italy'. *Oxford Bulletin of Economics and Statistics*, 64(2): 87–110.

—— 2004. 'The Dynamics and Inequality of Italian Men's Earnings: Permanent Changes or Transitory Fluctuations?' *Journal of Human Resources*, 39(2): 475–99.

—— 2006. 'Earnings Mobility among Italian Low Paid Workers'. *Journal of Population Economics*, 20(2): 465–82.

—— and JENKINS, S. P. 2004. 'Modelling Low Income Transitions'. *Journal of Applied Econometrics*, 19(5): 593–610.

CARD, D., and KRUEGER, A. B. 1994. 'Minimum Wages and Employment: A Case Study of the Fast-Food Industry in New Jersey and Pennsylvania'. *American Economic Review*, 84(4): 772–93.

—— —— 1995. *Myth and Measuremen: The New Economics of the Minimum Wage*. Princeton: Princeton University Press.

CARDOSO A. 2006. 'Wage Mobility: Do Institutions Make a Difference?' *Labor Economics*, 13: 387–404.

CONTINI, B., FILIPPI, M., and VILLOSIO, C. 1998. 'Earnings Mobility in the Italian Economy', in Asplund *et al.* (1998), 15–31.

DEDING, M. 2002. 'Low Wage Mobility in Denmark, Germany, and the United States'. The Danish National Institute of Social Research, Working Paper 33.

DELL'ARINGA, C., and LUCIFORA, C. 1994. 'Wage Dispersion and Unionism: Do Unions Protect Low Pay?' *International Journal of Manpower*, 15: 150–70.

DEVROYE, D., and FREEMAN, R. 2000. 'Does Inequality in Skills Explain Inequality of Earnings Across Countries?' Working Paper, Harvard University.

DICKENS, R. 2000. 'Caught in a Trap? Wage Mobility in Great Britain: 1975–94'. *Economica*, 67: 477–97.

——MACHIN, S., and MANNING, A. 1999. 'Effects of Minimum Wages on Employment: Theory and Evidence from Britain'. *Journal of Labor Economics*, 17(1): 1–22.

DINARDO, J., FORTIN, N., and LEMIEUX, T. 1996. 'Labor Market Institutions and the Distribution of Wages, 1973–1992: A Semi-parametric Approach'. *Econometrica*, 64(5): 1001–44.

DOERINGER, P. B., and PIORE, M. J. 1971. *Internal Labor Markets and Manpower Analysis*. Lexington, Mass.: D. C. Heath.

DUHAUTOIS, R., and KRAMARZ, F. 2006. 'Wage Bill Creation and Destruction'. Paper presented at 2006 International Comparative Analysis of Enterprises (Micro) Data Conference, Sept. 18–19. Chicago.

ELIAS, P., and BLANCHFLOWER, D. 1989. 'Occupational Earnings and Work Histories: Who Gets the Good Jobs?' Department of Employment, Research Paper no. 68.

ERIKSSON T. 1998. 'Long-Term Earnings Mobility of Low-Paid Workers in Finland', in Asplund *et al.* (1998), 32–46.

EUROPEAN COMMISSION 2004. 'Labor Market Transitions and Advancement: Temporary Employment and Low Pay'. *Employment in Europe: Recent Trends and Prospects*. Luxembourg: European Commission, 159–86.

FERNANDEZ, M., MEIXIDE, A., NOLAN, B., and SIMON, H. 2004. 'Low-Wage Employment in Europe'. PIEP Working Paper, Centre for Economic Performance, LSE.

FREEMAN, RICHARD, and SCHETTKAT, RONALD. 2001. 'Skill Compression, Wage Differentials, and Employment: Germany vs the US'. *Oxford Economic Papers*, 53: 582–603.

GITTLEMAN, M., and JOYCE, M. 1995. 'Earnings Mobility in the United States, 1967–91'. *Monthly Labor Review*, 118(9): 3–13.

GOOS, M., and MANNING, A. 2007. 'Lousy and Lovely Jobs: The Rising Polarization of Work in Britain'. *Review of Economics and Statistics*, 89(1): 118–33.

GOTTSCHALK, P. 1997. 'Inequality, Income Growth, and Mobility: The Basic Facts'. *Journal of Economic Perspectives*, 11(2): 21–40.

——and MOFFITT, R. 1994. 'The Growth of Earnings Instability in the U.S. Labor Market'. *Brookings Paper on Economic Activity*, 2: 217–54.

GREEN, F., MACHIN, S., and MANNING, A. 1996. 'The Employer Size-Wage Effect: Can Dynamic Monopsony Provide an Explanation?' *Oxford Economic Papers*, 48(3): 433–55

GREENHALGH, C. A., and STEWART, M. B. 1985. 'The Occupational Status and Mobility of British Men and Women'. *Oxford Economic Papers*, 37(1): 40–71.

GREGORY, M., and ELIAS, P. 1994. 'Earnings Transitions of the Low-Paid in Britain, 1976–91: A Longitudinal Study'. *International Journal of Manpower*, 15(2–3): 170–88.

————1996. 'Earnings Transitions of the Low-Paid in Britain, 1976–91: A Longitudinal Study'. *International Journal of Manpower*, 15(2–3): 170–88.

——and JUKES, R. 2001. 'Unemployment and Subsequent Earnings: Estimating Scarring among British Men 1984–94'. *Economic Journal*, 111(475): 607–25.

——SALVERDA, W., and BAZEN, S. (eds.) 2000. *Labor Market Inequalities: Problems and Policies of Low-Wage Employment in International Perspective*. Oxford: Oxford University Press.

——————and SCHETTKAT, R. (eds.) 2007. *Services and Employment: Explaining the US–European Gap*. Princeton: Princeton University Press.

GUSTAFSSON, B. 1994. 'The Degree and Pattern of Income Immobility in Sweden'. *Review of Income and Wealth*, 40(1): 67–86.

HOLZER, H. 2005. 'Employers in the Low-Wage Labor Market: Is Their Role Important?', in Bazen *et al.* (2005), 87–110.

IMMERVOLL, H. 2007. 'Minimum Wages, Minimum Labor Costs and the Tax Treatment of Low-Wage Employment'. OECD Social, Employment and Migration Working Papers no. 46, Paris.

INTERNATIONAL LABOR ORGANIZATION 1928. *General Conference of the International Labour Organisation* (C26 Minimum Wage-Fixing Machinery Convention). Geneva.

KEESE, M., PUYMOYEN, A., and SWAIM, P. 1998. 'The Incidence and Dynamics of Low-Paid Employment in OECD Countries', in Asplund *et al.* (1998), 223–65.

KOENIGER, W., LEONARDI, M., and NUNZIATA, L. 2007. 'Labor Market Institutions and Wage Differentials'. *Industrial & Labor Relations Review*, 60(3): 340–56.

KRUGMAN, P. 1994. 'Europe Jobless, America Penniless?', *Foreign Policy*, 95: 19–34.

LAM, K., ORMEROD, C., RITCHIE, F., and VAZE, P. 2006. 'Do Company Wage Policies Persist in the Face of Minimum Wages?' *Labour Market Trends*, Mar.: 69–82.

LEUVEN, E., OOSTERBEEK, H., and van OPHEM, H. 2004. 'Explaining International Differences in Male Skill Wage Differentials by Differences in Demand and Supply of Skill'. *Economic Journal*, 114 (495): 466–86.

LOHMANN, H. 2008. 'The Working Poor in European Welfare States: Empirical Evidence from a Multilevel Perspective', in Andresz and Lohmann (2008).

LOW PAY COMMISSION 1998. *The National Minimum Wage, First Report*. Cm. 3796. London: The Stationary Office.

LUCIFORA C. 2000. 'Labour Market Institutions and Low Wage Employment', in Gregory *et al.* (2000), 9–34.

——McKNIGHT, A., and SALVERDA, W. 2005. 'Low-Wage Employment in Europe: A Review of the Evidence'. *Socio-Economic Review*, 3: 259–92.

——and SALVERDA, W. (eds.) 1998. *Policies for Low-Wage Employment and Social Exclusion*. Milan: FrancoAngeli.

MACHIN, S., and MANNING, A. 1994. 'The Effects of Minimum Wages on Wage Dispersion and Employment: Evidence from the U.K. Wages Councils'. *Industrial and Labor Relations Review*, 47(2): 319–29.

——————and RAHMAN, L. 2003. 'Where the Minimum Wage Bites Hard: Introduction of Minimum Wages to a Low Wage Sector'. *Journal of the European Economic Association*, 1(1): 154–80.

——————and WOODLAND, S. 1993. 'Are Workers Paid their Marginal Product? Evidence from a Low Wage Labour Market'. CEP-London School of Economics, Discussion Paper no. CEPDP0158.

McKNIGHT, A. 1998. 'Low-Wage Mobility in a Working-Life Perspective', in Asplund *et al.* (1998), 47–76.

McKNIGHT, A. 2000. 'Trends in Earnings Inequality and Earnings Mobility, 1977–1997: The Impact of Mobility on Long-Term Inequality'. Department of Trade and Industry, Employment Relations Research Report no. 8.

MALTHUS T. R. 1798. *An Essay on the Principle of Population as it Affects the Future Improvement of Society, with Remarks on the Speculations of Mr. Godwin, M. Condorcet, and Other Writers*, 1st edn. London: J. Johnson.

MANNING, A. 1996. 'The Equal Pay Act as an Experiment to Test Theories of the Labour Market'. *Economica*, 63(250): 191–212.

——2000. 'Pretty Vacant: Recruitment in Low-Wage Labour Markets'. *Oxford Bulletin of Economics and Statistics*, 62: 747–70.

——2003. *Monopsony in Motion: Imperfect Competition in Labor Markets*. Princeton: Princeton University Press.

MARX, K. 1859. *Critique of Political Economy*. English translation by I. Stone. London: Charles H. Kerr Publishing, 1904.

MASON, G., and SALVERDA, W. 2009. 'Low Pay, Living Standards and Employment', in Schmitt *et al.* (2009).

MINCER, J., and JOVANOVIC, B. 1982. 'Mobility and Wages'. NBER Working Papers no. 357.

MISHEL, L., and BERNSTEIN, J. 1994. *The State of Working America: 1994–1995*. New York: Economic Policy and Cornell University Press.

——————and ALLEGRETTO, S. 2007. *The State of Working America 2006/2007*. New York: Economic Policy and Cornell University Press.

NEUMARK, D., and WASCHER, W. 2002. 'State-Level Estimates of Minimum Wage Effects: New Evidence and Interpretations from Disequilibrium Models'. *Journal of Human Resources*, 37(1): 35–62.

NICKELL, S. J., and BELL, B. 1996. 'Changes in the Distribution of Wages and Unemployment in the OECD Countries'. *American Economic Review*, 86, Papers and Proceedings: 3028.

——and LAYARD, R. 1999. 'Labour Market Institutions and Economic Performance', in O. Ashenfelter and D. Card (eds.), *Handbook of Labor Economics*, vol. 3. North-Holland: Elsevier.

NOLAN, B., and HUGHES, G. 2000. 'Low Pay, the Earnings Distribution and Poverty in Ireland, 1987–1994', in Gregory *et al.* (2000).

OECD 1996. *Employment Outlook*. Paris: OECD.

——1997. *Employment Outlook*, Paris: OECD.

——2006. *Employment Outlook*, Paris: OECD.

PEOPLES, J. 1998. 'Deregulation and the Labor Market'. *Journal of Economic Perspectives*, 12: 111–30.

PISSARIDES, C. 2000. *Equilibrium Unemployment Theory*, 2nd edn. Cambridge, Mass.: MIT Press.

PODGURSKY, M., and SWAIM, P. 1987. 'Job Displacement and Earnings Loss: Evidence from the Displaced Worker Survey'. *Industrial and Labor Relations Review*, 41(1): 117–29.

RICARDO, D. 1817. *On the Principles of Political Economy and Taxation*, 1st edn. London: John Murray.

ROBSON, P., DEX, S., WILKINSON, F., and SALIDA CORTES, O. 1999. 'Low Pay. Labor Market Institutions. Gender and Part-time Work: Cross-National Comparisons'. *European Journal of Industrial Relations*, 5(2): 187–207.

RUHM, C. J. 1991. 'Are Workers Permanently Scarred by Job Displacements?' *American Economic Review*, 81(1): 319–24.

SALVERDA, W., NOLAN, B., and LUCIFORA, C. (eds.) 2000. *Policy Measures for Low-Wage Employment in Europe*. Cheltenham: Edward Elgar.

———— MAITRE, B., and MÜHLAU, P. 2001. 'Benchmarking Low-Wage and High-Wage Employment in Europe and the United States'. Report to the European Commission DG Employment and Social Affairs, <http://ec.europa.ev/employment_social/docs/study.pdf>.

—— VAN KLAVEREN, M., and VAN DER MEER, M. (eds.) 2008. *Low-Wage Work in the Netherlands*. New York: Russell Sage.

SCHMITT, J., GAUTIÉ, J., BOSCH, G., MASON, G., MAYHEW, K., SALVERDA, W., and WESTERGÅRD-NIELSEN, N. (eds.) 2009. *Low-Wage Employment in the United States and Europe* (provisional title). New York: Russell Sage.

SCOTT, A., and NEUMARK, D. 2005. 'When Do Living Wages Bite?' *Industrial Relations*, 164–92.

SLOANE, P. J., and THEODOSSIOU, I. 1996. 'Earnings Mobility, Family Income and Low Pay'. *Economic Journal*, 106: 657–66.

———— 1998. 'Methodological and Econometric Issues in the Measurement of Low Pay and Earnings Mobility', in Asplund *et al.* (1998), 3–12

SPITZ-OENER, A. 2006. 'Technical Change, Job Tasks, and Rising Educational Demands: Looking Outside the Wage Structure'. *Journal of Labor Economics*, 24(2): 235–70.

STEWART, M. B. 2006. 'The Inter-related Dynamics of Unemployment and Low Pay'. *Journal of Applied Econometrics*, 22(3): 511–31.

—— and SWAFFIELD, J. K. 1999. 'Low Pay Dynamics and Transition Probabilities'. *Economica*, 66: 23–42.

———— 2004. 'The Other Margin: Do Minimum Wages Cause Working Hours Adjustments for Low-wage Workers?' Report to the UK Low Pay Commission, London.

STRENGMANN-KUHN, W. 2002. 'Working Poor in Europe: A Partial Basic Income for Workers?' Paper presented at BIEN 9th International Congress, Geneva. Sept. 12–14.

UNIVERSAL DECLARATION ON HUMAN RIGHTS 1948. General Assembly Resolution 217 A (III) of 10 December 1948. United Nations.

WESTERGÅRD-NIELSEN, N. 1989. 'Empirical Studies of the European Labour Market using Micro-economic Data Sets'. *European Economic Review*, 33: 389–94.

WILKINSON, F. (ed.) 1981. *The Dynamics of Labour Market Segmentation*. London: Academic Press.

WILKINSON, R. G., and PICKETT, K. E. 2007. 'The Problems of Relative Deprivation: Why some Societies do Better than Others'. *Social Science and Medicine*, 65: 1965–78.

CHAPTER 12

# GENDER AND ECONOMIC INEQUALITY

## MARY GREGORY

## 1. INTRODUCTION: WOMEN'S CHANGING STATUS

ECONOMIC inequality of women has featured since Old Testament times and doubt-less before that. The second half of the 20th century, however, brought a major transformation including, for the first time, the promotion of gender equality as a formal commitment on national and international political agendas. In the advanced economies the role of women in paid employment has expanded at an unprecedented rate, leading, in some countries, to near parity with the numbers of men in the labor force for the first time within the span of modern statistics. This feminization of the workforce in numerical terms has been paralleled by qualitative changes as women enter occupations and industries from which they were previously absent, or enter these in increasing numbers. This development is particularly marked in managerial positions and the professions. With this progres-sive shift of women's economic activity from household to market place women's

I would like to thank my discussant at Sevilla, Eugene Smolensky, other conference participants, and the editors for many helpful comments and suggestions; also Sara Connolly and Alison Booth for many previous conversations.

earnings are making an increasingly important contribution to the household's income, enhancing their status and bargaining power within it. These developments have brought women an unprecedented degree of financial independence, and they have been a key element in the transformation of their economic and social position.

But while women continue to make major strides towards economic equality, the transformation remains seriously incomplete. Their employment opportunities are still often inferior, and concentrated into a relatively narrow range of activities; they remain under-represented in prestige professions and 'top jobs'; they typically receive lower pay; and they feature disproportionately among the low-paid. Equality of outcomes in the labor market has not been achieved. Outside the labor market, largely unmeasured in economic statistics but of great practical importance, women still provide most of the care for children and the elderly, often curtailing their labor market participation to do so. Women's lower earnings in employment and shorter working lives bring lower lifetime earnings, reduced pension entitlements and a greater risk of poverty in old age, all accentuating their economic inequality.

The persistence of unequal outcomes, with the underutilization of female abilities and restriction of individual opportunities which it implies, is economically inefficient and socially inequitable. This has prompted the widespread introduction of anti-discrimination legislation, progressively strengthened and extended through provisions on equal opportunities and equal treatment, on occasion affirmative action, and, more recently, a range of measures aimed at supporting mothers in employment. Even after several decades of massive economic and social change, inequality in economic outcomes remains a significant issue. For some it is clear evidence of unequal treatment or discrimination. For others, unequal outcomes should not be unexpected and need not be unacceptable. If the labor market position of women is freely chosen then there is no cause for concern at its 'inferiority' and intervention would be distortionary. Others again have an uneasy feeling that genuinely equal opportunities are not on offer, but that the issue of advancing parity in the labor market is secondary to increasing parity in the home and in non-market work; the role of women in child-bearing and child-rearing poses a basic difference, or inequality, but should not lead to a lifetime's difference in economic status.

This chapter assesses the changing economic status of women, the forces driving it, and its implications for inequality between women and men and among women. Section 2 reviews women's growing labor market participation and its changing occupational structure. The extent and sources of the gender pay gap are analyzed in Section 3. Section 4 reviews two of the major drivers of recent economic change for women: the transformation of their educational status, and the impact of technology. The implications of women's rising employment and earnings for household inequality and their changing fertility patterns are addressed in Section 5. Section 6 examines the contribution of the legal framework to reducing inequality. Section 7 concludes with pointers to areas for further research.

# 2. THE GENDER GAP IN EMPLOYMENT

## Women's Employment Participation Rates

A generation ago just over 100 million women were in the labor force across the advanced economies. By 2005 this had risen to almost 180 million, in one of the most sustained and striking economic and social developments of the era. As Table 12.1 illustrates, the upward trend is almost universal, with women's employment growing at more than twice the (modest) growth rate for men. As a result the female share in OECD employment has risen from 37 to 45 percent, highest in the Nordic nations (over 48 percent in Finland) and lowest, just over 40 percent, in southern Europe.

This massive expansion in women's labor force participation has halved the gender employment gap, as measured by the difference in the employment/population ratios for men and women. Figure 12.1 shows the marked trend towards convergence, with participation rates growing particularly strongly in those countries where it was lowest (southern Europe) while remaining static, or even declining, where it had already reached high levels (Sweden; recently the USA). In spite of strong recent growth, women's participation in southern Europe remains below the level already attained in much of the rest of the OECD a generation ago. A major force driving this narrowing of the gender employment gap has been the rising employment among mothers now taking fewer and shorter breaks from employment; in the USA and the UK one out of two new mothers now returns to work before the baby's first birthday. In other countries, however, entry or re-entry into paid employment has been by women of all ages (Germany, Netherlands).[1]

The gender gap in employment on a headcount basis understates the gender gap in paid work done. Women working full-time work shorter weekly hours than men, reflecting differences in occupational mix. More significantly, women are much more likely to engage in part-time work; 26 percent of women but under 7 percent of men in OECD countries work part-time. The incidence of part-time work among women varies widely. By far the highest part-time share is in the Netherlands, 57 percent of women in employment, but it is also over 40 percent in the UK, Norway, Switzerland, and Australia; in the USA, Sweden and Italy, on the other hand, it is around 20 percent. It is noteworthy that no consistent relation

---

[1] For a detailed description of these developments see OECD (2002).

Table 12.1. Civilian labor force, OECD and selected countries, 1973–2005

| Country | Female civilian labor force (millions) | | | Females: average annual increase % | Males: average annual increase % | Female share in civilian labor force % | | |
|---|---|---|---|---|---|---|---|---|
| | 1973 | 1995 | 2005 | 1973–2005 | 1973–2005 | 1973 | 1995 | 2005 |
| France | 8.1 | 11.4 | 12.8 | 1.4 | 0.2 | 37.7 | 45.9 | 47.3 |
| Germany[1] | 10.2[1] | 16.8 | 18.4 | 1.9[1] | 0.9[1] | 37.8[1] | 43.1 | 45.1 |
| Italy | 6.2 | 8.4 | 9.8 | 1.5 | 0.1 | 30.3 | 37.2 | 40.5 |
| Sweden | 1.6 | 2.1 | 2.2 | 1.0 | 0.1 | 41.0 | 47.8 | 47.7 |
| United Kingdom | 9.4 | 12.5 | 13.6 | 1.2 | 0.0 | 37.1 | 44.7 | 46.4 |
| United States | 34.8 | 60.9 | 69.3 | 2.2 | 1.2 | 38.9 | 46.1 | 46.4 |
| Nordic countries[2] | 4.3 | 5.6 | 5.9 | 1.1 | 0.3 | 41.5 | 47.1 | 47.7 |
| Southern Europe[3] | 12.5[a] | 18.3 | 23.0 | 1.9[a] | 0.4[a] | 30.5[a] | 38.4 | 41.5 |
| Eastern Europe[4] | | 13.0 | 13.2 | 0.1[b] | 0.2[b] | | 45.5 | 45.3 |
| OECD | 102.9[a] | 159.1 | 178.6 | 1.7[a] | 0.7[a] | 37.2[a] | 43.6 | 44.9 |

Notes: [1] Prior to 1991 data refer to West Germany only (Federal Republic of Germany).
[2] Denmark, Finland, Norway, Sweden.
[3] Greece, Italy, Portugal, Spain.
[4] Czech Republic, Hungary, Poland, Slovakia.
[a] Greece and Portugal 1977.
[b] East Europe 1995–2005.

Source: OECD, Employment and Labor Market Statistics; Labor Force Statistics, summary tables, vol. 2006, release 03.

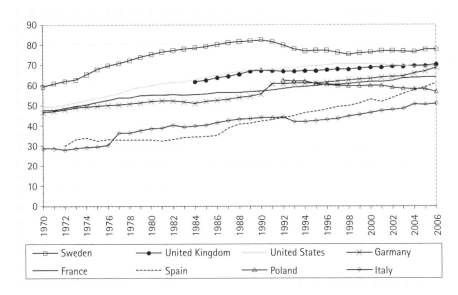

90
80
70
60
50
40
30
20
10
0

1970 1972 1974 1976 1978 1980 1982 1984 1986 1988 1990 1992 1994 1996 1998 2000 2002 2004 2006

—□— Sweden        —●— United Kingdom        United States        —✕— Garmany

——— France        ------ Spain        —▲— Poland        —◆— Italy

**Fig. 12.1. Women's labor force participation, ages 25–54; selected countries**

emerges between the level of women's labor force participation and share of part-time employment (OECD, 2002).

The advanced economies show equalizing but still unequal employment between men and women. But for the individual woman employment is a choice, with associated costs, including opportunity costs, and benefits; more is not necessarily better in welfare terms. Reported preferences, however, indicate that even among couples with a pre-school child actual employment rates for women are well below preferred levels, for both full- and part-time work, with the single bread-winner model preferred by only one-quarter of those actually following it (Jaumotte, 2003). In the light of this the European Union's Lisbon targets for increasing women's employment rates to 60 percent in all member countries may in fact be modest. At the same time the recent evidence of reversal in women's employment rates in Sweden and the USA suggests that women's preferences may set a ceiling to participation at a level noticeably short of parity with men's. Equality in welfare terms may not imply parity in numerical terms.

## The Occupational Distribution of Women's Employment

The occupational distribution of women's jobs has traditionally been seen as one of the major sources of labor market disadvantage, with women's jobs dispropor-tionately crowded into low-wage, low-status occupations. More recently, following women's rising educational attainment and labor market attachment, issues of promotions into top jobs and the glass ceiling have added a further dimension.

The distribution of employment across occupations is strongly gender-segmented. Using 50 to 80 occupational groups the OECD shows that between 60 and 80 percent of women are employed in the 'top ten' largest female occupations, which are remarkably similar across countries. These include clerical work, sales, teaching, nursing, and cleaning, although in the USA and Canada managerial occupations also feature (OECD, 1998). Male employment, on the other hand, is much more diversified, with under half in the top ten occupations. Trends in the oc-cupational structure of women's employment show a trans-Atlantic divide (Anker, 1998). In the USA it has become markedly more diversified, principally as the increasing presence of women has rebalanced the gender mix within occupations, a trend already under way in the 1970s, following the strong educational advancement of women from the 1960s (Blau *et al.*, 1998). The biggest changes in women's labor force participation continue to be their influx into non-traditional highly qualified professional careers (Costa, 2000). In Europe, on the other hand, change has been more sluggish, with segregation remaining high, including, strikingly, in the Scandinavian countries (Rubery *et al.*, 1996; Jonung and Persson, 1998); high participation does not necessarily end segregation. In a comparison of the EU with the USA Dolado *et al.* (2001) confirm the higher occupational segregation in the EU, including among highly educated women, and the weaker trend to desegregation. They find segregation to be particularly marked among women with low educa-tional attainment and those with children, and least among younger women, who are beginning to follow the US pattern of wider occupational and career choices as educational attainment rises.

The relationship between occupational segregation and inequality is not straight-forward. Horizontal segregation, with men and women holding different jobs at the same level, occurs at all occupational levels: professional (teachers), intermediate (secretaries), and low-skilled (counter assistants). Sorting by gender reflects differ-ing preferences, leading to over-representation of women in, for example, caring and other personal services. Or women may choose occupations where work prac-tices allow a better match to domestic constraints. On average, however, women are employed in lower-wage occupations, and 'female' occupations tend to be lower-paid. Occupational segregation will be to women's disadvantage if jobs are less well rewarded because they are held predominantly by women. The occupational crowding approach argues that restricted opportunities for women to enter 'male' occupations leads to their excess supply to available 'female' occupations, depress-ing wages there (Bergmann, 1989). More sharply, where women are restricted in their access to promoted positions, depriving them of career advancement, this vertical discrimination is both inequitable and inefficient. The issue is not whether segregation exists, but how far it adversely affects women's labor market outcomes. Identifying this through econometric estimates is a continuing challenge.

# 3. THE GENDER PAY GAP: ASSESSING UNEQUAL TREATMENT

the valuation shall be for the male ... fifty sheikels of silver ... and if it be a female then the valuation shall be thirty sheikels

(Leviticus, chapter 27, verses 1–4)

## Gender Pay Gaps

The gender pay gap is typically seen as the central issue in women's economic inequality. Separate pay rates for men and women as in the quote above are now illegal, and have been for half a century in the developed world. But the gender pay gap survives universally. The unweighted average of women's hourly pay across the OECD countries is estimated at 84 percent of men's, a pay gap of 16 percent. In the USA the gap is around 23 percent, and in EU countries between 10 and 25 percent; relatively low gaps characterize Belgium, Scandinavia, Australia, New Zealand, and Eastern Europe; gaps are higher in much of Western Europe, notably the UK (OECD, 2006). Overall, the pay gap has narrowed by approximately half since the 1960s, although this progress has recently faltered at both ends of the range, in the low-gap Scandinavian countries and the high-gap USA.

While the detailed pattern varies, the salient features of women's relative pay are common across countries. As illustrated for three leading economies in Figure 12.2, women's earnings are below those of men right across the earnings distribution. Women are concentrated at lower pay levels[2] and heavily outnumbered at high earnings. The earnings disadvantage applies across the life-cycle. Even as they enter the labor market women tend to be lower-paid; in their late 20s they experience a major loss of ground which persists over the remaining years of their working lives.

Pay gaps make headlines, but are, of course, very poor guides to the presence or otherwise of unequal treatment. Pay differentials reflect differences in individuals' productive characteristics (education, experience, ability, and motivation) and in the net advantages, including rents, of their workplaces. Discrimination arises only in the part of the pay gap due to unequal rewards for like characteristics, or unequal treatment due to unlike characteristics (gender) which are irrelevant to performance in the job. Assessing how far the gender pay gap represents unequal reward for equal productivity presents a major challenge.

---

[2] On women and low pay see Chapter 11.

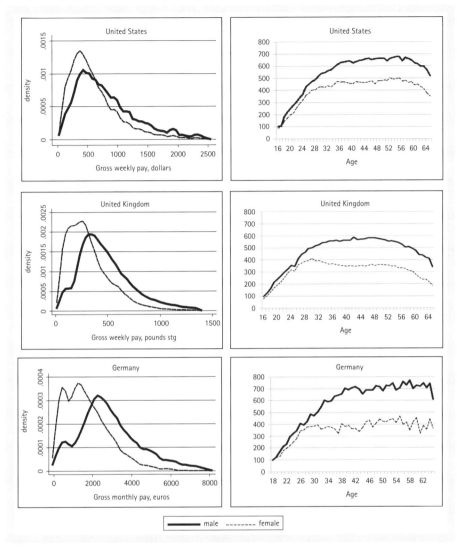

**Fig. 12.2. Male and female average earnings, USA, UK, and Germany, 2006**

*Note*: For earnings by age, male earnings at youngest age = 100.

*Sources*: USA, *Current Population Survey*; UK, *Annual Survey of Hours and Earnings*; Germany, *Socio-Economic Panel*.

## The Blinder-Oaxaca Decomposition

The traditional approach of the Blinder-Oaxaca decomposition,[3] still widely used, disaggregates the observed differential between men's and women's pay into the part which reflects differing characteristics relevant to productivity in work, and the part reflecting the differing rewards which they receive for these characteristics.

---

[3]  See Blinder (1973), Oaxaca (1973), and Oaxaca and Ransom (1994).

Denoting (the logarithm of) men's and women's pay as $w_M$ and $w_F$, and their productive characteristics as $X_M$ and $X_F$, pay for each group can be written:

$$w_M = X_M b_M$$

$$w_F = X_F b_F$$

where $b_M$ and $b_F$ denote the pay reward per unit of productive characteristics received by men and women respectively. The gender pay gap can then be decomposed as:

$$w_M - w_F = (X_M - X_F)b_F + X_M(b_M - b_F)$$

where $(X_M - X_F)$ gives the differences in the productive characteristics which men and women bring to the job, and $(b_M - b_F)$ measures the differing rewards to these attributes. The second term, the part of the earnings gap not explained by differences in productive characteristics, is taken as an estimate of discrimination.

There is a wide measure of agreement across a multitude of individual country studies[4] and the smaller number of international comparisons that the narrowing of the pay gap over recent decades has involved both dimensions. The gap in characteristics is narrowing, as rising educational attainment and employment continuity raise women's human capital; among younger cohorts this now closely matches men's, although a substantial gap remains among older cohorts. Estimates of the unexplained pay gap also indicate it has been declining over time. OECD (2002) summarizes international experience as showing that differences in characteristics are now of minor importance, while the unexplained component averages 15 percent of male earnings. Interpretation of the unexplained component as discrimination, however, depends crucially on the assumption that the measures of characteristics in the 'explained' part of the decomposition are unaffected by discrimination; if women's education or training are curtailed by actual or anticipated discrimination then the unexplained component is an underestimate. Particularly contentious is whether occupation is an explanatory characteristic.[5] To the extent that occupations are low-paid because they are 'female', occupational structure is a channel for discrimination. On the other hand, the estimate of discrimination as the residual after the 'explained' component implies that any omitted variables or errors of measurement or specification become attributed as discrimination; this would apply to, for example, any upgrading of women's unmeasured labor market skills (Blau, 1998).

---

[4]  Leading instances include Blau (1998) for the USA, Joshi and Paci (1998) for the UK and Clarke (2001) for EU countries; Jarrell and Stanley (2004) and Weichselbaumer and Winter-Ebmer (2005, 2007) report recent meta-analyses.

[5]  Following *et al.* (1980) the Blinder-Oaxaca decomposition can be extended to 'explained' and 'unexplained' components separately within and between occupations.

# The 'Family Gap'

As is clear from Figure 12.2, the emergence of a substantial gender pay gap correlates closely with women's childbearing and childcare years. The 'motherhood penalty' or 'family gap', and its contribution to the gender pay gap, is widely confirmed in studies using microdata. Childbearing interrupts employment, reducing the accumulation of human capital. Where it also brings a job separation there is the further loss of firm-specific human capital.[6] In addition mothers may receive lower returns to their characteristics, due to actual or perceived lowering of commitment or effort on the job—the 'mommy track'. Waldfogel (1998a, 1998b) finds that family status directly explains 40–50 percent of the gender gap in the USA and UK, with a further 30–40 percent attributable indirectly, through the effect of employment interruptions on human capital; these motherhood effects clearly dominate the gender gap.[7] While employment breaks reduce work experience permanently, maternity leave with job retention can avoid the depreciation of job-related human capital, preserving good job-matches. Waldfogel finds that the negative effect of children is partially offset when the availability of maternity leave encourages return to the previous employer. More strikingly, for Denmark, where job-protected maternity leave is mandatory, Datta Gupta and Smith (2002) find that the only adverse effect of children on mothers' earnings is through the loss of work experience; some depreciation of human capital occurs during child-related career interruptions, but the effect is small and temporary. For Germany, where women can take up to three years of job-protected maternity leave Beblo and Wolf (2002) estimate the depreciation of job-related human capital at 33 percent per year during an employment break but no depreciation with part-time work. The 'mommy track' appears not to apply in Sweden; mothers there do not suffer a wage loss for taking parental leave, although household time out of the labor market and unemployment spells carry a wage penalty (Albrecht et al., 1999).

# The Gender Gap across the Distribution

The Blinder-Oaxaca approach gives a single statistic based on the average. But the wider picture on women's relative earnings is much more nuanced. Quantile regression targeted across the whole distribution confirms the patterns suggested in the raw distributions in Figure 12.2: women receive lower returns to their characteristics throughout the distribution. For 11 countries available in the European Community

---

[6] Seminal early contributions are by Mincer and Polachek (1974), Corcoran (1977) and Mincer and Ofek (1982).

[7] Similar results are obtained for Australia by Chapman et al. (2001) and by Harkness and Waldfogel (2003) for seven countries, among many others. For the UK the 'motherhood penalty' often involves part-time work with occupational downgrading (Connolly and Gregory, 2008).

Household Panel, Arulampalam *et al.* (2007) find a statistically significant gap in every country at all quantiles of the distribution.

The quantile regressions also show that lower returns earned by women are most pronounced at higher earnings. In eight of the 11 countries the gap is wider at the 90th percentile than at the median; in six it increases at each percentile up the distribution; in only one (Spain) does it decrease. Women partially offset these adverse returns by superior characteristics. At the 10th percentile women in five countries have superior characteristics to men; this rises to seven countries at the 50th percentile, and to nine out of eleven at the 90th percentile (the exceptions are Denmark and Germany). Many women are better qualified than men at comparable points throughout the distribution, but this is insufficient to offset the lower rewards they receive for these characteristics. This disadvantage is particularly strong for women towards the upper end of the earnings distribution.

## Job Assignments and the Glass Ceiling

This distributional evidence obtrudes the issue of gender differences in job assignment, including promotions. Occupational segregation, in a vertical sense, will feature even within gender-mixed occupations as long as promoted positions remain male-dominated. As modeled by Lazear and Rosen (1990), where men and women are of equal ability and there is no male/female wage differential within narrow job categories, women are less frequently promoted because their comparative advantage in non-market activities leads to higher separation probabilities. Separation probability is clearly a potential source of statistical discrimination against women.

Establishing gender differences in job assignment and promotions requires a very specific context and suitably detailed data, usually personnel records within the firm.[8] Ransom and Oaxaca (2005) were able to access eleven years of employment data for a US regional grocery store chain facing a class-action lawsuit over gender discrimination. Modeling worker movements within the firm as a Markov process they find a pattern of initial job assignment and intra-firm mobility, including into supervisory and management positions, that generally penalized women. Even where appointments and promotions are subject to well-defined procedures, as typically in large organizations, placings within a specified scale depend on individual negotiation and employer discretion. Evidence tends to show a disadvantage for women in placing, promotion probabilities, and subsequent pay gains. For the USA, McCue (1996) finds lower promotion rates for women but comparable pay increases, while Cobb-Clark (2001) finds men to have higher promotion rates but women gain higher wage increases on promotion. Booth *et al.* (2003), using the British Household Panel Survey, find that women derive smaller pay gains

---

[8]   Seminal contributions here are Baker *et al.* (1994a, 1994b).

from promotion than men. Within the academic profession in the USA gender differences in salaries reflect women's lower promotions (Ginther and Hayes, 2003), findings corroborated for economists in UK universities (Blackaby *et al.*, 2005). Landers *et al.* (1996) in a study of two large US legal partnerships show that criteria for promotion including billable hours can lead to a 'rat race' equilibrium with inefficiently long hours worked; they further note: 'this selection process may have the effect, although not the intent, of keeping a disproportionate number of qualified women out of leadership positions in business and professional organizations'.

This tendency for women to fail to achieve career advancement comparable to men's, and for the wage gap to be much more pronounced among high earners, is the 'glass ceiling'. The seminal paper by Albrecht *et al.* (2003) for Sweden—a country conspicuous for its gender equality, including a low average gender pay gap—establishes that the strong acceleration in the raw gender gap into the upper tail of the earnings distribution substantially survives the introduction of explanatory controls. They find the most important of these to be occupation, the 107 occupations distinguished accounting for one-third of the explained gap at the top of the distribution. However they emphasize that they

do not view occupational, or more generally job, segregation as an explanation of the glass ceiling effect. Occupation and wages are jointly determined variables. In this sense, occupational segregation is the form in which the glass ceiling is manifested rather than an independent explanation of it.    (p. 163)

Albrecht *et al.* note that more equal wage distributions and relatively high wages at the bottom end make it difficult for career-minded women to purchase childcare for the very young, leading to mothers taking less demanding jobs, a point endorsed by Arulampalam *et al.* (2007). Inequality can support women's careers, while disadvantaging other women.

## National Inequalities in Earnings

A rather different extension to the Blinder-Oaxaca approach analyzes the gender pay gap in the context of the functioning of the labor market more widely. This has been developed in a series of papers by Blau and Kahn (1996, 1997, 2003) extending the work of Juhn *et al.* (1991, 1993). The national wage structure is given a central role, with the part of the wage differential not explained by characteristics decomposed between the effects of the overall wage distribution and the relative positions of men and women within it. The (log) wage equation for male worker $i$ in country $j$ can be written:

$$w_{ij} = X_{ij}b_j + \sigma_j\theta_{ij}$$

where the residual (unexplained) component of the wage is expressed in terms of the individual's percentile ranking $\theta_{ij}$ in country $j$'s distribution of residual wages for males measured by its dispersion $\sigma_j$. The gender wage gap in country $j$ is then

$$D_j \equiv w_{Mj} - w_{Fj} = \Delta X_j b_j + \sigma_j \Delta \theta_j$$

decomposed between differences related to observable characteristics $X$ and the residual component. The gender pay gap between two countries $j$ and $k$ can further be decomposed as:

$$D_j - D_k = (\Delta X_j - \Delta X_k) b_k + \Delta X_j (b_j - b_k)$$
$$+ (\Delta \theta_j - \Delta \theta_k) \sigma_k + \Delta \theta_j (\sigma_j - \sigma_k)$$

The first two terms comprise differences in observed characteristics and their rewards, as in Blinder-Oaxaca. The third term is the effect of the difference in the relative positions of men and women within the residual wage distribution in country $k$. The fourth is the component attributable to differing degrees of residual wage inequality between the two countries. The first and third terms are the gender-specific contributions to the pay gap, arising from gender differences in characteristics and in rankings in the residual wage distribution; the second and fourth terms reflect country-specific labor market features, the differences in rewards to observed characteristics and to the unobserved characteristics underlying residual wage inequality.

This approach brings to the fore the importance for the gender gap of national wage-setting institutions and the wage structures which they support. Blau and Kahn (1996), addressing the paradox that women's advancement has proceeded furthest in the USA while the gender gap there is one of the largest, conclude that if wage inequality in the USA matched its levels in Sweden or Australia the USA would match their relatively narrow gender pay gaps. More generally, they find that more egalitarian national wage structures reduce the gender wage gap (Blau and Kahn, 2003). Interpreting developments in the USA in the 1980s, Blau and Kahn (1997) conclude that women were swimming upstream successfully against the currents of rising wage inequality and higher skill premia, although these slowed their progress, 'reclaiming' up to 40 percent of the relative wage gains achieved through increased employment experience and improved occupational distribution. Similar offsetting effects, between women's rising skills and the growth of inequality, are identified for the UK by Harkness (1996). The balance between gender-specific gains and general labor market developments is, however, an empirical matter of time and place. For Denmark, historically a low-gap country with a strong commitment to gender equality, Datta Gupta et al. (2006) have recently established that women's relative wages have stalled, or even floated downstream, as their gains in education and experience have been offset by rising returns to these characteristics, particularly at the top end of the wage distribution where they are under-represented, and as pay in the public sector, where they are heavily over-represented, has slipped back.

## Matched Employer–Employee Data

Throughout these analyses the central issue is how to distinguish unequal treatment from observable and hard-to-observe differences in characteristics underpinning productivity. In the limit, precise evidence on this requires data that compare the pay of men and women in the same occupation or type of job in the same establishment. Important insights have been gained through studies of single establishments, but these lack generalizability. A fruitful recent development has been to exploit the increasing availability of matched employer–employee data to gain more precise control for individual productivity within the firm.[9] Meyersson Milgrom *et al.* (2001) use a dataset covering entire populations of private-sector establishments in several Swedish industries, where personnel records allow some 280 occupation-by-rank groupings ('occupations') to be distinguished. The raw wage gap between men and women in the same occupation with the same employer is found to be minimal, as is the residual gap after control for occupational (including vertical) segregation. Sweden is, however, untypical in the detailed collective bargaining provisions regulating pay even in the private sector. In a similar analysis for the USA, Bayard *et al.* (2003), matching long-form Census data for individuals with establishment data, find that, while segregation of women into lower-paying occupations, industries, establishments, and occupations-within-establishments all contribute, approximately one-half of the gender wage differential remains attributable to gender alone. Similarly for the UK, Mumford and Smith (2007), using matched employer–employee data from the Workplace Employment Relations Survey (WERS98), find that, while segregation by establishment is significant, over 40 percent of the gender pay gap is a gender differential. Like Bayard *et al.*, they conclude that these large remaining gender gaps indicate (in the absence of Swedish-style pay regulation through collective bargaining) a role for stronger enforcement of equal pay legislation.

# 4. The Fundamental Drivers: Education and Technology

## Women's Educational Attainment

The bedrock for the transformation in women's economic activity outside the home is the transformation in their relative educational attainment. This upsurge in their human capital accentuates the incentive to employment participation, and opens access to higher-skilled occupations with their greater rewards.

---

[9] See Chapter 9.

The advance of women in education has been remarkable in both scale and ubiquity. Across the developed economies females now surpass males in educational attainment in most subjects and at most levels. At school girls are outperforming boys in basic skills. The Programme for International Student Assessment (PISA), assessing attainment among secondary school pupils, shows girls to have strong superiority everywhere in reading, and often some advantage in mathematics and science. As recently as 1985 in only four of 17 OECD countries were more women than men attending college (France, Portugal, Sweden, USA). Now only in Turkey and Switzerland are more males enrolled, and even there women are narrowing the gap. In many countries the female lead in student enrollments is substantial; in the UK, for example, it is now 38 percent for men but 47 percent for women.[10]

Human capital acquisition and employment participation are strongly mutually reinforcing, notwithstanding the traditional distinction between discrimination before the labor market and discrimination within the labor market. Where opportunities for employment and career advancement are restricted, the incentive to acquire education and qualifications is blunted. Where educational attainment is weak, employment advancement is restricted. Increasingly, the reverse situation applies, with educated women leading the way in terms of higher female employment rates; 86 percent of women with tertiary-level education were economically active across the advanced economies, compared to 50 percent of women with less than secondary school qualifications (OECD, 2002). Women with higher educational attainment have access to better-paid jobs and are therefore more able to afford childcare. Absence from the labor market is more costly for them in future career advancement, accentuating the opportunity cost of a career break. They are therefore more likely to be in full-time employment and to take shorter breaks from it. This is most clear in the USA, where the upsurge of college education for women in 1960s introduced the transformation of women's participation in employment; the other advanced economies are following the same general pattern rather later and in their own particular ways.

It is clear that girls and young women in current cohorts are undertaking education in anticipation of a future involving a commitment to labor market participation. The challenging question is to explain why women have not simply caught up with men in college-going, but are so strongly surpassing them. Goldin *et al.* (2006) offer an answer in terms of the greater economic benefits of education to women, and greater economic costs to men. For American women the college wage premium is higher than for men. The rise in divorce, reinforced by her greater economic responsibility for children, creates incentives for women to invest in their own human capital to ensure financial self-sufficiency. Girls may have lower non-pecuniary (effort) costs of college preparation, building on their better high

[10] The comprehensive comparative database on this is the OECD Education Online Database at <http://www.oecd.org>. On the US Freeman (2004) is a further useful source. The PISA database is at <http://www.pisa.oecd.org>. See also Chapter 17.

school achievements, while boys are restrained by their slower social development and proneness to behavioral problems. How far these explanations are sufficient to explain the global outperformance by women remains for further research.

But women's rising educational attainment is not all good news for their labor market prospects. In choice of college major, women tend to specialize in humanities and the creative arts, which are less well rewarded in future earnings than the engineering and physical sciences disciplines which remain largely a male preserve. This choice of specialism is found to lead to wages for male graduates 2–4 percent higher than for females, contributing over one-quarter of the explained portion of the graduate wage gap (Machin and Puhani, 2003, for the UK and Germany; see also Brown and Corcoran, 1997, for the USA).

Since the female educational advantage is particularly marked in younger cohorts this will underpin rising participation rates for decades to come. Fortin (2005) makes the trenchant statement:

In all regression analyses, women's participation in higher education comes out overwhelmingly as the main determinant of favorable labor-market outcomes for women. Promoting women's access to higher education remains the primary policy instrument to foster women's equality in the labour market. (p. 417)

The group facing an unequal future may now be boys leaving education with limited qualifications.

## Technological Change

Where educational attainment provides the fundamental driver on the supply side, demand is also evolving in ways favorable to women's role in the labor market. Shifts in demand patterns are oriented towards services, which often feature the interpersonal 'soft' skills where women have a comparative advantage. Marketization, the shift to the market of work previously done in the home, mostly by women, is a particularly powerful process, simultaneously creating employment opportunities for women and releasing them from the constraints of home production (Gregory et al., 2007).[11] The demand for skills is rising, at a time when women's gains in educational attainment are qualifying them to meet it. At the same time, women have escaped much of the job destruction affecting male-dominated manual occupations as brain comes to be valued over brawn (Welch, 2000; Weinberg, 2000). This process is characterized by Galor and Weil (1996) as 'female-biased technical change'.

More subtly, technological change at the workplace is now emerging as the major new force expanding demands for women's skills. The ICT-based transformation of

---

[11] An insightful account of earlier structural changes affecting women's employment is Goldin (1990).

work is having a major impact on the evolution of men's and women's productivity and on the gender pay gap. In this relatively new research area the task-based framework developed by Autor *et al.* (2003) and applied by Spitz-Oener (2006) and Goos and Manning (2007) gives central place to workplace computerization as an underlying cause of changes in occupational skill requirements. In this framework the work performed in an occupation is broken down into a series of tasks, each of which can be characterized by its substitutability or complementarity with computers, changing the nature of jobs and the demands for skills. The major impact of technological change is to increase the role of non-routine analytical and interactive tasks, such as problem-solving, organization and management, while reducing routine cognitive work (audio-typing, book-keeping) and manual tasks (machine operating). Although not developed directly for it, the task-based approach adapts in a natural way to a gender dimension. Changes in job content have evolved differently for men and women. Routine tasks done by women have been sharply declining, as evidenced by the collapse in the numbers employed as typists and general office clerks, to be replaced by office positions with a larger executive and administrative content while routine component tasks are relegated to computers. For gender equality the major inference from this task-based approach is that up-skilling within the job has taken place in jobs predominantly held by women (where it may, of course, interact with their rising educational attainment) enhancing women's productivity in traditionally 'female' occupations. By contrast, the range of routine tasks more typically performed by men has not experienced comparable up-skilling. The testing of this approach is in its infancy, given the requirements for task-based data, but it offers potentially important new routes to understanding the changing nature of jobs and their gender implications.

# 5. Household Implications: Family Earnings and Female Fertility

Further dimensions of women's progress in the labor market are its 'family' implications, for household income and fertility behavior.

## Women's Role in Household Earnings Inequality[12]

With the growth of married women's employment and the rise in female earnings, wives are contributing a growing share of family incomes. Early approaches

---

[12] See also Chapter 18.

established that the move into employment, implying fewer wives with zero earnings, was reducing family income inequality (Cancian and Reed, 1998). Rising inequality, however, has prompted deeper analysis, unsurprisingly mostly in the USA. The key additional elements are assortative mating, the positive correlation of husband's and wife's earnings, potentially increasing household inequality, and women's labor supply responses to their own and their husband's wages. The contributions of these, however, remain contested.

The move of married women into paid employment is widely seen as significantly attenuating the inequality of family incomes generated by the increased inequality of male earnings (Pencavel, 2006; Daly and Valletta, 2006, particularly for low-income households). Devereux (2004) focuses on female labor supply directly, estimating the cross-wage elasticity to be negative and 'economically significant'; this moderates the impact of male wage changes on family inequality but is insufficient to maintain family incomes against substantial falls in male earnings, and is outweighed by the inequality-increasing effect of assortative mating. Hyslop (2001) focuses on the female own-wage elasticity, but in the context of household permanent income; he finds a significant labor supply response, contributing to both female and family earnings inequality, reinforcing assortative mating. Pencavel decomposes the (log) coefficient of variation of family earnings by age-group and cohort among male earnings dispersion, husband's share in family earnings, and a composite term involving the relative dispersion of husbands' and wives' earnings plus their correlation; his estimates suggest that the rise in women's relative earnings has stimulated their employment, reducing husbands' role in family earnings and household inequality. But, while noting that assortative mating has been increasing across cohorts, he rates its contribution to increased household inequality as unimportant.

## Fertility

Whether the biological differences between men and women constitute an inequality can be argued, but the implications of childrearing for women's labor market outcomes are undeniable. Equally clearly, women are now taking control of their fertility and using this to implement their choices over family and labor market roles.

At the core of the economic analysis of fertility and female labor supply is the effect of the market wage on the demand for children. As an analytical prediction the direction of this is ambiguous; a higher market wage raises the opportunity cost of time spent in childrearing, reducing the demand for children; it also increases household income, and therefore the demand for children (as long as they are not an inferior good) although investment in child quality may substitute for quantity

Table 12.2. Fertility rates and mean age of women at first birth, OECD and selected countries, 1970, 1995, and 2004

| Country | Total fertility rate | | | Mean age of mothers at first birth | | |
|---|---|---|---|---|---|---|
| | 1970 | 1995 | 2004 | 1970 | 1995 | 2004 |
| France | 2.47 | 1.70 | 1.91 | 24.4 | 28.1 | 28.4 |
| Germany | 2.03 | 1.25 | 1.36 | 24.0 | 27.5 | 29.0 |
| Italy | 2.42 | 1.18 | 1.33 | 25.0 | 28.0 | n.a. |
| Sweden | 1.92 | 1.73 | 1.75 | 25.9 | 27.2 | 28.6 |
| United Kingdom | 2.43 | 1.70 | 1.76 | n.a. | 28.3 | 29.5[a] |
| United States | 2.48 | 2.02 | 2.04 | 24.1 | 24.5 | 25.1[a] |
| Nordic countries[1] | 2.05 | 1.80 | 1.79 | 24.7[b] | 27.1 | 28.1[a] |
| Southern Europe[2] | 2.64 | 1.27 | 1.34 | 25.0[c] | 27.2 | 28.1[ad] |
| Poland | 2.20 | 1.61 | 1.23 | 22.8 | 23.8 | 25.6 |

*Notes:* [1] Denmark, Finland, Norway, Sweden.
[2] Greece, Italy, Portugal, Spain.
[a] UK, Finland, Greece, and Spain, 2003; USA, 2002.
[b] Denmark, Finland, and Sweden.
[c] Greece and Italy.
[d] Greece, Portugal, and Spain.
*Source:* OECD, Social Indicators, <http://www.oecd.org>.

in demand.[13] Increasing educational attainment, raising women's earnings, and narrowing of the gender wage differential strengthen the substitution effect, reducing fertility. Empirically, the substitution effect has clearly been dominant, with fertility decreasing as participation has risen. Declining fertility can be identified through two channels: a smaller number of children (the quantum effect) and later starts to family formation (the tempo effect). As shown in Table 12.2, fertility rates are everywhere lower, and the mean age of mothers at first birth higher, than a generation ago, often by substantial margins.

For most women smaller families and later childbearing are both now achieved through the contraceptive pill. Bailey (2006) uses variation in state consent laws to identify the contribution of fertility control to the boom in young women's market work in the USA, and Goldin and Katz (2002) trace the close association between the uptake of the pill and the expansion of female enrollment at Law, Business, and Medical Schools, as women use their control over the timing of births to support the establishment of a professional career before childbearing. The pill, however, merely provides an efficient means to fertility control. Fertility outcomes reflect choices, and these are now showing a more complex picture. In countries where participation is high, the decline in fertility predicted by women's rising educational attainment and career advancement appears to have halted, even reversed. At the same time the low participation countries (Germany, southern Europe) continue

[13] Seminal references include Willis (1973), Mincer (1985), and Becker (1991).

to be characterized by 'lowest-low' fertility.[14] The relationship across countries between fertility and female employment, previously strongly negative, has been reversed to a positive correlation, raising the possibility of two equilibria: high participation with high fertility, low participation with low fertility (Ahn and Mira, 2002).

Social norms toward families and working mothers are often invoked to explain varying employment and fertility patterns. For example, the World Values Survey shows the percentage of respondents believing that children are likely to suffer because the mother works ranging from 18 in Denmark to 80 in Italy and Spain, a divergence of attitude more extreme than their differing participation rates. However, social norms as well as choices are shaped by economic opportunities and constraints both across countries and over time (Esping-Andersen, 1999). Moreover, the modeling of fertility and labor market choices as jointly determined by women in a life-cycle context is well established (Hotz and Miller, 1988; Francesconi, 2002). On that view the significant recent development in many high-participation countries has been the expansion of 'family-friendly' policies, now central to strategies on gender equality.

# 6. IMPLEMENTING GENDER EQUALITY

## The Legal Framework

The legal framework for women's economic equality is based in the first instance in provisions on equal pay and the outlawing of sex discrimination. Legal proscription of gender-based pay scales can deliver substantial pay gains for women; in the UK the gender pay gap closed by 8 percentage points between 1974 and 1976 on the implementation of the Equal Pay and Sex Discrimination Acts. But the requirement to pay men and women equally is largely irrelevant in the face of gender segregation in jobs. To counter this, the EU has adopted the principle of 'comparable worth', equal pay for work 'of equal value'. 'Equal value' is not, however, easily implementable in law. Where men and women do different jobs, it requires evaluation of the skills and responsibilities involved, and the relative desirability of the jobs (their net advantages, following Adam Smith's famous discussion). This may at least in principle be attainable where the jobs are with a single employer, and has been

---

[14] All advanced countries are currently low-fertility, with rates below the 2.1 required for population replacement.

successfully contested in law,[15] but is not operational on an economy-wide basis. In much of the EU, however, it provides legal underpinnings for pay setting under collective agreements.

The law against sex discrimination has become a significant legal weapon. In the USA, although the vast majority of discrimination cases brought by employees are settled out of court, with the employer neither admitting nor found guilty of discrimination, recompense is paid, and a deterrent message is sent.[16] Sex discrimination provisions in EU law specifically cover indirect discrimination, where an apparently gender-neutral provision would differentially disadvantage persons of one sex; this has been used to give equal employment rights to part-time workers, who are predominantly women.[17]

The limitations of legislative action in promoting desired outcomes rather than merely proscribing undesirable ones prompted the introduction of programs of affirmative action in the USA in support of women's advancement in employment and education. In their comprehensive review, Holzer and Neumark (2000) give these qualified support, concluding that: significant discrimination persists; affirmative action programs redistribute employment (and university admissions) to women (and minorities), although the extent of the redistribution may not be large; there is virtually no evidence of weaker educational qualifications or job performance among females who benefit from affirmative action relative to males, especially within occupational grade. Affirmative action measures have, however, been increasingly challenged as themselves discriminatory, and are being ruled counter to the law.

While the law has provided a useful framework and signal, after the elimination of the rawest instances of discrimination its direct impact has been fairly limited.

## Family-Friendly Polices

The thrust of policies towards gender equality in most countries now centers on family support, in recognition of the pervasiveness of labor market participation by women, including mothers, and the dual-earner family. Policies vary widely, including in their balance of incentives between mothers' employment and fertility.[18] The heavy subsidization of good quality childcare in the Nordic countries is a strong incentive to both women's employment and fertility. Germany provides extended

---

[15]  A landmark case in the UK found the work of a female cook to be of equal value with that of her more highly paid male colleagues, a painter, an insulation engineer, and a joiner. She was awarded a pay rise of 31%.

[16]  In a leading instance in 2000, Voice of America agreed to pay $508m. for having rejected women applying for high-paying jobs.

[17]  Even this does not address occupational downgrading, where women move to a lower-level job in order to be able to work part-time; see Connolly and Gregory (2008).

[18]  OECD (2007) and Moss and O'Brien (2006) give comprehensive reviews.

maternity leave with job protection but only scarce and expensive pre-school child-care, influencing mothers towards providing childcare at home (Apps and Rees, 2004). In the USA the absence of statutory paid maternity leave and the sparseness of other maternity support prompt sustained employment particularly among low-income mothers. Part-time work is highly developed in the Netherlands and UK, leading to high participation rates, with the majority of mothers in employment working part-time (Gregory and Connolly, 2008). For many countries, survey evidence (World Values Survey, Eurobarometer) indicates that actual numbers of children now fall short of families' desired numbers, suggesting that, where labor market and family objectives are not fully compatible, the labor market is currently taking priority.

A major objective claimed for family-friendly policies, along with supporting women's employment and child well-being,[19] is promoting gender equity in employment (OECD, 2007). But their contribution in this direction is constrained by the presumption that mothers rather than fathers will take the main burden of childcare. This is the fundamental inequality. In all countries parental leave is directed predominantly to mothers; family leave for fathers is at best of short duration. The experience of Sweden is instructive. Paid parental leave for fathers was introduced in the 1970s with the objective of enhancing gender equality by enabling both parents to combine work and family, and involving fathers in childcare and household work; but the leave was transferable, and taken predominantly by mothers, supporting traditional gender roles. Sweden has now allocated two 'daddy months' of parental leave to fathers on a 'use it or lose it' basis to incentivize them to acquire human capital appropriate to household management and childcare.[20] 'Daddy months' imply restriction on choice within the family, and attitudes among the majority of fathers were initially negative; it is however reported that resistance has ebbed.[21] While only limited progress has been made towards modifying the gender division of domestic work and even less towards modifying the male career norm, it may be noted that time was required for the evolution of social norms towards mothers engaging in market work; even when the economic incentives are in place, a similar progressive adjustment must be expected for fathers' engagement in domestic work and absence from the workplace.[22]

Interventions imply that market outcomes will not be adequate. A 'business case' for family-friendly workplace support can be made, that it improves profitability

[19] Female employment and child development are complementary when additional household income reduces child poverty. But trade-offs are unavoidable, between the child's need for personal attention and the mother's presence at the workplace, or time spent nurturing and earning. The extensive literature on maternal employment and child's cognitive development includes Baum (2003), Ruhm (2004), James-Burdumy (2005), Gregg and Waldfogel (2005).

[20] Iceland has recently split parental leave entitlement into thirds, one to each parent and one transferable between them.

[21] On Swedish policy on parental leave see Duvander et al. (2005); also Gornick and Meyers (2003).

[22] See the discussion of household time-use in Chapter 14.

through enhanced productivity, and reduced absenteeism and turnover, although the costs to employers are undeniable. Evidence on this is typically inconclusive and rarely supportive, although family-friendly policies in place can attract female employees (Nielsen *et al.*, 2004), and the proportion of women in top management has been found to have positive effects on firm performance (Smith *et al.*, 2006, for 2,500 Danish firms), while Arthur and Cook (2004) identify abnormally large share price rises for large US firms on announcing the introduction of family-friendly policies.

# 7. CONCLUSIONS AND FURTHER RESEARCH

Much has been achieved towards economic equality for women, not least the recognition of gender equality and equal treatment as appropriate political objectives. Many impediments to women's economic and social status are now history, and seem quaint, even offensive: denial of equality in citizenship rights; the marriage bar in professional jobs; restricted rights in property ownership; and access to higher education and professional qualifications. Inequality and discrimination certainly still exist. Goldin and Rouse (2000) present striking evidence that auditioning before 'blind' judges increased female selection for major symphony orchestras. Neumark (1996) has pioneered a literature in hiring 'audits' showing female pseudo-applicants receiving lower job offers than males with similar résumés. MIT (1999) points to systematically adverse treatment of women faculty. Nonetheless, the major development across the developed world continues to be the reduction in inequality against women.

The period since the later 1970s in the US is characterized by Goldin (2006) as 'the quiet revolution' in the status of women. The 'revolution' is not so much in increased employment participation as in the nature of women's choices and decisions. She now makes her human capital investment in the expectation of sustained labor force involvement; she will define her identity at least in part through her own occupation or career; and her labor force participation decisions will be made autonomously or jointly with a partner, and not as a secondary earner. Labor force participation is the primary indicator of this revolution, but only one of many. To this can be added that much of women's progress made over recent decades is based in deep economic trends, with technology biasing labor demand in her favor and education underpinning her enhanced labor supply. These forces should prove durable, with men and women continuing to become increasingly similar as economic actors (Lundberg and Pollak, 2007; Blau and Kahn, 2007).

But these two fundamental drivers transforming women's labor market outcomes, educational achievement, and up-skilling through technological change at the workplace, are both imperfectly understood. The transformation of women's role in education is worldwide, but why they have so suddenly and pervasively outstripped men needs an explanation which is viable on a global basis. Similarly, the task-based interpretation of technological change and its gender implications are highly suggestive, but establishing a robust evidence base remains for future research.

The implications for the household of women's growing labor market success obtrude with increasing urgency. Only within the past generation has the two-earner household become the norm, but already one-quarter of married women in work are earning more than their husbands (Winkler *et al.*, 2005). This proportion seems set to rise. The narrowing of the gender wage gap has already largely undermined specialization by mothers into household work. How will household behavior adapt to further change in women's economic status, bargaining power, and opportunity costs in time-use?

More broadly, the basic research challenge continues to center on identifying when observed gender differences in labor market outcomes result from unequal treatment, justifying intervention, and how far they reflect fundamental differences between men and women. As Akerlof and Kranton (2000) emphasize, differing behavior across genders reflects 'identity', with men and women making different choices and accepting differing trade-offs which for each are also optimal responses. For women, education, labor market participation, and fertility are co-determined choices, and will jointly reflect 'identity' as well as constraints. The extent to which 'identity' and choices are deeply rooted in biological and psychological factors that make men and women different is an outstanding research issue. Much anecdotal commentary subscribes to the view that they are. Babcock and Laschever (2003) summarize this as 'women don't ask', giving many instances of women not bargaining, or bargaining less aggressively than men, on appointment. In similar vein, Blackaby *et al.* (2005) postulate a 'loyal servant' attitude on the part of women. Experimentalists are now seeking to establish whether men and women differ in systematic ways in responses which may affect their labor market outcomes, such as risk aversion and orientation towards competitive behavior; Gneezy *et al.* (2003), and others, have launched a research program toward this. With women's progress in the labor market already undermining the basis of the Beckerian approach to the division of labor within the household, economic analysis will increasingly need a new paradigm for analyzing gender equality.

# References

Ahn, N., and Mira, P. 2002. 'A Note on the Changing Relationship between Fertility and Female Employment Rates in Developed Countries'. *Journal of Population Economics*, 15: 667–82.

AKERLOF, G., and KRANTON, R. E. 2000. 'Economics and Identity'. *Quarterly Journal of Economics*, 115(3): 715–53.

ALBRECHT, J., BJORKLUND, A., and VROMAN, S. 2003. 'Is There a Glass Ceiling in Sweden?' *Journal of Labor Economics*, 21(1): 145–77.

—— EDIN, P.-A., SUNDSTROM, M., and VROMAN, S. B. 1999. 'Career Interruptions and Subsequent Earnings: A Reexamination Using Swedish Data'. *Journal of Human Resources*, 34(2): 294–311.

ANKER, R. 1998. *Gender and Jobs: Sex Segregation of Occupations in the World*. Geneva: International Labour Office,.

APPS, P., and REES, R. 2004. 'Fertility, Taxation and Family Policy'. *Scandinavian Journal of Economics*, 106(4): 745–63.

ARTHUR, M. M., and COOK, A. 2004. 'Taking Stock of Work-Family Initiatives: How Announcements of "Family-Friendly" Human Resource Decisions Affect Shareholder Value'. *Industrial and Labor Relations Review*, 57(4): 599–613.

ARULAMPALAM, W., BOOTH, A. L., and BRYAN, M. L. 2007. 'Is There a Glass Ceiling over Europe? Exploring the Gender Pay Gap Across the Wage Distribution'. *Industrial and Labor Relations Review*, 60(2): 163–86.

AUTOR, D. H., LEVY, F., and MURNANE, R. J. 2003. 'The Skill Content of Recent Technological Change'. *Quarterly Journal of Economics*, 118(4): 1279–333.

BABCOCK, L., and LASCHEVER, S. 2003. *Women Don't Ask: Negotiation and the Gender Divide*. Princeton: Princeton University Press

BAILEY, M. J. 2006. 'More Power to the Pill: The Impact of Contraceptive Freedom on Women's Life-Cycle Labor Supply'. *Quarterly Journal of Economics*, 121(1): 289–320.

BAKER, G., GIBBS, M., and HOLMSTROM, B. 1994a. 'The Internal Economics of the Firm: Evidence from Personnel Data'. *Quarterly Journal of Economics*, 109(4): 881–919.

—— —— —— 1994b. 'The Wage Policy of a Firm'. *Quarterly Journal of Economics*, 109(4): 921–55.

BAUM, C. L. 2003. 'Does Early Maternal Employment Harm Child Development? An Analysis of the Potential Benefits of Leave Taking'. *Journal of Labor Economics*, 21(2): 409–48.

BAYARD, K., HELLERSTEIN, J., NEUMARK, D., and TROSKE, K. 2003. 'New Evidence on Sex Segregation and Sex Differences in Wages from Matched Employer–Employee Data'. *Journal of Labor Economics*, 21(4): 887–922.

BEBLO, M., and WOLF, E. 2002. 'How Much Does a Year Off Cost? Estimating the Wage Effects of Employment Breaks and Part-Time Periods'. *Cahiers Economiques de Bruxelles*, 45(2): 191–217.

BECKER, G. S. 1991. *A Treatise on the Family*. Cambridge, Mass.: Harvard University Press.

BERGMANN, B. 1989. 'Does the Market for Women's Labor Need Fixing?' *Journal of Economic Perspectives*, 3(1): 43–60.

BLACKABY, D., BOOTH, A. L., and FRANK, J. 2005. 'Outside Offers and the Gender Pay Gap'. *Economic Journal*, 115, Feb.: F81–F107.

BLAU, F. D. 1998. 'Trends in the Well-Being of American Women 1970–1995'. *Journal of Economic Literature*, 36(1): 113–65.

—— and KAHN, L. M. 1996. 'Wage Structure and Gender Earnings Differentials: An International Comparison'. *Economica*, NS, 63(250), supplement: S29–S62.

—— —— 1997. 'Swimming Upstream: Trends in the Gender Wage Differential in the 1980s'. *Journal of Labor Economics*, 15(1): 1–42.

———— 2003. 'Understanding International Differences in the Gender Pay Gap'. *Journal of Labor Economics*, 21(1): 106–44.

———— 2006. 'The US Gender Pay Gap in the 1990s: Slowing Convergence'. *Industrial and Labor Relations Review*, 60(1): 45–66.

———— 2007. 'Changes in the Labor Supply Behavior of Married Women: 1980–2000'. *Journal of Labor Economics*, 25(3): 393–438.

—— SIMPSON, P., and ANDERSON, D. 1998. 'Continuing Progress? Trends in Occupational Segregation in the United States over the 1970s and 1980s'. *Feminist Economics*, 4(3): 29–71.

BLINDER, A. S. 1973. 'Wage Discrimination: Reduced Form and Structural Estimates'. *Journal of Human Resources*, 8: 436–55.

BOOTH, A. L., FRANCESCONI, M., and FRANK, J. 2003. 'A Sticky Floors Model of Promotions, Pay and Gender'. *European Economic Review*, 47(2): 295–322.

BROWN, C., and CORCORAN, M. 1997. 'Sex-Based Differences in School Content and the Male–Female Wage Gap'. *Journal of Labor Economics*, 15(3): 431–65.

BROWN, R. S., MOON, M., and ZOLOTH, B. S. 1980. 'Incorporating Occupational Attainment in Studies of Male–Female Earnings Differentials'. *Journal of Human Resources*, 15(1): 3–28.

CANCIAN, M., and REED, D. 1998. 'Assessing the Effects of Wives' Earnings on Family Income Inequality among Married Couples'. *Review of Economics and Statistics*, 80(1): 73–9.

CHAPMAN, B., DUNLOP, Y., GRAY, M., LIU, A., and MITCHELL, D. 2001. 'The Impact of Children on Lifetime Earnings of Australian Women: Evidence from the 1990s'. *Australian Economic Review*, 34(4): 373–89.

CLARKE, S. 2001. 'Earnings of Men and Women in the EU: The Gap Narrowing but only Slowly'. *Statistics in Focus: Population and Social Conditions*. Luxembourg: Eurostat.

COBB-CLARK, D. 2001. 'Getting Ahead: The Determinants of and Payoffs to Internal Promotion for Young US Men and Women', in S. W. Polachek (ed.), Worker Wellbeing in a Changing Labor Market. *Research in Labor Economics*, 20: 339–72.

CONNOLLY, S., and GREGORY, M. 2008. 'Moving Down: Women's Part-Time Work and Occupational Change in Britain 1991–2001'. *Economic Journal*, 118(526), Feb: F52–F76.

CORCORAN, M. E. 1977. 'Work Experience, Labor Force Withdrawals, and Women's Wages: Empirical Results Using the 1976 Panel of Income Dynamics', in C. B. Lloyd, E. S. Andrews, and C. L. Gilroy (eds.), *Women in the Labor Market*. New York: Columbia University Press.

COSTA, D. L. 2000. 'From Mill Town to Board Room: The Rise of Women's Paid Labor'. *Journal of Economic Perspectives*, 14(4): 101–22.

DALY, M. C., and VALLETTA, R. G. 2006. 'Inequality and Poverty in United States: The Effect of Rising Dispersion of Men's Earnings and Changing Family Behaviour'. *Economica*, 73, Feb.: 75–98.

DATTA GUPTA, N., OAXACA, R., and SMITH, N. 2006. 'Swimming Upstream, Floating Downstream: Comparing Women's Relative Wage Progress in the United States and Denmark'. *Industrial and Labor Relations Review*, 59(2): 243–67.

—— and SMITH, N. 2002. 'Children and Career Interruptions: The Family Gap in Denmark'. *Economica*, 69(4): 609–29.

DEVEREUX, P. J. 2004. 'Changes in Relative Wages and Family Labor Supply'. *Journal of Human Resources*, 39(3): 696–722.

DOLADO, J. J., FELGUEROSO, F., and JIMENO, J. F. 2001. 'Female Employment and Occupational Changes in the 1990s: How is the EU Performing Relative to the US?' *European Economic Review*, 45: 875–89.

DUVANDER, A.-Z., FERRARINI, T., and THALBERG, S. 2005. 'Swedish Parental Leave and Gender Equality: Achievements and Reform Challenges in a European Perspective'. Institute for Futures Studies, Copenhagen.

ESPING-ANDERSEN, G. 1999. *Social Foundations of Postindustrial Societies*. Oxford: Oxford University Press

FRANCESCONI, M. 2002. 'A Joint Dynamic Model of Fertility and Work of Married Women'. *Journal of Labor Economics*, 20(2), part 1: 336–80.

FORTIN, N. 2005. 'Gender Role Attitudes and the Labour-Market Outcomes of Women Across OECD Countries'. *Oxford Review of Economic Policy*, 21(3): 416–38.

FREEMAN, C. E. 2004. *Trends in Educational Equity of Girls and Women*. Washington: National Centre for Education Statistics, Institute of Education Science, US Department of Education.

GALOR, O., and WEIL, D. N. 1996. 'The Gender Gap, Fertility and Growth'. *American Economic Review*, 86: 374–87.

GINTHER, D. K., and HAYES, K. H. 2003. 'Gender Differences in Salary and Promotion for Faculty in the Humanities 1977–95'. *Journal of Human Resources*, 38(1): 34–73.

GNEEZY, U., NIEDERLE, M., and RUSTICHINI, A. 2003. 'Performance in Competitive Environments: Gender Differences'. *Quarterly Journal of Economics*, 118(3): 1049–74.

GOLDIN, C. 1990. *Understanding the Gender Gap: An Economic History of American Women*. Oxford and New York: Oxford University Press.

—— 2006. 'The Quiet Revolution that Transformed Women's Employment, Education and Family'. *American Economic Review*, 96(2): 1–21.

—— and KATZ, L. F. 2002. 'The Power of the Pill: Oral Contraceptives and Women's Career and Marriage Decisions'. *Journal of Political Economy*, 110(4): 730–00.

—— —— and KUZIEMKO, I. 2006. 'The Homecoming of American College Women: The Reversal of the College Gender Gap'. *Journal of Economic Perspectives*, 20(4): 133–56.

—— and ROUSE, C. 2000. 'Orchestrating Impartiality: The Impact of "Blind" Auditions on Female Musicians'. *American Economic Review*, 90(4): 715–41.

GOOS, M., and MANNING, A. 2007. 'Lousy and Lovely Jobs: The Rising Polarisation of Work in Britain'. *Review of Economics and Statistics*, 89(1): 118–33.

GORNICK, J. C., and MEYERS, M. K. 2003. *Families That Work: Policies for Reconciling Parenthood and Employment*. New York: Russell Sage Foundation.

GREGG, P., and WALDFOGEL, J. (eds.) 2005. 'Symposium on Parental Leave, Early Maternal Employment and Child Outcomes'. *Economic Journal*, 115(501): F1–F80.

GREGORY, M., and CONNOLLY, S. (eds.) 2008. 'The Price of Reconciliation: Part-Time Work, Families and Women's Satisfaction'. *Economic Journal*, 118, Feb.: F1–99.

—— SALVERDA, W., and SCHETTKAT, R. 2007. *Services and Employment: Explaining the US–European Gap*. Princeton: Princeton University Press.

HARKNESS, S. 1996. 'The Gender Earnings Gap: Evidence from the UK'. *Fiscal Studies*, 17(2): 1–36.

—— and WALDFOGEL, J. 2003. 'The Family Gap in Pay: Evidence from Seven Industrialised Countries'. *Research in Labor Economics*, 22: 369–414.

HOLZER, H., and NEUMARK, D. 2000. 'Assessing Affirmative Action'. *Journal of Economic Literaure*, 38(3): 483–568.

HOTZ, V. J., and MILLER, R. A. 1988. 'An Empirical Analysis of Life Cycle Fertility and Female Labor Supply'. *Econometrica*, 56(1): 91–118.

HYSLOP, D. R. 2001. 'Rising US Earnings Inequality and Family Labor Supply: The Covariance Structure of Intrafamily Earnings'. *American Economic Review*, 91(4): 755–77.

JAMES-BURDUMY, S. 2005. 'The Effect of Maternal Labor Force Participation on Child Development'. *Journal of Labor Economics*, 23(1): 177–211.

JARRELL, S. B., and STANLEY, T. D. 2004. 'Declining Bias and Gender Wage Discrimination? A Meta-Regression Analysis'. *Journal of Human Resources*, 39(3): 827–38

JAUMOTTE, F. 2003. 'Labour Force Participation of Women: Empirical Evidence on the Role of Policy and Other Determinants in OECD Countries'. *OECD Economic Studies*, 37: 51–108.

JONUNG, C., and PERSSON, I. (eds.) 1998. *Women's Work and Wages*. London: Routledge.

JOSHI, H., and PACI, P. 1998. *Unequal Pay for Women and Men: Evidence from the British Birth Cohort Studies*. Cambridge, Mass. and London: MIT Press.

JUHN, C., MURPHY, K. M., and PIERCE, B. 1991. 'Accounting for the Slowdown in Black–White Wage Convergence', in M. H. Kosters (ed.), *Workers and their Wages*. Washington: American Enterprise Institute.

——————— 1993. 'Wage Inequality and the Rise in the Return to Skill'. *Journal of Political Economy*, 101(3): 410–42.

LANDERS, R. M., REBITZER, J. B., and TAYLOR, L. J. 1996. 'Rat Race Redux: Adverse Selection in the Determination of Work Hours in Law Firms'. *American Economic Review*, 86(3): 329–48.

LAZEAR, E. P., and ROSEN, S. 1990. 'Male–Female Wage Differentials in Job Ladders'. *Journal of Labor Economics*, 8(1): S106–S23.

LUNDBERG, S., and POLLAK, R. A. 2007. 'The American Family and Family Economics'. *Journal of Economic Perspectives*, 21(2): 3–26.

MACHIN, S., and PUHANI, P. A. 2003. 'Subject of Degree and the Gender Wage Differential: Evidence from the UK and Germany'. *Economics Letters*, 79: 393–400.

McCUE, K. 1996. 'Promotions and Wage Growth'. *Journal of Labor Economics*, 14(2): 175–209.

Massachusetts Institute of Technology (MIT) 1999. *A Study on the Status of Women Faculty in Science at MIT*. Cambridge, Mass.: MIT.

MEYERSSON MILGROM, E. M., PETERSEN, T., and SNARTLAND, V. 2001. 'Equal Pay for Equal Work? Evidence from Sweden and a Comparison with Norway and the US'. *Scandinavian Journal of Economics*, 103(4): 559–83.

MINCER, J. 1985. 'Intercountry Comparisons of Labor Force Trends and of Related Developments'. *Journal of Labor Economics*, 3(1), part 2 'Trends in Women, Work and Education': S1–S32.

—— and OFEK, H. 1982. 'Interrupted Work Careers: Depreciation and Restoration of Human Capital'. *Journal of Human Resources*, 17, winter: 3–24.

—— and POLACHEK, S. 1974. 'Family Investments in Human Capital: Earnings of Women'. *Journal of Political Economy*, 82, supplement: S76–S110.

MOSS, P., and O'BRIEN, M. (eds.) 2006. *International Review of Leave Policies and Related Research*. Employment Relations Research Series no. 57. Department of Trade and Industry, London.

MUMFORD, K., and SMITH, P. 2007. 'The Gender Earnings Gap in Britain: Including the Workplace'. *The Manchester School*, 75(6): 653–72.

NEUMARK, D. 1996. 'Sex Discrimination in Restaurant Hiring: An Audit Study'. *Quarterly Journal of Economics*, 111(3): 915–41.

NIELSEN, H. S., SIMONSEN, M., and VERNER, M. 2004. 'Does the Gap in Family-Friendly Policies Drive the Family Gap?' *Scandinavian Journal of Economics*, 106(4): 721–44.

OAXACA, R. 1973. 'Male–Female Wage Differentials in Urban Labor Markets'. *International Economic Review*, 14(3): 693–709.

—— and RANSOM, M. 1994. 'On Discrimination and the Decomposition of Wage Differentials'. *Journal of Econometrics*, 61: 5–21.

OECD, *Education Online Database*; <http://www.oecd.org>.

—— *Labour Statistics*; <http://www.oecd.org>.

—— *Programme for International Student Assessment (PISA)*; <http://www.pisa.oecd.org>.

—— 1998. *The Future of Female-Dominated Occupations*. Paris: OECD.

—— 2002. 'Women at Work: Who are They, and How are They Faring?' *OECD Employment Outlook*.

—— 2006. *Women and Men in OECD Countries*. Paris: OECD.

—— 2007. *Babies and Bosses: Reconciling Work and Family Life*. Paris: OECD.

PENCAVEL, J. 2006. 'A Life-Cycle Perspective on Changes in Earnings Inequality among Married Men and Women'. *Review of Economics and Statistics*, 88(2): 232–42.

RANSOM, M., and OAXACA, R. 2005. 'Intrafirm Mobility and Sex Differences in Pay'. *Industrial and Labor Relations* Review, 58(2): 219–37.

RUBERY, J., FAGAN, C., and MAIER, F. 1996. 'Occupational Segregation, Discrimination and Equal Opportunity', in G. Schmidt, J. O'Reilly, and K. Schoenmann (eds.), *International Handbook of Labour Market Policy and Evaluation*. Cheltenham: Edward Elgar.

RUHM, C. J. 2004. 'Parental Employment and Child Cognitive Development'. *Journal of Human Resources*, 39(1): 155–92.

SMITH, N., SMITH, V., and VERNER, M. 2006. 'Do Women in Top Management Affect Firm Performance? A Panel Study of 2,500 Danish Firms'. *International Journal of Productivity and Performance Management*, 55(7): 569–93.

SPITZ-OENER, A. 2006. 'Technical Change, Job Tasks, and Rising Educational Demands: Looking Outside the Wage Structure'. *Journal of Labor Economics*, 24(2): 235–70.

WALDFOGEL, J. 1998a. 'The Family Gap for Young Women in the US and Britain: Can Maternity Leave Make a Difference?' *Journal of Labor Economics*, 16(3): 505–45.

—— 1998b. 'Understanding the "Family Gap" in Pay for Women with Children'. *Journal of Economic Perspectives*, 12(1): 137–56.

WEICHSELBAUMER, D., and WINTER-EBMER, R. 2005. 'A Meta-Analysis of the International Gender Wage Gap'. *Journal of Economic Surveys*, 19(3): 479–511.

—— —— 2007. 'International Gender Wage Gaps'. *Economic Policy*, Apr.: 237–87.

WEINBERG, B. A. 2000. 'Computer Use and the Demand for Female Workers'. *Industrial and Labor Relations Review*, 53(2): 290–308.

WELCH, F. 2000. 'Growth in Women's Relative Wages and in Inequality among Men: One Phenomenon or Two?' *American Economic Review*, 90(2): 444–9.

WILLIS, R. J. 1973. 'A New Approach to the Economic Theory of Fertility Behavior'. *Journal of Political Economy*, 81: S14–S64.

WINKLER, A. E., MCBRIDE, T. D., and ANDREWS, C. 2005. 'Wives Who Outearn Their Husbands: A Transitory or Persistent Phenomenon for Couples?' *Demography*, 42(3): 523–35.

# PART IV

## DIMENSIONS OF INEQUALITY

# CHAPTER 13

# ECONOMIC INEQUALITY, POVERTY, AND SOCIAL EXCLUSION

### BRIAN NOLAN

### IVE MARX

## 1. INTRODUCTION

POVERTY is the aspect of economic inequality that is most obviously a source of societal concern, both as a social problem in itself and because of the impact it can have on life-chances and quality of life for individuals, as well as on overall economic performance and social cohesion.[1] A large body of research on poverty in industrialized countries, much of it comparative in nature, has been produced since poverty was 'rediscovered' in various rich countries in the 1960s and 1970s (as reflected in the USA's 'War on Poverty', the impact of Abel-Smith and Townsend's study *The Poor and the Poorest* (1965) in the UK, and the 'Poverty Programmes' of the (then) European Communities). Even more than inequality, poverty is a focus for political debate and poverty research draws from and feeds into those debates.

[1] As discussed in other chapters in this Handbook, poverty may have a marked impact on health, education, earnings, inter-generational mobility, and is intimately related to gender, the labor market, demography and household formation, and migration.

The aim of this chapter is to provide an overview of the main approaches taken and the evidence produced by this research. The way poverty is conceptualized and measured is first discussed, followed by a review of the evidence about levels and trends in poverty measured in terms of low income. The types of person and household most at risk of poverty and the causal processes at work are then discussed. The factors underpinning differences in poverty levels across OECD countries are then explored, as is the relationship between poverty and economic inequality. The use of non-income information and the multidimensional nature of poverty and social exclusion are briefly discussed, and finally some key issues for policy and for future research are highlighted.

## 2. CONCEPTS AND MEASUREMENT

Poverty and social exclusion are intimately related to economic inequality but are distinct concepts. The definition of poverty most commonly applied in economically advanced societies is exclusion from the life of the society due to lack of resources (spelt out in depth in e.g. Townsend, 1979). This conceptualization underpins most recent research on poverty in Europe, and has also been very influential from a policy-making perspective, as evidenced by the definition adopted by the European Economic Communities in the mid-1980s:

The poor shall be taken to mean persons, families and groups of persons whose resources (material, cultural and social) are so limited as to exclude them from the minimum acceptable way of life in the Member State in which they live.[2]

This can be contrasted with the USA, where the existence of a long-standing official poverty line has fundamentally influenced how poverty is debated and research carried out. That standard goes back to the 1960s, when it was originally based on the cost of a nutritionally adequate diet, multiplied by a factor to take account of non-food spending, but its key feature is that it has subsequently been up-rated in line with consumer prices, rather than linked to average income or living standards.

To characterize this contrast as between 'relative' versus 'absolute' notions of poverty would be to over-simplify. In a developing country context, the notion of absolute poverty as inability to obtain the essentials for sustaining life has unarguable relevance. In that setting, current practice by the World Bank and others of measuring the 'extremely poor' as those who are living on no more than $1 per day

---

[2]  Similar definitions are also now commonly presented in official statements from different EU member states, notably in the National Action Plans prepared as part of the EU's Social Inclusion Process.

per person, and the 'poor' as those on less than $2, provides a basis for making comparisons across countries and monitoring progress over time (as discussed in detail in Chapter 26). However, poverty standards in developed countries are invariably strongly influenced by prevailing conditions and expenditure patterns. As Piachaud (1987) argued, 'close to subsistence level there is indeed some absolute minimum necessary for survival but apart from this, any poverty standard must reflect prevailing social standards: it must be a relative standard' (p. 148).

The key issue—both in making comparisons over time and across countries—is whether the poverty standard is fixed in terms of purchasing power, or varies with societal living standards. From both research and policy perspectives both clearly have value. Over time, as Lampman (1971) put it in a US context, in fighting a 'War on Poverty' one may want to monitor how well one is doing in meeting a fixed target rather than redefining the target as income changes. However, over any prolonged period where average living standards are rising, this may lose touch with the everyday understanding of poverty in the society. The official US poverty line has fallen from 49 percent of median income in 1959 to 28 percent in 2005, and a leading expert has argued that 'forty-three years after they were developed, the poverty thresholds are nonsensical numbers' (Blank, 2008). An influential expert panel reviewing the US official measure saw poverty in terms of insufficient resources for basic living needs, 'defined appropriately for the United States today' (Citro and Michael, 1995).[3] Similar arguments apply in making comparisons across countries at rather different levels of average income: neither purely country-specific relative measures nor common thresholds tell the whole story with respect to poverty. (In a European context this has been brought to the fore by the recent accession to the EU of countries with much lower levels of average income than the 'old' member states.)

Another contrast between Europe and the USA is that in the former, the concepts of social exclusion and social inclusion have come to be widely used alongside poverty in research and policy circles. Substantive claims have been made for the advantages of these concepts, which are seen to encompass multidimensional disadvantage, the dynamic nature of exclusionary processes, and inadequate social participation and lack of power in a way that 'poverty' does not. While this contrast is partly based on an unnecessarily narrow and static notion of poverty, there are underlying differences of substance and emphasis to which we return. What is interesting is that these concepts have so far had little purchase in the USA, where research and policy debate is still couched in terms of poverty rather than exclusion.

---

[3]  Few European countries have had 'official' poverty measures until recently, although some countries, e.g. the Netherlands, had official standards that were not actually called poverty standards but were widely interpreted as such. In the UK, progress toward the high-profile objective of eliminating child poverty is monitored with a combination of monetary and non-monetary indicators. The EU social inclusion indicators include both purely relative income poverty thresholds and ones anchored at a point in time and up-rated in line with prices.

The first requirement in carrying out research on poverty is a way of distinguishing the poor from the non-poor (Atkinson, 1987). While qualitative research methods can be very illuminating about the lives of the poor, most quantitative research employs income to distinguish the poor, identified as those falling below a certain threshold. Many different ways of establishing such a threshold have been proposed, for example by reference to what it costs to buy a specified basket of goods and services, to ordinary expenditure patterns, to standards implicit in social security support rates, or to views in the population about for example the income needed to 'get by'.[4] The most common practice in comparative research, though, has been to rely on relative income poverty lines.[5] These are derived as fixed proportions of mean or median incomes, with 50 or 60 percent of the median currently the most commonly used. The underlying rationale is that those falling more than a certain 'distance' below the average or normal income in their society are unlikely to be able to participate fully in it.

In distinguishing those below an income threshold the household is usually taken as the income recipient unit, as in the study of income inequality (Chapter 4), assuming that income is shared so members reach a common standard of living. Since a larger household will need more income than a smaller one to reach the same standard of living, size and composition are taken into account by setting the poverty threshold at different levels for different household types, or by 'equivalizing' household income using the equivalence scales employed in research on income inequality.

Two other important issues have featured in the research literature in recent decades. The first is how, having identified the poor, the extent of poverty can be summarized—what Sen termed the aggregation problem. The most straightforward and commonly used summary measure is the headcount, the number of persons falling below the poverty threshold, expressed as a proportion of the overall population. However, this fails to distinguish where a person is just below the poverty threshold versus very far below it, and faces the policy-maker with the perverse incentive to target the least poor, the easiest to lift above the threshold.

This provides the rationale for also taking into account the 'poverty gap'—how far people fall below the threshold. This can be done most simply by also calculating the average income shortfall of the poor. However, that will not be affected by whether they are all the same distance below the threshold, or some very close and some far below. Sen (1976) put forward a single poverty measure that incorporated the numbers below the threshold, the poverty gap, and the inequality among the poor (which he measured by the Gini coefficient). Alternative summary measures combining these three elements have been proposed, often derived—like

---

[4]  For a review of these different approaches see Nolan and Whelan (1996).
[5]  Examples include O'Higgins and Jenkins (1990), Buhmann et al. (1987), Förster and Pearson (2002), and Fritzell and Ritakallio (2004).

Sen's—from a set of axioms representing a priori notions of the properties such a measure should have, comparable to the axiomatic underpinnings of summary income inequality measures discussed in Chapter 3. (As in the inequality context, this is more problematic than it appears at first sight.) The Sen–Shorrocks–Thon measure captures three distinct aspects of poverty: the number of people below the poverty line, the depth of their poverty, and the extent of inequality among them. An attractive feature is that changes in poverty can be decomposed into these three dimensions (Osberg and Xu, 2000). The Foster et al. (1984) class of poverty measures are additively decomposable and, additionally, allow for different judgments regarding the importance attached to the extent of inequality among the poor. Although theoretically superior, such poverty measures that capture poverty intensity also suffer from greater sensitivity to measurement error, especially the presence of extreme low incomes which often reflects mis-reporting.[6] Myles (2000) argues that such measures also have had limited impact because their mathematical representation has made their meaning obscure to potential users.

Income-based poverty comparisons across countries or over time thus require the selection of a poverty line and equivalence scale to identify the poor, and a summary poverty measure; differing choices on any of these may lead to different results, as amply demonstrated in the empirical literature.[7] As in the income inequality literature, the robustness of poverty orderings has been a long-standing concern (Atkinson, 1987; Zheng, 2000), and dominance approaches developed for income inequality comparisons have been adapted for use in the poverty context (for a recent example see Duclos and Makdissi, 2005).

The other issue that has received a good deal of attention is whether relying on current income is a satisfactory way to identify the poor. As discussed in earlier chapters concerned with economic inequality more broadly, the measures of income that are generally available may not adequately represent living standards and control over economic resources for a variety of reasons. In the poverty context, it has been argued forcefully that low income may fail in practice to distinguish those experiencing distinctively high levels of deprivation or exclusion, and studies using direct measures of deprivation for a range of countries have lent some support to this assertion.[8] This mis-match arises partly because current income does not capture the impact of savings, debt, previous spending on consumer durables, (generally) owner-occupied housing, goods and services provided by the State, work-related expenses such as transport and child-care, and geographical variation

---

[6] The poverty gap measure advanced by Hills (2002), based on the distance between the threshold and the median income of the poor, is one response to that problem.

[7] See e.g. Buhmann et al. (1987), Coulter et al. (1992) on sensitivity to the equivalence scale employed.

[8] See e.g. Gordon et al. (2000) for Britain, Nolan and Whelan (1996) for Ireland, Muffels and Dirven (1998) with Dutch data, Halleröd (1995) for Sweden, Kangas and Ritakallio (1998) for Finland, and Mayer and Jencks (1988) for the USA.

in prices. Needs also differ in ways missed by conventional equivalence scales (e.g. in relation to disability). Finally, income from self-employment, home production, and capital are particularly difficult to measure accurately.

Research on poverty has taken a variety of directions in order to capture resources and living standards more comprehensively. One is to measure financial poverty in terms of consumption rather than income, on the basis that the transitory component is a great deal smaller. However, expenditure as measured in household budget surveys often covers only a short period and is not the same as consumption, while low expenditure may be associated with saving and does not necessarily capture constrained resources (see the discussion in Chapter 16). Other avenues have been to impute income from durables, owner-occupied housing, and non-cash benefits, to broaden the needs incorporated into equivalence scales, and to combine survey and other data to improve the measurement of income. It is, however, the exploitation of longitudinal data that has transformed poverty research. A dynamic perspective on income now plays a central role in research on poverty, and we will discuss the insights it offers in due course. A parallel development, embraced more enthusiastically in Europe than North America, seeks to incorporate non-income information into the identification of the poor: this is related to the growing emphasis on the multidimensionality of poverty and social exclusion, and is discussed in Section 9 below. Reflecting the literature, though, we devote most of our attention to poverty research based on income (the sole focus of the review by Jäntti and Danziger, 2000), and look first at the cross-sectional evidence about the extent of poverty across OECD countries.

# 3. A COMPARATIVE PERSPECTIVE ON POVERTY

Comparative poverty research, like that on income inequality, was for many years bedevilled by differences in definition and measures in the data available for different countries at national level. Recent research has relied heavily on two main sources of comparative data for this purpose: the Luxembourg Income Study (LIS) database covering many OECD countries, and figures produced by Eurostat for the EU countries. As discussed in Chapter 4, the LIS database has been constructed from data supplied by different countries from household surveys but then harmonized in so far as possible in terms of definitions and measures. On that basis poverty rates for different countries have been compared in for example Atkinson *et al.* (1995) and Fritzell and Ritakallio (2004). Using the data currently available from this source, we show in Table 13.1 the percentage of persons in households

Table 13.1. Income poverty rates in OECD countries around 2000

| Country | % below 50% of median income | % below 60% of median income |
|---|---|---|
| Australia (2001) | 13.0 | 21.6 |
| Austria (2000) | 7.7 | 13.4 |
| Belgium (2000) | 7.9 | 16.1 |
| Canada (2000) | 12.1 | 18.6 |
| Denmark (2000) | 5.4 | 13.1 |
| Estonia (2000) | 12.4 | 19.8 |
| Finland (2000) | 5.4 | 12.4 |
| France (2000) | 7.3 | 13.7 |
| Germany (2000) | 8.4 | 13.4 |
| Greece (2000) | 14.3 | 21.4 |
| Hungary (1999) | 6.7 | 13.4 |
| Ireland (2000) | 16.2 | 22.5 |
| Italy (2000) | 12.8 | 20.0 |
| Luxembourg (2000) | 6.1 | 12.4 |
| Mexico (2000) | 21.5 | 28.1 |
| Netherlands (1999) | 4.9 | 11.1 |
| Norway (2000) | 6.4 | 12.3 |
| Poland (1999) | 13.2 | 19.3 |
| Slovenia (1999) | 8.2 | 14.2 |
| Spain (2000) | 14.2 | 20.8 |
| Sweden (2000) | 6.5 | 12.3 |
| Switzerland (2000) | 7.6 | 14.4 |
| UK (1999) | 12.5 | 21.1 |
| USA (2000) | 17.7 | 24.2 |

Source: LIS.

falling below 50 and 60 percent of median (equivalized) disposable household income in 25 OECD countries around 2000.

We see that the poverty rate with the 50 percent of median threshold ranges from 5 percent in Denmark, Finland, and the Netherlands, all the way up to 18 percent in the USA and 22 percent in Mexico. With 60 percent of the median the range is from 11 up to 28 percent; there are some changes in the rankings of countries but considerable consistency in the groupings.

For EU member countries, Eurostat produces comparative statistics on 'poverty risk', now primarily drawn from EU Statistics on Income and Living Conditions (EU-SILC). The figures may differ from those in LIS for a variety of reasons, but the broad patterns in terms of the extent of variation across countries and where particular countries fit on the spectrum are reasonably consistent.

These figures are based on relative income thresholds that depend on median income in the country in question, and thus differ greatly across countries. Within the EU, for example, even when one takes differences in prices and purchasing power into account, the threshold in Germany is over four times as high as that in Latvia and Lithuania. (Whether available Purchasing Power Parities reliably capture such differences in purchasing power is a major concern in this context.) An alternative would be to use an income threshold that was the same across countries. The difference this would make can be illustrated by applying a common threshold set at 60% of median income across the EU as a whole. Analysis for around 2000 by Brandolini (2007) shows that this would re-classify most of the population of countries like Slovakia and Estonia as below the threshold, so the share of the EU's poor living in Eastern Europe goes up from 14 to 50 percent. (The difference made by applying a common threshold has also been demonstrated by studies using LIS data.)

# 4. TRENDS IN POVERTY

As well as reflecting differences in poverty across countries at a point in time, a key aim in measuring poverty is to see how it is changing over time. Trends in income poverty in OECD countries have been the focus of a number of national and comparative studies, notably Burniaux *et al.* (1998), Förster and Pearson (2002), Fritzell and Ritikallio (2004), Förster and d'Ercole (2005). Once again we look at what figures from the LIS suggest about these trends, Table 13.2 showing the percentage below 50 percent of the country's median income for selected years from the mid-1980s to around 2000. Over the whole period these rates have generally risen or stayed stable, with very few examples of significant falls. Over the 1995–2000 period rates were more stable and there were some reductions.

The most intensive examination of recent trends in poverty across countries was carried out by the OECD using data collected for the purpose from 20 countries (Förster and d'Ercole 2005). This shows that the average percentage below 50 percent of median income was 10.6 percent in 2000, compared with 9.4 percent in the mid-1980s and 10 percent in the mid-1990s. In the second half of the 1990s, the trend for working age people was generally upwards—often reflecting a decline in the poverty-reducing impact of taxes and transfers—but pensioners saw sizeable declines in many countries. So stability in the overall poverty rate can mask major underlying shifts for different groups.

National studies for various countries have also shed light on poverty trends and the factors at work, though given differences in methods and approaches it is more difficult to generalize from them. For the USA, for example, Hoynes *et al.* (2006) analyze trends in the official US poverty rate over 30 years. Like earlier studies (e.g. Blank, 1993) they highlight stagnant median wage growth, rising inequality,

Table 13.2. Trends in income poverty rates in OECD countries

| Country | % below 50% of median income | | | |
|---|---|---|---|---|
| | Around 1985 | Around 1990 | Around 1995 | Around 2000 |
| Australia | 11.8 | 12.2 | 11.4 | 13.0 |
| Austria | 6.7 | – | 10.6 | 7.7 |
| Belgium | 4.5 | 5.2 | 8.7 | 7.9 |
| Canada | 11.4 | 11.0 | 11.3 | 12.1 |
| Denmark | – | 5.2 | 5.2 | 5.4 |
| Finland | 5.4 | 5.7 | 4.2 | 5.4 |
| France | – | 8.9 | 8.0 | 7.3 |
| Germany | 7.9 | 5.8 | 8.2 | 8.4 |
| Greece | – | – | 15.4 | 14.3 |
| Hungary | – | 8.2 | 10.1 | 6.7 |
| Ireland | 11.1 | – | 12.9 | 16.2 |
| Italy | 10.5 | 10.4 | 14.0 | 12.8 |
| Luxembourg | 5.3 | 4.5 | 3.9 | 6.1 |
| Mexico | 20.8 | 21.1 | 21.8 | 21.5 |
| Netherlands | 4.7 | 6.3 | 8.1 | 4.9 |
| Norway | 7.2 | 6.4 | 6.9 | 6.4 |
| Poland | 9.7 | 7.7 | 11.6 | 13.2 |
| Russia | – | 19.4 | 20.1 | 18.7 |
| Spain | – | 10.1 | 13.7 | 14.2 |
| Sweden | 7.5 | 6.7 | 6.6 | 6.5 |
| Switzerland | – | 9.3 | – | 7.6 |
| UK | 9.1 | 14.6 | 13.4 | 12.5 |
| USA | 17.8 | 18.1 | 17.8 | 17.7 |

*Source*: LIS.

and the evolution of unemployment, with the changing wage distribution assigned a central role in explaining poverty trends. Note, however, that all these studies pertain to trends in the official 'absolute' US poverty line. As Dickens and Ellwood (2003) highlight in a comparative study of Britain and the United States, the factors influencing poverty trends can differ substantially between absolute and relative measures as well as countries.

The OECD comparative study also usefully documents trends in poverty taking a threshold 'anchored' at 50 percent of the median in the mid-1980s and then indexed to price changes. On this measure, all OECD countries achieved significant reductions in absolute poverty up to 2000. In countries like Ireland and Spain, which experienced very rapid income growth, poverty measured this way fell very sharply indeed over this period. The US poverty rate, customarily measured using an anchored measure, shows a decline from the mid-1980s up until 2000, but this decline was smaller than the average decline of the 15 OECD countries included in the study (Förster and d'Ercole, 2005). Smeeding (2006) shows than when the PPP equivalent of the US official poverty is applied in eight European countries (on data for around 2000), the USA still comes out as having comparatively high poverty, but the gap with other countries is smaller than when a relative measure is applied.[9]

# 5. INCOME POVERTY PERSISTENCE

Poverty measures are often based on the income of the household in a specific week, month, or year, but (even if measured accurately) income at a particular point in time may not be representative of the usual or longer-term income of the household. Longitudinal data tracking households and their incomes have now become much more widely available, allowing those who move in and out of low income to be distinguished from those who are persistently on low income, and a dynamic perspective on income now plays a central role in research on poverty. Bane and Ellwood (1986) pioneered research on the length of spells in poverty in the USA, and cross-country analysis was pioneered by Duncan *et al.* (1993). Comparative studies of income poverty dynamics since then include OECD (2001), Whelan *et al.* (2003), Fouarge and Layte (2005), and Valletta (2006).

Movements in and out of poverty are special cases of more general income mobility, discussed in Chapter 20, but mobility around the poverty threshold might well differ from other areas of the income distribution. Available studies show what the OECD (2001) has summarized as the seeming paradox that poverty is simultaneously fluid and characterized by long-term traps. Many spells in poverty are short and represent only transitory set-backs, and considerably fewer people are continually poor for an extended period of time than are observed in poverty at a point in time. On the other hand, the typical year spent in poverty is lived by someone who experiences multiple years of poverty and whose longer-term income is below the income poverty threshold on average. OECD (2001) looks at poverty dynamics over a three-year period across a range of countries using a 50 percent of median income threshold, and presents a variety of measures of poverty escape and persistence, reproduced in Table 13.3. The 'always poor' as a proportion of the 'ever poor', one summary indicator of persistence, is highest in the USA and lowest in the countries with the lowest cross-sectional poverty rates; yearly escape rates are also highest in the latter and lowest in the USA.

---

[9] Note, however, that the application of PPPs for cross-country poverty comparisons is fraught with difficulties.

Table 13.3. Poverty rates, exit rates, and poverty persistence in the European Union, Canada, and the USA, 1993–1995, 50 percent of median income threshold

| Country | (1) Annual poverty rate | (2) Yearly exit rate | (3) % poor at least once | (4) % always poor | (5) (4) as % of (3) (always poor as % of ever poor) |
|---|---|---|---|---|---|
| Belgium | 9.8 | 48.2 | 16.0 | 2.8 | 17.5 |
| Denmark | 4.7 | 60.4 | 9.1 | 0.8 | 8.8 |
| France | 9.6 | 46.9 | 16.6 | 3.0 | 18.1 |
| Germany | 12.1 | 41.1 | 19.2 | 4.3 | 22.4 |
| Greece | 14.5 | 38.8 | 25.1 | 6.5 | 25.9 |
| Ireland | 8.2 | 54.6 | 15.3 | 1.3 | 8.5 |
| Italy | 13.5 | 40.6 | 21.5 | 5.6 | 26.0 |
| Luxembourg | 7.8 | 47.4 | 12.7 | 2.2 | 17.3 |
| Netherlands | 7.8 | 55.7 | 12.9 | 1.6 | 12.4 |
| Portugal | 15.3 | 37.0 | 24.2 | 7.8 | 32.2 |
| Spain | 12.0 | 49.6 | 21.3 | 3.7 | 17.3 |
| UK | 12.1 | 58.8 | 19.5 | 2.4 | 12.3 |
| *ECHP average* | *11.7* | *46.1* | *19.2* | *3.8* | *19.8* |
| Canada | 10.9 | 36.4 | 18.1 | 5.1 | 28.2 |
| USA (1987–9) | 16.0 | 29.5 | 23.5 | 9.5 | 40.4 |

*Sources*: OECD (2001), tables 2.1 and 2.2, pp. 45 and 50, derived from European Community Household Panel (ECHP) Waves 1–3 except Canada and USA which are from the Survey of Labor and Income Dynamics (SLID) and the Panel Study of Income Dynamics (PSID) respectively.

Since the OECD study was completed, more data from the European Community Household Panel (ECHP) allow a longer horizon to be adopted.[10] Results using five waves, for example, show that the percentage exiting from poverty increases most rapidly as the observation window is lengthened in countries with low initial exit rates, so there is some convergence in five-year exits. The EU's social inclusion indicators also include a measure of persistent poverty, defined as the percentage below the relative poverty threshold in the current year and in at least two of the preceding three years. Once again countries with high cross-sectional rates tend to have a higher proportion of those persistently below the threshold.

Measurement error in survey income data may well affect not only cross-sectional poverty measures but also dynamics and persistence, with Breen and Moisio (2004) arguing that this may lead to an under-estimation of actual persistence. This is also relevant to econometric modeling of poverty dynamics, which seeks to link observed movements into or out of poverty over time to changes in the earnings, labor force participation, and composition of the household. A

[10] More recent exit rates for the USA drawn from the SIPP can also be found in US Census Bureau (2003).

distinction is often made between income 'events', such as changes in earnings or benefits, and demographic 'events' such as the arrival of a new child, partnership formation, death, marital dissolution, or offspring leaving home. The OECD study suggests that changes in household structure may be less important in poverty entries and escapes in European countries than in the USA. Changes in transfers as well as earnings were seen to be important in the EU and to a lesser extent in Canada, but much less so in the USA.

# 6. WHO IS POOR AND WHY

As well as measuring the extent of poverty and trends over time, research has focused on the characteristics associated with being in poverty and the underlying processes involved. This has been the subject of a very wide variety of studies for many countries, both descriptive and econometric. Broadly speaking, the types of individual or household seen as at particular risk include those with low levels of education and skills, the low paid, the unemployed, people with disabilities, lone parents, large families, the elderly, children, ethnic minorities, migrants, and refugees. However, there is substantial variation across countries in the profile of the poor, with implications for how the underlying processes are understood.

This is illustrated in Table 13.4, which uses LIS data to look at poverty rates for children and the elderly using the 50 percent of median relative income threshold. Children have above-average rates in about half the countries shown, with the gap being particularly wide in the UK and the USA, but in a substantial minority their rate is below average. The elderly have an above-average rate in most countries, with substantial variation in the size of the gap, and there are some where their rate is well below the average. A similar comparison across the EU 25 using data from EU-SILC shows similar patterns.

One sees similar variation when focusing on other groups which are generally thought of as vulnerable. For example, the unemployed face a significantly heightened risk virtually everywhere, but the gap between them and the employed varies widely. Similarly, lone parents often face much higher risks than couples with one or two children, but that gap varies a great deal. As OECD (2005) points out, in many countries it is not living in a single-parent household *per se* that increases risk, but rather the likelihood that parent is not in work.

Econometric studies of the characteristics associated with poverty in various countries also highlight age, gender, labor force status, and household composition, as well as such factors as education and labor force experience. Once again, though, a mix of commonality and variation across countries in the patterning of risk is seen, and this has major implications for how one understands the processes at

Table 13.4. Income poverty rates for children and elderly in OECD countries around 2000

| Country | % below 50% of median income | | |
| --- | --- | --- | --- |
| | All | Children (under 18) | Older persons (65+) |
| | % | % | % |
| Australia (2001) | 13.0 | 14.9 | 23.0 |
| Austria (2000) | 7.7 | 7.8 | 13.6 |
| Belgium (2000) | 7.9 | 6.7 | 14.8 |
| Canada (2000) | 12.1 | 15.2 | 5.8 |
| Denmark (2000) | 5.4 | 2.7 | 12.1 |
| Estonia (2000) | 12.4 | 13.6 | 11.0 |
| Finland (2000) | 5.4 | 2.8 | 8.5 |
| France (2000) | 7.3 | 7.9 | 8.5 |
| Germany (2000) | 8.4 | 9.0 | 10.4 |
| Greece (2000) | 14.3 | 12.7 | 26.8 |
| Hungary (1999) | 6.7 | 8.8 | 3.7 |
| Ireland (2000) | 16.2 | 15.8 | 36.8 |
| Italy (2000) | 12.8 | 16.6 | 14.3 |
| Luxembourg (2000) | 6.1 | 9.1 | – |
| Mexico (2000) | 21.5 | 24.8 | 27.9 |
| Netherlands (1999) | 4.9 | 6.3 | – |
| Norway (2000) | 6.4 | 3.4 | 11.9 |
| Poland (1999) | 13.2 | 18.5 | 7.0 |
| Slovenia (1999) | 8.2 | 6.9 | 17.9 |
| Spain (2000) | 14.2 | 16.0 | 23.3 |
| Sweden (2000) | 6.5 | 4.2 | 7.7 |
| Switzerland (2000) | 7.6 | 8.9 | 13.3 |
| UK (1999) | 12.5 | 17.0 | 17.2 |
| USA (2000) | 17.7 | 22.3 | 27.7 |

*Source:* LIS.

work. Individual characteristics such as limited education or skills, gender, ethnic background, migration, and ill health may predispose some people toward a relatively low level of income, as explored in the extensive economic research on these topics discussed in other chapters in this volume. However, the extent to which these individual characteristics, qualifications, or experiences manifest themselves in high poverty rates depends on the household, labor market, and institutional settings in which those 'disadvantages' are experienced.

Thus, for example, the position of the unemployed compared with others depends on whether they have dependants, whether there are others in the household at work, and how the welfare state and its institutions try to cushion the impact of unemployment, most importantly through social protection (Gallie and Paugam, 2000). The poverty status of low-paid individuals is strongly influenced by number of dependants and whether there are others in the household at work (Nolan and

Marx, 2000). The neighborhood one lives in has featured extensively in US poverty research in particular, but the degree of concentration of 'poor people in poor places' varies widely across countries, so one would not expect the independent effect of neighborhood—often difficult to identify with any precision—to be the same. The influence of social background and the inter-generational transmission of poverty have also been extensively studied, as discussed in depth in Chapter 20, with the importance of early childhood intervention a recent focus, but the extent to which context and institutional setting matter in this respect is still unclear. It is also worth emphasizing that the types of household identified as poor can themselves be sensitive to the choice of income threshold and equivalence scale— and, as we discuss in Section 8, to the use of income versus non-income information in identifying the poor.

# 7. UNDERSTANDING CROSS-COUNTRY VARIATION IN POVERTY

In seeking to understand cross-country variation in poverty rates, the numbers in what are generally high-risk demographic groups—for example, the numbers of single parents or older people—are one obvious focus. However, we have seen that it is not being a single parent *per se* that increases risk but the employment status of the parent. Cross-country differences in labor market performance and structure then seem a natural starting point (Burniaux *et al.*, 1998, Förster and D'Ercole, 2005), but at the country level employment rates—overall or for specific groups— are not in fact systematically linked to poverty rates. Burniaux *et al.* (2006) do find a relationship between female participation rates and poverty rates, but the relationship is not particularly strong and there are a number of notable outliers. Poverty rates are generally lower in low unemployment countries and vice versa, but there are notable exceptions and other factors than labor market performance seem to be driving this relationship. A high employment rate is clearly not a sufficient condition for low poverty among the working-age population. (This is of more than academic relevance since boosting labor market participation is at the heart of anti-poverty policy in many countries.) This is striking given that at the individual level those in work experience significantly less poverty than the unemployed, or the non-employed for that matter, in every country for which such information is available.

The working poor are not just an Anglo-Saxon phenomenon, although in-work poverty rates do tend to be higher there (Lohmann and Marx, 2008; Förster and d'Ercole, 2005). This does not simply reflect the extent of low-wage employment—

in fact, the overlap between low-paid work and household poverty is weak, because low-paid workers tend to live in multi-earner households (Nolan and Marx, 2000). Rather, it is associated with households' capacity to generate more than one income, which has become increasingly necessary to stay above the poverty threshold. Obstacles to multi-earnership relate not only to labor market regulation (minimum wages, restrictions on part-time and temporary employment etc.), but also to tax- and benefit systems (work-entry disincentives implied by benefits, dual-earner penalties in tax systems) as well as inadequate child care policies (Esping-Andersen, 1999; Immervoll et al., 2007).

So what matters, from a poverty perspective, is less how work is distributed across individuals than across households. The relationship between levels of household joblessness, or single-earnership for that matter, and working-age poverty is stronger than any of the relationships with individual-level labor market indicators (Burniaux et al., 2006; Förster and d'Ercole, 2005). On the basis of a shift-share exercise, Fritzell and Ritikallio (2004) find that some countries would have considerably lower poverty rates if they had a household labour participation (and socio-demographic) structure similar to Sweden's—the best-performing country. Interestingly, however, some countries like Germany or Canada would have higher rates. A similar exercise by Whiteford and Adema (2007) also showed that the impact of reducing household joblessness and increasing double earnership on child poverty would be generally favorable, but ranges from very strong in some countries to negligible elsewhere.

Employment growth does not always affect the distribution of work across households in such a way as to reduce poverty. For the period from the mid-1980s to the mid-1990s, some of the top performing countries in terms of employment growth actually saw relative poverty rates for the working-age population rise. (Very strong employment growth in the Netherlands, for example, was accompanied by a sharp increase in double earnership, but household joblessness dropped only modestly and more households on benefit fell below the poverty line (Marx, 2007).) Policies to boost work participation have aimed at improving incentives to work, but may reduce the adequacy of benefits in preventing poverty among those who fail to benefit from employment growth. As Förster and d'Ercole's (2005) analysis of working-age poverty trends during the second half of the 1990s shows, declines in the proportion of workless households generally contributed to lower levels of pre-transfer poverty, but this was in many cases partly offset by reductions in the effectiveness of benefits and transfers in preventing poverty.

While in principle low or moderate levels of social spending could produce low poverty rates if resources were well-targeted, there is a strong relationship at country level between the level of social spending and the incidence of poverty, especially for the non-retired population as illustrated in Figure 13.1. No advanced economy achieves a low (relative) poverty rate with a low level of social spending,

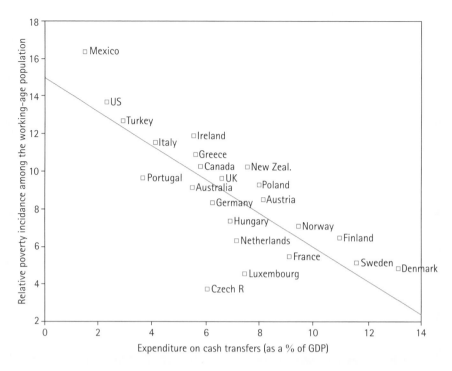

**Fig. 13.1. Expenditure on cash transfers (as % of GDP) and relative poverty incidence among working-age population**

*Source*: OECD database.

regardless of how well it does at maximizing employment—arguably one of the most robust findings of comparative poverty research (see e.g. Bradbury and Jäntti, 2001; Cantillon *et al.*, 2003; Förster and d'Ercole, 2005). The slope of the regression line in Figure 13.1 implies that an increase of 1 percentage point in the share of national income devoted to social spending is associated with a reduction in poverty of 1 percentage point.

This does not simply reflect the direct impact of transfers: high-spending countries have other institutional features that contribute, notably high levels of minimum wage protection and strong collective bargaining compressing wages (hence limiting overall inequality), more extensive public and subsidized employment, as well as active labor market programs, higher levels of public spending on education, and so on. Disentangling the effect of these various factors is inherently fraught with difficulties; simulation via tax-benefit models (notably the Euromod program designed for comparative analysis within the EU—see Immervoll *et al.*, 2006) is one helpful approach.[11] In comparative analysis countries are often simply grouped

---

[11]  Cantillon *et al.* (2003) show that increasing expenditures within the existing social transfer systems of nine EU countries would not always have a strong effect on poverty rates since additional

together into different 'welfare regimes', with a host of studies demonstrating the relationship between poverty outcomes and regime types (Esping-Andersen, 1999). As Tsakloglou and Papadopoulos (2002) bring out, the relationship between aggregate social spending and poverty levels also looks systematically different for the countries which joined the EU in 2004 versus the 'old' 15 members.

The direct effect of taxes and transfers on poverty differs substantially across countries. The best-performing countries succeed in lifting about two-thirds of their pre-tax/transfer poor above the threshold, while others only manage to move one-quarter above (Förster and d'Ercole, 2005). Some countries achieve better 'efficiency' (i.e. poverty is reduced more for each euro or dollar spent) through targeting more on low-income groups, and at the margin, means-tested systems are more efficient if it comes to reducing poverty. However, 'effort' and 'targeting' are negatively related, so targeted systems tend to have a weaker overall effect than universal systems (Korpi and Palme, 1998).

As far as child poverty is concerned, a fairly strong relationship with the level of child-contingent cash spending is seen. Corak *et al.* (2005) show that the best-performing countries tend to have systems of universal child benefits and tax concessions that are not particularly strongly targeted at low-income children.[12] Indeed, in the best-performing countries more tends to be spent on non-poor children than on the poor. Strikingly, countries like the UK and Ireland, which rank as above average spenders on child-contingent benefits, but target most by income, are among the worst-performing countries in terms of child poverty outcomes.

For the elderly, the effectiveness of public pension systems in preventing poverty varies very considerably across countries, with some countries coming close to a complete eradication of elderly poverty by the 50 percent of median threshold (though none do so with the 60 percent threshold). Country differences here are driven in particular by the scope and design of public pension systems. The best performing are basic pension systems as they exist in countries like Denmark, the Netherlands, and New Zealand, providing an income to the elderly regardless of work history or contribution record. Continental European countries mostly have Bismarckian pension systems, which are by design income insurance and status maintenance systems first and foremost, and are often only moderate performers when it comes to poverty prevention. Southern European countries stand out as having comparatively expensive systems that perform weakly at alleviating poverty. Other systems (including Beveridge-type ones) tend to be residual systems that rely heavily on means-testing, with quite widely varying poverty impact.

---

spending would end up disproportionally with those already above the poverty line—particularly in the pension-biased Southern European welfare states.

[12]  See also Bradbury and Jäntti (2001), Whiteford and Adema (2007).

# 8. POVERTY AND INCOME INEQUALITY

Relative income poverty is intrinsically linked to income inequality. In fact, a common criticism of relative poverty measures is that they are in effect inequality measures, and not necessarily valid indicators of the extent and depth of deprivation or exclusion in the society. Another notion that often recurs is that some level of relative income poverty is inevitable if we accept that incomes are not equally distributed. Theoretically, even a country with a very high degree of overall income inequality could have zero relative poverty if the redistributive mechanisms were in place to truncate the income distribution at or above the relative poverty line. The redistributive effort that would be required to truncate the distribution at a widely used threshold like 50 percent of median equivalent income is in fact a fraction of the actual redistributive flows that take place in most countries.[13] In practice, however, as Figure 13.2 shows, if inequality in disposable income is high (low) then relative income poverty rates tend to be high (low) as well, although similar inequality levels are in many cases associated with significantly different relative poverty levels. (The relationship between poverty and inequality in developing countries is among the issues discussed in Chapter 26.)

The fact that a substantial level of income inequality and a limited degree of relative poverty can go together is more evident if one looks at specific subgroups of the population. For example, countries like the Netherlands or New Zealand both have very substantial income inequality among their elderly populations, but the incidence of relative poverty among the elderly by the 50 percent threshold is close to zero in both countries,[14] reflecting the impact of public pensions.

# 9. SOCIAL EXCLUSION AND THE MULTIDIMENSIONALITY OF POVERTY

Up to this point, the research on poverty discussed in this chapter has been based on the identification of the poor via income, reflecting the dominant approach in the research literature on poverty and economic inequality. From a conceptual perspective, a focus on income can also be justified in terms of a person's right to a

---

[13] The aggregate poverty gap, expressed as a percentage of aggregate disposable income, is between 2 and 4% in most rich economies (see Förster and d'Ercole, 2005). Even in the USA it is less than 6%.

[14] In both cases, the elderly poverty rate increases dramatically once the threshold is shifted to 60% of median, indicating that many are in effect just above the 50% line.

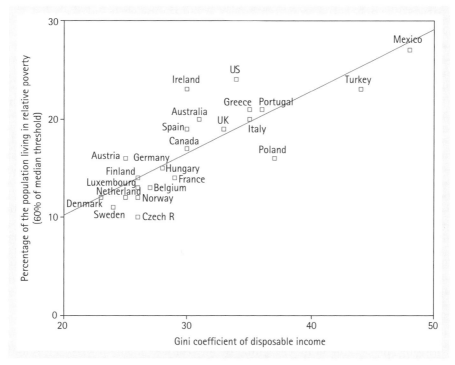

**Fig. 13.2. Gini coefficient for disposable income and relative income poverty (60% median)**

*Source*: OECD database.

minimum level of resources—as distinct from a concern with standard of living— as argued by Atkinson (1987). However, as we noted earlier there is a growing body of research on poverty that seeks to go beyond income, with a view to:

- identifying the poor more accurately and understanding the factors at work,
- capturing the multidimensional nature of poverty, and/or
- encompassing social exclusion conceived as something broader than 'financial poverty'.

Non-monetary indicators of deprivation have been used for many years to directly capture different aspects of living standards, what people have and are doing without. Townsend's (1979) landmark study of poverty in Britain, for example, relied heavily on such indicators, as have subsequent British studies of poverty and social exclusion such as Gordon *et al.* (2000). Various approaches to using such indicators to help identify the poor have also been developed, either on their own, combined with low income, or as the basis for distinguishing an income poverty threshold (see e.g. Townsend, 1979; Mack and Lansley, 1985: Nolan and Whelan, 1996: Halleröd, 1996). Even when longitudinal rather than just cross-sectional income data is available, using direct measures of deprivation may help to identify the poor more accurately as well as illustrating what it is like to be poor (see e.g. analysis of the ECHP by Whelan *et al.*, 2001). The key problems faced in doing so are how to select appropriate indicators, and how to distinguish those who are doing without because their resources are highly constrained as opposed to by choice.

Non-monetary indicators measured at micro-level are also increasingly being used in order to capture the multidimensional nature of poverty and of social exclusion more broadly. For example, analysis of deprivation items included in the ECHP and EU-SILC has identified distinct dimensions, which have been assigned labels such as 'basic deprivation', 'financial strain', housing deprivation, environmental problems, and so on[15]—remarkably, this structuring seems to be common across EU countries. The relationships between these dimensions and low income, and the extent of multiple deprivation across dimensions, have been investigated, and similar studies have been carried out in various countries. Both national and cross-country studies suggest that the numbers experiencing high levels of deprivation across a number of dimensions are often quite modest and that low income alone is not enough to predict who is experiencing different types of deprivation: poor housing, neighborhood deprivation, poor health and access to health services, and low education are clearly related to low income but are distinct aspects of social exclusion. The sizeable numbers falling below relative income poverty thresholds do not experience deprivation across all these dimensions, calling into question the notion that modern societies are increasingly characterized by a divergence between a 'comfortable' majority and an excluded minority: these studies suggest that the reality in OECD countries is rather more complex.

When different dimensions of deprivation or exclusion have been distinguished and one has measured whether people are deprived or excluded on each, how is such information to be summarized across dimensions? Tsui (2002) and Bourguignon and Chakravarty (2003) have explored this issue from a welfare-theoretic perspective. Tsui provides an axiomatic justification for aggregating across different deprivation dimensions into a single cardinal index, and distinguishing the poor as those above some threshold score on that index. Bourguignon and Chakravarty, on the other hand, seek to take into account that one may want to define a poverty threshold *for each dimension* or attribute. They provide a framework for counting the number of poor in different dimensions and combining that information into a statistic summarizing the overall extent of poverty. One can, for example, have a summary measure that counts as poor all those who are poor on *any* dimension. More sophisticated measures take into account different weightings of dimensions and the degree of substitutability one builds in between them. They show in particular how this can be linked to assumed properties of the social welfare

---

[15]  See e.g. Whelan *et al.* (2001), Eurostat (2003, 2005), Guio and Macquet (2007).

function. Atkinson (2003) contrasts what he terms 'social welfare' versus 'counting' approaches to summarizing multidimensional deprivation, emphasizing that each builds in strong assumptions about the underlying structure and interaction between the dimensions.

As well as household level, multidimensional indicators of poverty and social inclusion indicators at national level are increasingly being used to assess change over time and variation across countries.[16] A striking example is the adoption by the EU of an agreed set of indicators to allow progress in promoting social inclusion to be monitored (Atkinson *et al.*, 2002); countries such as the UK and New Zealand also now give a particularly prominent role to such indicators in assessing performance and progress. Comparative analysis highlights that the performance of countries can vary a great deal depending on the dimension and indicator chosen. Marlier *et al.* (2007) for example compare country rankings for the EU 25 on four indicators drawn from the agreed common set: income poverty risk, long-term unemployment, the proportion of working-age adults living in jobless households, and early school leavers. There are many substantial differences in rankings of member states on even just these four indicators—for example, the Czech Republic is ranked first on the poverty rate but 18th on long-term unemployment, while Poland ranks only 17th on the poverty rate but first on early school leavers.

Aggregation is also an issue when one is dealing with such batteries of national-level indicators, if one wants to use them to assess whether things are getting better or worse overall in a given country, or whether one country is doing better than another in some summary sense. Some take the position that the different dimensions are non-comparable and indicators relating to them should simply be presented separately and not aggregated. However, there has been a longstanding practice in the quality of life literature of summarizing across dimensions to produce a single quality of life index. In a development context the UNDP's summary Human Development Index (HDI), inspired by Sen's (1993) influential concept of capabilities, has received a great deal of attention, with a Human Poverty Index variant for developed countries now also produced. Proponents of summary measures of national performance aggregating across dimensions argue that they serve the twin functions of summarizing the overall picture and facilitating communication to a wide audience.[17] The problem is that this requires agreement not only on the best indicators to use but also on the weight to give different indicators/dimensions—the level of average income versus life expectancy, for example.

---

[16] Indicators at regional or local level are also widely employed to capture spatial variation in poverty and exclusion within countries.

[17] See e.g. Micklewright (2001), Hills (2002).

# 10. POVERTY POLICY AND FUTURE RESEARCH

Judging from the figures reported in Section 4, few countries have managed to make great headway in reducing poverty over recent decades, at least as captured by the numbers falling below relative income poverty thresholds. This is striking given that in many countries successive governments have highlighted the fight against poverty. In some cases policies have not had the intended impact—for example, employment growth has been achieved but has not had the hoped-for effect on poverty, at least in the short term. (Increased employment may however create the fiscal and political basis for subsequent action: simulations using Euromod demonstrate the very substantial fiscal costs of anti-poverty policies that have more than a symbolic impact (see Corak *et al.*, 2005; Sutherland, 2001).) Concerns about possible work and self-sufficiency disincentive effects of more adequate benefit systems have always proved a major obstacle to benefit improvements. As many studies show, effective marginal tax rates for people on benefits with limited earnings capacity can be prohibitive (Immervoll and Barber, 2005). Yet it is also clear that benefit adequacy and good labor market performance can go together. Denmark manages to combine one of the highest levels of minimum income protection, comparatively speaking, with a very high labor participation rate (Adema, 2006). Other Nordic countries demonstrate that high minimum income protection can co-exist with high labor participation and low unemployment, when combined with strictly imposed and socially sanctioned requirements regarding participation in training and job search programs, which, moreover, are extensive.

As Whiteford and Adema (2007) show, what does and does not work in fighting poverty depends heavily on context. They simulate the separate and combined effects of work-oriented and benefit-oriented strategies, specifically their impact on child poverty. Reforms to reduce household joblessness (and to get people in work at prevailing wages for those actually in work) would cause big drops in child poverty in some countries, but would hardly have any effect in other countries (notably in the USA). The same applies to policies aimed at reducing single earnership. Nowhere, however, would boosting employment suffice to bring child poverty down to the level of the best-performing countries. Countries that perform best are the countries that enjoy comparatively low 'before tax and transfer' child poverty levels (because of low household joblessness and high maternal employment), and that have tax and benefit systems that are comparatively effective at reducing these levels. Interestingly, there is a good deal of overlap in being a good performer in both respects. And here lies the problem for the worst-performing countries—these have the double hurdle to overcome of reducing pre-transfer/tax poverty levels and putting in place more effective tax/transfer systems.

It should of course be noted that the appropriate policies will also depend on how poverty itself is defined: if the focus is on income poverty thresholds held constant in purchasing power terms rather than linked to average incomes, then economic growth translated into increases in real incomes across the distribution has the major role to play. Even in that case, though, one cannot take this translation for granted—as demonstrated by the limited progress in reducing poverty as measured vis-à-vis the official 'anchored' poverty standard in the USA despite strong economic growth.

Both reviewing the recent literature and considering policy options points to some priorities for research. At the more practical level, the maintenance and improvement of data quality remain imperative. Some population groups prone to poverty and social exclusion remain underrepresented in surveys, migrants for example. Income and deprivation measurement generally needs to be further developed and refined, with panel data an essential ingredient despite the problems associated with attrition. The more fundamental challenges lie in deepening understanding of the processes at work at individual, household, national, and cross-national level. While much has been learned about the characteristics associated with poverty in different countries, the fact that this differs so widely across countries provides a window into the nature of the underlying processes that has not been fully exploited. In the same vein, studying the factors associated with change over time in a specific country is valuable but putting these changes in a comparative perspective adds another dimension. So a panel of countries approach has increasing potential as the statistical underpinning in terms of comparable data continues to be built. This can be complemented by continued development of the potential to carry out micro-simulation analysis in a comparative perspective; the challenge of incorporating behavioral responses into such analysis remains substantial (Immervoll et al., 2007). Exploiting the potential of panel data will continue to be a priority, for example to reliably distinguish those genuinely and persistently on low income, and understanding the barriers to income smoothing facing those on low income more transiently. Increasing recognition of the multidimensional nature of poverty and social exclusion points to the need to deepen understanding of the linkages between different forms of deprivation and exclusion, moving beyond descriptive analysis of the extent to which they go together to study the processes that underpin the underlying relationships between them—where once again a comparative perspective is invaluable—and also addressing the difficult conceptual issues involved. This relates to the broader issue of why one should be concerned with reducing relative poverty in rich societies—are lower levels of income poverty conducive to better outcomes on other dimensions than income, for example health or education outcomes, social cohesion, and trust, and are the economic efficiency arguments for combating poverty compelling?

## References

ADEMA, W. 2006. 'Social Assistance Policy Development and the Provision of a Decent Level of Income in Selected OECD Countries'. OECD Social, Employment and Migration Working Paper 38. Paris: OECD.

ATKINSON, A. B. 1987. 'On the Measurement of Poverty'. *Econometrica*, 55: 759–64.

—— 2003. 'Multidimensional Deprivation: Contrasting Social Welfare and Counting Approaches'. *Journal of Economic Inequality*, 1(1): 51–65.

—— CANTILLON, B., MARLIER, E., and NOLAN, B. 2002. *Indicators for Social Inclusion in the European Union*. Oxford: Oxford University Press.

—— RAINWATER, L., and SMEEDING, T. 1995. *Income Distribution in OECD Countries*. Paris: OECD.

BANE, M. J., and ELLWOOD, D. 1986. 'Slipping In and Out of Poverty: The Dynamics of Poverty Spells'. *The Journal of Human Resources*, 12: 1–23.

BLANK, R. 1993. 'Why were Poverty Rates So High in the 1980s?' in D. Papadimitreiou and E. Wolff (eds.), *Poverty and Prosperity in the Late Twentieth Century*. London: Macmillan.

—— 2008. 'How to Improve Poverty Measurement in the United States'. *Journal of Policy Analysis and Management*, 27(2): 233–54.

BOURGUIGNON, F., and CHAKRAVARTY, S. 2003. 'The Measurement of Multidimensional Poverty'. *Journal of Economic Inequality*, 1(1): 25–49.

BRADBURY, B., and JÄNTTI, M. 2001. 'Child Poverty across Twenty-Five Countries', in B. Bradbury, S. Jenkins, and J. Micklewright (eds.), *The Dynamics of Child Poverty in Industrialised Countries*. Cambridge: Cambridge University Press.

BRANDOLINI, A. 2007. 'The Measurement of Income Distribution in Supernational Entities: The Case of the European Union', in S. Jenkins and J. Micklewright (eds.), *Inequality and Poverty Re-Examined*. Oxford: Oxford University Press.

BREEN, R., and MOISIO, P. 2004. 'Poverty Dynamics Corrected for Measurement Error'. *Journal of Economic Inequality*, 2(3): 171–91.

BUHMANN, B., RAINWATER, L., SCHMAUS G., and SMEEDING, T. 1987. 'Equivalence Scales, Well-Being, Inequality and Poverty: Sensitivity Estimates across Ten Countries Using the Luxembourg Income Study (LIS) Database'. *Review of Income and Wealth*, 34: 115–42.

BURNIAUX, J.-M., DAN, T.-T., FORE, D., FÖRSTER, M., MIRA D'ERCOLE, M., and OXLEY, H. 1998. 'Income Distribution and Poverty in Selected OECD Countries'. OECD Economics Department Working Paper 189. Paris: OECD.

—— and MIRA D'ERCOLE, M. 2006. 'Labour Market Performance, Income Inequality and Poverty in OECD Countries'. OECD Economics Department Working Paper 500. Paris: OECD.

CANTILLON, B., MARX, I., and VAN DEN BOSCH, K. 2003. 'The Puzzle of Egalitarianism: The Relationship between Employment, Wage Inequality, Social Expenditure and Poverty'. *European Journal of Social Security*, 5(2): 108–27.

CITRO, C., and MICHAEL, R. 1995. *Measuring Poverty: A New Approach*. Washington: National Research Council, National Academy Press.

CORAK, M., LIETZ, C., and SUTHERLAND, H. 2005. 'The Impact of Tax and Transfer Systems on Children in the European Union'. IZA Discussion Paper 1589.

COULTER, F., COWELL, F., and JENKINS, S. 1992. 'Equivalence Scale Relativities and the Extent of Inequality and Poverty'. *Economic Journal*, 102: 1067–82.

DICKENS, R., and ELLWOOD, D. T. 2001. 'Whither Poverty in Great Britain and the United States? The Determinants of Changing Poverty and Whether Work Will Work'. NBER Working Paper no. W8253.

DUCLOS, J.-Y., and MAKDISSI, P. 2005. 'Sequential Stochastic Dominance and the Robustness of Poverty Orderings'. *Review of Income and Wealth*, series 51, no. 1: 63–87.

DUNCAN, G., GUSTAFSSON, B., HAUSER, R., SCHMAUS, G., MESSINGER, H., MUFFELS, R., NOLAN, B., and RAY, J.-C. 1993. 'Poverty Dynamics in Eight Countries'. *Journal of Population Economics*, 6(3): 215–34.

ESPING-ANDERSEN, G. 1999. *Social Foundations of Postindustrial Economies*. Oxford: Oxford University Press.

EUROSTAT 2003. *European Social Statistics: Income Poverty and Social Exclusion*, 2nd Report. Luxembourg: Office for Official Publications of the European Communities.

—— 2005. 'Material Deprivation in the EU', in A.-C. Guio, *Statistics in Focus*. Luxembourg: Office for Official Publications of the European Communities.

FÖRSTER, M., and MIRA D'ERCOLE, M. 2005. 'Income Distribution and Poverty in OECD Countries in the Second Half of the 1990s'. OECD Social Employment and Migration Working Papers no. 22. Paris: OECD.

—— and PEARSON, M. 2002. 'Income Distribution and Poverty in the OECD Area: Trends and Driving Forces'. *OECD Economic Studies*, 34: 7–39.

FOSTER, J., GREER, W. J., and THORBECKE, E. 1984. 'A Class of Decomposable Poverty Indices'. *Econometrica*, 52: 761–6.

FOUARGE, D., and LAYTE, R. 2005. 'Welfare Regimes and Poverty Dynamics: The Duration and Recurrence of Poverty Spells in Europe'. *Journal of Social Policy*, 34: 1–20.

FRITZELL, J., and RITAKALLIO, V.-M. 2004. 'Societal Shifts and Changed Patterns of Poverty'. Luxembourg Income Study Working Paper no. 393. Luxembourg: LIS.

GALLIE, D., and PAUGAM, S. (eds.) 2000. *Welfare Regimes and the Experience of Unemployment in Europe*. Oxford: Oxford University Press.

GORDON, D., ADELMAN, L., ASHWORTH, K., BRADSHAW, J., LEVITAS, R., MIDDLETON, S., PANTAZIS, C., PATSIOS, D., PAYNE, S., TOWNSEND, P., and WILLIAMS, J. 2000. *Poverty and Social Exclusion in Britain*. York: Joseph Rowntree Foundation.

GUIO, A.-C., and MACQUET, I. E. 2007. 'Material Deprivation and Poor Housing: What Can be Learned from the EU-SILC 2004 Data? How can EU-SILC be Improved in this Matter?' in *Comparative EU Statistics on Income and Living Conditions: Issues and Challenges, Proceedings of the EU-SILC conference, Helsinki, 6–8 November 2006*. Luxembourg: Office for Official Publications of the European Commission.

HALLERÖD, B. 1995. 'The Truly Poor: Direct and Indirect Measurement of Consensual Poverty in Sweden'. *Journal of European Social Policy*, 5(2): 111–29.

HILLS, J. 2002. 'Comprehensibility and Balance: The Case for Putting Indicators in Baskets'. *Politica Economica*, 1: 95–8.

HOYNES, H., PAGE, M., and STEVENS, A. 2006. 'Poverty in America: Trends and Explanations'. *Journal of Economic Perspectives*, 20(1): 47–68.

IMMERVOLL, H., and BARBER, D. 2005. 'Can Parents Afford to Work? Childcare Costs, Tax-Benefit Policies and Work Incentives'. OECD Social Employment and Migration Working Papers no. 31. Paris: OECD.

—— KLEVEN, H. J., KREINER, C. T., and SAEZ, E. 2007. 'Welfare Reform in European Countries'. *Economic Journal*, 117(516): 1–44

IMMERVOLL, H., LEVY, H., LIETZ, D., MANTOVANI, D., and SUTHERLAND, H. 2006. 'The Sensitivity of Poverty Rates in the European Union to Macro-level Changes'. *Cambridge Journal of Economics*, 30: 181–99.

JÄNTTI, M., and DANZIGER, S. 2000. 'Income Poverty in Advanced Countries', in A. B. Atkinson and F. Bourguignon (eds.), *Handbook of Income Distribution*. Amsterdam: Elsevier.

JARVIS, S., and JENKINS, S. 1998. 'How Much Income Mobility is there in Britain?' *Economic Journal*, 108: 428–43.

KANGAS, O., and RITAKALLIO, V.-M. 1998. 'Different Methods—Different Results? Approaches to Multidimensional Poverty', in H.-J. Andreß, *Empirical Poverty Research in Comparative Perspective*. Ashgate: Aldershot.

KORPI, W., and PALME, J. 1998. 'The Paradox of Redistribution and the Strategy of Equality: Welfare State Institutions, Inequality and Poverty in the Western Countries'. *American Sociological Review*, 63: 661–87.

LAMPMAN, R. 1971. *Ends and Means of Reducing Income Poverty*. Chicago: Markham-Rand McNally.

LOHMANN, H., and MARX, I. 2008. 'The Different Faces of In-Work Poverty in Europe', in H.-J. Andreß and H. Lohmann, *The Working Poor in Europe; Employment, Poverty and Globalization*. Cheltenham: Edward Elgar.

MACK, J., and LANSLEY, S. 1985. *Poor Britain*. London: Allen & Unwin.

MARLIER, E., ATKINSON, A. B., CANTILLON, B., and NOLAN, B. 2007. *The EU and Social Inclusion: Facing the Challenges*. Bristol: Policy Press

MARX, I. 2007. 'The Dutch Miracle Revisited: The Impact of Employment Growth on Poverty'. *Journal of Social Policy*, 34(1): 383–97.

MAYER, S., and JENCKS, C. 1988. 'Poverty and the Distribution of Material Hardship'. *Journal of Human Resources*, 24(1): 88–114.

MICKELWRIGHT, J. 2001. 'Should the UK Government Measure Poverty and Social Exclusion with a Composite Index?', in *Indicators of Progress: A Discussion of Approaches to Monitor the Government's Strategy to Tackle Poverty and Social Exclusion*. CASE Report no. 13, London School of Economics.

MUFFELS, R., and DIRVEN, H. J. 1998. 'Long-Term Income and Deprivation-Based Poverty among the Elderly', in H.-J. Andreß, *Empirical Poverty Research in Comparative Perspective*. Aldershot: Ashgate.

MYLES, J. 2000. 'Poverty Indices and Poverty Analysis'. *Review of Income and Wealth*, 46: 161–79.

NOLAN, B., and MARX, I. 2000. 'Low Pay and Household Poverty', in M. Gregory, W. Salverda, and S. Bazen (eds.), *Labour Market Inequalities: Problems and Policies of Low-Wage Employment in International Perspective*. Oxford: Oxford University Press, 100–19.

——and WHELAN, C. T. 1996. *Resources, Deprivation and Poverty*. Oxford: Clarendon Press.

O' HIGGINS, M., and JENKINS, S. 1990. 'Poverty in the EC: Estimates for 1975, 1980 and 1985', in R. Teekens and B. van Praag (eds.), *Analysing Poverty in the European Community*. Luxembourg: Eurostat.

ORGANISATION FOR ECONOMIC CO-OPERATION and DEVELOPMENT (OECD) 2001. 'When Money is Tight: Poverty Dynamics in OECD Countries'. *Employment Outlook 2001*. Paris: OECD, chapter 2.

OSBERG, L., and XU, K. 2000. 'International Comparisons of Poverty Intensity: Index Decomposition and Bootstrap Inference'. *Journal of Human Resources*, 35(1): 51–81.

PIACHAUD, D. 1987. 'Problems in the Definition and Measurement of Poverty'. *Journal of Social Policy*, 16(2): 147–64.

SEN, A. 1976. 'Poverty: An Ordinal Approach to Measurement'. *Econometrica*, 44: 219–31.

——1993. 'Capability and Well-Being', in M. Nussbaum and A. Sen (eds.), *The Quality of Life*. Oxford: Clarendon Press.

SMEEDING, T. 2006. 'Poor People in Rich Nations: The United States in Comparative Perspective'. *Journal of Economic Perspectives*, 20(1): 69–90.

SUTHERLAND, H. 2001. 'Reducing Child Poverty in Europe: What Can Static Microsimulation Tell Us?' Euromod Working Paper no. EM5/01.

TOWNSEND, P. 1979. *Poverty in the United Kingdom*. Harmondsworth: Penguin.

TSAKLOGLOU, P., and PAPADOPOULOS, F. 2002. 'Aggregate Level and Determining Factors of Social Exclusion in Twelve European Countries'. *Journal of European Social Policy*, 12(3): 211–25.

TSUI, K. 2002. 'Multidimensional Poverty Indices'. *Social Choice and Welfare*, 19: 69–93.

US CENSUS BUREAU 2003. *Dynamics of Economic Well-Being: Poverty 1996–1999*. Washington: US Census Bureau.

VALETTA, R. 2006. 'The Ins and Outs of Poverty in Advanced Economies: Government Policy and Poverty Dynamics in Canada, Germany, Great Britain and the United States'. *Review of Income and Wealth*, 52(2): 261–84.

WHELAN, C. T., LAYTE, R., and MAÎTRE, B. 2003. 'Persistent Income Poverty and Deprivation in the European Union'. *Journal of Social Policy*, 32(1): 1–18.

—— —— —— and NOLAN, B. 2001. 'Income, Deprivation and Economic Strain: An Analysis of the European Community Household Panel'. *European Sociological Review*, 17(4): 357–72.

WHITEFORD, P., and ADEMA, W. 2007. 'What Works Best in Reducing Child Poverty: A Benefit or Work Strategy?' OECD Social Employment and Migration Working Papers no. 51. Paris: OECD.

ZHENG, B. 2000. 'Poverty Orderings'. *Journal of Economic Surveys*, 14: 427–66.

# CHAPTER 14

# INEQUALITY AND TIME USE IN THE HOUSEHOLD

## NANCY FOLBRE

## 1. INTRODUCTION

INCOME is a measure of money that *comes into* a household. Consumption expenditures are a measure of money that *goes out*. Emphasizing the importance of this distinction, economists have long acknowledged that consumption might provide a better measure of living standards than income. Yet both measures, focusing on flows to and from the market economy, essentially ignore production and consumption *within* the household. As a result, both measures are seriously incomplete. Household members devote substantial time and energy to productive activities such as meal preparation, laundry, and child care that increase their overall consumption of goods and services and therefore represent implicit income (Becker, 1965). Household members also enjoy varying amounts of leisure that represent a distinctive form of consumption.

Time devoted to non-market work and leisure would matter little for estimates of inequality if it varied little over time or space. But as women's labor force participation has increased (see Chapter 12), the amount of time devoted to household production has decreased, and the amount of money devoted to purchases of services once produced at home has increased. Significant differences persist across countries—as well as across individual households—in the average amount of time devoted to both household production and leisure. As a result, there is no reason to assume that comparative measures of market income or market consumption provide an accurate picture of comparative living standards (the total amount of market and non-market goods and services consumed relative to needs). Nor is there any reason to assume that these comparative measures provide an accurate picture of comparative differences in utility or happiness.

Economists acknowledge that conventional measures are flawed by their failure to take household production and leisure into account. The recent advent of time-use surveys (now conducted by virtually all OECD countries) offers an important opportunity to address this flaw. Measures of the amount of time devoted to non-market work are now widely available, and the results of efforts to impute a value to this time show that they represent significant magnitude—between about 30% and 50% of conventionally measured Gross Domestic Product (Landefeld and McCulla, 2000). But economists have not yet reached a firm consensus on how best to incorporate analysis of household production and leisure into measurement of the level and distribution of economic well-being.

This chapter explores the implications of time use for measures of income and consumption inequality, summarizes relevant empirical resources and findings, and outlines an agenda for future research. It begins with an overview of the relationship between consumption, income, and time use, and then summarizes recent research on time allocation and its implications for relative well-being. Next, it summarizes research comparing differences in leisure time, assigning a market value to household production, and analyzing inequality among and within households. The final section explores some implications for analysis of poverty and public policy.

# 2. INCOME VERSUS CONSUMPTION

Income is typically measured as a flow of resources into households, the sum of earnings, interest, profits, and transfers. Consumption is typically measured as a flow of resources out of households—expenditures on capital goods such as housing, consumer durables, and direct consumption goods such as clothing and meals. Expenditures on capital goods that last more than a year are often amortized to arrive at a measure of annual consumption. Income is sometimes defined as the money value of goods and services consumed plus or minus any change in wealth or net worth.[1] Chapter 4 provides a more detailed discussion of income measures in the developed countries, while Chapter 24 emphasizes the importance of consumption measures for analysis of inequality in the developing world.

Neither measures of income nor consumption capture either of the two outcomes that economists claim to be most interested in: household living standards (what individuals consume relative to needs, discussed in more detail in Chapter 3) or household utility (the utility or satisfaction that individuals experience, discussed in more detail in Chapter 15). Both income and consumption are merely inputs into a household production process that combines purchased inputs of capital and raw materials with substantial amounts of non-market work and leisure time to produce what economists sometimes call 'full income'—the utility or subjective value of all goods and services consumed, including leisure (Becker, 1965). Furthermore, the relationships among income, consumption, and life satisfaction are surprisingly complicated, especially for mothers, who report subjective benefits from paid work outside the home (Booth and Ours, 2007).

From this perspective, income and consumption suffer from similar limitations. Both are typically based only on market transactions. Measures of income may not capture capital gains or increases in wealth that can potentially generate future income. Measures of consumption may omit past purchases of long-lived consumer durables that continue to generate a flow of consumption services. Both income and consumption typically exclude the value of publicly provided goods and services or natural assets as well as the value of household production and leisure time (Sen, 1989; Osberg and Sharpe, 2002). Income and consumption are also strongly linked to one another by all methods of standardizing household income to account for differences in the number and age of household members (see later discussion of equivalence scales, as well as Chapter 3).

In the last twenty years, considerable progress has been made in the development and administration of household surveys to more closely examine the relationship between income and consumption (Browning *et al.*, 2002) and better understand their implications for inequality (Crossley and Pendakur, 2003). We now have a better sense of how individuals change their consumption patterns in response to income changes (Browning and Collado, 2001). Development of comparable measures of consumption makes it possible to better track changes in consumption-based poverty over time and across countries, with important implications for public policy (Hagenaars *et al.*, 1998; Zaidi and de Vos, 2001).

Still, the traditional debate over income *versus* consumption as measures of well-being now seems less important than efforts to incorporate information regarding household production and leisure into both. Still, the traditional debate offers some

---

[1] The standard Haig-Simons approach defines income as consumption plus change in wealth. For a concise discussion see *Encyclopedia Britannica* at <http://www.britannica.com/eb/topic-763700/accrued-income>.

important lessons that could inform both design and analysis of more comprehensive measures of well-being. For instance, research on the relationship between income and consumption calls attention to variation over the lifecycle. Transient events such as unemployment affect income more strongly than consumption, which can be smoothed by borrowing and saving (Gottschalk and Moffitt, 1994; Slesnick, 2001). Home production provides a similar kind of buffer—in theory, individuals who lose a job have more time to devote to production of goods and services for own use. Life-cycle effects are also apparent: retirement from paid employment is accompanied by a slight increase in time devoted to household production, a factor that could help explain why consumption expenditures tend to drop more after retirement than a permanent income hypothesis predicts (Aguiar and Hurst, 2005).

Practical concerns and data availability often must take precedence over theoretical desirability. Income is easier to measure and to compare than consumption in an international context. Consumption expenditure surveys, typically highly disaggregated, cover a huge variety of expenditures. Expenditures on capital goods such as housing and durable goods can be amortized in a variety of ways. Both quantitative comparisons and qualitative studies suggest that income and consumption are systematically misreported, especially among low-income households (Slesnick, 2001; Edin and Lein, 1997). While proprietary databases increasingly use bar codes and radio transmitter devices to track consumer purchases, these are not yet effectively utilized for public data collection.[2]

Measurement problems also afflict time-diary surveys, which typically ask respondents to describe activities on only one or two randomly selected survey days.

Household income and consumption are distributed rather differently. Since savings tend to increase with household income, families at the top of the income distribution consume a smaller proportion of their income than those at the bottom. As a result, overall consumption inequality is almost always lower than income inequality, even when it follows similar trends over time (Johnson et al., 2005; Pendakur, 1998).

Responding to both methodological problems and empirical inconsistencies, recent research emphasizes that measures of income and consumption inequality should be seen as complements rather than substitutes. Each offers a different lens or prism on inequality (Johnson et al., 2005). The choice of which to use depends on what specific data is available and what specific questions are being asked.

Similarly, analysis of time devoted to household production and leisure can be seen as an important complement to measures of both income and consumption. When and where high quality time-use data is available, it should be used to supplement measures of both consumption and income.

---

[2]  See the website of the prominent marketing firm, A. C. Nielsen, at <http://www2.acnielsen. com/site/index.shtml>, accessed Feb. 4, 2008.

# 3. MEASURING NON-MARKET WORK

National statistical offices in most of the affluent countries (and many developing ones) now conduct regular time-diary surveys based on large, representative samples of the population, complementing earlier surveys often conducted on a smaller scale. Much of this survey data is available on-line in a harmonized format from the Multinational Time Use Survey (MTUS) and the Harmonized European Time Use Survey (HETUS).[3] The United States Bureau of Labor Statistics has been conducting the American Time Use Survey (ATUS) since 2003.

These surveys define non-market work in similar terms, as activities that someone could, in principle, be paid to perform (the so-called 'third person' criterion). This definition ignores the question of whether individuals derive satisfaction or utility from the activity. Many individuals report deriving considerable satisfaction or 'process benefits' from both paid and unpaid work activities (Juster and Stafford, 1985). Some social scientists argue that national accountants should measure reported happiness rather than merely income and consumption (Kahneman *et al.*, 2004). Direct measurement of subjective well-being raises issues very different from those under consideration here—the implications of forms of income and consumption that are obscured from view because they take place outside of market transactions.

The empirical time-use literature generally defines leisure as the sum of recreational activities such as watching television and socializing with friends. Personal care activities (such as sleep, bathing, and grooming) and educational activities are typically assigned to separate categories, rather than characterized as either work or leisure. While this categorization is widely accepted, it is problematic. Some forms of personal care (such as styling hair or manicuring nails) could be characterized as non-market work because many people pay for such services, and most students would describe studying as work.

Time-use surveys do a better job capturing specific activities such as cooking meals than more diffuse responsibilities such as care of children and the elderly, which may involve considerable supervisory time. Some surveys try to capture supervisory care directly; others treat it as a secondary activity, and others (e.g. the American Time Use Survey) ask stylized questions such as when 'was a child in your care?' during the day (Folbre and Yoon, 2007). National estimates of total time devoted to household production are highly sensitive to the way in which care activities are coded and measured (Ironmonger, 1996).

A recent United Nations Human Development report summarizes the average amount of market and non-market work per day (including weekends) performed

---

[3] The MTUS is available at <http://www.timeuse.org/mtus/access/levels/unrestricted.php>, the HTUS at <https://www.testh2.scb.se/tus/tus/StatMeanMact2.html>, and the ATUS at http://www.bls.gov/tus/home.htm>.

by men and women in twenty-seven countries in recent years (see Table 14.1). On average, women devote about two-thirds of their total work time to non-market work and men devote about one-third. For women, the percentage of time devoted to non-market work was highest in Mexico, at 70% and lowest in Latvia at 54%. The figure for the USA was close to that of Latvia, at 58%. The high for women was in Mexico, at about 70%. This percentage is inversely, but only weakly, correlated with the level of GDP per capita (R = −10). The range is far greater for men, from 46% in Belgium to 7% in Japan. Interestingly, the correlation with GDP per capita is positive, and larger (R = 0.23).

Level of development probably exercises less impact than demographic factors and public policies. In countries where a large percentage of the population is over age 65, retired persons devote considerable time to non-market work. Public policies such as universal child care and paid family leaves from work tend to encourage higher female labor force participation, which in turn tends to reduce the relative amount of non-market work (Gornick and Meyers, 2003).

Differences in the average amount of time devoted to paid employment have profound implications for comparisons of economic well-being (Parente *et al.*, 2000). Conventional measures of GDP per capita yield very different rankings than those based on GDP per hour of paid employment. On average workers in the European Union devote 16% fewer hours to paid employment per year than workers in the USA (Rosnick and Weisbrot, 2006: 2). A combination of higher taxes and collective bargaining has led to much longer vacation times in Europe than in the USA (Osberg, 2002).

One detailed comparison of the USA and Germany confirms that conventional measures overstate relative levels of consumption in the USA, because German women spend more time preparing meals and providing child care at home (Freeman and Schettkat, 2002). Within countries, average levels of time devoted to paid employment vary considerably across income deciles, confounding measures of inequality in living standards based on measures of consumption that ignore household production and leisure (Phipps and Burton, 2007).

# 4. LEISURE TIME AND CONSUMPTION

Economic theory emphasizes a labor/leisure tradeoff, in which individuals compare the utility generated by the additional income from an additional hour of paid employment with the disutility of work. Whether the tradeoff can be persuasively described in these terms or not (see Chapter 15), institutional rigidities and public policies often constrain individual choices. One panel study using German data

Table 14.1. Men's and women's average hours and minutes of total work and non-market work as percentage of total work in twenty-seven countries ranked by human development index

| HDI rank | Country | Year | GDP per capita (PPP) in 2003/04 | Women's avg. total work hours | Men's avg. total work hours | Women's non-market work as % of total | Men's non-market work as % of total | Ratio of women's total work to men's total work |
|---|---|---|---|---|---|---|---|---|
| 2 | Norway | 2000–01 | $37,357 | 7:13 | 7:23 | 59 | 39 | 97.7 |
| 3 | Australia | 1997 | $32,183 | 7:15 | 6:58 | 70 | 38 | 104.1 |
| 4 | Canada | 2005 | $31,600 | 7:57 | 7:51 | 60 | 41 | 101.3 |
| 5 | Ireland | 2005 | $30,583 | 6:38 | 6:10 | 70 | 28 | 107.6 |
| 6 | Sweden | 2000–01 | $28,639 | 7:32 | 7:43 | 58 | 41 | 97.6 |
| 8 | Japan | 1996 | $26,658 | 6:33 | 6:03 | 57 | 7 | 108.3 |
| 9 | Netherlands | 1995 | $28,901 | 5:08 | 5:15 | 73 | 31 | 97.8 |
| 10 | France | 1998–99 | $28,759 | 7:01 | 6:27 | 67 | 41 | 108.8 |
| 11 | Finland | 1999–00 | $25,736 | 7:20 | 6:58 | 62 | 41 | 105.3 |
| 12 | United States | 2005 | $39,535 | 8:06 | 7:54 | 58 | 36 | 102.5 |
| 13 | Spain | 2002–03 | $23,481 | 7:54 | 6:51 | 70 | 29 | 115.3 |
| 16 | United Kingdom | 2000–01 | $29,462 | 7:41 | 7:32 | 65 | 38 | 102.0 |
| 17 | Belgium | 1999–00 | $28,094 | 6:35 | 6:04 | 71 | 46 | 108.5 |
| 19 | New Zealand | 1999 | $26,097 | 7:00 | 6:57 | 68 | 40 | 100.7 |
| 20 | Italy | 2002–03 | $25,511 | 8:08 | 6:51 | 74 | 30 | 118.7 |
| 22 | Germany | 2001–02 | $28,074 | 7:00 | 6:49 | 70 | 45 | 102.7 |
| 26 | South Korea | 2004 | $19,354 | 7:30 | 6:51 | 60 | 14 | 109.5 |
| 27 | Slovenia | 2000–01 | $23,035 | 8:22 | 7:34 | 65 | 43 | 110.6 |
| 29 | Portugal | 1999 | $19,267 | 7:39 | 6:05 | 61 | 18 | 125.8 |
| 36 | Hungary | 1999–00 | $15,016 | 8:00 | 7:08 | 68 | 44 | 112.1 |
| 37 | Poland | 2003–04 | $10,484 | 7:55 | 7:25 | 69 | 41 | 106.7 |
| 43 | Lithuania | 2003–04 | $13,603 | 8:55 | 8:00 | 57 | 35 | 111.5 |
| 44 | Estonia | 1999–00 | $15,495 | 8:55 | 8:09 | 62 | 40 | 109.4 |
| 45 | Latvia | 2003–04 | $11,739 | 8:31 | 8:02 | 54 | 30 | 106.0 |
| 46 | Uruguay | 2002 | $10,718 | 7:20 | 6:56 | 67 | 32 | 105.8 |
| 52 | Mexico | 2002 | $8,883 | 8:10 | 6:25 | 77 | 22 | 127.3 |
| 65 | Mauritius | 2003 | $18,552 | 6:33 | 6:09 | 70 | 20 | 106.5 |
| | Average | | $23,586 | 7:30 | 6:58 | 65 | 34 | 107.8 |

*Sources: UN Human Development Report 2007–2008*, p. 114, available at <http://hdr.undp.org/en/media/hdr_20072008_tables.pdf>; data on GDP per capita from Penn World Tables version 6.2, at <http://en.wikipedia.org/wiki/List_of_countries_by_GDP_(PPP)_per_capita>

found many individuals reporting they would prefer to work less even at lower pay (Merz, 2002). Evidence suggests that many mothers of young children opt out of paid employment because they cannot find high quality part-time jobs (Gornick *et al.*, 2007). Parents working for pay—especially single parents—are most likely to report a 'time crunch'.

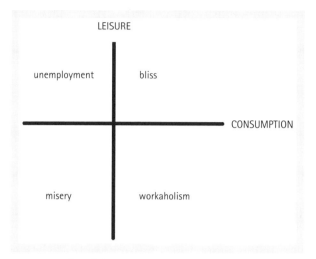

**Fig. 14.1. Possible relationships between leisure and consumption**

*Note*: Origin represents the median level of leisure and the median level of consumption

The relationship between leisure and other forms of consumption can be affected by income and by household production as well as by price effects with complex implications for living standards. Figure 14.1, where the origin represents median values for both, illustrates four different possible outcomes. In the upper right-hand quadrant individuals have greater than median values for leisure and other consumption, a region of 'economic bliss'. The mirror image of that quadrant can be aptly termed 'misery'—with leisure and other consumption both lower than the median values. In the other two quadrants, leisure and other forms of consumption counterbalance each other: those who have higher than median consumption but lower than median leisure may suffer from workaholism (or simply overwork), while those with the opposite combination represent the unemployed (or under-employed).

Empirical trends in leisure have been much debated in countries for which historical data are available, because empirical results are sensitive to definitions and time periods chosen (Aguiar and Hurst, 2006; Ramey and Francis, 2006). One historical study of the USA argues that low-earners worked longer hours for pay than high-earners around 1890, but that a century later the pattern was reversed, with high-earners working longer hours (Costa, 1998). As a result, monetary measures may overstate the relative standard of living of high-earners.

A recent international study compares actual hours worked to a hypothetical calculation of how much individuals would need to work to meet their basic needs, revealing considerable inequality in this measure (Goodin *et al.*, 2008). Another way of taking work time into account would be to develop a comprehensive estimate of labor productivity by calculating full income (market and non-market income) or full consumption (of market and non-market goods) per hour of work (both paid and unpaid). Such an estimate requires an estimate of the monetary value of non-market income and/or consumption.

# 5. THE MARKET VALUE OF NON-MARKET WORK

From the income side, time devoted to non-market work can be treated as a source of implicit income, using either a replacement-cost approach (what it would cost to hire a worker to provide comparable services) or an opportunity-cost approach (typically, what the worker could have earned in wage employment). From the consumption side, output valuation can ask what it would cost to purchase the good or service outside the household. Subtraction of capital costs and raw materials yields an estimate of the value of labor services. For instance, take the price of a hamburger at a restaurant, subtract the cost of the capital depreciation and raw materials required to cook the burger at home, and the residual represents an estimate of the value of the household labor devoted to preparing, cooking, and serving the hamburger.

The output-valuation method is superior because it includes consideration of household capital and technology. Ideally both input and output valuations should be performed and compared to one another as a cross-check (Abraham and Mackie, 2004). In practice, however, most national statistical offices assign a replacement cost valuation to household labor. The United Kingdom Statistical Office, however, has developed a set of experimental accounts based on output valuation (Holloway et al., 2002).

Household-level imputations typically vary more than the aggregate estimates provided by national statistical agencies. Some estimates value only time devoted to housework (Gottschalk and Mayer, 2002), while others include valuation of time devoted to child care (Frazis and Stewart, 2006). When child care is included, measures of secondary activity or time that children are 'in an adult's care' deserve valuation, rather than merely time that adults are engaged in direct activities such as feeding or reading aloud to children (Folbre and Yoon, 2008). Similar concerns apply to care of the disabled, sick, and elderly.

Imputations based on models of utility maximization typically use opportunity cost measures, reasoning that these capture the value that individuals themselves place on an activity (in more technical terms, the consumer surplus) (Apps and

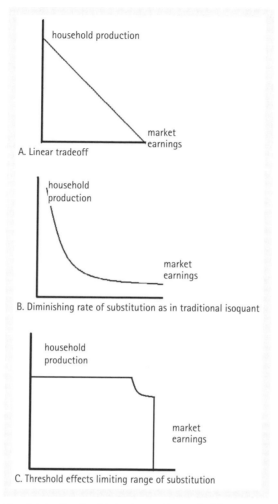

Fig. 14.2. Tradeoffs between household production and market earnings

Rees, 2002). Replacement cost estimates provide a measure more consistent with the assumptions of national income accounting (Abraham and Mackie, 2004). Replacement cost estimates can be misleading, however, as they imply a simple linear tradeoff between market work and any particular non-market activity (the slope of the line represents the ratio of the individual's wage to the replacement wage) (see Fig. 14.2.A). A standard production function with diminishing returns would yield a non-linear relationship characterized by diminishing returns, as illustrated in Figure 14.2.B. Even the continuous substitutability implied here is misleading. In a modern industrial economy most people lack the resources and the skills to successfully substitute home production for market-purchased goods.

They can purchase fewer restaurant meals or provide more family care at home, but seldom their own food, clothing, or shelter. A more realistic picture of limited substitutability with threshold effects is portrayed in Figure 14.2.C.

Interesting recent research analyzes differences in 'time-intensity', comparing the amounts of non-market work and consumption expenditures devoted to different types of consumption in the USA and Israel (Gronau and Hamermesh, 2006). Another accounting approach, outlined by Jonathan Gershuny (2005), uses information from aggregate input-output models to convert consumer expenditures into labor-time equivalents. In addition to showing how households combine purchased inputs with the goods and services they produce themselves, input-output matrices could include the value of government-provided services in total consumption, which is substantial. As Chapter 25 makes clear, government services such as child care and health care affect household consumption in ways that are not captured by standard measures. They are comparable, in this sense, to household production services.

# 6. HOUSEHOLD PRODUCTION AND INEQUALITY AMONG HOUSEHOLDS

Efforts to value non-market work generally find that imputations of its market value have an equalizing effect on the distribution of family 'full income', defined as the sum of market income and the imputed value of non-market work. Somewhat surprisingly, however, low-income households do not seem to devote significantly more time to household production (including child care) than high income households, and unemployed men don't perform significantly more housework than those who are employed (Frazis and Stewart, 2006). The equalizing effect of valuing household production results primarily from addition of a relatively large constant value to most household incomes (Frazis and Stewart, 2006; Gottschalk and Mayer, 2002; Aslaksen and Koren, 1996).

As Chapter 18 shows, increases in women's earnings have contributed to increases in household income inequality, because high-earning women tend to marry high-earning men. The effect on the inequality of household full income, taking the value of household production into account, has probably been even greater. Thirty years ago, fewer married women worked for pay, and most devoted more time to housework (Bianchi et al., 2006; Gauthier et al., 2004). The value of household production was probably greater relative to market income and its variance lower.

Chapter 18 also points out that historical decline in family size and increases in the percentage of children living with mothers alone has reduced income-sharing within households. This change in household structure also implies less sharing of household-produced services. While economists know little about the extent of economies of scale in household production, assumptions regarding their impact are built into standard equivalence scales, which assume that many can live more cheaply than one (see Chapter 3). There are almost certainly greater economies of scale in household production than in market purchases: the marginal cost of adding another person to the home dinner table is much smaller than that of adding them to a restaurant tab. Likewise, the marginal cost of putting a small child into paid child care is greater than the time cost of adding another child to the household. Hence, a shift away from household production towards market production probably reduces household economies of scale in consumption: another reason why household production may have a less equalizing effect than it once did.

Another dimension of household production, far more significant in the long run than the value of goods and services produced for household consumption, is the production of children's capabilities. In the USA, changes in household structure, as well as the stresses and strains of poverty, have contributed to concerns regarding growing inequality in child outcomes (McLanahan, 2004). Parental education tends to have a positive impact on both the quantity and quality of time that both mothers and fathers spend with children (Bianchi et al., 2006). Both factors hold special relevance for the issues of intergenerational income mobility discussed in Chapter 20.

Consideration of inputs into children also raises questions concerning inequality between parents and non-parents. Some economists treat childrearing as though it were simply a consumption activity. In a classic treatise of public finance published in 1938 Henry Simons wrote, 'it would be hard to maintain that the raising of children is not a form of consumption on the part of parents, whether one believes in the subsidizing of such consumption or not' (Simons, 1938: 140). From this perspective it does not make much sense to compare the well-being of households with and without children, any more than it makes sense to compare the well-being of households with and without pets (Ferreira et al., 1998).

But children obviously impose both financial and temporal costs on parents, and also yield benefits to society as a whole. In an explicit rebuttal of Henry Simons, William Vickrey wrote in 1947,

This reduction of children to a status comparable to that of a household pet is hardly acceptable. Almost everyone will concede that the community has a greater interest in the welfare of children than in the welfare of pets, even though there may be widespread disagreement as the nature of that interest. A more satisfactory approach, on the whole, is to regard minors and other dependents as citizens in their own right.    (Vickrey, 1947: 292)

If the money and time that parents devote to children are considered expenditures that reduce their own material standard of living, economic inequality between parents and non-parents becomes an issue (Folbre, 2008). Economists have not yet devoted much attention to this issue, but research on the distribution of income, consumption, and leisure within households could help bring it to the fore.

# 7. INTRAHOUSEHOLD INEQUALITY

Conventional approaches to inequality assume equal distribution within the household. Analysis of consumption and time use offers at least some opportunity to challenge this assumption. While many household consumption items such as expenditures on housing and utilities represent public goods, others such as diapers, toys, or clothing, are either age or gender-specific. A lifecycle approach calls attention to women's economic vulnerability: specialization in non-market work lowers lifetime earnings and reduces bargaining power within the household. Further, a large percentage of children in the OECD countries are now being raised by mothers alone. The money and time that lone parents devote to children may reduce their standard of living far more than suggested by standard per capita or equivalized income measures.

Bargaining models predict that the individuals with greater command over resources will claim a greater share of household consumption. Divorce-threat models put particular emphasis on fallback positions outside of marriage. Relatively high rates of divorce or dissolution of cohabiting relationships remain characteristic of many OECD countries, and women suffer far more adverse economic consequences from divorce than men. One study in the USA estimates a decrease in women's family incomes (adjusted for family size) of about 25%, compared to a slight increase for men (Hoffman and Duncan, 1988). While many European safety net policies are aimed at low-income families, not all effectively cushion the negative impact of divorce. A longitudinal analysis of German data shows gender-based inequalities of similar magnitude to those in the USA (Burkhauser et al., 1991).

As well as facing higher risks from divorce, women who contribute lower earnings than their partners have less direct control over household income. Some qualitative studies find that divorced women consider themselves better off financially after divorce even though their household income is lower, presumably because they have more control over spending (Graham, 1987). Several studies show that the share of household income a husband or wife contributes positively affects their share of private consumption goods (Browning et al., 1994; Phipps and Burton, 1998; Browning and Bonke, 2006). The causality is difficult to untangle, but one important study using data from the United Kingdom identifies the effect of an exogenous shift in control over income by examining the impact of a policy shift giving mothers, rather than fathers, control over the child family allowance. This change resulted in a small but significant increase in spending on women's and girls' clothing (Lundberg and Pollak, 1993).

Studies also reveal variations in the distribution of consumption between parents and children. In the USA, cohabiting couples with children spend proportionally less on them than married couples do (DeLeire and Kalil, 2005). Empirical evidence from the USA suggests that parents treat boys and girls differently (Lundberg and Rose, 2004). One might expect low-income families to devote a larger portion of their expenditures to children than high-income families that need not worry about meeting their children's basic needs, but few recent studies have explored this question.

More research on income sharing and consumption pooling within households is sorely needed, because it has important implications for social policy. Poverty among households is not the same as poverty among individuals (Jenkins, 1991). One simulation study of the effect of different possible sharing rules using Canadian data found that estimates varied between children and fathers experiencing the same incidence of poverty to children experiencing more than fifty times the incidence of their fathers' poverty (Phipps and Burton, 1995: 198). On the other hand, if single low-income parents devote a larger share of their expenditures to children than other parents, rates of poverty are lower among children—and higher among their mothers—than conventional measures suggest.

Analysis of leisure time also adds another dimension to consideration of intra-household inequality. Gender differences in leisure time depend heavily on the ways leisure is defined, and some economists argue that these differences are not significant in the developed countries (Burda et al., 2007). However aggregate data for the developed countries indicate that women still work longer total hours (paid and unpaid) than men (see Table 14.1). The ratio of women's work to men's ranges from a low of 97.6% in Sweden to a high of 125.8% in Portugal. The differences in daily averages may seem small, but a daily average of ten minutes a day comes to an hour and ten minutes per week, or more than 60 hours a year. Burda et al. (2007) argue that gender differences in work hours tend to diminish along with economic development. Analysis of the data in Table 14.1 bears out this observation: the correlation between GDP per capita and the ratio of women's to men's work is −0.53.

Differences in the quality of leisure also bear consideration. A spate of studies shows that adult men enjoy fewer interruptions of their leisure time, and are less likely to be encumbered by supervisory responsibilities for children (Phipps et al., 2001; Mattingly and Bianchi, 2003; Bittman and Wajcman, 2004). Women report higher levels of stress than men at balancing work/family responsibilities (Macdonald et al., 2005). The United Nations Statistical Office is considering the impact of leisure differences on national indicators of women's empowerment (Folbre, 2006).

Differences in consumption and time use can countervail one another. That is, the person who consumes a larger share of private goods in a household may also be the person who enjoys less leisure time. Analysis of a unique Danish data set that provides information on both suggests that both individual preferences and relative power influence intrahousehold allocation. Consumption may be more sensitive than leisure to relative power (Browning and Gortz, 2006). However, measurement problems remain significant. Future research should carefully examine time-use-survey treatment of secondary activities and responsibility for children. Efforts to calibrate quantitative surveys with qualitative ethnographic research could yield valuable insights.

# 8. POVERTY, TIME USE, AND POLICY

Poverty is typically measured either in terms of income or consumption, and both measures have limitations. An income-based definition fails to include people who have adequate income but extraordinary consumption needs, such as elderly households with large out-of-pocket expenditures on health. A consumption-based definition fails to include people who have inadequate income, such as the unemployed, as long as they are able to borrow money to cover their basic expenses. Both conventional definitions ignore the value of home production and leisure.

Most OECD countries define a poverty line in terms of relative income—such as families with equivalized income below 60% of the median income. But consumption poverty also receives attention. The satisfaction of basic human needs for food, shelter, education, and health hold special relevance for public policy. Eurostat collects data on living conditions, housing, social protection, and social cohesion indicators as well as household consumption expenditures. The current US poverty line is defined in terms of consumption needs, which also play a large role in the experimental poverty lines under discussion in recent years.

The European Community Household Panel, launched in 1994, collected microdata on living conditions. It was replaced, in 2003, by the European Union Statistics of Income and Living Conditions Survey (SILC). Private expenditures on health and child care are, obviously, less relevant in countries where these services are provided by the public sector. Perhaps as a result, European policy makers have focused more on indicators of social exclusion.

The original benchmarks for the US poverty line were set in the 1960s, based on a US Department of Agriculture estimate of the basic caloric needs of adults and children, combined with the observation that most low-income families at that time spent about one-third of their budget on food. These lines simply multiply an estimate of the cost of meeting basic caloric requirements by three. Women were weighted less than men until 1981, when the threat of prosecution for sex discrimination led to equalization (Ruggles, 1990: 87).

Most researchers agree that reliance on estimates of necessary food expenditures as a benchmark for poverty is conceptually incorrect. Further, the assumption that food expenditures represent one-third of household budgets is antiquated: studies show that low-income households now spend a smaller proportion of their budgets on food and more on necessities such as rent, health care, and transportation. Among other distortions, this assumption leads to lower poverty thresholds for elderly persons because their caloric needs are lower than those of other adults, ignoring the greater need the elderly often have for health care.

Other serious problems with the US poverty line include, on the income side, the omission of most of the value of the Earned Income Tax Credit and the value of in-kind transfers such as Food Stamps, and on the consumption side, the growing costs of child care and education. These omissions have the unfortunate effect of making it difficult to clearly discern the effects of important public policy measures on the well-being of families at the bottom of the income distribution.

Dissatisfaction with the official poverty line motivated a panel of experts convened by the National Academy of Science (NAS) to suggest an alternative approach (Citro and Michael, 1995; Short and Garner, 1999). A new set of experimental poverty measures defines food, clothing, shelter, and utilities as necessities and sets a threshold of need based on what most families spend. The minimum is set between 78% and 83% of the median expenditures on these items reported in the annual Consumer Expenditure Survey (CE). This threshold is multiplied by a number between 1.15 and 1.25 to account for other miscellaneous necessary expenditures.

The NAS approach subtracts many 'non-discretionary' expenditures, including taxes, from households' money and near-money income to arrive at a measure of disposable income available to meet the threshold described above. Expenditures on child care are considered 'non-discretionary' if they are a work-related cost; that is, if all parents living with the child are engaged in paid employment. Subtraction of these expenditures is capped at the level of the earnings of the lowest-earning parent. Other work-related costs such as transportation are also subtracted, as are out-of-pocket expenditures on health. The experimental measures also include various ways of taking into account both housing subsidies and the value of home ownership, which reduces the amount of rent that families must pay for shelter.

This approach represents a distinct improvement over the conventional US poverty line. But while treating expenditures on food, clothing, shelter, and necessities is better than relying entirely on expenditures on food as a marker of 'necessities', it reflects a similarly antiquated emphasis on goods rather than services. Many expenditures on food (such as restaurant meals) and clothing (such as fashionable athletic shoes) represent luxuries, while most families regard expenditures on health and education services as necessities, especially for children.

Another approach to measurement of consumption poverty would be to use the Consumer Expenditure Survey to measure the percentage of low-income households with medical expenditures or child-care expenditures over a certain threshold, or those who do and do not own a car (virtually everywhere, a necessity to maintaining paid employment). Surveys of reported hardships, such as not being able to obtain sufficient food, or not being able to pay utility bills in a given month, are also relevant.

Differences in time devoted to non-market work also have implications for measurement of poverty. Absolute poverty standards, such as the US poverty line, were constructed on the basis of family budgets, assuming the presence of a full-time homemaker (Vickery, 1977). Many fewer households in the highly developed countries enjoy the services of such a homemaker today, and as a result, their monetary cost of living has increased. Furthermore, lack of perfect substitutability between consumption goods and time—of particular relevance in consideration of emotionally laden, person-specific activities such as child care—suggests the need for an independent standard of 'time poverty' as well as income or consumption poverty (Citro and Michael, 1995).

Many of the trends noted above have unfortunate implications for the equivalence scales that are conventionally applied to measures of both consumption and income to adjust for differences in household size and composition. These equivalence scales embody assumptions regarding household economies of scale and the relative consumption needs of adults and children that remain largely unquestioned. If economies of scale in household production have declined over time and if the time that parents devote to child care is considered a cost that, like expenditures on child-specific goods, reduces adult living standards, then conventional equivalence scales overstate the well-being of households with children relative to those without. Empirical research shows that measures of both poverty and inequality are highly sensitive to equivalence scale adjustments, especially those that increase weights of children relative to adults (Phipps, 1993; Banks and Johnson, 1994). Consumption inequality in the USA appears to be especially high relative to income inequality among single parents and their children (Johnson et al., 2005).

Conventional equivalence scales may distort policy debates by making households with children appear to be better off than they actually are (Folbre, 2008). Such distortions could exacerbate a widely acknowledged problem. International comparisons show that children living with single parents, while economically disadvantaged in most countries, are particularly vulnerable in the USA (Christopher et al., 2001).

# 9. CONCLUSION

Both neoclassical and institutionalist economists acknowledge that measures of market income and spending on goods and services provide an incomplete picture of standards of living. The amount of leisure that individuals enjoy, as well as the value of the goods and services they produce outside the market, clearly affect their well-being. For many years, lack of conceptual attention to these issues could be justified by lack of empirical data to flesh them out. Today, the availability of time-use data has, in a sense, created the opposite problem: without greater conceptual consensus, new data cannot be put to effective use.

The traditional debate over whether income or consumption provides a better metric for analyzing inequality among households (see Chapters 4 and 24) is now overlaid by new concerns about leisure and valuation of household production. As with the traditional debate, there is no single answer—except that many metrics are probably better than one. The distribution of leisure time and the valuation of non-market work deserve more systematic attention. The potential of time-use surveys will be more fully realized when they are linked to surveys of consumer expenditure and measures of direct government service provision.

## REFERENCES

ABRAHAM, K., and MACKIE, C. 2004. *Beyond the Market. Designing Nonmarket Accounts for the United States.* Washington: The National Academies Press.

AGUIAR, M., and HURST, E. 2005. 'Consumption versus Expenditure'. *Journal of Political Economy*, 115(5): 919–48.

—————— 2006. 'Measuring Trends in Leisure: The Allocation of Time Over Five Decades'. National Bureau of Economic Research Working Paper 12082.

APPS, P., and REES, R. 2002. 'Household Production, Full Consumption, and the Costs of Children'. *Labour Economics*, 8: 621–48.

ASLAKSEN, I., and KOREN, C. 1996. 'Unpaid Household Work and the Distribution of Extended Income: The Norwegian Experience'. *Feminist Economics*, 2(3), Nov.: 65–80.

BANKS, J., and JOHNSON, P. 1994. 'Equivalence Scale Relativities Revisited'. *The Economic Journal*, 104(425), July: 883–90.

BECKER, G. 1965. 'A Theory of the Allocation of Time'. *Economic Journal*, 75: 493–517.

BIANCHI, S., ROBINSON, J. P., and MILKIE, M. A. 2006. *Changing Rhythms of American Family Life*. New York: Russell Sage.

BITTMAN, M., and WAJCMAN, J. 2004. 'The Rush Hour: The Quality of Leisure Time and Gender Equity', in N. Folbre and M. Bittman (eds.), *Family Time: The Social Organization of Care*. New York: Routledge.

BOOTH, A., and OURS, J. S. 2007. 'Job Satisfaction and Family Happiness: The Part-Time Work Puzzle'. Institute for Social and Economic Research Working Paper 2007-20, available at <http://www.iser.essex.ac.uk/pubs/workpaps/pdf/2007-20.pdf>.

BROWNING, M., and BONKE, J. 2006. 'Allocation Within the Household: Direct Survey Evidence'. Economics Series Working Papers 286, University of Oxford, Department of Economics.

——BOURGUIGNON, F., CHIAPPORI, P., and LECHENE, V. 1994. 'Incomes and Outcomes: A Structural Model of Intrahousehold Allocation'. *Journal of Political Economy*, 102(6): 1067–96.

——and COLLADO, D. 2001. 'The Response of Expenditures to Anticipated Income Changes: Panel Data Estimates'. *American Economic Review*, 91(3), June: 681–92.

——CROSSLEY, T. F., and WEBER, G. 2002. 'Asking Consumption Questions in General Purpose Surveys'. *Economic Journal*, 113(491), Nov.: F540–F567.

——and GORTZ, M. 2006. 'Spending Time and Money Within the Household'. Economics Series Working Paper 288, University of Oxford, Department of Economics.

BURDA, M., HAMERMESH, D. S., and WEIL, P. 2007. 'Total Work, Gender and Social Norms'. IZA Discussion Paper 2705.

BURKHAUSER, R. V., DUNCAN, G. J., HAUSER, R., and BERNTSEN, R. 1991. 'Wife or Frau, Women Do Worse: A Comparison of Men and Women in the United States and Germany After Marital Dissolution'. *Demography*, 28(3), Aug.: 353–60.

CHRISTOPHER, K., ENGLAND, P., ROSS, K., SMEEDING, T., and McLANAHAN, S. 2001. 'Gender Inequality in Poverty in Affluent Nations: The Role of Single Motherhood and the State', in K. Vleminckx and T. Smeeding (eds.), *Child Wellbeing, Child Poverty and Child Policy in Modern Nations*. Bristol: The Policy Press, 199–219.

CITRO, C., and MICHAEL, R. (eds.) 1995. *Measuring Poverty*. Washington: National Academy Press.

COSTA, D. 1998. 'The Unequal Work Day: A Long Term View'. *American Economic Review*, 88(2): 330–4.

CROSSLEY, T. F., and PENDAKUR, K. 2003. 'Consumption Inequality', in D. Green and J. Kesselman (eds.), *Dimensions of Inequality in Canada*. Vancouver: University of British Columbia Press.

DeLEIRE, T., and KALIL, A. 2005. 'How Do Cohabiting Couples with Children Spend their Money?' *Journal of Marriage and Family*, 67, May: 286–95.

EDIN, K., and LEIN, L. 1997. *Making Ends Meet: How Single Mothers Survive Welfare and Low-Wage Work*. New York: Russell Sage.

FERREIRA, M. L., BUSE, R. C., and CHAVAS, J. 1998. 'Is There a Bias in Computing Household Equivalence Scales?' *Review of Income and Wealth*, 44: 183–98.

FOLBRE, N. 2006. 'Measuring Care: Gender, Empowerment, and the Care Economy'. *Journal of Human Development*, 7(2), July: 183–200.

——2008. *Valuing Children: Rethinking the Economics of the Family*. Cambridge, Mass.: Harvard University Press.

——and YOON, J. 2007. 'What is Child Care? Lessons from Time Use Surveys of Major English-Speaking Countries'. *Review of Economics of the Household*, 5(3), Sept.: 223–48.

——————2008. 'The Value of Unpaid Child Care in the U.S. in 2003', forthcoming in Jean Kimmel (ed.), *How Do We Spend Our Time? Recent Evidence from the American Time-Use Survey*. Kalamazoo, MI: W. E. Upjohn Institute for Employment Research.

FRAZIS, H., and STEWART, J. 2006. 'How Does Household Production Affect Earnings Inequality? Evidence from the American Time Use Survey'. US Bureau of Labor Statistics Working Paper 393.

FREEMAN, R., and SCHETTKAT, R. 2002. 'Marketization of Production and the U.S.–Europe Employment Gap'. National Bureau of Economic Research Working Paper 8797.

GAUTHIER, A. H., SMEEDING, T. M., and FURSTENBERG, F. F. 2004. 'Are Parents Investing Less Time in Children: Trends in Selected Industrialized Countries'. *Population and Development Review*, 30(4), Dec.: 647–67.

GERSHUNY, J. 2005. 'Time Allocation and the Comprehensive Accounting of Economic Activity'. Institute for Social and Economic Research Working Paper no. 2005-8.

GOODIN, R. E., RICE, J. M., PARPO, A., and ERIKSSON, L. 2008. *Discretionary Time: A New Measure of Freedom.* London: Cambridge University Press.

GORNICK, J., HERON, A., and EISENBREY, A. 2007. 'The Work–Family Balance: An Analysis of European, Japanese and U.S. Work-Time Policies'. Briefing Paper no. 189. Washington: Economic Policy Institute.

——— and MEYERS, M. 2003. *Families that Work: Policies for Reconciling Parenthood and Employment.* New York: Russell Sage.

GOTTSCHALK, P., and MAYER, S. 2002. 'Changes in Home Production and Trends in Economic Inequality', in Daniel Cohen, Thomas Piketty, and Gilles Stain-Paul (eds.), *The New Economics of Rising Inequalities.* New York: Oxford University Press, 265–84.

——— and MOFFITT, R. 1994. 'The Growth of Earnings Instability in the US Labour Market'. *Brookings Papers on Economic Activity*, 2: 217–72.

GRAHAM, H. 1987. 'Being Poor: Perceptions and Coping Strategies of Lone Mothers', in Julia Brannen and Gail Wilson (eds.), *Give and Take in Families.* London: Allen and Unwin, 56–74.

GRONAU, R., and HAMERMESH, D. 2006. 'Time vs. Goods: The Value of Measuring Household Production Technologies'. *Review of Income and Wealth*, 52(1): 1–16.

HAGENAARS, A. J. M., DE VOS, K., and ZAIDI, M. A. 1998. 'Patterns of Poverty in Europe', in S. P. Jenkins, A. Kapteyn, and B. van Praag (eds.), *The Distribution of Welfare and Household Production: International Perspectives*, Aldi Hagenaars memorial volume. Cambridge: Cambridge University Press.

HOFFMAN, S. D., and DUNCAN, G. J. 1988. 'What are the Economic Consequences of Divorce?' *Demography*, 25(4), Nov.: 641–45.

HOLLOWAY, S, SHOR, S., and TAMPLIN, S. 2002. Household Satellite Account (Experimental). London: Office of National Statistics.

IRONMONGER, D. 1996. 'Counting Outputs, Capital Inputs and Caring Labor: Estimating Gross Household Product'. *Feminist Economics*, 2(3): 37–64.

JENKINS, S. (1991). 'Poverty Measurement and the Within-Household Distribution: Agenda for Action'. *Journal of Social Policy*, 20(4): 457–83.

JOHNSON, D. S., SMEEDING, T. M., and TORREY, B. B. 2005. 'Economic Inequality through the Prisms of Income and Consumption'. *Monthly Labor Review*, Apr.: 11–24.

JUSTER, T. F., and STAFFORD, F. 1985. 'Process Benefits and the Problem of Joint Production', in T. F. Juster and F. Stafford (eds.), *Time, Goods, and Well-Being.* Ann Arbor: ISR.

KAHNEMAN, D., KRUEGER, A. B., SCHKADE, D. A., SCHWARZ, N., and STONE, A. A. 2004. 'Toward National Well-Being Accounts'. *American Economic Review*, 94(2): 429–34.

LANDEFELD, S., and MCCULLA, S. 2000. 'Accounting for Nonmarket Household Production within a National Accounts Framework'. *Review of Income and Wealth*, 46(3): 289–307.

LUNDBERG, S., and POLLAK, R. A. 1993. 'Separate Spheres Bargaining and the Marriage Market'. *The Journal of Political Economy*, 101(6): 988–1010.

—— and ROSE, E. 2004. 'Investments in Sons and Daughters: Evidence from the Consumer Expenditure Survey', in A. Kalil and T. DeLeire (eds.), *Family Investments in Children: Resources and Behaviors that Promote Success*. Mahwah, NJ: Erlbaum.

MACDONALD, M, PHIPPS, S., and LETHBRIDGE, L. 2005. 'Taking its Toll: The Influence of Paid and Unpaid Work on Women's Wellbeing'. *Feminist Economics*, 11(1): 63–94.

McLANAHAN, S. 2004. 'Diverging Destinies: How Children are Faring under the Second Demographic Transition'. *Demography*, 41(4), Nov.: 607–27.

MATTINGLY, M. J., and BIANCHI, S. M. 2003. 'Gender Differences in the Quantity and Quality of Free Time: The U.S. Experience'. *Social Forces*, 81(3), Mar.: 999–1030.

MERZ, J. 2002. 'Time and Economic Well-Being: A Panel Analysis of Desired versus Actual Working Hours'. *Review of Income and Wealth*, 48(3): 317–46.

OSBERG, L. 2002. 'How Much Does Work Matter for Inequality? Time, Money, and Inequality in International Perspective'. Luxembourg Income Study Working Paper 326, Sept.

—— and SHARPE, A. 2002. 'An Index of Economic Well-Being for Selected OECD Countries'. *Review of Income and Wealth*, 48/3, Sept.: 291–316.

PARENTE, S., ROGERSON, R., and WRIGHT, R. 2000. 'Homework in Development Economics: Household Production and the Wealth of Nations'. *Journal of Political Economy*, 108(4), Aug.: 680–7.

PENDAKUR, K. 1998. 'Changes in Canadian Family Income and Family Consumption Inequality between 1978 and 1992'. *Review of Income and Wealth*, 44(2): 259–82.

PHIPPS, S. A. 1993. 'Measuring Poverty Among Canadian Households: Sensitivity to Choice of Measure and Scale'. *The Journal of Human Resources*, 28/1, winter: 162–84.

—— and BURTON, P. S. 1995. 'Sharing within Families: Implications for the Measurement of Poverty among Individuals in Canada'. *The Canadian Journal of Economics*, 28(1), Feb.: 177–204.

—— —— 1998. 'What's Mine is Yours? The Influence of Male and Female Incomes on Patterns of Household Expenditure'. *Economica*, 65: 599–613.

—— —— 2007. 'Families, Time, and Money in Canada, Germany, Sweden, the United Kingdom and the United States'. *Review of Income and Wealth*, 53(3), Sept.: 460–83.

—— —— and OSBERG, L. 2001. 'Time as a Source of Inequality within Marriage: Are Husbands More Satisfied with Time for Themselves than Wives?' *Feminist Economics*, 7(2), July: 1–21.

RAMEY, V., and FRANCIS, N. 2006. 'A Century of Work and Leisure'. National Bureau of Economic Research Working Paper 12264.

ROSNICK, D., and WEISBROT, M. 2006. 'Are Shorter Work Hours Good for the Environment? A Comparison of U.S. and European Energy Consumption'. Washington: Center for Economic and Policy Research.

RUGGLES, P. 1990. *Drawing the Line: Alternative Poverty Measures and their Implications for Public Policy*. Washington: Urban Institute Press.

SEN, A. 1989. *The Standard of Living*. New York: Cambridge University Press.

SHORT, K., and GARNER, T. I. 1999. 'A Decade of Experimental Poverty Thresholds, 1990 to 2000'. Current Population Reports, Consumer Income. Washington: US Census Bureau, 60–205.

SIMONS, H. 1938. *Personal Income Taxation: The Definition of Income as a Problem of Fiscal Policy.* Chicago: University of Chicago Press.

SLESNICK, D. T. 2001. *Consumption and Social Welfare: Living Standards and their Distribution in the United States.* New York: Cambridge University Press.

VICKERY, C. (1977). 'The Time Poor: A New Look at Poverty'. *Journal of Human Resources*, 12(1): 27–48.

VICKREY, W. 1947. *Agenda for Progressive Taxation.* New York: The Ronald Press Company.

ZAIDI, M. A., and DE VOS, K. 2001. 'Trends in Consumption-Based Poverty and Inequality in the European Union During the 1980s'. *Journal of Population Economics*, 14: 367–90.

# CHAPTER 15

# INEQUALITY AND HAPPINESS

## BERNARD VAN PRAAG
## ADA FERRER-I-CARBONELL

The principal motivating factor in our lives is the pursuit of happiness. In most cultures, when seeking this end, individuals place a high priority on income, and spend much of their waking time procuring this intermediate goal. The connection between income and happiness is by no means trivial, however.

(Rayo and Becker, 2007)

## 1. INTRODUCTION:
## THE CONCEPT OF HAPPINESS

THIS chapter deals with happiness and inequality. Happiness is not a traditional subject of economic science. Although some activity on this subject can be noticed in the 1970s, the term *happiness economics* was only introduced in the 1990s, and it is only in the last few years that there has been a steady and substantial flow of research. It is thus not surprising that up to now not much more than a handful of papers on happiness *and* inequality have been published.

There is no doubt that from the beginning of economics as a science it was realized that, in the words of Rayo and Becker (2007), 'the principal motivating factor in our lives is the pursuit of happiness'. Hence, a realistic approach to the description of human economic behavior should have been cast in terms of a 'happiness function' to be maximized over a constraint set. However, over the twentieth century it has proved difficult to operationalize the maximization concept in terms of a happiness function. The problem was of an empirical nature. How can individual happiness be measured if we are unable to construct a natural 'happiness' meter, by means of which the happiness of specific individuals can be measured and be made comparable on a cardinal scale which is the same for all individuals? Although in more theoretical parts of the body of welfare economics (Robbins, 1932; Sen, 1973), the not unimportant difference between income and well-being was acknowledged, it was taken as an axiom that well-being in theory, or at least in practice, is not measurable, and hence that a next-best solution is to consider income as a proxy for happiness. This has given rise to a large literature on the measurement of inequality using income or any modification of it, such as equivalent income.

Since the beginning of the 1990s, with some earlier work in the 1970s, economists have started rethinking the happiness issue and concluded that empirical instruments exist that can provide insight into the level of well-being of individuals. The main and characteristic instruments of this empirical literature are the subjective well-being questions, the answers to which are used as a proxy for an individual's welfare, happiness, or satisfaction with life,[1] With this proxy measure a new line of research has opened up, which includes the study of inequality. Nowadays the economics of happiness has become a well-established sub-field of economics with a literature that is growing exponentially. General surveys and overviews on the methods and applications are presented by Frey and Stutzer (2000 and 2002), Clark et al. (2007), DiTella and MacCulloch (2006), Kahneman and Krueger (2006), Layard (2005), Senik (2005), and Van Praag and Ferrer-i-Carbonell (2004 and 2007), Dolan et al. (2006). Not only economists, but also psychologists, sociologists, and political scientists, are involved. Being economists ourselves, we shall focus in this chapter on the contributions of economists. Contributions from other disciplines are reviewed in Cummins (2000), Kahneman et al. (2006), and Veenhoven (2005).

The role that subjective measurement can play in the measurement of inequality depends on whether one assumes cardinality or ordinality of measured utility. If ordinality is assumed, self-reported well-being can be used only to estimate the qualitative effect of income and the social distribution of income (or inequality) on

---

[1] We make no distinction between such terms as well-being, happiness, ophelimity, satisfaction, or utility.

individual happiness. If, however, cardinality is assumed, self-reported happiness can be used as an instrument for making welfare judgments in the same way that any other objective indicator of quality of life is used. The use of a proxy measure for well-being has the advantage of capturing all the information that is relevant to the individual instead of only using specific information on income or other variables considered relevant. If a cardinal happiness equation is estimated, it is possible to look not only at happiness inequalities but also at the question of which objective variables (such as income, employment status, age, and health) contribute the most to explaining these inequalities. This chapter describes the various approaches and reviews the still modest literature.

The structure of this chapter is as follows. Section 2 gives an explanation of the neo-classical negative attitude towards happiness as an operational concept, differentiating between ordinal and cardinal happiness. Section 3 introduces the happiness economics literature and the so-called Leyden School, which can be viewed as a forerunner of present-day happiness economics. Section 4 concentrates on the effect of income inequality in a given country on the individual's feelings of happiness. Section 5 will consider current attempts to characterize the inequality of the distribution of happiness and how that may be decomposed. Section 6 concludes.

## 2. THE (NON-)MEASURABILITY OF UTILITY OR HAPPINESS

Before we start with a constructive approach to modern happiness analysis it is worth dwelling in this section on the neo-classical presumption that happiness or utility is non-measurable. This is not only of historical interest—actually many economists are still convinced of this non-measurability—but also because an exposition and understanding of the problem, which haunted a good deal of twentieth-century economics, can pave the way for a new approach. Without refuting the neo-classical dogma of non-measurability of utility, this whole new literature—and therefore this chapter—would make little sense.

Nineteenth-century classical authors (Gossen, 1854; Edgeworth, 1881; and Cohen Stuart, 1889) started from the more or less tacit assumption that utility or ophelimity was something measurable. For instance, there is a famous quote by Samuelson (1945: 206): 'to Edgeworth utility was as real as his morning jam'. It was assumed that utility was derived from commodities and that utility could be translated into a specific degree of happiness or ophelimity for the individual who had that bundle at his disposal. These two concepts (utility and happiness) were considered identical by the classics.

If utility is measurable in a cardinal sense, such that it corresponds to everyday life concepts of welfare (happiness or well-being), one can define a Social Welfare Function (SWF) in which individual utilities of citizens are aggregated, using for example, their (weighted) average. This can be seen as a definition of *national* happiness. One may then look for an income distribution that maximizes SWF, given the capacities and endowments of the nation. This approach may take into account not only the contribution of income to each individual's happiness but also the effect of surrounding inequality on this happiness. Similarly, we may evaluate happiness *inequality* by applying to the happiness (or utility) distribution the usual measures developed for income inequality.

Around 1890, many economists had a rosy view of the socio-political relevance of economics in general and welfare theory in particular. Relevant application of the utility concept was hampered by the fact that, for the moment, there were no reliable estimates of neither the direct nor the indirect utility functions. However, this was thought to be just an empirical problem, to be solved in the near future. This outlook was cruelly disturbed by Pareto (1909) in his *Manuel*, when he demonstrated that one can not identify the utility function from observed demand behavior. The rather dramatic conclusion was then that the promising socio-political applications, hinted at above, cannot be based on demand data. Pareto, however, did not exclude the idea that there might exist other sources of information for identifying a cardinal utility curve.

Despite all this, the utility concept was maintained in the demand literature as a didactic tool. A utility function can be used to describe a system of indifference curves in commodity space. Such a utility function is called an *ordinal* utility function. It is obvious that we cannot assign any interpretation to an ordinal utility function as a happiness indicator, as many ordinal utility functions can describe the same system of indifference curves. What is needed for inequality comparisons is a unique utility concept, which cannot be inferred from observed demand behavior.

Later on prominent economists attempted to remove from the toolbox the whole utility concept (cardinal and ordinal) as unnecessary. This development was called the 'erosion of the utility concept'. Hicks and Allen (1934), Houthakker (1950), Samuelson (1945), and Debreu (1959) were important trend-setters (see Bruni and Sugden, 2007, for a recent discussion). This negative development did not prevent the sprouting of a whole body of literature in mainstream economics, where utility functions are the main tool for analysis, for example in welfare theory, savings, investment, risk and uncertainty, but here the specification of the utility function is based on intuition and on the mathematical attractiveness of the specification, for example the Cobb-Douglas, and the constant (CARA) and relative risk aversion (CRRA) utility functions (see e.g. Arrow, 1964 and Pratt, 1964).

# 3. THE LEYDEN SCHOOL AND MODERN HAPPINESS LITERATURE

Actually, the conclusion of mainstream economists in the 1950s seems a bit rash in retrospect. They did not realize that there might be other sources of information which would make it possible to estimate cardinal-utility happiness functions. The conclusion of non-measurability was justified under the hypothesis that only data derived from observed demand were valid data to base estimates on, discarding a whole body of other data—particularly information which may be gathered by interviewing people about their attitudes, or 'what they would do if'. The latter type of data is somewhat loosely classified as '*stated* preferences' or 'say-behavior' in contrast to '*revealed* preferences' or 'do-behavior'. 'Revealed preferences' were considered as the only source of valid information by mainstream economics until about 1990 (see also Van Praag and Frijters, 1999).

The new, subjective literature starts from the premise that one can derive information on the individual's well-being (or welfare, utility, enjoyment, pleasure, and happiness) from survey questions asking respondents to evaluate the degree of satisfaction with their life or certain aspects of it (e.g. health, job, financial situation, and family life). This was first attempted by Van Praag (1971) who posed a specific survey question to several thousands of respondents with the explicit aim of estimating a (cardinal) utility function of income on the basis of the responses. This so-called Income Evaluation Question (IEQ) is presented in Figure 15.1.

The IEQ asks the respondent to provide six money amounts that correspond, according to him/her, to the six utility levels represented by the verbal evaluations of the different levels of income. Van Praag stipulated an approximate relationship between the income amounts given by the respondent and the six utility levels, which

---

Whether you feel an income is good or not so good depends on your personal life circumstances and expectations.

In your case you would call your net household income:

*A very low income if it equaled $ _____*

*A low income if it equaled $ _____*

*A still insufficient income if it equaled $_____*

*A just sufficient income if it equaled $_____*

*A good income if it equaled $ _____*

*A very good income if it equaled $_____*

**Fig. 15.1. The Income Evaluation Question (IEQ)**

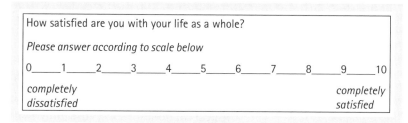

**Fig. 15.2. General Satisfaction Question**

was assumed to follow a lognormal distribution function (Van Praag, 1968). This led to the estimation of a utility function of income or, as it was called, an individual welfare function of income for each individual respondent separately. This was later followed by a host of publications by Van Praag and others, referred to as the Leyden School because of the authors' affiliation with Leyden University (compare Van Praag and Ferrer-i-Carbonell, 2004 and 2007, and Van Praag, 1985, 2007).

In the 1990s a new current of research on happiness economics[2] emerged, started by Clark and Oswald (1994), who considered the answer to a mental distress question module in the General Health Questionnaire as a proxy for happiness and utility. Their method is still at the basis of modern happiness economics. Most current research typically uses so-called satisfaction questions, which basically follow the format given in Figure 15.2.

The answers to such questions are termed self-reported or subjective satisfactions. These questions can be posed in terms of satisfaction with life (also called happiness) or with any life domain (e.g. satisfaction with health, job, or financial situation). This yields domain satisfactions, for health, finance, job satisfaction, etc. (Van Praag and Ferrer-i-Carbonell, 2004 and 2007).

At present, all existing empirical evidence indicates that happiness is measurable (it measures what we want) and commensurable (the happiness levels are interpersonally comparable). A very good account of the accumulated empirical evidence and the complete references can be found in Clark et al. (2008). A few examples are, first, that individuals seem to be fairly good at assessing the reported happiness level of other individuals they see in a picture or on a video (Sandvik et al., 1993; Diener and Lucas, 1999). Second, a relationship is found between reported happiness and physical reactions, such as facial expressions and all sorts of brain activity (Fernández-Dols and Ruiz-Belda, 1995). Third, there is a relationship between reported happiness and actual behavior. For example, individuals have a higher risk of terminating activities, such as marriage, if they have reported a negative relationship between satisfaction and the activity. Also the probability of quitting a job is correlated with reported job satisfaction, and unemployment duration with the intensity with which unemployment affects happiness (Clark

---

[2] Notice that the Leyden School avoided the term 'happiness' . They used the term individual welfare or well-being.

*et al.*, 1998; Clark, 2001 and 2003; Gardner and Oswald, 2006; Kahneman *et al.*, 1993; Frijters, 2000). Fourth, research has shown a positive relationship between good health and reported life satisfaction (see Clark *et al.*, 2008, for an overview).

Before turning to the applications of the subjective measures for the study of inequality, we address a criticism that is often made. Many have argued that using self-reported happiness as an instrument for making welfare judgments (mainly on poverty and inequality) has negative ethical connotations, because individuals tend to adapt to adverse circumstances. This adaptation phenomenon is known in the literature as *hedonic treadmill* (Brickman and Campbell, 1971), *preference drift* (Van Praag, 1971), or set-point theory (Kahneman, 1999). If individuals were able to adapt completely to adverse circumstances, the implication is that an extremely unequal society can go together with perfect equality in terms of subjective happiness. This means that using happiness as a measure might be providing the wrong signal about the true deprivation of individuals. Against this it can be argued, first, that adaptation is a mechanism for coping with adversity. If Nature is applying it to soften the impact of inequalities, it is paternalistic to deny its salutary influence in real life. Second, recent literature suggests that the adaptation phenomenon is less important than past empirical evidence suggested and that adaptation does not occur in all areas of life at the same size and speed (Clark *et al.*, forthcoming; DiTella *et al.*, 2007; Oswald and Powdthavee, 2007; Ferrer-i-Carbonell and Van Praag, 2008). Moreover, the use of subjective questions actually allows us to understand and quantify individuals' adaptation capacity, providing important information for this debate. Such knowledge would also enable the adaptation mechanism to be corrected. In order to make distributive welfare judgments, one needs to enter the realm of normative economics in which individuals are compared with each other on the basis of an index. For this, most traditional studies on inequality have looked at (equivalent) income or commodity bundles. However, this is only seemingly objective, as these are partial measures, which do not fully capture the differences in subjective perceptions of well-being.

Recent experiences with the General Satisfaction Question and similar domain questions open up new and meaningful alleys of economic research. The question is now what is the usefulness of these new tools for shaping socio-economic policy? The answer to this question depends again on the ordinality/cardinality issue. Let $U_1$, $U_2$ ... stand for responses to the satisfaction question (Fig. 15.2), ranging from zero to ten. Moreover, let us assume econometric estimation showing that these responses are determined by for example net income, number of children, health, and the level of public expenditure or, in short, a sequence of variables $X_1, X_2, \ldots, X_m$, some of which can be influenced by the individual, some of which are truly exogenous, and some of which can be affected by the public authorities. Then it becomes possible to explore the trade-off between private income and the level of public expenditure. If a specific type of public expenditure is cut for the purpose of lowering income tax, and the econometric estimation predicted a higher satisfaction level for specific individuals as a result, it implies a policy improvement from the standpoint of those individuals. Hence, ordinal evaluations of policy are possible. Clearly, but this is an evident caveat, we have to take into account that such econometric estimations, although giving strongly significant and plausible results, are invariably surrounded by huge error terms. Only average patterns are disclosed, with the possibility of considerable deviations for individuals.

So far, the satisfaction answers have been attributed only ordinal significance. Pushing the question further, can these welfare measurements per individual yield aggregate welfare indexes, say, of national happiness? Adding up satisfactions over different people does presuppose that satisfactions are cardinal measures. If, for instance, in one group the utilities are (4, 8) and in the other (5.9, 5.9). Average utility is larger in the first group, but at the cost of considerable inequality. In spite of these caveats, the national happiness index is not non-informative. It can be used to evaluate distributions, although in most instances it should be supplemented by a measure of utility inequality, of course a cardinal measure as well (see Easterlin, 1974; Kahneman and Krueger, 2006). If, finally, it is felt that a person with utility 8 is not twice as happy as another person with 4, but that there is some non-linearity, then it can be agreed by social convention that all answers $U$ are replaced by values $f(U)$, which are then used for social arithmetic.

Many happiness economists still adhere to the neo-classical ban on the possibility of utility or satisfaction measurement. Using satisfaction data they try to avoid cardinalism. However, in our opinion it is just a matter of time until the cardinal character of satisfaction (if necessary after a non-linear transformation) is explored to the full with the corresponding use of aggregate indexes. This is not to say that welfare or utility can be wholly characterized by one dimension, nor that there is not a lot of individual variation which will never be caught by sophisticated econometrics. However, as a next-best operational measure it will appear to be a very valuable tool that can no longer be ignored.

Although most economists working on happiness issues do not use subjective well-being measures in making welfare judgments (see for example the empirical work showing the relationship between inequality in a country and individual happiness), we will cover this in the chapter (Section 5).

## 4. HAPPINESS AND INEQUALITY: THE ORDINAL APPROACH

We first discuss happiness and inequality using the ordinal approach, meaning that the distances between the satisfaction categories do not convey information on the intensity of the differences. Under that assumption it can be stated that an individual $A$ with a reported satisfaction level 8 is happier than $B$ with a satisfaction level 4 but *not* that $A$ *is* twice as happy as $B$. With the outcomes of a satisfaction module, first, the percentage of the population below a threshold satisfaction level can be determined. We have to stress that the value of this information, when sticking to the ordinal assumption, is next to nothing. If it is a one point distribution one may conclude there is *no* inequality in happiness. However, if more than one response class is non-empty all one can say is that there is inequality in happiness (or satisfaction). However, as long as no meaning is assigned to *distances* between classes, it is impossible to attribute a level of inequality (low or high) to a distribution or compare different distributions.

Within the ordinal context, responses can also be related to characteristics $x$ of the respondents, allowing statements whether, for example, a higher income does or does not increase the probability of having a higher satisfaction level. This is indeed the mainstay of current modern happiness economics. Similarly, it can be established that individuals (dis)like income inequality or that they are affected by the income of the individuals around them (reference income). This type of analysis is usually done by ordered response models (see Greene, 2000; Ferrer-i-Carbonell and Frijters, 2004; and Maddala, 1983). Using this method actually implies estimating indifference curves. Examples abound: Clark (1997), Clark and Oswald (1994 and 1996), Clark *et al.* (2005), DiTella *et al.* (2001), Easterlin (1995, 2000 and 2001), Ferrer-i-Carbonell (2005), Ferrer-i-Carbonell and Frijters (2004), Ferrer-i-Carbonell and Van Praag (2002), Frey and Stutzer (2000 and 2002), Frijters, Shields and Haisken-DeNew (2004 and 2005), Oswald (1997), Senik (2004 and 2005), Van Praag and Baarsma (2005), and Van Praag and Ferrer-i-Carbonell (2004). Actually, a number of the important findings of *modern* happiness economics, notably with respect to adaptation and referencing, can be found already in the Leyden publications, which were generally unknown to the new 1990s generation of authors.

At this point, it is important to underline the essential difference between how indifference curves are estimated in the subjective literature and how they are derived in neo-classical demand theory. In the neo-classical paradigm indifference curves are estimated by assuming that the observed situation is the result of optimizing behavior. In the subjective literature no optimizing behavior is assumed and the indifference curve is observed *directly*. Indeed, it will be hard to maintain that individuals are continuously in an optimal situation. Clearly, at the moment of making house purchase decisions, job decisions, or even marriage choices, actors may believe *ex ante* that they make the best feasible decision. However, when time elapses they may find the result less than optimal, mostly because of changing circumstances or a change of preferences, but by then the transaction costs of undoing those past decisions will be prohibitive.

Linking individual satisfaction with inequality in society implies investigating if and how (domain) satisfactions are determined not only by individual variables but also by the circumstances of co-citizens. Indeed, it has been found that the individual's satisfaction or happiness is affected not only by the current income of the individual concerned, but also by the average income in his or her reference group and, more generally, by the income distribution of the society he or she lives in. The basic finding in the literature is that own income contributes positively to own happiness, while the opposite is true for the income of the reference group. In other words, the higher the reference income, the less satisfaction is derived from own income. The earlier evidence was found by the Leyden School based on the IEQ (Kapteyn *et al.*, 1978, and Hagenaars, 1986). In this tradition, a very interesting application was made by Kapteyn and Van Herwaarden (1980), who investigated how an income tax system is affected by reference effects. Despite the reference-income findings, empirical evidence suggests that individuals prefer to live in more equally distributed societies. One of the first investigations was provided by Morawetz *et al.* (1977), who compared two Israeli villages, one with about equal incomes (Isos) and one with a less egalitarian income distribution (Anisos). On the basis of self-reported happiness, they found that the 'Isos' were happier than the 'Anisos'.

Clearly, the problem is how to define the concept of an individual's reference group. Theoretically, the composition of the reference group and even the weighting of the individual members should vary over individuals. However, this is (as yet) empirically impossible. In practice, this problem of operationalizing the reference income has been solved using one of two main approaches:

(a) taking the average income of all individuals belonging to the same group as the individual, with respect to, for example, age, region, gender, or education (e.g. Stutzer, 2004). Luttmer (2005) proxied the reference group by administrative region (PUMAs). Ferrer-i-Carbonell (2005) defined it as those individuals in the same region and with the same age and level of education. In a European study Hagenaars (1986) considered the national populations as the reference groups. Van de Stadt *et al.* (1985) provide another example of this approach;

(b) using the individual's estimated income obtained from a wage or income regression (e.g. Senik, 2004). Clark and Oswald (1996) approximate reference income by the income predicted for the individual on the basis of an independently estimated earnings equation. The problem with this approach is that the reference income and own income tend to be strongly correlated.

Surprisingly, Senik (2004) finds with respect to a Russian population survey that the reference effect is positive. Following Hirschman (1973), Senik calls this a 'tunnel effect', reflecting positive expectations for the future. See also Dynan and Ravina (forthcoming).

Actually, the reference income does not wholly capture the income distribution of the reference group. Therefore, a further step is to include, in addition to the average income, a measure of the income inequality within the reference group. This was first done in an internationally comparative study by Van Praag *et al.* (1982) where the log-variance of the national income distribution was used as explanatory variable for financial satisfaction, as measured by the IEQ. The famous modern study that first employed the same idea to study happiness is by Alesina *et al.* (2004), who considered an amalgam of national surveys from various European countries and the USA. They included Gini inequality indices for the European countries and the separate states of the USA as additional variables and found that happiness is indeed negatively linked to rising inequality in the reference group. Moreover, they found that Europeans are more inequality-averse than Americans. They also found that individuals have a lower tendency to report themselves happy when inequality is high, even after controlling for individual income, a large set of personal characteristics, and year and country (or, in the case of the USA, state) dummies. The effect, however, is more precisely defined statistically in Europe than in the USA.

Thus, despite the fact that individuals dislike having peers who earn more, they also dislike seeing much income inequality around them. We see two possible explanations for this: (1) although individuals get unhappier from being poorer than their peers, they do not get happier from being richer (Ferrer-i-Carbonell, 2005), or (2) income inequality is correlated with variables that are not included in the model such as insecurity and conflict.

A similar study was done by Graham and Felton (2005) for 17 Latin American countries, a category with a strong cross-country variation in income inequality. The results are somewhat different from those of Alesina *et al.* (2004). This may be caused by the use of an 11-point wealth index as a proxy for the individual income variable assuming implicitly that there is a strong correlation between wealth and income, for which no data were available. Respondents in medium-level Gini countries are found to be happier than those in either low or high Gini countries, with the least happy respondents being found in the high Gini countries. The study is also interesting because it introduced education inequality as a second possible explanatory factor for happiness using the Theil (1967) index of inequality applied to education, taking education as a proxy for income and opportunity. Obviously education and income are correlated, but not completely so. The education scale allows for more variance, and the respondents in the upper ranks (completed university or higher technical degrees) are by far the highest income earners in the region. Graham and Felton found, unexpectedly, that respondents in countries with greater education inequality are happier (controlling, of course, for the usual socio-demographic traits). This finding holds with and without cluster controls, and whether or not they control for individual wealth in the regressions.

It is obvious that theoretically the reference group concept may be generalized from income to other variables such as education, health, and age. It may also be extended by not only considering satisfaction with life as a whole (happiness), but also focusing on specific domains of life, such as health satisfaction or job satisfaction.

## 5. HAPPINESS AND INEQUALITY: THE CARDINAL APPROACH

The results of Section 4 can all be obtained while only assuming ordinality. That is, indifference curves are observable, but one cannot assess the (absolute) magnitude of utility differences between them. As a consequence the ordinal approach does not permit further analysis, the main problem being that it does not permit calculating an 'average' happiness or any measure of 'dispersion' of happiness.

It is no surprise, then, that non-economists and even an increasing number of economists more or less reluctantly and more or less explicitly assume a cardinal approach. One of the earliest contributors in that vein was the pioneering contribution by Easterlin (1974). He calculated average happiness for a great number of countries and linked it to income per capita. He found that within a country income and happiness are positively correlated, while between countries all populations are about equally happy, irrespective of the absolute level of per capita income. This has become known as the Easterlin paradox. In later research this finding appeared to be not as general as was first thought (see Deaton, 2007; Veenhoven and Hagerty, 2005; Kahneman and Krueger, 2006).

The first possible exercise when assuming cardinality concerns the happiness distribution in different countries. Veenhoven (1995) set up a large international database on happiness, now covering more than 90 countries all over the world. Despite the fact that the survey questionnaires, originating from different sources, differ on some points, and that the quality and the underlying definitions of some variables also vary over countries, it is still the best data collection for internationally comparative happiness research. A special issue of *The Journal of Happiness Studies* (2005) was devoted to the inequality of happiness. Veenhoven and Kalmijn (2005; Kalmijn and Veenhoven, 2005) and Ott (2005) were among the first to consider the inequality in happiness proper. The former consider a list of inequality indices based on the zero to ten scale and conclude that standard deviations are to be preferred. Computing the standard deviation of happiness outcomes for 75 countries they conclude that there is no strong link between average happiness and inequality in happiness.

Another type of analysis was initiated by Van Praag (1977), who considered welfare inequality in the framework of the Leyden approach. He assumed, following Atkinson (1970), that inequality must be assessed in terms of a deviation from an optimal distribution, which was identified as the result of maximizing a Benthamite social welfare function. It follows that ideally *marginal* utilities $u_n$ should be equalized. This idea was applied and extended in Van Praag and Ferrer-i-Carbonell (2004) on the basis of the 'domain model' (see also Van Praag *et al.*, 2003).

The point of departure is that the evaluation of happiness or satisfaction on a bounded interval is described by a function of some happiness determinants. The cardinal happiness equation can be interpreted again as describing indifference curves. In fact, a comparison of the ordered response models with cardinal models shows that they give rise to similar trade-offs between coefficients (see Van Praag and Ferrer-i-Carbonell, 2004 and Ferrer-i-Carbonell and Frijters, 2004).

Along the same lines as Veenhoven one may consider the inequality of the satisfaction judgments, for instance, by calculating either the variance of the responses $U$ over the population, or if a non-linear transformation[3] is preferred, the variance of, for example, $\ln(U)$. Such indexes obtain operational and political significance when measured regularly so that they can be compared over time, or for various populations. It enables getting an idea of what is a large variance and what a small one. Moreover, it is stressed that all parties involved should agree as a matter of convention on which non-linear transform they use, if that is applied. We noticed before that econometrically one may estimate meaningful relationships between satisfaction $U$ and various objective observable variables $X_1, X_2, \ldots, X_m$, which are partly influenced by the individual, partly exogenous, and partly affected by the public authorities. Hence, if the relation $U = U(X_1, X_2, \ldots, X_m)$ is known, $U$ can be considered as an intermediate variable which can be eliminated. Then the variance is not characterized as a parameter of the distribution of $U$, but as a parameter of the multivariate distribution of the $X_1, X_2, \ldots, X_m$. However, in practice it is much easier to consider only the variance of one variable $U$. From this it is obvious that many distributions of $X$ are characterized by the same variance $var(U)$. We notice explicitly that instead of taking the variance of the distribution another index can be chosen (e.g. the Gini).

In addition, it is possible to decompose this inequality index $var(U)$. Consider a simple case, assuming that $U$ stands for financial satisfaction and that the empirical relationship $f(U) = \beta_1 \ln(y) + \beta_2 \ln(fs) + \beta_0 + \varepsilon$ is found where $f(.)$ stands for a suitable transform, $y$ for individual income, $fs$ for family size, and $\varepsilon$ for an error term. It includes $fs$ because it is established that families with more children are less satisfied with a specific income $y$ than families with fewer children. If $\beta_1 = 1$, $\beta_2 = 0$, $var(f(U))$ is just the variance of log-incomes. Now the variance can be

---

[3] In the following it is always understood that $U$ can either stand for the responses on the satisfaction question or for an agreed-upon non-linear transform of $U$.

decomposed as

$$\text{var}(u) = \beta_1^2 \text{var}(\ln(y)) + \beta_2^2 \text{var}(\ln(fs)) + 2\beta_1\beta_2 \text{cov}(\ln(y), \ln(fs)) + \sigma^2(\varepsilon)$$

This equation shows that the financial satisfaction inequality depends on the inequality in nominal income and in family size, the covariance between $\ln(y_n)$ and $\ln(fs)$, and the variance in a random component. This decomposition interprets the variance as caused by two factors *plus* a correction term, because the two factors are correlated. A similar formula holds for an arbitrary vector $x$ of explanatory variables (for a detailed exposition see Van Praag and Ferrer-i-Carbonell, 2004, chapter 14).

It is obvious that this approach can be reworked to define satisfaction inequality for other life domains yielding health satisfaction inequality, job satisfaction inequality, etc. It can even be applied to life domains where income does not play a role or to less-developed economies and even barter economies. In addition, the inequality definition is not derived from or restricted by any axiomatic preconditions. For instance, in the discussion of how to define income inequality it is frequently posited that an income transfer from a rich person to a poor person must reduce the inequality—the so-called Dalton condition (Dalton, 1920). Such a condition makes sense only if income and hence satisfaction is transferable from one person to another. It is obvious, however, that such transferability does not make sense for job satisfaction, health satisfaction, marriage satisfaction, or the all-inclusive concept of individual happiness.

Denoting the various life domains as $DS_1$, $DS_2$, ..., $DS_k$ and their combined vector as $DS = (DS_1, DS_2, ..., DS_k)$, this approach can be generalized to a multi-dimensional concept (Van Praag and Ferrer-i-Carbonell, 2004, table 14.4).

Finally, let us look at satisfaction with life as whole, denoted as General Satisfaction ($GS$). Van Praag and Ferrer-i-Carbonell (2004 and 2007) and Van Praag et al. (2003) explained $GS$ as an aggregate of the various (in this example eight) domain satisfactions, estimating

$$GS_n = a_{0,1}DS_{1,n} + \ldots + a_{0,8}DS_{8,n} + \gamma Z_n + C + \varepsilon_{0,n}$$

Again we refer to Van Praag and Ferrer-i-Carbonell (2004) for details. Using this $GS$ equation allows a breakdown of general satisfaction inequality. Such a breakdown is not unique as the $DS$ terms in the above equation are correlated. Hence, a specific ordering of the domains has to be chosen. The breakdown of General Satisfaction (Happiness) that was found for the UK is shown in Table 15.1.

This breakdown suggests that in the case of the British happiness inequality may be mainly assigned to three domains, namely job, marriage, and social life. The contribution of financial satisfaction is meager. However, we notice that this breakdown is not unique. The choice of another order of domains may lead to another breakdown.

Table 15.1. Decomposition of general satisfaction inequality (married individuals with job)

|                             | Variance | % Contribution |
|-----------------------------|----------|----------------|
| Job satisfaction            | 0.088    | 41.6           |
| Marriage satisfaction       | 0.040    | 19.2           |
| Social life satisfaction    | 0.049    | 23.1           |
| Financial satisfaction      | 0.012    | 5.6            |
| Health satisfaction         | 0.012    | 5.6            |
| Leisure amount satisfaction | 0.003    | 1.2            |
| Housing satisfaction        | 0.002    | 1.0            |
| Leisure use satisfaction    | 0.005    | 2.6            |
| z                           | 0.000    | 0.1            |
| Total                       | 0.211    |                |

*Note*: Data set used British Household Panel Survey, 1992–1997.
*Source*: Van Praag and Ferrer-i-Carbonell (2004, table 14.8).

# 6. CONCLUSIONS AND FURTHER RESEARCH

This chapter attempts to describe the present-day happiness approaches to inequality. The first point made is that the traditional aloofness of economists towards the concept 'happiness' or subjective satisfaction is no longer warranted. The happiness concept can be operationalized and observed. The subjective well-being literature provides a new opportunity for broadening the study of inequality while remaining within the welfare-utility framework. This approach is based on individual self-reported happiness.

If one accepts the idea that the subjective translation of inequality into feelings matters in the evaluation of the distribution of well-being in society, happiness concepts, as described above, are the primary candidates to be used as tools for this analysis. We show that in happiness economics there are two roads. The first maintains that happiness is only an ordinal concept. Then one may look at the effect of inequality (of income or any other variable such as education) on the feeling of happiness, but as usual in the ordinal approach, we can only get an indication of the sign of the effect. The second approach attributes a cardinal significance to responses to the happiness questions. Then, and only then, can one assess inequalities in happiness and also deal with happiness with life as a whole in a similar fashion as income inequality, and decompose happiness inequality into contributing factors. The cardinality assumption gives significance to the concept of happiness inequality and also makes it possible to distinguish why inequalities in happiness arise. Is it income inequalities that lead to happiness inequality? Is it any other individual situation related to economic circumstances, such as having a job? Or is it mainly dominated by non-economic explanations, such as being in good health or having a partner.

Finally, we notice that by extending the inequality concept to non-monetary factors, the road is open to defining inequalities for societies, such as less-developed countries or countries plagued by high inflation, where many commodities and amenities of life depend less on the availability of money than on physical and mental capacities, the availability of a social network, the availability of a garden and water, the existence of a well-developed barter economy, and so on and so forth.

Our main conclusion is that, although the happiness literature is still in its early years, it is entirely possible to add a happiness or satisfaction dimension to inequality studies. Actually, as in the end the individual and society act on reality as it is perceived, that is, not in terms of material dimensions but in terms of happiness and satisfaction, it seems that happiness analysis will become an essential ingredient in measuring and explaining inequalities and iniquities and the impact they may have on human beings.

## References

ALESINA, A., DITELLA, R., and MACCULLOCH, R. 2004. 'Inequality and Happiness: Are Europeans and Americans Different? *Journal of Public Economics*, 88: 2009–42.

ARROW, K. J. 1964. 'The Role of Securities in the Optimal Allocation of Risk-Bearing'. *Quarterly Journal of Economics*, 31: 91–6.

ATKINSON, A. B. 1970. 'On the Measurement of Inequality'. *Journal of Economic Theory*, 2: 244–63.

BRICKMAN, P., and CAMPBELL, D. T. 1971. 'Hedonic Relativism and Planning the Good Society', in M. H. Apley (ed.), *Adaptation-Level theory: A Symposium*. New York: Academic Press, 287–302.

BRUNI, L., and SUGDEN, R. 2007. 'The Road Not Taken: How Psychology was Removed from Economics, and How it might be Brought Back'. *Economic Journal*, 117: 146–73.

CLARK, A. E. 1997. 'Job Satisfaction and Gender: Why are Women So Happy at Work?' *Labour Economics*, 4: 341–72.

—— 2001. 'What Really Matters in a Job? Hedonic Measurement Using Quit Data'. *Labour Economics*, 8: 223–42.

—— 2003. 'Unemployment as a Social Norm: Psychological Evidence from Panel Data'. *Journal of Labor Economics*, 21: 323–51.

—— DIENER, E., GEORGELLIS, Y., and LUCAS, R. Forthcoming. 'Lags and Leads in Life Satisfaction: A Test of the Baseline Hypothesis'. *Economic Journal*.

—— ETILÉ, F., POSTEL-VINAY, F., SENIK, C., and VAN DER STRAETEN, K. 2005. 'Heterogeneity in Reported Well-Being: Evidence from Twelve European Countries'. *Economic Journal*, 115: C118–C132.

CLARK, A. E., FRIJTERS, P., and SHIELDS, M. A. 2008. 'Relative Income, Happiness and Utility: An Explanation for the Easterlin Paradox and Other Puzzles Relative Income, Happiness and Utility: An Explanation for the Easterlin Paradox and Other Puzzles'. *Journal of Economic Literature*, 46(1): 95–144.

——GEORGELLIS, Y., and SANFEY, P. 1998. 'Job Satisfaction, Wage Changes and Quits: Evidence from Germany'. *Research in Labor Economics*, 17: 95–121.

——and OSWALD, A. J. 1994. 'Unhappiness and Unemployment'. *Economic Journal*, 104: 648–59.

————1996. 'Satisfaction and Comparison Income'. *Journal of Public Economics*, 61: 359–81.

COHEN STUART, A. J., 1889. 'Bijdrage tot de theorie der progressieve belasting'. Den Haag: Martinus Nijhoff. ('Contribution to the Theory of Progressive Taxation', partially translated and reproduced in R. A. Musgrave and A. T. Peacock. 1958. *Classics in the Theory of Public Finance*. London: Macmillan.)

CUMMINS, R. A. 2000. 'Objective and Subjective Quality of Life: An Interactive Model'. *Social Indicators Research*, 52: 55–72.

DALTON, E. J. 1920. 'Measurement of the Inequalities of Income'. *Economic Journal*, 30: 348–61.

DEATON A. 2007. 'Income, Aging, Health and Wellbeing around the World: Evidence from the Gallup World Poll'. NBER Working Paper no. 13317.

DEBREU, G. 1959. *The Theory of Value: An Axiomatic Analysis of Economic Equilibrium*. New York: John Wiley & Sons.

DI TELLA, R., and MACCULLOCH, R. J. 2006. 'Some Uses of Happiness Data in Economics'. *Journal of Economic Perspectives*, 20: 25–46.

————and OSWALD, A. J. 2001. 'Preferences over Inflation and Unemployment: Evidence from Surveys of Subjective Well-Being'. *American Economic Review*, 91: 335–41.

————and HAISKEN-DE NEW, J. 2007. 'Happiness Adaptation to Income and to Status in an Individual Panel'. Working Paper.

DIENER, E., and LUCAS, R. E. 1999. 'Personality and Subjective Well-Being', in D. Kahneman, E. Diener, and N. Schwarz (eds.), *Well-Being: The Foundations of Hedonic Psychology*. New York: Russell Sage Foundation, chapter 11.

DOLAN, P., PEASGOOD, T., and WHITE, M. P. 2006. 'Review of Research on the Influences on Personal Well-Being and Application to Policy Making'. Project Report for Department of Environment Food and Rural Affairs (DEFRA) and to Government's Sustainable Development Unit, UK.

DYNAN, K. E., and RAVINA, E. Forthcoming. 'Increasing Income Inequality, External Habits, and Self-Reported Happiness'. *American Economic Review*.

EASTERLIN, R. A. 1974. 'Does Economic Growth Improve the Human Lot? Some Empirical Evidence', in P. A. David and M. W. Reder (eds.), *Nations and Households in Economic Growth: Essays in Honor of Moses Abramowitz*. New York: Academic Press, 89–125. (Also reprinted in R. A. Easterlin (ed.) 2002. *Happiness in Economics*. Cheltenham: Edward Elgar.)

——1995. 'Will Raising the Incomes of All Increase the Happiness of All?' *Journal of Economic Behavior and Organization*, 27: 35–47.

——2000. 'The Worldwide Standard of Living since 1800'. *The Journal of Economic Perspectives*, 14: 7–26.

—— 2001. 'Income and Happiness: Towards a Unified Theory'. *The Economic Journal*, 111: 465–84.

EDGEWORTH, F. Y. 1881. *Mathematical Psychics: An Essay on the Application of Mathematics to the Moral Sciences*. London: Kegan Paul.

FERNÁNDEZ-DOLS, J. M., and RUIZ-BELDA, M. A. 1995. 'Are Smiles a Sign of Happiness? Gold Medal Winners at the Olympic Games'. *Journal of Personality and Social Psychology*, 69: 1113–19.

FERRER-I-CARBONELL, A. 2005. 'Income and Well-being: An Empirical Analysis of the Comparison Income Effect'. *Journal of Public Economics*, 89: 997–1019.

—— and FRIJTERS, P. 2004. 'How Important is Methodology for the Estimates of the Determinants of Happiness?' *Economic Journal*, 114: 641–59.

—— and VAN PRAAG, B. M. S. 2002. 'The Subjective Costs of Health Losses due to Chronic Diseases. An Alternative Model for Monetary Appraisal'. *Health Economics*, 110: 709–22.

—— —— 2008. 'Do People Adapt? The Effect of Income Changes and other Life Events on Subjective Satisfaction'. Working Paper.

FREY, B. S., and STUTZER, A. 2000. 'Happiness, Economy and Institutions'. *The Economic Journal*, 110: 918–38.

—— —— 2002. 'What can Economists Learn from Happiness Research?' *Journal of Economic Literature*, 40: 402–35.

FRIJTERS, P. 2000. 'Do Individuals Try to Maximize General Satisfaction?' *Journal of Economic Psychology*, 21: 281–304.

—— SHIELDS, M. A., and HAISKEN-DENEW, J. P. 2004. 'Money Does Matter! Evidence from Increasing Real Incomes in East Germany following Reunification'. *American Economic Review*, 94: 730–41.

—— —— —— 2005. 'The Effect of Income on Health: Evidence from a Large Scale Natural Experiment'. *Journal of Health Economics*, 24: 997–1017.

GARDNER, J., and OSWALD, A. J. 2006. 'Do Divorcing Couples Become Happier by Breaking Up?' *Journal of the Royal Statistical Society*, 169: 319–36.

GOSSEN, H. H. 1854. *The Development of the Laws of Exchange among Men and of the Consequent Rules of Human Action*. Cambridge, Mass.: MIT Press, 1983.

GRAHAM, C., and FELTON, A. 2005. 'Does Inequality Matter to Individual Welfare? An Initial Exploration based on Happiness Surveys from Latin America'. CSED Working Paper no. 38. Washington: The Brookings Institution.

GREENE, W. H. 2000. *Econometric Analysis*, 4th edn. New Jersey: Prentice Hall Inc.

HAGENAARS, A. J. M. 1986. *The Perception of Poverty*. Amsterdam: North-Holland.

HICKS, J. R., and ALLEN, R. G. D. 1934. 'A Reconsideration of the Theory of Value'. *Economica*, 1: 52–76.

HIRSCHMAN A. O. 1973. 'Changing Tolerance for Income Inequality in the Course of Economic Development'. *Quarterly Journal of Economics*, 87: 544–66.

HOUTHAKKER, H. S. 1950. 'Revealed Preference and the Utility Function'. *Economica*, 17: 159–74.

KAHNEMAN, D. 1999. 'Objective happiness'. in D. Kahneman, E. Diener, and N. Schwarz (eds.), *Well Being: The Foundations of Hedonic Psychology*. New York: Russell Sage, 3–25.

—— FREDRICKSON, B. L., SCHREIBER, C. A., and REDELMEIER, D. A. 1993. 'When More Pain is Preferred to Less: Adding a Better End'. *Psychological Science*, 4: 401–5.

—— and KRUEGER, A. B. 2006. 'Developments in the Measurement of Subjective Well-Being'. *Journal of Economic Perspectives*, 20: 3–24.

KAHNEMAN, D., KRUEGER, A. B., SCHKADE, D., SCHWARZ, N., and STONE, A. A. 2006. 'Would You Be Happier If You Were Richer? A Focusing Illusion'. *Science*, 312: 1908–10.

KALMIJN, W. M., and VEENHOVEN, R. 2005. 'Measuring Inequality of Happiness in Nations: In Search for Proper Statistics'. *Journal of Happiness Studies*, 6: 357–96.

KAPTEYN, A., and VAN HERWAARDEN, F. G. 1980. 'Independent Welfare Functions and Optimal Income Distribution'. *Journal of Public Economics*, 14: 375–97.

—— VAN PRAAG, B. M. S., and VAN HERWAARDEN, F. G. 1978. 'Individual Welfare Functions and Social Preference Spaces'. *Economics Letters*, 1: 173–7.

LAYARD, R. 2005. *Happiness: Lessons from a New Science*. London: Allen Lane.

LUTTMER, E. F. P. 2005. 'Neighbors as Negatives: Relative Earnings and Well-Being'. *Quarterly Journal of Economics*, 120: 963–1002.

MADDALA, G. S. 1983. *Limited Dependent and Qualitative Variables in Econometrics*. Cambridge: Cambridge University Press.

MORAWETZ, D., ATIA, E., BIN-NUN, G., FELOUS, L., GARIPLERDEN, Y., HARRIS, E., SOUSTIEL, S., TOMBROS, G., and ZARFATY, Y. 1977. 'Income Distribution and Self-Rated Happiness: Some Empirical Evidence'. *The Economic Journal*, 87: 511–22.

OSWALD, A. J. 1997. 'Happiness and Economic Performance'. *Economic Journal*, 107: 1815–31.

—— and POWDTHAVEE, N. 2007. 'Does Happiness Adapt? A Longitudinal Study of Disability'. Working Paper.

OTT, J. 2005. 'Level and Inequality of Happiness in Nations: Does Greater Happiness of a Greater Number Imply Greater Inequality in Happiness?' *Journal of Happiness Studies*, 6: 397–420.

PARETO, V. 1909. *Manuel d'économie politique*. Paris: Giard & Briere.

PRATT, J. W. 1964. 'Risk Aversion in the Small and in the Large'. *Econometrica*, 32: 122–36.

RAYO, L., and BECKER, G. S. 2007. 'Habits, Peers, and Happiness: An Evolutionary Perspective'. *American Economic Review Papers and Proceedings*, 97: 487–91.

ROBBINS, L. 1932. *An Essay on the Nature and Significance of Economic Science*. London: Macmillan.

SAMUELSON, P. 1945. *Foundations of Economic Analysis*. Cambridge, Mass.: Harvard University Press.

SANDVIK, E., DIENER, E., and SEIDLITZ, L. 1993. 'Subjective Well-Being: The Convergence and Stability of Self and Non Self Report Measures'. *Journal of Personality*, 61: 317–42.

SEN, A. K. 1973. *On Economic Inequality*. Reprinted 1997. Oxford: Clarendon Press.

SENIK, C., 2004. 'When Information Dominates Comparison. Learning from Russian Subjective Panel Data'. *Journal of Public Economics*, 88: 2099–123.

—— 2005. 'What Can We Learn from Subjective Data? The Case of Income and Well-Being'. *Journal of Economic Surveys*, 19: 43–63.

STUTZER, A. 2004. 'The Role of Income Aspirations in Individual Happiness'. *Journal of Economic Behavior and Organization*, 54: 89–109.

THEIL, H. 1967. *Economics and Information Theory*. Amsterdam: North-Holland.

VAN DE STADT, H., KAPTEYN, A., and VAN DE GEER, S. 1985. 'The Relativity of Utility: Evidence from Panel Data'. *Review of Economics and Statistics*, 67: 179–87.

VAN PRAAG, B. M. S. 1968. *Individual Welfare Functions and Consumer Behavior: A Theory of Rational Irrationality*. Ph.D. Thesis. Amsterdam: North-Holland.

—— 1971. 'The Welfare Function of Income in Belgium: An Empirical Investigation'. *European Economic Review*, 2: 337–69.

—— 1977. 'The Perception of Welfare Inequality'. *European Economic Review*, 10: 189–207.

——— 1985. 'Linking Economics with Psychology: An Economist's View'. *Journal of Economic Psychology*, 6: 289–311.

——— 2007. 'Perspectives from the Happiness Literature and the Role of New Instruments for Policy Analysis'. CESifo Economic Studies, 53: 42–68.

——— and BAARSMA, B. E. 2005. 'Using Happiness Surveys to Value Intangibles: The Case of Airport Noise'. *Economic Journal*, 115: 224–46.

——— and FERRER-I-CARBONELL, A. 2004. *Happiness Quantified: A Satisfaction Calculus Approach*. Revised paperback edn. 2007. Oxford: Oxford University Press.

——— and FRIJTERS, P. 1999. 'Choice Behaviour and Verbal Behaviour: A Critical Assessment of their Relevance for Practical Policy', in M. M. G. Fase, W. Kanning, and D. A. Walker (eds.), *Economics, Welfare Policy and the History of Economic Thought: Essays in Honour of Arnold Heertje*. Cheltenham: Edward Elgar, 290–309.

——— ——— and FERRER-I-CARBONELL, A. 2003. 'The Anatomy of Well-Being'. *Journal of Economic Behavior and Organization*, 51: 29–49.

——— HAGENAARS, A., and VAN WEEREN, J. 1982. 'Poverty in Europe'. *Review of Income and Wealth*, 28: 345–59.

VEENHOVEN, R. 1995. 'World Database of Happiness'. *Social Indicators Research*, 34: 299–313.

——— 2005. 'Return of Inequality in Modern Society?' *Journal of Happiness Studies*, 6: 457–87.

——— and HAGERTY, M. 2006. 'Rising Happiness in Nations 1946–2004: A Reply to Easterlin'. *Social Indicators Research*, 79: 421–36.

——— and KALMIJN, W. 2005. 'Inequality-Adjusted Happiness in Nations: Egalitarianism and Utilitarianism Married in a New Index of Societal Performance'. *Journal of Happiness Studies*, 6: 421–55.

# CHAPTER 16

# HEALTH AND ECONOMIC INEQUALITY*

ANDREW LEIGH

CHRISTOPHER JENCKS

TIMOTHY M. SMEEDING

## 1. INTRODUCTION

MORE than 100 articles have been published over the past two decades on whether changes in economic inequality lead to changes in health (Lynch *et al.*, 2004a).[1] A somewhat smaller literature has looked at whether changes in health affect economic inequality. An even smaller literature looks at whether economic inequality predicts the size of health disparities between educational or economic groups.

This chapter first reviews the most common hypotheses about how inequality might affect health and vice versa. Hypotheses about how income inequality might affect health fall into three broad classes: those that focus on the implications of diminishing marginal health benefits from increases in individual income, those that focus on relative deprivation, and those that focus on society-wide effects of

* We are grateful to Eugene Smolensky, seminar participants at the Handbook conference in Seville, and the editors for feedback on an earlier draft. Susanne Schmidt and Elena Varganova provided outstanding research assistance.

[1] For a recent review from a more sociological perspective see Neckerman and Torche (2007).

income inequality. Theories about how health might affect inequality also focus on three potential mechanisms: labor market effects, educational effects, and marriage market effects.

The chapter then turns to assessing empirical evidence for a link between health and inequality. Although most of this literature is motivated by the hypothesis that inequality affects health, it often employs the same empirical techniques that one would use to detect a causal impact of health on inequality. We therefore regard many of these studies as effectively testing only the hypothesis that the two measures are causally linked in some way, without investigating the direction of the causal arrow.[2] Since both hypotheses predict a negative relationship between inequality and health, studies that find no relationship between inequality and health can be regarded as evidence against both hypotheses (at least insofar as these hypotheses assume relatively immediate effects). If studies find a significant negative relationship between inequality and health, however, it is usually necessary to probe further to determine the direction of causation.

Because income inequality and health are likely to have common causes that cannot all be measured, the cross-sectional relationship between inequality and health is quite likely to provide a biased estimate of how changes in income inequality affect health. Until relatively recently, data limitations (particularly on economic inequality) led many researchers to analyze the relationship at a single point in time. With better data, however, the empirical literature has now largely moved beyond cross-sectional and time series studies to use panel data techniques. Such panel studies are now available for US states, European regions, and rich countries.

Most of these studies use mortality or expected longevity to measure population health, but some use self-reported health.[3] While self-reports of poor health are a fairly strong predictor of subsequent mortality, poor health and death are not identical and may not have the same relationship to income inequality. Self-reported health does, however, predict other outcomes that individuals care about, such as their happiness (see Chapter 17). The individual-level outcomes of death are, in contrast, completely speculative.

We should also emphasize at the outset that assessing the effects of economic inequality is not the same as assessing the effects of poverty. Furthermore, even if economic inequality does not affect health, poverty may well do so (and in extreme cases clearly does so). There is a strong negative relationship between health and absolute poverty[4] and this may also hold for relative poverty (Eibner and Evans,

---

[2]  Smith (2004) tries to unravel these simultaneous effects.

[3]  As more surveys begin to collect data on both biomarkers and socioeconomic measures from the same respondents, studies using these biomarkers as proxies for health are also likely to become more common.

[4]  Some of the best known of these include writings of Alan Williams, Alan Maynard, A. Donabedian, A. J. Culyer, and Julian Le Grand. See the references in van Doorslaer *et al.* (1993), Wolfe (1994), the *Future of Children* (1998, vol. 8, no. 2, on Children and Managed Health Care) and *Health Affairs* (2004, vol. 23. no. 5, on Child Health: A Progress Report), Smith (1999), Adler and Newman (2002), Mullahy *et al.* (2004), Institute of Medicine (2004) and Phipps *et al.* (2006). See also

2005). There is evidence that poverty and poor health limit intergenerational mobility (Case and Paxson, 2006). But high levels of absolute poverty are often found in poor countries where incomes are relatively equal. Even in rich countries high levels of inequality are not invariably linked to high levels of poverty, although the two measures are in most cases strongly correlated.

To preview our conclusions, we argue that although there are plausible reasons for anticipating a relationship between inequality and health (in either direction), the empirical evidence for such a relationship in rich countries is weak. A few high-quality studies find that inequality is negatively correlated with population health, but the preponderance of evidence suggests that the relationship between income inequality and health is either non-existent or too fragile to show up in a robustly estimated panel specification. The best cross-national studies now uniformly fail to find a statistically reliable relationship between economic inequality and longevity. Comparisons of American states yield more equivocal evidence.

## 2. HYPOTHESES ABOUT INEQUALITY AND HEALTH

### The Effect of Inequality on Health

Epidemiologists and social scientists have proposed numerous mechanisms by which income inequality might affect an individual's health.[5] We group these mechanisms under three broad headings: absolute income, relative income, and society-wide effects of income inequality.

*The absolute income hypothesis*

If health depends on individual income, standard economic models predict that the health gains from an extra unit of income will diminish as an individual's income rises. Figure 16.1 shows a stylized version of such a relationship. A mean-preserving transfer from the richer individual (R) to the poorer individual (P) raises the health of P by more than it lowers the health of R. Holding total income constant, therefore, a more equal distribution of income should improve population health.

the review of evidence on poverty and poor health in Gould *et al.* (2005). The majority of these studies are based on correlations with some controls for exogenous influences. Few try to identify the causal effects of health on poverty, but that is typical of the vast literature.

[5] This section draws on Leigh and Jencks (2007).

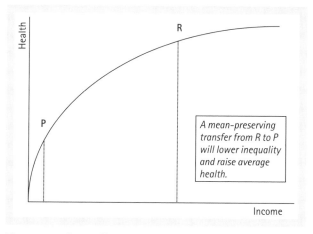

Fig. 16.1. A nonlinear relationship between income
and health

When one compares countries, the relationship between *average* income and *average* health follows the pattern in Figure 16.1. Figure 16.2 shows the relationship for OECD countries. (For ease of comparison, we reverse the scale for infant mortality, so a move up the y-axis always represents better health.) We exclude the three poorest OECD nations (Mexico, Poland, and Turkey) and the richest (Luxembourg) and weight the remaining countries equally when we estimate the slope. Using either life expectancy or infant mortality as a measure of population health, the protective effect of income on health appears substantial as countries move from about $15,000 to $25,000 US dollars per capita, but appears small or non-existent above that point.[6]

When one compares individuals within the USA, the relationship between family income and age-specific mortality also exhibits a pattern similar to Figure 16.1 (Backlund *et al.*, 1996). However, neither the comparisons of countries nor the comparisons of individuals take account of all the factors that could affect both income and health.[7] Furthermore, the nonlinear relationship between income and health at both the country level and the individual level could be driven by a strong nonlinear effect of health on income rather than a strong nonlinear effect of income on health. Thus while there are strong theoretical reasons for expecting additional income to have less effect on health as income rises, the empirical evidence supporting this assumption is not conclusive.

[6] The apparent downturn in longevity when per capita GDP exceeds $35,000 is largely attributable to one country, namely the USA, which is an outlier on many measures besides per capita GDP.

[7] Deaton (2006), for example, concludes that there is no evidence economic growth alone will reduce infant and child mortality on a global scale unless growth is accompanied by additional education and higher-quality public health institutions, which presumably affect both future growth and health.

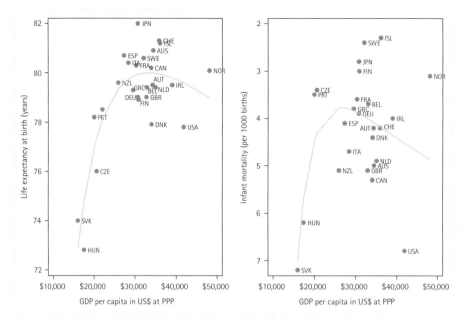

## Fig. 16.2. GDP and mortality in OECD countries (c.2005)

*Note:* Infant mortality is scaled in reverse, to allow comparability with life expectancy. We exclude the three poorest countries in the OECD (Mexico, Poland, and Turkey), and the richest (Luxembourg).

*Source:* OECD health data (2007).

### The relative income hypothesis

Holding individual income constant, the income of others can affect people's health if they evaluate either their income or their lives as a whole by comparing themselves to others. The relative income hypothesis assumes that, at least in the economic domain, upward comparisons are more salient than downward comparisons and that upward comparisons are more likely to be stressful than soothing.[8] Wilkinson (1997) argues, for example, that if individuals assess their well-being by comparing themselves to others with more income than themselves, increases in economic inequality will engender '[l]ow control, insecurity, and loss of self esteem'. When upward economic comparisons are distressing, they are said to produce 'relative deprivation'. The most frequently suggested physical mechanism linking relative deprivation to mortality is chronic stress, which appears to lower resistance to many forms of disease in a variety of species.[9]

One potential objection to this hypothesis is that most studies of relative deprivation suggest that social comparisons are most stressful when they involve

---

[8] Upward comparisons can be soothing if they lead people whose current economic circumstances are stressful to think that their future circumstances could be better. We are not aware of any persuasive evidence on whether upward economic comparisons are more salient than downward comparisons or on whether they are more often upsetting than soothing.

[9] Marmot (2005) provides numerous references.

people who have a lot in common, such as co-workers, relatives, and neighbors.[10] Income differences within such reference groups are likely to be much smaller than differences between random members of national populations. Nonetheless, when income inequality changes in society as a whole, it is also likely to change in the same direction within reference groups composed of co-workers, relatives, or neighbors. If such changes lead to increases in chronic stress, higher inequality at the national level could increase mortality and lower inequality could decrease mortality.[11]

## Society-wide effects of inequality

### Violent crime

Violent crime accounts for a tiny fraction of all deaths in developed countries, but it could have larger second-order effects on mortality if it increases chronic stress among those who worry that they or their kin may become victims of violence in the future. The empirical literature on inequality and violent crime has produced mixed findings. Cross-sectional studies tend to report a positive association across countries, but panel studies produce mixed results.

Fajnzylber et al. (2002) use changes in various measures of inequality from the Deininger–Squire dataset to predict changes in homicide and robbery for 20 industrialized countries and 19 middle-income countries between 1965 and 1994. To measure change they use average levels of inequality and crime for non-overlapping five-year periods in each country.[12] They find a robust relationship within countries between trends in inequality, homicide, and robbery with a variety of controls. This relationship holds up regardless of how they measure inequality. They also report a strong serial correlation between measures of violent crime in successive five-year periods. The estimated half-life of a sudden change in violent crime is 17 years. This finding suggests that modeling the relationship between inequality and violent crime requires close attention to the possibility of very long lags.

More recently, Leigh and Jencks (2007) found no positive relationship between the income share of the richest decile and homicide using panel data on developed countries. That could be because, unlike Fajnzylber et al., they had no data on inequality within the bottom 90 percent of the income distribution, because they focused on lags of five years or less, or because of other methodological differences. However, Brush (2007) also failed to find a positive relationship between changes in inequality and changes in violent crime across US counties over a ten-year period.

---

[10]  Martin (1981) provides some relevant references for earnings. See also Eibner and Evans (2005).

[11]  The relative income hypothesis also comes in a more extreme variant, where all that matters is ordinal rank, not the distance between ranks. In that variant any income hierarchy in which every individual has a unique income has the same effect as any other.

[12]  Not all countries have data for all of the six possible periods.

## Public spending

If the Meltzer–Richard theorem is correct, greater economic inequality among voters should make the median voter more inclined to support government spending on health (Meltzer and Richard, 1981). Szreter (1988) shows, for example, that clean water was made available in much of the UK only after the franchise was extended to include the less affluent, for whom public spending on sanitation provided large health benefits at little cost to themselves.[13] However, Alesina et al. (1999) show that the average value of public goods to members of a community will decrease when heterogeneity increases. If income inequality makes voters' preferences more heterogeneous, that could lower government spending on health. In addition, increases in economic inequality may allow the rich to buy more political influence, which could lead to reductions in government spending on health. Schwabish et al. (2006) use cross-national data to show that the larger the distance between the 90th and 50th percentiles in market incomes, the less the rich support public expenditures. However the mechanisms accounting for this relationship are not well understood (see also Neckerman and Torche, 2007).

## Social capital and trust

Comparing American states, Kawachi et al. (1997) find negative cross-sectional relationships both between inequality and social capital and between social capital and mortality. Other studies have also found that people in more unequal places tend to be less trusting (Knack and Keefer, 1997; Alesina and La Ferrara, 2002; Leigh, 2006). Low trust may make voters more skeptical about the claim that public spending will improve health. Low trust may also be linked to thinner friendship networks, which are associated with higher age-specific mortality (Berkman and Syme, 1979).

## The Effect of Health on Inequality

The theoretical literature on how health might affect economic inequality is less developed than that on how economic inequality might affect health, but a number of plausible hypotheses have been proposed. We divide these into three broad categories: labor market effects, educational effects, and marriage market effects.[14]

---

[13]   The social capital and public expenditure channels do not posit any specific link between an individual's position in the income distribution and his or her health. Instead, they suggest that greater variance of incomes will adversely affect population health. This impact could conceivably affect individuals anywhere in the distribution.

[14]   Other inequality-related mechanisms, such as neighborhood location, may also affect infant mortality adversely (Mayer and Sarin, 2005), but the three categories in the text encompass the vast majority of the research on this issue.

*Labor market effects*

Poor health can make it more difficult for prospective workers to search for jobs, less likely that employers will hire them, and more physically or mentally costly to work. Illness may also increase absenteeism and harm job performance, which can affect earnings, increase the probability of dismissal, and reduce the chance of promotion. Employers may also discriminate against workers who have a physical or mental disability even when their performance is satisfactory. Finally, poor health might reduce earnings if sicker workers tend to have sicker children who are more likely to require care at times when the parent is supposed to be at work.

*Educational effects*

Poor health in childhood can also affect educational outcomes through direct physiological channels, since health in the womb and in the early years can affect brain development. Health may also affect school performance through reduced school attendance or inability to concentrate while at school. Haas (2006) reviews much of this evidence.

*The marriage market*

As we shall see, healthier members of a given population are more likely to marry and less likely to divorce. We have not found evidence on whether this pattern also holds at the population level, but if it does, an adverse shock to a population's health will lower the marriage rate and thereby alter the level of household income inequality. Likewise, adverse health shocks to economically disadvantaged subgroups are likely to lower these groups' household income and increase household income inequality.

# 3. EMPIRICAL EVIDENCE

Most studies of the relationship between income inequality and health rely on aggregate data. Under normal circumstances such studies cannot distinguish empirically between the absolute income hypothesis, the relative income hypothesis, and hypotheses about society-wide effects of inequality.[15] Our discussion of empirical evidence therefore focuses largely on reduced-form models that estimate the

---

[15] See Gravelle *et al.* (2002) or Leigh and Jencks (2007) for a mathematical treatment. Miller (2001) has shown that the argument in the text holds only if the second-order approximation in Leigh and Jencks's equation 1 is exact. However, while the second-order approximation is unlikely to be exact, investigators would need much better data than they normally have to distinguish the two effects.

net effect of a change in income inequality on population health or vice versa. For the most part, the panel studies that we discuss (and the new evidence we present) assume that the effects occur without much lag. However, including lags does not generally change the conclusions, at least in the panel studies discussed below.

## Data Quality

Poor data on inequality has been a major problem in studies of the relationship between income inequality and health. As Judge *et al.* (1998: 569) note in their review of the literature:

Many of the studies use multiple sources of income distribution data and/or data from a wide range of years, which makes comparability between countries questionable. Only five of the studies [available in 1998] use data based on a measure of equivalent disposable income. In fact, we believe it is the generally poor quality of the income data that poses the most serious weakness in most of the studies we have reviewed.

Most cross-national studies have used measures of inequality from the Deininger–Squire dataset (Deininger and Squire, 1996) or the World Income Inequality Database (WIID). Atkinson and Brandolini (2001) have shown that using higher-quality inequality data can substantially alter results based on these two sources. The Luxembourg Income Study (LIS) provides a more consistent and appropriate measure of income inequality for comparing countries and years, namely disposable household income adjusted for household size. However, while the LIS dataset is expanding, it still covers a relatively small number of nations and years, reducing the number of degrees of freedom in statistical analyses.

Leigh and Jencks (2007), in contrast, use data on the income share of the richest 10 percent to measure inequality. Such data are now available on an annual basis for a dozen rich countries, sometimes going back to the early 20th century. The disadvantage of this approach is that some theories about how inequality affects health and most theories about how health affects income predict a stronger relationship between health and inequality in the bottom part of the income distribution than in the top part, and the income share of the top decile is an imperfect proxy for inequality in the bottom half of the distribution. Most investigators therefore prefer measures of inequality like the Gini coefficient, which is sensitive to income disparities throughout the distribution. Still other studies use a commonly constructed panel dataset for two or more countries to examine differences both within and across nations (Banks *et al.*, 2006a, 2006b).

A number of studies have also compared US states, where income data collected by the decennial census provide comparable measures of state-level inequality.

Income surveys of the European Union can also be used to create consistent national and sub-national inequality measures (e.g. Hildebrand and Van Kerm, 2005). The drawback of looking at the sub-national level in either the USA or the EU is that some theories about the relationship between inequality and health (e.g. public health expenditure, relative comparisons) may be more applicable at the national than the state or regional level. There is also considerably more migration between sub-national jurisdictions than between nations, making long-term effects of inequality on health harder to detect in sub-national jurisdictions.

Measuring population health also poses numerous problems. Mortality rates are generally thought to be quite well measured in developed nations, but mortality rates do not capture variation in the health status of the living except insofar as the two are correlated at the aggregate level. One alternative is to use 'quality adjusted' or 'disability adjusted' life years (often called QALYs and DALYs respectively), but such measures are not available for many countries and are seldom available as far back in time as data on mortality or life expectancy.

Subjective health measures, such as 'How is your health in general: excellent, good, fair, or poor?', have sometimes been used to fill this gap, but they implicitly require respondents to compare their health to some benchmark, which may be either the respondent's past health, the health of other people the respondent knows, or some mixture of these and other benchmarks. Those who report that their health is 'excellent' are therefore likely to mean different things in different times and places and at different ages. These implicit benchmarks may also be affected by changes in economic inequality. Suppose that Type A and Type B people live in the same community, have the same initial distribution of income, and are used to comparing themselves to one another. Now suppose that some exogenous shock doubles the income of Type A people, raising inequality. Type A people spend part of their extra income on improving their health. On all objective measures, Type B people are just as healthy as before. However, even if their objective health is unchanged, the improved health of some people in their reference group may cause them to rate their health lower than before.

Johnston et al. (2007) identify another problem with relying on subjective measures. Comparing objective and subjective measures of hypertension they find that the poor are no more likely than the affluent to report hypertension but are much more likely to test positive for hypertension when examined by a medical professional. This suggests that the health gradient with respect to income can be quite sensitive to whether an objective or a subjective measure is utilized. If that is the case, and if higher income inequality mainly affects the health of those with lower incomes, the estimated correlation between income inequality and the prevalence of hypertension in the population as a whole will be weaker in studies that rely on self-reports than in studies that rely on health exams.

## Cross-Country Evidence

Judge *et al.* (1998), Deaton (2003), and Lynch *et al.* (2004a) have all done careful reviews of the cross-country relationship between inequality and health. They all conclude that while the evidence is not conclusive, studies with better data on inequality and better methods tend to observe a weak or non-existent relationship.

Because unobserved factors can affect both health and inequality, we focus here on studies that look at changes over time in multiple countries or regions. Econometrically, this means that we only review estimates that include country and year fixed effects. Country fixed effects capture stable differences between countries in both health and inequality, including stable differences in the way health and inequality are measured. Year fixed effects capture the influence of shocks that affect health in multiple countries at the same time. Examples of the latter might include major influenza epidemics, the spread of HIV/AIDS, the introduction of new vaccines, and the diffusion of antibiotics.[16] Country and year fixed effects cannot, of course, eliminate all possible sources of omitted variable bias, but they are more likely to do so than either time series studies of a single country or cross-sectional studies of multiple countries at a single point in time.[17]

A number of studies have compared the UK and the USA. Analyzing the last decades of the 20th century in the USA and the UK, Wilkinson (1996) argues that rising inequality during the 1980s was the main reason why the decline in infant mortality slowed after 1985. Deaton and Paxson (2004), in contrast, find no systematic relationship between inequality and health in either the UK or the USA from the mid-1970s to the mid-1990s.

Leigh and Jencks (2007) look at the relationship between inequality and mortality for a panel of 12 developed nations between 1920 and 2000. They find no evidence that the income share of the top decile has any effect on population health. However, relying exclusively on a measure of upper-tail inequality is not ideal. Top income shares are quite strongly related to the Gini coefficient in recent years, but the relationship may not be as strong in earlier periods. And even the Gini coefficient may not be an ideal measure of inequality if inequality in the lower tail of the distribution is what affects health.

Using income inequality data from the Luxembourg Income Study, Judge *et al.* (1998) find no evidence that changes in inequality are negatively related to changes in life expectancy or positively related to changes in infant mortality. This remains true whether they measure inequality using the Gini, the 90/10 ratio, or the share of income going to the poorest 60 percent of the population.

---

[16] Technological innovations do not, of course, reach all developed countries in exactly the same year. Deaton and Paxson (2004) argue, for example, that technological innovations tend to affect the UK about four years later than the USA.

[17] For a discussion of the same issue in a different context, see Acemoglu *et al.* (2005).

Judge *et al.*'s data are mostly drawn from the 1980s, so we update their analysis, looking at changes in inequality and mortality from around 1980 to around 2000. Health measures are drawn from OECD Health Data 2007, while inequality measures are drawn from the Luxembourg Income Study. We choose the interval 1980–2000 because it is the longest span for which we can obtain LIS inequality data for a reasonably large number of countries. Because there is no consensus in the literature on the best measure of income inequality for predicting changes in health, we use the Gini coefficient, the 50/10 ratio, and the 90/50 ratio. The Gini is sensitive to all points of the distribution. The 50/10 is a measure of relative poverty. The 90/50 is a measure of top income inequality. Note that because our analysis looks at changes in both inequality and population health over the same period (1980–2000), it does not explicitly allow for the possibility of longer lags.

Figure 16.3 shows the pattern across OECD countries over this period (again, we reverse the scale for infant mortality, so a move up the vertical axis always represents better health). We find no significant relationship between changes in inequality and changes in mortality. Indeed, all three charts for life expectancy show that it rose more in countries where inequality rose more; and all three panels for infant mortality suggest that it fell more in countries where inequality rose more. (Again, we exclude Poland, Mexico, and Luxembourg, and we do not have data on Turkey. Adding back the three omitted countries does not change the slope of the fitted line in the infant mortality plots, but it does make the relationship between changes in life expectancy and changes in inequality upward-sloping only for the 90/50 measure, and essentially flat for the Gini and 50/10.)

## Cross-Regional Evidence

Although several studies have estimated the relationship between inequality and population health across US states, few use a fixed effects approach. Across US states and Metropolitan Statistical Areas (MSAs), controlling for census region effects, Mellor and Milyo (2002) find no significant relationship between changes in inequality and changes in self-reported health status. Deaton and Lubotsky (2003) also exploit variation across MSAs and find that after controlling for racial composition, there is no significant relationship between changes in inequality and mortality. Perhaps the most robustly estimated results are those of Miller and Paxson (2006), who estimate a fixed effects model of mortality and inequality across metropolitan areas (PUMAs). They find no evidence that having wealthier neighbors is harmful to one's health. A less formal analysis of mortality trends across US regions (Lynch *et al.*, 2004b) also shows little evidence of a causal relationship between income inequality and mortality.[18]

---

[18]  Clarkwest (2008) argues that if income inequality slows either the rate at which new ideas diffuse in a state or the medical profession's commitment to high quality care for all residents of the

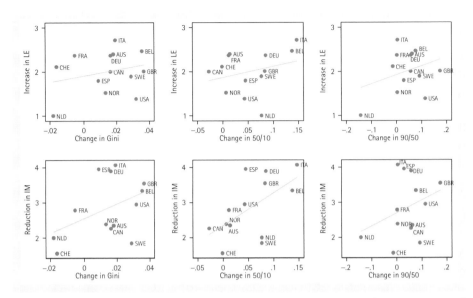

**Fig. 16.3. Changes in inequality and mortality in OECD countries (c.1980–c.2000)**

*Notes*: Changes in infant mortality are scaled in reverse, to allow comparability with life expectancy measures. LE is life expectancy at birth (years). IM is infant mortality (deaths per 1,000). All changes are expressed on a 'per decade' basis (i.e. annualized and multiplied by 10). We exclude the three poorest countries in the OECD (Mexico and Poland; and Turkey for lack of data), and the richest (Luxembourg). Countries and years covered are Australia (AUS) 1981–2001, Belgium (BEL) 1985–2000, Canada (CAN) 1981–2000, France (FRA) 1981–2000, Germany (DEU) 1981–2000, Italy (ITA) 1986–2000, Netherlands (NLD) 1983–99, Norway (NOR) 1979–2000, Spain (ESP) 1980–2000, Sweden (SWE) 1981–2000, Switzerland (CHE) 1982–2000, the United Kingdom (GBR) 1979–99, and the United States (USA) 1979–2000.

*Sources*: LIS Key Figures (as at Aug. 13, 2007) and OECD health data (2007). Mortality figures for the UK in 1979 are from the Human Mortality Database (<http://www.mortality.org>) and cover only England and Wales.

We are only aware of one other panel study of inequality and population health that uses intra-country variation with region fixed effects. Exploiting differences in inequality and population health across European regions over the period 1994–2001, Hildebrand and Van Kerm (2005) find a robust negative relationship between income inequality and self-reported health on a five-point scale, although the magnitude of the estimated effect is very small.[19]

state, the way to detect this effect is to regress the change in longevity over a given period on the initial level of inequality, not to regress the change in longevity on the change in inequality during the same period. Using this setup, which implicitly assumes fairly long lags, he finds a negative and statistically significant relationship between initial inequality and subsequent changes in longevity for US states between 1970 and 2000, as well as cross-sectional evidence that the negative association between inequality and longevity can be explained by between-state differences in adoption of health-enhancing medical innovations.

[19] Using a random effects specification, with the same dataset and time period, Etienne *et al.* (2007) find the same result across 14 European countries.

# Health and the Distribution of Income

As we have noted, the literature on the relationship between health and inequality is largely presented as a test of the hypothesis that inequality affects health. However, in a specification that looks at levels or changes in the same time period, the studies discussed above can also be regarded as a test of the hypothesis that health affects inequality, as argued for example by Smith (1999, 2004). Accordingly, if most panel studies conclude that the dispersion of income does not have a robust impact on the level of health, they also imply that the level of health does not have a robust impact on the dispersion of income. (In theory, the effects could cancel each other out, but virtually all theories assume that both relationships are negative.)

However, in addition to the studies discussed in the two previous sub-sections, a number of papers have looked specifically at the effect of health on income, education, and labor market outcomes.

## Income effects of poor health

Currie and Madrian (1999) review the literature on the relationship between health and labor income. They find studies that report a strong negative association between labor income and arthritis, asthma, hypertension, physical disabilities, psychiatric disorders, and self-reported health. These studies, although very numerous, seldom try to separate the effect of health on labor income from the effect of labor income on health. However, those that try to determine the direction of causation also tend to find an adverse effect of poor health on labor market outcomes. For example, Ettner *et al.* (1997) use parents' mental health as an instrument for children's mental health and find a reduced but still negative impact of mental health on employment and earnings. Similarly, Black *et al.* (2007) use variation in twins' birth weight in a specification that includes twin-pair fixed effects, and find that heavier babies which are typically healthier at birth, also tend to have higher earnings as adults.

## Disability

Economists have also studied the effects of disability benefits on economic outcomes. Since disability benefits are usually conditional on medical evidence that the claimant cannot work, the direction of causality might seem clear-cut. But because workers only claim disability benefits if they expect to be better off in some broad sense, those with low potential wages are more likely to claim benefits than those with high potential wages.

Studies of US disability applicants in the 1970s and 1980s (Bound, 1989; Gruber and Kubik, 1997) suggested that tougher disability standards did not lead to large increases in employment among rejected applicants. Nonetheless, generous policies with regard to sickness and early retirement due to disability do reduce labor supply among workers who have reached middle age (Autor and Duggan,

2003). Similarly, laws barring discrimination against disabled workers, such as the Americans with Disabilities Act (ADA) in the USA, are often counterproductive and may even reduce work (Acemoglu and Angrist, 2001; Hotchkiss, 2004).[20] Spending on disability benefits as a share of GDP rose during the 1990s in most OECD countries (OECD, 2003). If disability benefits do not fully replace earnings, and if such programs have a negative impact on labor supply, then the growth of disability benefits and anti-discrimination laws could strengthen the link between ill health and economic inequality—a result that is probably the opposite of what advocates for such laws intended.

### Educational effects of poor health

A significant literature also explores the relationship between health status and educational outcomes. Most of these studies focus on how education affects health.[21] However, several studies also analyze the impact of health on education. Wolfe (1985) estimates a simultaneous model and finds that both physical illness and psychological disorders have a causal impact that reduces years of schooling. In a lagged specification using a rich dataset from Finland, Koivusilta et al. (1998) find that poor health behaviors as a teenager are associated with lower educational attainment among respondents in their late 20s. Using a structural model, Gan and Gong (2007) find that having a serious illness before age 21 decreases the individual's education by 1.4 years. Together, the effect of early-onset ill health and disability can lead to a 'double penalty' involving both lower educational attainment and lower lifetime labor force participation (Burkhauser et al., 1993). Haas (2006) shows that sibling differences in childhood health predict subsequent differences in both educational attainment and labor market success.

### Marriage market effects of poor health

Numerous studies have analyzed the impact of marriage on health (see Ribar, 2004, and Wilson and Oswald, 2005, for recent reviews). But those who marry also tend to be healthier before they marry than those who remain single (Waldron et al., 1996; Fu and Goldman, 1996). Likewise, those who divorce tend to be less healthy before they divorce than those who remain married (Joung et al., 1998). However, we are not aware of any work on whether changes in population health lead to changes in marriage rates, much less on whether the resulting changes in marriage rates affect the distribution of income.

---

[20]  On the other hand, European laws that require large employers hire the disabled, such as those in Germany, tend to increase work for the disabled (Aarts et al., 1992).

[21]  Grossman and Kaestner (1997) and Cutler and Lleras-Muney (2006) review the literature on education's effect on health. For recent debates on the effects of exogenous changes in education on health status in the UK see Oreopoulos (2006) and Clark and Royer (2007). For the US debate see Lleras-Muney (2005) and Mazumder (2007).

# 4. CONCLUSIONS

The theoretical literature has suggested three main ways in which inequality might adversely affect health: through diminishing returns to increases in absolute income, through relative income, and through society-wide effects of income inequality. Conversely, health can affect inequality by affecting earnings, educational attainment, and the probability of being married.

Empirical work on inequality and health has been hampered by both low-quality data on inequality and limited knowledge about the prevalence and correlates of health problems that affect household income. Data problems have, in turn, made it hard to use the best available methods to eliminate spurious correlations and identify causal impact. For developed countries, however, this appears to be changing. Setting aside natural experiments, the most convincing way to test for an effect of inequality on health is to use panel data econometrics, in which we observe the relationship between changes in inequality and changes in health for a number of countries or regions. Accordingly, we have focused primarily on these kinds of studies.

Unfortunately, these methods are not likely to detect effects of inequality that take a long time to manifest themselves. Suppose, for example, that economic inequality affects a society's institutional arrangements for providing high-quality medical care to those with below-average incomes. Since hypotheses of this kind do not tell us how long it takes for inequality to affect institutional arrangements, it is not easy to test this hypothesis with a change-on-change model. If the hypothesis is true and the effects are large relative to other sources of variation in health, we may observe some cross-national association between inequality over long periods, institutional arrangements for the prevention and treatment of illness, and longevity. But even that is chancy.

Our reading of the evidence is that most studies of health and inequality find no statistically significant relationship either across countries or over time. However, the confidence intervals in many of these studies include both positive and negative values large enough to be of considerable practical importance. Precisely estimated zeros are the exception, not the rule. Drawing firm negative conclusions may therefore be premature. This is a field with too many theories for the number of available data points. In psychology, which also suffers from this problem at times, meta-analysis has often managed to reduce the range of uncertainty substantially, and the same might be possible for inequality and health. A formal meta-analysis of studies on inequality and health could be very valuable, especially if it tried to model the effect of different methods, data sources, and dependent variables on the point estimates for the coefficient of inequality reported in the literature.

Thus while the currently available evidence suggests to us that the relationship between inequality and health is either small or inconsistent, readers should bear in mind that not everyone agrees, especially social epidemiologists. Achieving more consensus will require more work with better data and better methods than have been usual in the past.

# APPENDIX

......................................................................................................................

## Table A16.1. Income and mortality c.2005

| Country | Year used | GDP per capita (US$, PPP) | Life expectancy at birth | Infant mortality per 1,000 births |
|---|---|---|---|---|
| Australia | 2005 | $34,484 | 80.90 | 5.00 |
| Austria | 2005 | $34,394 | 79.50 | 4.20 |
| Belgium | 2004 | $33,021 | 79.40 | 3.70 |
| Canada | 2004 | $34,057 | 80.20 | 5.30 |
| Czech Republic | 2005 | $20,633 | 76.00 | 3.40 |
| Denmark | 2005 | $34,110 | 77.90 | 4.40 |
| Finland | 2005 | $30,911 | 78.90 | 3.00 |
| France | 2005 | $30,350 | 80.30 | 3.60 |
| Germany | 2005 | $30,776 | 79.00 | 3.90 |
| Greece | 2005 | $29,578 | 79.30 | 3.80 |
| Hungary | 2005 | $17,484 | 72.80 | 6.20 |
| Iceland | 2005 | $36,183 | 81.20 | 2.30 |
| Ireland | 2005 | $39,019 | 79.50 | 4.00 |
| Italy | 2005 | $28,401 | 80.40 | 4.70 |
| Japan | 2005 | $30,777 | 82.00 | 2.80 |
| Korea | 2005 | $22,098 | 78.50 | |
| Luxembourg[a] | 2005 | $70,600 | 79.30 | 2.60 |
| Mexico[a] | 2005 | $10,537 | 75.50 | 18.80 |
| Netherlands | 2005 | $35,112 | 79.40 | 4.90 |
| New Zealand | 2005 | $25,963 | 79.60 | 5.10 |
| Norway | 2005 | $48,162 | 80.10 | 3.10 |
| Poland[a] | 2005 | $13,915 | 75.10 | 6.40 |
| Portugal | 2005 | $20,030 | 78.20 | 3.50 |
| Slovak Republic | 2005 | $15,983 | 74.00 | 7.20 |
| Spain | 2005 | $27,400 | 80.70 | 4.10 |
| Sweden | 2005 | $32,111 | 80.60 | 2.40 |
| Switzerland | 2005 | $35,956 | 81.30 | 4.20 |
| Turkey[a] | 2005 | $7,711 | 71.40 | 23.60 |
| United Kingdom | 2005 | $32,896 | 79.00 | 5.10 |
| United States | 2004 | $41,827 | 77.80 | 6.80 |

*Notes*: These data are used to create our Fig. 16.2.
[a] Not shown.
*Source*: OECD health data (2007).

Table A16.2. Changes in inequality and mortality from about 1980 to about 2000

| Country | Year | Gini | 50/10 | 90/50 | Life expectancy at birth | Infant mortality per 1000 births |
|---|---|---|---|---|---|---|
| Australia | 1981 | 0.28 | 2.11 | 1.86 | 74.90 | 10.00 |
| Australia | 2001 | 0.32 | 2.14 | 1.99 | 79.70 | 5.30 |
| Belgium | 1985 | 0.23 | 1.68 | 1.62 | 74.60 | 9.80 |
| Belgium | 2000 | 0.28 | 1.89 | 1.74 | 78.30 | 4.80 |
| Canada | 1981 | 0.28 | 2.22 | 1.83 | 75.50 | 9.60 |
| Canada | 2000 | 0.31 | 2.17 | 1.93 | 79.30 | 5.30 |
| France | 1981 | 0.29 | 1.81 | 1.88 | 74.50 | 9.70 |
| France | 2000 | 0.28 | 1.83 | 1.88 | 79.00 | 4.40 |
| Germany | 1981 | 0.24 | 1.70 | 1.69 | 73.50 | 11.80 |
| Germany | 2000 | 0.28 | 1.87 | 1.80 | 78.00 | 4.40 |
| Italy | 1986 | 0.31 | 2.04 | 1.98 | 75.80 | 10.20 |
| Italy | 2000 | 0.33 | 2.25 | 1.99 | 79.60 | 4.50 |
| Luxembourg[a] | 1985 | 0.24 | 1.71 | 1.72 | 74.30 | 9.00 |
| Luxembourg[a] | 2000 | 0.26 | 1.76 | 1.85 | 78.00 | 5.10 |
| Mexico[a] | 1984 | 0.44 | 3.02 | 2.86 | 69.10 | 42.70 |
| Mexico[a] | 2000 | 0.49 | 3.14 | 3.31 | 74.10 | 23.30 |
| Netherlands | 1983 | 0.26 | 1.58 | 1.86 | 76.30 | 8.40 |
| Netherlands | 1999 | 0.23 | 1.70 | 1.63 | 77.90 | 5.20 |
| Norway | 1979 | 0.22 | 1.75 | 1.58 | 75.50 | 8.80 |
| Norway | 2000 | 0.25 | 1.76 | 1.59 | 78.70 | 3.80 |
| Poland[a] | 1986 | 0.27 | 1.99 | 1.77 | 71.00 | 21.10 |
| Poland[a] | 1995 | 0.32 | 2.14 | 1.89 | 72.00 | 13.60 |
| Spain | 1980 | 0.32 | 2.17 | 2.02 | 75.60 | 12.30 |
| Spain | 2000 | 0.34 | 2.26 | 2.08 | 79.20 | 4.40 |
| Sweden | 1981 | 0.20 | 1.61 | 1.51 | 76.10 | 6.90 |
| Sweden | 2000 | 0.25 | 1.76 | 1.68 | 79.70 | 3.40 |
| Switzerland | 1982 | 0.31 | 1.84 | 1.85 | 76.00 | 7.70 |
| Switzerland | 2000 | 0.28 | 1.84 | 1.82 | 79.80 | 4.90 |
| United Kingdom | 1979 | 0.27 | 1.96 | 1.80 | 73.38 | 12.90 |
| United Kingdom | 1999 | 0.34 | 2.13 | 2.15 | 77.40 | 5.80 |
| United States | 1979 | 0.30 | 2.50 | 1.86 | 73.90 | 13.10 |
| United States | 2000 | 0.37 | 2.60 | 2.10 | 76.80 | 6.90 |

Notes: These data are used to create our Fig. 16.3.
[a] Not shown.

Sources: LIS Key Figures (as at Aug. 13, 2007) and OECD health data (2007). Mortality figures for the UK in 1979 are from the Human Mortality Database (<http://www.mortality.org>) and cover only England and Wales.

## References

AARTS, L., BURKHAUSER, R. V., and DeJONG, P. 1992. 'The Dutch Disease: Lessons for the United States'. *Regulation*, 15(2): 75–86.

ACEMOGLU, D., and ANGRIST, J. 2001. 'Consequences of Employment Protection? The Case of the Americans with Disabilities Act'. *Journal of Political Economy*, 109(5): 915–57.

——— JOHNSON, S., ROBINSON, J., and YARED, P. 2005. 'From Education to Democracy?' *American Economic Review*, 95(2): 44–9.

ADLER, N. E., and NEWMAN, K. 2002. 'Socioeconomic Disparities in Health: Pathways and Policies'. *Health Affairs*, 21(2): 60–76.

ALESINA, A., BAQIR, R., and EASTERLY, W. 1999. 'Public Goods and Ethnic Divisions'. *Quarterly Journal of Economics*, 114: 1243–84.

——— and LA FERRARA, E. 2002. 'Who Trusts Others?' *Journal of Public Economics*, 85: 207–34.

ATKINSON, A., and BRANDOLINI, A. 2001. 'Promise and Pitfalls in the Use of "Secondary" Data-Sets: Income Inequality in OECD Countries as a Case Study'. *Journal of Economic Literature*, 39: 771–99.

AUTOR, D., and DUGGAN, M. 2003. 'The Rise in Disability Recipiency and the Decline in Unemployment'. *Quarterly Journal of Economics*, 118(1): 157–205.

BACKLUND, E., SORLIE, P., and JOHNSON, N. 1996. 'The Shape of the Relationship between Income and Mortality in the United States: Evidence from the National Longitudinal Mortality Survey'. *Annals of Epidemiology*, 6(1): 12–20.

BANKS, J., MARMOT, M., OLDFIELD, Z., and SMITH, J. 2006a. 'The SES Health Gradient on Both Sides of the Atlantic'. London: Institute for Fiscal Studies WP07/04. Dec.

——— ——— ——— ——— (2006b). 'Disease and Disadvantage in the United States and in England'. JAMA, 295(17): 2037–45.

BERKMAN, L., and SYME, L. 1979. 'Social Networks, Host Resistance, and Mortality: A Nine-Year Follow-Up Study of Alameda County Residents'. *American Journal of Epidemiology*, 109: 186–204.

BLACK, S., DEVEREUX, P., and SALVANES, K. 2007. 'From the Cradle to the Labor Market? The Effect of Birth Weight on Adult Outcomes'. *Quarterly Journal of Economics*, 122(1): 409–39.

BOUND, J. 1989. 'The Health and Earnings of Rejected Disability Insurance Applicants'. *American Economic Review*, 79(3), June: 482–503.

BRUSH, J. 2007. 'Does Income Inequality Lead to More Crime? A Comparison of Cross-Sectional and Time-Series Analyses of United States Counties'. *Economics Letters*, 96: 264–8.

BURKHAUSER, R. V., HAVEMAN, R., and WOLFE, B. 1993. 'How People with Disabilities Fare When Public Policies Change'. *Journal of Policy Analysis and Management*, 12(2): 429–33.

CASE, A., and PAXSON, C. 2006. 'Children's Health and Social Mobility'. *The Future of Children*, 16(2): 151–73.

CLARK, D., and ROYER, H. 2007. 'The Effects of Education on Adult Mortality: Evidence from the United Kingdom'. University of Florida, Department of Economics and Case Western Reserve University Department of Economics, July 20.

CLARKWEST, A. 2008. 'Neo-materialist Theory and the Temporal Relationship between Income Inequality and Longevity Change'. *Social Science and Medicine*, 66(9): 1871–81.

CURRIE, J., and MADRIAN, B. C. 1999. 'Health, Health Insurance and the Labor Market', in O. Ashenfelter and D. Card (eds.), *Handbook of Labor Economics*, vol. 3. Amsterdam: Elsevier, 3309–416.

CUTLER, D., and LLERAS-MUNEY, A. 2006. 'Education and Health: Evaluating Theories and Evidence'. NBER Working Paper 12352. Cambridge, Mass.: NBER.

DEATON, A. 2003. 'Health, Inequality, and Economic Development'. *Journal of Economic Literature*, 41: 113–58.

——— 2006. 'Global Patterns of Income and Health: Facts, Interpretations and Policies'. NBER Working Paper 12735. Cambridge, Mass.: NBER.

——— and LUBOTSKY, D. 2003. 'Mortality, Inequality and Race in American Cities and States'. *Social Science and Medicine*, 56: 1139–53.

——— and PAXSON, C. 2004. 'Mortality, Income, and Income Inequality over Time in Britain and the United States', in D. A. Wise (ed.), *Perspectives on the Economics of Aging*. Chicago: University of Chicago Press, 247–80.

DEININGER, K., and SQUIRE, N. 1996. 'A New Data Set Measuring Income Inequality'. *World Bank Economic Review*, 10(3): 565–91.

EIBNER, C., and EVANS, W. 2005. 'Relative Deprivation, Poor Habits and Mortality: A Call to Action'. *New England Journal of Medicine*, 340(9), Mar. 4: 722–8.

ETIENNE, J., SKALLI, A., and THEODOSSIOU, I. 2007. 'Do Economic Inequalities Harm Health? Evidence from Europe'. Centre for European Labour Market Research Discussion Paper 2007-13.

ETTNER, S. L., FRANK, R. G., and KESSLER, R. C. 1997. 'The Impact of Psychiatric Disorders on Labor Market Outcomes'. *Industrial and Labor Relations Review*, 51(1): 64–81.

FAJNZYLBER, P., LEDERMAN, D., and LOAYZA, N. 2002. 'Inequality and Violent Crime'. *Journal of Law and Economics*, 45(1): 1–40.

FU, H., and GOLDMAN, 1996. 'Incorporating Health into Models of Marriage Choice: Demographic and Sociological Perspectives'. *Journal of Marriage and the Family*, 58(3): 740–58.

GAN, L., and GONG, G. 2007. 'Estimating Interdependence between Health and Education in a Dynamic Model'. NBER Working Paper 12830. Cambridge, Mass.: NBER.

GOULD, E., SMEEDING, T., and WOLFE, B. 2005. 'Trends in the Health of the Poor and Near Poor: Have the Poor and Near Poor Been Catching Up to the Non Poor in the Last 25 Years?' Presented to the APPAM Conference, Washington, Nov.

GRAVELLE, H., WILDMAN, J., and SUTTON, M. 2002. 'Income, Income Inequality and Health: What Can We Learn from Aggregate Data?' *Social Science and Medicine*, 54: 577–89.

GROSSMAN, M., and KAESTNER, R. 1997. 'Effects of Education on Health', in J. R. Behrman and N. Stacey (eds.), *The Social Benefits of Education*. Ann Arbor: University of Michigan Press, 69–122.

GRUBER J., and KUBIK, J. D. 1997. 'Disability Insurance Rejection Rates and the Labor Supply of Older Workers'. *Journal of Public Economics*, 64(1): 1–23.

HAAS, S. 2006. 'Health Selection and the Process of Social Stratification: The Effect of Childhood Health on Socioeconomic Attainment'. *Journal of Health and Social Behavior*, 47: 339–54.

HILDEBRAND, V., and VAN KERM, P. 2005. 'Income Inequality and Self-Rated Health Status: Evidence from the European Community Household Panel'. CEPS/INSTEAD, IRISS Working Paper 2005-01, available at <http://www.ceps.lu/iriss>.

HOTCHKISS, J. L. 2004. 'A Closer Look at the Employment Impact of the Americans with Disabilities Act'. *Journal of Human Resources*, 39: 887–911.

Institute of Medicine-National Research Council (IOM-NRC) (2004). 'Children's Health, The Nation's Wealth: Assessing and Improving Child Health'. Institute of Medicine, National Academies.

JOHNSTON, D. W., PROPPER, C., and SHIELDS, M. A. 2007. 'Comparing Subjective and Objective Measures of Health: Evidence from Hypertension for the Income/Health Gradient'. IZA Discussion Paper 2737.

JOUNG, I. M. A., VANDEMHEEN, H. D., STRONKS, K., *et al.*, 1998. 'A Longitudinal Study of Health Selection in Marital Transitions'. *Social Science and Medicine*, 46: 425–35.

JUDGE, K., MULLIGAN, J., and BENZEVAL, M. 1998. 'Income Inequality and Population Health'. *Social Science and Medicine*, 46(4–5): 567–79.

KAWACHI, I., KENNEDY, B. P., LOCHNER, K, and PROTHROW-STITH, D. 1997. 'Social Capital, Income Inequality, and Mortality'. *American Journal of Public Health*, 87(9): 1491–8.

KOIVUSILTA, L., RIMPELA, A., and RIMPELA, M. 1998. 'Health Related Lifestyle in Adolescence Predicts Adult Educational Level: A Longitudinal Study from Finland'. *Journal of Epidemiology and Community Health*, 52: 794–801.

KNACK, S., and KEEFER, P. 1997. 'Does Social Capital Have an Economic Payoff? A Cross-Country Investigation'. *Quarterly Journal of Economics*, 112(4): 1251–88.

LEIGH, A. 2006. 'Does Equality Lead to Fraternity?' *Economics Letters*, 93: 121–5.

—— and JENCKS, C. 2007. 'Inequality and Mortality: Long-Run Evidence from a Panel of Countries'. *Journal of Health Economics*, 26(1): 1–24.

LLERAS-MUNEY, A. 2005. 'The Relationship between Education and Adult Mortality in the United States'. *Review of Economic Studies*, 72: 189–221.

LYNCH, J., SMITH, G. D., HARPER, S., HILLEMEIER, M., ROSS, N., KAPLAN, G. A., and WOLFSON, M.. 2004a. 'Is Income Inequality a Determinant of Population Health? Part 1. A Systematic Review'. *Milbank Quarterly*, 82(1): 5–99.

—— —— —— —— 2004b. 'U.S. National and Regional Trends in Income Inequality and Age- and Cause-Specific Mortality'. *Milbank Quarterly*, 82(2): 355–400.

MARMOT, M. 2005. *The Status Syndrome: How Social Standing Affects our Health and Longevity*. New York: Times Books, Henry Holt.

MARTIN, J. 1981. 'Relative Deprivation: A Theory of Distributive Injustice for an Era of Shrinking Resources'. *Research in Organizational Behavior*, 3: 53–107.

MAYER, S. E., and SARIN, A. 2005. 'Some Mechanisms Linking Economic Inequality and Infant Mortality'. *Social Science and Medicine*, 60(3): 439–55.

MAZUMDER, B. 2007. 'How Did Schooling Laws Improve Long-Term Health and Lower Mortality?' Federal Reserve Bank of Chicago, WP 2006-23 (revised Jan. 24, 2007). Chicago.

MELLOR, J. M., and MILYO, J. 2002. 'Income Inequality and Health Status in the United States: Evidence from the Current Population Survey'. *Journal of Human Resources*, 37: 510–39.

MELTZER A., and RICHARD, S. 1981. 'A Rational Theory of the Size of Government'. *Journal of Political Economy*, 89(5): 914–27.

MILLER, D. 2001. 'Income Inequality and Mortality in the US: Aggregate Data and Micro Relationships'. Mimeo. University of California, Berkeley.

—— and PAXSON, C. 2006. 'Relative Income, Race, and Mortality'. *Journal of Health Economics*, 25: 979–1003.

MULLAHY, J., ROBERT, S., and WOLFE, B. 2004. 'Health, Income and Inequality: Review and Redirection', in K. Neckerman (ed.), *Social Inequality*. New York: Russell Sage Foundation, 523–44.

NECKERMAN, K., and TORCHE, F. 2007. 'Inequality: Causes and Consequences', in K. Cook and D. Massey (eds.), *Annual Review of Sociology*, 33: 335–57.

OECD 2003. *Transforming Disability into Ability: Policies to Promote Work and Income Security for Disabled People*. Paris: OECD.

——2007. *Sickness, Disability and Work: Breaking the Barriers Department of Social Affairs*. Paris: OECD.

OREOPOULOS, P. 2006. 'Estimating Average and Local Average Treatment Effects of Education when Compulsory School Laws Really Matter'. *American Economic Review*, 96(1): 152–75.

PHIPPS, S., BURTON, P., OSBERG, L., and LETHBRIDGE, N. 2006. 'Poverty and the Extent of Child Obesity in Canada, Norway and the United States'. *Obesity Reviews*, 7: 5–12.

RIBAR, D. C. 2004. 'What Do Social Scientists Know About the Benefits of Marriage? A Review of Quantitative Methodologies'. IZA Discussion Paper 998.

SCHWABISH, J., SMEEDING, T. M., and OSBERG, L. 2006. 'Income Distribution and Social Expenditures: A Cross-National Perspective', in D. B. Papadimitriou (ed.), *The Distributional Effects of Government Spending and Taxation*. Northampton, Mass.: Edward Elgar Publishing, 247–88.

SMITH, J. P. 1999. 'Healthy Bodies and Thick Wallets: The Dual Relation between Health and Economic Status'. *Journal of Economic Perspectives*, 13(2): 145–66.

——2004. 'Unraveling the SES: Health Connection'. *Population and Development Review*, 30: 108–32.

SZRETER, S. 1988. 'The Importance of Social Intervention in Britain's Mortality Decline c.1850–1914: A Reinterpretation of the Role of Public Health'. *Social History and Medicine*, 1: 1–37.

VAN DOORSLAER, E., WAGSTAFF, A., and RUTTEN, F. (eds.). 1993. *Equity in the Finance and Delivery of Health Care: An International Perspective*. Oxford: Oxford Medical Publications.

WALDRON, I., HUGHES M. E., and BROOKS, T. L. 1996. 'Marriage Protection and Marriage Selection—Prospective Evidence for Reciprocal Effects of Marital Status and Health'. *Social Science and Medicine*, 43(1): 113–23.

WILKINSON, R. G. 1996. *Unhealthy Societies: The Affliction of Inequality*. London: Routledge.

——1997. 'Socioeconomic Determinants of Health: Health Inequalities: Relative or Absolute Material Standards?' *British Medical Journal*, 314: 591–5.

WILSON, C. M., and OSWALD, A. J. 2005. 'How Does Marriage Affect Physical and Psychological Health? A Survey of the Longitudinal Evidence'. IZA Discussion Paper 1619.

WOLFE, B. 1985. 'The Influence of Health on School Outcomes: A Multivariate Approach'. *Medical Care*, 23: 1127–38.

——1994. 'Reform of Health Care for the Nonelderly Poor', in S. Danziger, G. Sandefur, and D. Weinberg (eds.), *Confronting Poverty*. Cambridge, Mass.: Harvard University Press.

CHAPTER 17

# EDUCATION AND INEQUALITY

## STEPHEN MACHIN

## 1. INTRODUCTION

THE focus of this chapter is on education acquisition and inequality, the impact of education on economic and social outcomes and on how changes in education, together with the pattern of demand for skills, affect earnings and income distributions. In the recent past these have become big areas of research, especially amongst labor economists, as it has become evident that education has become more important for getting jobs and more highly valued in the labor markets of many countries.

Education acquisition itself is linked to inequality, particularly family background (e.g. parental income and education) and aspects of economic and social disadvantage experienced across the life course. I therefore begin my review of work on education and inequality by considering research that looks at connections between education acquisition and inequality at different stages of the life cycle. This is undertaken in Section 2 of this chapter.

It is long established that education raises earnings, and the earnings equation first derived by Mincer (1958, 1974) has become a basic tool for analyzing earnings

This chapter draws on and further develops a number of my other papers in this area, especially Machin (2005) for Section 2, Machin and McNally (2006) and Machin (2008) for Section 3, and Machin (2003) and Machin and Van Reenen (2008) for Section 4. I would like to thank my discussant at the Seville Conference, Susan Mayer, and other participants in the Conference for some very helpful comments and suggestions.

premia generated by increased schooling or educational qualifications. The interpretation of educational earnings or wage differentials as 'returns' has, however, been scrutinized closely, as has the notion that more education directly causes higher earnings. I will discuss these issues in Section 3 of the chapter, together with a discussion of heterogeneity of returns to education in terms of observable characteristics and how there can be differential returns at different points of the education distribution.

The other main area I consider is how changes in education have altered the distribution of wages and employment and affected labor market inequality. I consider this research in Section 4 of the chapter. This has become a very large research area, with evidence from many settings showing that education matters more for labor market outcomes than it did in the past. This arises from combinations of the changing demand and supply of more and less highly qualified workers. In the last 25 years or so, in a number of countries either the relative wage or relative employment (or in some places both) of more educated versus less educated workers has risen and I discuss why this has happened.

Finally, I will end in Section 5 by offering some conclusions about research in this area and briefly linking it to contemporary discussions about education policy.

# 2. Education Acquisition and Inequality

Education is linked to economic and social inequalities experienced throughout an individual's life span. This includes their time in pre-primary education, in the compulsory schooling system during their childhood years, as young adults in post-compulsory education, and during the years of adulthood. In this section I consider empirical evidence on the connections between education and inequality for each of these life phases in turn. The aim of this section is to discuss and summarize the evidence on learning experiences and inequality during the life course.

## Early Childhood Education

Gaps in cognitive and non-cognitive skills arise before children go to school. A huge, and sometimes contentious, research literature looks at many of the links between early child development and inequality or social disadvantage. Much of the empirical work by economists and social policy researchers relates early age test scores of children to family background and uncovers important correlations.

Some of the work, like that on early childhood programs like Head Start (see the discussion in Currie, 2001), is of an experimental nature in that some children participate in a program whereas others do not. The analysis thus compares a 'treatment' group (those in the program) with a 'control' group (those not in the program) to evaluate the impact of the program.

It is clear from this literature that test score gaps emerge across children from different family backgrounds at early ages. For example, a recent review by Meyers *et al.* (2004) documents sizable disparities in pre-school enrollment between children from high and low education parental backgrounds. Evidence shows that early childhood education programs narrow test score gaps between ethnic minority children and whites in the United States (Currie, 2001); and that attendance at pre-school confers a cognitive advantage on children before they enter school (see Magnusson *et al.*, 2004, for the United States and Sammons *et al.*, 2002, for the United Kingdom).

Thus inequality in the cognitive and non-cognitive skills of individuals can be tracked to the early years and it can be argued that these early age skills are key drivers of subsequent economic and social success or failure (Cameron and Heckman, 2001; Heckman *et al.*, 2006). Significant gaps in cognitive and non-cognitive skills arise early on, even before school, and these gaps are strongly linked to social disadvantage and income inequalities.

## Compulsory Education

Test score gaps evident in the early years continue to develop and widen in the school years. In academic work and in the policy arena the links between education experiences and measures of childhood disadvantage have long been recognized. Empirical research has often linked observable measures of educational achievement to various aspects of disadvantage. These include (among others): child poverty; parental education and income; parental attitudes; neighborhood factors. There is a by now sizable body of evidence (Currie, 1995; Gregg and Machin, 1999, 2001; Mayer, 1997) that educational achievement is significantly lower for children from disadvantaged backgrounds. This includes a higher probability of dropping out of school, lower qualification attainment, and lower test scores at various ages through the school years. These gaps are present even in studies that condition on the early age (pre-school or at or near school starting ages) test scores of children.

There is a lot of evidence showing that children from relatively disadvantaged backgrounds do worse in terms of educational attainment through the school years or in terms of education levels achieved at the compulsory school-leaving age. Much of this comes from studies based upon single countries. However, with some of the data sources on international test scores of school-age children one can draw some

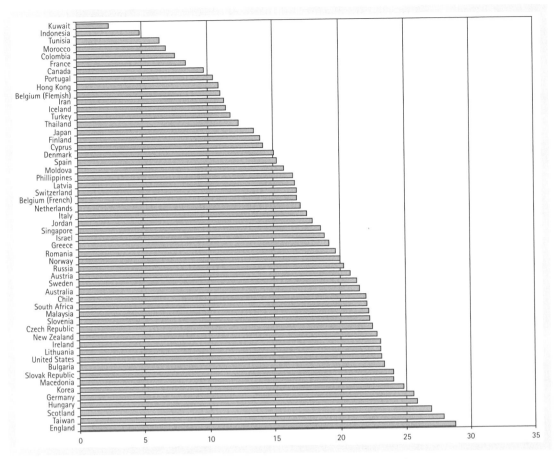

**Fig. 17.1. Estimated effects of family background on students' test scores across countries**

*Notes*: Family background effects are based on reported measures of the number of books at home; test scores are average maths and science scores from TIMSS. The family background effects are estimated from statistical regressions explaining standardized test scores based on the number of books at home. As standardized test scores have an international standard deviation of 100, these effects can be interpreted as percentages of an international standard deviation by which test achievement increases if the number of books is raised by one category. The authors validate these estimates by also looking at other measures of family background from the 2001 Progress in International Reading Literacy Survey (PIRLS).

*Source*: Schuetz *et al.* (2005).

international comparisons to illustrate the almost universal strong links between pupil achievement and family background. Figure 17.1 shows family background effects on test scores from an interesting recent paper by Schuetz *et al.* (2005). This uses cross-country data from the Third International Mathematics and Science Study (TIMSS) from 1995 and its repeat survey from 1999. In 53 out of 54 countries the family background effect (in this study measured by the number of books at home[1]) is statistically significant and the implied gaps in test scores are large. Moreover, the estimates are internationally comparable and show very large family background effects in some countries. The largest family background effects are in England and, whilst all show an important family background gradient, there is a fairly wide range of estimates.[2]

## Post-Compulsory Education

Inequality and social disadvantage continue to matter for the phase of post-compulsory education, where it is evident that educational inequalities linked to family background tend to persist and become larger (Feinstein, 2004). The like-lihood of staying on after the compulsory school-leaving age is linked to family background and social disadvantage in many countries. Since participation in higher education enhances life chances and success as an adult, this compounds the already wide inequalities linked to social disadvantage that arise in the childhood years.

There are a range of issues pertaining to the way in which inequality and disadvantage lower the probability of participating in higher education (or push people from such backgrounds into the lower quality end of the spectrum). Work looking at participation in higher education, or more specifically university attendance, has shown that people from lower income backgrounds have significantly lower participation rates (two recent examples are Blanden and Gregg, 2004, for the United Kingdom; and Black and Sufi, 2002, for the United States). Whilst there are problems of comparability across countries, owing to data differences and to the different nature of higher education systems, Figure 17.2 shows difference in participation in tertiary education by parents' level of education for a range of countries. In all of them there are sizable gaps between participation rates of those from families with parents who themselves have tertiary levels of education as compared to parents with lower education levels.

Another feature of post-compulsory education and its connection to social disadvantage is that people from poorer backgrounds who do participate tend to enrol on courses, or in institutions, that yield lower economic and social benefits. This includes a lower likelihood of studying at 'elite' universities (Chevalier and Conlon, 2003) and also a higher probability of studying for a vocational qualification rather than an academic qualification (Conlon, 2002).

---

[1]  One may worry about the use of the 'books at home' variable as a measure of family background. The authors spend a long time discussing this in their paper, most importantly showing results from a different data source which contains income and the books at home variable, albeit for a smaller sample of countries. Reassuringly they show similar results for this reduced sample whether one uses income or books at home.

[2]  Of course, some of the relative positions may well be sensitive to the use of TIMSS data as compared to other survey data on pupil achievement.

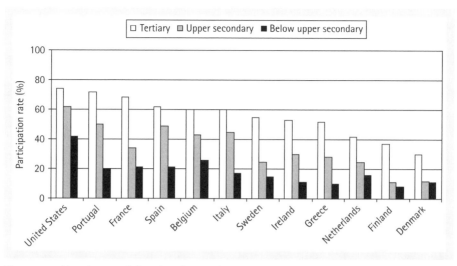

**Fig. 17.2. Youths participating in tertiary education by educational attainment of their parents, 1994–1995**

*Note*: Participation rates of 18–24-year-olds.
*Source*: EURYDICE (1997).

## Adult Education and Lifelong Learning

Social disadvantages experienced earlier in life also impact strongly on adult life chances (Bynner and Feinstein, 2004). This is clearly bad for those affected individuals and for national prosperity, and research has shown that education is an important factor in explaining why basic skills deficiencies (like poor literacy and numeracy skills) arise. Studying the characteristics of the low basic skills group amongst the adult population shows them very clearly to be those who left the school system at the compulsory school-leaving age, who typically have no educational qualifications, and who come from poorer and more disadvantaged social backgrounds.

Figure 17.3 shows rates of attendance in adult education by educational attainment. Participation rates are higher in all countries for the most educated. The lifelong learning process evidently is biased towards those that already have more education, and this has a reinforcing effect on the educational inequalities. Without exception, even in the Scandinavian countries where the adult education and training gap is narrower by education group, there seems less scope to alleviate problems linked to low educational levels and/or poor basic skills that emerge from the adult education system.

These cross-country differences also raise the question of academic versus vocational education and training. Some research (e.g. Hanushek and Woessmann, 2006) shows that countries which track individuals into academic or vocational

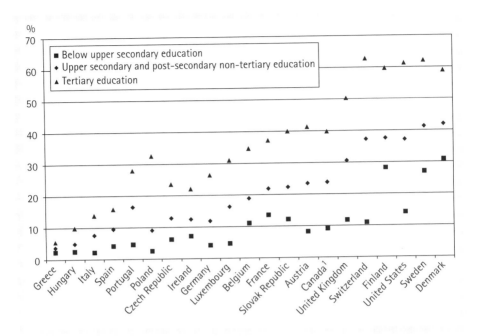

**Fig. 17.3. Participation rate in non-formal job-related continuing education and training for the labor force, 25–64, by level of educational attainment, 2003**

*Notes:* Countries are ranked, from left to right, in ascending order of the participation rates in non-formal continuous education and training, for all levels of education, within a 12-month period.
[1] Data refer to 2002.
*Source:* OECD (2005). *Education at a Glance.* Paris.

routes at earlier ages have higher levels of educational inequality.[3] This tends to confirm the importance of the nature of educational systems and that the way in which they are differently organized across countries has implications for educational inequality. It is evident that education policy differences from the different organization of education systems matters in this regard. For example, the presence of vocational training systems can impact upon educational inequalities by deterring individuals on the vocational track from participating in higher education (see, *inter alia*, Hillmert and Jacob, 2002).

## Summary

The persistence of skills problems through adult life is not only bad news for the individuals concerned (in terms of unemployment, deprivation, and so on) but also for their families, their children's educational performance, and for the

---

[3] Hanushek and Woessmann (2006) study the dispersion of PISA educational attainment and how that varies by age of tracking/selection.

communities in which they live. Inequality and social disadvantage clearly have much wider and far-reaching implications since cycles of disadvantage can run across generations and through families and communities. Some of the discussion here, on education at different ages acting as a transmission mechanism that underpins the persistence of intergenerational inequalities, links closely to Chapter 20 on intergenerational mobility (by Björklund and Jäntti).

There is also the highly relevant question about whether it is low income/poverty or inequality of the whole distribution which matters for this discussion. This certainly matters for the policy implications one might wish to draw. However, general conclusions from research in this area are currently not forthcoming enough to draw strong conclusions on this question. It nonetheless remains an important research question to inform the scope that social policy has to affect educational opportunities and the distribution of educational achievement. This is especially marked for the important question of why poor households in many countries tend to 'under-invest' in education.

# 3. WAGES AND EDUCATION

What about the economic impact of education? It is well established that more education is associated with higher wages and better job prospects. Much of the empirical work in this area has its roots in some of the highly influential and path-breaking work done in the economics of education field by American economists in the 1960s. During this period a number of highly influential economists (like Becker, 1964; Mincer, 1958; and Schultz, 1961, 1963) conducted major, innovative research applying economics to education questions.[4] This included the development of human capital theory, work on general versus specific training and the derivation of the earnings function that relates labor market earnings to schooling levels.

## Earnings Functions

The earnings function has become an almost ubiquitous tool used by labor economists (and others). Mincer's (1958, 1974) highly influential work developed the earnings function (the Mincer earnings equation) that relates log(earnings) to years

---

[4] Of course, one can trace economic questions to do with education and earnings potential back to well before this time (e.g. the potential importance of education for raising the productive capacity of society was raised by Adam Smith in *The Wealth of Nations* in 1776). See the discussion of how the economics of education once again became a thriving research field in the recent past in Machin (2008).

Table 17.1. Earnings differentials between tertiary education and post-secondary non-tertiary levels of education (aged 30–44, men and women, in 2005)

| Country | Earnings differentials |
| --- | --- |
| Australia | 0.34 |
| Austria | 0.48 |
| Belgium | 0.34 |
| Denmark | 0.22 |
| Finland | 0.38 |
| France | 0.48 |
| Germany | 0.50 |
| Ireland | 0.59 |
| Italy | 0.43 |
| Korea | 0.48 |
| The Netherlands | 0.47 |
| Spain | 0.30 |
| Sweden | 0.22 |
| UK | 0.61 |
| USA | 0.75 |

Source: OECD (2007). *Education at a Glance*. Paris.

of schooling and experience and is one of the most widely used tools amongst empirical economists. It lies at the cornerstone of a vast array of empirical research done in many areas of economics.[5] The typical specification is:

$$\log w = a + bS + c_1 X + c_2 X^2 + u$$

where w is earnings, S measures schooling, X denotes years of experience, and u is a random error term.

Earnings equations of this form almost invariably show a monetary 'return' to schooling (i.e. b is estimated to be positive). Thus people who acquire more education get paid more (and get better jobs). This is, of course, a return that is private to the individual making the investment.

Table 17.1 shows OECD evidence on educational wage differentials that accrue to people with tertiary education levels relative to post-secondary non-tertiary levels in 15 countries. The existence of sizable gaps in earnings is seen for all countries.

---

[5] This includes many micro-based empirical applications that focus on the core elements of the Mincer equation, like Card's (1999) discussion of a large body of work on the causal impact of education on earnings, or the work on wage returns to experience or job tenure (see, *inter alia*, Jacobson *et al.*, 1993; Topel, 1991; Angrist, 1990; or Dustmann and Meghir, 2005). Other work relies upon extended or augmented Mincerian equations to look at the determinants of individual earning power. There are numerous examples of this, like work on gender wage discrimination (see Altonji and Blank, 1999) or the huge literature on estimating union non-union wage differentials (see Lewis, 1986).

According to these earnings differentials, acquisition of more education leads to significantly higher earnings.


## Causality

Many commentators have noted that interpretation of positive earnings differentials for the more educated as a causal impact of education may not be correct due to differential selection into higher education groups by more able individuals and those from higher income families (as discussed in Section 2). As such it may be that higher ability/income people select into education more so that the positive coefficient on education in a wage equation is actually upward biased. The existence of ability bias of this form has been studied in detail, from the highly influential work of Griliches (1977) onwards, and confirmed in research since empirically it is the case that the education coefficient falls once ability proxies are included (this is because ability is positively correlated with both earnings and education).

On the other hand, one may think that the education variable included in the earnings function may not be measured perfectly. This causes a downward bias in the estimated coefficient of education variables in earnings equations. Card (1999, 2001) studies the respective roles of ability bias and measurement error in affecting estimates of the earnings impact of education. He very carefully considers just what particular estimates of education effects are picking up and compares and contrasts the standard least squares estimates with those from instrumental variable estimation approaches that should (under the assumption that the instruments are legitimate) purge endogeneity and measurement error bias.

In the recent literature addressing these issues, a number of what Card (2001) refers to as 'supply-side' instruments are used to identify the causal impact of education.[6] Table 17.2 summarizes some of the key papers in the field: in all cases the 'causal' impacts, where researchers try and ensure variations in education are driven by factors that do not directly impact on wages, are above the 'basic' uncorrected differentials. Moreover, differences between the basic and causal returns are of similar magnitudes for the studies considered in the table (they, of course, differ across studies owing to different data, different countries, and so on). Hence, there is robust cross-country evidence that the more educated get higher monetary rewards in the labor market.

From this, we can have a degree of confidence that education is causally associated with higher earnings. Moreover, it seems that the simple least squares

---

[6] Examples are changes in compulsory school leaving laws and differences in the accessibility of schools. Formally these enter an education equation, but not the earnings equation, and so their impact on earnings is assumed to operate only through education acquisition.

Table 17.2. Evidence on the causal impact of education on earnings

| Study | Data | Basic return | Causal return | Means to generate causal estimate |
|---|---|---|---|---|
| Angrist and Krueger (1991) | US Census | 5–7% | 6–11% | Variations in years of education generated by different quarter of birth |
| Card (1995) | 1966 Cohort of Young Men, United States | 7% | 13% | Variation in years of education from proximity to college when growing up |
| Conneely and Uusitalo (1997) | Finnish men in the army in 1982 | 8% | 11% | Variation in years of education from proximity to college when growing up |
| Harmon and Walker (1995) | Family Expenditure Survey, United Kingdom | 6% | 15% | Variation in education induced by raising of compulsory school leaving age |
| Ashenfelter and Rouse (1998) | 1991–93 Princeton Twins Survey | 7% | 9% | Variation in education within twin pairs |
| Miller et al. (1995) | Australian Twins Register | 3% | 5% | Variation in education within twin pairs |

Note: Examples taken from Card's (1999) review.

regressions which estimate human capital earnings functions give a pretty good idea of how big the education effects on earnings actually are. From this it seems reasonable to conclude that there is a significant and sizable average rate of return to education.

## Variations over Observed Characteristics

There are significant variations around the average return to education. This can be linked to a whole host of observable characteristics. Table 17.1 has already shown differences across countries. Table 17.3 shows further examples based on UK and US data (the 2000 US Census and the 2007 UK Labour Force Survey), reporting estimated educational differentials across gender and age groups. Clearly there are variations in estimated earnings returns across demographics.

Education-related differentials also vary significantly for different aspects of study. For example, different degree subjects pay off to varying degrees in the labor market. Table 17.4 shows subject of degree differentials for the United Kingdom and United States, broken down by gender. It is evident that, amongst graduates, there are systematic variations in wage differentials for different types of graduate investments.

Table 17.3. Variations in weekly earnings differentials—demographics

|  | UK Labour Force Survey, 2007 Degree/A Levels differentials | US Census, 2000 College (16 years)/High School (12 years) differentials |
|---|---|---|
| All | 0.419 (0.014) | 0.601 (0.001) |
| Men | 0.417 (0.018) | 0.564 (0.001) |
| Women | 0.425 (0.023) | 0.630 (0.001) |
| Men < 40 | 0.352 (0.026) | 0.492 (0.002) |
| Men ≥ 40 | 0.467 (0.026) | 0.607 (0.002) |
| Women < 40 | 0.342 (0.029) | 0.587 (0.002) |
| Women ≥ 40 | 0.526 (0.039) | 0.636 (0.002) |

Notes: Standard errors in parentheses. Sample sizes: UK—all 5,017, men 3,041, women 1,976, men < 40 1,377, men ≥ 40 1,664, women < 40 1,210, women ≥ 40 766; USA—all 3,278,162, men 1,754,414, women 1,523,748, men < 40 835,688, men ≥ 40 918,726, women < 40 708,625, women ≥ 40 815,123.

A sizable, but sometimes misleading literature, also discusses over- and under-education. This is the idea that there is some degree of mismatch between people's jobs and their education levels: 'over' education means people have too much education (e.g. graduates doing non-graduate jobs) and 'under' education the opposite. Inclusion of indicators for these variables into earnings equations does, for example, show a penalty for over-education. That is to say, in the case of graduates doing non-graduate jobs, the earnings return to being a graduate is lower for those in non-graduate jobs than for those matched to graduate jobs. The problem here is that the over-education variable is almost certainly proxying for unobserved characteristics of individuals and their educational qualifications: for example, ability, degree subject, and institution where a degree was obtained from.

Table 17.4. Variations in graduate earnings differentials (2000)—degree subject

|  | Differentials (Relative to arts degree) | | |
|---|---|---|---|
|  | Science/Engineering/ Technology | Social Science | Rest/Combined (incl. Medicine, Education) |
| UK men | 0.25 | 0.21 | 0.17 |
| UK women | 0.16 | 0.10 | 0.18 |
| US men | 0.35 | 0.34 | 0.16 |
| US women | 0.18 | 0.14 | 0.02 |

Notes: Based on UK General Household Survey, US National Survey of College Graduates. From Machin and Puhani (2006). Sample sizes: UK men 2,868, UK women 1,881, US men 36,557, US women 24,300.

Table 17.5. Quantile regression estimates (0.1, 0.5, 0.9 quantiles)

|  | UK Labour Force Survey, 2007 Degree/A Levels differentials | US Census, 2000 College (16 years)/High School (12 years) differentials |
|---|---|---|
| Men, 0.1 | 0.308 (0.029) | 0.421 (0.002) |
| Men, 0.5 | 0.465 (0.019) | 0.539 (0.001) |
| Men, 0.9 | 0.437 (0.034) | 0.739 (0.001) |
| Women, 0.1 | 0.412 (0.029) | 0.510 (0.003) |
| Women, 0.5 | 0.438 (0.038) | 0.669 (0.001) |
| Women, 0.9 | 0.392 (0.038) | 0.668 (0.001) |

Notes: As for Table 17.3.

## Variation over Unobserved Characteristics—Heterogeneous Returns

It is clear that the rather simple earnings functions that are used to identify earnings gaps between people with differing levels of education and schooling do not contain the full set of variables that, in the real world, relate to earnings potential. However, rather than looking at average differentials that accrue to education, or returns to observable characteristics, we can also consider other unobserved factors across the earnings and education distribution. Quantile regressions are increasingly being used to look at effects at different quantiles of the distribution rather than at the average (see e.g. Angrist et al., 2006, or Autor et al., 2008). This can help us understand more about effects of education on the distribution of earnings, rather than just at the average.

Some examples are given in Table 17.5 for the US Census and UK Labour Force Survey data considered above. They show education coefficients for quantile regressions at the 10th, 50th, and 90th quantiles of the distribution. The effects are evidently of different magnitude at these three quantiles in both cases. In particular, for both countries the impact of education tends to be lower at the bottom end of the distribution, showing a lower return to education amongst lower earners (especially for men). In the United States returns for men at the top are also higher. Angrist et al. (2006) note this in their study of US Census data for 1980, 1990, and 2000 showing there to be much more heterogeneous returns to schooling in 2000, and noting that this increased variation in schooling returns is one of the features of rising US wage inequality.

## Social Outcomes

Returns to individuals in terms of higher wages are only one part of the story in which education affects inequality. Investment in education can clearly impact on other outcomes, and generate externalities that can cause the private and social returns to diverge from one another. One way of thinking about this is to consider the impact of education on other non-wage economic and social outcomes.

Social science researchers have considered the wider benefits of education by studying connections between education and outcomes like health, crime, civic engagement, and intergenerational effects on children's outcomes. There is evidence of important externalities, in that education significantly improves health outcomes (Grossman and Kaestner, 1997; Kitagawa and Hauser, 1973; Lleras-Muney, 2005), is associated with lower crime levels (Lochner and Moretti, 2004; Feinstein and Sabates, 2005; Machin and Vujic, 2005), and enhances the extent of civic engagement and participation (Brehm and Rahn, 1997; Bynner and Egerton, 2001; Bynner and Parsons, 1997; Dee, 2004). Moreover, there are important intergenerational effects of education of adults on the education of their children (Black, Devereux and Salvanes, 2005).

# 4. CHANGES IN WAGE INEQUALITY AND EDUCATION

One feature of contemporary society is that more people acquire higher educational qualifications than did in the past. For example, Figure 17.4 shows recent OECD numbers (from 2005) on the percentage of the 25–34 and 45–54 populations of a number of countries who have attained tertiary education. In almost all countries there is a larger percentage for the 25–34 year olds, and often by some distance.

It turns out that this has had important implications for labor market inequality and how it has evolved over time, since education now matters more for labor market outcomes than it did in the past.[7] I consider these links between education changes and changes in inequality in this section.

## Increases in Education Supply and Demand and Relative Wages

According to standard market economics it is normally thought that, starting from a position where the demand and supply are perfectly equalized (in a competitive market), a boost in the supply of graduates should, *ceteris paribus*,

---

[7] The evidence from recent data is that the advantage provided by education has been increasing over time. Of course, the opposite has occurred in other past periods, like the 1970s in the UK or USA where the wage advantage from higher education actually fell in the face of rapid supply increases.

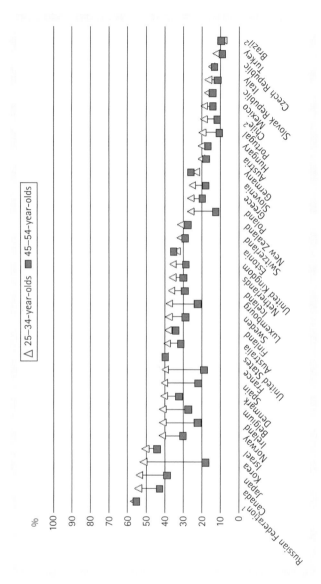

Fig. 17.4. International education levels, 2005

Notes: [1] Year of reference 2003.
[2] Year of reference 2004.
Countries are ranked in descending order of the percentage of 25–34-year-olds who have attained tertiary education.
Source: OECD (2007). Education at a Glance. Paris.

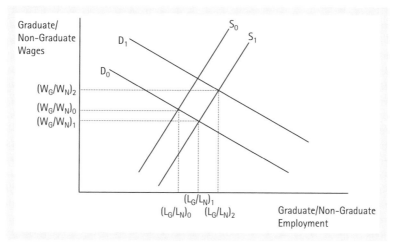

**Fig. 17.5. Relative supply–demand framework**

lead to a reduction in the relative wage between graduates and non-graduates because employers have a wider range of similarly qualified people to choose from.

To see this, consider Figure 17.5 which shows a labor market with two types of labor—graduates (G) and non-graduates (N). The wages of graduates and non-graduates are denoted by $W_G$ and $W_N$, and their employment levels are respectively $L_G$ and $L_N$. In the usual economic model we have an initial equilibrium at the intersection of the initial relative demand and supply curves, $D_0$ and $S_0$ respectively, with associated relative wages $(W_G/W_N)_0$ and relative employment $(L_G/L_N)_0$. The clear prediction from this model is that, if an increase in the supply of graduates occurs, and so the supply curve shifts to the right (from $S_0$ to $S_1$) then the relative employment rate rises (to $(L_G/L_N)_1$) and the relative wage falls. Thus the supply shock dampens down the relative wage of graduates.

However, reductions in relative wages need not occur if demand for graduates is also rising and, in fact, they could rise if relative demand outpaces relative supply. If, for whatever reason, employers demand more tertiary graduates, then the expansion may not cause a fall in the wage premium that graduates receive. In fact, if demand is increasing faster than supply, the wage premium can increase, that is, although the number of graduates is rising, graduate-level jobs are increasing at a faster rate and so are commensurate with a higher relative wage.

Figure 17.5 shows this, keeping the relative supply curve fixed (schedule $S_1$) but allowing for such a relative demand shift by moving the demand curve to the right (from $D_0$ to $D_1$). In this case the relative demand shift outweighs the supply shift and the relative wage rises above the initial level to relative wage level $(W_G/W_N)_2$. In this example, both the relative wages and employment levels of tertiary graduates are higher after the expansion. An intuitive way of thinking about this

Table 17.6. Aggregate trends in graduate/non-graduate employment and wages, UK and USA

| | UK | | USA | |
|---|---|---|---|---|
| | % Graduate share of employment | Relative weekly wage (full-time) | % Graduate share of employment | Relative weekly wage (full-time) |
| 1980 | 5.0 | 1.48 | 20.8 | 1.41 |
| 1985 | 9.8 | 1.50 | 24.2 | 1.53 |
| 1990 | 10.2 | 1.60 | 25.7 | 1.60 |
| 1995 | 14.0 | 1.60 | 31.8 | 1.65 |
| 2000 | 17.2 | 1.64 | 31.8 | 1.69 |
| 2004 | 21.0 | 1.64 | 34.2 | 1.66 |
| Changes: | | | | |
| 1980–2004 | 16.0 | .16 | 13.4 | .25 |
| 1980–1990 | 5.2 | .12 | 4.9 | .19 |
| 1990–2000 | 7.0 | .04 | 6.1 | .09 |
| 2000–2004 | 3.8 | .00 | 2.4 | −.02 |

*Notes*: UK—derived from General Household Survey (GHS) and Labour Force Survey (LFS); USA—derived from Current Population Survey data. UK—updated from Machin and Vignoles (2005). Sample is all people aged 18–64 in work and earning, except for relative wages which are defined for full-time workers. The relative wage ratios are derived from coefficient estimates on a graduate dummy variable in semi-log earnings equations controlling for age, age squared, and gender (they are the exponent of the coefficient on the graduate dummy).

supply–demand approach is in terms of an economic model where the wages and employment of graduates and non-graduates are the outcomes of a race between supply and demand. That is, demand and supply curves are shifting and the question is which curve has moved the most.

The simple supply–demand framework we have just set out has been widely used in academic research on changing labor market inequality (see Katz and Murphy, 1992, for a more formal derivation and the earlier discussion in Freeman, 1976). In fact, large increases in the demand for graduates are the only way to rationalize constant (or increasing) wage premiums that have been observed in the face of the expansion of tertiary education in many countries. For example, much work has been done to understand what lies behind the increase in the demand for educated workers in the United States and the United Kingdom. In both countries, wage premia have risen (or remained constant—in more recent years) despite a massive expansion in the supply of graduates with a tertiary education.

In Table 17.6, for example, the percentage of graduates grew from 21 percent in 1980 to 34 percent in 2004 in the United States.[8] The equivalent figures from the United Kingdom were even more dramatic—the growth in graduates was from 5 to 21 percent over the same time period. But at the same time the relative wages of

---

[8]  In the US numbers the graduate measure is having a bachelor's degree or higher (i.e. excluding people with some college education who do not get a degree).

graduates have risen (very fast in the 1980s, but with no fall in the 1990s and 2000s despite the supply changes). The only way to reconcile these facts in the standard model is through an outward shift in the relative demand curve for graduates. Put differently, the recent patterns of change showing simultaneously rising relative wages and relative employment of graduates mean that the relative demand for graduates has outstripped the relative supply, despite the latter rising rapidly.

This discussion also makes it clear that adjustment to changing conditions affecting demand and supply can be reflected in employment or unemployment probabilities as well as in wages. In fact, if there are wage rigidities (created e.g. by labor market institutions), adjustment through employment may occur instead of adjustment through wages (Nickell and Bell, 1995). It has been hypothesized that the fall in the relative demand for unskilled labor manifests itself in Anglophone countries as a rise in wage inequality whereas in some countries of continental Europe (e.g. Germany), it is reflected in the rise of unemployment (the 'Krugman hypothesis', Krugman, 1994). Some evidence to support the hypothesis has been found for Germany (Puhani, 2003). This argument is also made by Goux and Maurin (1997) in relation to France.

The evidence thus suggests that, as education supply has risen education demand has risen faster, so that the relative wages of the more educated have gone up, or the relative employment rates of the more educated have risen, or in some countries both have occurred. In the latter case, as in the United Kingdom and United States, rising educational wage differentials have been important aspects of rising wage inequalities (Katz and Autor, 1999).

## Explanations of Relative Demand Shifts

A key question has been to ask what caused the relative demand shift in favor of more educated workers. The weight of the evidence is behind 'skill biased technology change' (sbtc) as the key driver. There is good evidence for the importance of sbtc internationally as opposed to competing explanations such as increased globalization (Berman *et al.*, 1998; Katz and Autor, 1999; Machin and Van Reenen, 2008).

The skill-biased technology change hypothesis is founded upon the notion that employers' demand for more skilled workers has been shaped by the kinds of new technologies that are permeating into modern workplaces. The critical idea is that these new technologies lead to higher productivity, but that only some workers possess the necessary skills to use them. As such, employers are prepared to increase the wages of the skilled workforce who are complements with the new technology. But at the same time less skilled workers do not possess enough skills to operate the new technologies and their wages are lowered or they lose their jobs. Relative wages and/or employment of the more skilled therefore rise.

There is now abundant empirical evidence that suggests that sbtc is an important and international phenomenon (e.g. see the survey in Bond and Van Reenen, 2006). One (frequently used) way in which researchers have formally tested this is to estimate cost-share equations that relate changes in the skilled wage bill/employment share in a given industry to observable measures of technology. A typical specification (Berman et al., 1994; Machin and Van Reenen, 1998), measured for industry j in year t, is:

$$\Delta(\text{Skilled wage bill share})_{jt} = \alpha + \beta\Delta \log(\text{Capital}_{jt}) + \delta\Delta \log(\text{Output}_{jt})$$
$$+ \phi \, \text{TECH}_{jt} + \varepsilon_{jt} \tag{1}$$

where this cost-share equation can be generated from a translog cost function with two labor inputs (skilled and unskilled) and assuming capital to be a quasi-fixed factor. The focus in these equations then becomes whether the coefficient $\phi$ on the technology indicator TECH is estimated to be positive.

Table 17.7 summarizes the US and UK estimates of $\phi$. It is clear that for a range of time periods, different levels of aggregation, and technology measures, there exists a positive association between industry shifts in skilled wage bill or employment shares and observable technology measures. Put differently, it appears to be the technologically more advanced industries where one has seen faster increases in the relative demand for skilled workers. This has been taken in some quarters as evidence in line with the hypothesis that skill-biased technology changes lie behind the demand shifts favoring relatively skilled and more educated workers.

There are several other sources of evidence on sbtc. Berman et al. (1998) report evidence of faster skill demand shifts occurring in the same sorts of industries in different countries and one may view this as informing the sbtc hypothesis (to the extent that similar industries in different countries utilize similar technologies). A less used alternative to test for sbtc is to regress the adoption of technologies on skill prices (i.e. when skilled workers wages rise relative to unskilled workers this should depress the incentive to adopt new technologies) or skilled labor supply—some evidence for this method is in Caroli and Van Reenen (2001) and Doms and Lewis (2006) and also supports sbtc. A third method is to directly estimate the production function or the cost function underlying the factor demand equation given above. This has also tended to uncover evidence of skill-technology complementarity (e.g. Bresnahan et al., 2002). Finally some authors have directly regressed individual wages on computer use or controlling for other factors (e.g. Krueger, 1993). This is a rather unsatisfactory test of sbtc, however, as computers are likely to be allocated to more productive workers as has been found by several studies (Chennells and Van Reenen, 1997; DiNardo and Pischke, 1997). This method therefore conflates selection and sbtc and does not offer any causal evidence.

This literature has not been without controversy. Indeed, the wider consequences for general patterns of change in wage inequality are still being discussed and

Table 17.7. Regression correlations of skill demand changes and technology measures

| Study | Unit of analysis | Time period | Skill demand measure | Technology measure | Estimate of $\phi$ (standard error) | Controls |
|---|---|---|---|---|---|---|
| Autor et al. (1998) | 140 US industries | 1990–96 1980–90 1970–80 1960–70 | College wage bill share | Industry computer use (1984–93) | .289 (.081) .147 (.046) .127 (.031) .071 (.025) | None |
| | 123 US industries | 1960–90 | | Computer investment per FTE | .130 (.027) | Change in log(capital/labor), decade dummies |
| Berman et al. (1994) | 450 US manufacturing industries | 1959–89 | Non-production wage bill share | Computer investment/ investment | .027 (.007) | Change in log(capital/output), Change in log(output) |
| | 143 US manufacturing industries | 1979–87 | Non-production wage bill share | Computer investment/ investment R&D/Sales | .028 (.006) .097 (.021) | Change in log(plant/output), Change in log(equipment/output), Change in log(output) |
| Machin (1996) | 16 UK manufacturing industries | 1982–89 | Non-production wage bill share | R&D/Sales | .065 (.026) | Change in log(capital), Change in log(real sales), 1 digit industry dummies |
| | 16 UK manufacturing industries | 1980–85 | | Innovation Count from 1970s | .092 (.053) | |
| | 398 British workplaces | 1984–90 | Managers, senior technical and professional employment share | Micro computers introduced | .044 (.022) | Dummy for employment decline, 1 digit industry dummies |
| Machin and Van Reenen (1998) | 15 UK manufacturing industries | 1973–89 | Non-production wage bill share | R&D/Value added | .026 (.009) | Change in log(capital), Change in log(output), year dummies |

are high on the current research agenda (see e.g. the recent expansion of work revisiting the area in Autor *et al.*, 2006, 2008; Lemieux, 2006; and Machin and Van Reenen, 2008). Part of the controversy has been an objection by some (most notably Card and DiNardo, 2002) that skill-biased technology change cannot be the sole explanation for the observed changes.

## More Recent Developments

Due to this, there is now acknowledgment that the simple sbtc explanation needs to be expressed in a more nuanced manner. Most researchers still think sbtc has been the prime driver of the increased demand for education and skills seen over the longer term. However, recent patterns of changes in wage inequality and education returns have meant that the way in which technical change has an impact has had to be considered more carefully.

Autor *et al.* (2003) offer a more sophisticated version of the sbtc hypothesis, arguing that computerization reduces the demand for routine tasks (for manual and non-manual workers) but results in an increase in demand for analytic or non-routine skills. Thus routine non-manual tasks (e.g. clerical work) may be replaced by computers, whilst some non-routine tasks done by manual workers (like cleaning) are largely unaffected. Thus one sees increased demand for workers with the skills and capabilities to do jobs involving non-routine tasks. Again this shows that education that confers these skills on workers is likely to have a bigger payoff in the labor market and generate earnings returns.

# 5. CONCLUSIONS AND FURTHER RESEARCH

In this chapter I have considered connections between education and inequality. I have done so in three (related) stages, in turn examining education acquisition and inequality, the labor market returns to education, and the contributions of increased education demand and supply to patterns of change in wage inequalities. All of these show that education and inequality are closely linked. Under certain circumstances education can provide the route out of disadvantage by enabling people from poorer backgrounds to escape poverty. In other circumstances education reinforces already existent inequalities and can result in increased inequality. What is very clear from the evidence in this area is that education has been becoming more important for labor market outcomes and that those left behind with low levels of educational attainment are penalized more heavily in the modern labor market. An important methodological aspect of these findings is that the causal links between returns to education and education accumulation are quite well understood and, because of this, there is now a broad consensus on the issue of the existence of positive economic returns to education.

This makes consideration of the possible inequality effects of educational policies, at all stages of the education sequences, all the more important. There is a need to link the design of public policy to the observed trends in the skill structure of international labor markets. In particular, the worsening labor market position of less skilled workers stresses the need for government policy to devote resources towards increased and improved skill formation and education acquisition. Education and training policy need to be formulated with this in mind so as to ensure that future generations of workers entering the labor market (and current workers requiring training) possess the skills needed to utilize modern-day technologies in the workplace.

# REFERENCES

ALTONJI, J., and BLANK, R. 1999. 'Race and Gender in the Labor Market', in O. Ashenfelter and D. Card (eds.), *The Handbook of Labor Economics*. Amsterdam: Elsevier Science.

ANGRIST, J. 1990. 'Lifetime Earnings and the Vietnam Era Draft Lottery: Evidence from Social Security Administrative Records'. *American Economic Review*, 80: 313–36.

—— CHERNOZHOKOV, V., and FERNANDEZ-VAL, I. 2006. 'Quantile Regression under Misspecification, with an Application to the US Wage Structure'. *Econometrica*, 74: 539–63.

—— and KRUEGER, A. 1991. 'Does Compulsory School Attendance Affect Schooling and Earnings'. *American Economic Review*, 106: 979–1014.

ASHENFELTER, O., and ROUSE, C. 1998. 'Income, Schooling and Ability: Evidence from a new Sample of Twins'. *Quarterly Journal of Economics*, 113: 253–84.

AUTOR, D., KATZ, L., and KEARNEY, M. 2006. 'The Polarization of the U.S. Labor Market'. *American Economic Review*. Papers and Proceedings, 96: 189–94.

—— —— —— 2008. 'Trends in U.S. Wage Inequality: Re-Assessing the Revisionists'. *Review of Economics and Statistics*, 90: 300–23.

—— —— and KRUEGER, A. 1998. 'Computing Inequality: Have Computers Changed the Labor Market?' *Quarterly Journal of Economics*, 113: 1169–214.

—— LEVY, F., and MURNANE, R. 2003. 'The Skill Content of Recent Technological Change: An Empirical Investigation'. *Quarterly Journal of Economics*, 118: 1279–333.

BECKER, G. 1964. *Human Capital: A Theoretical Analysis with Special Reference to Education*. New York: Columbia University Press.

BERMAN, E., BOUND, J., and GRILICHES, Z. 1994. 'Changes in the Demand for Skilled Labor within U.S. Manufacturing Industries: Evidence from the Annual Survey of Manufacturing'. *Quarterly Journal of Economics*, 109: 367–98.

—— —— and MACHIN, S. 1998. 'Implications of Skill-Biased Technological Change: International Evidence'. *Quarterly Journal of Economics*, 113: 1245–80.

BLACK, S., DEVEREUX, P., and SALVANES, K. 2005. 'Why the Apple Doesn't Fall Far: Under-standing the Intergenerational Transmission of Education'. *American Economic Review*, 95: 437–49.

—— and SUFI, A. 2002. 'Who Goes to College? Differential College Enrolment by Race and Family Background'. NBER Working Paper 9310.

BLANDEN, J., and GREGG, P. 2004. 'Family Income and Educational Attainment: A Review of Approaches and Evidence for Britain'. *Oxford Review of Economic Policy*, 20: 245–63.

BOND, S., and J. VAN REENEN 2006. 'Micro-Econometric Models of Investment and Em-ployment', in J. Heckman and E. Leamer (eds.), *Handbook of Econometrics*, Volume VI. Amesterdam: North-Holland.

BREHM, J., and RAHN, W. 1997. 'Individual-Level Evidence for the Causes and Consequences of Social Capital'. *American Journal of Political Science*, 41: 999–1023.

BRESNAHAN, T., BRYNJOLFSSON, E., and HITT, L. 2002. 'Information Technology, Workplace Organization and the Demand for Skilled Labor: Firm-Level Evidence'. *Quarterly Journal of Economics*, 117: 339–76.

BYNNER, J., and EGERTON, M. 2001. *The Wider Benefits of Higher Education*. London: Higher Education Funding Council For England.

—— and FEINSTEIN, L. 2004. 'The Importance of Developmental Trajectories in Mid-Childhood: Effects on Adult Outcomes in the UK 1970 Birth Cohort'. *Child Development*, 75: 1329–39.

—— and PARSONS, S. 1997. *It Doesn't Get Any Better: The Impact of Poor Basic Skills on the Lives of 37 year Olds*. London: Basic Skills Agency.

CAMERON, S., and HECKMAN, J. 2001. 'The Dynamics of Educational Attainment for Black, Hispanic and White Males'. *Journal of Political Economy*, 109: 455–99.

CARD, D. 1995. 'Using Geographic Variation in College Proximity to Estimate the Return to Schooling', in L. Christofides, E. Grant, and R. Swidinsky (eds.), *Aspects of Labor Market Behaviour: Essays in Honour of John Vanderkamp*. Toronto: University of Toronto Press.

—— 1999. 'The Causal Effect of Education on Earnings', in O. Ashenfelter and D. Card (eds.), *Handbook of Labor Economics*, vol. 3. Amsterdam: Elsevier-North Holland.

—— 2001. 'Estimating the Return to Schooling: Progress on Some Persistent Problems'. *Econometrica*, 69: 1127–60.

—— and DiNARDO, J. 2002. 'Skill-Biased Technological Change and Rising Wage Inequality: Some Problems and Puzzles'. *Journal of Labor Economics*, 20: 733–83.

CAROLI, E., and VAN REENEN, J. 2001. 'Skill-Biased Organizational Change? Evidence from a Panel of British and French Establishments'. *Quarterly Journal of Economics*, 116: 1449–92.

CHENNELLS, L., and VAN REENEN, J. 1997. 'Technical Change and Earnings in British Estab-lishments'. *Economica*, 64: 587–604.

CHEVALIER, A., and CONLON, G. 2003. 'Does it Pay to Attend a Prestigious University?' Centre for the Economics of Education (CEE) Discussion Paper P0033.

CONLON, G. 2002. 'The Determinants of Undertaking Academic and Vocational Qualifica-tions in the UK'. Centre for the Economics of Education Discussion Paper 20.

CONNEELY, K., and UUSITALO, R. 1997. 'Estimating Heterogeneous Treatment Effects in the Becker Schooling Model'. Mimeo.

CURRIE, J. 1995. *Welfare and the Well-Being of Children*. Fundamentals of Pure and Applied Economics no. 59. Chur, Switzerland: Harwood Academic Publishers.

—— 2001. 'Early Childhood Intervention Programs: What do we Know?' *Journal of Eco-nomic Perspectives*, 15: 213–38.

DEE, T. 2004. 'Are there Civic Returns to Education?' *Journal of Public Economics*, 88: 1697–720.

DiNARDO, J., and PISCHKE, S. 1997. 'The Returns to Computer Use Revisited: Did Pencils Change the Wage Structure Too?' *Quarterly Journal of Economics*, 112: 291–303.

DOMS, M., and LEWIS, E. 2006. 'Labor Supply and Personal Computer Adoption'. Federal Reserve Bank of Philadelphia Research Paper 06-10, June.

DUSTMANN, C., and MEGHIR, C. 2005. 'Wages, Experience and Seniority'. *Review of Economic Studies*, 72: 77–108.

FEINSTEIN, L. 2004. 'Mobility in Pupils' Cognitive Attainment during School Life'. *Oxford Review of Economic Policy*, 20: 213–29.

—— and SABATES, R. 2005. 'Education and Youth Crime: Effects of Introducing the Education Maintenance Allowance Programme'. Centre for Research on the Wider Benefits of Learning Research Report no. 14.

FREEMAN, R. 1976. *The Overeducated American*. New York: Academic Press.

GOUX, D., and MAURIN, E. 1997. 'La Déclin del la Demande de Travail non Qualifié: Une Méthode d'Analyse Empirique et son Application au Cas de la France'. *Revue Économique*, 48(5): 1091–114.

GREGG, P., and MACHIN, S. 1999. 'Childhood Disadvantage and Success or Failure in the Labour Market', in D. Blanchflower and R. Freeman (eds.), *Youth Employment and Joblessness in Advanced Countries*. Cambridge, Mass: National Bureau of Economic Research.

—— —— 2001. 'The Relationship Between Childhood Experiences, Subsequent Educational Attainment and Adult Labour Market Performance', in K. Vleminckx and T. Smeeding (eds.), *Child Well Being in Modern Nations: What do we Know?* Bristol: Policy Press.

GRILICHES, Z. 1977. 'Estimating the Returns to Schooling: Some Econometric Problems'. *Econometrica*, 45: 1–22.

GROSSMAN, M., and KAESTNER, R. 1997. 'Effects of Education on Health', in J. Behrman and N. Stacey (eds.), *The Social Benefits of Education*. Ann Arbor: University of Michigan Press.

HANUSHEK, E., and WOESSMANN, L. 2006. 'Does Educational Tracking Affect Performance and Inequality? Differences-in-Differences Evidence across Countries'. *Economic Journal*, 116: C63–C76.

HARMON, C., and WALKER, I. 1995. 'Estimates of the Economic Return to Schooling for the United Kingdom'. *American Economic Review*, 85: 1278–86.

HECKMAN, J, STIXRUD, J., and URZUA, S. 2006. 'The Effects of Cognitive and Noncognitive Abilities on Labor Market Outcomes and Social Behavior'. *Journal of Labor Economics*, 24: 411–82.

HILLMERT, S., and JACOB, M. 2002. 'Social Inequality in Higher Education: Is Vocational Training a Pathway to or Leading From University'. *European Sociological Review*, 19: 319–34.

JACOBSON, L., LALONDE, R., and SULLIVAN, D. 1993. 'Earnings Losses of Displaced Workers'. *American Economic Review*, 83: 685–709.

KATZ, L., and AUTOR, D. 1999. 'Changes in the Wage Structure and Earnings Inequality', in O. Ashenfelter and D. Card (eds.), *Handbook of Labor Economics*, vol. 3. Amsterdam: North-Holland.

—— and MURPHY, K. 1992. 'Changes in Relative Wages, 1963–87: Supply and Demand Factors'. *Quarterly Journal of Economics*, 107: 35–78.

KITIGAWA, E., and HAUSER, P. 1973. *Differential Mortality in the United States: A Study in Socio-economic Epidemiology*. Cambridge: Harvard University Press.

KRUEGER, A. 1993. 'How Computers Have Changed the Wage Structure: Evidence From Microdata, 1984–1989', *Quarterly Journal of Economics*, 108: 33–60.

KRUGMAN, P. 1994. 'Past and Prospective Causes of High Unemployment'. *Economic Review*, Federal Reserve Bank of Kansas City, 23–43.

LEMIEUX, T. 2006. 'Increasing Residual Wage Inequality: Composition Effects, Noisy Data, or Rising Demand for Skill?' *American Economic Review*, 96: 461–98.

LEWIS, H. G. 1986. *Union Relative Wage Effects: A Survey*. Chicago: University of Chicago Press.

LLERAS-MUNEY, A. 2005. 'The Relationship between Education and Adult Mortality in the United States'. *Review of Economic Studies*, 72: 189–221.

LOCHNER, L., and MORETTI, E. 2004. 'The Effect of Education on Criminal Activity: Evidence from Prison Inmates, Arrests and Self-Reports'. *American Economic Review*, 94: 155–189.

MACHIN, S. 1996. 'Changes in the Relative Demand for Skills in the UK Labor Market', in A. Booth and D. Snower (eds.), *Acquiring Skills: Market Failures, Their Symptoms and Policy Responses*. Cambridge: Cambridge University Press.

—— 2003. 'Skill-Biased Technical Change in the New Economy', in D. Jones (ed.), *New Economy Handbook*. Amsterdam: Elsevier Academic Press.

—— 2005. 'Social Disadvantage and Education Experiences'. Report for OECD.

—— 2008. 'The New Economics of Education: Methods, Evidence and Policy'. *Journal of Population Economics*, 21: 1–19.

—— and MCNALLY, S. 2006. 'Tertiary Education Systems and Labour Markets'. Report for OECD.

—— and PUHANI, P. 2006. 'The Contribution of Degree Subject to the Gender Wage Gap for Graduates'. Mimeo. University College London.

—— and VAN REENEN, J. 1998. 'Technology and Changes in Skill Structure: Evidence From Seven OECD Countries'. *Quarterly Journal of Economics*, 113: 1215–44.

—— —— 2008. 'Changes in Wage Inequality', in S. Durlauf and L. Blume (eds.), *The New Palgrave Dictionary of Economics*, 2nd edn. London: Palgrave Macmillan.

—— and VIGNOLES, A. 2005. *What's The Good of Education?* Princeton: Princeton University Press.

—— and VUJIC, S. 2005. 'Crime and Education in the United Kingdom'. Draft paper, Centre for Economic Performance.

MAGNUSON, K., MEYERS, M., RUHM, C., and WALDFOGEL, J. 2004. 'Inequality in Preschool Education and School Readiness'. *American Educational Research Journal*, 41: 115–57.

MAYER, S. 1997. *What Money Can't Buy: Family Income and Children's Life Chances*. Cambridge, Mass.: Harvard University Press.

MEYERS, M., ROSENBAUM, D., RUHM, C., and WALDFOGEL, J. 2004. 'Inequality in Early Childhood Care and Education: What do we Know?' in K. Neckerman (ed.), *Social Inequality*. New York: Russell Sage Foundation.

MILLER, P., MULVEY, C., and MARTIN, N. 1995. 'What do Twins Studies Reveal about the Economic Returns to Schooling? A Comparison of Australian and US Findings'. *American Economic Review*, 85: 86–599.

MINCER, J. 1958. 'Investment in Human Capital and Personal Income Distribution'. *Journal of Political Economy*, 66: 281–302.

—— 1974. *Schooling, Experience and Earnings*. New York: Columbia University Press, NBER.

NICKELL, S., and BELL, B. 1995. 'The Collapse in Demand for the Unskilled and Unemployment Across the OECD'. *Oxford Review of Economic Policy*, 11: 40–62.

PUHANI, P. A. 2003. 'Transatlantic Differences in Labour Markets: Changes in Wage and Non-Employment Structures in the 1980s and the 1990s'. IZA Discussion Paper 764.

SAMMONS, P., SYLVA, K., MELHUISH, E., SIRAJ-BLATCHFORD, I., TAGGART, B., and ELLIOT, K. 2002. 'Measuring the Impact of Pre-School on Children's Cognitive Progress Over the Pre-School Period'. Technical Paper 8A. The Effective Provision of Pre-School Education Project, Institute of Education, London.

SCHUETZ, G., URSPRUNG, H., and WOESSMANN, L. 2005. 'Education Policy and Equality of Opportunity'. CESifo Working Paper 1518.

SCHULTZ, T. 1961. 'Investment in Human Capital'. *American Economic Review*, 51: 1–17.

—— 1963. *The Economic Value of Education*. New York: Columbia University Press.

TOPEL, R. 1991. 'Specific Capital, Mobility and Wages: Wages Rise with Job Seniority'. *Journal of Political Economy*, 99: 145–76.

# PART V

## THE DYNAMICS
## OF INEQUALITY

CHAPTER 18

# DEMOGRAPHIC TRANSFORMATION AND ECONOMIC INEQUALITY

## GARY BURTLESS

## 1. INTRODUCTION

DEMOGRAPHIC change has profoundly affected the population age structure and family living arrangements of most countries. In many industrialized nations cross-border migration has also produced a gradual transformation in the ethnic composition of the population. The shifts in the age structure have led to an outpouring of commentary by journalists, scholars, and policymakers on the affordability of public programs to support the aged. Many now believe that increases in the percentage of the population past retirement age will eventually impose intolerable burdens on workers and public budgets.

Shifts in demography will not only present challenges to public budgets, they can also affect income inequality and poverty. As the population past retirement age grows larger, an increasing percentage of adults will depend solely on pensions and public transfers for support. A shrinking percentage will derive most of their income from current labor earnings. Since pensions and transfers are typically lower than pre-retirement wages, the annual incomes of many families will be relatively small. To remain solvent, public pension systems in many countries must raise the benefit-claiming age, which will reduce or eliminate pensions for people who are in late middle age. Most affected workers will work a little longer, but those who cannot keep or find jobs may experience considerable income loss, pushing up inequality. Other changes in the composition of the population have had notable effects on inequality. Family structure in rich countries has changed enormously over the past half century. A growing percentage of non-elderly adults and children live in families with only a single adult head, where they are more likely to be poor than they would be in families headed by a married couple or by two adults in a marriage-like relationship. Smaller households have one important advantage. It takes fewer resources to support such households than it does to support households with more members. Thus, income requirements are smaller. Households with children that contain only one adult face formidable challenges in earning income, however. It is difficult for a single adult to combine simultaneously the duties of child caretaker and breadwinner. The result in most countries is that one-parent households experience higher poverty rates than two-parent households containing the same number of children.

This chapter assesses the impact of changing demography on inequality and poverty. This topic should be of broad interest, to both voters and scholars, because demographic shifts have both direct and indirect effects on the distribution of well-being. Many of these, including the impact of immigrants on the incomes of the native-born, are hotly debated in rich countries. This chapter first considers how household living arrangements affect personal economic well-being and its distribution across the population. If all members of the population lived alone and depended solely on their own earnings for support, the distribution of economic well-being would depend on the distribution of individual earnings. Most adults and children live as members of families, however. Since family members who live together pool their incomes, the distribution of well-being depends not only on the distribution of earnings but also on how members of the population are distributed in income-sharing family units. This depends in turn on the marriage and fertility choices of adults and on how those choices interact with the distribution of earnings and other sources of income.

Section 3 considers recent evidence on the inequality effects of demographic trends. One important trend already noted is the rise of cross-border migration with its attendant effects on native workers' wages and the ethnic composition of the population. Another is population ageing. This trend has been largely driven by the long-term decline of fertility in rich countries, a trend that affected the composition and income needs of younger households many decades before it increased the percentage of households headed by a retirement-age adult. A number of social trends have also affected the composition, incomes, and income needs of non-elderly households. These include delays in first marriage and first births, increases in the rate of divorce, rising female employment rates, and changes in the correlation of husbands' and wives' earnings. Several scholars have estimated the effects of these trends on inequality or poverty. The chapter concludes with a brief discussion of unresolved issues in assessing the impact of demography on trends in inequality.

# 2. HOUSEHOLD LIVING ARRANGEMENTS

Shifts in living arrangements can have a decisive influence on both the distribution and the trend in economic well-being. In a society that does not offer generous transfers, individuals who have poor income prospects will enjoy a more comfortable existence if they live and share incomes with relatives who have better prospects. A person who is too young, too old, or too disabled to work will enjoy higher consumption as a member of a family with a working breadwinner than as an unrelated individual who lives alone. The person with poor prospects obtains two advantages from living in a larger household. The obvious one is access to the income earned by a better-paid relative. Less obvious is the gain that occurs as a result of economies of scale in household consumption. Two people who live together need fewer kitchens, bathrooms, and household appliances than two people who live in separate dwellings.

The first advantage can be captured by assuming that all family members share equally in the income received by the family, regardless of the identity of the actual income recipient. The second advantage can be taken into account by calculating 'equivalent' incomes for households of different sizes. Economists estimate equivalent incomes by determining the change in expenditure that is required to hold living standards constant when a household gets larger or smaller.

Now consider two kinds of societies. In a society containing many large, income-sharing households, individuals with poor earnings prospects will be more likely to have access to the incomes of better-paid relatives and to enjoy economies of scale in consumption. In contrast, in an atomized society people with poor prospects are more likely to live alone and on very meager incomes. At the personal level, disparities in economic well-being are likely to be smaller in the first society than the second. Of course, the difference between the two societies hinges on the way in which individuals sort themselves into households. If people with poor income prospects have relatives who also have very poor prospects, living in income-sharing households will allow them to enjoy economies of scale in consumption but will not give them access to better earnings.

To see the impact of different household composition patterns when there is wide disparity in earnings prospects, consider the distribution of earned income

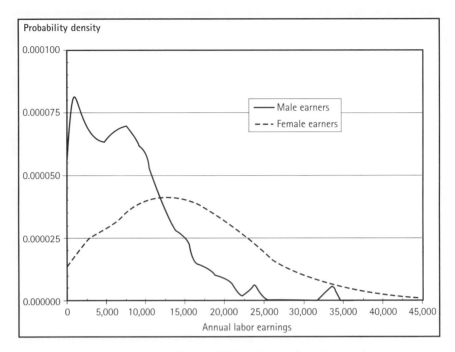

**Fig. 18.1. Probability distributions of US male and female earnings, 1979**

*Source*: Author's estimates based on March 1980 Current Population Survey.

among men and women. Figure 18.1 shows the 1979 distribution of labor earnings among US men and women who were between 20 and 64 in that year. The estimates include the earnings of people who worked even briefly or on part-time schedules during the year, but they exclude all the zero earnings amounts of adults who did not earn any labor income. The figure shows that men typically earned more wages and self-employment income than women. The average labor income of men was about 215 percent of the average for women. Standard measures of inequality show that earnings inequality was higher among women than it was among men. For example, the Gini coefficient of 1979 male earnings was 0.356; the Gini coefficient of female earnings was 0.418. Suppose there were an identical number of male and female earners. The Gini coefficient of the combined earnings distribution would be 0.427, indicating somewhat more inequality than in either the male or female earnings distributions when they are evaluated separately.

Now consider the impact of marriage on the distribution of economic well-being in this population. If each female earner sets up a household with one of the male earners, the economic well-being of the members of the new households will be affected by income sharing and economies of scale in consumption. Figure 18.2 shows the resulting distribution of personal equivalent income under two extreme assumptions regarding marriage partners. Under one assumption, each woman

Probability density

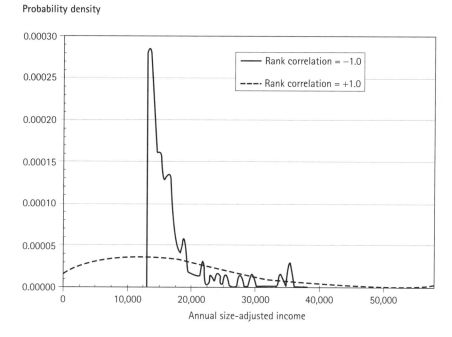

Annual size-adjusted income

**Fig. 18.2. Probability distribution of married–couple household income under alternative assumptions about rank correlation of husband and wife earnings**

*Source*: Author's simulation estimates as explained in text.

with a given rank in the female earnings distribution marries the man who holds the same rank in the male earnings distribution. That is, the highest female earner marries the highest male earner, the second highest female earner marries the second highest male earner, and so on. In this case, the rank correlation of husbands and wives in their respective earnings distributions is 1.0. Not surprisingly, this marriage pattern produces a very unequal distribution of income, indicated by the lower line in Figure 18.2. The Gini coefficient of household size-adjusted personal income is 0.376. This is more unequal than the distribution of male labor earnings (Gini = 0.356), but it is less unequal than the distribution of female earnings (Gini = 0.418) or of combined male and female earnings (Gini = 0.427). Pooling income improves average well-being because it increases the average level of equivalent income per person, and it equalizes well-being because by assumption it equalizes the incomes of husbands and wives who live together. If men and women both had identical earnings distributions and men and women paired off following the rule just described, there would of course be no effect on inequality.

Under an alternative assumption about marriage patterns among male and female earners, suppose the woman with the lowest earnings rank in the female distribution marries the man with the highest earnings rank in the male distribution,

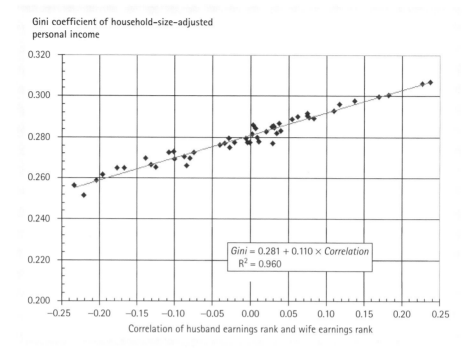

**Fig. 18.3. Simulated impact of husband–wife earnings rank correlation on household-size-adjusted personal income inequality**

*Source:* Author's simulation estimates as explained in text.

the woman with the second lowest rank marries the man with the second highest earnings rank, and so on. There is a perfect inverse correlation of male and female earnings ranks in married couple pairs. Not surprisingly, this marriage pattern dramatically reduces overall inequality (see the higher spiked line in Fig. 18.2). The Gini coefficient of household size-adjusted personal income is just 0.122.

It is improbable that men or women choose marriage partners based on either of the rules just described. Suppose men and women select marriage partners independently of the partner's earnings rank. The distribution of economic well-being would nonetheless be affected by the actual correlation of husbands' and wives' earnings. To see this, consider a population consisting of 100 men and 100 women who have the earnings distributions shown in Figure 18.1. Suppose each person marries and selects a marriage partner at random from among those of the opposite sex who are still unmarried. The expected correlation of the earnings ranks of marriage partners will be zero. Figure 18.3 shows the results of performing this experiment 50 times. Each point represents the combination of marriage partners' earnings rank correlation and the Gini coefficient of income inequality that results from a single repetition of the experiment. Across all 50 experiments the average correlation of husbands' and wives' earnings ranks is close to zero. The average Gini coefficient of household size-adjusted personal income is 0.280. Note that when the simulated matching of partners produces a higher correlation of spouse earnings, inequality is also higher. Even so, economic inequality is substantially lower when adults combine their earnings in married-couple households than when they live independently.

Not everyone marries or lives with an adult partner. Inequality in economic well-being depends on the earnings capacity of adults who choose to marry as well as on the relative earnings of marriage partners. In 1979 about one-third of Americans between 20 and 64 were never married or were widowed, separated from their spouse, or divorced; two-thirds were married and living with a spouse. If we assume that unmarried men and women are randomly distributed across the male and female earnings distributions and that marriage partners select one another independently of their earnings ranks, we can simulate the marriage pairs that form. To calculate the inequality of well-being, it is necessary to estimate the household size-adjusted income of each adult in the population. No household size adjustment is needed for single people. For married people, the earnings of the two partners are added and the resulting sum of earnings is then adjusted so that each partner's income is equivalent to that of a person living alone. The adjustment made in this simulation is to divide total household income by the square root of 2, the number of people who share a married couple's income. Once again, consider a population consisting of 100 men and 100 women who have the earnings distributions shown in Figure 18.1. Two-thirds of them marry and one-third remains unmarried. When the marriage partners are selected at random from the population and those who remain unmarried are also selected at random, the Gini coefficient of personal size-adjusted income averages 0.333. This is notably higher than the Gini coefficient when all people marry (0.280), but it is considerably lower than the Gini when all earners live alone (0.427). Inequality is typically higher as the percentage of married people declines and as the correlation of partners' incomes increases. Inequality also tends to be higher when low-income earners are disproportionately likely to remain unmarried.

This discussion underlines the importance of household formation in the determination of income disparities. Except under unrealistic assumptions, income-sharing within households reduces inequality compared with the situation in which income recipients live independently of one another. The amount of equalization that occurs when income recipients pool their incomes depends critically on the relative income positions of the household partners. If the pre-marriage positions of the two partners are similar, inequality will fall less than would be the case if the positions of the two are very dissimilar. This discussion ignores many of the real-world factors that affect household formation and dissolution. A sizeable percentage of households contains children and other dependents, who have few if any income sources of their own. The presence of children and disabled dependents in a household can affect the ability of nondisabled adults to earn income. If the dependents are cared for by an unmarried working-age adult, the responsibility of providing care can make it impossible for the adult to work full time or to work at all. In married-couple households, one spouse may give up paid employment or scale back working hours in order to provide care to the dependents who are too young, too old, or too disabled to work.

The discussion highlights a number of channels through which demographic change can influence the distribution of economic well-being. Most rich countries have experienced common long-term trends that affect household living arrangements and the age structure of their populations. Among these are declining fertility, increased life expectancy at birth and at age 65, delays in the age of first marriage, increased rates of divorce, and rising rates of childbearing outside of marriage. Past declines in the fertility rate have slowed labor force growth in most rich countries and may have encouraged many of them to reduce old barriers to immigration.

In many rich countries it is now less common for people to live in households containing members of more than two generations, and it is more common for old people to live separately from their younger relatives. Rising incomes and wealth permit more adults to live alone, apart from other relatives. Yet there remain important differences across industrial countries in the prevalence of households where adults from two generations live together. In southern Europe it is more common for young adults to live in a parent's household than it is in northern Europe and North America. This will obviously affect estimates of income inequality when these are based on equivalent personal incomes and the assumption that household members share incomes equally. The increased generosity of public and employer-provided pensions has allowed many retired workers and their spouses to live independently of their younger relatives. The drop in fertility means that young adults have fewer siblings and cousins than was the norm in earlier generations, and it means that adults are now more likely to reach middle age without having any children. The trends in marriage, fertility, and divorce have reduced average household size. Part of the decline stems from the shrinking number of children in families containing a working-age adult. Because households now contain a smaller number of dependent children, there is less reason for adults in working-age households to remain at home. Indeed, a major economic development of the past half century has been the substantial rise in labor force participation among 20–54-year-old adults, driven entirely by the increase in the fraction of women who work outside the home. This trend is partly due to the decline in labor market discrimination against women. Since the contributions of women are now more highly valued in the job market, many of them may now place less emphasis on bearing and rearing children and on the contributions they can make in the home.

Some of the atomization of households has been spurred by changes in access to income on the part of households that contain no working breadwinners. Public and private pensions and transfers targeted on the aged allow old people to live comfortably without sharing the earnings of a working relative. Governments are nowadays also more generous in providing transfers to the disabled and long-term unemployed and to one-parent families containing dependent children. These developments have provided protection to workerless households, insuring them against the risk of acute poverty and lessening inequality. However, these innovations also have encouraged adults to choose household living arrangements where the risk of poverty is higher.

## 3. EMPIRICAL EVIDENCE

Many scholars have attempted to assess the impact of demographic change on trends in the distribution of earned income and economic well-being. Three demographic factors that have drawn particular attention are changes in the age structure of the population, changes in household living arrangements, and changes in the racial or ethnic composition of the national population, driven either by immigration or differences in birth rates across racial and ethnic groups. Table 18.1 shows trends in income, relative population size, and income inequality along these dimensions for the United States. The tabulations cover the period from 1979 to 2004, a quarter century in which US inequality increased noticeably after a long period of relative stability or decline. The first two columns in the table show average income levels in 1979 and 2004. Income is measured on a per person basis using equivalent (household-size-adjusted) income. Gross household income includes wages, self-employment earnings, interest, dividends and other property income, public and employer-provided pensions, and government transfers, including food stamps and the implicit rent subsidies provided to residents of public housing. Estimated tax liabilities for income and payroll taxes are subtracted from gross income to form an estimate of after-tax and after-transfer household income. The resulting estimate of net household income is then divided by the square root of the number of household members to form an estimate of equivalent income per person in the household.

Measured in constant prices, average size-adjusted income increased almost one-third between 1979 and 2004. Income rose more slowly among people in households headed by adults under 35. The smallest gains were achieved by people in households headed by someone under 25. People in childless households headed by a single adult also saw slower than average income growth. Among racial and ethnic groups, Hispanic Americans experienced the slowest income gains. (The racial and ethnic identity of a household is determined by the identity of the person who heads the household.) In both 1979 and 2004 a large percentage of Hispanics were new

Table 18.1. Population shares and inequality of size-adjusted personal income in selected US subpopulations, 1979 and 2004

| Population group | Average size-adjusted income[a] ($) | | | Proportion of population | | | Gini coefficient | | |
|---|---|---|---|---|---|---|---|---|---|
| | 1979 | 2004 | Change (%) | 1979 | 2004 | Change (%) | 1979 | 2004 | Change (%) |
| All households | 22,866 | 30,093 | 32 | 1.00 | 1.00 | — | 0.295 | 0.354 | 20 |
| Age of household head | | | | | | | | | |
| Under age 25 | 17,845 | 19,461 | 9 | 0.07 | 0.06 | -10 | 0.306 | 0.374 | 23 |
| 25–34 | 21,264 | 25,628 | 21 | 0.24 | 0.20 | -20 | 0.281 | 0.353 | 26 |
| 35–44 | 22,915 | 30,496 | 33 | 0.24 | 0.26 | 8 | 0.271 | 0.333 | 23 |
| 45–54 | 26,277 | 35,426 | 35 | 0.19 | 0.22 | 16 | 0.266 | 0.320 | 20 |
| 55–64 | 26,794 | 35,804 | 34 | 0.13 | 0.13 | -1 | 0.293 | 0.350 | 20 |
| Age 65 or older | 19,345 | 26,319 | 36 | 0.13 | 0.14 | 6 | 0.337 | 0.369 | 9 |
| Household composition | | | | | | | | | |
| Couples with children | 22,383 | 30,668 | 37 | 0.50 | 0.40 | -20 | 0.248 | 0.312 | 26 |
| Couples without children | 28,598 | 38,463 | 34 | 0.24 | 0.24 | 0 | 0.273 | 0.322 | 18 |
| Singles with children | 14,015 | 18,534 | 32 | 0.11 | 0.15 | 38 | 0.346 | 0.383 | 11 |
| Singles without children | 21,755 | 27,672 | 27 | 0.15 | 0.20 | 40 | 0.338 | 0.374 | 11 |
| Race/ethnicity | | | | | | | | | |
| White, not Hispanic | 24,248 | 33,213 | 37 | 0.81 | 0.68 | -15 | 0.278 | 0.331 | 19 |
| Black, not Hispanic | 16,085 | 21,913 | 36 | 0.11 | 0.12 | 2 | 0.337 | 0.387 | 15 |
| Hispanic | 17,643 | 21,071 | 19 | 0.06 | 0.13 | 126 | 0.311 | 0.366 | 18 |
| Other | 21,264 | 30,501 | 43 | 0.02 | 0.07 | 242 | 0.311 | 0.357 | 15 |

Notes: [a] Size-adjusted income consists of cash and near-cash income, after subtracting income and payroll taxes, adjusted to reflect differences in household size. The inequality estimates in the table reflect income differences between persons, where each person in a household is assumed to have the same size-adjusted (or 'equivalent') income. Incomes in both years are measured in 2004 prices.

Sources: Author's tabulations of 1980 and 2005 March Current Population Survey files.

entrants to the United States. Many of them had less education than native-born US residents. The combined handicaps of limited schooling and poor English-speaking skills meant that many of these immigrants worked in poorly paid jobs. The racial and ethnic category labeled as 'other' includes residents of Asian and American Indian ancestry as well as many non-Hispanic residents who decline to identify a race.

The fourth and fifth columns in Table 18.1 show proportions of the US population in each subpopulation in 1979 and 2004. People in households headed by a householder under 35 represented a smaller percentage of the population in 2004 than in 1979, and people in households headed by a person between 35 and 54 represented a bigger percentage of the population in the later year. As noted in the previous section, households containing a married couple have become relatively less common, while households headed by a never-married, separated, divorced, or widowed person have become more common. Families containing children have also become relatively less common. People in married-couple households containing children accounted for 50 percent of the population in 1979 but just 40 percent of the population in 2004. Single-parent families containing children have become relatively more important, however. The seventh and eighth columns show estimates of the Gini coefficient for the populations and subpopulations just described. For the population as a whole, inequality as measured by the Gini coefficient increased 20 percent between 1979 and 2004. Inequality also rose within every subpopulation shown in the table, with the biggest increases occurring in households headed by young working-age adults and in households with married couples that contain children.

Even without an elaborate analysis of the numbers displayed in Table 18.1 it is evident that increases in income inequality *within* each subpopulation accounted for much of the rise in US inequality between 1979 and 2004. The Gini coefficient rose 20 percent or more within each age group of households where the family head was under 65. The Gini coefficient also increased 11 percent or more in each category of household classified by the marital status of the head and the presence or absence of children, and it rose by at least 15 percent within every racial and ethnic group. Still, it would be interesting to know whether any of the demographic changes contributed to the growth in inequality and, if so, how big the contribution was. The way many scholars approach this question is to calculate the population weights of interesting subpopulations in some benchmark year and then ask how inequality in later years would have developed if the weights of these subpopulations had remained unchanged in later years. This calculation rests on the assumption that a change in population shares would not affect two other factors that contribute importantly to overall inequality, namely, the amount of inequality within subpopulations and the difference in average income between the subpopulations.

Under these assumptions, the demographic shifts shown in Table 18.1 had a very modest impact on the development of US inequality between 1979 and 2005. Had the 1979 age structure of the population remained unchanged but within-group and between-group income differences developed as observed, the Gini coefficient in 2004 would have been 0.356 instead of 0.354. This suggests that the shift in the age distribution of household heads slightly reduced the rise in inequality. The opposite is true of the changes in household composition and the racial and ethnic composition of the population. If the subpopulation weights had remained unchanged between 1979 and 2004, the Gini coefficient would have been somewhat lower under a fixed distribution of household types and under a fixed race and ethnic mix. In this case, the demographic shifts produced faster growth in inequality than would have occurred under a fixed demographic structure. The differences are not very large, however. In each case, about 85 percent of the observed rise in the Gini would have occurred even if the demographic structure had remained unchanged. (The results are very similar using an alternative measure of inequality, the Theil index.) Thus, an overwhelming share of the increase in inequality occurred as a result of inequality changes within and between the subpopulations identified in Table 18.1, at least under the assumptions of this exercise.

The same is not necessarily true in other countries or in other time periods, and it may not be true if we consider other indicators of relative well-being or deprivation. However, a number of analysts examining the experiences of different countries have reached broadly similar conclusions. Mookherjee and Shorrocks (1982) analyzed the trend in UK income inequality between 1965 and 1980 seeking to clarify the contribution of changes in the population age structure. Overall household inequality increased over the period and the age structure also changed, but the main factors pushing up inequality were the growing differences in mean income between age groups and in inequality within age groups. The shift in the age structure by itself played essentially no role in the trend in inequality (Mookherjee and Shorrocks, 1982: 901).

Analyzing a somewhat later period, Jenkins (1995) reaches a nearly identical conclusion about the impact of changes in the UK population age structure. He also analyzed the shift in household living arrangements by dividing households into ten groupings classified by the number of adults and children in the household and, where no children were present, by the age of the household head (younger or older than age 65). Over the period from 1971 to 1986, the influence of the changing shares of the population in each type of household had virtually no impact on the trend in UK inequality. Instead, inequality varied over time because of changes in inequality within each type of household and to a lesser extent because of changes in the relative incomes of each group. The change in within-group inequality was mainly due to changes in earned income inequality and the employment status of working-age adults.

Using somewhat different methods, Johnson and Wilkins (2003) obtain a basic-ally similar result when analyzing Australian income distribution changes between 1982 and 1998. Like the United Kingdom and the United States, Australia saw a rise in pre-tax, pre-transfer inequality over this period. The question is, how much of the rise can be attributed to demographic change and how much to other factors? Dividing Australian households into the same four living arrangement categories shown in Table 18.1, into the same age groups, into the foreign- and native-born, and into four educational attainment groups, the authors conclude that the shift in household living arrangements may have accounted for between a fifth and a quarter of the increase in market income inequality, but this effect was approximately offset by the other demographic trends they consider—changes in population age structure, the percentage of foreign-born, and the share of the population with differing levels of school attainment. Changes in the distribution of dependent children had virtually no effect on inequality. Mirroring Jenkins's (1995) findings for the United Kingdom, Johnson and Wilkins (2003) find that changes in labor force status account for more than half of the rise in inequality.

Jäntti (1997) used cross-nationally comparable micro-census data from five rich countries to assess changes in income inequality using consistent methods for all the countries. His analysis covered a relatively short span of years, just four to seven years in the early to mid-1980s, so it may be unrealistic to think demographic changes will play a big role in explaining inequality changes. Inequality of post-tax, post-transfer income was relatively stable in two of the countries, Canada and the Netherlands, while it increased noticeably in the other three, Sweden, the United Kingdom, and the United States. The influence of demographic trends was measured after dividing households into the same four living arrangement groups shown in Table 18.1 as well as into fairly narrow age groups. Jäntti also examined labor market factors by dividing households into four groups according to the number workers in the household (0, 1, 2, and 3 or more). He concluded that changes in the age structure and family living arrangements fail to explain the changes in overall income inequality in those countries where inequality rose. Instead, inequality rose within the demographic groups defined in his analysis and, in a few cases, between these demographic groups as well. With only a few exceptions, the biggest contributor to higher inequality was the growth in earnings inequality among household heads. In a few cases, earnings inequality among spouses of the household heads also contributed to the growth in inequality.

Karoly and Burtless (1995), Burtless (1999), and Daly and Valletta (2006), have assessed the impact of rising earnings inequality and demographic trends on US inequality over much longer periods than evaluated by Jäntti. Karoly and Burtless analyzed the 30-year period after 1959; Burtless examined income changes in the 17 years after 1979; and Daly and Valletta examined the period between 1969 and 1998. These periods are long enough so that even comparatively slow demographic changes should have observable effects if those effects are important determinants of income inequality.

To understand the role of labor market and family composition changes on the income distribution, Karoly and Burtless (1995) decomposed the change in the Gini coefficient in a way that allowed them to see how trends in individual income components contributed to the overall change in inequality. Two income sources that are especially important are the earned incomes of the male head of family and the female head of family. These income sources are unequally distributed across the population for three reasons. Families with a working male head can have unequal male head earnings because some working men earn higher incomes than others. The amount of this inequality will rise or fall depending on the inequality of male labor incomes. Second, some households that contain a male head of family may see his earnings disappear if he ceases to work. This will typically raise inequality. Finally, as a result of changes in family formation and dissolution, some households that would once have contained a male family head may no longer have one, depriving household members of the potential earnings of a male family head. Of course, the same reasoning applies to the labor earnings of a female family head. One important difference is that in the past far fewer than half of female family heads worked for pay, so the earnings contributions of female heads were very unequally distributed across the population. As more female heads of household entered the labor force, female head earnings became more equally distributed across households, producing a reduction in overall inequality. In contrast, a very high percentage of working-age male family heads earned labor incomes.

In the three decades analyzed by Karoly and Burtless, the overall trends in inequality and the sources of change in inequality varied notably from one decade to the next. Male earnings inequality fell in the 1960s. In that same decade, increases in female employment rates meant that female head earnings were more equally distributed across households. Both factors helped reduce income inequality among households headed by a working-age person. In the 1970s there was an acceleration in the trend toward household dissolution, and this trend deprived a growing percentage of the population of access to a male head's earnings. In addition, some working-age men withdrew from the labor force, increasing the percentage of households with no male earnings. Both these trends tended to push up inequality, though the change in overall change was small in the 1970s. In the 1980s, male earnings inequality soared, contributing directly and substantially to rising household income inequality. In addition, the correlation in the earned incomes of male and female household heads increased sharply. As we have seen, this change in the relationship between a male head's and a female head's earnings can cause inequality to rise. The analysis suggests that different factors have influenced inequality trends in different eras. The demographic factor with the biggest long-term effect was the atomization of US households, which tended to boost inequality over the entire 30-year analysis period, though most strongly in the 1970s. In periods when there were big changes in overall inequality, however, the major source of change was likely to be a labor market development. In the 1960s male earnings became less unequal and in the 1980s they became sharply more unequal. In the 1970s, employment rates among working-age men fell, boosting inequality.

Burtless (1999) and Daly and Valletta (2006) tried to directly assess the impact of selected demographic trends, rising earned income inequality, and changes in the relationship of husband and wife earnings on US inequality. Both studies conclude that changes in the earnings inequality produced by far the biggest impact on household inequality, though family structure changes also contributed to increased inequality during the periods analyzed. Burtless's analysis focused narrowly on the contribution of higher earned income inequality among family heads with earnings and on the effects of the growing positive association between husbands' and wives' earnings. Daly and Valetta viewed earnings inequality more broadly and took into account changes in the proportion of family heads who had any earned income at all. For that reason, Daly and Valetta find a bigger impact of labor market developments on the final distribution of income. Both studies agree, however, that changes in family living arrangements and other demographic characteristics account for one-quarter or less of the upward trend in American inequality.

When analysts focus on narrower population groups or other measures of inequality and deprivation, they sometimes find a bigger impact of demographic developments. A long-standing controversy in the United States centers on the impact of single-parent families on the child poverty rate and the distribution of children's well-being. For reasons mentioned earlier, adults and children who live in one-parent households face elevated risks of receiving low labor incomes. Inequality in such households is typically much greater than it is in married-couple or two-partner households, where income pooling on the part of family heads can reduce the likelihood of very low earnings. The increasing share of children living in one-parent households can contribute directly to higher rates of relative deprivation among children.

How much has the trend toward one-parent households contributed to child poverty? As Robert Lerman notes, 'One simple way to analyse the issue is to assume that poverty rates remained constant over the period *within* categories and to calculate how much change in child poverty would have taken place if the only change was the proportion of children in each category' (Lerman, 1996: S121). In the period he analyzes, 1970–89, he concludes that virtually all the rise in US child poverty rates can be attributed to the change in the family structure of households that contain children.

The calculations rest on an assumption that Lerman finds implausible, namely, that the hypothetical shift in the distribution of households to an earlier family structure would leave the characteristics of one-parent and two-parent families unchanged. This is unlikely to be true, if only because the hypothetical husbands and wives in the newly created married-couple households are likely to differ from the family heads who are currently married. In the United States, single-parent households are typically headed by adults who have less schooling and potential earnings than parents in married-couple households. When they marry, they are likely to marry a person who has similar characteristics—that is, similar age, educational attainment, race or ethnicity, and earnings capacity. Under these circumstances, it is unrealistic to expect that the hypothetical marriage partners will have the same distribution of earned income and other income as currently married couples. The incomes of the new married couples are likely to increase the inequality and child poverty rates of married-couple households compared with the levels among current married couple families.

To remedy this flaw in standard shift-share analysis, Lerman (1996) used simulation to identify marriage partners for single parents up to the number of partnerships needed to achieve a target ratio of single-parent and married-couple households. Hypothetical marriage partners were selected to have similar ages, educational attainments, and ethnicity as the single parents to whom they were attached. Lerman makes one other adjustment to the incomes of hypothetical marriage partners. Because men tend to earn higher wages as a married parent than they do as a single person, he adjusts upward their earnings to reflect this marriage effect. However, he subtracts any social assistance benefits that the single parent may have received when calculating the combined income of the simulated new household. Even ignoring the predicted earnings responses of the new husbands, Lerman's simulation suggests that a higher marriage rate would have substantially eliminated the 3-percentage-point rise in child poverty rate experienced by black and white youngsters between 1971 and 1989. If the hypothesized earnings gain among new husbands is also included in the simulation, Lerman predicts child poverty would have fallen slightly rather than increased. When child inequality is measured with the Gini coefficient of size-adjusted personal income rather than the poverty rate, the decline in inequality resulting from a higher marriage rate seems less impressive. Using the income-to-needs ratio as a measure of child well-being, Lerman finds that the actual Gini coefficient increased from 0.335 in 1971 to 0.384 in 1989, a rise of about 15 percent. If the proportion of children in two-parent families had remained constant, the Gini coefficient would have increased to only 0.375, a rise of about 12 percent. Taking into account the possible earnings gains among new husbands, the Gini coefficient would have risen to just 0.366, an increase of about 9 percent. These estimates imply that many of the inequality-reducing effects of a higher marriage rate would be concentrated in the lower ranks of the income distribution, where the main effects on child poverty would be concentrated.

The contribution of cross-border migration to the distribution of well-being is the subject of intense debate, in both the scholarly community and the wider public. Immigrants represent a growing percentage of the population in all rich countries where it is possible to measure this statistic. The entry of immigrants into wealthy countries arouses controversy, mainly because of natives' fear that the new entrants will threaten their living standards. If immigrants had work skills that were exactly like those of natives, their arrival would probably have little impact on the distribution of income and earnings. In recent years it is common for immigrants to come from poor countries and to bring limited job skills when they arrive in rich countries. When immigrants are less skilled than natives, their entry will add to the ranks of workers competing for low-skill jobs. Even in this case, however, the distribution of income will only change if the ratio of immigrants to natives changes or if the skill gap between the two groups changes. This is precisely what has happened in many rich countries. In 1970 less than 5 percent of the resident US population had been born abroad, and recent immigrants earned 17 percent less than natives. By the end of the 1990s, 11 percent of the US population had been born abroad, and recent immigrants earned 34 percent less than natives (Borjas, 1999: 28).

American poverty statistics provide a simple illustration of how immigration can affect distributional statistics. The poverty rate for households headed by native-born Americans did not change between 1979 and 1998, but both the number of immigrant households and their poverty rate rose. As a result, the poverty rate for all residents, both native- and foreign-born, increased from 11.7 to 12.7 percent (Burtless and Smeeding, 2001). This calculation assumes that the entry of less-skilled immigrants had no impact on the distribution of income among natives. Opponents of immigration do not think this is true, but economists are divided on the issue. If competition from immigrants depressed the wages or employment rates of unskilled natives, the overall effect of immigration on poverty and inequality was greater than implied by the simple calculation performed by Burtless and Smeeding. Borjas *et al.* (1997) find evidence that rising numbers of less skilled immigrants in the US labor market hurt the wages of low-skill American workers, widening pay disparities and contributing to the inequality trends documented by other researchers. Card (2005) finds little evidence, either in time series data or in regional wage patterns, to support the view that increased unskilled immigration has contributed to poor labor market outcomes for native unskilled workers. While immigration has almost certainly added to the ranks of low-wage workers and low-income households, all of the addition may be among the immigrants themselves. Since an overwhelming share of the immigrants enjoy higher incomes as a result of moving to a rich country, it is not obvious whether the wider inequality that is due to immigration represents an important welfare problem. The answer to this question depends crucially on whether immigration has hurt the incomes of low-skill natives, and this question is so far unresolved.

# 4. Conclusions and Unresolved Issues

The simulation results of Lerman (1996) remind us that it is difficult to analyze the impacts of demographic change without reference to other social and economic shifts, both those that induce demographic change and those that are a possible byproduct of demographic change. Along with most other analysts who examine income distribution changes over a long span of years, he concludes that changes in household structure have had a nontrivial effect on the trend in economic inequality, with particularly powerful effects on the well-being of children at the bottom of the income distribution. Although the potential size of this effect is straightforward to calculate under stylized assumptions, Lerman recognizes that those assumptions are unlikely to be true. In particular, it is unrealistic to believe that a sizeable increase in the marriage rate could occur without any change in the income distributions of the married and unmarried populations. Unusually for economists who analyze the effects of demographic factors on the trend in inequality, Lerman tries to make plausible adjustments in the married and unmarried populations before calculating the ultimate effects of demographic change on the income distribution.

Lerman goes still further by asserting that entry into marriage can actually increase the earnings of men who would otherwise be single. There is some evidence to support this view (Lerman, 1996 and 2002). There is also evidence that the decline in marriage has disproportionately affected men who have a low rank in the earnings distribution (Burtless, 1999: 856). One interpretation is that the decline in marriage has reduced the necessity of work for many prime-age men, increasing the probability they will be jobless for part or all of a year. This increases the likelihood that they will have low annual earnings, which in turn boosts male earnings inequality. Another interpretation is that a change originating in the labor market has reduced the demand for workers who have limited skills. This lowers their market wages and their attractiveness as marriage partners. It reduces their chances of marrying or remaining married. Without knowing which of these interpretations is correct, it is difficult to say whether the rise in income inequality and child poverty is due to a social and demographic change—the shift in attitudes towards marriage—or a labor market change—the rise in male earnings inequality.

Similarly, the debate over the role of immigration in the determination of wages highlights the importance of considering the indirect as well as the direct influence of a demographic phenomenon. If the influx of unskilled immigrants has reduced the earnings and household incomes of native workers, it is crucial to trace out the size of these effects before offering estimates of the impact of immigration on inequality.

None of the income distribution studies weighs relevant evidence that would allow us to decide whether observed distributional changes are associated with pure demographic shifts or some other kind of economic or social change. A common finding in many studies is that demographically induced changes in inequality are more likely to account for a large portion of the total change in inequality only when the change in overall inequality is comparatively small. When countries experience changes in the income distribution that are large enough to attract popular notice, demographic shifts are almost never the main source of change. Most peacetime demographic shifts, including population ageing and changes in marital and childbearing behavior, occur at a gradual pace. This is particularly true when they are compared with changes in involuntary unemployment, profits, government tax and transfer policy, and relative wages. Each of these economic or political determinants of inequality can change dramatically in a short span of years, producing noticeable changes in the relative well-being of workers, property owners, taxpayers, and pensioners.

Demographic shifts are more likely to be associated with large changes in the income distribution when the income distribution is evaluated over a lengthy period. A problem in sorting out the effects of demographic change over long periods is calculating the full effect of the change, including its indirect effects through economic variables, such as wages. Many labor economists believe that changes in the relative supply of workers in different skill classes can have a major influence on the relative wages of workers in different classes and the disparity of wages within a given skill class. A widely accepted explanation for the drop in relative wages earned by young American men in the 1970s was entry of the large baby-boom generation into the labor market (Welch, 1979). This demographic development clearly could have affected the overall distribution of household incomes by depressing the relative incomes of households headed by young adults. In nearly all industrialized countries, young adults head households which have below-average equivalent incomes (see Table 18.1). If the standard supply–demand story of wage formation is correct, the entry of the baby-boom generation into the labor market affected the income distribution through its direct effect on the relative population weights of different age groups and also through its indirect effect on the relative earnings of workers in different age and skill groups. Researchers have yet to perform a study that traces out the full direct and indirect effects of this demographic development on the income distribution.

More recently Thomas Lemieux has argued that the ageing of the workforce in combination with senior workers' rising average skill has increased the predictable dispersion of wages. 'Wage dispersion among narrowly defined groups of workers is substantially larger for older and more educated workers than for younger and less educated workers. As a result, ... a large fraction of the increase in residual wage inequality is a spurious consequence of the fact that the work force has grown older and more educated since the 1980s' (Lemieux, 2006: 462). If this interpretation is correct, part of the growth in overall wage inequality is due to workforce ageing and part is due to increases in average worker educational attainment and skill *within* age groups. Although it should be possible to trace out the impact of these wage developments on overall income inequality, this has not yet been done.

Shifts in demography can play a major role in long-term inequality trends. Most research so far has focused on obtaining fairly straightforward estimates of the direct effects of demography under simple and sometimes unrealistic assumptions.

One major challenge for social scientists is developing more realistic assumptions for performing these calculations. In particular, researchers are still in the early stages of formulating plausible methods for tracing out the indirect as well as direct influences of demographic change.

# References

BORJAS, G. 1999. *Heaven's Door: Immigration Policy and the American Economy*. Princeton: Princeton University Press.

——FREEMAN, R. B., and KATZ, L. 1997. 'How Much Do Immigration and Trade Affect Labor Market Outcomes?' *Brookings Papers on Economic Activity*, 1997(1): 1–67.

BURTLESS, G. 1999. 'Effects of Growing Wage Disparities and Changing Family Composition on the US Income Distribution'. *European Economic Review*, 43(4–6) (Apr.): 853–65.

——and SMEEDING, T. M. 2001. 'The Level, Trend, and Composition of Poverty', in S. Danziger, R. Haveman, and B. Wolfe (eds.), *Understanding Poverty: Progress and Problems*. Cambridge, Mass.: Harvard University Press.

CARD, D. 2005. 'Is the New Immigration Really So Bad?' *The Economic Journal*, 115(507), Nov.: F300–23.

DALY, M. C., and VALLETTA, R. G. 2006. 'Inequality and Poverty in United States: The Effects of Rising Dispersion of Men's Earnings and Changing Family Behavior'. *Economica*, 73(289), Feb.: 75–98.

JÄNTTI, M. 1997. 'Inequality in Five Countries in the 1980s: The Role of Demographic Shifts, Markets, and Government Policies'. *Economica*, 64(255), Aug.: 415–40.

JENKINS, S. P. 1995. 'Accounting for Inequality Trends: Decomposition Analyses for the UK, 1971–86'. *Economica*, 62(242), Feb.: 29–63.

JOHNSON, D., and WILKINS, R. 2003. 'The Effects of Changes in Family Composition and Employment Patterns on the Distribution of Income in Australia: 1982 to 1997–98'. Melbourne Institute Working Paper no. 19/03. Melbourne: Melbourne Institute of Applied Economic and Social Research.

KAROLY, L., and BURTLESS, G. 1995. 'Demographic Change, Rising Earnings Inequality, and the Distribution of Personal Well-Being, 1959–1989'. *Demography*, 32(3), Aug.: 379–405.

LEMIEUX, T. 2006. 'Increasing Residual Wage Inequality: Composition Effects, Noisy Data, or Rising Demand for Skill?' *American Economic Review*, 96(3), June: 461–98.

LERMAN, R. 1996. 'The Impact of Changing US Family Structure on Child Poverty and Income Inequality'. *Economica*, 63(250): S119–39.

——2002. 'Marriage and the Economic Well-Being of Families with Children: A Review of the Literature'. Urban Institute Working Paper. Washington: Urban Institute.

MOOKHERJEE, D., and SHORROCKS, A. 1982. 'A Decomposition Analysis of the Trend in UK Income Inequality'. *The Economic Journal*, 92(368), Dec.: 886–902.

WELCH, F. 1979. 'Effects of Cohort Size on Earnings: The Baby Boom Babies' Financial Bust'. *Journal of Political Economy*, 87(5, part 2), Oct.: S65–97.

CHAPTER 19

...............................................................................................

# INTERNATIONAL MIGRATION, ETHNICITY, AND ECONOMIC INEQUALITY

...............................................................................................

## MARTIN KAHANEC

## KLAUS F. ZIMMERMANN

Our review of economic research finds immigrants not only help fuel the Nation's economic growth, but also have an overall positive effect on the income of native-born workers.

US Council of Economic Advisers Chairman Edward P. Lazear

## 1. INTRODUCTION

...............................................................................................

INTERNATIONAL and national migration is a momentous phenomenon driving the fortunes of large numbers of people.[1] The issue of labor flows is also an important

Financial support from Volkswagen Foundation for the IZA project on 'The Economics and Persistence of Migrant Ethnicity' is gratefully acknowledged. We thank Deborah A. Cobb-Clark, Amelie F. Constant, Stephen J. Nickell, Brian Nolan, Wiemer Salverda, Timothy M. Smeeding, and Mutlu Yuksel for helpful comments on earlier drafts.

[1] According to United Nations (UN) estimates, the share of international migrants in the total world population was 2.4% in 1965, 2.3% in 1985, and reached 3.0% in 2005. In more developed

part of any textbook in economics. Why do people move, and what happens to their welfare and that of the receiving and sending countries when they do? A widely accepted answer is that immigration helps to achieve a more efficient allocation of resources, and hence improves the welfare of nations. However, the rise in allocative efficiency is often considered to be fairly small.[2] The controversy starts with concerns about the distributional effects of immigration: (i) Is immigration detrimental, that is, do immigrants depress the wages and increase the unemployment of the natives, often enter into poverty within the receiving countries, and deprive the sending regions of their most motivated and talented workers? (ii) Is it possible that immigration is just not large and significant enough to cause such damage to be noticeable? Or: (iii) Is immigration *de facto* beneficial, because most empirical studies fail to identify any negative effects on the natives, immigrants are typically doing better in the receiving countries than at home, and the sending countries' population benefits from remittances and their labor force from the induced scarcity in the home labor markets? And: (iv) What is actually the objective—equality among natives or among natives and immigrants together?

This chapter uses a well-defined setting to suggest an optimistic view about the distributional effects of immigration. We apply well-established concepts from the allocative debate to investigate the inequality issues, and extend the analysis to cover the role of ethnicity and ethnic identity for the labor market. For the empirical investigation, we use data from the OECD countries. Conceptually, we adopt the 'no-job, job, good job' approach to the concept of economic inequality and the 'unskilled–skilled paradigm' of labor migration. We discuss the issues of economic absorption (or assimilation) over time and across generations and consider selection through immigration and emigration choices and immigrant admission policies. We also deal with the impacts of ethnic identity on economic performance, and hence inequality.

Section 2 provides a general picture of the native–immigrant differences in labor force participation, unemployment, and occupational and educational attainment, taking skill levels and years since immigration into account. Section 3 investigates the inequality impact of immigration by summarizing the potential labor market impacts and the wage and employment consequences. Assuming immediate and full adjustment by immigrants, our stylized model suggests that skilled immigration is largely positive for the host economy, as inequality measured by the Gini coefficient improves for the most part. This model conjecture is supported by empirical evidence. Section 4 deals with the potentially slow integration of

regions, including Europe, Northern America, Australia, New Zealand, and Japan, the corresponding share reached 9.5% in 2005. See United Nations, Department of Economic and Social Affairs, World Migrant Stock: The 2005 Revision Population Database.

  [2]  See Borjas (1999b) for equilibria situations. However, Bauer and Zimmermann (1997) have pointed out that the increase or decrease in allocative efficiency can be very large under particular disequilibrium conditions.

immigrants into the labor market of the host country, as well as with the role that self-selection and selection through politically set admission rules can play for the performance in the labor market. We also consider cultural or ethnic identity as an independent factor potentially affecting economic success and discuss the consequences for inequality. Section 5 concludes.

# 2. SOME EMPIRICAL FACTS

The empirically measured association between inequality and the presence of immigrants in the economy reflects many aspects of mutual influence. On the one hand, migrants carry different amounts and forms of capital with them and represent different types of labor, thereby directly affecting the distribution of income in host societies. Furthermore, they have an indirect impact through changing the productivity of incumbent production factors as well as impinging on the redistributive policies in the host societies. On the other hand, different migrants select into countries with different degrees of inequality. As shown in Table 19.1, New World countries with a high share of foreign-born population, such as the USA or Australia, also have higher income inequality. Post-transition OECD members, such as Poland or Slovakia, have very low shares of foreign population and low Gini coefficients. Western European countries are in between.

This comparison is misleading, however. The three groups of countries differ in terms of their economic institutions, redistribution policies, as well as the nature, type, and history of immigration. For example, the post-transition countries have low inequality and low shares of foreign population due to their history as closed command economies. The New World countries, at the other end of the spectrum, have a history of liberal immigration and economic policies. Therefore, it is appropriate to deal with these groups of countries separately to characterize the relationship between inequality and immigration.

In Figure 19.1 we therefore concentrate on European countries that share similar histories of immigration and economic institutions, focusing on the relationship between the Gini coefficient and the share of foreigners in the labor force. We observe no clear-cut relationship. In Figure 19.2, however, when we drop the outlier countries Luxembourg and Switzerland, the predicted values of a line plot of the nonparametric locally weighted regression of Gini values on the share of foreign labor suggest a distinct negative relationship. But such a finding could be affected by the quality composition of the foreign labor force. Only if it were the same across countries, might one safely predict declining inequality with rising shares of foreign labor.

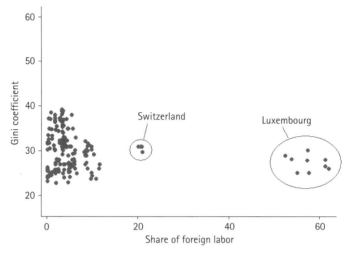

**Fig. 19.1. Scatter plot of the Gini coefficient as a function of the share of foreign labor**

*Notes*: Data on Gini coefficients are from the WIID 2007 database. Foreign labor force as a share of total labor force; the OECD. Stat database, 1995–2004. Western European OECD members; see Table 19.1.

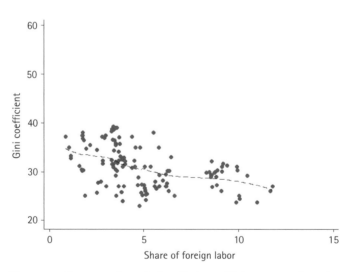

**Fig. 19.2. Scatter plot of the Gini coefficient as a function of the share of foreign labor with a locally weighted line plot**

*Notes*: Western European OECD members; see Table 19.1, excluding Switzerland and Luxembourg. The dashed line represents a line plot of the nonparametric locally weighted regression of Gini values on the share of foreign labor. See Fig. 19.1 on data sources.

Table 19.1. Share of foreign population and the Gini coefficient

| Country | Foreign population | Gini coefficient |
|---|---|---|
| New World: | | |
| Australia | 23.3 | 30.9 |
| Canada[e] | 17.5 | 29.1 |
| United States | 11.8 | 46.2 |
| Western Europe | | |
| Austria[a] | 8.8 | 23.7 |
| Belgium[a] | 8.2 | 29.3 |
| Germany | 8.9 | 31.7 |
| Greece | 7.0 | 32.3 |
| Denmark | 4.9 | 39.0 |
| Finland | 2.0 | 30.2 |
| France[c] | 5.6 | 27.0 |
| Ireland[a] | 4.0 | 28.9 |
| Italy | 2.6 | 36.4 |
| Luxembourg[a] | 37.5 | 26.6 |
| The Netherlands | 4.3 | 27.0 |
| Norway | 4.3 | 27.0 |
| Portugal[a] | 3.4 | 37.1 |
| Spain | 3.1 | 31.0 |
| Sweden | 5.3 | 25.7 |
| Switzerland | 19.9 | 30.9 |
| United Kingdom | 4.5 | 35.0 |
| Post-transition: | | |
| Czech Republic | 2.3 | 27.3 |
| Hungary | 1.1 | 38.6 |
| Poland | 0.1 | 34.9 |
| Slovakia | 0.5 | 26.0 |
| Other OECD | | |
| Japan[d] | 1.2 | 31.9 |
| Korea[d] | 0.3 | 37.2 |
| Mexico[b] | 0.4 | 53.5 |

*Notes*: Data on Gini coefficients are from the WIID 2007 database. Foreign population as a share of total population; the OECD.Stat database, 2002 data.
[a] 2001; [b] 2000; [c] 1999; [d] 1998; [e] 1996.
No data for Iceland, New Zealand, and Turkey.

Therefore, to identify some of the key mechanisms driving the relationship between immigration and labor market inequality we focus on three specific integration issues that govern the economic success of immigrants. First, labor market participation rates of the working-age immigrant population characterize the economic activity of immigrants and their earnings prospects. Second, immigrants' unemployment rates mirror immigrants' chances of being employed and measure immigrants' earnings prospects conditional on their labor market participation.

Third, the occupational attainment of immigrants depicts immigrants' chances of obtaining well-paid jobs, conditional on employment.

While a number of member states of the European Union[3] (EU) are still significantly behind the employment objectives stipulated in the Lisbon Agenda,[4] the standing of immigrants is often even more adverse in many respects. This disparity suggests that one use natives as a benchmark to identify to what extent immigrants integrate in terms of their labor market outcomes. There are a number of factors that determine individual economic attainment and drive the economic gap between immigrants and natives. Among these, perhaps the most significant is human capital. Immigrants' labor market success is a function of their skills as well as the transferability of those skills into the new economic environment of the destination country. Furthermore, as immigrants face new incentives to adjust and invest in skills specific to their new economic environment, such as acquisition of language skills, the time that they have spent in the host country matters for their economic attainment.

We report here statistics for the working-age population on labor market participation, unemployment, and occupational attainment for the categories natives, immigrants with at least 10 years of experience in the host country, immigrants in general, and three skill categories for both natives and immigrants pooled together, defined as third (high), upper secondary (medium), and lower secondary (low) level of highest educational attainment.[5] We consider the EU25 as a whole and the traditional European destination countries (EU15) separately to highlight some of the salient stylized patterns of immigrant–native labor market gaps and the role of human capital and adjustment in driving these gaps.[6]

---

[3]  For a detailed discussion of the Lisbon strategy see Sapir *et al.* (2004), for instance.

[4]  Set out in March 2000, the Lisbon Agenda of the EU stipulates, among other ambitious targets, that the overall employment rate and the female employment rate, which reflect the above-mentioned participation and unemployment margins, should reach 70% and 60%, respectively, by 2010.

[5]  Statistics are based on the EU Labour Force Survey 2005. A high level of education includes ISCED 5 and 6 levels. ISCED 5 denotes first-stage tertiary programs having an educational content more advanced than those offered by secondary levels. They do not lead to the award of an advanced research qualification and must have a cumulative duration of at least two years. ISCED 6 denotes second-stage tertiary education leading to an advanced research qualification and requiring original research contribution in the form of a thesis or dissertation. A medium level of education includes ISCED 3 and 4 levels, which denote education that typically begins at the end of full-time compulsory education and involves higher qualification and specialization than the ISCED 2 level. ISCED 3 level education is often designed to provide direct access to ISCED 5. ISCED 4 serves to broaden the knowledge achieved in ISCED 3 but is not regarded as tertiary. A low level of education includes ISCED 0, 1, and 2 levels. These include pre-primary, primary, and lower secondary or second stage of primary education. The end of ISCED 2 often coincides with the end of compulsory schooling where it exists. For further details see UNESCO (1997).

[6]  The EU denotes the 25 member states of the European Union in 2005 except for Malta for which no data are available. Romania and Bulgaria joined the EU in 2007 and are not included. The EU15 denotes the 15 member states prior to the 2004 enlargement.

Table 19.2 reports participation rates. The rates of natives vary from 45% in Italy up to 78% in Sweden. In the Netherlands and Sweden, immigrants have fairly similar rates to natives, although natives have the highest participation rates, followed by immigrants with a long-term presence and then immigrants in general. This is consistent with the hypothesis that immigrants need some time to assimilate into the labor market and to adjust to the natives' way of working or living. The numbers for Austria, Spain, Ireland, Italy, and Luxembourg suggest the opposite: immigrants there have higher participation rates than natives, and these rates seem to be even higher for newcomers. This observation is consistent with the selection hypothesis, whereby it is the people with strong labor market potential, economic motives, and a desire to work who migrate. They only slowly adapt to the lower participation levels of the natives.

Another interpretation is based on cohort effects. In the 1960s and early 1970s immigrants in Western and Northern Europe were labor migrants selected to work through immigration policies. After the 1973 general halt on recruitment there were periods of political and refugee immigration as well as family reunification, resulting in migrants with lower work incentives. Southern Europe and Ireland turned into immigration destination areas only in the last decade, where stronger growing economies and the opening of the Eastern bloc were attracting larger numbers of labor immigrants. Such cohort effects may also explain the situation in Germany, the UK, France, and other countries where immigrants with long-term presence have lower participation rates than their recent counterparts (or natives). In these countries, however, immigrants are less active than the natives. This observation may reflect negative selection of immigrants to these countries. In Portugal, Greece, Finland, Denmark, and the EU25 as a whole, immigrants are more active than natives, especially if they have been in the respective economy for more than 10 years. Such a finding may be due to positive selection and beneficial effects of experience in the destination country.

A consistent picture across the columns of Table 19.2 is that educational levels and participation rates are positively associated. That is, more educated individuals exhibit much higher labor market participation rates than lower educated individuals. In general, immigrants in Europe are much less educated than in the USA or Australia. In some European countries, this has been fostered for many decades by immigration policies as outlined above that had focused on the immigration of blue-collar workers before the recession in 1973, as discussed by Zimmermann (2005b).

Table 19.3 contains unemployment rates. The results here provide a clear-cut picture: tenure in the country and education do matter; they are associated with lower unemployment rates.[7] New immigrants have higher unemployment rates

---

[7] The only exception is Greece, where experienced immigrants have higher unemployment than more recent immigrants. Nevertheless, natives do better than immigrants.

Table 19.2. Labor market participation rates of natives, immigrants, and skill groups

| | EU25 | AT | BE | DE | DK | ES | FI | FR | GR | IE | IT | LU | NL | PT | SE | UK |
|---|---|---|---|---|---|---|---|---|---|---|---|---|---|---|---|---|
| Natives | 56.49 | 58.62 | 56.66 | 58.09 | 66.28 | 51.89 | 63.26 | 53.65 | 48.32 | 59.07 | 45.29 | 47.42 | 76.17 | 56.88 | 78.45 | 61.07 |
| Immigrants 10+ | 60.73 | 59.61 | 51.61 | 47.92 | 76.31 | 61.02 | 72.63 | 50.25 | 68.23 | 62.52 | 59.58 | 58.41 | 69.43 | 72.62 | 73.82 | 55.71 |
| Immigrants | 57.14 | 60.14 | 54.12 | 51.29 | 74.83 | 72.52 | 67.84 | 50.98 | 67.90 | 68.79 | 61.99 | 64.08 | 68.10 | 72.00 | 71.62 | 60.53 |
| Education: | | | | | | | | | | | | | | | | |
| High | 81.00 | 77.00 | 80.01 | 73.61 | 83.18 | 80.70 | 81.16 | 75.22 | 80.22 | 81.76 | 75.75 | 76.33 | 86.77 | 84.04 | 88.56 | 89.94 |
| Medium | 68.42 | 66.49 | 64.82 | 61.72 | 72.59 | 65.18 | 73.25 | 64.36 | 62.31 | 70.22 | 65.33 | 55.06 | 80.18 | 64.22 | 82.57 | 80.00 |
| Low | 38.00 | 35.49 | 34.60 | 36.28 | 41.30 | 40.95 | 37.53 | 34.74 | 34.39 | 40.69 | 31.63 | 37.29 | 61.06 | 53.84 | 57.76 | 57.09 |

*Notes:* Own calculations using data from the EU Labour Force Survey for civilians over 14 years of age. The values for the EU cover all the 25 member states of the European Union in 2005 except for Malta for which no data is available. *Immigrants* denotes people who were not born in the respective country. *Immigrants 10+* are those immigrants who have been in the respective country for at least 10 years. *Natives* are those born to mothers residing in the respective country. High level of education includes ISCED 5 and 6 levels. ISCED 5 denotes first-stage tertiary programs having an educational content more advanced than those offered by secondary levels. They do not lead to the award of an advanced research qualification and must have a cumulative duration of at least two years. ISCED 6 denotes second-stage tertiary education leading to an advanced research qualification and requiring original research contribution in the form of a thesis or dissertation. Medium level of education includes ISCED 3 and 4 levels, which denote education that typically begins at the end of full-time compulsory education and involves higher qualification and specialization than the ISCED 2 level. ISCED 3 level education is often designed to provide direct access to ISCED 5. ISCED 4 serves to broaden the knowledge achieved in ISCED 3 but is not regarded as tertiary. Low level of education includes ISCED 0, 1, and 2 levels. These include pre-primary, primary, and lower secondary or second stage of primary education. The end of ISCED 2 often coincides with the end of compulsory schooling where it exists. For further details see UNESCO (1997).

Table 19.3. Unemployment rates of natives, immigrants, and skill groups

| | EU25 | AT | BE | DE | DK | ES | FI | FR | GR | IE | IT | LU | NL | PT | SE | UK |
|---|---|---|---|---|---|---|---|---|---|---|---|---|---|---|---|---|
| Natives | 7.32 | 3.80 | 7.42 | 9.25 | 5.47 | 8.91 | 6.51 | 9.11 | 9.44 | 4.07 | 7.81 | 3.48 | 3.30 | 7.21 | 5.62 | 4.55 |
| Immigrants 10+ | 9.64 | 8.20 | 14.79 | 13.91 | 5.65 | 9.91 | 10.77 | 13.76 | 11.14 | 5.30 | 9.15 | 4.08 | 7.25 | 8.31 | 9.81 | 6.19 |
| Immigrants | 10.81 | 9.70 | 16.47 | 16.45 | 9.35 | 11.01 | 14.54 | 15.97 | 10.35 | 6.20 | 11.27 | 5.41 | 8.52 | 9.11 | 12.03 | 7.64 |
| Education: | | | | | | | | | | | | | | | | |
| High | 4.42 | 2.29 | 4.78 | 5.03 | 5.04 | 6.62 | 3.31 | 6.54 | 7.79 | 2.47 | 6.52 | 3.43 | 2.29 | 6.50 | 4.17 | 2.54 |
| Medium | 7.67 | 4.11 | 8.40 | 10.22 | 5.38 | 8.59 | 7.35 | 9.13 | 11.99 | 4.02 | 7.56 | 3.90 | 3.33 | 8.19 | 6.01 | 5.16 |
| Low | 10.49 | 8.36 | 14.18 | 18.10 | 8.15 | 10.84 | 11.21 | 14.19 | 7.86 | 6.66 | 8.99 | 5.95 | 5.81 | 7.29 | 11.54 | 8.94 |

Notes: See Table 19.2.

than natives and than those immigrants who are longer in the host country, which is consistent with the assimilation hypothesis of slow adaptation to the host labor market. In comparison to natives, immigrants do particularly poorly in Belgium, Finland, and Germany, and fairly well in Greece, Luxembourg, Portugal, and Spain.[8] Immigrants' unemployment rates are about the same as those of all the low educated for example in the EU25 and Spain, but substantially larger for Finland and the Netherlands.

Table 19.4 summarizes the occupational attainment[9] of immigrants. Like the participation picture, it exhibits a mixed pattern. While in most countries natives do significantly better than immigrants, in the UK and Portugal immigrants' attainment is higher. Tenure in the destination country pays off, especially in Spain, Ireland, and Denmark, where it actually helps immigrants to outperform the natives. The occupational attainment of the low educated is below that of immigrants, and close only in the case of Spain and Greece.

The educational composition of immigrants might explain the observed native–migrant labor market gaps. Table 19.5 provides only limited support for this conjecture. While immigrants are on average less educated than natives in some countries, including France and the Netherlands, in the EU25 as a whole and in a number of countries the evidence is less conclusive as the percentage of highly educated individuals is highest among immigrants. We can conjecture that the differences in education do not suffice to explain differences in labor market outcomes between natives and immigrants.

Turning to the other OECD countries, in the USA the foreign-born population had a higher participation rate than the natives (67.7% against 65.8%) and a lower unemployment rate (4.6% against 5.2%) in 2005.[10] This finding may reflect positive selection of immigrants into the USA and the liberal institutions that reward active participation in the labor market. The evidence is fairly mixed in the post-transition OECD members, perhaps due to the short history of immigration.[11] While participation rates are for most countries smaller for immigrants, unemployment rates are higher in the Czech Republic and Slovakia, lower in Poland, and almost equal in Hungary. The Australian experience highlights the role of institutional immigrant selection mechanisms. Table 19.6 reveals that (i) tenure in Australia in general is positively associated with immigrants' participation and negatively with their unemployment rates, (ii) immigrants who came through streams that select on skills and economic aptitude perform better than those who came through other streams, and (iii) immigrants who faced more stringent immigration rules in 1999 and 2000 perform better than the cohorts of the early 1990s.

[8]   Measured by the unemployment rate gap.
[9]   At least rank 3 of the ISCO88 classification (1: Legislators, senior officials, and managers; 2: Professionals; 3: Technicians and associated professionals). For further details see ILO (1990).
[10]   The data are from the 2005 US Bureau of Labor Statistics.
[11]   We base this on unreported statistics from the 2005 EU Labour Force Survey.

Table 19.4. Occupational attainment of natives, immigrants, and skill groups

| | EU25 | AT | BE | DE | DK | ES | FI | FR | GR | IE | IT | LU | NL | PT | SE | UK |
|---|---|---|---|---|---|---|---|---|---|---|---|---|---|---|---|---|
| Natives | 39.02 | 38.18 | 45.58 | 45.12 | 46.05 | 32.79 | 43.86 | 39.95 | 33.14 | 38.41 | 39.38 | 46.85 | 48.25 | 24.41 | 44.65 | 40.73 |
| Immigrants 10+ | 36.58 | 25.13 | 42.46 | 30.68 | 46.78 | 33.99 | 39.31 | 35.46 | 14.57 | 48.58 | 32.92 | 35.24 | 43.70 | 39.61 | 38.58 | 49.69 |
| Immigrants | 33.36 | 26.07 | 42.56 | 30.02 | 40.83 | 12.02 | 41.23 | 34.24 | 9.42 | 36.58 | 23.74 | 42.59 | 41.88 | 30.09 | 40.59 | 45.85 |
| Education: | | | | | | | | | | | | | | | | |
| High | 80.15 | 77.65 | 77.64 | 78.20 | 85.88 | 65.98 | 82.93 | 80.21 | 81.72 | 70.53 | 87.41 | 95.74 | 86.30 | 88.20 | 87.62 | 77.79 |
| Medium | 30.40 | 32.52 | 30.75 | 33.67 | 28.89 | 25.48 | 24.76 | 27.35 | 24.52 | 25.24 | 44.65 | 35.04 | 41.21 | 35.62 | 29.63 | 27.22 |
| Low | 13.14 | 9.76 | 16.48 | 16.80 | 12.85 | 11.20 | 18.46 | 16.40 | 10.05 | 22.07 | 14.54 | 6.19 | 14.72 | 12.46 | 15.12 | 12.70 |

*Notes*: Percentages of individuals over 14 years of age with occupational attainment at least rank 3 of the ISCO88 classification (1: Legislators, senior officials, and managers; 2: Professionals; 3: Technicians and associated professionals). For details on the ISCO88 classification see ILO (1990). See also Table 19.2.

Table 19.5. Educational attainment of natives and immigrants

| | EU25 | AT | BE | DE | DK | ES | FI | FR | GR | IE | IT | LU | NL | PT | SE | UK |
|---|---|---|---|---|---|---|---|---|---|---|---|---|---|---|---|---|
| **Natives** | | | | | | | | | | | | | | | | |
| High | 17.33 | 13.18 | 25.95 | 20.18 | 26.75 | '20.58 | 26.32 | 19.53 | 13.28 | 20.85 | 8.43 | 15.44 | 26.13 | 7.72 | 24.73 | 26.30 |
| Medium | 41.03 | 27.82 | 39.68 | 25.14 | 28.63 | 62.33 | 33.53 | 42.81 | 54.95 | 45.73 | 60.44 | 32.92 | 33.18 | 80.83 | 21.78 | 13.97 |
| Low | 41.64 | 59.00 | 34.37 | 54.68 | 44.62 | 17.09 | 40.16 | 37.65 | 31.77 | 33.41 | 31.13 | 51.64 | 40.69 | 11.45 | 53.49 | 59.73 |
| **Immigrants 10+** | | | | | | | | | | | | | | | | |
| High | 19.88 | 12.47 | 20.69 | 16.20 | 34.66 | 25.78 | 24.02 | 16.07 | 16.57 | 33.60 | 12.33 | 19.68 | 23.02 | 22.06 | 24.07 | 31.62 |
| Medium | 39.63 | 40.07 | 51.96 | 41.52 | 23.31 | 48.71 | 28.86 | 59.31 | 44.31 | 33.70 | 47.70 | 45.95 | 31.48 | 53.86 | 25.01 | 19.18 |
| Low | 40.49 | 47.46 | 27.35 | 42.29 | 42.02 | 25.51 | 47.11 | 24.62 | 39.12 | 32.70 | 39.97 | 34.37 | 45.50 | 24.07 | 50.92 | 49.20 |
| **Immigrants** | | | | | | | | | | | | | | | | |
| High | 21.94 | 14.18 | 22.94 | 17.36 | 33.86 | 21.33 | 21.80 | 18.06 | 13.72 | 39.79 | 11.72 | 27.51 | 23.28 | 18.83 | 28.50 | 27.70 |
| Medium | 38.32 | 39.46 | 49.46 | 41.73 | 27.89 | 46.76 | 33.74 | 57.47 | 47.74 | 26.58 | 49.80 | 39.93 | 31.69 | 54.72 | 23.86 | 18.45 |
| Low | 39.74 | 46.36 | 27.59 | 40.91 | 38.25 | 31.92 | 44.46 | 24.47 | 38.54 | 33.64 | 38.48 | 32.56 | 45.03 | 26.45 | 47.64 | 53.85 |

*Notes:* Percentages of individuals over 14 years of age with high, medium, and low educational attainment. See also Table 19.2.

Table 19.6. Immigrant adjustment and selection in Australia

| Months after arrival | Participation rates LSIA 1 | | | Unemployment rates LSIA 1 | | | Participation rates LSIA 2 | | Unemployment rates LSIA 2 | |
|---|---|---|---|---|---|---|---|---|---|---|
| | 6 | 18 | 42 | 6 | 18 | 42 | 6 | 18 | 6 | 18 |
| Skill Stream: | | | | | | | | | | |
| Business skills | 61 | 84 | 88 | 10 | 3 | 1 | 54 | 80 | 8 | 0 |
| Employer nomination scheme | 95 | 99 | 98 | 1 | 3 | 2 | 99 | 100 | 0 | 0 |
| Independent | 88 | 91 | 93 | 25 | 9 | 4 | 89 | 92 | 8 | 7 |
| Skilled Australia Sponsored | 80 | 85 | 90 | 35 | 18 | 10 | 85 | 87 | 21 | 6 |
| Family Stream: | | | | | | | | | | |
| Family | 49 | 55 | 58 | 38 | 19 | 17 | 53 | 62 | 22 | 13 |
| Humanitarian | 48 | 58 | 67 | 85 | 52 | 33 | 18 | 32 | 71 | 43 |

Notes: Participation and unemployment rates in percent for immigrants arriving in Australia through different selection streams, 6, 18, and 42 months after arrival. LSIA 1 denotes Longitudinal Survey of Immigrants to Australia that arrived in Australia between September 1993 and August 1995 and were interviewed three times. LSIA 2 covers immigrants that arrived between September 1999 and August 2000, and were interviewed twice. Tables from the Australian Department of Immigration and Citizenship, Fact Sheet 14.

These empirical observations suggest that immigrant adjustment is an important factor driving immigrants' labor market outcomes vis-à-vis the native population. While experience in the host society seems to reduce the observed gaps, it may also dissipate the positive effects of self-selection of economic immigrants on participation rates in some countries. The changing composition of immigrant flows, often due to policy changes, may be another important factor driving the immigrant–native labor market gaps. While education is an important determinant of labor market outcomes, it does not seem to be the sole driver of the observed gaps.

# 3. THE INEQUALITY IMPACT OF MIGRATION

## State of the Literature

International flows of people fuel relocation of production factors and wealth attached to migrants and thus affect the allocation of the world income. Zlotnik (1999) and Chiswick and Hatton (2003) report that migrant flows to the developed countries have increasingly involved migrants from less developed countries. Besides the perceived positive effects on world income equality, these migration flows affect also intra-national income distribution in sending and receiving countries. The literature on the effects of emigration from rural areas of poor countries dates back to Lipton (1977), who argues that such emigration increases interpersonal and inter-household inequality within and between rural villages. A rich empirical literature has found mixed evidence on the inequality-effects of emigration, especially when remittances are taken into account.[12]

The impact of immigration on the destination labor market has been modeled by a number of studies, including Chiswick et al. (1992) and Chiswick (1980, 1998). Empirical studies include Borjas (1987a), Card (1990), and DeNew and Zimmermann (1994). These are summarized in more detail by Borjas (1999a), Zimmermann (2005b) and Kahanec and Zimmermann (2008a). Typically, the effects of migration on income inequality in receiving countries largely depend on the socio-economic and demographic characteristics of the immigrant and native populations as manifested by the substitutability or complementarity of their labor. The conclusion obtained is that immigration is largely beneficial for the receiving countries. There can be phases of adjustment, but there is no overall evidence that natives' wages are strongly depressed or that unemployment is substantially increased as a consequence of immigration. The labor market integration of immigrants has been slow, but steady, and their impact on the natives in total has not been very strong, but is mostly beneficial. However, with globalization and the particular

---

[12]  See Kahanec and Zimmermann (2008a) for a more detailed overview.

pressure on low-skilled workers and the rising demand for the high skilled, the observed patterns are changing. Most importantly, the economic position of the new immigrants has become weaker. A selective immigration policy seems to be more important than before.

An important issue is the composition of immigrant inflows and the (self-)selection of immigrants. Another important aspect of immigrants' labor market success is the transferability of their skills to the host society. Dustmann *et al.* (2007) provide evidence that immigrants temporarily downgrade to less skilled occupations than they are qualified for due to incomplete transferability of their skills upon arrival. We further discuss the issues of selection and adaptation in Section 4.

## A Stylized Model of the Labor Market Impacts of Immigration

This section provides a simple theoretical setting[13] in which to investigate the impacts of labor migration on the economy of the host country. Let us start with a very simple economy where labor is homogeneous and capital is the only other production factor. Then, the standard textbook model using a competitive market framework is illustrated in Figure 19.3 with a fixed labor supply and a downward-sloping labor demand curve. Denoting the quantity of labor $L$ and the wage level $w$, the equilibrium values are $w^0$ for the wage and $\bar{L}^0$ for employment. Additional employed workers (or immigrants) of size AB depress the wage level down to $w^1$. They migrate because they receive higher wages than at home (their income is the rectangle $\bar{L}^0\bar{L}^1$BA), and are better off. Pre-migration labor loses the rectangle AD$w^0w^1$ to capital, which also takes the total welfare gain for the economy, ABD. However, wages may not be downward flexible, perhaps due to restrictions established by unions.[14] Then immigration may cause unemployment up to a maximum of AB, given we started at full employment. Gains by immigrants and capital are thus associated with either lower wages, higher unemployment, or both, depending on the degree of wage flexibility. This is often the picture behind the public debate about the impact of labor immigration.

Extending this simple equilibrium framework to the immigrants' countries of origin, the response there is symmetric: capital loses at first at the expense of labor. The countries of origin will further gain from parts of $\bar{L}^0\bar{L}^1$ BA in the form of remittances. Migration, therefore, helps to reduce inequality across the world. We also learn that, if migrants stay, they become first immigrants and then even citizens, and this may change the calculation of inequality measures: at what stage

---

[13]  Our conceptual reasoning is in line with Bauer and Zimmermann (1997) and Blau and Kahn, Chapter 8, this volume.

[14]  See Schmidt *et al.* (1994) for a theoretical treatment of this issue.

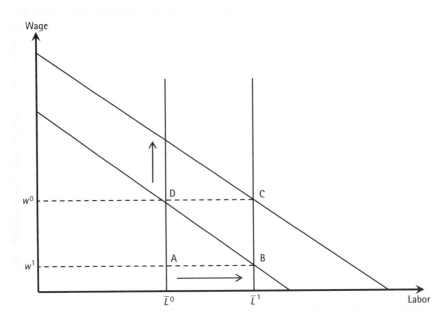

**Fig. 19.3. Gains from immigration: homogeneous labor**

do immigrants count in the evaluation of inequality, and how? Do the gains of capital justify redistribution efforts to compensate labor and to share the welfare gain ABD fairly?

As suggested above, there might be a union wage equal to $w^0$, imposing a threat of unemployment of level AB. However, in the face of competitive international markets with labor, capital, and technologies, unions might be under substantial pressure to reduce the union wage and allow the welfare gain to occur.

A further and important issue is that the assumption of an invariant labor demand curve during the phase of immigration might be unfounded. This curve might shift due to migrants' additional demand for goods, the inflow of capital, or both. Assume that immigrants are economically identical to natives upon arrival, they are perfectly assimilated in the labor market and supply the same labor and bring same amount of capital per person as the natives. A strict neoclassical world with a constant returns production function would then lead to point C with a shift in the labor demand function, full employment, and additional production equal to the rectangle $\bar{L}^0 \bar{L}^1$ CD all absorbed by the immigrants. Native labor and capital would both receive zero gains (or losses), since their parameters would remain unchanged. Immigrants, therefore, need to be 'different' to have an economic impact.

As we have seen in Section 2, an important part of reality is that labor is heterogeneous, which brings the analysis to a different level. Immigration typically involves inflows of people who are on average more or less skilled than the native workers. As a result, it has important consequences for the distribution of skills in the economy. Furthermore, it affects the equilibria in the markets for skilled and unskilled labor and thus the distribution of income in the economy. To highlight the mechanisms that drive the effects of immigration on the host economy and to provide a powerful analytical instrument to study these mechanisms it is sufficient to concentrate on two types of labor only, the skilled $S$ and the unskilled $L$.[15] Therefore, we make a simplifying assumption that immigrant and native labor is homogeneous within skill categories which we relax in Section 4.

In line with standard production functions and empirical evidence, we can assume that skilled and unskilled workers are complements.[16] We also assume for simplicity that the output price is constant. The key issues for the evaluation of the wage and employment effects of immigrant labor are then (i) whether the new workers are substitutes or complements to skilled or unskilled natives and (ii) what the equilibrium conditions are in the markets for skilled and unskilled labor in the host country. The first issue is about the share of skilled persons among the stock of immigrant workers, which is driven by immigration policies and self-selection. The answer to the second issue provides information on whether both markets can be considered to be in a competitive equilibrium or have excess supply of low-skilled workers (as in the USA) or to be in equilibrium or have excess demand for the high skilled (as in Europe). Whichever is the case, skilled immigration reduces the wages of skilled people and increases wages and employment of the unskilled. Hence, skilled immigration is 'good' not only in an allocative sense (it provides an increase of general welfare as in the homogeneous labor case), but it also improves equality in a heuristic sense. The 'poor' fare better while the 'rich' get less. For unskilled immigration we find the reverse situation.

Let us first illustrate the situation for unskilled immigration by use of Figure 19.4. While the labor market of the skilled is characterized by competitive conditions and equilibrium $A^0$, we find a union wage $w_l^0$ higher than the equilibrium wage $w_l^1$ in the market for unskilled labor. This has generated unemployment at level $\bar{L}^0 - L^0$ for the unskilled in the partial equilibrium $B^0$. Then an inflow of unskilled migrant workers may just cause additional unemployment of size $\bar{L}^1 - \bar{L}^0$, and nothing will happen in the market for skilled labor. The economic position of the (poor) unskilled will deteriorate, however. Only if the union wage declines in the face of the additional competition from the immigrants, and the wage falls from $w_l^0$ to $w_l^1$, will this lead to more unskilled employment and through complementarity also to a higher demand for skilled workers. Consequently, wages of the high skilled move

---

[15] We use the terms *skilled* and *educated* interchangeably to describe workers' level of human capital. We, however, recognize the difference between the two terms; skills being the result of the learning process involving formal education as well as experience and practice, while education refers to the time spent in formal educational institutions. Thus, while in the theoretical part we prefer to use the broader term *skills*, in the empirical part we use the available measures of *education*.

[16] See Hamermesh (1993).

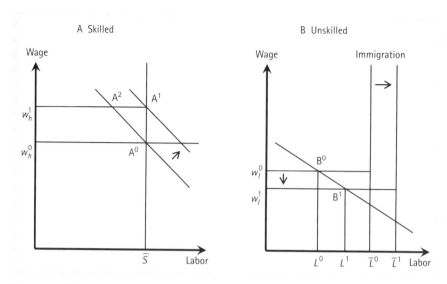

**Fig. 19.4. Heterogeneous labor markets: unskilled immigration**

up from $w_h^0$ to $w_h^1$ from equilibrium point $A^0$ to $A^1$. This effect is the stronger the more competitive is the market for unskilled labor. In sum, rising unemployment or falling wages for the poor (or both) and rising wages for the skilled workers mark a reduction in the relative economic position of the poor, and provide an indication of increasing inequality.[17]

The evaluation of the immigration of skilled workers is even more obvious. The rise in the stock of skilled workers (see the shift in the supply curve from $\bar{S}^0$ to $\bar{S}^1$ in Fig. 19.5A) moves the equilibrium point down from $C^0$ to $C^1$. The demand for unskilled workers increases due to complementarity (see the shift of the demand curve in Fig. 19.5B) and under a competitive unskilled market, unskilled wages rise from $w_l^3$ to $w_l^2$ at the full employment level $\bar{L}$. Under a rigid union wage $w_l^0$, the demand increase generates a higher level of employment of unskilled workers, whether ($D^0$ to $D^1$) or not ($D^0$ to $D^2$) the union wage decreases to $w_l^1$. Due to the complementarity of skilled and unskilled labor, the implied rise in unskilled employment ($L^0$ to $L^2$ or $L^1$) causes an upward shift in the demand for skilled workers and partly counteracts the original wage decline, raising the skilled wage from $w_h^1$ to $w_h^2$. Hence, immigration of skilled labor is likely to cause a decline in skilled wages and a rise in unskilled employment, and in the case of a competitive equilibrium in the unskilled market, also a rise in low-skilled wages. This provides a strong rationale for the conjecture that skilled immigration reduces inequality.

[17] In practice it is often difficult to provide evidence of negative effects of unskilled immigration. This might have to do with the fact that immigrants provide different types of services and talents than even unskilled natives so that they are complements to both skilled and unskilled natives.

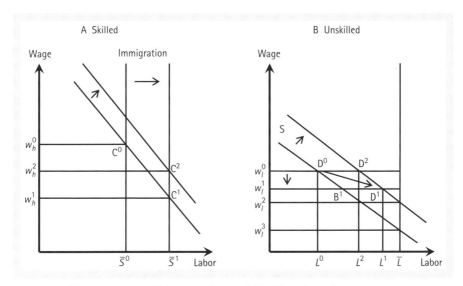

**Fig. 19.5. Heterogeneous labor markets: skilled immigration**

## High-Skilled Immigration Decreases Inequality

We further investigate this issue in an analytical labor market model that relates inequality to skill composition of the labor force and then explicate its predictions for the inequality effects of migration. Consider an economy of size one with $L$ low-skilled and $S = 1 - L$ high-skilled workers earning wages $w_l$ and $w_h$, respectively.[18] The graphical representation of the Gini coefficient as a measure of inequality in this economy is quite straightforward. Figure 19.6 plots the share of income accruing to the $\lambda$ poorest individuals in the economy, where we normalize income to unity, $w_l L + w_h (1 - L) = 1$, and order individuals from the poorest to the most affluent. The Gini coefficient is the area between the line of perfect equality, the 45 degree line, and the Lorenz curve $z(\lambda)$, depicting the share of the economy's income accruing to the $\lambda$ poorest individuals, divided by the area between the line of perfect equality and the line of perfect inequality. The line of perfect inequality attains zero for any $\lambda \in [0, 1)$ and $z(1) = 1$. Given the assumptions above, if the economy starts at point A the Gini coefficient is calculated as the size of the triangle 0A1 divided by the triangular area below the line of perfect equality, 01. The slopes of the lines 0A and A1 are $\theta/(\theta L^1 + (1 - L^1))$ and $1/(\theta L^1 + (1 - L^1))$, respectively, where $\theta = w_l/w_h$.

How does the Gini coefficient change when wages or skill composition in the economy change? Consider an increase in the relative wage $\theta$ that might occur with an inflow of highly skilled migrants who depress the relative wages of the skilled

---

[18]  That is, we normalize the size of the labor force to unity and $L$ denotes also the share of low-skilled workers.

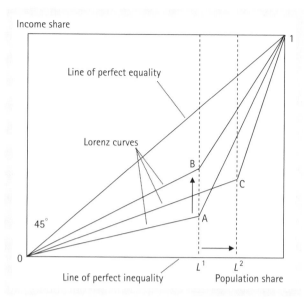

**Fig. 19.6. The effects of a rise in the relative wages of the low skilled on the Gini coefficient by share of skilled labor**

natives. We still hold $L$ constant at $L^1$ in this analysis, assuming for the moment that our population of interest for measuring inequality are the incumbent natives only. Increasing $\theta$ increases the slope of the Lorenz curve for $\lambda \in [0, L^1]$ and decreases it for $\lambda \in [L^2, 1]$, such that the economy moves to point B. Clearly, the triangle 0B1 is smaller than 0A1 and the Gini coefficient decreases, indicating a decrease in inequality. The increase in the share of low-skilled workers from $L^1$ to $L^2$, holding wages constant at the original level, has more intricate effects, as it is not obvious how the triangles 0A1 and 0C1 compare.

These issues can be tackled analytically. Kahanec and Zimmermann (2008a) show that the Gini coefficient in this economy is always decreasing in $\theta$ for admissible values of $L$ and $\theta$, confirming the geometric analysis in Figure 19.6: the rise in the relative wages of unskilled labor caused by skilled immigration causes a decrease in inequality among the natives. However, if one considers both natives and migrants together, one needs to account for the changes in the working population that immigration brings about. Based on Kahanec and Zimmermann (2008a), Figure 19.7 plots the Gini coefficient as a function of $1 - L$ and Figure 19.8 illustrates the effects of immigration for an exogenously given wage ratio, as might be the case in some Western European countries with strong union regulation. For example, an inflow of immigrants who are on average more skilled than the natives lowers $L$ in the economy. If the share of low skilled workers in the economy is low and/or the wage gap is large such that $L < 1/(1 + \sqrt{\theta}) \equiv L^0$, this decrease in $L$ decreases inequality measured by the Gini coefficient. This is the case in the upper

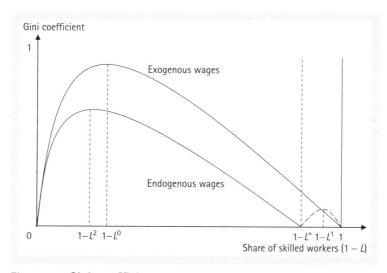

**Fig. 19.7. Gini coefficient as a function of the share of skilled workers**

right triangle in Figure 19.8. The inflow of low-skilled immigrants that increases $L$ has corresponding converse effects.[19]

The effects of immigration on inequality in a more realistic setup, where skilled and unskilled wages adjust, can then be considered. Let $\theta = \theta(L)$ and, for the sake of simplicity, consider a specific case with the Constant Elasticity of Substitution (CES) production function $C = (L^{1-\rho} + (aS)^{1-\rho})^{\frac{1}{1-\rho}}$, where $\rho = 1/\varepsilon$ and $\varepsilon > 0$ is the (finite) elasticity of substitution of high- and low-skilled labor in a competitive industry and $a > 1$ is the efficiency shift factor of skilled relative to unskilled labor. Under these assumptions $\theta = (L/(a(1 - L)))^{-\rho}$ and the earnings of an unskilled relative to a skilled worker are $\theta/a$. Where the earnings of high-skilled workers are higher than those of low-skilled ones, $\theta/a < 1$, Kahanec and Zimmermann (2008a) show that the Gini coefficient is

$$G(L) = \frac{L\,(1 - L)\left(a - (a\,(1 - L))^\rho \big/ L^\rho\right)}{a - aL + (a\,(1 - L))^\rho \big/ L^{\rho-1}}$$

and that there is a nondegenerate range $L^1 L^2$ within the interval $[0, 1]$ where $G(L)$ is increasing in $L$. In fact, whenever $\varepsilon \in (0, 1]$, $dG(L)/dL > 0$ for any $L \in (0, 1)$. For $\varepsilon > 1$, $G(L)$ is increasing within and decreasing outside of $L^1 L^2$, that is, for very low and very high values of $L$. It turns out that the range $L^1 L^2$ tends to be quite large.[20] Parametric values determine which $L \in (0, 1)$ are admissible with respect to the condition $\theta/a < 1$ and which are not. We denote $L^*$ the value

[19] The effects on the source countries are the mirror image of those on the destination countries.

[20] For example, if the substitutability of skilled and unskilled labor is about 2.5, as estimated by C. U. Chiswick (1978), and high-skilled labor is twice as productive as its low-skilled counterpart, the corresponding values are $L^1 = 0.07$ and $L^2 = 0.83$.

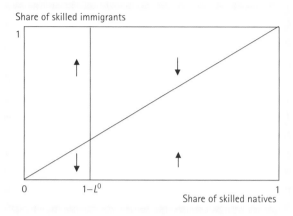

**Fig. 19.8. The effects of immigration on the Gini coefficient by shares of skilled labor among natives and immigrants: the case of inflexible wages**

of $L$ at which $\theta/a = 1$. One can show that $L^* = a^{1-1/\rho}/(1 + a^{1-1/\rho})$, $L^1 < L^* < L^2$, and $\theta/a < 1$ for any $L \in (L^*, 1)$ and $\theta/a > 1$ for any $L \in (0, L^*)$.[21] It turns out that for the values of $L \in (0, L^*)$ the Gini coefficient equals $-G(L)$. Figure 19.7 shows the Gini coefficient as a function of the share of *skilled* labor, $1 - L$, in case of endogenous wages and for $\varepsilon > 1$. Note that for OECD economies with a large share of skilled labor, the relevant segment of $G(L)$ is decreasing in $1 - L$ for the most part.

This result enables us to consider the effects of changes in $L$ that occur when immigrants of different skill composition (vis-à-vis the natives) enter (leave) the economy under the conditions of flexible wages. In Figure 19.9 the arrows indicate the effects of immigration on inequality in the economy, for various combinations of shares of skilled and unskilled labor among the natives and immigrants. For example, in the upper central trapezoid for $L \in (L^*, L^2)$ an inflow of immigrants who are on average more skilled than the natives decreases inequality in the economy.[22]

To summarize, theory predicts that skilled immigration decreases inequality in advanced economies such as the OECD countries where skilled labor is abundant. Accounting for the endogeneity of wages confirms this result, predicting that inequality is decreasing with skilled immigration for moderate to high values and may be increasing for very high values of the share of skilled labor, $1 - L$. We examine this theoretical result empirically in the next section.

---

[21]  See Kahanec and Zimmermann (2008a). Note, that if $\varepsilon > 1$ ($\varepsilon \in (0, 1)$), it must be that $L < 0.5$ ($L > 0.5$) for $\theta/a < 1$ to hold. $L^* = 0.26$ under the assumptions of the previous footnote.

[22]  Note that we consider the case $\varepsilon > 1$ in the figure.

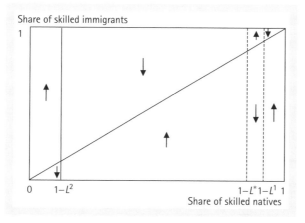

**Fig. 19.9. The effects of immigration on the Gini coefficient by shares of skilled labor among natives and immigrants: the case of flexible wages**

## The Gini Coefficient and the Educated Labor Force

As discussed in the previous section, theory predicts a negative relationship between inequality and the share of skilled labor in the labor force, which is itself a function of immigrants' skills, for advanced economies where skilled labor is abundant. We, therefore, analyze here the empirical relationship between inequality and educational attainment levels in the labor force.[23] We combine data on education, labor force characteristics, and other national indicators from the OECD Statistical Compendium 2007 with the Gini measures reported in the World Income Inequality Database (WIID 2007) version 2.0b compiled by the WIDER institute at the United Nations University and published in May 2007.

The WIID 2007 dataset reports Gini coefficients for a large number of countries covering many years of collection and estimation of this inequality indicator. In those cases where WIID 2007 reports multiple Gini coefficients per year and country, we prefer those of the highest quality if based on gross rather than net takings and earnings rather than broader measures of income to quantify those components of economic inequality that stem from the labor market as precisely as possible.[24] The combined dataset covers 29 OECD member states and provides 154

[23] As mentioned earlier, education measures a certain type of skills.

[24] It needs to be acknowledged that whether earnings inequality is measured at the individual or household level is a non-trivial issue in the context of measuring the relationship between inequality and immigration. In particular, immigrants often have larger households and different family structures than natives. As a result, measures of inequality based on individual and household earnings may give different pictures of inequality. The analysis of this complex relationship is beyond the scope of this chapter, however. Nevertheless, we control for the level (individual vs. household) at which the Gini coefficient was measured in our empirical analysis.

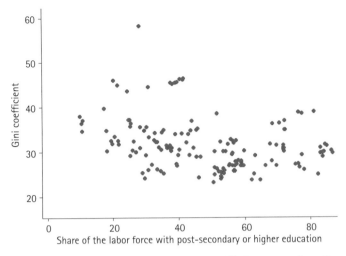

**Fig. 19.10. Scatter plot of the Gini coefficient as a function of the share of labor force with post-secondary or higher education**

*Notes*: OECD members except for Iceland. Data on Gini coefficients are from the WIID 2007 database. Data on the shares of the labor force with given education are from the OECD Compendium, 1992–2003.

observations with non-missing information on the Gini coefficient and the shares of the labor force with post-secondary or higher education.

Figure 19.10 plots the Gini coefficient against the shares of educated labor at work measured by the variables described above. We observe a U-shaped relationship that is downward sloping for most of the observed data. To investigate the properties of these relationships more precisely, we compute the predicted values of a locally weighted regression of the Gini coefficient on the measures of educational attainment in the labor force. Figure 19.11 confirms the U-shaped character of the observed relationships. Indeed, this relationship is negative for about 80% of the observations.

However, there are factors other than the distribution of educational levels in the labor market that may influence this relationship. For example, Katz and Murphy (1992) argue that increased demand for skilled workers and females as well as changes in the allocation of labor between industries contributed to increasing inequality in the USA in recent years. Gustafsson and Johansson (1999) find that the share of industry in employment, per capita gross domestic product, international trade, the relative size of the public expenditures, as well as the demographic structure of the population affect inequality measured by the Gini coefficient across countries and years. Topel (1994) provides evidence that technological and economic developments determine economic inequality. A regression

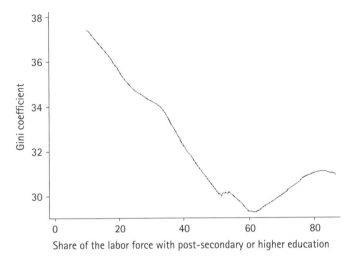

**Fig. 19.11. Line plot of the nonparametric locally weighted regression of the Gini coefficient as a function of the share of labor force with post-secondary or higher education**

*Notes:* OECD members except for Iceland. For data sources see Fig. 19.10. 1992–2003.

analysis by Kahanec and Zimmermann (2008b) using the covariates mentioned in the literature confirms that the observed U-shaped, predominantly negative, relationship is robust and significant over a number of model specifications, including models with weighing by data quality and country size, clustering, and random and fixed country effects. These empirical findings are consistent with our theoretical prediction of a generally negative relationship between the quality of labor force and inequality.

# 4. IMMIGRANT ABSORPTION, SELECTION, AND ETHNICITY

## Demand, Supply, and Policy Measures

There are many channels through which immigration affects the host economy. Immigration brings in new people with diverse characteristics and economic aptitudes, it affects the economic prospects of the native population, and it impinges on the decisions of important economic and policy actors. The labor market status of immigrants is a principal measure of immigrants' success in the destination economy. After proper adaptation to the host country, immigrants can fully utilize their skills, possibly turning from low- into high-skilled labor. As shown in the previous section, the skill level of immigrants affects inequality. Therefore, the degree of immigrants' labor market assimilation is in turn an important determinant of economic inequality in the host society.

One reaction to concerns about the limited absorption of immigration is immigrant selection based on clear admission criteria and immigration policies (Zimmermann, 2005a, 2005b; Constant and Zimmermann, 2005 for an evaluation of immigration policies across countries). Constant and Zimmermann (2005) aim to understand the impact of the legal status of the migrant at the time of entry into the host country (work permit, refugee, and kinship) on work participation and earnings using individual survey data for Denmark and Germany. Their results suggest that non-economic migrants are less qualified for the labor market and exhibit lower earnings even having controlled for skill level. Arriving through family reunion or as asylum seekers or refugees affects paid-employment earnings negatively in both Germany and Denmark. However, while the effect is of about the same size for both groups in Denmark, refugee/asylum status is more harmful in Germany than family reunion status. Individuals arriving with work status in Germany are more likely to earn less when changing to self-employment than when arriving through another channel. These estimates suggest that there are long-lasting effects of legal status at entry into a country on the earnings potential of immigrants. Hence, a selective immigration policy might be helpful in ensuring the attraction of more talented individuals.

There is some confusion about how best to study immigrant absorption into the host country's society and economy. Economists typically have discussed 'assimilation' as the process where (i) immigrant earnings each year come closer to the earnings of an equivalent native (B. R. Chiswick, 1978) or (ii) among two observationally equivalent immigrants the one with the longer presence in the host country earns more (LaLonde and Topel, 1992: 75). As Borjas (1999a: 1721) has pointed out, it is important to stress in the analysis what the relevant reference group is. In our context it is important to deal with the question of how immigrants become economically like natives. They might earn less upon arrival, but converge with time spent in the country after adapting to the host country labor market. This economic absorption, however, does not have to be complemented by cultural absorption, that is, the ethnic identity of the immigrant might evolve separately and exhibit an independent effect on economic performance. We, therefore, distinguish here between economic assimilation and cultural or ethnic assimilation.[25]

---

[25] According to Webster's Collegiate Dictionary assimilation is 'the process whereby individuals or groups of differing ethnic heritage are absorbed into the dominant culture of a society'.

## Economic Assimilation

The pioneering work of B. R. Chiswick (1978) investigates the economic assimilation of immigrants defined as earnings parity between immigrants and natives and their age–earnings profiles in a cross-sectional setting. The typical pattern observed in cross-sectional data features three distinct attributes. First, upon arrival, immigrants' earnings are significantly below those of natives, holding observable skills constant. This finding is typically ascribed to immigrants' lack of certain unobservable skills, non-transferability of their skills, and their lack of information specific to the host economy, including language, educational qualifications, and general information about the host labor market. Second, with experience in the host economy, however, immigrants acquire the missing skills and information and catch up with the natives.

Finally, the evidence in the USA is that after a certain period of converging to the native level of earnings, immigrants seem to earn more than natives. The standard human capital model does not offer simple explanations for this finding. The typical explanation offered by economists is selection, the innate (unobservable) ability of immigrants, and their drive and determination to succeed in the new country. Since the decision to migrate involves weighing the costs and benefits of migration, people with stronger economic prospects in the destination economy are more likely to migrate and, therefore, after a period of adjustment, on average outperform the representative native population.

The cross-sectional analysis could thus explain why immigrants who migrated in the more distant past earn more than their more recent counterparts. However, the cross-sectional data may hide certain cohort effects as argued by Borjas (1985). In particular, more recent immigrants can be inherently different to those who arrived some years ago. If these more recent arrivals are unobservably less skilled than the older cohorts, cross-sectional data cannot distinguish these cohort effects from the assimilation hypothesis described above. Cohort effects may be driven by changes in the immigration policy of the host country or by institutional and political changes in the source countries. For example, refugees from the Soviet bloc to Germany were typically highly skilled professionals. After the fall of the Berlin Wall, however, migration barriers were lessened and a much more varied sample of people decided to migrate to the West.

The empirical evidence on these cohort effects suggests that these effects may be quite large.[26] Borjas (1995) provides evidence that the educational attainment of immigrant cohorts in the USA declined by 1.8 years of schooling between 1960 and 1990 and that the age–earnings profiles of the 1950–59 cohort are higher than those of the 1970–79 cohort throughout the life cycle. In particular, while the earlier cohort's age–earnings profiles are above those of the natives, the more recent immigrants' profiles are inferior to the natives'. These cohort effects suggest

---

[26] Borjas (1994) surveys the early literature.

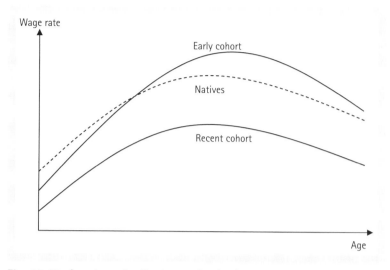

Fig. 19.12. Immigrant adjustment in the host economy

that more recent arrivals will hardly assimilate and never fully catch up with the natives.

Figure 19.12 compares the hypothetical age–earnings profiles of two immigrant cohorts with the natives. According to the assimilation hypothesis, the early cohort of immigrants quickly catches up with the natives, surpassing them after some adjustment time. On the other hand, the more recent immigrant cohort has poor labor market characteristics that drive their age–earnings profiles below those of the natives and the earlier immigrant cohort throughout the life cycle and full assimilation does not occur.

Immigrant assimilation has important consequences for inequality in the host economy. Under the assimilation hypothesis, immigration affects earnings inequality in the host economy in two ways. First, fresh immigrants earn below average wages and thus increase the number of low-paid workers. After a certain assimilation period, however, positively selected immigrants earn more than the average native and thus increase the number of high-paid workers. Given our earlier theoretical results, if immigrants first behave as low-skilled and then, after an adjustment period, as high-skilled, immigration eventually lowers earnings inequality. The exact magnitude of this effect is importantly determined by the speed of the assimilation process. The cohort effect hypothesis, on the other hand, predicts that immigration invariably contributes to the number of low-paid workers and that these effects are invariant over time and immigrants' life cycle.

The literature has identified a single most important factor driving the declining relative skills across immigrant waves: the changing composition of immigrants in terms of their country of origin.[27] For the USA, Borjas (1990) reports a significant shift in the composition of new arrivals, Latin American and Asian immigrants replacing those of European origin. The relatively facile transferability of human capital between developed countries as compared to the transfer from less developed to developed countries and this increase in the share of immigrants from less developed countries explains why more recent immigrants have lower skills. The higher opportunity costs of migration in high-GDP countries leading to selection of only immigrants with the best economic prospects further explains why immigrants from less developed countries are less skilled.

This selection argument can be extended to different skill groups within and between source countries.[28] The character of the earnings distribution in the source country affects the migration incentives of high- and low-skilled workers differently. In a country that has a relatively flat earnings distribution the opportunity costs of migration are higher for the low-skilled workers who enjoy wealth redistribution in their favor. On the other hand, in a country with a relatively steep income distribution it is the high skilled who enjoy high returns to skills and have high opportunity costs of migration (Borjas, 1985). As a result, we can expect that high-skilled (low-skilled) migrants will move from countries that have a flatter (steeper) income distribution than the destination country. The logic of this argument can easily be explained using the Roy model.[29] Consider people in the source country making their migration decision based on the expected wage in the source and destination countries. Assume that earnings are determined solely by individual skills such that

$$w_s = a_s + \gamma_s s \tag{1}$$

$$w_d = a_d + \gamma_d s \tag{2}$$

where $w$ denotes wages, $a$ is the shift factor, and $\gamma$ denotes the returns to skills $s$. Subscripts $s$ and $d$ denote the source and destination country, respectively. The migration decision is illustrated in Figure 19.13. Panel A depicts skill–earnings profiles (1) and (2) in the situation where the source country is more egalitarian than the destination country. After the breakeven point $b_p$ migration becomes an attractive option and immigrants are positively selected on skills. In panel B, on the other hand, it is the destination country that is relatively more egalitarian and $b_p$ marks the breakeven point of skill-driven negative migrant selection. According to

---

[27] Chiswick (1999) discusses the theoretical approaches to self-selection, noting that especially migrants whose main reason to migrate is economic opportunities tend to be favorably self-selected.

[28] Another extension would be the self-selection of migrants who decide to return to their home countries, or to third countries. See e.g. Borjas (1989), Constant and Massey (2003), Dustmann (2003), and Galor and Stark (1991).

[29] Roy (1951) and Borjas (1987b).

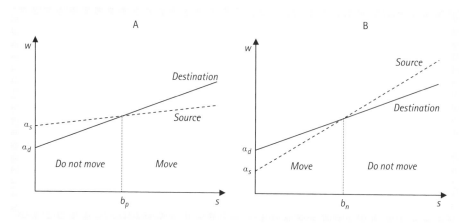

**Fig. 19.13. Inequality as a determinant of the migration decision**

this model, it is not the average income level in the source and destination country that drives skill-based selection of migrants. Rather, it is the relative distribution of income.[30]

The Roy model has important implications for income distribution in the source and destination countries as a function of immigrants' self-selection. It predicts that the more (less) egalitarian the destination country is, the higher the likelihood that it attracts low (high) skill immigrants. In effect, egalitarian (non-egalitarian) destination countries are prone to earnings inequality with a concentration of immigrants at the lower (upper) tail of the earnings distribution. On the other hand, egalitarian (non-egalitarian) source countries are likely to experience an uneven distribution of earnings with a thin upper (lower) tail.

These distributional aspects highlight the role of immigration policy for earnings inequality between and within immigrant and native groups in the host society. Focusing on Europe, and Germany and Denmark in particular, Constant and Zimmermann (2005) provide evidence that these countries could benefit from more pro-active policies aimed at recruitment and integration of immigrants with strong economic prospects. An example of such a policy is selection of qualified immigrants using observable and measurable criteria. Such policies would lower the shares of immigrants with inferior economic aptitude in the host economy. Depending on the selection criteria, such polices have real potential to reduce income inequality and immigrant poverty in the destination countries.

---

[30]  See Chiswick (1999) for a more general treatment of self-selection. Chiquiar and Hanson (2005) provide evidence inconsistent with the negative selection hypothesis hypothesized by Borjas (1987b).

## Ethnicity and Ethnic Identity

There is a growing and related literature studying the evolution of culture and ethnic identity and its role in economic outcomes.[31] Constant *et al.* (2006a) define ethnic identity as the balance between the commitment to or self-identification with the culture and society of the origin and host countries. They conjecture that a migrant who arrives in the host country moves along a plane formed by two axes representing commitment to the home and host countries. On the horizontal axis they measure commitment to and self-identification with the country of origin, and on the vertical axis they measure commitment to and self-identification with the host country.

Confronted with both cultures, which combination of commitments do migrants choose to uphold? The two-dimensional *ethnosizer*, a measure of the intensity of a person's ethnic identity, deals with this question and conceptualizes the position of migrants in the positive orthant of commitment combinations. As illustrated in Figure 19.14, the *ethnosizer* contains four measures or regimes of ethnic identity differentiated by the strength of cultural and social commitments. *Assimilation* (A) is a strong identification with the host culture and society, coupled with a firm conformity to its norms, values, and codes of conduct, and a weak identification with ancestry; *Integration* (I) is achieved when an individual combines, incorporates, and exhibits both strong dedication to the origin and commitment and conformity to the host society; *Marginalization* (M) is a weak dedication to or strong detachment from either the dominant culture or the culture of origin; and *Separation* (S) is an exclusive commitment to the culture of origin even after years of emigration, paired with weak involvement in the host culture and country realities. Starting at point $(1, 0)$, a migrant can undergo a more complicated journey through the various states, leaving separation towards integration, assimilation, or marginalization, or remaining separated.

The *ethnosizer* is empirically constructed by using individual data with information on the following elements: language, culture, societal interaction, history of migration, and ethnic self-identification (Constant *et al.*, 2006a). We briefly summarize some recent findings about the effects of ethnic identity on economic behavior.[32] The two-dimensional *ethnosizer* is added to standard regressions to

[31]  Ottaviano and Peri (2006) and Guiso *et al.* (2006) deal with the mixed impact of culture. Kahanec (2007) investigates how the interaction of social relationships and ethnicity drive ethnic competition and specialization in the labor market. Theories of ethnic identity (Darity *et al.*, 2006; Austen-Smith and Fryer, 2005; Chiswick, 2006; Battu *et al.*, 2007) and empirical studies (Mason, 2004; Constant *et al.*, 2006a and 2006b) provide a better understanding of societal and economic behavior.

[32]  Constant and Zimmermann (2008) provide an overview of this research and present evidence that the measures of ethnic identity (the *ethnosizer*) are exogenous. Constant *et al.* (2006b) deal with the probability to work, Zimmermann (2007) with earnings, and Constant *et al.* (forthcoming) with homeownership.

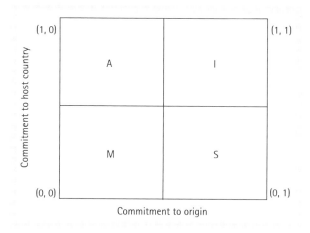

**Fig. 19.14. The two-dimensional non-negative** *ethnosizer*

*Note:* See Constant *et al.* (2006a).

examine the particular contribution of ethnic identity. Consistently, it is found that ethnicity matters significantly for economic performance and that the findings are very robust with respect to the concrete model specification. Assimilation and integration have a positive effect on economic performance, while separation and marginalization do not.

As discussed above, the economic literature on assimilation considers economic assimilation, which suggests that immigrants may finally converge to the economic behavior and performance of natives. The issue is the speed of this process. The ethnicity literature considers ethnic identity as cultural capital that may emerge and develop, but in all likelihood persists over time and exhibits comparative advantages and disadvantages for the economic process. This approach may help to explain why different ethnic groups can be observed to exhibit very different positions in the distribution of income and why some stay at the lower tail of income distribution while others move up and close the gap vis-à-vis the natives.

# 5. CONCLUSIONS AND FURTHER RESEARCH

The analysis in this chapter suggests that skilled labor immigration has a substantial potential to reduce inequality in the receiving countries. An important channel is the rise in relative wages of the unskilled with respect to the wages of the skilled. Unskilled immigration seems to generally increase inequality, but under specific circumstances it may decrease it. For instance, if migrant adaptation overcomes downgrading, immigrants may turn from low- to high-skilled workers.

But the relationship between inequality and the presence of immigrants in the economy is not trivial. Complementarities between skilled and unskilled (immigrant) labor and ethnic capital, or the role of skilled and unskilled immigrants in satisfying the taste for variety in the host economy, may affect inequality in complex ways. One has to be aware also of the different institutional and social histories of immigration and inequality across countries. Immigrants differ across countries, not only in terms of ethnic origin but also in terms of educational attainment, ethnic identity, and societal and economic aspirations.

The flow of labor migration depends on incentives, but also on inequality in the sending and receiving countries. The relative inequality in the source and destination countries affects the prospects of immigrants with different skill levels differently, and thus feeds into the selection of immigrants across destination countries. Many immigrants do not remain migrants forever. Some of them assimilate, some integrate, some return, and some remain trapped to different degrees in social and labor market exclusion. The dynamics of the allocation of immigrants across these states importantly affects their labor market position as well as that of the natives and thus inequality.

With the rising excess demand for skilled labor worldwide, and the positive consequences of labor migration for allocative and distributional purposes, there is significant potential for an international policy regime of unrestricted temporary and circular skilled labor migration. Highly skilled workers could obtain a global green card to work in their country of choice depending on the availability of a work contract. This could contribute to global welfare and more equality, since such a temporary and circular migration regime makes the best use of scarce brains and ensures that both sending and receiving regions receive their share of the gains of migration.

Given the complexity of the effects and causes that the relationship between migration and inequality involves, research on the causal effects of migration on inequality in the host and sending countries as well as on world inequality is urgently required. We understand already many parts of this link, but the big picture is unclear, partly due to the lack of data. Some of the specific issues that need further attention include (i) the effects on sending countries generated by the brain drain, (ii) the inter-relationships between immigration, immigration policy, attitudes towards immigrants, and immigrants' labor market outcomes, and (iii) the interactions between immigrant assimilation, ethnic capital, and immigrants' labor market outcomes.

## References

Austen-Smith, D., and Fryer Jr., R. G. 2005. 'An Economic Analysis of "Acting White"'. *Quarterly Journal of Economics*, 120: 551–83.

Battu, H., Mwale, M., and Zenou, Y. 2007. 'Oppositional Identities and the Labour Market'. *Journal of Population Economics*, 20: 643–67.

Bauer, T., and Zimmermann, K. F. 1997. 'Integrating the East: The Labour Market Effects of Immigration', in S. W. Black (ed.), *Europe's Economy Looks East: Implications for the EU and Germany*. Cambridge: Cambridge University Press, 269–306.

Borjas, G. J. 1985. 'Assimilation, Changes in Cohort Quality, and the Earnings of Immigrants'. *Journal of Labour Economics*, 3: 463–89.

——1987a. 'Immigrants, Minorities, and Labour Market Competition'. *Industrial and Labour Relations Review*, 40: 382–92.

——1987b. 'Self-Selection and the Earnings of Immigrants'. *American Economic Review*, 77: 531–53.

——1989. 'Immigrant and Emigrant Earnings: A Longitudinal Study'. *Economic Inquiry*, 27: 21–37.

——1990. *Friends or Strangers: The Impact of Immigrants on the US Economy*. New York: Basic Books.

——1994. 'The Economics of Immigration'. *Journal of Economic Literature*, 32: 1667–717.

——1995. 'Assimilation and Changes in Cohort Quality Revisited: What Happened to Immigrant Earnings During the 1980s?' *Journal of Labour Economics*, 13: 201–45.

——1999a. 'Economic Analysis of Immigration', in O. C. Ashenfelter and D. Card (eds.), *Handbook of Labour Economics*, vol. 3A. Amsterdam: Elsevier, 1697–760.

——1999b. *Heaven's Door: Immigration Policy and the American Economy*. Princeton: Princeton University Press.

Card, D. 1990. 'Impact of the Mariel Boatlift on the Miami Labour Market'. *Industrial and Labour Relations Review*, 43: 245–57.

Chiquiar, D., and Hanson, G. H. 2005. 'International Migration, Self-Selection, and the Distribution of Wages: Evidence from Mexico and the United States'. *Journal of Political Economy*, 113: 239–81.

Chiswick, B. R. 1978. 'The Effect of Americanization on the Earnings of Foreign-Born Men'. *Journal of Political Economy*, 86: 897–921.

——1980. '*An Analysis of the Economic Progress and Impact of Immigrants, Employment and Training Administration*'. US Department of Labour. National Technical Information Service, PB80-200454.

——1998. 'The Economic Consequences of Immigration: Application to the United States and Japan', in Myron Weiner and Tadashi Hanami (eds.), *Temporary Workers or Future Citizens? Japanese and U.S. Migration Policies*. New York: New York University Press, 177–208.

——1999. 'Are Immigrants Favorably Self-Selected?' *American Economic Review*, 89: 181–5.

——and Hatton, T. J. 2003. 'International Migration and the Integration of Labour Markets', in M. Bordo, A. Taylor, and J. Williamson (eds.), *Globalization in Historical Perspective*. NBER Conference Report, 65–119.

Chiswick, C. U. 1978. 'The Growth of Professional Occupations in U.S. Manufacturing, 1900–73', in I. Sirageldin (ed.), *Research in Human Capital and Development*. Greenwich, Conn.: JAI Press, 191–217.

—— 2006. 'The Economic Determinants of Ethnic Assimilation'. IZA Discussion Paper no. 2212.

—— CHISWICK, B. R., and KARRAS, G. 1992. 'The Impact of Immigrants on the Macroeconomy'. *Carnegie-Rochester Conference Series on Public Policy*, 37: 279–316.

CONSTANT, A., GATAULLINA, L., and ZIMMERMANN, K. F. 2006a. 'Ethnosizing Immigrants'. IZA Discussion Paper no. 2040.

—— —— —— 2006b. 'Gender, Ethnic Identity and Work'. IZA Discussion Paper no. 2420.

—— and MASSEY, D. S. 2003. 'Self-Selection, Earnings, and Out-Migration: A Longitudinal Study of Immigrants to Germany'. *Journal of Population Economics*, 16: 631–53.

—— ROBERTS, R., and ZIMMERMANN, K. F. forthcoming. 'Ethnic Identity and Immigrant Homeownership'. *Urban Studies*.

—— AND ZIMMERMANN, K. F. 2005. 'Immigrant Performance and Selective Immigration Policy: A European Perspective'. *National Institute Economic Review*, 194: 94–105

—— —— 2008. 'Measuring Ethnic Identity and its Impact on Economic Behavior'. *Journal of the European Economic Association*, 6: 424–33.

DARITY, W. A., MASON, P. L., and STEWART, J. B. 2006. 'The Economics of Identity: The Origin and Persistence of Racial Identity Norms'. *Journal of Economic Behavior and Organization*, 60: 283–305.

DE NEW, J. P., and ZIMMERMANN, K. F. 1994. 'Native Wage Impacts of Foreign Labour: A Random Effects Panel Analysis'. *Journal of Population Economics*, 7: 177–92.

DUSTMANN, C. 2003. 'Return Migration, Wage Differentials, and the Optimal Migration Duration'. *European Economic Review*, 47: 353–69.

—— FRATTINI, T., and PRESTON, I. 2007. 'A Study of the Migrant Workers and the National Minimum Wage and Enforcement Issues'. Research Report for the Low Pay Commission. University College London.

GALOR, O., and STARK, O. 1991. 'The Probability of Return Migration, Migrants' Work Effort and Migrants' Performance'. *Journal of Development Economics*, 35: 399–405.

GUISO, L., SAPIENZA, P., and ZINGALES, L. 2006. 'Does Culture Affect Economic Outcomes?' NBER Working Paper no. 11999.

GUSTAFSSON, B., and JOHANSSON, M. 1999. 'In Search of Smoking Guns: What Makes Income Inequality Vary over Time in Different Countries?' *American Sociological Review*, 64: 585–605.

HAMERMESH, D. S. 1993. *Labour Demand*. Princeton: Princeton University Press.

ILO (1990). *International Standard Classification of Occupations (ISCO-88)*. Geneva: International Labour Office.

KAHANEC, M. 2007. 'Ethnic Competition and Specialization'. IZA Discussion Paper no. 3167.

—— and ZIMMERMANN, K. F. 2008a. 'International Migration, Ethnicity and Economic Inequality'. IZA Discussion Paper no. 3450.

—— —— 2008b. 'Migration, the Quality of the Labour Force and Economic Inequality'. IZA Discussion Paper no. 3560.

KATZ, L. F., and MURPHY, K. M. 1992. 'Changes in Relative Wages, 1963–1987: Supply and Demand Factors'. *The Quarterly Journal of Economics*, 107: 35–78.

LALONDE, R. J., and TOPEL, R. H. 1992. 'The Assimilation of Immigrants in the U.S. Labor Market', in G. J. Borjas and R. B Freeman (eds.), *Immigration and the Work Force: Economic Consequences for the United States and Source Areas*. Chicago: University of Chicago Press.

LIPTON, M. 1977. *Why Poor People Stay Poor: Urban Bias in Developing Countries.* London: Temple Smith.

MASON, P. L. 2004. 'Annual Income, Hourly Wages, and Identity among Mexican-Americans and other Latinos'. *Industrial Relations,* 43: 817–34.

OTTAVIANO, G. I. P., and PERI, G. 2006. 'The Economic Value of Cultural Diversity: Evidence from US Cities'. *Journal of Economic Geography,* 6: 9–44.

ROY, A. D. 1951. 'Some Thoughts on the Distribution of Earnings'. *Oxford Economic Papers,* 3: 135–46.

SAPIR, A., AGHION, P., BERTOLA, G., HELLWIG, M., PISANI-FERRY, J., ROSATI, D., VIÑALS, J., WALLACE, H., BUTI, M., NAVA, M., and SMITH, P. M. 2004. *An Agenda for a Growing Europe: The Sapir Report.* Oxford: Oxford University Press.

SCHMIDT, C. M., STILZ, A., and ZIMMERMANN, K. F. 1994. 'Mass Migration, Unions, and Government Intervention'. *Journal of Public Economics,* 55: 185–201.

TOPEL, ROBERT H. 1994. 'Regional Labour Markets and the Determinants of Wage Inequality'. *The American Economic Review, Papers and Proceedings of the Hundred and Sixth Annual Meeting of the American Economic Association,* 84: 17–22.

UNESCO 1997. *International Standard Classification of Education. ISCED 1997.* <http://portal.unesco.org/education/en/files/9405/10371902320ISCED_A_word.doc/ISCED_A%2Bword.doc>, retrieved on Jan. 29, 2008.

ZIMMERMANN, K. F. 2005a. 'European Labour Mobility: Challenges and Potentials'. *De Economist,* 153: 425–50.

—— 2005b. *European Migration: What Do We Know?* Oxford and New York: Oxford University Press.

—— 2007. 'Migrant Ethnic Identity: Concept and Policy Implications'. *Ekonomia, The Cyprus Economic Society Annual Lecture in Economics 2007.* Forthcoming.

ZLOTNIK, H. 1999. 'Trends of International Migration since 1965: What Existing Data Reveal'. *International Migration,* 37: 21–61.

# CHAPTER 20

# INTERGENERATIONAL INCOME MOBILITY AND THE ROLE OF FAMILY BACKGROUND

ANDERS BJÖRKLUND

MARKUS JÄNTTI[1]

## 1. INTRODUCTION

How a person's income is related to her family background is a topic of great interest in academic circles, political debate, and everyday conversations among people. There are many reasons to be interested in the association between income and family background. To illustrate, consider two hypothetical societies. The first is

[1] Björklund acknowledges financial support from the Swedish Council for Working Life and Social Research. Jäntti's work is supported by the Russell Sage Foundation and a grant from the Academy of Finland. The authors thank Robert Erikson, Susan Mayer, Cheti Nicoletti, and Gary Solon for useful comments on earlier versions of the chapter.

characterized by strong income associations between parents and children as well as between siblings, so knowing a person's family background makes it easy to predict her adult income. In the second society, the association between family members' income is weak, so family background is a poor predictor of future income. In the first society, a person's income is largely predetermined by factors not chosen by herself. Arguably, there is less equality of opportunity in the first society.

Strong family income associations can have other societal consequences, as illustrated by this example from the sociological literature on social class mobility. In the 1800s, the USA was conjectured to be a highly mobile society, especially compared to Europe. The higher US mobility implied that fathers and sons more often came to belong to different social groups than in Europe, which is why Europeans formed stronger class solidarity. This in turn would explain why left-wing political parties and unions became stronger in Europe than in the USA.[2]

Strong income persistence across generations is cause for concern also if parental income has *direct causal effects* on offspring. For example, poor parents might be unable to invest in their children's human capital. If there are causal effects of parental income, public interventions that weaken the transfer of inequality from one generation to the next may be called for.

Although some central issues in this research field are 'only' descriptive in kind— for example, comparing the correlation between fathers' and sons' income in two countries—empirical measurement is non-trivial and, in particular, requires sophisticated data. First, data are needed for different family members. Analysis of the intergenerational associations, such as between fathers and sons, requires incomes for two generations to be measured during two different time periods. Accurate parental income data are unlikely to be obtained by asking retrospective questions about fathers' incomes decades before the sons'. Retrospective questions are more reliable for finding out fathers' main occupation and social class, which probably explains why sociological intergenerational social class analysis has a longer history than intergenerational income analysis. Second, family associations are only meaningfully measured using *long-run*, ideally lifetime income. Intergenerational analysis requires good estimates of the long-run income of two generations.

Representative data sets that satisfy these requirements have only recently become available. Research in this field got a major boost in 1992, when the *American Economic Review* published two papers on US intergenerational income mobility. Solon (1992) and Zimmermann (1992) took the data requirements seriously and found, using different data sources, much less mobility than suggested by (the few) previous US studies. Solon (1999) comprehensively surveyed the first wave of research stimulated by these studies and previous work. Building on his survey, we focus on recent developments in the literature.

---

[2]  See e.g. Erikson and Goldthorpe (1992, ch. 1).

We continue in Section 2 with a theoretical discussion of the mechanisms that may explain the associations between income and family background. In Section 3, we discuss the income concepts used in this research. We explain in Section 4 the measures used to describe family associations in income and offer in Section 5 a cross-national overview of recent estimates of family associations. Section 6 presents evidence on whether parental income has a causal impact on offspring, and in Section 7 we report results from a variety of approaches to uncover what underlies associations between income and family background. Section 8 concludes and offers some advice for future research.

# 2. THEORY

The approach to intergenerational mobility and family associations surveyed here is largely empirical. Although most studies have estimated simple measures of association between parents' and offsprings' income, researchers recognize that many complex mechanisms in need of theoretical treatment underlie those associations.

The most commonly cited theoretical background is the Becker–Tomes model (Becker and Tomes, 1979, 1986), an approach that is lucidly discussed by Goldberger (1989). Solon (2004) develops a stylized and strongly parameterized version of the Becker–Tomes model, which highlights important channels for intergenerational persistence. Parents derive utility from own consumption and their child's adult well-being and use a limited budget to finance private investment in their child's human capital and their own consumption. A child's realized human capital has two additive sources. One is human capital investment, which should be interpreted broadly and might include health as well as education. Such investments are made by the parents and the public sector, which in Solon's version are perfect substitutes. The other source is 'endowments', which are mechanically (and costlessly) transmitted across generations. Becker and Tomes (1979: 1158) write that these are 'determined by the reputation and "connections" of their families, the contribution to the ability of race, and other characteristics of children from the genetic constitutions of their families, and the learning, skills, goals, and other "family commodities" acquired through belonging to a particular family culture'. Finally, the child's adult income depends on the return to and amount of her human capital.

Assuming it is always optimal for parents to invest in their children's education, Solon derives the parents' optimal investment, taking public investments as given. Public investments partly, but not completely, crowd out private investments. Solon derives a linear relationship between the log of the child's and the log of the parent's pre-tax incomes. The relationship is derived under steady-state conditions with equal income variances in both generations and the coefficient is both an elasticity and a correlation. The coefficient is a function of four parameters: it is *higher* the greater the extent of (1) the automatic heritability of human capital endowments, (2) the productivity of human capital investments, (3) the income or earnings return to human capital, and *lower* in (4) the degree of progressivity of public education spending.

As both endowments and investments are broadly interpreted, the model encompasses many mechanisms and their interactions. Since all parameters can vary across countries and time, differences and changes in generational persistence may reflect those differences in parameters.

Solon goes on to investigate what the model tells us about cross-sectional income inequality, finding that the variance of the natural logarithm (ln) of income and the intergenerational correlation increase in the same parameters. Cross-sectional inequality and intergenerational immobility may therefore be positively correlated across time and countries, so these two different dimensions of inequality may reinforce rather than conflict with each other.

The Becker–Tomes model has been used to generate hypotheses about the impact of parental borrowing constraints on the intergenerational income relationship. In Solon's version, parents cannot borrow to finance educational investments that would be paid back by the child, the only source of finance being reduced parental consumption. Becker and Tomes distinguish between two cases. With perfect capital markets, all parents invest optimally in their child so the intergenerational relationship is solely driven by the mechanically inherited endowments. With constrained credit, parental income additionally and more directly affects the offspring's income, strengthening the observed intergenerational relationship. Becker and Tomes argue that direct income effects are more common among low-income parents, who are more likely to face credit constraints. They predict the intergenerational association is concave, that is, is stronger at the bottom than at the top of the parental income distribution under credit constraints. This is an interesting and testable policy-elevant hypothesis, but credit constraints may lead to the opposite result. Grawe (2004b) and Bratsberg *et al.* (2007) argue that if the optimal level of investment is higher for high-ability parents and all families are credit constrained for high levels of investment, the relationship might be convex.

The design of schooling institutions is a policy topic in which equality of opportunity and mobility play a role. The Backer–Tomes model includes public education financing and its interaction with parental behavior. Conclusions very much depend on the assumptions. Davies *et al.* (2005), for example, formulate a theoretical model in which a public policy can impose equality of 'input of goods in education' and find that mobility and cross-sectional equality are positively correlated. By contrast, Checchi *et al.* (1999) construct a model to account for their empirical finding that the centralized and egalitarian Italian school system generates more equality but less occupational and educational intergenerational mobility than the more decentralized and inegalitarian US school system. In their model, schooling is a sorting instrument and the schooling decision is based on each person's belief in his own talent. They argue that the US system stimulates more of the low-income group to invest in education and increase their income.

Intergenerational mobility plays a role in models that integrate parental child investments within the macroeconomic literature. It makes substantive sense to include skill accumulation due to parental educational investments in models of economic growth. It makes methodological sense to go beyond the partial nature of the Becker–Tomes framework and allow for markets for skilled and unskilled labor with endogenous wages. Recently, Hassler *et al.* (2007) develop a model in which parental child investments, via changes in supply, affect the market wages for skilled and unskilled workers. Their model determines inequality and mobility simultaneously and is used to examine the impact of labor-market institutions and educational policies. Differences in education subsidies lead to equality and mobility being positively correlated, whereas differences in labor-market institutions lead to a negative correlation.

To sum up, economic theory suggests there are many causal processes behind intergenerational income associations. Further, the different processes likely interact in many ways that can only be captured in very complex models. For example, parental behavior in the presence of public education programs likely depends on whether these are substitutes or complements. It is therefore unsurprising that different theoretical models offer different predictions about the relationship between intergenerational mobility and cross-sectional inequality and the impact of public education programs. Ideally, the models should be subjected to empirical tests, but they are often far too complex and data demanding for structural estimation and testing. Indeed, one of Goldberger's (1989) critical comments about the Becker–Tomes approach is that some of the critical parameters are unidentifiable. By offering a rich set of stylized facts, empirical research can tell us what mechanisms are important, which can in turn sharpen future theoretical research.

# 3. THE INCOME CONCEPT

Although data availability has often governed the actual choice of income concept, the underlying purpose of the study should ideally guide the income concept that is employed. Most studies have used (annual or hourly pre-tax) *labor* earnings, which captures earnings power in the labor market. In some data sets, however, information about self-employment earnings is missing or measured less accurately, limiting the value of the analysis. *Total factor income* has been used frequently. This broader measure of income-generating power includes capital income that can be inherited.

Both labor earnings and total factor income can be pooled across spouses to provide *family earnings* or *family income*. One advantage of pooling income is that both parents' resources are accounted for, although mothers' income is often absent. It is important to bear in mind that intergenerational associations in family resources are affected by assortative mating. If spouses have similar family background, combined income is more strongly associated with each of their parents' than if mating is more random (see Chadwick and Solon, 2002 and Raaum *et al.*, 2007).

A few studies have used *disposable household income*, a concept that takes into account taxes and transfers, and often also the economic needs of the household as measured by an equivalence scale. Disposable income is closely related to household members' consumption standard, which according to many economists corresponds to economic welfare. Intergenerational analysis of disposable income thus comes closer to measuring the transmission of well-being. Also, in the Becker–Tomes framework parents spend out of their disposable income on their child's human capital accumulation. However, the 'needs' of the household, as defined by the equivalence scale, depend on family structure. Thus, intergenerational mobility in disposable income might reflect both the transmission of family structure and income.

There is a vast literature on intergenerational transmission of *educational attainment*. Our focus is on income, not educational mobility. However, education is a potentially central mediating mechanism as parents can more easily influence their offspring's education than their income. One of our goals is to examine the empirical importance of education in intergenerational income mobility.

Whatever income concept is used, it needs to be measured over a reasonably long time period, because current income is affected by various temporary factors. Such factors can render estimates of the association between, say, sons' income in 2007 and fathers' income in 1975 weak or non-existent. Thus, the proper focus is on family associations in long-run income.

Nonetheless, short-run income fluctuations around a long-run level are relevant for assessing equality of opportunity. Such variations are associated with uncertainty and thus welfare losses. Income volatility might be correlated within families. Indeed, sociologists studying class mobility point out that the working class is more exposed to income vulnerability than the service classes (see e.g. Goldthorpe and McKnight, 2006).

There is no simple answer to the question of what is a reasonable measure of long-run income for intergenerational income mobility studies. The answer depends on how one wants to measure mobility, a question examined next.

# 4. DESCRIBING FAMILY ASSOCIATIONS IN INCOME

We review in this section measures of family associations in income, starting with the intergenerational relationship between parent and offspring income. We then turn to the sibling income correlation, emphasizing the relationship between the parent–child correlation and the sibling correlation.

## Intergenerational Association

Denote the long-run, or over-time average of the natural logarithms (ln) of parent and offspring income in family $i$ as $y_{fi}$ and $y_{si}$, measured as deviations from generational means, with generational variances $\sigma_f^2$ and $\sigma_s^2$. Given the bivariate distribution of parent and offspring income, what succinct ways can be used to summarize the extent of mobility in that distribution? This depends, among other things, on how much information one has access to.

The prototypical approach, which has relatively low data requirements, is to estimate the regression of the son's ln income on that of the father's. This regression coefficient is the intergenerational elasticity, that is, it measures the percentage differential in the son's expected income with respect to a marginal percentage differential in the income of the father. It is the coefficient of the 'regression to the mean' model defined in terms of ln incomes:

$$y_{si} = \alpha + \beta y_{fi} + \varepsilon_i. \tag{1}$$

Although informative and interpretable, its size depends on income dispersion in the two generations. If income inequality rises from one generation to the next, a larger coefficient is needed to account for the larger income differentials in the second generation. Arguably, the intergenerational correlation coefficient, which equals the elasticity multiplied by the ratio of the standard deviations of father's to son's income, may be preferable:

$$\varphi = \beta(\sigma_f/\sigma_s). \tag{2}$$

The correlation coefficient tells us how many standard deviations the son's income would change in response to a small change in the standard deviation of the father's income. The correlation is independent of the marginal distributions in the two generations and is therefore arguably more suitable for comparing mobility across countries, especially if the marginal distributions have changed in different ways across the countries.

How can $\beta$ or $\varphi$ be estimated from available data? We are unaware of any data set that provides access to the lifetime incomes for two consecutive generations.

Instead, we must consider how far we can get with data covering shorter periods. Jenkins (1987) identifies two sources of bias or inconsistency for intergenerational associations. Transitory errors around long-run income is one source. Incomes measured at stages in the life-cycle that systematically deviate from long-run income is another.

As is well-known, random errors have different effects on the estimated regression coefficient depending on whether they affect the son's or the father's income. Because the son's income is the dependent variable in equation (1), $\beta$ can be consistently estimated using an indicator of $y_{si}$ that, while subject to transitory factors and measurement errors, has expected value equal to $y_{si}$. Because the father's income is the independent variable, even classical measurement errors lead to inconsistent estimates of $\beta$. This 'attenuation bias' can be reduced by using a long-run average of fathers' ln income.

Over how long a period must income be measured to yield a reasonable estimate? The answer depends on the longitudinal parental income process. Mazumder (2005) illustrates the inconsistency under alternative assumptions about the income process and the number of years over which averaging takes place ($T$). Assuming, plausibly, that the transitory variance is half of the total income variance, with no autocorrelation, the attenuation factor goes from 0.50 to 0.91 when $T$ goes from 1 to 10; with an autocorrelation of 0.7, the corresponding numbers are 0.5 and 0.71. Even with $T$ as large as 30, the attenuation factor only goes to 0.85 if the autocorrelation coefficient is 0.7.[3]

All estimates based on time-averaging are thus more or less downwards inconsistent. Therefore, some studies have used an instrumental-variable approach to deal with transitory errors in parental income. Parental education and occupation are typically used as instruments in these applications so the estimates of $\beta$ are probably upwards inconsistent.[4]

Biased measurement of long-run income is a problem that needs careful attention for both fathers and sons. Building on Jenkins's analytical framework, Grawe (2006) shows the empirical importance of the age at which both generations' incomes are measured. Grawe's results suggest that estimation inconsistencies are primarily driven by life-cycle biases rather than transitory fluctuations, being particularly sensitive to the life-cycle stage of father's income observations.

To deal with life-cycle biases, which affect both the elasticity and correlation, we need to know at what ages annual incomes are unbiased indicators of long-run

---

[3] Björklund *et al.* (2007), using an AR(1) model, find an autocorrelation coefficient around 0.6 for Sweden.

[4] A special case of IV estimation of intergenerational elasticities is so-called two-sample IV (TSIV), which has lower data requirements than the other approaches. TSIV relies on one sample for sons with reports about the father's occupation and education during the son's childhood and another sample that is used to estimate predicted income for fathers with the given characteristics during the time period of the son's childhood. This does not require matched fathers and sons. Three out of eleven studies (Australia, France, and Italy) reported in Fig. 20.1 below, apply this technique.

income. Haider and Solon (2006) and Böhlmark and Lindquist (2006), with US and Swedish data respectively, address that question. They find that for men in these two countries, annual incomes around ages 34–40 are good proxies for long-run income. For women there is no such simple rule. Their results imply that using the son's income at lower or higher ages may lead to quite substantial inconsistencies.

Recall that the correlation coefficient is related to the elasticity by the ratio of parental to offspring standard deviations. In the USA, Gottschalk and Moffitt (1998) estimate this ratio between 1969 and 1991 to be about 0.70, that is, the standard deviation of sons' permanent earnings is higher than that of fathers. By contrast, Gustavsson's (forthcoming) findings suggest that during the same period the permanent earnings variance in Sweden decreased and this ratio exceeds one. Such differences in the changes in the marginal distributions strengthen the case for comparing countries in terms of the correlation, not the more common elasticity.

The differential impact on the estimated intergenerational relation of measurement errors in the two generations applies to the elasticity. For the correlation coefficient $\varphi$, long-run income is needed for both generations. US studies in the early 1990s tended for this reason to emphasize elasticities, as the sons in US data sets (PSID and NLS) were quite young.

Next, we might ask if the log-linear functional form is a suitable representation for the father–son relationship. This can be studied using non-parametric regression. A spline function is a discrete version of the non-parametric technique in that the researcher (in more modern versions a software algorithm) chooses 'knots' at which the regression slope is allowed to change. A simple approach is to include a higher-order polynomial, for example, including quadratic and cubic terms, in parental income in the estimating equation (1).

The information contained in the full bivariate distribution can also be summarized using quantile regressions of the son's income on the father's income. A quantile regression of, say, the 10th percentile of the son's ln income on the father's ln income allows the researcher to express the 10th percentile of the son's ln income as a function of the father's income. The coefficient on the father's ln long-run income measures the elasticity of the particular quantile of the son's long-run income with respect to the father's. Differences across the quantiles tell us how sensitive different parts of the son's conditional distribution are to small changes in the father's income.

A transition matrix, yet another summary of the bivariate distribution, can reveal asymmetries in mobility and the probability of both small and large transitions. The matrices are commonly defined in terms of quantiles of the marginal distributions.[5] While such analyses can be illuminating, studies that examine transition

[5] There are, of course, many different ways to define the income classes. An alternative is to defire classes based on different bands constructed around the median income in each marginal distribution or in terms of absolute incomes. Quantile-based approaches are more likely to be

probabilities rarely address the problem that the probabilities can be fairly impre-cisely estimated, especially in the tails of the distribution with the most interesting information (see Jäntti et al., 2006). Transition matrices can be summarized into mobility indices, which for example Bartholomew (1982) reviews. A simple example is the normalized trace of the matrix, that is, the normalized sum of probabilities that sons are found in their fathers' income class. Most summary indices are sym-metric in upwards and downwards mobility, but it is possible to construct indices that measure particular kinds of asymmetries. Atkinson (1983, chapter 3) explores dominance conditions for mobility matrices.

The close attention paid within the regression framework to problems caused by transitory errors and life-cycle biases is rarely found in the analysis of income mobility tables. For instance, autocorrelated and heteroscedastic transitory errors around long-run income may lead to serious and intractable biases and inconsist-encies for the estimation of mobility tables. O'Neill et al. (2007) study the impact of classical measurement error on transition matrices and summary measures, finding that estimation biases are quite substantial, especially in the tails.

## Sibling Associations

The importance of family background for income can also be measured by the degree of sibling similarity. Arguably, this provides a fuller account of the impact of family and community background on economic status than does a comparison of parents' and their offsprings' characteristics. Namely, siblings share also part of what parents transfer to their children that is not directly related to income, such as values and aspirations.

The correlation could be measured by drawing pairs of siblings. An alternative is to use a random-effects model, which captures the role of shared family factors in the incomes of siblings.[6] Such a model can include covariates with associated coefficients, consisting typically of a polynomial in age and year dummies. The parameters of interest are the variances of the random effects for the family, $\sigma_a^2$ and the individual, $\sigma_b^2$.

The importance of family background for the distribution of long-run income is measured by the share of the variance of long-run income (the sum of the individual and family effect variances) that is attributable to family background

---

invariant to differences in measurement across generations or countries. In part, different approaches to discretization reflect similar differences in class mobility measurement in sociology (Erikson and Goldthorpe, 1992).

[6] The consensus in the statistical literature, following Laird and Ware (1982), is that variance-components models should be estimated using restricted maximum likelihood (REML). Other estimation approaches are available, including ANOVA, which was applied in early studies, and generalized method of moments (GMM). To apply GMM, a researcher would not need to rely on specific distributional assumptions about the individual and family effects. Mazumder (2007) compares approaches using US data and finds only small differences.

(the variance of the family effect):

$$\rho = \frac{\sigma_a^2}{\sigma_a^2 + \sigma_b^2} \tag{3}$$

This 'sibling correlation' is related to the intergenerational correlation by:[7]

Sib corr = (intergenerational correlation)$^2$

+ shared factors unrelated to par income.

Because the square of the intergenerational correlation is the explanatory power of parental income, equation (4) suggests that a sibling's income generally provides a fuller account of own income than parental income does. Nonetheless, because siblings share only part of the family and community background factors that influence income, the sibling resemblance provides a lower bound on the impact of those factors on income.

Both life-cycle effects and transitory fluctuations may also confound estimates of the sibling correlation. Siblings' incomes need to be observed at sufficiently long periods at stages of the life-cycle that allow for unbiased measurement of long-run incomes. The analytical models for life-cycle effects and transitory fluctuations may be observationally false. In comparing estimates from very different populations, such as different countries, different violations of these assumptions can have a very large effect on the estimated difference in the sibling correlations. An advantage of using the sibling correlation is that reasonably narrowly spaced siblings are drawn from the same marginal distribution. This allows for 'cleaner' cross-country comparisons, as the problems caused by differential structural change across two generations are not an issue.

# 5. THE CROSS-NATIONAL PATTERNS IN FAMILY ASSOCIATIONS

We now report results from research on intergenerational and family associations. We start with results from comparable studies from several countries. A cross-national overview helps us evaluate the theoretical framework discussed in Section 2 and can provide clues about the underlying mechanisms.

We start by reporting results from estimates of father–son associations. We are aware of such estimates for eleven developed countries. Some authors have striven for explicit cross-national comparisons by choosing similar sample definitions and time periods. Most cross-national comparisons stick to the standard constant-elasticity model presented above, partly because comparisons become

---

[7] For a formal derivation, see Solon (1999).

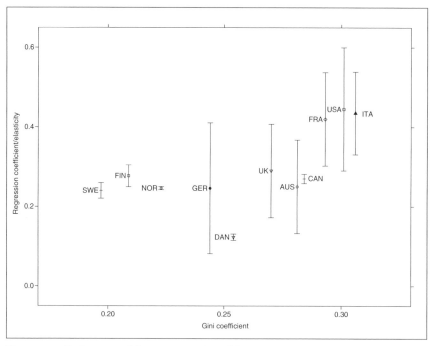

**Fig. 20.1. Estimates of intergenerational income elasticities for fathers and sons and cross-sectional disposable income Gini coefficients in 11 developed countries**

*Notes*: (1) We have aimed at choosing estimates using (i) earnings, (ii) studies measuring sons' earnings at ages 30–40 years and using sons born in the 1950s or early 1960s, (iii) studies using long-run measures of fathers' earnings when the child was living home. (2) For Australia we picked Leigh's own correction of his estimates to make them comparable to US estimates. (3) Italian earnings are measured net of taxes. (4) The Canadian estimate is adjusted upwards by a factor of 1.2 to account for the low age of sons (around age 30). (5) The elasticity estimates are shown with their 95% confidence intervals.

*Sources*: See appendix, available on the Handbook website. Australia: Leigh (2007), Canada: Corak and Heisz (1999), Denmark: Hussain *et al.* (2008), Finland: Pekkarinen *et al.* (2006), France: LeFranc and Trannoy (2005), Germany: Vogel (2008), Italy: Piraino (2007), Norway: Aakvik *et al.* (2006), Sweden: Björklund and Chadwick (2003), UK: Nicoletti and Ermisch (2007), USA: Mazumder (2005). GINI coefficients are taken from Luxembourg Income Study (LIS) Wave 1 or 2 (around 1980 if available, around 1985 if the wave 1 data are not available). See <http://www.lisproject.org/keyfigures.htm>.

more complicated with more elaborate measures of association, partly because data in some countries only permit estimation of this model.

In Figure 20.1, we show our preferred intergenerational elasticity estimates, along with the estimated 95 percent confidence intervals (CI).[8] We relate the estimates to the Gini coefficient of annual disposable income in or close to the prime age of the parental generation. There is a weak tendency for high inequality of disposable income to be related to a high elasticity. The country ordering has some surprises— for instance, the elasticity in Germany is quite low. Elasticities in France and Italy

---

[8] We have chosen from among a set of estimates a representative one for the figure. The full set of estimates and our stated reason for each choice is available in a data appendix from the authors on request.

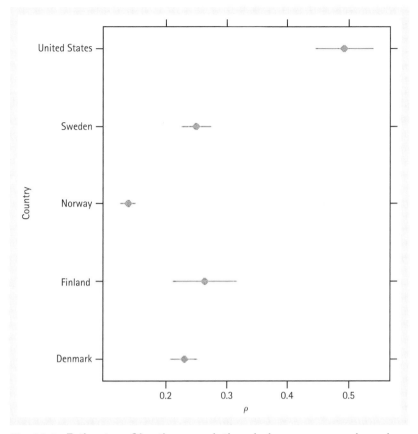

**Fig. 20.2. Estimates of brother correlations in long-run annual earnings for five countries**

*Note*: The errors bars show the 95% confidence interval. More detailed information is available from the authors.
*Sources*: USA: Mazumder (2008); Björklund *et al.* (2002) for all others.

are quite close to the US numbers at the low end of mobility. Australia and Canada, by contrast, along with Germany, have low elasticities, in the range of the Nordic country estimates, with the UK in between. However, the estimated confidence intervals tend to be very wide, especially when based on survey data, so the robustness of any ordering is open to debate. The Australian elasticity, for instance, is at the same level as the Nordic ones but its CI overlaps with those of the USA and Italy. Moreover, as we argued above, the comparison should preferably be done using the correlation coefficient, since the elasticities are sensitive to differences in the change in cross-sectional inequality across generations.

To the best of our knowledge, sibling correlation estimates only exist for the four Nordic countries and the USA, shown in Figure 20.2. The correlation is much larger in the USA than in the Nordic countries, among which Norway stands out as having a much smaller correlation than Denmark, Finland, or Sweden; 0.14 for Norway compared to around 0.25 for the other countries. While the confidence interval in the USA is substantial, it does not overlap with any of the Nordic estimates. These results suggest family background is more important in the USA than in the Nordic countries.

These results are confined to men, giving father–son elasticities and brother correlations. The literature on fathers and daughters and for sisters or mixed-gender siblings is smaller but growing. The general impression from these studies is that intergenerational elasticities and sister correlations are lower, but that the overall cross-national pattern remains. It is important to note that women's life-cycle earnings pattern is both more complicated and more varied across countries than that for men. As noted in Section 4, there is no simple rule for the age at which women's income is a useful proxy for long-run income, which is one reason why we do not present estimates for women here.

We have presented results only for earnings. It is sometimes claimed that inter-generational associations in broader income concepts, such as total individual or family income, tend to be stronger. However, systematic comparisons are needed to rationalize these claims.

# 6. INTERGENERATIONAL INCOME EFFECTS: CAUSALITY

Intergenerational elasticities are often interpreted as estimates of the *effect* of parental income on an offspring's income. However, the *causal* effect of parental income is conceptually different and much more difficult to estimate. A causal effect relates to a thought intervention in the income determination process: what would the offspring's income be if parental income was changed from X to Y? There are as many causal effects as there are possible interventions. An additional complication compared to descriptive intergenerational analysis is that both long-run *and* transitory parental income might have long-run effects on offspring. For example, a spell of poverty during a sensitive period in a child's life might have lasting consequences. There are thus potentially a large number of interesting causal parameters.

Even if a causal parameter is well defined, it can be very difficult to estimate. As we explained in Section 2, parental influences on children's income work through many channels, many of which are hard or impossible to observe but may be correlated with income. A descriptive intergenerational elasticity captures much more than just the causal income effect.

Recent research has used a variety of approaches to disentangle causal effects from intergenerational income associations. One approach has been to estimate intergenerational coefficients for children and parents related by adoption. The relationship between adoptive parents' income and their adopted children's outcomes is not confounded by genetic, non-causal effects. Björklund *et al.* (2006), using a large set of Swedish adoptees and their adoptive parents, find the coefficients for adoptive parents to be around two-thirds of those for biological parents. This result holds when they control for non-random adoption by including the characteristics of biological parents in the adoptee regressions. Sacerdote (2007), using data on Korean-born children adopted into US families who were approximately randomly placed, estimates separate intergenerational income coefficients for adopted and biological children in the same families. The coefficients for adopted children are about two-thirds of those for biological children, but are imprecisely estimated. Plug and Vijverberg (2005) apply the approach to a small US data set but get rather imprecisely estimated coefficients.

A second approach is to use differences between family members, thereby eliminating the unobserved factors they share. Blau (1999) studies the impact of parental income on a set of child development indicators using this approach. In some specifications he finds significant but small effects of parental income. To illustrate that the impact is small, he applies his largest estimate—obtained from a between-cousin specification that eliminates family factors shared by cousins—to some US family policy reforms. The estimates imply that 'it would take an unprecedentedly large income transfer to relatively poor households in order to have a substantial impact on child development'.

A third approach is to exploit only variations in income that reflect an effect of only income, not the innate ability a policy intervention would not affect. Mayer (1997) uses measures of parental income taken *after* a child's outcome is observed, arguing that future income is exogenous with respect to previously measured income. This identification strategy requires parental investment in the child to be unaffected by the anticipation of future income. Shea (2000) uses income variation induced by cross-sectional variation in fathers' earnings due to union status, industry wage differentials, and involuntary job loss as an instrument to estimate the impact on children of the resulting parental earnings variation. Although this income variation may well be related to innate ability, the estimates are insignificant.

Oreopoulos *et al.* (2005), using Canadian data, and Bratberg *et al.* (forthcoming) with Norwegian data, estimate the direct effect of parental job loss on children's income. Interestingly, the Canadian study convincingly finds that such a parental labor market shock lowers children's income by 9 percent, whereas the Norwegian study finds no effects, which points to possible country differences in the consequences of such labor market shocks. However, it is not clear what policy intervention in the income determination process is being mimicked by such studies.

The closely related literature on the causal effect of parental education on children's education faces the same methodological problems as the studies on income effects with the thought intervention being in educational policy. To illustrate the complexities involved, Holmlund *et al.* (2006) compare the three methods discussed above using Swedish register data. They relate educational differences between same-sex twins to educational differences in education between their children, that is, differences between cousins, eliminating genetic effects shared by cousins with same-sex twin parents. Their use of adoption data relies on assumptions discussed above. Their IV method exploits the variation in parental education generated by the Swedish comprehensive school reform which lengthened compulsory education by two years and was quasi-experimentally implemented across regions. Their results suggest there may be positive causal effects of parental education, but they are substantially smaller than the descriptive intergenerational coefficients. Importantly, however, the authors stress that their three approaches identify different causal parameters. Adoptions tend to take place in the upper half of the educational distribution so this approach identifies effects at the top of the distribution. The school reform exploits variation and identifies an effect at the bottom of the educational distribution. Twins are evenly distributed across the parental income distribution, so their use identifies yet another parameter. In conclusion, parental income may have causal effects on children, but these are likely much smaller than the descriptive intergenerational associations.

## 7. MECHANISMS BEHIND FAMILY ASSOCIATIONS

We now turn to another causal question: what are the causal mechanisms behind the observed family associations? A variety of approaches to this question have been used. No estimates of a model that encompasses all the mechanisms of Becker and Tomes (1986) and that uses exogenous variation in all the background factors exist. However, some useful partial evidence is available, so the literature offers some clues as to which mechanisms are more important than others.

### Trends

Trends in the association between family background and income are interesting in themselves, and can point to important mechanisms. Recent years have seen a wave of such trend studies. Ferrie (2005) addresses the question of whether the USA in the 19th century was an unusually mobile society. He offers new evidence on this classical question using occupational data from historical US and British censuses that recently have become available for research. He reports so-called fluidity measures of occupational mobility which control for the fact that the marginal distributions of occupations change over time and differ between countries. The USA exhibited more mobility than Britain during the 19th century, but US mobility fell during the 20th century, so for the cohorts born around

1940s the US advantage has disappeared. Although these results pertain to mobility between four to six broad occupational groups, they place recent work based on income in an interesting long-run perspective.

Changes in intergenerational income mobility for post-World War II US cohorts are also of great interest. For example, learning how intergenerational mobility responded to the rise in cross-sectional inequality in the 1980s would help us evaluate the theoretical predictions discussed above. Unfortunately, changes in intergenerational mobility are difficult to estimate precisely using US survey data. Some point estimates that suggest large changes may be due to high sampling variability. Lee and Solon (forthcoming) and Hertz (2007) have tried to use the PSID efficiently but do not find major changes for the cohorts born between 1952 and 1975.

Blanden et al. (2004) examine the change in intergenerational mobility in the UK for children born in 1958 and 1970. To achieve intertemporal comparability, they confine themselves to using parents' post-tax family income, and offspring earnings and family income. They find a substantial increase in intergenerational elasticities and correlations of some 0.05–0.12 points, depending on specification. They attribute the decline during this rather short period of time to rapid educational upgrading that benefited those with well-to-do parents the most. Using other data and another estimation technique, Nicoletti and Ermisch (2007) find that both elasticities and correlations were stable for cohorts born between 1950 and 1960. For the 1961 to 1972 cohorts, elasticities rose somewhat but correlations were stable. These results are only partly in agreement with those of Blanden et al., so there is some uncertainty about the trend in the UK.

Cohorts in the Nordic countries born in the 1950s and early 1960s had weak family associations in income. It is of interest to know if the associations were stronger for earlier cohorts who grew up before the rise of the ambitious Nordic welfare states. The large register-based datasets in these countries allow for changes to be estimated with high precision.

Björklund et al. (2007) estimate brother correlations in long-run income for Swedish men born between 1932 and 1968. The correlations were as high as 0.34 for cohorts born in the early and mid-1930s and stabilized around 0.23 from 1950 onward, a sizeable decline taking place during a period of many political reforms. Education can account for part of the decline, but more research is needed to find what educational changes were important and to assess the relative importance of changes in the return to and the distribution of education.

Pekkala and Lucas (2007) estimate intergenerational elasticities for Finnish cohorts born between 1930 and 1970, using census data on annual earnings for offspring and family income for parents. The intergenerational elasticities declined substantially; for sons from over 0.30 to around 0.20, and for daughters from 0.25 to around 0.15 for cohorts born in 1930 to those born in 1950 and later. The Norwegian trend studies have focused on the post-1950 cohorts. Bratberg et al. (2007) find a small decline in father–son and father–daughter elasticities from 1950 to 1965 cohorts. Hansen (2007), however, finds that this result does not hold when using the income of both parents. Instead, she finds a small increase in the elasticities for the 1955–70 cohorts. This difference suggests an increasing role for mothers, which has not been much explored in the literature.

The trend studies suggest that both intergenerational associations and sibling correlations can change substantially during quite short periods of time, and that the changes can often be traced to changes in education. Further analysis of the role of education seems to be a productive path for future research.

## Evidence on Non-linearities

Many lessons can be learned from the functional form of the generational dependence. The functional form of the intergenerational relation may reveal interesting empirical patterns, which may have implications for what theoretical models are plausible. The evidence must be interpreted with caution relative to the theoretical models.

Using a flexible polynomial in parental income, Bratsberg *et al.* (2007) find that in Denmark, Finland, and Norway, the regression slope of sons' income on fathers' is flat for low levels of parental income and increasing thereafter. For the USA, the log-linear regression appears to fit the data.[9] For the UK, they find only weak evidence for non-linearity.[10] Corak and Heisz (1999) use non-parametric regression to examine departures from log-linearity in the father–son relationship in Canada. The elasticity varies substantially and non-monotonically across fathers' earnings, being negative across a large part of fathers' earnings distribution.

Consider next the quantile regressions. Eide and Showalter (1999) find using PSID data that the US elasticities decrease across the son's distribution. Their 10th, 50th, and 90th percentiles' slopes are 0.77, 0.37, and 0.17, compared to a regression coefficient of 0.34, suggesting that sons' income distribution conditional on fathers' income gets more compressed as fathers' income increases. Bratberg *et al.* (2007) report a similar pattern for Norway, as does Grawe (2004a) for Canada. But Grawe finds a spreading out for Germany and the UK. His US results vary depending on whether PSID or NLS data are used and how the sample is defined, but mostly suggest a narrowing of the son's conditional distribution.

There is thus evidence that deviations of son's income from the regression slope are heteroscedastic (as the shape of the conditional distribution changes across father's income). This heteroscedasticity varies across countries.

Grawe (2004b) critically examines the evidence from non-linearities for the credit constraints hypotheses. He uses Canadian data to estimate quantile

---

[9]  Couch and Lillard (2004) get somewhat different results for the USA and Germany but have data on quite young sons.

[10]  Björklund and Chadwick (2003) get similar results for Sweden.

regressions that include a spline function in father's income, allowing the slope of the regression to vary. He finds convex relationships between son's and father's income for quantiles above the median and S-shaped relationships up to and including the median. This, he argues, points away from credit constraints as being the driver of the non-linearities and suggests that other elements of the standard Becker–Tomes model, such as government expenditures on human capital, may be responsible (see Section 2).

Corak and Heisz (1999) also estimate transition matrices, defined using quartiles and deciles of the marginal distributions, which suggest mobility patterns are, indeed, non-symmetric. Because they use register data, the usual impediment to looking at mobility across many groups, small sample size, is not an issue for them. Moreover, Corak and Heisz take an overtime average of both fathers' and sons' earnings in constructing the transition matrices, so biases caused by transitory errors in sons' income are less of an issue. Jäntti et al. (2006) estimate transition matrices defined for quintile groups using data for Denmark, Finland, Norway, Sweden, the UK, and the US. While their main results do not average across parental income, their results indicate statistically significant cross-country differences in the income persistence for men at the bottom and the top, with the USA displaying most such persistence. The evidence also suggests that large moves out of the lowest income quintile group are least likely in the USA.

# The Explanatory Power of Parental Income versus The Sibling Correlation

The sibling correlation can be interpreted as the fraction of income inequality attributable to the factors siblings share, including parental income (see Section 4). The sibling correlation is also approximately the intergenerational elasticity squared plus the explanatory power of non-income factors. We now use these properties and the estimates reported in Section 5.

For the Nordic countries, we reported intergenerational elasticities in the range 0.15–0.25—suggesting explanatory power of 0.0225 to 0.0625—and sibling correlations in the range 0.20–0.25 (see Figs. 20.1 and 20.2). For the USA, both intergenerational elasticities and sibling correlations tend to be in the range 0.40–0.45, which implies that parental income accounts for about half of what the shared non-income factors do.

These comparisons suggest that focusing on parental income in investigating how family background affects income during adulthood is almost like focusing on the tip of an iceberg. The challenge is to identify the factors under the water that account for more than half of what siblings share. One such factor is the neighborhood.

## The Neighborhood or the Family?

Siblings share both the family and the neighborhood in which they grew up. It would be useful to know their relative importance. Empirical attempts to disentangle the factors are complicated by the fact they are strongly correlated; children who grow up in communities with schools, peers, and role models that lead to favorable adult outcomes also live in families with favorable characteristics. Distinguishing between family and neighborhood factors is intrinsically difficult.

Solon *et al.* (2000) compare the magnitude of estimated sibling and neighborhood correlations to learn about the relative importance of family and community factors. The sibling correlation captures shared factors originating from the family and the neighborhood. With suitable data, it is also possible to estimate the correlation among unrelated children from the same neighborhood. That correlation captures both pure neighborhood factors and family traits that are (likely positively) correlated within the neighborhood. Thus, a raw neighborhood correlation provides an upper bound on the importance of neighborhood factors. The neighborhood correlation can be purged of the observed family characteristics of the neighborhood yielding a tighter upper bound.

Empirical implementation of this approach requires data that are only rarely available. Solon *et al.* use the cluster design of the original PSID survey which sampled households in the same vicinity, usually within a block or two of each other. They use the clusters to estimate both a sibling correlation and a 'purged' neighborhood correlation in years of schooling. The former was above 0.5 and the latter around 0.1, thus suggesting that neighborhood factors at most account for one-fifth of the factors that siblings share.

Page and Solon (2003a, 2003b) apply the same approach to the long-run earnings of brothers and sisters. Similar conclusions follow from these studies, although the upper bound on the importance of neighborhood factors for brothers' long-run earnings was higher, around one-half of the sibling correlation. Raaum *et al.* (2006) apply this approach to Norwegian census data with detailed neighborhood information. They find that neighborhood correlations in years of schooling and in long-run earnings account for less than a third of the sibling correlations.

These studies suggest that family is more important than the neighborhood. It is also notable that the results are so similar for two so different types of societies as the highly unequal US and egalitarian Norway. We now turn to the family to try to understand what in the family is important.

## Learning from Different Family Types

One research approach, with roots in quantitative genetics, is based on estimating family associations in income between relatives with different genetic and environmental connectedness. With additional modeling assumptions, it is possible to infer the relative importance of genetic ('nature') and environmental ('nurture') factors for income inequality and for intergenerational associations.[11]

Income correlations for different sibling types can be used to disentangle such effects in the overall variation in income. Consider the following very simple model of the determinants of long-run income $Y$:

$$Y = gG + sS + uU, \tag{4}$$

where $G$ represents genetic factors, $S$ environmental factors that may be shared between siblings, and $U$ individual factors not shared by siblings and thus not correlated with either $G$ or $S$; $g$, $s$, and $u$ are the corresponding factor loadings. This model is very simple with its additive structure that rules out interaction effects between $G$ and $S$. If we add the strong assumption that $G$ and $S$ are uncorrelated, we get the much-discussed decomposition of the variation in $Y$ into nature and nurture components. This decomposition is more transparent when $Y$, $G$, $S$, and $U$ are all standardized to have mean 0 and variance 1. We then get

$$\text{Var}(Y) = 1 = g^2 + s^2 + u^2. \tag{5}$$

Estimating the components of equation (6) requires information on more than one sibling type. For example, the correlation between monozygotic (identical) twins, who have the same genes and likely share as much environment as any siblings, gives us $g^2 + s^2$, since for them $\text{Corr}(G, G') = \text{Corr}(S, S') = 1$. For dizygotic (fraternal) twins we assume half of the genes are shared so $\text{Corr}(G, G') = 0.5$ and also that their environmental influences are fully shared so $\text{Corr}(S, S') = 1$ and $\text{Corr}(Y, Y') = 0.5g^2 + s^2$. These two correlations then identify $g^2$ and $s^2$. A model that uses these strong assumptions is the prototypical model in much research on the influence of nature and nurture.

It is also possible to estimate $g^2$ separately from a correlation between identical twins who have been reared in different environments, if we are also willing to assume that these environments are independent and the twin siblings were separated immediately after birth. Such twin pairs are very rare. Even with a reasonable sample, one could strongly doubt that the necessary assumptions are fulfilled. In a similar fashion, $s^2$ could be estimated using a correlation between adopted siblings who share only the same environment. Such sibling pairs are also rare and have in general not shared the same environment throughout their childhoods.

Björklund et al. (2005) use nine different sibling types, namely monozygotic twins, dizygotic twins, full siblings, half-siblings (all types split into those reared together and reared apart), and adoptive siblings. Variation across sibling types allows testing for the assumptions of the underlying prototypical model; it was clearly rejected by the data. Of the more general models that imposed weaker assumptions,

---

[11] The concepts pre- and post-birth factors are more appropriate since there is no certain way to separate pure genetic effects from environmental effects in the womb and during delivery.

the only model not rejected by the data was one that allowed a different degree of shared environments to reared-together monozygotic and dizygotic twins and allowed the environments of siblings reared apart to be correlated. Using that model, they estimated $g^2 = 0.20$ and $s^2 = 0.16$ for brothers (for sisters the estimates were 0.13 and 0.18), suggesting approximately equal importance for genetic factors and shared environment as determinants of earnings. But importantly, most earnings variation is attributable to the idiosyncratic component $u^2$, that is, environmental factors not shared within the family.

Another approach to disentangling intergenerational associations relies on adopted children and their parents. Björklund *et al.* (2006) and Björklund *et al.* (2007) use Swedish register data on adopted children and their biological and adoptive parents to estimate models with both types of parents' income and education as explanatory variables. In this race among parental variables, all are positive and generally significant and of about the same magnitude. Björklund *et al.* (2006) also include interactions between adoptive and biological parents. The interactions are positive, but not always significantly so. Interaction effects imply that a straightforward decomposition into 'nature' and 'nurture' is not possible. Sacerdote's (2007) results reported above in Section 6 also have relevance here. When he estimates separate intergenerational income coefficients for adopted and biological children in the very same families, he gets coefficients for adopted children that are about two-thirds of those for biological children.

What overall conclusions can be drawn from this research? 'Nature' (or pre-birth) factors and 'nurture' (or post-birth) factors each account for about half of the family associations. This holds when family background's share is assessed using sibling correlations as well as when it is measured using regression coefficients for biological and rearing parents' income or education. Any comprehensive theory for the impact of family background must then incorporate both nature and nurture components. Any theory that focuses on only one of these will be incomplete. The conclusion about the substantive importance of both types of factors is reinforced by the presence of interactions between nature and nurture. It does *not* follow that policies can only affect the part of the family correlation that is associated with nurture. Most likely, different types of policies are needed to affect different sources of the impact of family background. Identifying these policies requires a quite different type of analysis.

## The Role of Education

It is likely that family background affects offspring's income by influencing her educational attainment. In the Becker–Tomes model, the intergenerational income association is mediated by both the earnings return to education and parental investment in their offspring's education. The model also emphasizes an additional

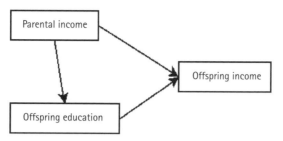

Fig. 20.3. A simple path model of intergenerational effects

mechanism, a direct link between parental and offspring's income. Of course, the importance of both the earnings return to education and the quantity of education for family associations in income has been recognized in earlier work.

Given this relation, we want to know the relative importance of education in the family association versus the direct effect of parental income. So-called path analysis allows for the quantification of the direct and indirect effects of parental income (see Fig. 20.3)

Conventional estimates of intergenerational associations combine direct and indirect effects. The two effects could be disentangled by estimating an intergenerational equation with offspring's education as well as income as explanatory variables.[12] The coefficient for income is purged of the indirect effect of parental income via education and could be interpreted as the direct effect. Some attempts have recently been made to separate the total 'effect' into direct and indirect effects. An early empirical application is by Eide and Showalter (1999) using US data. Their main finding is that the intergenerational elasticity falls from 0.34 to 0.24 when entering years of schooling as an additional variable, a decline driven by both the quantity of education and its return. The importance of education as a channel has also been pursued using decomposition techniques, which can be applied to both intergenerational and sibling associations in income; see Österbacka (2001) for an application.

These approaches are appealing since they show what we *want* to know about the underlying mechanism. Nonetheless, It is important to stress that the approaches rely on strong econometric assumptions. In particular, for OLS-estimates of the path coefficients to be consistent, the error terms in the two structural equations that underline the figure must be uncorrelated. This assumption, which is very difficult to test empirically appears to us to be strong. Another way to learn about the role of education is to examine the total effect of school reforms that have been implemented quasi-experimentally, a topic we turn to in the next section.

---

[12]  This approach is explored at length by Bowles and Gintis (2002).

## Lessons from Policy Interventions

Substantial policy differences across time or regions, or a combination thereof, can generate powerful research. We would for research purposes ideally have access to policies that have been randomly assigned across regions and time. Some comprehensive school reforms in the Nordic countries come quite close to such randomized policy interventions.

Sweden implemented comprehensive school reform in the 1950s and early 1960s in a quasi-experimental way, namely by introducing the reform in different regions at different periods of time. Using differences-in-differences estimates with controls, analyses have shed light on the reform's impact on intergenerational mobility. Meghir and Palme (2005) found that the reform had a positive impact on the earnings of the offspring of low-education fathers but not on average, which suggests that intergenerational mobility increased. Holmlund (2007) also investigated the reform and found a significant decline in the intergenerational family income elasticity, by some 0.03 points from around 0.20.

Pekkarinen *et al.* (2006) examine the impact of a Finnish school reform affecting cohorts born 1961–65. The reform, which also was implemented gradually across the country, increased the length of compulsory schooling from eight to nine years, postponed the age when students are channeled into academic and vocational schooling from 11 to 16, and reduced quality differentials between schools. They estimate the reform to have reduced the intergenerational income elasticity by 0.07 (standard error 0.02) from 0.30 to 0.23. This is a sizeable impact by a single education reform. The Swedish and Finnish school reforms, designed in part to equalize schooling, are in stark contrast to the findings of Checchi *et al.* (1999) that more equality would be associated with less mobility.

Mayer and Lopoo (2008) exploit inter-state variation in US government expenditures to examine their impact on intergenerational income elasticities. They find that states with higher expenditures tend to have lower income elasticities and higher income mobility. The interaction effect is robust across different specifications and identification strategies, but its precision is low.

Taken together, these results support the view that public policies may affect intergenerational mobility. The results from single policy interventions within a country are in conformity with the cross-national results reported above.

## Health, Skills, Personality Traits, and Accounting for the Sibling Correlation

In the basic economic model for intergenerational transmission, parents invest in their child's human capital. This investment model should be broadly interpreted and income capacity can be inherited via characteristics such as health, non-cognitive skills, and personality traits. A substantial part of the intergenerational income elasticity likely reflects transmission via characteristics other than schooling and cognitive skills. A large literature has documented strong intergenerational transmission of health. Eriksson *et al.* (2005) find, by controlling for offspring's health in intergenerational earnings equations, that around 25 percent of the intergenerational earnings elasticity in Denmark can be accounted for by transmission through offspring's health. Blanden *et al.* (2007) find using British data that the elasticity of 0.32 falls to 0.26 when a set of non-cognitive skills are entered into the equation, to 0.23 on adding cognitive test scores, and to 0.14 on further adding educational attainment. Dohmen *et al.* (2006) find strong intergenerational transmission in income-enhancing personality traits such as risk and trust attitudes. Thus, intergenerational income transmission most likely takes place also through such characteristics.

Another challenge is to learn more about what factors account for the sibling correlation, and especially those that are uncorrelated with parental income. Mazumder (2008) explores this, starting from an estimated brother correlation in long-run earnings of 0.49. He asks what variables account for the family component in earnings. Parental income accounts for 36 percent of it, which is consistent with an estimated intergenerational income elasticity of slightly above 0.4: equation (4) implies $(0.4)^2 = 0.16$, which is about 36 percent of 0.49. Mazumder next examines which characteristics brothers share that explain their similar earnings. He finds that, conditional on parental income, siblings' human capital, measured as years of schooling and test scores in the upper teens, accounts for an additional 25 percent of the family component. Psychological characteristics measured with indices of self-control and self-esteem account for an additional 8 percent. Height, weight, and body mass index hardly matter at all. An interesting extension of this approach would be to explore what *parental* characteristics other than income account for the sibling correlation.

All these results are correlational rather than causal, but they do suggest cognitive skills and non-cognitive personality traits might serve important roles in the intergenerational process.

# 8. CONCLUSIONS AND FURTHER RESEARCH

Recent research on income and family background has produced several valuable insights. We know that family background, in a broad sense that encompasses community and neighborhood influences, is important for income during adulthood. Estimates of sibling correlations show that family and/or community background factors that siblings share account for a sizeable fraction of variation in long-run income. The US estimates suggest that as much as 40–50 percent of long-run income inequality is accounted for by such factors, while estimates in the Nordic countries suggest a range of 15–25 percent. Since siblings do not share all family and community background influences, these numbers are only lower bounds on their share.

There are also substantial differences in the importance of family background across countries and substantial intertemporal changes within countries. The intergenerational earnings elasticities we showed in Figure 20.1 range from around 0.12–0.25 in the Nordic countries to about 0.42 in the USA. The elasticities changed by some 0.10 units in some countries in only 10–15 years; Swedish brother correlations also fell from over 0.34 to 0.23 in 15 years. In several studies, changes in the importance of family have been traced to changes in the educational system. These differences and changes suggest that the impact of family background is not a given constant but is susceptible to cultural and political differences and changes. We should add a note of caution. Arguably, intergenerational correlations rather than elasticities are most useful for cross-country comparisons, but there is very little good evidence on correlations, in part because such estimates require averaging across offspring incomes as well as parents'.

Further, we know that some background factors are not as important as one might think. For example, comparisons of neighborhood and sibling correlations show that the family is much more important than the neighborhood. What then is it in the family that is important? Once again, it is easier to say what is *not* important than to put one's finger on the decisive causal mechanisms. Because parental income has relatively low explanatory power in regressions explaining offsprings' adult incomes, the sibling association mainly works through factors that are uncorrelated with parental income. Attempts to disentangle the true causal effect of parental income from the statistical correlation between parents' and offsprings' income suggest that the causal effect accounts for no more than at most half the correlation. These results—suggesting a minor role for the neighborhood and small causal effects of parental income—do not rule out that policy interventions in the neighborhood or parental income can be effective. But such interventions should not be expected to generate substantial changes in the relationship between family background and income.

A major challenge for future research is to find out what in the family other than income is important for the future of children. Maybe the now very active research in behavioral economics and neuroeconomics will provide a deeper understanding of the causes of strong family income associations. We also beleive that more interaction between economist and sociologists would be beneficial.

Very little is known about the cross-national importance of family background for women's economic status, in part because women's labor markets have changed in different ways across countries. The sibling approach allows for meaningful cross-country comparisons also for women.

Future research can benefit from a better understanding of longitudinal income processes and the association between lifetime income and annual income at different life-cycle stages. A new wave of studies that build on these insights, use better and updated data, and choose mobility measures suited to the data at hand would improve upon the estimates we have surveyed and allow for better cross-country comparisons of the extent to which economic status is associated with family background.

# REFERENCES

AAKVIK, A., NILSEN, Ø. A., VAAGE, K., and JACOBSEN, K. Å. 2006. 'Sources of Measurement Errors in Earnings Data: New Estimates of Intergenerational Mobility in Norway'. Mimeo.

ATKINSON, A. B. 1983. *Social Justice and Public Policy*. Cambridge, Mass.: MIT Press.

BARTHOLOMEW, D. J. 1982. *Stochastic Model for Social Processes*. London: Wiley & Sons.

BECKER, G. S., and TOMES, N. 1979. 'An Equilibrium Theory of the Distribution of Income and Intergenerational Mobility'. *Journal of Political Economy*, 87(6): 1153–89.

————1986. 'Human Capital and the Rise and Fall of Families'. *Journal of Labor Economics*, 4(3): S1–39.

BJÖRKLUND A., and CHADWICK, L. 2003. 'Intergenerational Income Mobility in Permanent and Separated Families'. *Economics Letters*, 80(2): 239–46.

——ERIKSSON, T., JÄNTTI, M., RAAUM, O., and ÖSTERBACKA, E. 2002. 'Brother Correlations in Denmark, Finland, Norway and Sweden Compared to the United States'. *Journal of Population Economics*, 15(4): 757–72.

——JÄNTTI, M., and LINDQUIST, M. J. 2007. 'Family Background and Income during the Rise of the Welfare State: Brother Correlations in Income for Swedish Men Born 1932–1968'. IZA Discussion Paper 3000.

————and SOLON, G. 2005. 'Influences of Nature and Nurture on Earnings Variation: A Report on a Study of Sibling Types in Sweden', in S. Bowles, H. Gintis, and M. Osborne (eds.), *Unequal Chances: Family Background and Economic Success*. New York: Russell Sage Foundation.

——————2007. 'Nature and Nurture in the Intergenerational Transmission of Socioeconomic Status: Evidence from Swedish Children and their Biological and Rearing Parents'. *Berkeley Electronic Journal of Economic Analysis and Policy (Advances)*, 7(2): article 4.

——LINDAHL, M., and PLUG, E. 2006. 'The Origins of Intergenerational Associations: Lessons from Swedish Adoption Data'. *Quarterly Journal of Economics*, 121(3): 999–1028.

BLANDEN, J., GOODMAN, A., GREGG, P., and MACHIN, S. 2004. 'Changes in Intergenerational Mobility in Britain', in M. Corak (ed.), *Generational Income Mobility in North America and Europe*. Cambridge: Cambridge University Press.

BLANDEN, J., GREGG, P., and MACMILLAN, L. 2007. 'Accounting for Intergenerational Income Persistence: Noncognitive Skills, Ability and Education'. *The Economic Journal*, 117, Mar.: C43–60.

BLAU D. M. 1999. 'The Effect of Income on Child Development'. *The Review of Economics and Statistics*, 81(2): 261–76.

BÖHLMARK, A., and LINDQUIST, M. J. 2006. 'Life-Cycle Variations in the Association between Current and Lifetime Income: Replication and Extension for Sweden'. *Journal of Labor Economics*, 24(4): 879–96.

BOWLES, S., and GINTIS, H. 2002. 'The Inheritance of Inequality'. *Journal of Economic Perspectives*, 16(3): 3–30.

BRATBERG, E., NILSEN, Ø. A., and VAAGE, K. 2007. 'Trends in Intergenerational Mobility across Offspring's Earnings Distribution in Norway'. *Industrial Relations*, 46(1): 112–28.

—— —— —— Forthcoming. 'Job Losses and Child Outcomes'. *Labour Economics*.

BRATSBERG, B., RØED, K., RAAUM, O., NAYLOR, R., JÄNTTI, M., ERIKSSON, T., and ÖSTERBACKA, E. 2007. 'Nonlinearities in Intergenerational Earnings Mobility: Consequences for Cross-Country Comparisons'. *Economic Journal*, 117(519): C72–92.

CHADWICK, L., and SOLON, G. 2002. 'Intergenerational Income Mobility among Daughters'. *American Economic Review*, 92(1): 335–44.

CHECCHI, D., ICHINO, A., and RUSTICHINI, A. 1999. 'More Equal but Less Mobile? Education Financing and Intergenerational Mobility in Italy and in the US'. *Journal of Public Economics*, 74(3): 351–93.

CORAK, M., and HEISZ, A. 1999. 'The Intergenerational Earnings and Income Mobility of Canadian Men: Evidence from Longitudinal Income Tax Data'. *Journal of Human Resources*, 34(3): 504–33.

COUCH, K., and LILLARD, D. 2004. 'Non-linear Patterns of Intergenerational Mobility in Germany and the United States', in M Corak (ed.), *Generational Income Mobility in North America and Europe*. Cambridge: Cambridge University Press.

DAVIES, J., ZHANG, K., and ZENG, J. 2005. 'Intergenerational Mobility under Private vs. Public Education'. *Scandinavian Journal of Economics*, 107(3): 399–417.

DOHMEN, T., FALK, A., HUFFMAN, D., and SUNDE, U. 2006. 'The Intergenerational Transmission of Risk and Trust Attitudes'. IZA Discussion Paper no. 2380.

EIDE, E. R., and SHOWALTER, M. H. 1999. 'Factors Affecting the Transmission of Earnings across Generations: A Quantile Regression Appoach'. *Journal of Human Resources*, 34(2): 253–67.

ERIKSON, R., and GOLDTHORPE, J. H. 1992. *The Constant Flux: A Study of Class Mobility in Industrial Societies*. Oxford: Clarendon Press.

ERIKSSON, T., BRATSBERG, B., and RAAUM, O. 2005. 'Earnings Persistence across Generations: Transmission through Health?' Working Paper.

FERRIE, J. P. 2005. 'The End of American Exceptionalism? Mobility in the United States Since 1850'. *Journal of Economic Perspectives*, 19(3): 199–215.

GOLDBERGER, A. S. 1989. 'Economic and Mechanical Models of Intergenerational Transmission'. *American Economic Review*, 79(3): 504–13.

GOLDTHORPE J., and MCKNIGHT, A. 2006. 'The Economic Basis of Social Class', in S. L. Morgan, D. B. Grusky, and G. S. Fields (eds.), *Mobility and Inequality*. Stanford, Calif.: Stanford University Press.

GOTTSCHALK, P. T., and MOFFITT, R. A. 1998. 'Trends in the Variances of Permanent and Transitory Earnings in the U.S. and their Relation to Earnings Mobility'. Unpublished paper. Johns Hopkins University and Boston College.

GRAWE, N. D. 2004a. 'Reconsidering the Use of Nonlinearities in Intergenerational Earnings Mobility as a Test for Credit Constraints'. *Journal of Human Resources*, 39(3): 813–27.

——2004b. 'Intergenerational Mobility for Whom? The Experience of High- and Low-Earnings Sons and Daughters in Intergenerational Perspective', in M. Corak (ed.), *Generational Income Mobility in North America and Europe*. Cambridge: Cambridge University Press.

——2006. 'Life-Cycle Bias in Estimates of Intergenerational Earnings Persistence'. *Labour Economics*, 13(5): 551–70.

GUSTAVSSON, M. Forthcoming. 'A New Picture of Swedish Earnings Inequality: Persistent and Transitory Components'. *Review of Income and Wealth*.

HAIDER, S., and SOLON, G. 2006. 'Life-Cycle Variations in the Association between Current and Lifetime Income'. *American Economic Review*, 96(4): 1308–20.

HANSEN, M. N. 2007. 'Change in Intergenerational Economic Mobility in Norway. Conventional versus Joint Classifications of Economic Origin'. Mimeo.

HASSLER, J., RODRIGUES, J. V., and ZEIRA, J. 2007. 'Inequality and Mobility'. *Journal of Economic Growth*, 12(3): 221–59.

HERTZ, T. 2007. 'Trends in the Intergenerational Elasticity of Family Income in the United States'. *Industrial Relations*, 46(1): 22–50.

HOLMLUND, H. 2007. 'Intergenerational Mobility and Assortative Mating: Effects of an Educational Reform'. Mimeo.

——LINDAHL, M., and PLUG, E. 2006. 'Estimating Intergenerational Schooling Effects: A Comparison of Methods', in H. Holmlund (2006), *Education and the Family*. Dissertation no. 68. Swedish Institute for Social Research, Stockholm University.

HUSSAIN, M. A., MUNK, M. D., and BONKE, J. 2008. 'How Sensitive is Intergenerational Earnings Mobility to Different Measures?' The Danish National Centre for Social Research. Working Paper 07:2008.

JÄNTTI, M., BRATSBERG, B., ROED, K., RAAUM, O., NAYLOR, R., ÖSTERBACKA, E., and BJÖRKLUND, A. 2006. 'American Exceptionalism in a New Light: A Comparison of Intergenerational Earnings Mobility in the Nordic Countries'. IZA Discussion Paper no. 1938.

JENKINS, S. 1987. 'Snapshots versus Movies: "Lifecycle Biases" and the Estimation of Intergenerational Earnings Inheritance'. *European Economic Review*, 31, July: 1149–58.

LAIRD, N., and WARE, J. H. 1982. 'Random-Effects Models for Longitudinal Data'. *Biometrics*, 38(4): 963–74.

LEE, C., and SOLON, G. Forthcoming. 'Trends in Intergenerational Income Mobility'. *Review of Economics and Statistics*.

LEFRANC A., and TRANNOY, A. 2005. 'Intergenerational Earnings Mobility in France: Is France more Mobile than the U.S.?' *Annales d'Économie et de Statistiques*, 78: 57–78.

LEIGH, A. 2007. 'Intergenerational Mobility in Australia'. *Berkeley Journal of Economic Analysis and Policy*, 7(2), Contributions: article 6.

MAYER, S. E. 1997. *What Money Can't Buy: Family Income and Children's Life Chances*. Cambridge, Mass.: Harvard University Press.

——and LOPOO, L. M. 2008. 'Government Spending and Intergenerational Mobility'. *Journal of Public Economics*, 92: 139–58.

MAZUMDER, B. 2005. 'Fortunate Sons: New Estimates of Intergenerational Mobility in the United States Using Social Security Data'. *Review of Economics and Statistics*, 87(2): 235–55.

MAZUMDER, B. 2008. 'Sibling Similarities and Economic Inequality in the US'. *Journal of Population Economics*, 21(3): 685–701.

MEGHIR, C., and PALME, M. 2005. 'Educational Reform, Ability, and Family Background'. *American Economic Review*, 95(1): 414–24.

NICOLETTI, C., and ERMISCH, J. F. 2007. 'Intergenerational Earnings Mobility: Changes across Cohorts in Britain'. *Berkeley Journal of Economic Analysis and Policy*, 7/2, Contributions: article 9.

O'NEILL, D., SWEETMAN, O., and VAN DE GAER, D. 2007. 'The Effects of Measurement Error and Omitted Variables when Using Transition Matrices to Measure Intergenerational Mobility'. *Journal of Economic Inequality*, 5(2): 159–78.

OREOPOULOS, P., PAGE, M., and HUFF STEVENS, A. 2005. 'The Intergenerational Effects of Worker Displacement'. Working Paper.

ÖSTERBACKA, E. 2001. 'Family Background and Economic Status in Finland'. *Scandinavian Journal of Economics*, 103(3): 467–84.

PAGE, M. E., and SOLON, G. 2003a. 'Correlations between Brothers and Neighboring Boys in their Adult Earnings: The Importance of Being Urban'. *Journal of Labor Economics*, 21(4): 831–55.

—————— 2003b. 'Correlations between Sisters and Neighboring Girls in their Subsequent Income as Adults'. *Journal of Applied Econometrics*, 18: 545–62.

PEKKALA, S., and LUCAS, R. E. B. 2007. 'Differences across Cohorts in Finnish Intergenerational Income Mobility', *Industrial Relations*, 46(1): 81–111.

PEKKARINEN, T., PEKKALA, S., and UUSITALO, R. 2006. 'Educational Policy and Intergenerational Mobility: Evidence from the Finnish Comprehensive School Reform'. IFAU Working Paper no. 2006:13.

PIRAINO, P. 2007. 'Comparable Estimates of Intergenerational Income Mobility in Italy'. *Berkeley Journal of Economic Analysis and Policy*, 7/2, Contributions: article 1.

PLUG, E., and VIJVERBERG, W. 2005. 'Does Family Income Matter for Schooling Outcomes? Using Adoption as a Natural Experiment'. *Economic Journal*, 115(506): 880–907.

RAAUM, O., BRATSBERG, B., ROED, K., ÖSTERBACKA, E., ERIKSSON, T., JÄNTTI, M., and NAYLOR, R. A. 2007. 'Marital Sorting, Household Labor Supply, and Intergenerational Earnings Mobility across Countries'. *Berkeley Electronic Journal of Economic Analysis and Policy (Advances)*: article 7.

—— SALVANES, K.-G., and SØRENSEN, E. 2006. 'The Neighborhood is Not What it Used to Be'. *Economic Journal*, 116(508): 200–22.

SACERDOTE, B. 2007. 'How Large are the Effects from Changes in Family Environment? A Study of Korean American Adoptees'. *Quarterly Journal of Economics*, 122(2): 119–57.

SHEA, J. 2000. 'Does Parents' Money Matter?', *Journal of Public Economics*, 77(2): 155–84.

SOLON, G. 1992. 'Intergenerational Income Mobility in the United States'. *American Economic Review*, 82(3): 393–408.

—— 1999. 'Intergenerational Mobility in the Labor Market', in O. Ashenfelter and D. Card (eds.), *Handbook of Labor Economics*, vol. 3A. Amsterdam: Elsevier North-Holland.

—— 2004. 'A Model of Intergenerational Mobility Variation over Time and Place', in M. Corak (ed.), *Generational Income Mobility in North America and Europe*. Cambridge: Cambridge University Press.

——PAGE, M., and DUNCAN, G. 2000. 'Correlations between Neighboring Children in their Subsequent Educational Attainment'. *Review of Economics and Statistics*, 82(3): 383–92.

VOGEL, T. 2008. 'Reassessing Intergenerational Mobility in Germany and the United States: The Impact of Differences in Lifecycle Earnings Patterns'. Mimeo.

ZIMMERMANN, D. J. 1992. 'Regression Toward Mediocrity in Economic Stature'. *American Economic Review*, 82(3): 409–29.

# CHAPTER 21

# INTRA-GENERATIONAL INEQUALITY AND INTERTEMPORAL MOBILITY

RICHARD V. BURKHAUSER

KENNETH A. COUCH[1]

## 1. INTRODUCTION

THE level of average income (as well as wages, wealth, and consumption), its distribution at a given time (income inequality), and how they change over time are among the important indicators used to evaluate and compare the quality of life in modern societies.[2] Previous chapters have explored how inequality changes

[1] Lisa M. Dragoset, Gary S. Fields, and Joachim R. Frick as well as the authors and editors of this volume provided useful feedback on preliminary versions of this chapter. We thank them for their comments and Jessica O'Day for excellent editorial assistance with the manuscript.
[2] Income is only one measure of economic well-being but is the most common used in the intragenerational mobility literature. Thus, we primarily focus our discussion on it. The methods developed to measure intragenerational income mobility are also applicable to wages, wealth, consumption, etc.

over time using repeated cross-sectional measures for different countries. Here, we discuss the literature which uses panel data to measure the income patterns of individuals over their lifetimes, that is, intragenerational mobility.

Some market-oriented societies like the United States are seen as accepting higher levels of cross-section inequality, not only to achieve more rapid economic growth over time, but also to allow greater mobility, and thus to have less permanent inequality, than societies more willing to restrict competitive forces. A major achievement of the modern intragenerational mobility literature has been to precisely define mobility so that it can be empirically measured for various purposes. One of the first uses of these mobility measures was to determine whether a tradeoff exists between increased cross-sectional inequality (permanent and transitory inequality) and mobility (less permanent inequality) across countries. More recently a new measure has been developed that takes into consideration the role of economic expansions and recessions. It can be decomposed into the portion of mobility due to income growth versus changes in individual positions. Others have sought simply to measure the extent of permanent inequality within the distribution of income. All of these measures are useful in cross-national comparisons of different societal rules.

But the intragenerational mobility literature has also looked at individuals within societies to determine the degree that their initial place in the income distribution influences mobility. These studies have been motivated by an interest in whether those at the top and bottom of society are differentially mobile but also by an interest in the degree to which spells in poverty impact future movement up the income distribution.[3]

Finally, a parallel literature, primarily focusing on changes in labor earnings, has attempted to identify the extent of permanent and transitory variance in individual labor earnings as a way of considering the consequences of social institutions on the volatility of wages over time. A variation of this literature in the United States has attempted to determine whether large downward income fluctuations have increased among American households and if so, whether reduced government and private sector insurance protection is the cause.

We begin this chapter with a detailed explanation of the most common methods used to calculate intragenerational mobility and the empirical problems of doing so across countries using panel data. Although other chapters have avoided technical detail by referring to the discussion of cross-sectional measures of inequality contained in Chapter 3, it is necessary for us to review some of this detail in our discussion of the link between single and multi-period measures of inequality. In doing so, we describe the relationship between the data used in studies of mobility

---

[3] Erikson and Nolan (2006) provide an excellent discussion of the relationship of income mobility to persistent poverty. Whether there is a poverty trap in Britain is discussed in Dickens (2000) and Gardiner and Hills (1999).

and the conceptual content of the research; major findings in the literature, and, finally, what remains to be learned.

# 2. BASIC MEASURES

Intragenerational mobility refers to observed differences in the economic circumstances of individuals over time. The mobility we examine is within a generation since the research observes specific people over time who, when aggregated, loosely form a generation. We do not consider the role parents play in determining their children's subsequent position in the income distribution, leaving that to the intergenerational mobility Chapter 20. We begin by reviewing the properties of cross-sectional income inequality measures because the earliest measures of intragenerational mobility developed from them.

## Cross-Sectional Inequality

The most widely used measure of intragenerational mobility (Shorrocks R) incorporates standard classes of inequality indices as an element in its calculation. Thus, to fully understand the intragenerational mobility literature it is important to know the properties of these cross-sectional income inequality measures. Because these measures are discussed in Chapter 3, we focus on how they relate to the intragenerational mobility literature.

Theil (1967) provides an early method of calculating income inequality that satisfies desirable formal properties while retaining intuitive interpretations—the general entropy class of indices. Entropy is the loss of information in the transmission of a signal. Theil (1967) considers the issue of how strong a signal population shares provide in describing the observed distribution of well-being. If the distribution of well-being is unequal relative to population weights, there is entropy in the system.

Theil (1967) is important because he considers whether methods of measuring inequality satisfy basic useful properties applied analysts agree should be met. The underlying properties of those indices are more fully explored in Shorrocks (1980).[4] The developments of inequality indices by Shorrocks (1980) and Theil (1967) are similar to the axiomatic approach used in microeconomic theory to develop utility functions. Shorrocks (1980) first states formal properties (axioms) desirable in an

---

[4] Shorrocks places a stronger set of restrictions on potential measures than Theil.

inequality measure. He then proves Theil (1967) indices can be derived from the equations representing those axioms.[5]

Shorrocks (1980) argues four properties are desirable for a cross-sectional inequality measure. The first is *symmetry*. In measuring inequality for some income level, equal absolute deviations from above or below should make the same contribution to the sum of inequality.

To ease interpretation, it is also useful to construct inequality measures that have a reference value for no inequality; this norms the index relative to that limiting value. To norm an index means to give an interpretation to its maximum or minimum, so that other values can be interpreted relative to it. A value of zero, or no inequality, is usually associated with distributions where every individual income is equal to the mean. So, the measure has a *norm of zero*.

Third, if the measure is going to be useful, it needs to be calculable across all valid levels of income. So, the measure is assumed to be characterized by *continuity*. That is, it is everywhere calculable and does not increase or decrease in discontinuous jumps.

Finally, it would be helpful if an aggregate measure is decomposable into the amount coming from each separate group as well as cross-group components.[6] Decomposability is a useful feature of an inequality measure. For instance, a country's overall inequality can be disaggregated into components within demographic groups and across them (Karoly and Burtless, 1995). Likewise total world inequality can be disaggregated within and across nations (Berry *et al.*, 1983; Bourguignon and Morrisson, 2002). Shorrocks (1980) assumes that the class of indices to be considered is *additively decomposable*.

He then proves that the only index that satisfies these four properties is:

$$I(y; n) = \frac{1}{\theta(\mu, n)} \sum_i [\phi(y_i) - \phi(\mu)]. \tag{1}$$

The inequality index, $I$, is a function of the relevant measure of well-being and the number of individuals. The index includes a proportional weight, $1/\theta$, where $\theta$ is also a function of the mean of the measure of well-being and the sample size. The weight is multiplied by the sum of a weighted measure of individual levels of well-being less the mean, $\mu$.

In addition to the above axioms, the cross-sectional inequality literature argues that additional properties should be satisfied. One is the Pigou–Dalton principle

[5] Similar approaches can be found in the work of Bourguignon (1979) and Cowell (1985). Cowell (1985) uses an axiomatic approach to develop a set of Kolm indices which subsume the Theil and Atkinson indices as special cases. Bourguignon (1979) considers a similar set of conditions to those found in Shorrocks (1978a) and draws a similar conclusion.

[6] Bourguignon (1979), Cowell (1980), and Shorrocks (1980, 1982, and 1984) each consider decomposable inequality indices in addition to Theil (1967). Theil (1967) shows that the Gini is not mathematically decomposable.

of transfers which states that when income goes from someone above to someone below average well-being while preserving the mean, it should reduce inequality. Shorrocks (1980) shows that equation (1) satisfies this property. A second is that the measure should not vary if all values in a given population are replicated and combined with the original distribution so that the count of its members is doubled. Indices described by equation (1) will satisfy this condition as long as the weights used in calculating the index take a specific form. A third is mean independence. If two distributions have the same variability of income but a different level, the measures of their inequality should be equal.

Shorrocks (1980) shows that only inequality indices that take the form below can simultaneously satisfy all of these properties:

$$I(y; n) = \frac{A_n}{c(c-1)} \sum_i \left[ \left( \frac{y_i}{\mu} \right)^c - 1 \right] \quad \text{when} \quad c \neq 0, 1$$

$$I(y; n) = \frac{1}{n} \sum_i \log\left( \frac{\mu}{y_i} \right) \quad \text{when} \quad c = 0, \quad \text{and}$$

$$I(y; n) = \frac{1}{n} \sum_i \frac{y_i}{\mu} \log\left( \frac{\mu}{y_i} \right) \quad \text{when} \quad c = 1. \tag{2}$$

This equation is a one parameter index because the value of c determines the analytical form used to calculate the inequality indices and is identical to the one developed by Theil (1967). The Theil indices are abbreviated as $I_c(y)$ where $I_0(y)$ refers to the form shown above when c = 0. This measure is the average difference (in logs) between individual measures of well-being and the average in the sample. It's the average (geometric) proportional difference between each person's measure relative to the sample average. $I_1(y)$ is the same geometric mean difference weighted by the proportional difference in the income received by each individual relative to the average.

Because the weighting across observations changes with the value of c, different versions of the Theil indices emphasize different parts of the distribution.[7] Because the upper range of most survey measures of well-being include a few very large values, weighting each observation equally places more emphasis on lower values since they represent a greater share of the population. Hence the $I_1(y)$ measure places a greater emphasis on higher values because it weights the contribution of each person based on the income received relative to the average.

Even though the Gini index does not satisfy the condition of decomposability, it is often used in inequality research. We present its formula taken from Theil

[7] Foster and Shorrocks (1987) provides a useful discussion of this issue. The Atkinson Index (Atkinson, 1975) requires that a researcher explicitly set a parameter which determines the weights placed on different parts of the distribution.

(1967: 121) in equation (3) since it is often imbedded within measures of mobility.

$$G^* = \frac{1}{2} \sum_{i=1}^{n} \sum_{j=1}^{n} x_i x_j \left| \frac{y_i}{x_i} - \frac{y_j}{x_j} \right| \tag{3}$$

where $x$ is the population share of the group indexed while $y$ is the income share of the group. The Gini is one-half of a weighted average of all absolute differences between the deflated per capita incomes, the weights being the products of the corresponding population shares.

## Decomposability and Intragenerational Mobility

### Measures using individual data

Theil (1967) shows the usefulness of the decomposability property of entropy indexes in the cross-sectional literature by using them to calculate within and between inequality values by race, across states, and nations. Shorrocks (1982, 1984) does so for income and demographic subgroups. Bourguignon (1979) and Cowell (1980) independently provide alternative analytical approaches to deriving decomposable indices discussed above. But most importantly for our purposes, Shorrocks (1978a) recognized the potential of applying decomposable indices in the dimension of time.

Shorrocks (1978a) poses his concept of intragenerational mobility as a comparison between a static or one-period measure of inequality and a dynamic one. High frequency events such as monthly earnings are less volatile if aggregated over a year. Hence in moving from a one-period measure at any time to a longer sampling frame, those observed in the worst position initially should be in an improved position later and vice versa. Thus, Shorrocks argued that multi-period measures of inequality provide a contrast between static positions and movement over time and hence are measures of mobility. 'In essence, mobility is measured by the extent to which the income distribution is equalized as the accounting period is extended' (Shorrocks, 1978a: 378).

His formal analysis focuses primarily on indices taking the form:

$$I[Y] = g\left(\frac{Y}{\mu}\right) \tag{4}$$

where $g$ is a strictly convex function. This includes the Theil (1967) inequality indices as well as those developed in Atkinson (1970, 1975). By the definition of convexity, if a measure of inequality is calculated using multiple periods of data, it must be less than or equal to the measures for individual years.

Shorrocks (1978a) benchmarks his analysis to the state where relative incomes never change, to get a measure which takes complete immobility (or perfect rigidity) as its limiting value. In this conceptual model, equalization of incomes over time requires variation or mobility over time. So, societies with more variability in incomes should also be more equalizing in the long run.

He proposes a measure of rigidity, $R$, with an upper limiting value of 1. The computational formula for the Shorrocks $R$ is:

$$R = \frac{I[Y]}{\sum_{k=1}^{m} w_k I[Y^K]} \tag{5}$$

where $w_k = \mu_k/\mu$; $m$ refers to the number of periods over which the measure is computed. The numerator of $R$ is the measure of inequality over all periods of the sample while the denominator is calculated as the sum over individual years. The weights in the denominator are the shares of income received in each year relative to the multi-period total.[8] Burkhauser and Poupore (1997), in the first paper to employ the measure within a cross-national framework, provide a detailed discussion of its calculation.

### Measures based on transition tables

Many studies of mobility provide transition probability matrices from the data rather than a Shorrocks R scalar measure of it. Comparing these matrices across studies to draw inferences about which country or time period is characterized by more mobility is difficult. Shorrocks (1978b) considers how these transition probability matrices could be converted into summary measures of mobility similar to $R$.

Probability matrices contain the conditional probability that a person who starts in one group in period 1 will be observed there or in a different category later. When viewing these square matrices, the diagonal elements provide the probabilities that a person who starts in one group remains there. Hence they are indicators of immobility.

Shorrocks (1978b) summarizes the information contained in these transition matrices by devising a measure of mobility that is confined to the [0, 1] interval and requires that it increase in value as the probabilities in the off-diagonal elements rise. He also requires the measure equal 0 if all the off-diagonal elements are zero and refers to this as perfect immobility. Perfect mobility occurs when there is no systematic relationship between where a person starts and finishes. This concept is referred to as origin independence in the intragenerational mobility literature. Origin independence requires that all values in the probability transition matrix

---

[8]  Goebel (2007) modifies the Shorrocks R to measure persistent poverty rather than inequality and provides an empirical application comparing the USA and Germany from 1984–2002 using the PSID and GSOEP.

are equal. Shorrocks (1978b) requires the index to take the value of 1 in this case.

Shorrocks (1978b) notes that it is desirable for the value of a mobility index to increase monotonically as the off-diagonal probabilities rise in value. This implies that when the off-diagonal elements have a value of one, the index itself is at its maximal value. Shorrocks (1978b) also notes that it is desirable for the mobility index to take its maximum value when all elements in the matrix are identical. But he shows that it is not mathematically possible for a single index to have both properties.

This conflict in how to norm (assign the interpretation attached to) the upper value of a mobility index is a recurring theme in this literature.[9] Shorrocks (1978b) resolves this conflict by restricting his measure to realistic cases. One is where the probabilities in the diagonal elements of the transition matrix are always greater or equal to the probability of transitioning to any other state so that the measure has a unique upper limiting value of 1. Shorrocks (1978b: 1017) notes other restrictions that can be imposed for this property to hold.

Given this restriction, Shorrocks (1978b) proposes the mobility measure:

$$M(P) = \frac{n - trace(P)}{n - 1} \tag{6}$$

In the case of a perfectly mobile transition probability matrix $trace(P)$ will be 1 and $M(P)$ will take the value of 1 indicating perfect mobility.

## An alternative axiomatic approach

There are different notions of what mobility implies. Fields and Ok (1999) use an axiomatic approach which allows the portion of income increases due to economic growth to be incorporated in a measure of mobility. The measure can also be decomposed into the portions of mobility due to income growth and to changes in individual positions.

We have already discussed three of the conditions Fields and Ok (1999) impose on their measure: scale invariance, symmetry, and subgroup decomposability. The other is multiplicative path separability. This condition allows growth in incomes over time to be decomposed. Using their notation, if from time 0 to 1, incomes grow at a rate of $\beta$, and from time 1 to 2 at a rate $\alpha/\beta$, then growth from period 0 to 2 equals $\alpha$ or $(\beta^*(\alpha/\beta))$. As long as income paths decompose in this manner, the condition of multiplicative path separability is satisfied.

---

[9]  Both Dragoset and Fields (2006) and Jenkins and Van Kerm (2006) consider different indices which estimate these concepts separately. Gottschalk and Spolaore (2002) also provide methodological advances regarding this measurement issue.

Fields and Ok (1999) prove that only income movement measures of this form satisfy these properties:

$$m(x, y) = c \left( \frac{1}{n} \sum_{i=1}^{N} |\log y_i - \log x_i| \right) \tag{7}$$

where $c$ is a constant greater than zero, and $x$ and $y$ are a person's income at two points in time. Setting $c = 1$ yields the average absolute value of proportional income changes. This mobility measure treats positive and negative changes in the same manner; they are movements. Because positive movements imply welfare increases and negative ones decreases, Fields and Ok (1999) also develop a directional measure so that positive and negative changes over time are treated differently; however, the functional form is similar to the mobility measure they propose:

$$d_n(x, y) = c \left( \frac{1}{n} \sum_{i=1}^{N} (\log y_i - \log x_i) \right). \tag{8}$$

Again setting $c = 1$, the directional mobility measure is the average (geometric) proportional change in individual incomes. A positive value means that total income movements have been welfare increasing. Using their mobility measure, Fields and Ok (1999) also decompose all percentage changes in income into components due to growth or changes in position:

$$m_n^*(x, y) = \left( \frac{1}{n} \sum_{i=1}^{N} (\log y_i - \log x_i) \right) + \left( \frac{2}{n} \sum_{i \in L} (\log y_i - \log x_i) \right). \tag{9}$$

The first term on the left represents the average welfare change due to growth and the second captures transfers from losers (those whose income declines) to gainers.

## Welfare interpretations

The best-known measures of inequality are not derived from the class of standard utility functions used in microeconomic theory. However, studies of the relationship of social utility functions to measures of inequality are common. Atkinson (1970) provides the first formal examination of the relationship of social inequality measures to social welfare functions. He shows that since the mathematical properties imposed on measures of social inequality are similar to those underlying utility functions, in many cases, they have a welfare interpretation. Chapter 3 considers this issue in more detail.

## Intragenerational mobility, permanent and transitory inequality

The Shorrocks R is the ratio of a multi-period measure of inequality which reduces the influence of short-term or transitory phenomena to a weighted average of

single-period measures which fully reflect both permanent and transitory influences on inequality. At a conceptual level, the Shorrocks R can be thought of as the
ratio of permanent to total inequality.

A largely separate empirical literature which incorporates these same concepts
has sought to identify the extent of permanent and transitory variance in individual
labor earnings. In its best-known formulation (Gottschalk and Moffitt, 1994), this
literature seeks to understand for each individual how much of their earnings
variation is due to a permanent component versus transitory error. The permanent
component is the average observed for each individual in the sample over the time
frame of the study. The transitory components are the deviations of each observation from the individual averages. The variance due to the permanent component is
calculated using the individual averages. The variance of the transitory components
is computed using all of the individual deviations in the sample.

Given the importance of this literature, we provide the basic formulas used to
calculate the permanent and transitory variances by Gottschalk and Moffitt (1994)
so that the reader can see the differences relative, for example, to the formula
for permanent variance imbedded in the Shorrocks R as used by Burkhauser and
Poupore (1997).

In equation (10), $v$ is the transitory component of labor earnings and in equation
(11) $\mu$ is the permanent component of labor earnings. The outcome values, $y$, are in
natural logs.

$$\sigma_v^2 = \frac{1}{N} \sum_{i=1}^{N} \frac{1}{(T-1)} \sum_{t=1}^{T_i} (y_{it} - \bar{y}_i)^2 \tag{10}$$

$$\sigma_\mu^2 = \frac{1}{N-1} \sum_{i=1}^{N} (\bar{y}_i - \bar{y})^2 - (\sigma_v^2/\bar{T}) \tag{11}$$

Loosely, Shorrocks R can be written as

$$R \approx \frac{\sigma_\mu}{\sigma_\mu + \sigma_v}. \tag{12}$$

Conceptually, this observation provides a link between studies which are primarily
interested in changing volatility of the permanent and transitory components of
earnings and measures of intragenerational mobility. Although Gottschalk and
Moffitt (1994) provide estimates of $\sigma_\mu^2$ and $\sigma_v^2$ that can be used to infer the value
of Shorrock's R, caution should be used in doing this because they pre-adjust
observations of labor earnings used in their calculations for position in the age–
earnings profile to make them more comparable.

Baker and Solon (2003) extend the framework of Gottschalk and Moffitt (1994)
to more fully specify the sources of transitory variation. By fully modeling the
transitory error to consist of both systematic shocks and random errors, they reduce

the portion of overall variance considered transitory. Their model also allows for the permanent and transitory components to change over time.

# 3. DATA REQUIREMENTS, RESEARCH FOCUS, AND CHOICE OF MEASURES

Empirical studies of inequality require appropriate data. Since the 1960s the applied intragenerational mobility literature has experienced major advances. Those advances were made possible by the development of panel data and the increased ability of researchers to process these data with modern computers.

The first and best-known panel data set, the Panel Study of Income Dynamics (PSID), was launched in 1968. It was more than a decade before similar large-scale panel surveys began in Europe. Today, there are several ongoing European panel data sets and this has fostered the development of cross-national applied research on intragenerational mobility. But panel data sets that resurvey individuals over time are still relatively less common than cross-sectional surveys.

A very practical consideration in cross-national comparative research is that for the analysis to be valid the data, either as initially collected (ex ante) or adjusted later (ex post) must reflect the same conceptual content. But reconciling the differences across surveys and data sources so that they reflect similar conceptual content is a difficult, time-consuming task.

One example of a useful approach to obtaining equivalent data for cross-national comparisons of intragenerational mobility is the Cross National Equivalency File (CNEF). This ongoing ex post effort by researchers at Cornell University takes separately fielded country panel data (the United States PSID, the German Socio-Economic Panel (SOEP), the British Household Panel Study (BHPS), the Canadian Survey of Income and Labor Participation (SLID) and the Household Income and Labor Dynamics Study of Australia (HILDA)) and provides researchers with comparably recoded versions of key variables for analysts to use in cross-national research. See Frick, Jenkins et al. (2007) for a fuller discussion of CNEF.[10]

A different approach can be found in the ex ante effort begun in 1994 to field the European Community Household Panel (ECHP) via simultaneously collected equivalent panel data in all European Union countries by the Statistical Office of the European Communities. While in principle this is a better way of providing

---

[10]  The first major attempt to systematically gather data across countries and organize them into a comparable format did not occur until 1983 when the Luxembourg Income Study (LIS) was launched. Atkinson and Brandolini (2001) discuss issues researchers using cross-sectional data sets on individual countries to compare levels of income inequality and its trends must consider.

a harmonized family of country data sets, in practice the ECHP ran into early problems of attrition which led it to drop its efforts in Germany, Great Britain, and Luxembourg and replace those data with ongoing panel studies—the GSOEP, the BHPS, and the Panel Study, Living in Luxembourg (PSELL) respectively. There were additional concerns as well regarding the timeliness of cross-sectional information that could be obtained from panel surveys. Ultimately, these concerns led to the ECHP being discontinued in 2001. For those still interested in using the ECHP data because of its potential for multi-period analysis, the critical issue is differential attrition bias that is known to exist in the country panels.

Even when data are harmonized across sources of income, in their treatment of sharing units, and in the other characteristics considered in Lillard (2007), differences can arise that will bias cross-national comparisons.[11] One is top-coding.[12] To preserve confidentiality, surveys often top code reported labor earnings and other sources of income. Over time, if these top codes are not systematically adjusted, inflation as well as economic growth will push an increasing share of the highest values above the top codes. The majority of those with top-coded sources of income are in the top percentiles of the overall income distribution, but because these top codes are on individual sources of income, others with top-coded income sources are scattered among household incomes percentiles throughout the income distribution. Therefore these top codes will not only impact measured trends in mean household income and in scalar measures of overall household income inequality but they will also impact comparisons of points in the household income distribution over time such as 90/10 ratios. Burkhauser *et al.* (2007) document this problem in the Current Population Survey which is the most common data used to track income inequality in the United States both internally and in the context of cross-national comparisons. Hence in a comparative international context, the challenge is to adjust for differential top codes across the components of income as they occur in multiple surveys across countries. This is important since top codes themselves, by impacting the underlying distribution of the measure of economic well-being being considered, can directly impact measures of inequality and the cross-national inferences being made (see Levy and Murnane, 1992 and more recently Burkhauser *et al.*, 2007 and Larrimore *et al.*, 2008).

Within both cross-sectional and panel data sets, a wide variety of measures of economic well-being are available for use by researchers. However, in individual studies, researchers commonly only consider one. Their choice to use only one measure or to contrast several is related directly to the study's goals. In past studies, researchers have focused on hourly wage rates, labor earnings, household

---

[11]   For instance, Frick and Grabka (2007) show the sensitivity of inequality estimates to different methods of imputation of missing data across surveys.

[12]   Comparative results have also been shown to vary with the use of purchasing power parity adjustments (Brandolini, 2007b).

size-adjusted income and its public and private subcomponents, including taxes and transfers. Here, we briefly discuss this issue.[13]

The most basic inquiries examine the market reward for work by asking how much inequality is associated with rewards from an hour's work (hourly wage and its dispersion). Abstracting from global economic conditions, differences in inequality in market wage rates across countries are used as a marker of those societies' acceptance of differential market rewards and their willingness to reduce it via laws or social conventions. Gottschalk (1993) provides an excellent study which considers wage inequality across countries as well as its contribution to income inequality.

While wage rates are important in determining consumption possibilities for any individual, people must also decide how many hours to work. That choice is impacted by a broad array of social influences. But when the analysis is widened to consider the interaction of the wage rate with hours of work, individual choice can be an important influence on total labor income. Thus, if a study examines both wages and individual labor earnings across countries, it can make statements regarding the degree of inequality in rewards across countries while differentiating between the basic influences of market rewards and work choices.

The vast majority of individuals live in households. The first consideration in assessing consumption opportunities of individuals living in households is that there are more potential wage earners; however, income must be shared among more people. As individuals are added to a household, the associated expenses do not increase linearly. While it requires an assumption about the returns to scale of households of different sizes, equivalence scales can be used to adjust the consumption power of individual incomes.[14] Moreover, the inclusion of private sources of non-labor income allows analysts to examine the impact of private wealth holdings as an influence on current income.

An additional consideration beyond the particular measure (wages, labor income, household equivalent income) of well-being used in the study is the role of government. Considering any of these measures in the absence of either government transfers or taxes informs us about some of the variation generated by the market. However such measures are not a pure reflection of the impact of the market because to literally believe them is to accept the counterfactual that government's presence has no impact on individual behavior.

Nonetheless, it is of value to look at the ability of individuals and families to generate resources for themselves and then as a first approximation use these values to examine the role of government. If one were going to fully integrate the role of government into the analysis, the data should be adjusted for both taxes and

---

[13]  Gottschalk (1997) provides a similar discussion to the one presented here in the context of cross-sectional inequality measurement.

[14]  Burtless and Karoly (1995) and Burkhauser *et al.* (1996) provide useful discussions of the impact of different methods of calculating equivalent family income on resulting measures of inequality.

transfers. Many data sets now have post-tax, post-transfer measures of household income available for analytical use—disposable income.

# 4. THE LITERATURE ON INTRAGENERATIONAL MOBILITY

In Table 21.1 we characterize empirical research on intragenerational mobility by whether a study considers one outcome measure (labor earnings, equivalent household income, etc.) or provides a contrast across several as well as by whether the study considers one country or provides a cross-national comparison. We identify the specific countries, time periods, and measures of well-being considered in each study.

Virtually all of the studies in Table 21.1 begin with a cross-sectional examination of inequality. This is not a perfunctory exercise since the panel data used in these mobility studies require respondents to be present for many years. So, demonstrating that the sample drawn for longitudinal study exhibits similar patterns of inequality to those found in cross-sectional analysis using the full sample reinforces the validity of the remainder of the study.

One major question in the empirical literature on intragenerational mobility is whether greater cross-sectional inequality is associated with larger intragenerational mobility. Do the most heavily market-orientated countries with relatively large cross-sectional levels of inequality such as the United States have greater rates of mobility and hence less permanent inequality?

Most studies find no strong relationship between cross-sectional inequality and mobility. Burkhauser *et al.* (1997a, 1997b, and 1997) draw this conclusion using measures of labor earnings, equivalent pre-government household-size-adjusted income, and post-government household-size-adjusted (disposable) income based on harmonized CNEF data for Germany and the United States. These findings have been examined in subsequent studies which confirm their findings. Gottschalk and Spolaore (2002) use the same data and draw the same conclusion although their study only considers post-government household-size-adjusted income. Similarly, Maasoumi and Trede (2001) confirm this finding using pre- and post-government household-size-adjusted income as do Jenkins and Van Kerm (2006) examining post-government equivalent income.

Ayala and Sastre (2002) further consider post-government household-size-adjusted income, using data from some of the ECHP countries (UK, Spain, France, and Germany) and the PSID (USA), to address this question and conclude (p. 31) that, 'the most significant result is the absence of any clear relationship between

Table 21.1. Studies of intragenerational mobility

| Author (Year) | Data (Years) | Countries | Income Measure |
|---|---|---|---|
| Aaberge et al. (2002) | LDB<br>IDS, TAF<br>Level of Living Surveys, PSID | Denmark<br>Norway<br>Sweden<br>USA | Labor earnings, market income, post-government equivalent household income (Head and partner) |
| Auten and Gee (2007) | Tax Filings (1987, 1996) | USA | Total income and size adjusted for joint tax filings |
| Ayala and Sastre (2002) | ECHP (1993–97) | UK, Spain, France, Germany, USA | Post-government equivalent household income |
| Burkhauser et al. (1997a) | PSID (1992–96)<br>GSOEP (1984–89) | Germany, USA | Pre-government labor earnings |
| Burkhauser et al. (1997b) | PSID (1984–89)<br>GSOEP (1984–89) | Germany, USA | Labor earnings, pre-government equivalent family income, post-government equivalent family income |
| Burkhauser and Poupore (1997) | PSID (1984–89)<br>GSOEP (1984–89) | Germany, USA | Labor earnings, pre-government equivalent family income, post-government equivalent family income |
| Dahl et al. (2007) | SSA (1980–2003), SIPP (1991–93) | USA | Labor earnings |
| Dickens (2000) | NES (1975–94)<br>BHPS (1991–94) | Britain | Labor earnings |
| Dragoset and Fields (2006) | SIPP–SSA PUF (1990, 1991, 1992, 1993, 1996 SIPP panels covering 1990–99 inclusively) | USA | Labor earnings |
| Fields and Ok (1999) | PSID (1969–86) | USA | Pre-government post-tax household income |
| Gangl (2005) | CNEF (1992–97)<br>ECHP (1994–99) | Belgium, Denmark, France, Germany, Greece, Ireland, Italy, Netherlands, Portugal, Spain, UK, USA | Post-government equivalent household income |

| Study | Dataset | Country (years) | Income concept |
|---|---|---|---|
| Gittleman and Joyce (1999) | PSID (1968–92) | USA | Pre-tax, post-transfer equivalent family income |
| Gottschalk (1997) | PSID (1974–91) | USA | Labor earnings |
| Gottschalk and Spolaore (2002) | PSID (1984–93), GSOEP (1984–93) | Germany, USA | Post-government equivalent family income |
| Gustafsson (1994) | Sweden Tax Register (1971–80), Sweden Household Income Surveys (1980–81) | Sweden | Individual post-tax income, Post-government equivalent income |
| Jarvis and Jenkins (1998) | BHPS (1991–94) | Britain | Post-government equivalent household income |
| Jenkins and Van Kerm (2006) | CNEF (1980–2000) | USA (1981–92), Germany (1985–99) | Post-government equivalent household income |
| Maasoumi and Trede (2001) | CNEF (1984–88) | USA (1984–88), Germany (1984–88) | Pre and post-government equivalent family income |
| Schiller (1978) | LEED–SSA (1957–71) | USA | Individual earnings |
| Van Kerm (2004) | CNEF (1985–97), SEP (1985–97) | USA, Germany (1985–97), Belgium (1985–97) | Post-government equivalent household income |
| Kopczuk et al. (2007) | CWHS (1937–2004), LEED–SSA (1957–2004) | USA (1937–2004) | Individual labor earnings |
| Zaidi et al. (2005) | GSOEP (1990–2000), BHPS (1990–99) | Germany, Britain | Post-government equivalent household income |

inequality and mobility'. Aaberge *et al.* (2002) compare inequality and mobility across Denmark, Sweden, Norway, and the United States in the period from 1980–90. They use data from the Longitudinal Data Base (LDB) for Denmark, the Income Distribution Survey (IDS) and Tax Assessment Files (TAF) for Norway, and the Level of Living Surveys (LOL) for Sweden. They similarly conclude that there is 'no evidence of a *positive* relationship between inequality and mobility'. Gangl (2005), using data from the ECHP and CNEF, considers the largest set of countries (Belgium, Denmark, France, Germany, Greece, Ireland, Italy, Netherlands, Portugal, Spain, UK, USA). He also focuses on post-government household-size-adjusted income and similarly concludes that cross-sectional inequality in the United States is relatively high but that intragenerational mobility is not.

Researchers using the CNEF to focus on the relationship between cross-sectional inequality and intragenerational mobility in Germany and the United States, as well as researchers using additional countries from the ECHP, and even researchers such as Aaberge *et al.* (2002) who use both national registers and panel data sources draw similar conclusions. Countries with relatively large inequality do not appear to have systematically higher mobility.[15]

A second but related question in the empirical literature on intragenerational mobility is the degree to which inequality falls in a country when multiple periods of data are used rather than one. All Table 21.1 studies regardless of their measure of welfare or countries considered find that inequality falls as the time frame expands. Most of the decline usually occurs in the first few years. For example, Gittleman and Joyce (1999) find that approximately two-thirds of the reduction in inequality they observed over the 10 years of their study occurred in the first five years. Gustafsson (1994: 85), who considers a 10-year panel (1971–80) of tax register data on individual post-tax incomes, similarly concludes that, 'The pace by which immobility decreases over time is not constant but decreases'.

Few of the Table 21.1 studies test the sensitivity of their results using alternative measures of well-being. Nonetheless, initial evidence suggests that the size of the decline in inequality over time systematically varies with the measure of income used. Burkhauser *et al.* (1997b) and Burkhauser and Poupore (1997) in their studies of Germany and the United States each consider labor earnings as well as pre- and post-government equivalent household income. These studies find that cross-section inequality is greatest for labor earnings, less so for pre-government equivalent income, and least for post-government equivalent income. However,

---

[15]  While the results across studies are in accord, it should be noted that the attrition rates in some of the countries included in the ECHP countries raise concerns. For example, a comparison of income inequality rates in the ECHP survey of Italy compared with those found over the same years by the Bank of Italy's Survey of Household Income and Wealth in Brandolini (2007a) provides evidence regarding the impact of attrition problems in the ECHP survey of Italy on empirical inequality research.

when inequality in labor earnings is computed over time, its level of inequality falls, by approximately one-quarter. In contrast, the level of pre-government equivalent income inequality falls by approximately one-third and that of post-government equivalent household income by one-tenth over time.

Summary measures of mobility consistently find that the majority of the cross-sectional inequality, 60 to 90 percent, in most societies is persistent. A related topic of interest is whether there is differential mobility across the distribution of well-being within the countries included in Table 21.1. The finding that the majority of cross-sectional inequality is persistent over time is consistent with findings of the individual studies that there is very little economic mobility from the very bottom of the distribution to the top. The majority of economic mobility occurs over fairly small spans of the distribution of well-being and those at the top of the distribution are less likely to move down. The most recent evidence on this issue for the United States can be found in two studies based on administrative records (Auten and Gee, 2007 and Kopczuk et al., 2007). Auten and Gee (2007) make use of tax filings in their calculations while Kopczuk et al. (2007) look at mobility in earnings in Social Security records as did Schiller (1978). Dragoset and Fields (2006) provide evidence that mobility estimates using administrative records such as those employed in these two studies yield estimates similar to those obtained from panel survey data. Jarvis and Jenkins (1998) provide evidence for Britain. Comparative evidence on mobility from different points in the distribution for Germany and the United States can be found in Burkhauser et al. (1997a, 1997b).

A more recent topic of interest is whether mobility has changed over time. Gittleman and Joyce (1996) use the PSID from 1968–92 to examine patterns of US mobility in pre-tax, post-transfer equivalent family income and conclude that mobility was fairly constant. Similarly, Dahl et al. (2007) examine US individual labor earnings from 1980–2003 using Social Security program data and conclude that the trend in income variability has been flat. This was during a period of widening cross-sectional inequality. Kopczuk et al. (2007) also use US Social Security program data to examine individual earnings mobility but do so since 1937. They also conclude that trends in long-term mobility over the past several decades have been essentially unchanged. Dickens (2000) uses the New Earnings Survey (1975–94) and the BHPS (1991–94) to examine wage mobility in Great Britain. He concludes that British inequality has risen over time and that mobility has declined. This area of research is relatively new and suggests that long-term trends of mobility in US household income and labor earnings have been stable over the past two decades. However, given the scant international evidence, we view this as a fruitful area of future research.

A final issue in the empirical literature on intragenerational mobility is whether the welfare of the typical citizen improves with economic growth. As discussed above, the Fields and Ok (1999) index of income movement allows one to consider this question.

In the cross-sectional inequality literature, Burkhauser *et al.* (2004), use descriptive graphical methods to plot distributions of household size-adjusted incomes over time and find that over the 1990s business cycle in the United States (1989–2000) overall cross-sectional inequality increased but the entire distribution of income improved. In real terms, the average person at every decile of the distribution earned more. In contrast, Burkhauser *et al.* (1999), using similar methods, found that over the 1980s business cycle in the United States (1979–89) overall cross-sectional inequality increased but there was a decline in the size-adjusted incomes of those at the bottom of the distribution. Calculations using the Fields and Ok (1999) mobility index can capture these types of changes over different time periods.

Fields and Ok (1999) consider total movement of equivalent pre-tax post-transfer incomes from 1969–76 and 1979–86 using US PSID data. They report more total income movement in the later period, a time of increasing cross-sectional inequality. Using their directional measure, they find that the increased movement of incomes from 1979 to 1986 was welfare reducing.

Also, the use of the Fields and Ok mobility measure may change relative rankings across countries in the degree of permanent inequality. Van Kerm (2004) uses panel data from the German SOEP, the Belgian Socio-Economic Panel, and the US PSID from 1985–97 to examine intragenerational mobility in post-government equivalent income by computing the Shorrocks R and finds that the United States has the greatest degree of permanent inequality. However, when he computes the Fields and Ok mobility measure, the United States has the largest amount of income movement. This larger movement is most associated with re-rankings of individuals within the US distribution.

In a conceptually similar paper, Zaidi *et al.* (2005) consider the mobility of incomes among older residents of Germany and Britain. Using both Shorrocks R and the Fields and Ok index of total income movement, they find that older British citizens experience more economic instability. Thus, the use of the Fields and Ok index does not always change rankings based on the Shorrocks R.

# 5. CONCLUSIONS AND FUTURE RESEARCH

The maturing of individual-based panel studies first in the United States and more recently in European Community countries has spawned an empirical literature on intragenerational mobility resulting in plausible evidence on how it varies over time and across countries as well as how cross-sectional inequality is related to mobility. While more research is needed, a picture is emerging:

- Most studies find no clear relationship between greater cross-sectional inequality and greater intragenerational mobility.
- All studies find that inequality falls as the time frame expands regardless of the measure of welfare or countries considered, and that most of the reduction usually occurs in the first few years. But a large degree of permanent inequality remains.
- While the evidence is sparser, studies using alternative measures of well-being suggest that the decline in inequality systematically varies with the measure of income used.
- The few studies looking at trends in long-term mobility find little change over the past several decades in the United States.

Despite this progress, the field of intragenerational mobility research is relatively undeveloped in comparison to the cross-sectional inequality literature, due in part to more stringent data requirements. High quality person-based panel data is still relatively rare. And past efforts to assemble uniform ex ante panel data sets across countries have met with mixed success. Enhancing current country-based panel data and building new ones in other countries is necessary for better understanding of economic mobility over time as well as other types of dynamic social processes.

Despite their relative scarcity, greater use of existing panel data for cross-national comparative purposes is still possible. Few studies have used multiple measures of well-being across countries. Contrasting different measures of well-being within and across countries in integrated studies should increase our understanding of the role of different institutions (labor markets, family, and government) in contributing to mobility over time and in the reduction of inequality.

A consistent finding in the intragenerational mobility literature is that inequality declines (due to mobility) as years are added to the analysis. Nonetheless, these studies find that the majority of initial economic inequality remains. The best evidence indicates that between 10 to 40 percent of cross-sectional inequality is transitory. The percentage reduction in inequality is largest for pre-government equivalent household income followed by labor earnings and then by post-government equivalent income.

As existing panel data sets have matured and administrative files have become more accessible, the intragenerational mobility literature has begun to examine whether mobility has changed over time. This literature is progressing rapidly in the United States. Few studies exist for European Community countries and no comparative international study has explored temporal patterns of mobility.

Because the basic methodologies for measuring mobility are well developed, intragenerational mobility researchers have a common language to describe their findings. Despite the very high quality of the early work which developed the most common measures of mobility, the discussion of what is meant by the word mobility continues. The ongoing importance of this topic as an area of research is demonstrated by the recent work of Fields and Ok (1999) which identifies the role of economic growth in income mobility.

The largest gap in the intragenerational mobility literature is the lack of systematic attempts to relate mobility to policy-relevant variables. Studies focusing on patterns of mobility across demographic subgroups have examined the role of taxes and transfers. Extending these studies to explore the roles of specific public programs and behavioral mechanisms would provide a major advance within the literature on intragenerational mobility.

# References

AABERGE, ROLF, BJORKLUND, ANDERS, JÄNTTI, MARKUS, PALME, MARTEN, PEDERSEN, PEDER J., SMITH, NINA, and WENNEMO, TOM. 2002. 'Income Inequality and Income Mobility in the Scandinavian Countries Compared to the United States'. *Review of Income and Wealth*, 48(4): 443–69.

ATKINSON, ANTHONY B. 1970. 'On the Measurement of Inequality'. *Journal of Economic Theory*, 2: 241–63.

——1975. *The Economics of Inequality*. Oxford: Clarendon Press.

——and BRANDOLINI, ANDREA. 2001. 'Promise and Pitfalls in the Use of "Secondary" Data Sets: Income Inequality in OECD Countries as a Case Study'. *Journal of Economic Literature*, 39(3): 771–99.

AUTEN, GERALD E., and GEE, GEOFFREY. 2007. 'Income Mobility in the U.S.: Evidence from Income Tax Returns'. Office of Tax Analysis Paper 99, US Department of Treasury.

AYALA, LUIS, and SASTRE, MERCEDES. 2002. 'Europe Versus the United States: Is There a Trade-Off Between Mobility and Inequality?' Working Paper 19/2002 European Economy Group.

BAKER, MICHAEL, and SOLON, GARY. 2003. 'Earnings Dynamics and Inequality Among Canadian Men, 1976–1992: Evidence from Longitudinal Income Tax Records'. *Journal of Labor Economics*, 21(2): 289–321.

BERRY, ALBERT, BOURGUIGNON, FRANCOIS, and MORRISON, CHRISTIAN. 1983. 'Changes in the World Distribution of Income Between 1950 and 1977'. *The Economic Journal*, 93(370): 331–50.

BOURGUIGNON, FRANCOIS. 1979. 'Decomposable Income Inequality Measures'. *Econometrica*, 47(4): 901–20.

——and MORRISSON, CHRISTIAN. 2002. 'Inequality Among World Citizens: 1820–1992'. *American Economic Review*, 92(4): 727–44.

BRANDOLINI, ANDREA. 2007a. 'Income Inequality and Poverty in Italy: A Statistical Compendium'. Bank of Italy Working Paper.

——2007b. 'Measurement of Income Distribution in Supranational Entities: The Case of the European Union', in Stephen Jenkins and John Micklewright (eds.), *Inequality and Poverty Re-Examined*. Oxford: Oxford University Press.

BURKHAUSER, RICHARD V., COUCH, KENNETH A., HOUTENVILLE, ANDREW J., and ROVBA, LUDMILA. 2004. 'Income Inequality in the 1990s: Re-Forging a Lost Relationship?' *Journal of Income Distribution*, 12(3–4): 8–35.

——CUTTS, AMY CREWS, DALY, MARY C., and JENKINS, STEPHEN P. 1999. 'Testing the Significance of Income Distribution Changes over the 1980s Business Cycle: A Cross-National Comparison'. *Journal of Applied Econometrics*, 14(3): 253–72.

——FENG, SHUAIZHANG, and JENKINS, STEPHEN. 2007. 'Using a P90/P10 Ratio to Measure Inequality Trends with the Public Use Current Population Survey: A View from Inside the Census Bureau Vaults'. ISER Working Paper 2007-14, June.

——HOLTZ-EAKIN, DOUGLAS, and RHODY, STEPHEN E. 1997a. 'Labor Earnings Mobility and Inequality in the United States and Germany During the Growth Years of the 1980s'. *International Economic Review*, 38(4): 775–94.

——————1997b. 'Mobility and Inequality in the 1980s: A Cross-National Comparison of the United States and Germany', in Stephan Jenkins, Arie Kapteyn and Bernard van Praag (eds.), *The Distribution of Welfare and Household Production: International Perspectives*, Cambridge, Mass.: 111–75.

——and POUPORE, JOHN G. 1997. 'A Cross-National Comparison of Permanent Inequality in the United States and Germany'. *The Review of Economics and Statistics*, 79(1): 10–17.

——SMEEDING, TIMOTHY M., and MERZ, JOACHIM. 1996. 'Relative Inequality and Poverty in Germany and the United States Using Alternative Equivalency Scales'. *The Review of Income and Wealth*, 42(4), Dec.: 381–400.

COWELL, FRANK A. 1980. 'On the Structure of Additive Inequality Measures'. *Review of Economic Studies*, 47(3): 521–31.

——1985. 'Measures of Distributional Change: An Axiomatic Approach'. *Review of Economic Studies*, 52(1): 135–51.

DAHL, MOLLY, DELEIRE, THOMAS, and SCHWABISH, JONATHAN. 2007. 'Trends in Earnings Variability over the Past 20 Years'. Congress of the United States, Congressional Budget Office, mimeograph.

DICKENS, RICHARD. 2000. 'Caught in a Trap? Wage Mobility in Great Britain: 1975–1994'. *Economica*, 67(268): 477–98.

DRAGOSET, LISA M., and FIELDS, GARY S. 2006. 'U.S. Earnings Mobility: Comparing Survey-Based and Administrative-Based Estimates'. Mimeograph.

ERIKSON, ROBERT, and NOLAN, BRIAN. 2006. 'Intragenerational Income Mobility: Poverty Dynamics in Industrial Societies'. World Bank, mimeograph.

FIELDS, GARY S., and OK, EFE A. 1999. 'Measuring Movement of Incomes'. *Economica*, 66(264): 455–71.

FOSTER, JOHN E., and SHORROCKS, ANTHONY F. 1987. 'Transfer Sensitive Inequality Measures'. *Review of Economic Studies*, 54(3): 485–97.

FRICK, JOACHIM R., and GRABKA, MARKUS W. 2007. 'Item Non-Response and Imputation of Annual Labor Income in Panel Surveys from a Cross-National Perspective'. SOEP Papers on Multidisciplinary Panel Data Research, DIW, Berlin.

——JENKINS, STEPHEN P., LILLARD, DEAN R., LIPPS, OLIVER, and WOODEN, MARK. 2007. 'The Cross-National Equivalent File (CNEF) and its Member Country Household Panel Studies'. *Schmoller's Jahrbuch (Journal of Applied Social Science Studies)*, 127(4): 627–54.

GANGL, MARKUS. 2005. 'Income Inequality, Permanent Incomes, and Income Dynamics'. *Work and Occupations*, 32(2): 140–62.

GARDINER, KAREN, and HILLS, JOHN. 1999. 'Policy Implications of New Data on Income Mobility'. *The Economic Journal*, 109(453): F91–111.

GITTLEMAN, MAURY, and JOYCE, MARY. 1999. 'Have Family Income Mobility Patterns Changed?' *Demography*, 36(3): 299–314.

GOEBEL, JAN. 2007. 'Methodological Issues in the Measurement of Poverty and Inequality'. Doctoral Dissertation, Techniseben Universität Berlin.

GOTTSCHALK, PETER. 1993. 'Changes in Inequality of Family Income in Seven Industrialized Countries'. *American Economic Review: Papers and Proceedings*, 83(2): 136–42.

—— 1997. 'Inequality, Income Growth, and Mobility: The Basic Facts'. *The Journal of Economics Perspectives*, 11(2): 21–40.

—— and MOFFITT, ROBERT 1994. 'The Growth of Earnings Instability in the United States'. *Brookings Papers on Economic Activity*, 2.

GOTTSCHALK, PETER, and SPOLAORE, ENRICO. 2002. 'On the Evaluation of Economic Mobility'. *Review of Economic Studies*, 69(1): 191–208.

GUSTAFSSON, BJORN. 1994. 'The Degree and Pattern of Income Immobility in Sweden'. *Review of Income and Wealth*, 40(1): 67–86.

JARVIS, SARAH, and JENKINS, STEPHEN P. 1998. 'How Much Income Mobility is there in Britain?' *The Economic Journal*, 108(447): 428–43.

JENKINS, STEPHEN P., and VAN KERM, PHILIPPE. 2006. 'Trends in Income Inequality, Pro-Poor Income Growth, and Income Mobility'. *Oxford Economic Papers*, 58: 531–48.

KAROLY, LYNN A., and BURTLESS, GARY. 1995. 'Demographic Change, Rising Earnings Inequality, and the Distribution of Personal Well-Being'. *Demography*, 32(3): 379–405.

KOPCZUK, WOJCIECH, SAEZ, EMMANUEL, and SONG, JAE. 2007. 'Uncovering the American Dream: Inequality and Mobility in Social Security Earnings Data since 1937'. NBER Working Paper no. 13345.

LARRIMORE, JEFF, BURKHAUSER, RICHARD V., FENG, SHUAIZHANG, and ZAYATZ, LAURA. 2008. 'Consistent Cell Means for Topcoded Incomes in the Public Use March CPS (1976–2005)'. Mimeograph. Department of Policy Analysis and Management, Cornell University, Feb.

LEVY, FRANK, and MURNANE, RICHARD J. 1992. 'U.S. Earnings Levels and Earnings Inequality: A Review of Recent Trends and Proposed Explanations'. *Journal of Economic Literature*, 30: 1333–81.

LILLARD, DEAN R. 2007. 'Cross-National Harmonization of Household Panel Data: Concept, Practice, and Philosophy'. Mimeograph. Department of Policy Analysis and Management, Cornell University. Oct.

MAASOUMI, ESFANDIAR, and TREDE, MARK. 2001. 'Comparing Income Mobility in Germany and the United States Using Generalized Entropy Mobility Measures'. *Review of Economics and Statistics*, 83(3): 551–9.

SCHILLER, BRADLEY R. 1978. 'Relative Earnings Mobility in the United States'. *American Economic Review*, 67(5): 926–41.

SHORROCKS, ANTHONY F. 1978a. 'Income Inequality and Income Mobility'. *Journal of Economic Theory*, 19: 376–93.

—— 1978b. 'The Measurement of Mobility'. *Econometrica*, 46(5): 1013–24.

—— 1980. 'The Class of Additively Decomposable Inequality Measures'. *Econometrica*, 48(3): 613–25.

——1982. 'Inequality Decomposition by Factor Components'. *Econometrica*, 50(1): 193–211.

——1984. 'Inequality Decomposition by Population Subgroup'. *Econometrica*, 52(6): 1369–85.

THEIL, HENRI. 1967. *Economics and Information Theory*. Amsterdam: North-Holland.

VAN KERM, PHILIPPE. 2004. 'What Lies Behind Income Mobility? Reranking and Distributional Change in Belgium, Western Germany, and the USA'. *Economica*, 71: 223–39.

ZAIDI, ASGHAR, FRICK, JOACHIM R., and BUECHEL, FELIX. 2005. 'Income Mobility in Old Age in Britain and Germany'. *Aging and Society*, 25: 543–65.

# PART VI

············································

# GLOBAL
# PERSPECTIVES
# ON INEQUALITY

············································

CHAPTER 22

......................................................................................

# INEQUALITY AND ECONOMIC GROWTH

......................................................................................

## SARAH VOITCHOVSKY[1]

## 1. INTRODUCTION

......................................................................................

MOST chapters in this book have examined the role of economic or institutional forces as determinants of the evolution of income, wage, or wealth inequality. This chapter, however, looks at the reverse direction of causality, and investigates how inequality may affect a country's rate of economic growth, as well as undermine its institutions.

Relative to the empirical literature on this topic, theoretical arguments have a longer history and suggest numerous transmission channels through which inequality may affect aggregate production. Moreover, the alternative channels considered by the theoretical literature may imply different influences of inequality on growth. Perhaps unsurprisingly therefore, recent empirical efforts to capture the overall effect of inequality on growth using cross-country data have generally proven inconclusive.

[1] I am grateful to Mary Gregory, Justin van de Ven, the editors of this volume, and seminar participants at the Russell Sage Foundation in New York for helpful comments and suggestions. I would also like to thank Tony Atkinson and Steve Bond for valuable comments on early drafts of the research published here. Any errors remain my own.

In this chapter, we attempt to summarize the principal issues that have been raised in both the theoretical and empirical strands of the literature that is concerned with the influence of inequality on economic growth. It is important to note that this survey is not meant to be comprehensive. Rather, its aim is to provide an introductory overview of several key theoretical and empirical aspects of the research in this field.

The review starts, in Section 2, by discussing a selection of transmission mechanisms that have been explored in the theoretical literature. A critical assumption that underlies much of this literature concerns the nature of the disparities that are observed in the economy. That is, income or asset inequality is considered to reflect inequities of opportunities. This conjecture is particularly prevalent in studies that consider inequality in the lower part of the distribution, and argue that poverty may prevent individuals from participating fully in the productive process.

The discussion is organized primarily around the influence of alternative parts of the distribution. Indeed, a closer look at this literature reveals that in different studies the term 'inequality' may be used to refer to the economic situation of specific income groups, or to the distance between different groups. Organizing the literature in this way reveals that most of the detrimental effects of inequality on growth are associated with inequality at the bottom end of the distribution (poverty), or with extreme overall inequality. In contrast, the beneficial influences of inequality are mostly found in mechanisms where inequality refers to a strong middle class, or to income or wealth concentration. While data constraints continue to limit the type of empirical analyses that can be undertaken, investigations that focus on specific channels generally provide more robust conclusions than evidence from reduced-form analyses. The constraints of the current chapter, however, prevent the empirical analysis of specific channels from being discussed systematically. Related discussion can be found in many of the contributions that are reviewed.

The second part of the review, Section 3, turns to the literature that tries to identify the empirical effect of inequality on growth is, reduced-form from analyses. This section presents a selection of studies to illustrate several dimensions of the research in this literature. These studies are summarized in Table 22.1. Based on this table, the review then discusses some of the estimation and specification issues that currently characterize research in this field, and which could explain the lack of conclusive findings that are reported. The last section concludes.

Note that following the terminology commonly used in this literature, the term 'growth' may refer to growth during the convergence process, growth in the steady state, or to income levels in the steady state, depending on the context. Furthermore, unless otherwise specified, the word 'inequality' may be taken to describe disparities of any financial concept (e.g. income, human capital, wealth), and among any unit of analysis (households, individuals).

Other reviews are related to and complement the survey undertaken in this chapter. For a more detailed discussion of certain mechanisms see, for example, Aghion *et al.* (1999), Thorbecke and Charumilind (2002), and the World Development Report (2006) for a survey with a focus on developing countries. The reader is also referred to Bertola (2000) and Bertola *et al.* (2006) for a technical discussion of the assumptions that underlie different parts of this literature, and detailed coverage of endogeneity issues associated with the evolution of the income distribution and economic growth. Moreover, certain aspects of the material covered in this chapter naturally overlap with the discussion of other chapters of this book, and are referred to in several places.

# 2. Transmission Channels from Inequality to Economic Growth

The theoretical literature suggests two main ways in which inequality may influence aggregate production. The first effect refers to the fact that different income groups are likely to behave differently, in economic terms. The second effect arises when the distance between different income groups affects the way in which people interact, and in turn impinges on future growth prospects. In an effort to simplify the current discussion, this section is organized around this split, into which the literature naturally falls. The first three sub-sections look at mechanisms where the situation of specific income groups is at the origin of the effect of inequality on growth, and distinguishes between influence of the bottom, middle, and top ends of the distribution. Channels where the distance between different income groups defines the effect of inequality on growth are reviewed in the last sub-section.

Most mechanisms discussed below could apply to both rich and poor economies, subject to certain nuances. For example, studies that focus on poor countries often refer to absolute poverty, while relative poverty concepts appear to be more relevant in the analysis of richer countries. Similarly, labor supply mechanisms typically refer to self-employment or employment in the informal sector in the context of developing countries, but to formal employment in developed countries. Institutions also differ between rich and poor countries, and may imply that the importance of certain channels varies with the level of development. The fertility channel, however, seems particularly relevant to poor countries. The link between household income and fertility decisions appears to be much less clear-cut in richer countries.

Before moving on to the core of the review, however, a few qualifications regarding the structure and content of this section are required. First, the classification that is adopted here highlights important implicit distinctions in this literature, but cannot always reflect the diversity of the large literature under review. The redistribution channel, for example, which has traditionally been associated with the economic situation of the median voter—and is reviewed here under the middle-class sub-heading—has been criticized by several recent studies, which suggest that the decisive voter could be located elsewhere in the distribution. Second, for each channel discussed (e.g. the effect of inequality on growth, via its impact on human capital), other studies could be mentioned that explore different directions of causality (e.g. the effect of human capital on growth via inequality, or the joint effect of human capital and growth on inequality). While the complexity and endogeneity of each channel is acknowledged, this review tries to assess the direction of causality that runs from inequality to economic growth.

To sum up, the review in this section starts by discussing transmission channels where inequality is associated with the circumstances of the poor. The next sub-section examines channels where inequality defines the size of the middle class. In the following sub-section, the mechanisms presented mainly refer to inequality as a measure of income or wealth concentration. The last sub-section looks at mechanisms where the term inequality is used to describe the distance between different income groups within the distribution.

## Inequality Refers to the Circumstances of the Poor

People located at the lower end of the income distribution may be too poor to contribute to the accumulation process efficiently. If these households and their descendants are unable to escape from poverty as the economy grows, the country may end up stuck at a sub-optimal production level with persistent inequality. The literature on this argument further stresses the multi-dimensional aspect of poverty. Several papers show how poverty mechanisms may interact with each other within and between generations, for example, high fertility rates and low human capital (de la Croix and Doepke, 2003; Moav, 2005), or low health and a low educational attainments (Chakraborty and Das, 2005). Taking into account the possible interrelations between poverty mechanisms, therefore, not only highlights the difficulty that individual households may face when trying to escape the combined poverty traps, but also reinforces the long-term dimension of the detrimental effects of bottom-end inequality on growth. This discussion is echoed in Chapter 13 on inequality, poverty, and exclusion.

The mechanisms reviewed in this section are: credit constraints and indivisibilities in investment, effort and the effective labor supply, property crime,[2] and fertility rates.

---

[2] Note that crime committed by the rich, referred to as rent-seeking or corruption in this literature, is reviewed below.

## Credit constraints and indivisibilities in investment

The basic credit constraint argument states that owing to imperfect credit (or insurance) markets, households with a low initial wealth do not have access to higher (riskier) return investments and remain trapped in poverty. Studies in this literature have looked in particular at the role of forgone opportunities of investment in human capital. By raising labor productivity, education could ensure a wage premium in later life. Instead, poverty implies that individuals remain unskilled at the minimum subsistence wage. Moreover, as investment at the individual level may exhibit diminishing returns to scale, for example, if investment in primary education is more productive than secondary or tertiary education, the most productive investment opportunities are not undertaken, with an adverse impact on output.

With intergenerational transfers like bequests, initial distributional conditions also determine the convergence properties of the model, that is, the size of each class, the average income and education level in the economy, and possibly the social organization or occupational structure of the society in equilibrium. See, for example, Scheinkman and Weiss (1986), Galor and Zeira (1993), Banerjee and Newman (1993), Fishman and Simhon (2002), Ghatak and Jiang (2002), Moav (2002), Mookherjee and Ray (2003). For more discussion and evidence regarding the interactions between inequality and education in particular, see also Chapter 17.

## Effort and the effective labor supply

Individuals' productivity may be affected by the unobservable level of effort that they supply. The effort supplied, however, will depend on its expected (fair) rate of return. Several papers have shown how individuals at the bottom end of the distribution are likely to receive a lower rate of return for their effort, and end up being less productive as a result.

Suppose that indivisibilities in investment mean that for small wealth holdings borrowing is required. Furthermore, the gross return to individuals' investment depends on their unobservable level of effort. Poor people (who need to borrow in order to invest) see a share of the return to their effort appropriated by the lender, as debt repayment. The charge levied by the lender reduces the incentives to supply effort, resulting in a lower probability of success of poor individuals. Lenders anticipate this outcome and prefer not to lend, or lend at a higher interest rate, to poor agents—a situation of credit rationing due to moral hazard (Aghion and Bolton, 1997; Piketty, 1997). Nevertheless, if owing to hard work, poor individuals are able to bypass the non-linearity associated with credit market imperfections and get a high rate of return on their investment, poverty could imply a higher level of effort supplied (e.g. Ghatak et al., 2001). The debate at the core of this literature therefore concerns the return to effort function, and whether, as a result, hard work may allow poor people to escape the poverty trap.

Similar concerns regarding poverty and productivity arise in the labor literature. Agents retain control over their labor supply by adjusting their effort level. Several papers explain how shirking by low-paid workers can then be prevented by a wage premium. A higher wage may reduce workers' feelings of frustration and unfairness (Akerlof and Yellen, 1990) or increase the cost of being caught and fired (Shapiro and Stiglitz, 1984).[3] As an example of empirical evidence, the analysis by Goldsmith *et al.* (2000) using data from the US National Longitudinal Survey of Youth suggests that receiving an efficiency wage premium encourages effort, and that a higher effort supplied increases the wage received. For more discussion, the study of Goldsmith *et al.* (2000) provides a good survey of this literature. Related issues are also discussed in Chapter 11 on low pay.

## Property crime

Individuals are considered to engage in criminal activities if the return from crime is higher than the return from legal activities, or from investment in education. For poor people, the net gain from illegal activities may be higher than an income from the legal sector, when wages are low or unemployment rates are high. Moreover, as the rich get richer, the expected return on burglary increases (Chiu and Madden, 1998). A higher crime rate is likely to reduce the return to legal activities and provides further incentives for individuals to seek illegal income, with an adverse effect on investment and individual human capital accumulation (e.g. Josten, 2003; Burdett *et al.*, 2003).

With data for US metropolitan counties, the investigation of Kelly (2000) reports that property crime is strongly correlated with poverty, but not with inequality. In contrast, inequality explains violent crime, which has no financial return. The interpretation of these findings is that property crime is consistent with the low opportunity cost of the poor. Violent crime is probably more related to frustration theories.[4] With data for England and Wales, Machin and Meghir (2004) also report a strong negative relation between changes in wages at the bottom end of the distribution and property crime. More evidence of a significant positive effect of inequality on property crime (and violent victimization) is reported in studies based on data at the individual, regional, or county level (e.g. Fajnzylber *et al.*, 2002; Van Wilsem *et al.*, 2003).

## Fertility rates

The fertility mechanism mainly works through the low opportunity cost of children, a child's prospective labor earnings, or the lack of old-age insurance in poor

---

[3]  Arguably, inequality at the lower end of the wage distribution could also represent an incentive structure for a downwardly flexible wage system. Nevertheless, a reward structure may have to be balanced against insurance concerns especially when employees are risk averse (Aghion *et* al. 1999).

[4]  See below for discussion of arguments where inequality, rather than poverty, may explain social tensions.

households. Poor households (with low wages and low education in this case) not only tend to have a higher fertility rate but also provide a lower level of education for each child.[5] Additionally, assuming the wage rate is an increasing function of the educational level, higher fertility rates reinforce the poverty trap situation of poor households.

At the macro level, high fertility rates tend to dilute the average level of human capital and increase the supply of unskilled relative to skilled workers, or of labor to capital. There is downward pressure on uneducated workers' wages and a high level of inequality with poverty and high fertility rates is perpetuated (Morand, 1999; Kremer and Chen, 2002; de la Croix and Doepke, 2003; Moav, 2005). Education subsidies can provide a way out of this poverty trap by raising poor households' incomes as well as the opportunity cost of children. Another option may be to raise the cost of children for poor households directly, for example, by regulating the child labor market (Moav, 2005). The negative relation between inequality and growth via fertility rates appears in many empirical studies (Barro, 2000; de la Croix and Doepke, 2003; Kremer and Chen, 2002).

## Inequality Defines the Size and Income of the Middle Class

This section examines two channels—redistribution via the median voter mechanism, and the size of demand—where the effect of inequality on output crucially depends on the size and/or economic situation of the middle class.

### Taxation, redistribution, and the median voter mechanism

In several recent papers, the pivotal function of the middle class in the growth process stems from the fact that these individuals may determine the level of redistribution in a democracy, through a median voter mechanism. The standard median voter redistribution model focuses on the difference between the median and mean income—the lower the median income relative to the mean income, the stronger the median voter's preference for redistribution and vice versa. By affecting the distance between the median and mean income, the level of inequality affects the degree of taxation in the economy. Different redistribution levels in turn have different impacts on individuals' incentives for accumulation. The aggregate impact of taxation ultimately depends on the balance between the reactions of the contributors and beneficiaries of the redistributive system.

Assuming that growth is entirely driven by the savings of the rich, while poor households consume their income, a redistributive system that taxes savers (the rich) in favor of consumers (the poor) will lower the growth rate. In this case,

---

[5]  In contrast, wealthy (educated) households, choose fewer children and have a comparative advantage in providing them with education; see Moav (2005), de la Croix and Doepke (2003).

inequality has a clear adverse effect on growth—that is, if rising inequality reduces the median/mean ratio[6] (see e.g. Bertola, 1993; Persson and Tabellini, 1994). Instead, economic growth would be improved by a middle class that is sufficiently wealthy to vote for a low level of redistribution. Although regularly referred to as an explanation for the negative correlation between inequality and growth that was reported in the early empirical literature, this political economy argument has since been subject to wide-ranging criticism, and is not well supported by a broader analysis of the evidence (e.g. Perotti, 1996; Saint Paul and Verdier, 1996; Arjona *et al.*, 2003).

To start with, the pivotal voter may not correspond to the median voter, even in democracies. Many studies explain why the decisive voter is likely to be located elsewhere in the distribution, and therefore that assuming a uniform repercussion of inequality on the level of redistribution may be too restrictive.[7] Moreover, countries with a traditionally generous redistribution system could also exhibit a lower level of pre-transfer income inequality (see also Chapter 27). Disparity measures like wage earnings inequality are likely to reflect the influence of (past) labor policies and the fact that people may adjust their behavior in response to changes in taxation (Cusack and Beramendi, 2006).

Finally, if taxes are used for public and private investments, for example in education, the effect of redistribution on growth may become ambiguous. The negative incentive effect on net taxed agents at the top end may be compensated by the productive impact of poor agents' investments, of government spending (Perotti, 1993; Saint Paul and Verdier, 1993, 1996; Alesina and Rodrik, 1994; Lee and Roemer, 1999; Aghion *et al.*, 1999), or of reduced instability (Alesina and Perotti, 1996).

This channel remains contentious, empirically and theoretically. This could be explained in part by the tenuous link between inequality and redistribution. Indeed, although inequality in these models is considered to affect the degree of taxation, the ultimate effect of redistribution on growth also depends on the type of policies that are implemented, the ways in which they are financed, and who the beneficiaries are.

## The size of demand

One of the many implications of poverty is a small domestic demand for manufactured or technologically advanced goods, which limits incentives for investment and innovation (Nurkse, 1953; Rosenstein-Rodan, 1943; Zweimüller, 2000; Mani, 2001; Foellmi and Zweimüller, 2006). Although poverty is usually associated with restricted capital availability, that is, the poor may be poor because they cannot save,

---

[6] This is not necessarily the case, as discussed in Saint Paul and Verdier (1996).

[7] For alternative outcomes on how the level of inequality may translate into redistribution, see Persson and Tabellini (1994), Bénabou (1996, 2000), or Li and Zou (1998); see in particular Osberg *et al.* (2004) for more discussion.

a low demand together with poverty may persist even in the presence of a savings capacity in the economy. As Nurkse (1953: 9) summarizes it: capacity to buy means capacity to produce.

Assuming for simplicity that the poor only cover their basic needs while the wealthy mainly consume luxuries, the aggregate demand for manufactured goods will depend on the size of the middle class. The importance of a local demand for domestic industry is reinforced when exporting is not a feasible alternative due for example to trade barriers or competitive disadvantage; see Murphy *et al.* (1989). Furthermore, a strong (expected) demand contributes to productivity gains in production (Matsuyama, 2002) and encourages R&D and innovation (Zweimüller, 2000), which in turn lower prices, raise wages, and expand the size of the market. This process can happen with each new good introduced into the market. Initially only richer consumers can afford new and expensive goods. As their increasing demand starts driving the price–wage ratio down due to economies of scale, mass consumers slowly start entering the market.

Thus, the optimal income distribution in these models usually consists of a small wealthy class to motivate the development of new products and a large middle class to soak up the additional capacity generated by economies of scale in production. With high inequality and poverty, the economy ends up trapped in an equilibrium with low wages, low human capital, and low growth, which reinforces the lack of demand.

## Inequality as a Measure of Income or Wealth Concentration

According to one of the oldest economic arguments linking inequality and aggregate production, the industry of wealthy entrepreneurs may drive a country's investment and capital accumulation. If the rich do save (relatively) more or if large investments are more productive, some income or wealth concentration may encourage faster growth. Moreover, the wealth accumulated by the rich may benefit the rest of the economy through trickle-down effects.

Extreme income or wealth concentration, however, may lead to undesirable distortions and reduced growth when associated with rent-seeking and corruption. While this adverse influence of wealth concentration may be mitigated by strong institutions, high levels of inequality also undermine a country's institutions. High inequality and weak institutions are therefore likely to perpetuate one another, and vice versa for low inequality and strong institutions (Chong and Gradstein, 2007). Assuming richer economies are better able to afford good institutions, they should be less sensitive to inequality via rent-seeking and corruption than poor economies, where the high inequality/weak institutions situation is more likely to hold. This section first looks at the savings and trickle-down channels, before addressing the rent-seeking argument.

## Savings and investment

If the propensity to save is increasing with income (e.g. Pasinetti, 1962), higher (top end) inequality may be associated with higher average savings or physical capital accumulation (Bourguignon, 1981). This positive association may be especially relevant in the presence of limited borrowing possibilities, initial set-up costs, or when large investments are better suited to risky and high return opportunities (Bhattacharya, 1998).

One of the earliest empirical studies to consider the link between savings and income in the upper income groups was conducted by Kuznets, using different data sources for the USA, over the period 1929–50. His analysis reported that the saving–income ratio is increasing with income but at a decreasing rate (Kuznets, 1953). Moreover, savings from the upper income groups appeared generally less sensitive to business cycles and followed different investment routes. Upper income savings were mainly made through dividends while individuals in lower income groups save through interest-bearing assets or equities in small businesses.

With recent micro data, Dynan et al. (2004) corroborate this observation. They report that rich US households not only save more but also have a higher propensity to save. Also, Smith (2001) reports a positive effect of inequality on private savings,[8] using cross-sectional and panel analyses with data for developed and developing countries. His analysis further suggests that the positive effect of inequality may be linked to the presence of credit market imperfections. Evidence from macro studies, however, is usually not as clear-cut. Arguably, a major limitation of macro studies is the difficulty of getting reliable and comparable measures of aggregate inequality and saving (Schmidt-Hebbel and Serven, 2000). Additionally, variations in aggregate savings following a change in distribution might be difficult to spot in aggregated data (Dynan et al., 2004), as an increase in inequality at the top end of the distribution may be offset by an increase in the number of individuals falling below the savings threshold.

## The trickle-down process

Higher inequality at the top end of the distribution may promote economic growth, as it boosts the overall level of savings available for investment. Furthermore, following an initial period during which the rich are getting richer and inequality widens, wealth may trickle down the distribution and allow poor people to participate in production. The trickle-down process may take place through the average wage rate or return to education (Galor and Tsiddon, 1996, 1997; Banerjee and Newman, 1993; Maoz and Moav, 1999; Fishman and Simhon, 2002), via the market return to capital (Aghion and Bolton, 1997; Matsuyama, 2000), or through redistributive policies (Perotti, 1993; Galor et al., 2006).

---

[8] Note that private savings do not include human capital investments.

Therefore, the improvement in the global economic situation due to investment by the rich may render individual constraints less binding and allow the lower classes to gradually catch up. A weak trickle-down process, in contrast, could imply inequality and low growth in the long term. For example, the median voter might become relatively wealthy and suddenly choose a level of redistribution that is too low to ensure full convergence (e.g. Perotti, 1993).

### Lobbying, corruption, and misallocation of resources

The pursuit of the wealthy elite's economic interests, however, may sometimes be at odds with aggregate production, or with the process of development. The rich may use their economic power to subvert the legal and political institutions by rent-seeking and corruption, appropriate the country's resources or public services (Easterly, 2001; Glaeser *et al.*, 2003; Gradstein, 2003), slow the process of democratization and prevent the implementation of economic reforms or other policies—like health care, education, infrastructure, or the development of financial markets—that are not in their interest (Falkinger and Grossmann, 2005; Fogel, 2006; Galor *et al.*, 2006).[9]

Even in the absence of corrupt bureaucrats, but when credit constraints are binding, wealthy agents may have an advantage over productive agents at lobbying the government, leading to the misallocation of public resources (e.g. Esteban and Ray, 2000, 2006). Another consequence of wealth concentration is the rich pulling out of publicly funded services, like health care, education, or the protection of property rights. This literature also argues that the rich are likely to benefit from, and therefore promote, weak institutions at the expense of investment and economic growth (Glaeser *et al.*, 2003; Sonin, 2003; Chakraborty and Dabla-Norris, 2006; Fogel, 2006; Gradstein, 2007).

## When the Overall Distance between Individuals also Matters

Inequality is also considered to affect incentives to cooperate between (political representatives of) agents from different income groups, and as a result affects future economic growth prospects. Compared to the discussion in previous sections, inequality now refers to the distance between different parts of the distribution, for example the economic distance between the rich and poor.

The mechanisms reviewed in this section are: social capital and trust, polarization and social conflict, and macroeconomic volatility. Similar to the arguments on rent-seeking and lobbying discussed above, the quality of institutions plays a major

---

[9]  See in particular Fogel (2006) for a review of this argument, and Bardhan (1997) for a review of the effect of corruption on growth and development.

role in shielding the economy from the potentially adverse effects of inequality, while inequality simultaneously tends to weaken these institutions.

## Trust and social capital

The concept of social capital[10] refers to the (unquantifiable) resources available through social networks, trust, and reciprocity. The growing literature on this topic argues that social capital fosters cooperation within communities, reduces transaction costs, promotes civic engagement, social cohesion, government efficiency, and growth as a result. At the firm level, social capital can facilitate exchange of information regarding the reliability of prospective business partners or employees, and the adoption of new technologies. At the household level, community-based social capital is found to be conducive to better health and importantly to higher investment in education (see Coleman, 1988; Putnam, 2000; or Josten, 2004).

Empirically, Knack (2003) finds no robust impact of 'group memberships' (a variable constructed from the World Value Surveys to measure social capital) on growth or investment in a cross-section of countries, but reports strong effects of group memberships and inequality on trust, which are positive and negative respectively.[11] This literature, nevertheless, remains controversial in many respects, including on the definition and measurement of social capital, and value of the empirical evidence; see Stolle and Hooghe (2005) for more discussion.

## Polarization, unrest, and social conflicts

When disparities are high, the cost of cooperation between classes might outweigh the benefits of a deviation to appropriate a larger share of the economic pie. Both ends of the distribution might be tempted to expropriate the opposing end. The resulting political instability, social unrest, and reduced protection of property rights increase production costs—for instance, transportation costs, spending on security for staff and factories. See, for example, Alesina and Perotti (1996) or Easterly (2001) for evidence on inequality and instability. As argued by Collier and Hoeffler (2002), if wages are constrained at the bottom, the full cost of insecurity will be borne by capital, with direct implications for aggregate accumulation.

In certain cases, the rich may agree to redistribution—for example by funding public education—to ease the expropriation pressures on their wealth or take advantage of an educated workforce, and therefore indirectly pave the way to democracy and prosperity (Bourguignon and Verdier, 2000; Galor *et al.*, 2006).

---

[10] This concept is usually attributed to the work of Putnam (e.g. *Bowling Alone: The Collapse and Revival of American Community*, 2000) or to Coleman (e.g. 'Social Capital in the Creation of Human Capital', 1988).

[11] See also Helliwell (2003) for a cross-country analysis of the determinants of well-being.

In other cases, social tension may degenerate into revolt, violence, and civil war (Benhabib and Rustichini, 1996; Esteban and Ray, 1999).

### Macroeconomic volatility and shock management

Social polarization can lead to a policy environment where shifts in policies, such as property protection policies, become more likely, increasing economic uncertainty (Keefer and Knack, 2002). Woo (2003, 2005) explores the situation when social polarization (due to ethnic division or income inequality) leads to policy coordination failure. Coordination failure happens when different ministers have very different objective functions (e.g. left and right wing). In that case, each policymaker pursues an individually rather than collectively rational policy, leading to overspending of current government resources, increased deficit, and procyclicality of fiscal policies. This volatile fiscal path is found to reduce growth in the short term as well as at the steady state. Similarly, some studies report that higher inequality is associated with greater inflation (e.g. Albanesi, 2007).

An unequal distribution of resources is also found to weaken the institutions of conflict management and the ability of a country to deal with economic shocks, like the oil shocks in the 1970s (Rodrik, 1999). Anbarci *et al.* (2005) develop a similar argument in the context of natural disasters, by investigating the death toll of large earthquakes worldwide, between 1960–2002. Their study suggests that inequality undermines the collective action required to mitigate the impact of earthquakes, by failing to enforce construction norms for example.

# 3. EVIDENCE FROM REDUCED-FORM GROWTH REGRESSIONS

Over the last decade, and following the release of several datasets on inequality—starting with the Deininger and Squire (1996) dataset (DS)—the debate regarding the overall effect of inequality on growth has been fostered by a growing empirical literature. Yet, in spite of a large number of studies on this topic, the contemporary empirical literature has so far failed to reach any substantive conclusions regarding the overall influence of inequality on economic performance.

Several reasons have been suggested to account for the lack of an empirical consensus, like data quality and comparability, or the appropriateness of econometric technique considered. Table 22.1 presents a selection of recent reduced-form studies, based on data for multiple countries, to illustrate several aspects of this literature where differences between studies may help explain differences in results obtained.

# Table 22.1. Selection of representative studies from the recent empirical literature (in alphabetical order)

| Study | Estimation techniques | Length of growth spell(s); overall period | Sample no. of countries and/or obs. | Inequality dataset + quality level (if DS un/adjusted) Income concept on which ineq. is based | Inequality indices Estimated sign and significance of coefficient(s) 's' refers to the length of growth spells | Highlights of the sensitivity analysis | Main claim/conclusion on the effect of income inequality on growth |
|---|---|---|---|---|---|---|---|
| Banerjee and Duflo (2003) | Random effect Kernel regressions | 5-year periods 1965–95 | DCs and LDCs 45 countries 128 obs. | DS HQ (adjusted) *Several income concepts* | *Table 3 col. (1)* $\Delta$ Gini$_{t-s}$ + and $\Delta$ Gini$^2_{t-s}$ –$^*$ *Figure 1, kernel regression:* inverted U-relation between $\Delta y_t$ and $\Delta$Gini$_{t-s}$, with max. close to zero. | Results shown for regressions with Perotti (1996) controls—broadly similar results with Barro (2000) controls, on 98 obs. Gini$_{t-s}$ alone insignif. Non-linear relation between $\Delta$Gini$^2_t$ and Gini$_{t-s}$ | Growth rate is an inverted U-shape function of net changes in inequality. Non-linearity as a possible explanation for different results obtained when using different estimators |
| Barro (2000) | Three-stage LS (with random effects) | 10 year periods 1965–95 | DCs and LDCs 146 obs. | DS LQ (unadjusted) *Several income concepts* | *Table 4, growth regressions* Gini$_{t-s}$ + Gini$_{t-s}$ –$^{***}$ and Gini $_{t-s}$ $^*$ $y_{t-s}$ +$^{***}$ Gini RICH$_{t-s}$ + and Gini POOR$_{t-s}$ –$^{**}$ | When fertility is omitted, Gini coeff becomes neg. and signif. The relationship robust to other ineq. indices like top, middle, or bottom quintile shares | Little effect of inequality on growth or investment in overall sample; but inequality dis/encourages growth in poor/rich countries |
| Castello and Domenech (2002) | OLS | Whole period 1960–2000 | DCs and LDCs Countr./obs. (a) 67 (b) 83 | Self-assembled dataset on HC ineq., based on Barro and Lee (2001) Other Ginis from DS HQ—*Several income concepts* | *Table 3 cols. (1–2) 'Income'* Gini measured as avg. over the period. (a) HC Gini$_{t-s}$ –$^{***}$ and Gini$_t$ +$^{**}$ (b) HC Gini$_{t-s}$ –$^{***}$ | 'Income' Gini alone: neg. signif., but not robust to incl. of regional dummies. (a) and (b) robust to excl. of atypical obs., HC Q3 instead of HC Gini, DCs sub-sample only | More robust—negative effect—of HC inequality than income inequality. HC inequality is also found to reduce physical capital investment |
| Deininger and Squire (1998) | OLS | Whole period 1960–1992 | DCs and LDCs Countr./obs. (a) 87 (b) 67 (c) 55 | DS HQ *Several income concepts* FAO World Census of Agric.—*land inequality* | *Table 3 cols. (1, 3, 5) 'Income'* Gini measured as avg. over the period. (a) Gini$_t$ –$^{***}$ (b) Land Gini$_{t-s}$ –$^{***}$ (c) Gini$_t$ – and Land Gini$_{t-s}$ –$^{***}$ | With regional dummy: Gini insignif.; land Gini signif. at 10%; (c) similar results in LDCs sub-sample on 27 obs. Neg. effects of income and land inequality disappear in democratic sub-sample | Strong negative effect of land inequality on growth, weak effect of income inequality. Support for credit constraint channel—limits HC invest.—rather than median voter channel |

| Forbes (2000) | First-difference GMM | 5-year periods 1970–95 | DCs and LDCs 45 countries 135 obs. | DS HQ (adjusted) *Several income concepts* | *Table 3, equation 4* $Gini_{t-s}$ +*** | Pos. effect, robust to other ineq. indices and set of X vars, but sensitive to data quality; effect weaker when looking at 10-year periods. Neg. signif effect of ineq. with OLS on single 25-year spell | Positive short to medium-term effect of inequality on growth. Omitted variable bias potentially important in cross-country studies |
|---|---|---|---|---|---|---|---|
| Knowles (2005) | OLS | Whole period 1960–90 | DCs and LDCs count./obs. (a) 40 (b) 40 (c) 27 (d) 30 | WIID 'Reliable' obs that apply to whole pop (a) *unadjusted* (b) *adjusted* (c) *gross individual income only* (d) *expenditure only* | *Table 1 cols. (1, 3, 4); Table 3 col. (1) Ineq indices in (a) & (b): net/gross individual/household income, or individual/household expenditure* (a) $Gini_{t-s}$ –** (b) $Gini_{t-s}$ –** (c) $Gini_{t-s}$ – (d) $Gini_{t-s}$ –* | Possible sample effects; in (c) sample is mostly the consistent sub-sample of (a). In (d), sample of LDCs apart from Portugal. Similar results when education omitted from X vars. | Role of measurement error when estimating effect of inequality on growth. No effect of gross income ineq., but neg. signif. effect of expenditure ineq. Different income concepts may capture different channels. |
| Voitchovsky (2005) | System GMM | 5-year periods 1975–2000 | DCs 21 countries 81 obs. | LIS *Individual weighted net equivalised income* | *Table 2 cols. (1, 4) and (6)* (a) $Gini_{t-s}$ – (b) $Gini_{t-s}$ –*** and $90/75_{t-s}$ +*** (c) $50/10_{t-s}$ –*** and $90/75_{t-s}$ + | Robust to inclusion of Eastern European countries; other top & bottom ineq. indices. Coefficients on $90/75_{t-s}$ and $50/10_{t-s}$ insignif. when alone. | Opposite effects of inequality from top and bottom ends of the distribution. Single index, e.g. Gini, likely to capture average of these effects |

*Notes:* \*\*\*, \*\*, \* indicates that the coefficient is significantly different from 0 at the 1, 5, and 10 percent significance levels, respectively.

Dependent variable: average growth rate (of GDP or GNP), usually per capita, sometimes annualized over the length of the growth spell (reported in col. 3). It is often defined as $\Delta y_t$ where $y_t$ is the log of income per capita in period $t$.

- DCs and LDCs = developed and less developed countries.
- DS = Deininger and Squire dataset. HQ refers to high quality data only, and LQ implies that high quality as well as low quality indices have been considered in the analysis. 'adjusted' mentions if the inequality indices have been (at least partially) adjusted for differences in sources and definitions—see main text or Deininger and Squire (1996).
- 'Gini' refers to net/gross income, expenditure, or consumption (as opposed to land Gini or human capital Gini). The exact notion of income, if specified, is mentioned in the fifth or sixth column. When nothing is specified, indices may be based on a mix of several definitions of income or expenditure, applied to individuals or households.
- Gini RICH and Gini POOR are abbreviations for 'Gini indices in sample of rich countries' and 'Gini indices in sample of poor countries', respectively.
- HC = human capital
- LIS = Luxembourg Income Study dataset.
- WIID = World Income Inequality Database, compiled by UNDP and WIDER.
- X var(s) = explanatory variable(s).

The characteristics considered here are the estimation technique, the sample of countries included in the analysis, the quality and comparability of inequality statistics, and the specification that is used to capture the effect of inequality on growth. For each of these aspects, this section introduces the main issues and explanations that have been suggested in the literature as well as referring to further studies for detailed discussion.

The DS dataset, whatever its shortcomings (Székely and Hilgert, 1999; Atkinson and Brandolini, 2001), represented a significant advance on previous compilations and is used here to define the data quality benchmark for the selection of papers included in Table 22.1. These studies are therefore either based on DS data (and its subsequent updates, like the World Income Inequality Database), or on other cross-country datasets of at least comparable quality, for example, the Luxembourg Income Study (LIS) dataset.

### Estimation technique

Until the late 1990s, results from the empirical literature generally indicated that more inequality hinders future growth prospects. A negative effect of inequality was usually obtained from a cross-sectional OLS estimation of growth rates, measured over a single long interval of 20 to 30 years, as a function of several variables (measured at the start or the period or as period averages), including a measure of inequality. A review of this early literature can be found in Bénabou (1996).

With the introduction of the larger and better quality Deininger and Squire (1996) dataset (DS), the empirical literature has evolved to include the latest panel estimation methods—like fixed-effects (FE) and first-difference GMM panel estimators—following other developments in the growth literature. With a panel approach, a set of repeated growth observations in several countries (usually over short periods of time, e.g. five or ten years) is estimated as a function of time-varying variables. This approach also allows the control of unobserved time-invariant country-specific characteristics. Studies that estimate short growth spells with FE or first-difference GMM, however, tend to report a positive effect of inequality on growth.[12]

The two approaches—that is, the estimation of a single long growth spell with a cross-sectional technique or of repeated short growth spells with panel estimation techniques—are exemplified by the studies of Deininger and Squire (1998) and Forbes (2000), respectively, which are reported in Table 22.1. There currently exist several concurring explanations for this commonly observed split between the negative and positive effects of inequality reported in studies that are based on different specifications, as described above.[13] They are briefly discussed in turn.

---

[12]  See also Banerjee and Duflo (2003) for similar conclusions on this literature.

[13]  No such clear-cut negative versus positive pattern of effects emerges from studies that look at the effect of asset inequality (measured as human capital or land inequality) or that focus on data for

One argument states that the neglect of time-invariant omitted variables in cross-sectional studies biases the estimated coefficient on inequality downwards. The bias would then come from omitted time-invariant variables that are simultaneously associated with growth and inequality, but in the opposite direction, for example, corruption, fertility rates, or the quality of government policies on health and education (see Forbes, 2000, for more discussion). Moreover, the negative effect reported in cross-sectional studies is usually found to be sensitive to the inclusion of regional dummies, of other explanatory variables, or to sample composition. This feature of the results has often been considered as evidence for the existence of an omitted variable bias in cross-sectional analyses (Deininger and Squire, 1998).

The impact of measurement error on estimation results is another factor that has been suggested. Studies which report a positive effect of inequality on growth using panel methods also rely on the more limited time-series variation in the data. This approach is likely to be more sensitive to measurement error,[14] particularly when the variable is persistent and the time structure considered is short (Barro, 2000; Durlauf et al., 2005). In contrast, the negative effect reported in cross-sectional analyses could also reflect country- or regional-specific measurement error in inequality statistics (Knowles, 2005).

Banerjee and Duflo (2003) argue instead that this sign pattern could be explained by the misspecification of the linear effect of inequality that is commonly estimated. They show how, if the real effect of inequality on growth is non-linear as their evidence suggests, a linear specification is likely to report a negative effect of inequality with a cross-sectional estimation method, and a positive effect in a fixed-effects analysis. See their study for more details.

Another possible reason is that the short lag structure (used in panel estimations) and the long lag structure (used in cross-sectional analyses) capture the short- and long-term effects of inequality on growth. These effects are expected to be positive and negative respectively. Knowles (2005), Banerjee and Duflo (2003), and Forbes (2000) also discuss this argument. Nevertheless, even assuming that different time structures may capture alternative effects of inequality, the current approach that considers a single inequality parameter forces the short-term and long-term influences to have the same sign and magnitude; see also Pritchett (2000). With enough variation in the data, or enough years of data available, it would be possible to identify these short-term and long-term effects of inequality using different parameters at different lags.

---

a single country (not discussed here). The discussion in this section refers to multi-country studies that test for a linear effect of income inequality (defined as net/gross income or expenditure inequality, as is common with DS data) on growth.

[14] Note that this depends on the nature of measurement error. Permanent measurement error is eliminated by differencing, and independently and identically distributed measurement error is relatively easy to control by using appropriate instrumental variables.

All these explanations seem plausible but may only be part of the story. Due to the scarcity of inequality data, there may be a trade-off between different sources of bias and precision in these studies. This reflects a fundamental problem with the data on which current studies are based, and caution is therefore required with the conclusions of both approaches. Many of the estimation issues faced by the inequality-growth literature, however, are common to growth regressions more generally (Bond *et al.*, 2001; Durlauf *et al.*, 2005). A wider outlook could therefore also help to advance the inequality-growth debate.

## Sample selection

According to the theoretical explanations reviewed in Section 2, inequality may encourage or hamper growth in rich as well as in poor countries. Different mechanisms, however, may be more relevant at different levels of development (Galor and Moav, 2004). Yet, in light of existing data constraints most empirical studies tend to select a sample of countries as large as the availability of inequality data permits. The resulting samples usually include data for sets of developed and developing countries.

Several studies, however, report that the effect of inequality varies greatly between different samples of countries, although not always in a systematic way. The study of Barro (2000), for example, reports a positive effect of inequality in rich countries and an adverse effect in poor countries. Similarly, in Deininger and Squire (1998) the negative effect of inequality disappears in the democratic sub-sample. Yet, further studies report reverse or unrelated effects of inequality on growth in rich and/or in poor countries (Forbes, 2000; Castello and Domenech, 2002; Voitchovsky, 2005). Other factors may also cloud comparisons; for example, inequality could be higher and/or measurement error greater in data for poorer countries in general (Durlauf *et al.*, 2005).

## Measurement error in inequality statistics

A great improvement in inequality data quality and availability has been the introduction of the Deininger and Squire dataset (DS) in the mid-1990s. Since then, most studies on the subject of inequality have relied on this dataset or on its subsequent extensions (e.g. the World Income Inequality Database (WIID)).

The DS dataset includes inequality indices from several sources, for a set of developed and developing countries. To be considered in the high quality (DS HQ) sub-sample, inequality measures have to meet three quality criteria: data must be drawn from household surveys, be representative of the national population, and be based on a comprehensive definition of income. A set of inequality indices comprising both high quality and non-high quality measures is usually referred to as low quality (DS LQ) data.[15] Nevertheless, the inequality indices included in the DS HQ sample may be based on different income concepts (net income, gross income, expenditure) or unit definitions (individual or household income). These discrepancies may result in serious inconsistencies in the series over time as well as across countries. Atkinson and Brandolini (2001) give a detailed assessment of DS inequality indices.

To reduce the effect of mixing statistics based on different definitions, Deininger and Squire suggest further adjustments to the data (e.g. adding 6.6 points to Gini coefficients based on expenditure to render them more comparable with Gini coefficients based on gross income). Most studies that use DS data follow some (or all) of these recommendations, which are referred to as 'un/adjusted' in column (5) of Table 22.1. These adjustments, however, do not appear to have a significant impact on the results (Deininger and Squire, 1998; Barro, 2000; Knowles, 2005; Székely and Hilgert, 1999). Knowles (2005) further argues that these adjustments may be ineffective because they are inappropriate.[16]

Although commonly acknowledged as a likely source of bias, it is difficult to assess what is the exact impact of measurement error on estimated results in the current empirical literature. Moreover, few options for adjustment are available when using secondary datasets like the DS dataset. In an attempt to limit measurement error further, several studies based on DS data have opted for a selection of indices based on a consistently defined inequality concept (e.g. gross income), or used period averages rather than start of period indices. The use of instrumental variable methods has also been considered. On a more positive note, however, the significance of this problem is likely to decrease as more reliable data becomes available.

## Specification of the effect of inequality

In the theoretical literature, each mechanism connecting inequality to growth involves a specific definition of the concept of inequality. For instance, in models that explore the political or median voter argument, pre-tax income inequality determines the level of redistribution. On the other hand, the borrowing ability of an individual is likely to be linked to the collateral available. Ideally, therefore, accurately defined indices should be used when investigating specific links between inequality and growth.

Empirically, findings appear to be sensitive to the income concepts on which the inequality is based, like gross income, net income, or expenditure inequality

[15]  See Forbes (2000) for a study that also investigates the impact of data quality on reported results, by comparing results estimated on DS HQ and DS LQ data.

[16]  'This approach may be valid if there is relatively little deviation around the mean difference of 6.6, but unfortunately this is not the case'; Knowles (2005: 142).

(Knowles, 2005; Székely and Hilgert, 1999). Nevertheless, differences between estimations, like sample of countries or econometric techniques, make it difficult to identify a clear pattern of effects associated with different concepts of 'income' inequality. In contrast, findings from papers that look at 'asset' inequality provide a more consistent story. Empirical testing from several cross-sectional and panel analyses reveals that land and human capital inequality indices are more robust as determinants of growth than measures of income inequality. Moreover, asset inequality is always found to be adversely related to subsequent growth (Deininger and Squire, 1998: Castello and Domenech, 2002; Deininger and Olinto, 2000).[17]

Another aspect of the specification of the effect of inequality concerns the (combination of) statistics that are included in the regressions. Traditionally, the effect of inequality on growth has been investigated using a single linear inequality index, like the Gini coefficient. This choice has mostly been dictated by data availability and facilitates comparison with the existing literature. Several studies also report findings that are robust to replacing one overall inequality index by another—like substituting the Gini coefficient by a quintile share (Barro, 2000; Forbes, 2000).

Yet, as discussed in Section 2, different inequality mechanisms may simultaneously have an inhibiting and stimulating influence on economic performance. At the aggregate level, their combined effect is likely to be ambiguous and highly non-linear. The analysis of Banerjee and Duflo (2003), which also discusses these issues in greater detail, reports strong evidence of a non-linear effect of inequality on growth. Furthermore, a large part of the theoretical literature associates the adverse effect of inequality with relative or absolute deprivation. Some of the mechanisms explored in this context include credit constraints on investment in human and physical capital, lower individual labor productivity, lower effort supplied, higher fertility rates, and higher crime rates. Instead, some degree of income or wealth concentration may promote savings and investment, which eventually benefits the rest of the economy. This reading of the literature suggests that inequality located in different parts of the distribution may relate to growth differently and therefore that statistics that are sensitive to changes in inequality in different parts of the distribution may capture alternative mechanisms of inequality on growth.

My own investigation on a sample of wealthy countries (Voitchovsky, 2005) shows that when captured by a single index—for example, the Gini coefficient, the 90/75 or 50/10 percentile ratios—inequality is not significantly related to economic growth. However, when a measure of top-end inequality is simultaneously included in a regression with a measure of bottom-end inequality or overall inequality (e.g. Gini), inequality at the top end appears to be positively related to growth while inequality further down the distribution is adversely related to growth.

---

[17]  Nevertheless, land or human capital inequality could be better measured than income inequality since easier to observe, and therefore the non-robustness of results usually obtained with income inequality could also be attributable to measurement error.

The positive influence from inequality at the top end of the distribution may reflect the beneficial mechanisms mentioned above. Inequality outside that top range and lower down the income distribution—captured by the Gini coefficient or 50/10 percentile ratio once the 90/75 percentile ratio is controlled for—may be associated with other channels, such as credit constraints on investment in human capital. These opposing effects from inequality in different parts of the income distribution can help explain why any single measure of inequality is not found to be significant when included on its own, given that the different inequality measures are positively correlated with each other. Székély and Hilgert (1999) and Gobbin *et al.* (2007) present more related evidence on how different inequality indices may capture different types of channels of inequality on growth.

# 4. DISCUSSION AND CONCLUSION

This chapter reveals a complex and multi-dimensional effect of inequality on growth. The theoretical literature suggests that inequality can both facilitate and retard growth. Furthermore, most of the positive mechanisms can be linked to inequality at the top end of the distribution while many of the detrimental effects can be traced to bottom-end inequality, or to high overall inequality. The ultimate effect of inequality on the economy will therefore depend on the relative strengths of the positive and negative influences that are identified. In theory, this balance will be affected by the overall level of inequality in a country, together with the strength of its institutions. Additionally, different levels of inequality may be conducive to growth at different levels of development.

However, the empirical literature that investigates the effect of inequality on growth has traditionally relied on estimating a single coefficient on inequality, linearly, in a growth regression. Based on data for rich and/or poor countries, alternative papers have reported widely divergent effects of inequality on economic growth. Moreover, these findings appear generally sensitive to several aspects of the analysis, notably to the econometric method employed and the data considered.

The discrepancy between theoretical complexities and the prevailing empirical specification has largely been ignored in the empirical literature, presumably on pragmatic grounds. Nevertheless, the inconsistency of reported empirical findings could reflect the gap between the intricacy of the relationship, as expressed in the theoretical literature, and the simple relations that are commonly estimated. While data availability may still be the biggest obstacle to the type of empirical investigations that can be undertaken, a closer integration of the theoretical arguments in empirical testing may be a fruitful avenue for further research.

# References

Aghion, P., and Bolton, P. 1997. 'A Theory of Trickle-Down and Development'. *Review of Economic Studies*, 64: 151–72.

——Caroli, E., and Garcia-Penalosa, C. 1999. 'Inequality and Economic Growth: The Perspective of the New Growth Theories'. *Journal of Economic Literature*, 37: 1615–60.

Akerlof, G. A., and Yellen, Y. L. 1990. 'The Fair Wage-Effort Hypothesis and Unemployment'. *Quarterly Journal of Economics*, 105: 255–83.

Albanesi, S. 2007. 'Inflation and Inequality'. *Journal of Monetary Economics*, 54: 1088–114.

Alesina, A., and Perotti, R. R. 1996. 'Income Distribution, Political Instability, and Investment'. *European Economic Review*, 40: 1203–28.

——and Rodrik, D. 1994. 'Distributive Politics and Economic-Growth'. *Quarterly Journal of Economics*, 109: 465–90.

Anbarci, N., Escaleras, M., and Register, C. A. 2005. 'Earthquake Fatalities: The Interaction of Nature and Political Economy'. *Journal of Public Economics*, 89: 1907–33.

Arjona, R., Ladaique, M., and Pearson, M. 2003. 'Growth, Inequality and Social Protection'. *Canadian Public Policy-Analyse de Politiques*, 29: S119–39

Atkinson, A. B., and Brandolini, A. 2001. 'Promises and Pitfalls in the Use of "Secondary" Data-Sets: Income Inequality in OECD Countries as a Case Study'. *Journal of Economic Literature*, 39: 771–99.

Banerjee, A. V., and Duflo, E. 2003. 'Inequality and Growth: What Can the Data Say?' *Journal of Economic Growth*, 8: 267–99.

——and Newman, A. F. 1993. 'Occupational Choice and the Process of Development'. *Journal of Political Economy*, 101: 274–98.

Bardhan, P. 1997. 'Corruption and Development: A Review of Issues'. *Journal of Economic Literature*, 35: 1320–46.

Barro, R. J. 2000. 'Inequality and Growth in a Panel of Countries'. *Journal of Economic Growth*, 5: 5–32.

——and Lee, J.-W. 2001. 'International Data on Educational Attainment, Updates and Implications'. *Oxford Economic Papers*, 3: 541–63.

Bénabou, R. 1996. 'Inequality and Growth', in B. S. Bernanke and J. J. Rotemberg (eds.), *NBER Macroeconomics Annual*. Cambridge, Mass.: MIT Press.

——2000. 'Unequal Societies: Income Distribution and the Social Contract'. *American Economic Review*, 90: 96–129.

Benhabib, J., and Rustichini, A. 1996. 'Social Conflict and Growth'. *Journal of Economic Growth*, 1: 125–42.

Bertola, G. 1993. 'Factor Shares and Savings in Endogenous Growth'. *American Economic Review*, 83: 1184–98.

——2000. 'Macroeconomics of Distribution and Growth', in A. B. Atkinson and F. Bourguignon (eds.), *Handbook of Income Distribution*, vol. 1. Amsterdam and Oxford: Elsevier Science.

Bertola, G., Foellmi, R., and Zweimüller, J. 2006. *Income Distribution in Macroeconomic Models*. Princeton and Oxford: Princeton University Press.

Bhattacharya, J. 1998. 'Credit Market Imperfections, Income Distribution, and Capital Accumulation'. *Economic Theory*, 11: 171–200.

BOND, S. R., HOEFFLER, A., and TEMPLE, J. 2001. 'GMM Estimation of Empirical Growth Models'. Centre for Economic Policy Research (London) Discussion Paper no. 3048.

BOURGUIGNON, F. 1981. 'Pareto Superiority of Unegalitarian Equilibria in Stiglitz Model of Wealth Distribution with Convex Saving Function'. *Econometrica*, 49: 1469–75.

——and VERDIER, T. 2000. 'Oligarchy, Democracy, Inequality and Growth'. *Journal of Development Economics*, 62: 285–313.

BURDETT, K., LAGOS, R., and WRIGHT, R. 2003. 'Crime, Inequality, and Unemployment'. *American Economic Review*, 93: 1764–77.

CASTELLO, A., and DOMENECH, R. 2002. 'Human Capital Inequality and Economic Growth: Some New Evidence'. *Economic Journal*, 112: C187–200.

CHAKRABORTY, S., and DABLA-NORRIS, E. 2006. 'Rent-Seeking'. *IMF Staff Papers*, 53: 28–49.

——and DAS, M. 2005. 'Mortality, Human Capital and Persistent Inequality'. *Journal of Economic Growth*, 10: 159–92.

CHIU, W. H., and MADDEN, P. 1998. 'Burglary and Income Inequality'. *Journal of Public Economics*, 69: 123–41.

CHONG, A., and GRADSTEIN, M. 2007. 'Inequality and Institutions'. *The Review of Economics and Statistics*, 89: 454–65.

COLEMAN, J. S. 1988. 'Social Capital in the Creation of Human Capital'. *American Journal of Sociology*, 4: S95–120.

COLLIER, P., and HOEFFLER, A. 2002. 'On the Incidence of Civil War in Africa'. *Journal of Conflict Resolution*, 46: 13–28.

CUSACK, T. R., and BERAMENDI, P. 2006. 'Taxing Work'. *European Journal of Political Research*, 45: 43–73

DEININGER, K., and OLINTO, P. 2000. 'Asset Distribution, Inequality, and Growth'. Macro-economics and Growth Policy Research Working Paper 2375.

——and SQUIRE, L. 1996. 'A New Data Set Measuring Income Inequality'. *World Bank Economic Review*, 10: 565–91.

————1998. 'New Ways of Looking at Old Issues: Inequality and Growth'. *Journal of Development Economics*, 57: 259–87.

DE LA CROIX, D., and DOEPKE, M. 2003. 'Inequality and Growth: Why Differential Fertility Matters'. *American Economic Review*, 93: 1091–13.

DURLAUF, S. N., JOHNSON, P. A., and TEMPLE, J. R. W. 2005. 'Growth Econometrics', in P. Aghion and S. Durlauf (eds.), *Handbook of Economic Growth*, 1st edn., vol. 1. Amsterdam and Oxford: Elsevier Science.

DYNAN, K. E., SKINNER, J., and ZELDES, S. P. 2004. 'Do the Rich Save More?' *Journal of Political Economy*, 112: 397–444.

EASTERLY, W. 2001. 'The Middle Class Consensus and Economic Development'. *Journal of Economic Growth*, 6: 317–35.

ESTEBAN, J., and RAY, D. 1999. 'Conflict and Distribution'. *Journal of Economic Theory*, 87: 379–415.

————2000. 'Wealth Constraints, Lobbying and the Efficiency of Public Allocation'. *European Economic Review*, 44: 694–705.

————2006. 'Inequality, Lobbying, and Resource Allocation'. *American Economic Review*, 96: 257–79.

FAJNZYLBER, P., LEDERMAN, D., and LOAYZA, N. 2002. 'What Causes Violent Crime?' *European Economic Review*, 46: 1323–57.

FALKINGER, J., and GROSSMANN, V. 2005. 'Institutions and Development: The Interaction between Trade Regime and Political System'. *Journal of Economic Growth*, 10: 231–72.

FISHMAN, A., and SIMHON, A. 2002. 'The Division of Labor, Inequality and Growth'. *Journal of Economic Growth*, 7: 117–36.

FOGEL, K. 2006. 'Oligarchic Family Control, Social Economic Outcomes, and the Quality of Government'. *Journal of International Business Studies*, 37: 603–22.

FOELLMI, R., and ZWEIMÜLLER, J. 2006. 'Income Distribution and Demand-Induced Innovations'. *Review of Economic Studies*, 73: 941–60.

FORBES, K. J. 2000. 'A Reassessment of the Relationship between Inequality and Growth'. *American Economic Review*, 90: 869–87.

GALOR, O., and MOAV, O. 2004. 'From Physical to Human Capital Accumulation: Inequality and the Process of Development'. *Review of Economic Studies*, 71: 1001–26.

—————— and VOLLRATH, D. 2006. 'Inequality in Land Ownership, the Emergence of Human Capital Promoting Institutions, and Great Divergence'. Working Papers 2006-14. Brown University, Department of Economics.

—— and TSIDDON, D. 1996. 'Income Distribution and Growth: The Kuznets Hypothesis Revisited'. *Economica*, 63: S103–17.

—————— 1997. 'The Distribution of Human Capital and Economic Growth'. *Journal of Economic Growth*, 2: 93–124.

—— and ZEIRA, J. 1993. 'Income-Distribution and Macroeconomics'. *Review of Economic Studies*, 60: 35–52.

GHATAK, M., and JIANG, N. N. H. 2002. 'A Simple Model of Inequality, Occupational Choice, and Development'. *Journal of Development Economics*, 69: 205–26.

—— MORELLI, M., and SJOSTROM, T. 2001. 'Occupational Choice and Dynamic Incentives'. *Review of Economic Studies*, 68: 781–810.

GLAESER, E. L., SCHEINKMAN, J., and SHLEIFER, A. 2003. 'The Injustice of Inequality'. *Journal of Monetary Economics*, 50: 199–222.

GOBBIN, N., RAYP, G., and VAN DE GAER, D. 2007. 'Inequality and Growth: From Micro Theory to Macro Empirics'. *Scottish Journal of Political Economy*, 54: 508–30.

GOLDSMITH, A. H., VEUM, J. R., and DARITY, W. 2000. 'Working Hard for the Money? Efficiency Wages and Worker Effort'. *Journal of Economic Psychology*, 21: 351–85.

GRADSTEIN, M. 2003. 'The Political Economy of Public Spending on Education, Inequality and Growth'. World Bank Policy Research Working Paper no. 3162.

—— 2007. 'Inequality, Democracy and the Protection of Property Rights'. *Economic Journal*, 117: 252–69.

HELLIWELL, J. F. 2003. 'How's Life? Combining Individual and National Variables to Explain Subjective Well-Being'. *Economic Modelling*, 20: 331–60.

JOSTEN, S. D. 2003. 'Inequality, Crime and Economic Growth. A Classical Argument for Distributional Equality'. *International Tax and Public Finance*, 10: 435–52.

—— 2004. 'Social Capital, Inequality, and Economic Growth'. *Journal of Institutional and Theoretical Economics—Zeitschrift Für Die Gesamte Staatswissenschaft*, 160: 663–80.

KEEFER, P., and KNACK, S. 2002. 'Polarization, Politics and Property Rights: Links between Inequality and Growth'. *Public Choice*, 111: 127–54.

KELLY, M. 2000. 'Inequality and Crime'. *Review of Economics and Statistics*, 82: 530–9.

KNACK, S. 2003. 'Groups, Growth and Trust: Cross-Country Evidence on the Olson and Putnam Hypotheses'. *Public Choice*, 117: 341–55.

KNOWLES, S. 2005. 'Inequality and Economic Growth. The Empirical Relationship Reconsidered in the Light of Comparable Data'. *Journal of Development Studies*, 41: 135–59.

KREMER, M., and CHEN, D. L. 2002. 'Income Distribution Dynamics with Endogenous Fertility'. *Journal of Economic Growth*, 7: 227–58.

KUZNETS, S. 1953. 'Shares of Upper Income Groups in Income and Savings'. National Bureau of Economic Research, New York.

LEE, W. J., and ROEMER, J. E. 1999. 'Inequality and Redistribution Revisited'. *Economics Letters*, 65: 339–46.

LI, H. Y., and ZOU, H. F. 1998. 'Income Inequality is not Harmful for Growth: Theory and Evidence'. *Review of Development Economics*, 2: 318–34.

MACHIN, S., and MEGHIR, C. 2004. 'Crime and Economic Incentives'. *Journal of Human Resources*, 39, 958–79.

MANI, A. 2001. 'Income Distribution and the Demand Constraint'. *Journal of Economic Growth*, 6: 107–33.

MAOZ, Y. D., and MOAV, O. 1999. 'Intergenerational Mobility and the Process of Development'. *Economic Journal*, 109: 677–97.

MATSUYAMA, K. 2002. 'The Rise of Mass Consumption Societies'. *Journal of Political Economy*, 110: 1035–70.

MOAV, O. 2002. 'Income Distribution and Macroeconomics: The Persistence of Inequality in a Convex Technology Framework'. *Economics Letters*, 75: 187–92.

——— 2005. 'Cheap Children and the Persistence of Poverty'. *Economic Journal*, 115: 88–110.

MOOKHERJEE, D., and RAY, D. 2003. 'Persistent Inequality'. *Review of Economic Studies*, 70: 369–93.

MORAND, O. F. 1999. 'Endogenous Fertility, Income Distribution, and Growth'. *Journal of Economic Growth*, 4: 331–49.

MURPHY, K. M., SHLEIFER, A., and VISHNY, R. 1989. 'Income-Distribution, Market-Size, and Industrialization'. *Quarterly Journal of Economics*, 104: 537–64.

NURKSE, R. 1953. *Problems of Capital Formation in Underdeveloped Countries*. Oxford: Blackwell.

OSBERG, L., SMEEDING, T. M., and SCHWABISH, J. 2004. 'Income Distribution and Public Social Expenditure: Theories, Effects, and Evidence', in K. Neckerman (ed.), *Social Inequality*. New York: Russell Sage Foundation, 821–59.

PASINETTI, L. 1962. 'Rate of Profit and Income Distribution in Relation to the Rate of Economic Growth'. *Review of Economic Studies*, 29: 267–79.

PEROTTI, R. 1993. 'Political Equilibrium, Income-Distribution, and Growth'. *Review of Economic Studies*, 60: 755–76.

——— 1996. 'Growth, Income Distribution and Democracy: What the Data Say'. *Journal of Economic Growth*, 1: 149–87.

PERSSON, T., and TABELLINI, G. 1994. 'Is Inequality Harmful for Growth'. *American Economic Review*, 84: 600–21.

PIKETTY, T. 1997. 'The Dynamics of the Wealth Distribution and the Interest Rate with Credit Rationing'. *Review of Economic Studies*, 64: 173–89.

PRITCHETT, L. 2000. 'Understanding Patterns of Economic Growth: Searching for Hills among Plateaus, Mountains, and Plains'. *World Bank Economic Review*, 14: 221–50.

PUTNAM, R. D. 2000. *Bowling Alone: The Collapse and Revival of American Community*. New York and London: Simon & Schuster.

RODRIK, D. 1999. 'Where Did All the Growth Go? External Shocks, Social Conflict, and Growth Collapses'. *Journal of Economic Growth*, 4: 85–412.

ROSENSTEIN-RODAN, P. N. 1943. 'Problems of Industrialisation of Eastern and South-Eastern Europe'. *The Economic Journal*, 53: 202–11.

SAINT PAUL, G., and VERDIER, T. 1993. 'Education, Democracy and Growth'. *Journal of Development Economics*, 42: 399–407.

————1996. 'Inequality, Redistribution and Growth: A Challenge to the Conventional Political Economy Approach'. *European Economic Review*, 40: 719–28.

SCHEINKMAN, J. A., and WEISS, L. 1986. 'Borrowing Constraints and Aggregate Economic-Activity'. *Econometrica*, 54: 23–45.

SCHMIDT-HEBBEL, K., and SERVEN, L. 2000. 'Does Income Inequality Raise Aggregate Saving?' *Journal of Development Economics*, 61: 417–46.

SHAPIRO, C., and STIGLITZ, J. E. 1984. 'Equilibrium Unemployment as a Worker Discipline Device'. *American Economic Review*, 74: 433–44.

SMITH, D. 2001. 'International Evidence on How Income Inequality and Credit Market Imperfections Affect Private Saving Rates'. *Journal of Development Economics*, 64: 103–27.

SONIN, K. 2003. 'Why the Rich may Favor Poor Protection of Property Rights'. *Journal of Comparative Economics*, 31: 715–31.

STOLLE, D., and HOOGHE, M. 2005. 'Review Article: Inaccurate, Exceptional, One-Sided or Irrelevant? The Debate about the Alleged Decline of Social Capital and Civic Engagement in Western Societies'. *British Journal of Political Science*, 35: 149–67.

SZÉKÉLY, M., and HILGERT, M. 1999. 'What's Behind the Inequality we Measure: An Investigation using Latin American Data'. Inter-American Development Bank, Research Department Working Paper no. 409.

THORBECKE, E., and CHARUMILIND, C. 2002. 'Economic Inequality and its Socio-economic Impact'. *World Development*, 30: 1477–95.

VAN WILSEM, J., DE GRAAF, N. D., and WITTEBROOD, K. 2003. 'Cross-National Differences in Victimization: Disentangling the Impact of Composition and Context'. *European Sociological Review*, 19: 125–42.

VOITCHOVSKY, S. 2005. 'Does the Profile of Income Inequality Matter for Economic Growth?' *Journal of Economic Growth*, 10: 273–96.

WOO, J. 2003. 'Economic, Political, and Institutional Determinants of Public Deficits'. *Journal of Public Economics*, 87: 387–426.

——2005. 'Social Polarization, Fiscal Instability and Growth'. *European Economic Review*, 49: 1451–77.

World Development Report. 2006. *Equity and Development*. New York: The World Bank and Oxford University Press.

ZWEIMÜLLER, J. 2000. 'Schumpeterian Entrepreneurs Meet Engel's Law: The Impact of Inequality on Innovation-Driven Growth'. *Journal of Economic Growth*, 5: 185–206.

CHAPTER 23

....................................................................

# GLOBALIZATION AND INEQUALITY

....................................................................

## RICHARD B. FREEMAN

## 1. INTRODUCTION

....................................................................

GLOBALIZATION has been the most widely publicized economic phenomenon in recent times. Googling the term in 2008 turned up more references to globalization than to economic or income inequality, recession, or Alan Greenspan.[1] Books, research articles, media reports, and everyday life bring home to people the pervasiveness of global economic transactions. In the USA a large proportion of manufactured consumer items are imported, immigrant workers are found in large numbers in the least skilled jobs and in the most skilled jobs, international students fill graduate school classes, especially in science and engineering, and US-based corporations define themselves as multinational or global, sourcing labor and locating production around the world, rather than as American.

It is almost impossible that globalization of the magnitudes observed in the 1990s and 2000s would not impact the distribution of earnings and incomes in the USA and elsewhere. There are many ways for globalization to alter the distribution of incomes. While most attention has traditionally been on international trade, trade is only part of the globalization story. Capital flows, immigration, and technology transfers also affect incomes around the world, in most cases impacting inequality

---

[1] On January 18, 2008 there were 19 million links for globalization, 2 million for Alan Greenspan, 8 million for inequality, but many of these were for mathematics; economic inequality had 0.5 million and income inequality 0.6 million.

in the same direction as trade. Given that labor demand for workers with different skills has changed due to skill-biased technical change and the changing industrial mix of goods and services, and that relative supply of educated persons has changed, and that collective bargaining, minimum wages, tax and welfare state spending, and other institutional and policies as well as the business cycle also affect the distribution of earnings and incomes, globalization is surely not the only determinant of inequality, but it is also not a minor determinant either.

What do we know about how globalization affects inequality and how do we know it? What are the main issues about which we are uncertain and how might we research them? What policies might spread the benefits of globalization more broadly?

This chapter argues that the impact of globalization on labor markets and inequality has increased since globalization rose to national attention in the USA in the early 1990s debate over the North American Free Trade Agreement (NAFTA). China, India, and the ex-Soviet bloc have expanded their presence in the world economy. Advances in information technology permit offshoring and fragmentation of economic activities that makes more jobs subject to overseas competition than ever before. The combination of digitalization and globalization partially moots the debate over whether trade or skill-biased technical change drives inequality more: offshoring and digitalization go together. And the rapid expansion of mass higher education in developing countries has allowed low-wage countries to compete in high-tech sectors, weakening the comparative advantage of advanced countries in these sectors.

Comparing inequality during the period of rapid globalization with inequality in the preceding period, and comparing inequality between countries or industries subject to greater or lesser global pressures, and before and after episodes of trade liberalization, shows that recent globalization has been associated with reduced income inequality worldwide but with greater inequality within countries. These results do not fit with the traditional Heckscher-Ohlin model that makes given factor endowments the driving force in trade. The expansion of high-tech industries and university graduate level work to low income countries runs counter to technology-based models in which advanced countries dominate high-tech sectors by having a relatively more skilled work force. The facts have forced analysts to modify the models to fit historic experience.

While our inability to predict the patterns of the past two decades or so makes one leery of looking into the future, globalization appears to have set the world onto a path toward a single global labor market that in the long run is likely to lower inequality worldwide. It will do this by bringing wages and living standards in low income countries toward the levels in the advanced countries. The transition to a global labor market is, however, unlikely to occur smoothly, in part because pressures for greater inequality within countries risk setting off a backlash against globalization in advanced countries and social instability in developing countries.

Even in the global labor market of the future, moreover, there will be substantial income differences among countries, just as there are substantial differences among regions in the USA and other countries.

# 2. Globalization for Real

At the end of the 20th century globalization became a more powerful driver of labor market outcomes than before, for reasons that are largely independent of the details of trade treaties on which most of the debate over globalization had focused. Indeed, the past three decades have shown that both the optimistic claims that NAFTA, the various global trade negotiations, and formation of the European Common Market would spark new eras of prosperity and growth, and the pessimistic counterclaims that they would create economic and social disasters proved to be exaggerated (Freeman, 2004). NAFTA did not destroy large numbers of jobs in the USA nor did it induce a job-creating burst in economic growth. It did not deliver the promised huge job creation in Canada. Similarly, the Common Market did not spur Europe to outdo the USA or Japan in the world economy. The failure of the Multilateral Agreement on Investment in the mid-1990s had no discernible effect on global capital flows.

Treaties aside, three developments in the 1990s and 2000s increased international economic interactions between low-wage developing countries and advanced countries in ways that have greater potential to impact inequality than did the trade among similarly situated economies that dominated the world economy through most of the 20th century.

The first development was the approximate *doubling of the number of workers in the world economy* brought about by China's shift to market capitalism, India's market reforms and entry into the global trading system, and the collapse of Soviet communism. Before those countries embraced global capitalism, the world economy encompassed half of the world's population: the OECD countries, Latin America, the Caribbean, Africa, some parts of Asia and the Middle East. The other half lived in separate economic spaces. Workers in the USA and other higher-income countries and in market-oriented developing countries did not face competition from low-wage Chinese or Indian workers nor from workers in the Soviet empire. Entry of these economies into the world trading system in the 1990s increased the labor pool available to global capitalism from approximately 1.46 billion workers to 2.93 billion workers, motivating my use of the term 'Great Doubling' (Freeman, 2005a and 2005b). The upper panel of Table 23.1 shows the figures for this change.

Table 23.1. Estimated effects of the entry of China, India, and the ex-Soviet bloc on the global work force and the global capital/labor ratio

|  | Before | After | Ratio |
|---|---|---|---|
| Panel A: Millions of Economically Active Persons, 2000 | | | |
| Global total | 1460 | 2930 | |
| Advanced | 460 | 460 | |
| Developing | 1000 | 1000 | |
| New | – | 1470[1] | |

Notes: [1] China, 760; India, 440; Ex-Soviet, 260.
Source: Tabulated from ILO, <http://laborsta.ilo.org/>.

| Panel B: Global Capital/Labor Ratio, 2000 | | | |
|---|---|---|---|
| 2000 | $61,300 | $37,600 | 0.61 |

Source: Calculated using Penn World Tables, with perpetual inventory method based on investment (no distinction between buildings, equipment, housing, etc.). But China investment rate in current currency and ex-Soviet bloc based on K/L ratio of 15% of the USA.

The impact of the doubling on the income distribution in advanced and traditional market-oriented developing countries depends in part on its effect on the global capital/labor ratio. To see how the entry of China, India, and the ex-Soviet bloc affected the labor ratio, I estimated the global capital stock by applying the perpetual inventory method of cumulating investments per year from Penn World Table data to obtain capital stocks for countries and summing the estimates for 1990 and 2000. In these calculations, I used two different depreciation rates, a 5% rate and a 10% rate. The 5% rate gives investments a longer life and thus produces a higher amount of capital than does the 10% depreciation rate. Because investments in the communist period produced less useful capital in the Soviet bloc than this methodology indicates, I made some adjustments for that. The investment share of GDP in China is much lower in the Penn tables than in the World Bank and other sources, so I also adjusted the data for that. None of my changes affects the overall pattern of results.

The lower panel of Table 23.1 shows that the doubling of the global work force reduced the ratio of capital to labor in the global economy by 40% as of 2000. The reason for the reduction is that China, India, and the ex-Soviet bloc did not have much capital to bring with them when they joined the global economy. The labor force doubled but the capital stock did not. Since the bulk of the work force in China and India had little education, moreover, there was a similar drop in the ratio of skilled to unskilled labor.

Economics has a strong prediction about how a lower capital/labor ratio and a lower skilled-to-unskilled-labor ratio should affect the distribution of income. In the advanced capitalist countries and in developing countries that were already part of the global economy, it should increase inequality. It gives firms in those countries the option to shift capital to the low-wage, highly populous new entrants to the global economy, or alternatively to threaten to move operations overseas unless domestic workers make concessions on wages and working conditions. By contrast, the capital/labor ratio in the new entrants to the global economy should rise, reducing inequality and raising the incomes of lower-paid workers.

The second development boosting the economic impact of the global economy is the spread of *modern information and communication technology*, particularly digitalization of white-collar work and worldwide access to the Internet. These innovations increased the scope over which global economic forces operate. In 1980s economists drew sharp demarcations between traded goods, notably manu-facturing, natural resources, and agriculture, and seemingly non-tradable services. The growing share of the labor force in services limited the direct effects of trade to a declining proportion of workers, which arguably reduced the effect of trade on the overall work force, albeit subject to the general equilibrium spillover of effects on the traded goods sector to other sectors.

Digitalization of work and modern communication and technology has out-moded this assessment. It created opportunities to offshore services at all levels of labor skills, from call centers to computer programming to research and develop-ment. As the British Institute of Directors declared (2006),

the availability of high-speed, low-cost communications, coupled with the rise in high-level skills in developing countries meant offshoring has become an attractive option outside the manufacturing industry. Britain has first seen call centers and IT support move away from Britain, but now creative services such as design and advertising work are also being outsourced. There is more to come. *In theory, anything that does not demand physical contact with a customer can be outsourced to anywhere on the globe.* For many UK businesses this presents new opportunities, for others it represents a serious threat. But welcome it or fear it, it is happening anyway, and we had better get used to it.

In part because government statistics were not designed to measure offshoring phenomena (Houseman, 2007), economists initially were uncertain whether off-shoring was a large development that merited attention or a small phenomenon blown out of proportion. That debate is over. Offshoring may not be Alan Blinder's (2006) 'new industrial revolution' but few would now deny that it has greatly extended the impact of trade on demand for labor (Collins and Brainerd, 2005). Lori Kletzer and Brad Jensen (2005) use the geographic distribution of employ-ment in the US to obtain an objective measure of the potential for US jobs to be offshored. They argue that service-sector jobs that are geographically concen-trated in the US—away from direct customer contact—could just as easily be concentrated outside the country. On the basis of the uneven distribution of jobs in the USA, they estimate that about 30% of US employment is vulnerable to offshoring. Surveys show that American workers are highly concerned about the phenomenon.[2]

Advances in information communication and transportation technology have also changed the global division of labor by allowing for the fragmentation of production in manufacturing. Low-wage parts of manufacturing that might have remained in advanced countries as part of producing a high-tech good are now done in low-wage countries and assembled there or elsewhere into a final product. The result is global sourcing of intermediate goods. Trade in parts and components increased more rapidly in the 1990s than intra-industry trade (Jones *et al.*, 2005), which in turn increased more rapidly than total trade and world GDP. Analyses suggest that fragmentation could affect the distribution of income much as does trade in the Heckscher-Ohlin model, reducing inequality in low-income countries that can compete for low-productivity parts of production and raising inequality in high-income countries that concentrate on high-productivity sectors (Jones and Kierzkowski, 2005). But there is only limited evidence on its actual effects (Kierzkowski, 2005; Feenstra and Hanson, 1996).

The third way in which globalization has become a more powerful determinant of economic outcomes is by increasing the speed of transfer of modern knowledge and technology from advanced countries to developing countries. One reason for this is that university enrollments have increased rapidly in developing countries. Data from UNESCO show that the developing country share of tertiary enrollments increased from 54% in 1970 to 61% in 1990 and then jumped to 72% in 2005. Four-fifths of the growth on tertiary enrollments in 1990–2005 was in developing countries (Freeman, 2008). In 2006, China alone graduated over 4 million bachelors, largely in science and engineering. By 2010 China will graduate more Ph.D.s in science and engineering than the USA (Freeman, 2006). I have called the huge investments that China and other highly populous developing countries make in higher education 'human resource leapfrogging' because it allows them to compete at the scientific and technical frontier despite having many fewer university graduates per person than advanced countries. This is because scale not factor proportions matters in technological prowess.

Another reason knowledge has spread rapidly is that multinationals investing in developing countries usually use the most modern production processes and knowledge. As of 2006, multinationals had established over 700 research and

---

[2] In 2004 an Employment Law Alliance survey found that 6% of American workers claimed to have lost a job because their work was sent overseas; 10% said that they feared losing their job due to it being sent to an overseas subcontractor; and 30% reported that someone they knew had lost a job due to offshoring. An Associated Press-IPSOS survey in the same year reported that 20% of Americans said that they, a family member, or someone they knew personally lost their job due to offshoring (<http://www.danieldrezner.com/archives/001355.html>).

Table 23.2. Indicators of the increased technological and scientific prowess of developing countries

(1) Georgia Tech indicator of technological competitiveness of larger developing economies relative to USA

| | 1993 | 2007 |
| --- | --- | --- |
| USA | 100 | 100 |
| China | 55 | 76 |
| India | 51 | 64 |
| Mexico | 45 | 56 |
| Russia | 49 | 62 |
| Indonesia | 49 | 51 |
| Brazil | 63 | 53 |

(2) Developing country share of S&E articles

| | 1995 | 2005 |
| --- | --- | --- |
| | 8.8% | 18.4% |

(3) Developing country share of high–tech manufacturing production

| | 1985 | 1996 | 2005 |
| --- | --- | --- | --- |
| Value added | 14.5% | 18.6% | 29.4% |
| Gross revenues | 13.1% | 21.5% | 38.1% |
| Exports | 31.4% | 49.8% | 64.6% |

(4) Developing country share of high–tech services production

| | 1985 | 1996 | 2005 |
| --- | --- | --- | --- |
| Value added | 12.5% | 14.4% | 16.9% |

Notes: (1) NSF Science and Engineering Indicators, 2008, appendix table 6–26.
(2) NSF Science and Engineering Indicators, 2008, appendix table 5-34.
(3) NSF Science and Engineering Indicators, 2008, appendix table 6-9, 6–15.
(4) NSF Science and Engineering Indicators, 2008, appendix table 6-5.
Source: Georgia Tech Technology Policy and Assessment Center, available at <http://tpac.gatech.edu/>.

development centers in China and hundreds in India, which will move these countries to the forefront of innovation as well as production of high-tech goods.

Table 23.2 documents the extent to which developing countries have raised their scientific and technological competence. Part 1 of the table records the overall indicator of technological competitiveness that the Georgia Tech Technology Policy and Assessment Center produces for the US National Science Foundation. Between 1993 and 2007, most large developing economies drew closer to the USA in technological prowess, with China in particular making huge advances. Part 2 of the table shows that between 1995 and 2005 developing countries more than doubled their share of scientific publications. Data for individual countries (not reported in the table) document that China increased its proportion particularly rapidly. Turning to high-tech manufacturing, we see in part 3 a twofold increase in the developing country share of value added and a nearly threefold increase in the developing country share of gross revenues—which reflects the increased role of these countries in the global chain of production in high-tech manufacturing. By contrast, part 4 shows a modest change in the share of value added in high-tech services in 1985, 1996, and 2005, though it is possible that this modest change reflects the inadequacy of statistics on offshoring.

In sum, expansion of the global work force, extension of the scope of globalization via offshoring and fragmentation, and transmission of modern technological knowledge through education and tech transfers within multinational firms have boosted the likely impact of globalization on economic outcomes worldwide. By allowing developing countries to grow more rapidly, these factors are likely to reduce inequality among countries, which all else the same will lower inequality worldwide.

## 3. TRADE AND FACTOR FLOWS BETWEEN ADVANCED AND DEVELOPING COUNTRIES

Traditional measures of globalization—trade, immigration, and capital flows—show substantial increases in international transactions in the past half-century or so. Between 1970 and 2005, one measure of trade, the ratio of exports to world GDP, rose from 0.12 to 0.27. Most important in terms of potential impacts on income inequality across and within countries is the huge increase in trade between developing countries and advanced countries. The share of US imports from non-OPEC developing countries provides one measure of this pattern. Between 1990 and 2006, this share increased from 32% to 48% (Council of Economic Advisors, 2008). Including OPEC countries as part of the developing country group raises the developing country share of imports to about 55%. Worldwide, the developing country share of trade has risen. WTO data show that it reached an all-time high of 36% in 2006 (<http://www.wto.org/english/news_e/pres07_e/pr472_e.htm>).

Immigration follows a similar pattern (Freeman, 2006). In 2000, 2.9% of persons in the world lived in a country other than the one in which they were born. Two-thirds of the immigrants resided in advanced countries where they made up nearly 9% of workers. The USA was the single biggest recipient of immigrants. From 1970 to 2005 the share of immigrants nearly tripled, with the result that in the latter year roughly one in five workers aged 25–39 was foreign-born. As a result of the flow of highly educated workers from lower-income countries to higher-income countries, one in ten persons from a developing country with a 'tertiary' (post-secondary) education lives in an advanced country. In some cases the *brain drain* is massive—40% of the university educated from Turkey and Morocco reside in OECD countries and over half of university graduates from Caribbean countries live in advanced countries, primarily North America and the United Kingdom.

The way in which the statistician accounts for the earnings of immigrants can affect estimates of the impact of globalization on income inequality. When the earnings of highly educated workers who have moved from a lower-income country to a higher-income country are counted as part of the income of the low-income country, income in the lower-income country rises, which reduces inequality among countries. At the same time inequality within the low-income country rises. Contrarily, when the incomes of these highly educated immigrants are counted as income in the advanced country, income inequality among countries rises while inequality within the low-income country falls.

Foreign direct investment, which had been 2–3% of global gross capital formation in the 1970s, rose to 7–20% of gross capital formation in the 1990s–2000s, varying greatly with the business cycle and other economic and political conditions. The share of foreign equities in investors' equity portfolios increased from negligible numbers to about 15% in the early 2000s. Capital flows, however, show one great peculiarity, largely due to the US trade deficit. In the 1970s high-income countries had surpluses on their current accounts while lower-income countries had deficits. Because capital flows are by definition the opposite of trade flows, the implication is that capital was moving from higher-income countries to developing countries. But in the 1990s, the reverse was true (Zagha *et al.*, 2006). Capital flowed to the USA as many developing countries bought US treasury notes. Some developing country firms bought US businesses (vide the Lenovo purchase of IBM's laptop production). Increasingly, government 'sovereign wealth funds' composed of financial assets such as stocks, bonds, foreign currency, and the like, have invested in bank equity and ownership stakes in other companies.

# 4. THEORY

The workhorse theories of international trade give clear predictions about how globalization *should* affect inequality.

*Heckscher–Ohlin*[3] (H-O) theory takes country factor endowments (labor, human capital, natural resources, capital) as given and examines how these differences affect trade, capital flows, and immigration, and through them prices, wages, and returns to capital. Identifying skilled labor, unskilled labor, capital, and natural resources as the relevant factors of production, trade patterns between advanced

[3]  <http://en.wikipedia.org/wiki/Heckscher-Ohlin_model>

and developing countries fit the H-O model as a first approximation.[4] Countries with abundant skilled labor, such as the USA, export goods produced by skilled workers, and import goods made by low-skilled labor while countries with natural resources export those resources and import goods and services made with other inputs. But H-O models are silent on the huge volumes of usually intra-industry trade among advanced countries with similar factor endowments.[5]

The H-O theory also predicts that trade between advanced countries and developing countries will raise inequality in advanced countries and reduce it in developing countries. This is because advanced countries have relatively more skilled workers than unskilled workers, which should lead them to import products made by less-skilled workers and export products made by skilled workers. This reduces demand for less-skilled workers and increases demand for skilled workers, which raises income inequality. The theory predicts the opposite pattern for developing countries, so that trade reduces inequality.

The theory further predicts that less-skilled workers will immigrate into advanced countries, where they are in relatively short supply while skilled workers will immigrate into lower-income countries where they are in relatively short supply. These flows ought to increase inequality in advanced countries and reduce it in developing countries. As for capital, it should flow from advanced countries with high capital/labor ratios to developing countries with low capital/labor ratios. This raises the return on capital in advanced countries relative to wages and lowers the return on capital relative to wages in developing countries. Given the high income of capital owners, this should increase inequality in advanced countries and lower it in developing countries. In fact, inequality increased in advanced countries during the period of rapid globalization but also increased in developing countries; and skilled labor moved from developing countries to advanced countries (brain drain) rather than in the predicted direction.

*Ricardian trade* models treat differences in technology as the fundamental determinant of trade and factor flows and examine how investments in technology create comparative advantage. Again, trade among advanced countries has no clear impact on inequality while trade between advanced and developing countries should produce greater inequality in the former and less in the latter countries. In contrast to the Heckscher-Ohlin model, trade and factor mobility are complements in this model. A technologically advantaged sector that uses, say, highly skilled labor or capital will attract highly skilled immigrants and capital to help it expand. Factor mobility will magnify differences in factor endowments as labor and capital move to economies where the technological advantage creates greater demand for them. Advanced countries increase their share of 'good jobs' while developing countries increase their share of 'bad jobs'. The flow of factors should

---

[4]  Debaere (2003) gives a reasonably favorable reading of the H-O model while Trefler (1995) is more critical.

[5]  Ruffin, 'Roy 1999'.

reduce earnings inequality in advanced countries and increase it in lower income countries.

In the 'North-South' or product-cycle version of the technology models (Krugman, 1979), the difference in income per capita between advanced countries and lower-income countries depends on the rate of innovation in the advanced country, which increases its productivity and income edge over the lower-income country, and the speed with which the lower-income countries adopt new technologies, which reduces the gap between them and advanced countries. The flow of knowledge across borders allows economies to improve their technical prowess and operate along the global production possibility frontier even when they lack the scientific base to expand the frontier. With labor paid different wages among countries, firms have incentives to offshore some jobs to foreign countries, including service-sector jobs that had been historically non-tradable. Moreover, by creating greater competition in high-tech sectors, the transfer of technology can reduce the income of advanced countries by cutting their gains to trade (Gomory and Baumol, 2000; Samuelson, 2004). It is possible that the advanced countries will lose comparative advantage in high tech, though the citizens of the advanced country benefit from the lower prices of high-tech goods (Ruffin and Jones, 2007).

Critics of the standard economic analysis of globalization offer another perspective on its effects on inequality. In the 1960s through the 1980s critics feared that globalization would impoverish lower-income countries by closing off opportunities to develop comparative advantage in industries that have knowledge spillovers and potential for improving productivity, leaving them stuck producing natural resources for more advanced countries. Critics have also worried that the brain drain would reduce the opportunity for developing countries to advance in higher value-added sectors. They stress that many farmers or peasants in developing countries cannot compete with the highly technological and often highly subsidized agriculture sectors of advanced countries. Finally, the critics feared a race to the bottom in labor standards, where the cost advantages of countries with low wages and poor working conditions force other countries to reduce wages and working conditions.

None of the theories fits experience well. As noted, inequality has risen in developing countries and skilled workers have migrated to advanced countries, contrary to the H-O model. Models that stress technological differences among countries predict factor flows better, but have little to say about the changing competence of lower-income populous countries in high-tech sectors. Reviewing the relation between these models and the facts, Easterly (2004) concludes that models based on 'productivity differences are more relevant than [models based] on factor endowments in some circumstances, whereas factor endowments dominate in other situations' (p. 70). A more direct way of saying this is that both theories fail in important ways. As for the critics of globalization, their fears of divergence of incomes among countries run counter to the rapid growth of the highly populous India and

Table 23.3. Ratio of earnings in detailed occupations in the top 20% of countries relative to earnings in the bottom 20% of countries, c.2000

| Occupation | Exchange rates | Purchasing power parity |
|---|---|---|
| Physicians | 15.6 | 5.1 |
| Insurance agents | 8.1 | 3.2 |
| Computer programmer | 12.7 | 3.5 |
| Clicker cutter | 11.5 | 4.3 |
| Logger | 13.5 | 7.2 |

Source: Freeman and Oostendorp (2001).

China, while labor standards have risen rather than fallen with globalization (Elliott and Freeman, 2003; Freeman, 2008).

## 5. WAGE DIFFERENTIALS REMAIN LARGE

There is a striking difference between the variation in the prices of goods and the cost of capital between advanced and developing countries and the variation in the wages of nominally similarly skilled labor between advanced and developing countries. The prices of many goods and services differ only moderately across countries. For instance, in 2004 the price of a McDonald's Big Mac sandwich showed a narrow distribution across countries—a 1.9:1 spread between the 80th percentile of Big Mac prices among 65 countries and the 20th percentile of Big Mac prices, for example.[6] Similarly, estimates of international differences in the cost of capital show a ratio of costs at the top 25th percentile of countries to costs at the bottom 25th percentile of 1.43.[7] By contrast, the variation of wages in the same occupation is huge. The 1998–2002 Occupational Wages Around the World data on wages in five occupations in Table 23.3 show that wages at the top quintile (20%) point of the earnings distribution for a *given narrowly defined* occupation are eight to 16 times the wages at the bottom quintile point of earnings distribution using exchange rates to compare currencies and are four to five times greater at the top quintile point than at the bottom quintile point using purchasing power parity units to compare currencies (Freeman and Oostendorp, 2001, 2003).

[6] <http://www.economist.com/markets/bigmac/displayStory.cfm?story_id=2708584>. <http://www.skfriends.com/big_mac_index.htm> with data for 65 countries.
[7] This averages estimates from five different sources from Hail and Leuz (2004).

Only a small part of this variation is due to differences in the education and skill of workers in the same occupation in advanced and developing countries: barbers make markedly more in advanced countries than in lower-income countries. The offshoring of computer programming and call centers to India in the 2000s highlights the fact that even among highly skilled occupations, what differentiates workers in lower-income countries from those in more advanced countries is not what they can do, but what they are paid for what they do.

The greater cross-country dispersion of wages than of prices or the cost of capital suggests that globalization has impacted the price of labor less than other prices. One possible reason is that international migration is smaller relative to the work force than is trade relative to world production or flows of capital relative to capital formation. This explanation requires that trade and capital flows affect directly the prices of goods/services and the cost of capital more than they indirectly affect wages.

# 6. Changes in Relative and Absolute Inequality among Countries

Analysts disagree about whether global inequality—defined by a Gini coefficient or some other measure of the incomes of all persons in the world—increased or decreased during the period of rapid globalization. On the one side, Milanovich (2002) has estimated incomes for persons around the world using survey data and found that inequality rose from 1988 to 1993. On the other side, Sala-i-Martin (2006) has combined measures of inequality within countries with estimates of country differences in incomes to argue that inequality fell from 1970 to 2000.

My analysis, summarized in Table 23.4, shows that global inequality among countries fell from 1980 to 2000 after having risen from 1960 to 1980. I further estimate that this decline in inequality among countries was sufficiently large to dominate any plausible increase in inequality within countries, so that inequality among all persons in the world fell in relative terms, as Sala-i-Martin argues. For my calculations I measure inequality by the variance of the log of incomes. I use this metric largely because the variance of the log has a simple additive decomposition of income inequality between and within countries. In addition, the lognormal fits income distributions reasonably well except at very high incomes where the Pareto distribution does better. In labor economics the lognormal is widely used, due in part to the interpretation of the regression coefficients on education as indicators of the return to schooling.

Table 23.4. Changes in inequality in GDP per capita among countries, measured by the variance of log GDP per capita in purchasing parity price units

| | Ln income gap between advanced and developing countries | Variance due to difference in income among advanced countries | Variance due to difference in income among developing countries | Share of advanced countries in world population | Variance of log income among countries |
|---|---|---|---|---|---|
| | (1) | (2) | (3) | (4) | (5) |
| 1960 | 2.09 | 0.16 | 0.32 | 0.22 | 1.04 |
| 1980 | 2.33 | 0.04 | 0.50 | 0.18 | 1.24 |
| 2000 | 2.05 | 0.04 | 0.44 | 0.15 | 0.92 |

*Notes:* (1)  This is the ln of income in advanced countries relative to income in developing countries, using population weights.
(2)  This is the variance of ln incomes among advanced countries where the mean of ln incomes is the weighted average.
(3)  This is the variance of ln incomes among developing countries where the mean of ln incomes is the weighted average.
(4)  This is the share used in the decomposition formula.
(5)  This is the sum of column 1 squared and multiplied by the share in column 4 x (1 minus that share in column 4); plus column 2 times column 4; plus column 3 times (1 minus the share in column 4).

1960–1980 inequality rises despite convergence among advanced countries because China and India fall behind; 1980–2000 drop in world inequality of 0.32 ln points because China and India reduce ln gap between advanced countries and LDC. The 0.32 drop in ln variance dominates any conceivable within-country rise in inequality.

*Source:* Tabulated from Penn World Tables data, as described in text.

I decompose the variance of the log of incomes into five parts, each weighted by the relevant population, to reflect their impact on global inequality.

Three parts of the decomposition measure inequality among countries in GDP per capita in purchasing power parity units: (1) the square of the difference between the log income per capita in all advanced countries taken as a group compared to the log income per capita in developing countries taken as a group; (2) the variance in the log income among advanced countries, which measures the extent to which average incomes vary between, say, the USA, Japan, and European countries; (3) the variance in the log income among developing countries. The underlying data for these calculations are Penn World Table estimates of per capita income across countries.

Two parts of the decomposition measure *within country* inequality of incomes: (4) the variance of log incomes within advanced countries; (5) the variance of log incomes within developing countries. The underlying data for these calculations are Gini coefficients based on household survey data from World Bank and UN sources, described in the section on within-country inequality.

Table 23.4 presents calculations of the contribution to changes in inequality due to changes in incomes per capita between advanced countries and developing countries and changes in incomes per capita among countries in the two groups. The dominant term is the difference in incomes between advanced countries and developing countries (column 1). In 1960–80, this term increases, primarily because China and India, which were among the lowest-income countries, lost ground relative to advanced countries. From 1980 through the 1990s, by contrast, the rapid growth of these countries reduced the log income difference between advanced countries and developing countries. This produces the decline in inequality worldwide among countries in the table. Inequality among advanced countries (column 2) fell in the 1960s and 1970s when Europe and Japan were catching up in income per capita with the USA and was stable in the 1980s and 1990s. Inequality among developing countries (column 3) increased in the 1960s and 1970s when China and India had poor growth experiences relative to other developing countries and decreased when they grew rapidly.

The data underlying these estimates are imperfect. National accounts provide only crude measures of income per capita in developing countries with large informal sectors and subsistence agriculture. Purchasing power parity (PPP) price indices are problematic. Changes in inequality worldwide show different directions with exchange rate adjustments than with purchasing power price indices (Dowrick and Akmal, 2005). Revisions in estimated PPPs can produce large changes in the share of world output in developing countries. For instance, in 2008 the IMF reduced its estimate of China's share of 2007 global output from 15.8% at 10.9% and reduced its estimate of India's share of 2007 global output from 6.4% to 4.6%, due to new and improved purchasing power price indices (<http://imf.org/external/pubs/ft/survey/so/2008/RES018A.htm>).

Still, accepting the income accounts and purchasing power measures as approximately correct, they tell a clear story: inequality measured in relative terms decreased in the era of rapid globalization due to the improved economic performance of developing countries, notably India and China, who together make up one-third of the world's population.

The log variance measures of inequality used in Table 23.4 do not, however, tell the full story about changes in income inequality among countries. For some purposes, we may want to consider measures of absolute inequality, which can move differently than measures of relative inequality. If the initial absolute difference in incomes between two countries is large, even large declines in relative inequality can coincide with increases in absolute income inequality. The reason is that small percentage changes in large numbers can exceed large percentage changes in small numbers, though if differences in percentage changes go on ad infinitum, eventually relative and absolute differences must move in the same direction.

In the situation at hand, the huge differential in incomes between advanced countries and developing countries produces a different pattern of change in inequality measured in absolute income terms than in relative income terms. Table 23.5 illustrates this by comparing the growth rates and the absolute change

Table 23.5. Growth rates of annual GDP per capita and absolute growth in GDP per capita in purchasing power parity prices, USA versus China, 1990–2006

| Country | % annual growth rate 1990–2006 | Change in absolute income in purchasing power parity prices, 1990–2006 |
| --- | --- | --- |
| USA | 1.9 | 11,300 |
| China | 8.9 | 5,700 |

*Source*: Tabulation using the following data:
• 2006: incomes per capita in USA and China, from IMF as reported in Wikipedia <http://en.wikipedia.org/wiki/List_of_countries_by_GDP_(PPP)_per_capita>;
• 1990: incomes per capita, Penn World Tables, PWT6.2. Alan Heston, Robert Summers, and Bettina Aten, Penn World Table Version 6.2, Center for International Comparisons of Production, Income and Prices at the University of Pennsylvania, September 2006.

in incomes per capita between China and the USA from 1990 to 2006. In 1990, the USA had approximately 16 times the income per capita of China. From 1990 to 2006 income per capita grew at 1.9% in the USA compared to 8.9% in China. This reduced the relative income gap between the two countries to about 6:1. But as the table shows, the absolute income gap between the USA and China grew substantially over the period. The revised purchasing power parity price indices referred to earlier would amplify this difference. To the extent that the incentive for persons in lower-income countries to immigrate to advanced countries depends on absolute income differences, the pattern of change in incomes per capita around the world has increased rather than reduced the economic motivation for workers to move from the lower-income countries to the high-income countries.

# 7. INEQUALITY AND LABOR'S SHARE WITHIN COUNTRIES

Finding a sizeable decline in relative inequality among countries is only part of the story of inequality during the period of rapid globalization. Global inequality depends on inequality within countries as well as among countries. The most frequently used measures of inequality within countries are Gini coefficients. Increasingly, however, economists also compare earnings at different percentiles of distributions—for instance earnings at the 90th percentile versus earnings at the 10th percentile. Deininger and Squire (1996) first calculated Gini coefficients from household survey data for many countries over time. The United Nations' Human Development Report regularly publishes estimated Gini coefficients figures and the UN's World Institute for Development Research maintains a large database of Gini coefficients for different countries and surveys. World Bank economists have also mined these data to produce Gini coefficients for developing and advanced economies over time.

The measures of inequality are fraught with data problems. Different surveys sometimes give surprisingly different estimates in the same country. They also differ across countries depending on how surveys treat the self-employed in agriculture or the informal urban sector; whether the data come from income surveys or consumption surveys, and rates of response to surveys. Finally, there is sufficient noise in the data that estimated Gini coefficients or income ratios can vary depending on how analysts treat incomes at the extremes of the distribution.

Data problems notwithstanding, the measures of inequality from percentile wage ratios to Gini coefficients tell a fairly consistent story about within-country income inequality during the period of rapid globalization. Within countries, inequality rose in most cases. Ratios of wages for different percentiles of wage distributions for OECD countries show rising inequality in labor market earnings in nearly all advanced countries in the 1990s, following a mixed pattern of change in earlier periods (OECD, 2004, 2006). The earnings data also show huge differences in the inequality by country, for instance between the Nordic countries and the US. Gini coefficients for developing countries also show a general pattern of rising inequality. And inequality rose from exceedingly low levels in the ex-Soviet bloc economies and in China.

Inequality in income overall depends on the division of output between capital and labor as well as on inequality in labor incomes. Since most citizens rely on earnings from the labor market for their incomes while few rely on earnings from capital, a higher share of GDP going to capital in a country tends to be associated with higher inequality in the distribution of income in total. National income accounts data show that the share of GDP going to capital has risen in many countries while labor's share has fallen (Harrison, 2002; Guscina, 2006; Chapter 5, this volume), which is consistent with increased inequality within countries.

Have increases in inequality of incomes within countries been large enough to counterbalance the decreased inequality of incomes among countries shown in Table 23.4 to produce a rise in inequality among persons worldwide?

One way to answer this question is to take the available Gini coefficients for countries and estimate their change over time. Between 1980 and 2000, I estimate that the Gini coefficient for within-country inequality rose among the developing countries that dominate the world's population, on average, by 0.08 points. I transformed this estimate into changes in inequality in a log income metric and obtained an estimated increase in the standard deviation of the log of incomes of 0.16.[8] This falls far short of the decrease in the standard deviation of log incomes of 0.32 shown in Table 23.4.

To check the robustness of the conclusion, I turned the question around and asked if there were plausible levels of within-country inequality that, with the estimated change in the variance of log incomes, could produce rising inequality. The calculation described in the footnote shows that inequality would have to have been massively larger than statistics show to reverse the conclusion.[9] The narrowing income gap between advanced countries and developing countries due to the growth of China and India is simply too great for any plausible increase in within-country inequality to produce a rise in global inequality.

Why has inequality in developing countries increased counter to the prediction of the H-O model?

A large literature seeks to answer this question. One possible reason for rising inequality in lower-income countries is that skilled workers in developing countries are more comparable in their skills to unskilled workers in advanced countries, so that when developing countries export products previously made by unskilled workers in advanced countries, it raises demand for skilled workers in the developing world. Another possible reason is that developing countries have adopted new technologies from advanced countries, which use skilled workers, rather than unskilled workers. The unskilled may be displaced by the new technologies and end up in low-paid informal sector work. Kremer and Maskin (2003) model this idea by stressing the globalization of the production process rather than globalization of trade in produced goods. But there may be other factors at work as well.[10]

# 8. GLOBALIZATION OR SOMETHING ELSE?

The analysis has focused on patterns of change in inequality during the period of rapid globalization. Given that other factors also determine inequality, the question remains as to whether globalization was a major or minor contributor to the

---

[8]  In the range of measures, the change in standard deviation of lognormal is about twice the change in the Gini, so this turns out to be a simple adjustment.

[9]  Assume an initial $\sigma$ of 0.30 (a reasonable standard deviation of log earnings), then raise it by 0.16 to 0.46. This increases the variance $\sigma^2$ by 0.12 (= $0.46^2 - 0.30^2$) compared to the fall in the variance of 0.32 in Table 23.4. With a smaller initial standard deviation of within-country earnings, the increase in $\sigma^2$ is smaller. Solving the equation $(\sigma + 0.16)^2 - \sigma^2 = 0.32$ shows that it would take an implausibly huge initial $\sigma$ of 0.91 for the 0.16 increase in within-country inequality to be greater than the decrease in cross-country inequality. Thus, no conceivable rise in within-country inequality could overcome the 0.32 drop.

[10]  Zhu and Trefler, 2005.

observed patterns (or perhaps even worked weakly to change inequality in the opposite direction to that observed). Analysts have sought to deal with this possibility and to pin down the magnitude of the effect of globalization on inequality using a range of more detailed calculations and tests.

During the NAFTA debate, Borjas *et al.* (1997) used factor content calculations to assess how much trade shifted demand for unskilled labor and compared the estimated effect of trade with that of immigration. These calculations show that importing goods made by less-skilled workers in developing countries and exporting products made with skilled labor shift the demand–supply balance in favor of skilled workers. Given estimates of responses of relative wages to such shifts, Borjas *et al.* calculated that trade had a modest impact on raising skill differences in the USA and that immigration had a bigger impact. But this was before the 1990s–2000s increased trade with developing countries enlarged the trade impact. While one might expect that increased trade with developing countries in the 2000s would increase labor market pressures on low-paid workers, Mishel *et al.*'s (2007) factor content analysis for the 2000s tells a different story: a more even impact of trade on workers with different skills. This is associated with rapid increases in imports from high-wage industries (Lawrence, 2008) and with the increased competence of developing countries in high-tech sectors (see Table 23.2). By contrast, if one assumes that US firms would use relatively more lesser-skilled workers to produce imported goods than they use to produce domestic goods in the same sector, trade would account for perhaps 20% of the rise in the college to non-college earnings ratio since the 1979.

Diverse studies use cross-country regression models to assess the effect of globalization on inequality and labor's share of income. Many of these studies measure globalization in terms of trade volumes. In their review of the literature, Milanovic and Squire (2007) cite three studies that find little relation between changes in inequality within countries and openness, and four studies that find that increased openness increases inequality, particularly in lower-income countries. No studies find increased openness reducing inequality. Similarly, Harrison (2002) and Guscina (2006) find that higher trade shares are associated with lower shares of labor and that exchange-rate crises also reduce labor's share, though other factors also matter substantively. Harjes (2007) argues that changes in unionization offer a better explanation of changing labor shares than does globalization.

Another set of studies analyze the impact of trade-related policy innovations, such as reductions in tariffs, on inequality within particular countries, often focusing on the changes in sectors or regions most immediately impacted by the policy innovation with changes in other sectors. This assumes that general equilibrium spillovers occur over a longer period than that encompassed in the study. Analyses of this type find that trade increased inequality in Mexico (Hanson and Harrison, 1999; Robertson, 2000), Chile (Beyer *et al.*, 1999), and Brazil (Arbache *et al.*, 2003). In their reviews, Robbins (2003) and Goldberg and Pavcnik (2006) conclude that the research has shown that increased trade and trade barriers are associated with rising inequality in Latin America. But there is disagreement about whether this generalization applies to Brazil. Gonzaga *et al.* (2006) argue that trade reduced skill differences in Brazil while Ferreira *et al.* (2007) argue that trade-induced flows of labor across sectors were one mechanism by which trade reduced inequality. Changes in inequality in Mexico over time also raise questions about the way in which trade has contributed to inequality (Robertson, 2007). The studies for East Asia reviewed by Robbins (2003) do not yield clear results on the impact of trade on inequality in that part of the world.

In sum, while the evidence that trade has contributed to within-country inequality has led trade economists to reject the Heckscher-Ohlin model as a guide to the impact of trade on inequality, there is no consensus on the magnitude of the trade impact and arguments that it has different effects in different countries.

## 9. CONCLUSIONS AND FUTURE RESEARCH

Barring economic or social disaster, the forces of globalization—immigration, trade, education, the transfer of technology and business practices, and capital flows—should move the world towards a global labor market that will over the long run compress country differences in earnings and living standards and thus reduce economic inequality. But the transition to a global labor market is likely to be long and bumpy. Western Europe and Japan needed 30–40 years post-World War II to reach rough parity with the USA; and it took Korea 50 or so years to rise from extreme poverty to the second rung of advanced economies. The large peasant populations in China, India, and in other developing countries make it harder for their labor markets to generate wages and salaries close to those of advanced countries, save for some particular groups. Continued growth of within-country inequality could generate a backlash against globalization in advanced democracies;[11] and could produce political instability in developing countries, particularly those with non-democratic regimes. Concerns over national security and international political disputes could lead some governments to seek to curb flows of labor, capital, and knowledge, as well as trade, and abort the process.

Assuming that the benefits of a global labor market outweigh the costs, policies in advanced and developing countries should lean against the pressures toward

---

[11] The Pew Global Attitudes Project (2007) of opinion around the world shows 'less enthusiasm for trade' among advanced countries and substantial opposition to immigration. Micro-data shows that more highly skilled workers in advanced countries are more favorable to globalization than lower-skilled workers (O'Rourke, 2003).

higher within-country inequality associated with globalization. The international financial institutions and organizations that help set the tone in world policy discourse should rethink their traditional emphasis on protecting capital and de-regulating labor markets in favor of finding ways to protect labor. With so many workers in developing countries in the informal sector, it is important to determine how globalization affects them and to find ways to extend to them social benefits (pensions, occupational health and safety, training, etc.) traditionally associated with formal sector employment.

The unexpected fragmentation of production and growth of offshoring calls for research on measuring the new phenomenon and modeling the incidence of their effects on workers. Going behind trade, I am impressed by the multiple ways in which globalization affects inequality that economists, concerned largely with trade, have not explored intensively: changes in the bargaining power of labor within firms, transfer of technology, immigration, and capital flows. I suspect that the globalization of knowledge will in the long run be more important than trade in goods and services in global economic outcomes. If this is the case, we need to focus on the diffusion of knowledge across locales, of the ways firms transform knowledge into products and activities of economic value, and of how intellectual property rights, pure research and development, education and training impact these processes. If in the knowledge economy, knowledge is the key determinant of outcomes, then globalization of knowledge should lie at the heart of analyses of how globalization affects inequality.

# References

Antràs, P., and Helpman, E. 2004. 'Global Sourcing'. *Journal of Political Economy*, 112(3): 552–80.

Arbache, J., Dickerson, A., and Green, F. 2003. 'A Picture of Wage Inequality and the Allocation of Labor Through a Period of Trade Liberalization: The Case of Brazil'. *World Development*, 29(11): 1923–39.

Arndt, S., and Kierzkowski, H. (eds.) 2001. *Fragmentation: New Production and Trade Patterns in the World Economy*. Oxford: Oxford University Press.

Atkinson, T. 2007. 'The Distribution of Earnings in OECD Countries'. *International Labour Review*, 146(1–2): 41–61.

Beyer, H., Rojas, P., and Vergera, R. 1999. 'Trade Liberalization and Wage Inequality'. *Journal of Development Economics*, 59: 103–23.

Blinder, A. S. 2006. 'Offshoring: The Next Industrial Revolution?' *Foreign Affairs*, Mar./Apr: 113–128.

Borjas, G., Freeman, R. B., and Katz, L. F. 1997. 'How Much Do Immigration and Trade Affect Labor Market Outcomes?' *Brookings Papers on Economic Activity*, 1997(1): 1–90.

COLLINS, S. and LAEL B. 2005. Brookings Trade Forum 2005; Offshoring White-Collar Work: The Issues and Implications. Brookings Institution, Washington DC.

COUNCIL OF ECONOMIC ADVISORS 2008. Economic Report of the President 2008; Washington DC, February 11, 2008.

CRAGG, M. I., and EPELBAUM, M. 1996. 'Why Has Wage Dispersion Grown in Mexico? Is It the Incidence of Reforms or the Growing Demand for Skills?' *Journal of Development Economics*, 51(1): 99–116.

DEBAERE, P. 2003. 'Relative Factor Abundance and Trade'. *Journal of Political Economy*, 111: 589–610.

DEININGER, K. and LYN S. 1996. 'A New Data Set Measuring Income Inequality'. *World Bank Economic Review* 10: 565–91.

DOWRICK, S., and AKMAL, M. 2005. 'Contradictory Trends in Global Income Inequality: A Tale of Two Biases'. *Review of Income and Wealth*, 52(2): 201–29.

EASTERLY, W. 2004. 'Channels from Globalization to Inequality: Productivity World versus Factor World'. *Brookings Trade Forum*, 39–81.

ELLIOTT, K., and FREEMAN, R. 2003. *Can Labor Standards Improve Under Globalization?* Peterson Institiute of Intenational Economics, Washington DC, June 2003.

FEENSTRA, R. C., and HANSON, G. H. 1996. 'Globalization, Outsourcing, and Wage Inequality'. *American Economic Association Papers and Proceedings*, 86(2): 240–5.

——— 1999. 'The Impact of Outsourcing and High-Technology Capital on Wages: Estimates for the United States, 1979–1990'. *Quarterly Journal of Economics*, August, 114(3): 907–40.

FELICIANO, Z. 2001. 'Workers and Trade Liberalization: The Impact of Trade Reforms in Mexico on Wages and Employment'. *Industrial and Labor Relations Review*, 55(1): 95–115.

FERREIRA, F. H. G., LEITE, P. G., and WAI-POI, M. 2007. 'Trade Liberalization, Employment Flows and Wage Inequality in Brazil'. World Bank Policy Research Working Paper 4108, Jan.

FREEMAN, R. B. 2004. 'Trade Wars: The Exaggerated Impact of Trade in Economic Debate'. *The World Economy*, 27(1): 1–23.

——— 2005a. 'The Great Doubling: America in the New Global Economy'. Usery Lecture, Apr. 8, 2005. Georgia State University.

——— 2005b. 'What Really Ails Europe (and America): The Doubling of the Global Workforce'. *The Globalist*, June 3. <http://www.theglobalist.com/StoryId.aspx?StoryId=4542>.

——— 2006. 'People Flows'. *Journal of Economic Perspectives*, 20(2), spring: 145–70.

——— 2008. 'What does the Growth of Higher Education Overseas Mean for the US', conference paper in Charles Clotfelter (ed.), *NBER Conference on American Universities in a Global Market*.

——— and OOSTENDORP, R. H. 2001. 'The Occupational Wages around the World Data File'. *International Labour Review*, 140(4): 379–401.

——— 2003. Occupational Wages Around the World database. 2003 data. <http://www.nber.org/oww/>.

GARRETT, G. 2001. 'The Distributive Consequences of Globalization'. Leitner Working Paper 2001-02. Yale University Leitner Program in International and Comparative Political Economy.

GOLDBERG, P. K., and PAVCNIK, N. 2007. 'Distributional Effects of Globalization in Developing Countries'. *Journal of Economic Literature*, 45(1), Mar: 39–82.

GOMORY, R., and BAUMOL, W. 2000. *Global Trade and Conflicting National Interest.* Cambridge, Mass.: MIT Press.

GONZAGA, G., MENEZES-FILHO, N., and TERRA, C. 2006. 'Trade Liberalization and the Evolution of Skill Earnings Differentials in Brazil'. *Journal of International Economics*, 68(2): 345–67.

GROSSMAN, G. M., and ROSSI-HANSBERG, E. 2006. 'Trading Tasks: A Simple Theory of Offshoring'. NBER Working Paper 12721, Dec.

GUSCINA, A. 2006. 'Effects of Globalization on Labor's Share in National Income'. IMF Working Paper WP06/294.

HAIL, L., and LEUZ, C. 2004. 'International Differences in the Cost of Equity Capital: Do Legal Institutions and Securities Regulation Matter?' University of Pennsylvania, Dec. <http://papers.ssrn.com/sol3/papers.cfm?abstract_id=641981>.

HANSON, G. 2006. 'Globalization, Labor Income, and Poverty in Mexico', in Ann Harrison, *Globalization and Poverty*. NBER.

—— and HARRISON, A. 1999. 'Trade and Wage Inequality in Mexico'. *Industrial* and *Labor Relations Review*, 52: 271–88.

HARJES, T. 2007. 'Globalization and Income Inequality: A European Perspective'. IMF Working Paper no. 07/169, July. Available at SSRN: <http://ssrn.com/abstract=1007918>.

HARRISON, A. 2002. 'Has Globalization Eroded Labor's Share: Cross Country Evidence'. NBER. University of California at Berkeley, Oct.

—— (ed.) 2006. *Globalization and Poverty*, National Bureau of Economic Research Conference volume. Chicago: University of Chicago Press.

HOUSEMAN, S. 2007. 'Outsourcing, Offshoring, and Productivity Measurement in US Manufacturing'. *International Labour Review*, 146(1–2,): 61–82.

JONES, R. W., and KIERZKOWSKI, H. 2005. 'International Trade and Agglomeration: An Alternative Framework'. *The Journal of Economics*, Jan., supplement 10: 1–16.

—— —— and LURONG, C. 2005. 'What Does Evidence Tell Us About Fragmentation and Outsourcing?' in Kierzkowski (2005).

KIERZKOWSKI, H. (ed.) 2005. 'Outsourcing and Fragmentation: Blessing or a Threat?' *International Review of Economics and Finance*, special issue, May.

KLETZER, L., and JENSEN, B. 2005. 'Tradeable Services: Understanding the Scope and Impact of Services Offshoring', in S. Collins and L. Brainerd, Brookings Trade Forum 2005, Offshoring White-Collar Work: The Issues and Implications.

KREMER, M., and MASKIN, E. 2003. 'Globalization and Inequality'. Harvard University, Department of Economics Working Paper.

KRUGMAN, P. 1979. 'A Model of Innovation, Technology Transfer, and the World Distribution of Income'. *The Journal of Political Economy*, 87(2), Apr.: 253–66.

LAWRENCE, R. 2008. 'Blue-Collar Blues: Is Trade to Blame for Rising US Income Inequality?' Peterson Institute for International Economics, Jan.

LI, H., SQUIRE, L., and ZOU, H. 1998. 'Explaining International and Intertemporal Variations in Income Inequality'. *Economic Journal*, 108(446): 26–43.

LUNDBERG, M., and SQUIRE, L. 2003. 'The Simultaneous Evolution of Growth and Inequality'. *Economic Journal*, 113(487): 326–44.

MARKUSEN, J. 2005. 'Modeling the Offshoring of White-Collar Services: From Comparative Advantage to the New Theories of Trade and FDI', in S. Collins and L. Brainerd, Brookings Trade Forum 2005, Offshoring White-Collar Work: The Issues and Implications.

MILANOVIC, B. 2002. 'True World Income Distribution, 1988 and 1993: First Calculation Based on Household Surveys Alone'. *Economic Journal*, 112: 51–92.

—— 2005 'Can We Discern the Effect of Globalization on Income Distribution? Evidence from Household Surveys'. *World Bank Economic Review*, 191: 21–44.

—— and SQUIRE, L. 2006. 'Does Tariff Liberalization Increase Wage Inequality?' in A. Harrison, (ed.), *Globalization and Poverty*. Chicago: Chicago University Press.

MISHEL, L., BERNSTEIN, J., and ALLEGRETTO, S. 2007. *The State of Working America 2006/2007*. Washington and Ithaca, NY: Economic Policy Institute and Cornell University Press.

OECD. 2004. *Employment Outlook, 2004*. Paris: OECD, table 3.2.

—— 2006. *Society at a Glance*, 2006 edition, Table EQ2.1, p. 71.

O'ROURKE, K. 2003. 'Heckscher-Ohlin Theory and Individual Attitudes Toward Globalization'. NBER Working Paper 9872, July.

PEW GLOBAL ATTITUDES PROJECT 2007. Oct. 4. <http://pewglobal.org/reports/pdf/258.pdf>.

ROBBINS, D. 1996. 'HOS Hits Facts: Facts Win. Evidence on Trade and Wages in the Developing World'. Cambridge, Mass.: Harvard University Institute for International Development.

—— 2003. 'The Impact of Trade Liberalization upon Inequality in Developing Countries'. ILO Working Paper 13.

ROBERTSON, R. 2000. 'Trade Liberalisation and Wage Inequality: Lessons from the Mexican Experience'. *The World Economy*, June 23(6): 827–49.

—— 2007. 'Trade and Wages: Two Puzzles from Mexico' *The World Economy*, 30(9) Sep.: 1378–98.

RUFFIN, R. 1999. 'The Nature and Significance of Intra-Industry Trade'. Dallas Federal Reserve Bank. <http://www.dallasfed.org/research/efr/1999/efr9904a.pdf>.

—— and Jones, R. 2007. 'International Technology Transpher: Who Gains and Who Loses?' *Review of International Economics*, 15(2), May: 209–22.

SALA-I-MARTIN, X. 2006. 'The World Distribution of Income: Falling Poverty and . . . Convergence, Period'. *Quarterly Journal of Economics*, 121(2), May: 351–97.

SAMUELSON, P. 2004. 'Where Ricardo and Mill Rebut and Confirm Arguments of Mainstream Economists Supporting Globalization'. *Journal of Economic Perspectives*, 18(3), summer: 135–46.

TREFLER, D. 1995. 'The Case of the Missing Trade and Other Mysteries'. *The American Economic Review*, 85(5), Dec.: 1029–46.

WOOD, A. 1997. 'Openness and Wage Inequality in Developing Countries: The Latin American Challenge to East Asian Conventional Wisdom'. *World Bank Economic Review*, 11: 33–57, 1997.

ZAGHA R., NANKINI, G., and GILL, I. 2006. 'Rethinking Growth'. *Finance and Development*, Mar.

ZHU, S. C., and TREFLER, D. 2005. 'Trade and Inequality in Developing Countries: A General Equilibrium Analysis'. *Journal of International Economics*, 65 Jan.: 21–48.

CHAPTER 24

........................................................................

# POVERTY AND INEQUALITY: THE GLOBAL CONTEXT

........................................................................

## FRANCISCO H. G. FERREIRA

## MARTIN RAVALLION[1]

THE previous chapters in this Handbook have focused primarily on inequality in developed countries. The approximately five billion people who live in low and middle-income countries figured only fleetingly in the plot, as a huge (and possibly a little frightening) cast of extras, who produce cheap internationally tradable goods (Chapter 23) and are potential migrants to richer countries (Chapter 19). Yet, developing countries account for over 80% of the world's population, and experience levels of absolute poverty—and often of inequality too—much greater than those found in developed countries.

This chapter summarizes the recent evidence on global poverty and inequality, including both developed and developing countries. It draws on two main compilations of distributional data created at the World Bank, both of which are

[1] We are grateful to the editors (Brian Nolan, Wiemer Salverda, and Tim Smeeding) and to Branko Milanovic, Berk Ozler, and participants in a symposium at the Russell-Sage Foundation in New York City for helpful comments on an earlier version. Thanks are also due to François Bourguignon, Shaohua Chen, and Branko Milanovic for kindly allowing us to draw on earlier work that we (either one or both of us) co-authored with them in the past, as well as to Phillippe Leite and Prem Sangraula for able assistance and very useful suggestions. However, we alone are responsible for any errors. Furthermore, the opinions expressed in this chapter are those of the authors, and should not be attributed to the World Bank, its Executive Directors, or the countries they represent.

built up from country-specific nationally representative household surveys, generally fielded by national statistical offices. First is the *PovcalNet* data set, which comprises some 560 surveys for 100 low and middle-income countries, representing some 93% of the developing world's population.[2] Where necessary, the *PovcalNet* data set is complemented with information from the *World Development Report* 2006 household survey database, which has a somewhat broader geographical coverage (including many developed countries), but a more limited time-span.

In the first part of the chapter we discuss our poverty and inequality data and present evidence on levels and recent trends in poverty and inequality around the world. Global and regional poverty aggregates are also discussed here. Section 2 turns to the issues involved in aggregating inequality indices across countries, in order to construct a meaningful measure of global inequality. It reviews the main results from the literature that has sought to measure global income inequality, and briefly summarizes some of the evidence on global inequalities in health and education. Section 3 discusses the empirical relationship between economic growth, poverty, and inequality dynamics. Here we present what we see as the three key stylized facts to emerge from these data: the absence of a correlation between growth rates and changes in inequality among developing countries; the strong (positive) correlation between growth rates and rates of poverty reduction, and the importance of inequality to that relationship. In Section 4, in a more speculative mode, we turn to the likely economic determinants of poverty and inequality changes. Section 5 offers some conclusions, and points to some promising research themes within this general topic.

# 1. Poverty and Inequality around the World: A Bird's Eye View

There has been a remarkable expansion in the availability of household surveys in developing countries over the last 25 years. These surveys, which are typically designed and fielded by national statistical agencies, have the measurement of living standards in the population as one of their key objectives. Although clearly there are measurement errors in such data, it is also widely accepted that these data generally represent the best available source of information on the distribution of living standards for any country where they have been conducted.

---

[2] See <http://iResearch.worldbank.org/PovcalNet/jsp/index.jsp>.

Our poverty and inequality measures are constructed for the distributions of household income or consumption per capita, as captured by these surveys. This choice of indicator prompts three caveats. First, by focusing on income or consumption, we end up effectively taking a one-dimensional approach to measuring welfare. It would clearly be desirable to include other important dimensions of welfare not already included in consumption or income (at least directly), such as health status, cognitive functioning, civil and personal freedoms, and environmental quality.[3] Even short of a fully multidimensional approach to welfare, it might well be desirable to include in the aggregate indicator of well-being some measure of the value of access to public and publicly provided goods (such as education and health services, personal security, and access to local infrastructure). But extending welfare measurement in either of these two directions in a manner that allows international comparisons is impossible on the basis of the information available to date. As in most of the preceding chapters in this Handbook, we restrict our attention to the narrow realm of people's ability to consume private goods, as measured by their income or consumption expenditures.

Second, income is not the same thing as consumption. Although over the long run consumption should come quite close to permanent income (except for the limited number of lineages where bequests are important), there can be considerable deviations in the short run, as households either save or dissave. Consumption is thus generally considered a better measure of current welfare than income.[4] In addition, and perhaps of greater practical importance, the questionnaires for income and consumption are perforce quite different, and yield different types of measurement error; see Deaton (1997). As a result of both higher measurement error and of the variance of the transitory component,[5] income inequality tends to be higher than inequality in consumption expenditures in a given population. In the description that follows, we use consumption distributions to construct our poverty and inequality measures wherever possible. Only when consumption data are unavailable in the survey do we report income-based indicators. The type of indicator is noted for each country in Table 24.1.

Third, by looking at the distribution of income or consumption per capita, we are effectively making two strong assumptions, neither of which is likely to hold perfectly. First, we ignore intra-household inequality. Following common practice,

---

[3] The Human Development Index (HDI) is a well-known example of how one can construct an aggregate index that combines income and certain 'non-income' dimensions of welfare. The HDI does not directly reflect inequality within countries and also imposes some questionable aggregation conditions (including trade-offs); for further discussion see Ravallion (1997a). Grimm et al. (2006) provide an ambitious attempt to differentiate the HDI by income groups.

[4] It is sometimes claimed that this argument carries less weight in developed countries, but for a counter-argument see Slesnick (1998).

[5] There tend to be more people dissaving than saving at the bottom of the income distribution, and more people saving than dissaving at the top.

Table 24.1. Poverty and inequality measures for individual countries, 1990s and 2000s

| No. | Country | World Bank's regional classification[N] | GDP per capita, PPP (constant 2000 international $)** | Survey year | y/c | International poverty line | | Inequality | | |
|---|---|---|---|---|---|---|---|---|---|---|
| | | | | | | Population below $1 a day % | Population below $2 a day % | Gini index | MLD | Source* |
| 1 | Albania | ECA | 4,955.27 | 1997 | c | 0.10 | 11.30 | 0.291 | 0.141 | 1 |
| | | | | 2004 | | 0.30 | 9.30 | 0.311 | 0.163 | |
| 2 | Algeria | MNA | 6,375.64 | 1995 | c | 1.10 | 14.40 | 0.353 | 0.215 | 1 |
| | | | | — | | — | — | — | — | |
| 3 | Argentina | LAC | 13,652.41 | 1996 | y | 1.10 | 9.80 | 0.486 | 0.429 | 1 |
| | | | | 2003 | | 6.60 | 17.40 | 0.513 | 0.510 | |
| 4 | Armenia | ECA | 5,011.03 | 1996 | c | 6.80 | 31.80 | 0.444 | 0.343 | 1 |
| | | | | 2003 | | 1.70 | 30.30 | 0.338 | 0.198 | |
| 5 | Australia | HI | 30,677.86 | 1994 | y | — | — | 0.320 | — | 2 |
| | | | | — | | — | — | — | — | |
| 6 | Austria | HI | 30,735.78 | — | y | — | — | — | — | 3 |
| | | | | 2000 | | — | — | 0.290 | — | |
| 7 | Azerbaijan | ECA | 5,953.36 | 1995 | c | 11.50 | 45.80 | 0.350 | 0.211 | 1 |
| | | | | — | | — | — | — | — | |
| 8 | Bangladesh | SAR | 1,916.20 | 1996 | c | 32.90 | 81.90 | 0.330 | 0.185 | 1 |
| | | | | — | | — | — | — | — | |
| 9 | Belarus | ECA | 7,809.61 | 1995 | c | 1.40 | 13.00 | 0.288 | 0.143 | 1 |
| | | | | 2002 | | 0.00 | 1.40 | 0.297 | 0.147 | |
| 10 | Belgium | HI | 30,004.20 | — | y | — | — | — | — | 2 |
| | | | | 2000 | | — | — | 0.260 | — | |
| 11 | Bolivia | LAC | 2,579.16 | — | y | — | — | — | — | 1 |
| | | | | 2002 | | 24.00 | 42.90 | 0.602 | 0.709 | |
| 12 | Bosnia & Herzegovina | ECA | — | — | c | — | — | — | — | 2 |
| | | | | 2001 | | — | — | 0.250 | — | |
| 13 | Botswana | SSA | 11,313.27 | 1994 | c | 28.50 | 56.10 | 0.610 | 0.673 | 1 |
| | | | | — | | — | — | — | — | |
| 14 | Brazil | LAC | 7,825.78 | 1995 | y | 10.50 | 23.30 | 0.615 | 0.756 | 1 |
| | | | | 2004 | | 7.60 | 19.80 | 0.570 | 0.617 | |
| 15 | Bulgaria | ECA | 8,753.89 | 1994 | c | 0.00 | 1.30 | 0.243 | 0.099 | 1 |
| | | | | 2003 | | 0.00 | 6.40 | 0.292 | 0.146 | |
| 16 | Burkina Faso | SSA | 1,142.93 | 1994 | c | 51.40 | 80.10 | 0.507 | 0.441 | 1 |
| | | | | 2003 | | 28.70 | 71.30 | 0.396 | 0.267 | |
| 17 | Burundi | SSA | 629.81 | 1992 | c | 44.10 | 85.10 | 0.333 | 0.183 | 1 |
| | | | | — | | — | — | — | — | |
| 18 | Cambodia | EAP | 2,628.83 | 1994 | c | 82.00 | 96.20 | 0.383 | 0.252 | 1 |
| | | | | 2004 | | 66.00 | 89.80 | 0.429 | 0.307 | |
| 19 | Cameroon | SSA | 2,079.40 | 1996 | c | 35.80 | 71.80 | 0.468 | 0.375 | 1 |
| | | | | — | | — | — | — | — | |
| 20 | Canada | HI | 30,277.87 | — | y | — | — | — | — | 2 |
| | | | | 2000 | | — | — | 0.330 | — | |
| 21 | Cape Verde | SSA | 5,381.04 | — | c | — | — | — | — | 1 |
| | | | | 2001 | | 1.90 | 19.00 | 0.510 | 0.446 | |
| 22 | Central African Rep. | SSA | 1,111.49 | 1993 | c | 66.60 | 84.00 | 0.613 | 0.741 | 1 |
| | | | | — | | — | — | — | — | |
| 23 | Chile | LAC | 10,938.57 | 1994 | y | 0.90 | 10.80 | 0.552 | 0.548 | 1 |
| | | | | 2003 | | 0.50 | 5.60 | 0.549 | 0.539 | |

Table 24.1. (*Continued*)

| No. | Country | World Bank's regional classification[N] | GDP per capita, PPP (constant 2000 international $)[**] | Survey year | y/c | International poverty line | | Inequality | | |
|---|---|---|---|---|---|---|---|---|---|---|
| | | | | | | Population below $1 a day % | Population below $2 a day % | Gini Index | MLD | Source[*] |
| 24 | China | EAP | 6,620.67 | — | c | — | — | — | — | 3 |
| | | | | 2004 | | 9.90 | 34.90 | 0.470 | — | |
| 25 | Hong Kong, China | HI | 32,901.35 | 1996 | | — | — | 0.430 | — | 3 |
| | | | | — | | — | — | — | — | |
| 26 | Colombia | LAC | 6,886.04 | 1995 | y | 3.10 | 16.30 | 0.572 | 0.611 | 1 |
| | | | | 2003 | | 7.60 | 19.40 | 0.588 | 0.669 | |
| 27 | Costa Rica | LAC | 9,646.49 | 1996 | y | 3.60 | 13.30 | 0.471 | 0.419 | 1 |
| | | | | 2003 | | 1.80 | 9.60 | 0.498 | 0.459 | |
| 28 | Côte d'Ivoire | SSA | 1,470.76 | 1995 | c | 12.30 | 49.40 | 0.367 | 0.227 | 1 |
| | | | | 2002 | | 15.70 | 48.40 | 0.484 | 0.409 | |
| 29 | Croatia | ECA | 12,164.04 | — | c | — | — | — | — | 1 |
| | | | | 2001 | | 0.00 | 0.50 | 0.310 | 0.159 | |
| 30 | Czech Rep. | HI | 19,699.53 | 1993 | y | 0.00 | 0.00 | 0.266 | 0.121 | 1 |
| | | | | — | | — | — | — | — | |
| 31 | Denmark | HI | 31,422.48 | 1997 | y | — | — | 0.270 | — | 2 |
| | | | | — | | — | — | — | — | |
| 32 | Dominican Republic | LAC | 7,617.82 | 1996 | y | 1.80 | 11.70 | 0.487 | 0.426 | 1 |
| | | | | 2004 | | 2.80 | 16.20 | 0.516 | 0.476 | |
| 33 | Timor-Leste | EAP | — | — | c | — | — | — | — | 2 |
| | | | | 2001 | | — | — | 0.370 | — | |
| 34 | Ecuador | LAC | 3,981.58 | 1994 | y | 16.80 | 37.40 | 0.520 | 0.511 | 1 |
| | | | | — | | — | — | — | — | |
| 35 | Egypt, Arab Rep. | MNA | 4,031.03 | 1995 | c | 3.80 | 47.00 | 0.326 | 0.179 | 1 |
| | | | | — | | — | — | — | — | |
| 36 | El Salvador | LAC | 4,775.52 | 1995 | y | 20.80 | 47.10 | 0.499 | 0.454 | 1 |
| | | | | 2002 | | 20.40 | 40.50 | 0.523 | 0.541 | |
| 37 | Estonia | HI | 15,885.01 | 1995 | c | 0.40 | 6.90 | 0.301 | 0.155 | 1 |
| | | | | 2003 | | 1.00 | 6.70 | 0.358 | 0.220 | |
| 38 | Ethiopia | SSA | 1,030.17 | 1995 | c | 31.30 | 76.40 | 0.400 | 0.278 | 1 |
| | | | | — | | — | — | — | — | |
| 39 | Finland | HI | 30,420.32 | — | y | — | — | — | — | 2 |
| | | | | 2000 | | — | — | 0.300 | — | |
| 40 | France | HI | 28,876.53 | 1995 | y | — | — | 0.330 | — | 3 |
| | | | | — | | — | — | — | — | |
| 41 | Gambia, The | SSA | 1,744.87 | 1992 | c | 53.70 | 84.00 | 0.478 | 0.402 | 1 |
| | | | | — | | — | — | — | — | |
| 42 | Georgia | ECA | 3,303.92 | 1996 | c | 0.00 | 8.50 | 0.371 | 0.240 | 1 |
| | | | | 2003 | | 6.40 | 25.80 | 0.404 | 0.288 | |
| 43 | Germany | HI | 27,437.59 | — | y | — | — | — | — | 2 |
| | | | | 2000 | | — | — | 0.280 | — | |
| 44 | Ghana | SSA | 2,299.10 | 1992 | c | 47.30 | 84.00 | 0.381 | 0.243 | 1 |
| | | | | — | | — | — | — | — | |
| 45 | Greece | HI | 21,674.64 | — | y | — | — | — | — | 3 |
| | | | | 2000 | | — | — | 0.340 | — | |

(*cont.*)

Table 24.1. (*Continued*)

| No. | Country | World Bank's regional classification[N] | GDP per capita, PPP (constant 2000 international $)** | Survey year | y/c | Population below $1 a day % | Population below $2 a day % | Gini Index | MLD | Source* |
|-----|---------|-----------|------------|------|-----|------|------|------|------|------|
|     |         |           |            |      |     | **International poverty line** | | **Inequality** | | |
| 46 | Guatemala | LAC | 4,150.21 | — | y | — | — | — | — | 1 |
|    |           |     |          | 2002 |   | 13.90 | 32.60 | 0.553 | 0.581 | |
| 47 | Guinea | SSA | 2,107.90 | 1993 | c | — | — | 0.400 | — | 2 |
|    |        |     |          | — |   | — | — | — | — | |
| 48 | Guyana | LAC | 4,203.60 | 1993 | y | 8.10 | 27.00 | 0.516 | 0.499 | 1 |
|    |        |     |          |   |   |   |   |   | — | |
| 49 | Haiti | LAC | 1,479.34 | — | y | — | — | — | — | 1 |
|    |       |     |          | 2001 |   | 52.90 | 77.60 | 0.600 | 0.675 | |
| 50 | Honduras | LAC | 3,170.33 | 1994 | y | 23.70 | 48.20 | 0.552 | 0.573 | 1 |
|    |          |     |          | 2003 |   | 14.10 | 36.00 | 0.539 | 0.523 | |
| 51 | Hungary | ECA | 16,927.87 | 1993 | c | 0.00 | 0.80 | 0.279 | 0.134 | 1 |
|    |         |     |           | 2002 |   | 0.00 | 0.70 | 0.268 | 0.119 | |
| 52 | India | SAR | 3,307.95 | — | c | — | — | — | — | 3 |
|    |       |     |          | 2004 |   | 33.50 | 80.00 | 0.368 | — | |
| 53 | Indonesia | EAP | 3,570.06 | 1993 | c | 17.40 | 64.20 | 0.344 | 0.193 | 1 |
|    |           |     |          | 2002 |   | 7.80 | 52.90 | 0.343 | 0.197 | |
| 54 | Iran, Islamic Rep. | MNA | 7,405.16 | 1994 | c | 0.40 | 7.00 | 0.430 | 0.322 | 1 |
|    |           |     |          | — |   | — | — | — | — | |
| 55 | Ireland | HI | 36,237.93 | — | y | — | — | — | — | 2 |
|    |         |    |           | 2000 |   | — | — | 0.310 | — | |
| 56 | Israel | HI | | — | y | — | — | — | — | 2 |
|    |        |    | | 2000 |   | — | — | 0.310 | — | |
| 57 | Italy | HI | 26,495.73 | — | c | — | — | — | — | 2 |
|    |       |    |           | 2001 |   | — | — | 0.350 | — | |
| 58 | Jamaica | LAC | 3,907.43 | 1993 | c | 4.90 | 27.50 | 0.357 | 0.221 | 1 |
|    |         |     |          | 2004 |   | 0.50 | 14.40 | 0.455 | 0.357 | |
| 59 | Japan | HI | 27,991.92 | 1993 | c | — | — | 0.248 | — | 3 |
|    |       |    |           | 2004 |   | — | — | 0.450 | — | |
| 60 | Jordan | MNA | 5,175.99 | 1992 | c | 0.60 | 10.60 | 0.434 | 0.323 | 1 |
|    |        |     |          | 2002 |   | 0.10 | 7.50 | 0.389 | 0.255 | |
| 61 | Kazakhstan | ECA | 7,652.20 | 1993 | c | 0.40 | 17.50 | 0.327 | 0.179 | 1 |
|    |            |     |          | 2003 |   | 0.90 | 17.10 | 0.339 | 0.194 | |
| 62 | Kenya | SSA | 1,137.37 | 1994 | c | 26.50 | 62.30 | 0.445 | 0.345 | 1 |
|    |       |     |          | — |   | — | — | — | — | |
| 63 | Kuwait | HI | | 1998 | y | — | — | 0.320 | — | 2 |
|    |        |    | | — |   | — | — | — | — | |
| 64 | Kyrgyz Republic | ECA | 1,749.30 | 1993 | c | 8.00 | 17.30 | 0.537 | 0.586 | 1 |
|    |           |     |          | 2003 |   | 0.40 | 23.50 | 0.303 | 0.152 | |
| 65 | Lao PDR | EAP | 2,012.94 | 1992 | c | 18.60 | 74.90 | 0.304 | 0.158 | 1 |
|    |         |     |          | 2002 |   | 27.40 | 74.20 | 0.347 | 0.202 | |
| 66 | Latvia | ECA | 13,724.49 | 1995 | c | 0.00 | 7.00 | 0.310 | 0.167 | 1 |
|    |        |     |           | 2003 |   | 0.50 | 4.40 | 0.377 | 0.247 | |
| 67 | Lebanon | MNA | 4,876.22 | 1995 | c | — | — | 0.630 | — | 2 |
|    |         |     |          | — |   | — | — | — | — | |
| 68 | Lesotho | SSA | 3,104.77 | 1995 | c | 36.40 | 56.00 | 0.631 | 0.840 | 1 |
|    |         |     |          | — |   | — | — | — | — | |

Table 24.1. (*Continued*)

| No. | Country | World Bank's regional classification[N] | GDP per capita, PPP (constant 2000 international $)** | Survey year | y/c | Population below $1 a day % | Population below $2 a day % | Gini Index | MLD | Source* |
|-----|---------|-----------|-----------|------|-----|-----|-----|-----|-----|-----|
| 69 | Lithuania | ECA | 14,020.39 | 1994 | c | 2.50 | 16.00 | 0.373 | 0.242 | 1 |
|    |          |     |           | 2003 |   | 0.60 | 7.50 | 0.360 | 0.224 |   |
| 70 | Macedonia, FYR | ECA | 6,579.66 | – | c | – | – | – | – | 1 |
|    |          |     |           | 2003 |   | 0.20 | 3.30 | 0.390 | 0.263 |   |
| 71 | Madagascar | SSA | 840.15 | 1993 | c | 46.30 | 80.00 | 0.461 | 0.373 | 1 |
|    |          |     |           | – |   | – | – | – | – |   |
| 72 | Malawi | SSA | 631.45 | – | c | – | – | – | – | 1 |
|    |          |     |           | 2004 |   | 20.80 | 63.00 | 0.390 | 0.258 |   |
| 73 | Malaysia | EAP | 10,090.96 | 1995 | y | 0.90 | 13.50 | 0.485 | 0.416 | 1 |
|    |          |     |           | – |   | – | – | – | – |   |
| 74 | Mali | SSA | 942.05 | 1994 | c | 72.30 | 90.60 | 0.505 | 0.437 | 1 |
|    |          |     |           | – |   | – | – | – | – |   |
| 75 | Mauritania | SSA | 2,160.64 | 1993 | c | 49.40 | 81.90 | 0.501 | 0.436 | 1 |
|    |          |     |           | – |   | – | – | – | – |   |
| 76 | Mexico | LAC | 9,967.30 | 1995 | c | 8.40 | 26.00 | 0.537 | 0.528 | 1 |
|    |          |     |           | 2004 |   | 1.90 | 12.50 | 0.461 | 0.379 |   |
| 77 | Moldova | ECA | 2,151.04 | 1992 | c | 7.30 | 31.80 | 0.343 | 0.201 | 1 |
|    |          |     |           | 2003 |   | 1.10 | 20.80 | 0.351 | 0.207 |   |
| 78 | Mongolia | EAP | 2,033.98 | 1995 | c | 13.30 | 48.90 | 0.332 | 0.188 | 1 |
|    |          |     |           | 2002 |   | 10.80 | 44.80 | 0.328 | 0.184 |   |
| 79 | Morocco | MNA | 4,346.35 | 1998 | c | 0.60 | 14.30 | 0.390 | 0.264 | 1 |
|    |          |     |           | – |   | – | – | – | – |   |
| 80 | Mozambique | SSA | 1,162.36 | – | c | – | – | – | – | 1 |
|    |          |     |           | 2002 |   | 36.20 | 74.10 | 0.471 | 0.386 |   |
| 81 | Namibia | SSA | 7,037.76 | 1993 | y | 34.90 | 55.80 | 0.743 | 1.132 | 1 |
|    |          |     |           | – |   | – | – | – | – |   |
| 82 | Nepal | SAR | 1,379.11 | 1996 | c | 34.40 | 77.90 | 0.377 | 0.239 | 1 |
|    |          |     |           | 2003 |   | 24.70 | 64.80 | 0.473 | 0.382 |   |
| 83 | Netherlands | HI | 31,305.98 | – | y | – | – | – | – | 2 |
|    |          |     |           | 1999 |   | – | – | 0.290 | – |   |
| 84 | New Zealand | HI | 23,109.26 | 1997 | y | – | – | 0.370 | – | 2 |
|    |          |     |           | – |   | – | – | – | – |   |
| 85 | Nicaragua | LAC | 3,538.94 | 1993 | c | 47.90 | 77.90 | 0.504 | 0.452 | 1 |
|    |          |     |           | – |   | – | – | – | – |   |
| 86 | Niger | SSA | 700.29 | 1994 | c | 54.80 | 86.10 | 0.415 | 0.291 | 1 |
|    |          |     |           | – |   | – | – | – | – |   |
| 87 | Nigeria | SSA | 1,008.09 | 1993 | c | 59.20 | 85.30 | 0.450 | 0.374 | 1 |
|    |          |     |           | 2003 |   | 71.20 | 92.30 | 0.436 | 0.331 |   |
| 88 | Norway | HI | 37,667.33 | – | y | – | – | – | – | 2 |
|    |          |     |           | 2000 |   | – | – | 0.270 | – |   |
| 89 | Pakistan | SAR | 2,206.29 | 1993 | c | 8.50 | 63.00 | 0.303 | 0.157 | 1 |
|    |          |     |           | 2004 |   | 9.00 | 59.50 | 0.312 | 0.165 |   |
| 90 | Panama | LAC | 7,234.06 | 1995 | y | 7.40 | 17.40 | 0.571 | 0.645 | 1 |
|    |          |     |           | 2003 |   | 6.00 | 16.80 | 0.561 | 0.603 |   |
| 91 | Papua New Guinea | EAP | 2,321.83 | 1996 | c | – | – | 0.509 | – | 3 |
|    |          |     |           | – |   | – | – | – | – |   |

(*cont.*)

Table 24.1. (Continued)

| No. | Country | World Bank's regional classification[N] | GDP per capita, PPP (constant 2000 international $)[**] | Survey year | y/c | International poverty line | | Inequality | | |
|---|---|---|---|---|---|---|---|---|---|---|
| | | | | | | Population below $1 a day % | Population below $2 a day % | Gini Index | MLD | Source[*] |
| 92 | Paraguay | LAC | 4,368.11 | 1995 | y | 19.40 | 38.50 | 0.591 | 0.687 | 1 |
| | | | | 2003 | | 13.60 | 29.80 | 0.584 | 0.660 | |
| 93 | Peru | LAC | 5,725.07 | 1994 | y | 9.40 | 31.60 | 0.449 | 0.350 | 1 |
| | | | | 2003 | | 10.50 | 30.60 | 0.520 | 0.489 | |
| 94 | Philippines | EAP | 4,730.58 | 1994 | c | 18.10 | 52.70 | 0.429 | 0.306 | 1 |
| | | | | 2003 | | 13.50 | 43.90 | 0.445 | 0.332 | |
| 95 | Poland | ECA | 13,349.33 | 1993 | c | 4.10 | 11.80 | 0.324 | 0.208 | 1 |
| | | | | 2002 | | 0.10 | 1.50 | 0.341 | 0.197 | |
| 96 | Portugal | HI | 18,965.97 | 1994–97 | y | <2 | < 2 | 0.390 | – | 2 |
| | | | | – | | – | – | – | – | |
| 97 | Romania | ECA | 8,721.79 | 1994 | c | 2.80 | 27.40 | 0.282 | 0.136 | 1 |
| | | | | 2003 | | 1.10 | 12.60 | 0.311 | 0.169 | |
| 98 | Russian Federation | ECA | 10,349.98 | 1993 | c | 6.10 | 22.70 | 0.483 | 0.420 | 1 |
| | | | | 2002 | | 0.70 | 13.50 | 0.399 | 0.273 | |
| 99 | Rwanda | SSA | 1,104.69 | – | c | – | – | – | – | 1 |
| | | | | 2000 | | 60.30 | 87.80 | 0.470 | 0.378 | |
| 100 | Senegal | SSA | 1,598.65 | 1995 | c | 24.00 | 65.70 | 0.414 | 0.296 | 1 |
| | | | | – | | – | – | – | – | |
| 101 | Serbia & Montenegro | ECA | – | – | c | – | – | – | – | 2 |
| | | | | 2003 | | – | – | 0.280 | – | |
| 102 | Sierra Leone | SSA | 752.51 | 1989 | c | 57.00 | 74.20 | 0.630 | 0.732 | 1 |
| | | | | – | | – | – | – | – | |
| 103 | Singapore | HI | 28,305.42 | 1998 | y | – | – | 0.430 | – | 2 |
| | | | | – | | – | – | – | – | |
| 104 | Slovak Rep. | ECA | 15,408.87 | 1992 | y | 0.00 | 0.00 | 0.195 | 0.066 | 1 |
| | | | | – | | – | – | – | – | |
| 105 | Slovenia | HI | 20,890.20 | 1993 | c | 0.00 | 0.00 | 0.292 | – | 2 |
| | | | | – | | – | – | – | – | |
| 106 | South Africa | SSA | 10,337.77 | 1995 | c | 6.30 | 32.20 | 0.566 | 0.564 | 1 |
| | | | | – | | – | – | – | – | |
| 107 | Spain | HI | 24,680.95 | – | y | – | – | – | – | 2 |
| | | | | 2000 | | – | – | 0.350 | – | |
| 108 | Sri Lanka | SAR | 4,391.40 | 1996 | c | 6.60 | 45.40 | 0.344 | 0.199 | 1 |
| | | | | 2002 | | 5.80 | 41.50 | 0.402 | 0.271 | |
| 109 | St. Lucia | LAC | 6,482.11 | 1995 | y | 25.20 | 59.60 | 0.426 | 0.316 | 1 |
| | | | | – | | – | – | – | – | |
| 110 | Swaziland | SSA | 4,440.13 | 1995 | c | 68.20 | 87.40 | 0.607 | 0.688 | 1 |
| | | | | – | | – | – | – | – | |
| 111 | Sweden | HI | 30,392.45 | – | y | – | – | – | – | 2 |
| | | | | 2000 | | – | – | 0.250 | – | |
| 112 | Switzerland | HI | 32,775.22 | – | y | – | – | – | – | 3 |
| | | | | 2000 | | – | – | 0.340 | – | |
| 113 | Tajikistan | ECA | 1,256.90 | – | c | – | – | – | – | 1 |
| | | | | 2003 | | 7.00 | 42.50 | 0.326 | 0.179 | |
| 114 | Tanzania | SSA | 649.53 | – | c | – | – | – | – | 1 |
| | | | | 2000 | | 57.00 | 90.20 | 0.350 | – | |

Table 24.1. (*Continued*)

| No. | Country | World Bank's regional classification[N] | GDP per capita, PPP (constant 2000 international $)** | Survey year | y/c | International poverty line | | Inequality | | |
|---|---|---|---|---|---|---|---|---|---|---|
| | | | | | | Population below $1 a day % | Population below $2 a day % | Gini Index | MLD | Source* |
| 115 | Thailand | EAP | 8,065.13 | 1992 | c | 6.00 | 37.50 | 0.462 | 0.357 | 1 |
| | | | | 2002 | | 0.90 | 25.80 | 0.420 | 0.297 | |
| 116 | Trinidad & Tobago | HI | 14,708.07 | 1992 | y | 5.10 | 23.20 | 0.403 | 0.288 | 1 |
| | | | | – | | – | – | – | – | |
| 117 | Tunisia | MNA | 7,758.15 | 1995 | c | 1.00 | 12.70 | 0.417 | 0.301 | 1 |
| | | | | – | | – | – | – | – | |
| 118 | Turkey | ECA | 7,842.15 | 1994 | c | 2.40 | 18.00 | 0.415 | 0.299 | 1 |
| | | | | 2003 | | 3.20 | 19.40 | 0.437 | 0.335 | |
| 119 | Turkmenistan | ECA | – | 1993 | c | 20.70 | 59.10 | 0.354 | 0.209 | 1 |
| | | | | – | | – | – | – | – | |
| 120 | Uganda | SSA | 1,312.82 | 1992 | c | 90.30 | 98.10 | 0.426 | 0.319 | 1 |
| | | | | 2002 | | 82.30 | 95.70 | 0.458 | 0.364 | |
| 121 | Ukraine | ECA | 6,605.20 | 1995 | c | 2.10 | 14.80 | 0.393 | 0.267 | 1 |
| | | | | 2003 | | 0.20 | 5.00 | 0.281 | 0.133 | |
| 122 | United Kingdom | HI | 30,237.16 | – | y | – | – | – | – | 2 |
| | | | | 1999 | | – | – | 0.340 | – | |
| 123 | United States | HI | 38,165.25 | – | y | – | – | – | – | 2 |
| | | | | 2000 | | – | – | 0.380 | – | |
| 124 | Uruguay | LAC | 9,897.78 | 1996 | y | 0.60 | 4.60 | 0.438 | 0.344 | 1 |
| | | | | 2004 | | 0.00 | 9.20 | 0.461 | 0.378 | |
| 125 | Uzbekistan | ECA | 1,942.35 | 1993 | c | 3.30 | 26.50 | 0.333 | 0.189 | 1 |
| | | | | 2003 | | 0.00 | 1.80 | 0.367 | 0.230 | |
| 126 | Venezuela, RB de | LAC | 6,485.33 | 1995 | y | 9.40 | 28.80 | 0.468 | 0.402 | 1 |
| | | | | 2003 | | 18.70 | 40.20 | 0.482 | 0.461 | |
| 127 | Vietnam | EAP | 2,924.84 | 1993 | c | 14.60 | 58.20 | 0.357 | 0.214 | 1 |
| | | | | 2004 | | 0.60 | 21.90 | 0.371 | 0.229 | |
| 128 | Yemen, Rep. | MNA | 857.68 | 1992 | c | 3.40 | 19.90 | 0.395 | 0.268 | 1 |
| | | | | – | | – | – | – | – | |
| 129 | Zambia | SSA | 949.10 | 1993 | c | 73.60 | 90.70 | 0.526 | 0.518 | 1 |
| | | | | 2004 | | 60.00 | 84.90 | 0.507 | 0.467 | |
| 130 | Zimbabwe | SSA | 1,738.57 | 1995 | c | 56.10 | 83.00 | 0.501 | 0.433 | 1 |
| | | | | – | | – | – | – | – | |

*Notes*: [N] The World Bank classifies countries regionally and among income groups according to 2006 nominal GNI per capita, calculated using the World Bank Atlas method. High-income countries have GNI per capita of $11,116 or more. ECA = Eastern Europe and Central Asia; MNA = Middle-East and North Africa; EAP = East Asia and the Pacific; SAR = South Asia; SSA = Sub-Saharan Africa; LAC = Latin America and Caribbean; HI = High Income. y = income; c = consumption;

* 1 = PovcalNet; 2 = WDR 06; 3 = WDI;

** *Source*: the World Bank Indicators, reference year 2006.

such inequality is simply assumed away from our computations. Secondly, even if one is forced to use a single indicator for each household, it is not clear that the per capita definition is the most appropriate. There are differences in needs across age groups (and possibly genders), and there may well be certain fixed costs or 'household public goods' that generate economies of scale in consumption at the household level.[6] Both of these considerations have led many analysts to use some measure of 'equivalent income' as their welfare indicator for each household. However, these variables turn out to be quite sensitive to the different assumptions made in identifying specific equivalence scales from observed demand behavior, and there is no agreement on which particular scale should be used.[7] There is likely to be more agreement, in fact, with the statement that different scales may be appropriate for different settings (such as, say, South Korea and Togo). All this implies that seeking to introduce sensitivity to household size and composition in the context of international comparisons is, given the present state of knowledge, likely to contribute to less, not more, clarity.

Having agreed on the choice of welfare indicator, the next challenge is the aggregation of the national distributions into scalar poverty or inequality indices. This is a much easier problem in the case of relative inequality measures that are, by construction, scale-invariant.[8] Since these measures do not depend on mean incomes or on the currency in which income is expressed, a number of vexing issues to do with Purchasing Power Parity (PPP) exchange rates and with the relevance of national account means to welfare measurement (to which we return below when discussing poverty measures) can be safely ignored. The inequality indices reported in Table 24.1 are therefore simple Gini indices and mean log deviations (MLD), computed over the original distribution of household consumption (or income) per person in each country's nominal currency, in each year. Unlike the Gini index, MLD is additively decomposable into between-group and within-group inequality components (Bourguignon, 1979).

Absolute poverty measures, on the other hand, summarize the extent of deprivation in a distribution with respect to a specific welfare threshold, given by the poverty line. This implies that scale matters, and so does the choice of mean (e.g. mean income from a household survey, or GDP per capita) and exchange rate when making inter-country comparisons or aggregations. It has been argued that misreporting of incomes in household surveys would justify scaling up the income distribution so that its mean equaled per capita consumption in the Private Consumption account in the National Accounts System (NAS).[9] But such an approach ignores the fact that the Private Consumption account includes components of institutional consumption as well as personal consumption, which could introduce a systematic overstatement of household welfare levels. Things are even worse if the scaling up is to GDP per capita itself, rather than only to per capita consumption from the NAS.

---

[6]  See Lanjouw and Ravallion (1995).

[7]  See Coulter *et al.* (1992) and Chapter 3 of this Handbook.

[8]  Absolute inequality measures, which may well be relevant for the discussion of global trends, are scale-sensitive. We return to absolute measures of inequality in Section 2 below.

[9]  See e.g. Sala-i-Martin (2006).

In addition, in economies with substantial subsistence agriculture and other forms of production for own consumption, it is not clear that the national accounts system provides a more accurate portrayal of real consumption than the surveys, which typically include information on consumption from own production at the household level. Finally, it is unlikely that income under-reporting or selective compliance in surveys is distribution-neutral.[10] If richer households under-report more than middle-income or poorer households, then the uniform re-scaling that is proposed would result in an unwarranted under-estimation of poverty. It appears likely that richer households are also less likely to participate in surveys. This has theoretically ambiguous implications for inequality, although there is evidence (for the USA) that it entails a non-negligible under-estimation of overall inequality (Korinek et al., 2006). In what follows we do not use National Accounts information to re-scale mean incomes or consumption from the surveys (although NAS data are used in the interpolation method of Chen and Ravallion, 2004a, which is used for 'lining up' household surveys with the reference years used in Tables 24.2 and 24.3).

In this chapter, we report poverty measures with respect to the World Bank's 'standard' international poverty line of about $1 a day (or, more precisely, $32.74 per month, at 1993 international PPP exchange rates).[11] This is a deliberately conservative definition of 'poverty', being anchored to the poverty lines typical of low-income countries. It is also one that has acquired considerable currency in international policy discussions: The first Millennium Development Goal (MDG1), for example, is to halve the 1990 '$1 a day' poverty rate by 2015. To gauge sensitivity, we also use a line set at twice this value, $65.48 per person per month. Following common practice we refer to these as the '$1 a day' and '$2 a day' lines ($1.08 and $2.15 would be more precise). The higher line is more representative of what 'poverty' means in middle-income developing countries.

These international lines are converted to local currencies using the Bank's 1993 PPP exchange rates for consumption, and each country's consumer price index (CPI). PPP exchange rates adjust for the fact that non-traded goods tend to be cheaper in poorer countries. There is more than one way to calculate PPP exchange rates. The Geary–Khamis (GK) method used by the Penn World Tables (PWT) uses quantity weights to compute the international price indices. For our purposes, this method gives too high a weight to consumption patterns in richer countries when measuring poverty globally. The Elteto–Kones–Sculc (EKS) method—a multilateral extension of the usual bilateral Fisher index—attempts to correct for this bias. Since 2000, the World Bank's global poverty and inequality measures have been based on the Bank's PPP rates, which use the EKS method.[12] At the time of writing, new PPP

---

[10]  See e.g. Banerjee and Piketty (2005) and Korinek et al. (2006).

[11]  See Chen and Ravallion (2001) for a detailed description of how this line was constructed.

[12]  For further discussion of the difference between these two methods and the bearing on poverty measurement see Ackland et al. (2006).

Table 24.2. Poverty measures for $1 a day: world and regional averages

| Region | 1981 | 1984 | 1987 | 1990 | 1993 | 1996 | 1999 | 2002 | 2004 |
|---|---|---|---|---|---|---|---|---|---|
| **(a) Percentage of population** | | | | | | | | | |
| East-Asia and Pacific (EAP) | 57.73 | 39.02 | 28.23 | 29.84 | 25.23 | 16.14 | 15.46 | 12.33 | 9.05 |
| Of which China | 63.76 | 41.02 | 28.64 | 32.98 | 28.36 | 17.37 | 17.77 | 13.79 | 9.90 |
| Eastern-Europe + Central Asia (ECA) | 0.70 | 0.51 | 0.35 | 0.46 | 3.60 | 4.42 | 3.78 | 1.27 | 0.94 |
| Latin America + Caribbean (LAC) | 10.77 | 13.07 | 12.09 | 10.19 | 8.42 | 8.87 | 9.66 | 9.09 | 8.64 |
| Middle East + North Africa (MNA) | 5.08 | 3.82 | 3.09 | 2.33 | 1.87 | 1.69 | 2.08 | 1.69 | 1.47 |
| South Asia (SAS) | 49.57 | 45.43 | 45.11 | 43.04 | 36.87 | 36.06 | 34.92 | 33.56 | 30.84 |
| Of which India | 51.75 | 47.94 | 46.15 | 44.31 | 41.82 | 39.94 | 37.66 | 36.03 | 34.33 |
| Sub-Saharan Africa (SSA) | 42.26 | 46.20 | 47.22 | 46.73 | 45.47 | 47.72 | 45.77 | 42.63 | 41.10 |
| Total | **40.14** | **32.72** | **28.72** | **28.66** | **25.56** | **22.66** | **22.10** | **20.13** | **18.09** |
| Total excl. China | 31.35 | 29.69 | 28.75 | 27.14 | 24.58 | 24.45 | 23.54 | 22.19 | 20.70 |
| **(b) Number of people** | | | | | | | | | |
| EAP | 796.40 | 564.30 | 428.76 | 476.22 | 420.22 | 279.09 | 276.54 | 226.77 | 169.13 |
| China | 633.66 | 425.27 | 310.43 | 374.33 | 334.21 | 211.44 | 222.78 | 176.61 | 128.36 |
| ECA | 3.00 | 2.27 | 1.61 | 2.16 | 16.94 | 20.87 | 17.90 | 6.01 | 4.42 |
| LAC | 39.35 | 50.90 | 50.00 | 44.60 | 38.83 | 42.96 | 49.03 | 48.13 | 47.02 |
| MNA | 8.81 | 7.26 | 6.41 | 5.26 | 4.53 | 4.38 | 5.67 | 4.88 | 4.40 |
| SAS | 455.18 | 445.05 | 471.14 | 479.10 | 436.74 | 452.91 | 463.40 | 469.55 | 446.20 |
| India | 363.72 | 359.41 | 368.60 | 376.44 | 376.14 | 378.91 | 376.25 | 377.84 | 370.67 |
| SSA | 167.53 | 199.78 | 222.80 | 240.34 | 252.26 | 286.21 | 296.07 | 296.11 | 298.30 |
| Total | **1470.28** | **1269.56** | **1180.73** | **1247.68** | **1170.17** | **1087.81** | **1108.61** | **1051.46** | **969.48** |
| Total excl. China | 836.62 | 844.29 | 870.30 | 873.35 | 835.96 | 876.37 | 885.83 | 874.85 | 841.12 |

*Source:* Chen and Ravallion (2007). The set of countries are the Part 2 member countries of the World Bank, which is essentially all low and middle-income countries, which the Bank currently defines as having average GDP per capita over 2004–6 of no more than $11,115.

Table 24.3. Poverty measures for $2 a day: world and regional averages

| Region | 1981 | 1984 | 1987 | 1990 | 1993 | 1996 | 1999 | 2002 | 2004 |
|---|---|---|---|---|---|---|---|---|---|
| (a) Percentage of population | | | | | | | | | |
| EAP | 84.80 | 77.17 | 68.53 | 69.73 | 65.04 | 52.49 | 49.34 | 41.68 | 36.58 |
| China | 88.12 | 79.00 | 68.64 | 72.16 | 68.13 | 53.34 | 50.05 | 40.94 | 34.89 |
| ECA | 4.60 | 3.93 | 3.08 | 4.31 | 16.53 | 17.97 | 18.57 | 12.88 | 9.79 |
| LAC | 28.45 | 32.25 | 29.57 | 26.25 | 24.09 | 25.24 | 25.31 | 24.76 | 22.17 |
| MNA | 29.16 | 25.59 | 24.24 | 21.69 | 21.41 | 21.40 | 23.62 | 21.09 | 19.70 |
| SAS | 88.53 | 87.01 | 86.57 | 85.62 | 82.22 | 82.12 | 80.41 | 79.73 | 77.12 |
| India | 88.92 | 87.89 | 86.98 | 86.30 | 85.33 | 84.12 | 82.67 | 81.37 | 80.36 |
| SSA | 74.52 | 76.98 | 77.36 | 77.05 | 76.09 | 76.42 | 75.85 | 73.81 | 71.97 |
| Total | 66.96 | 64.25 | 60.73 | 60.79 | 59.44 | 55.52 | 54.24 | 50.69 | 47.55 |
| Total excl. China | 59.08 | 58.87 | 57.89 | 56.78 | 56.43 | 56.26 | 55.63 | 53.85 | 51.58 |
| (b) Number of people (millions) | | | | | | | | | |
| EAP | 1169.74 | 1115.97 | 1040.71 | 1112.93 | 1083.21 | 907.83 | 882.70 | 766.26 | 683.83 |
| China | 875.77 | 819.11 | 744.07 | 819.11 | 802.86 | 649.47 | 627.55 | 524.24 | 452.25 |
| ECA | 19.78 | 17.38 | 14.03 | 20.07 | 77.83 | 84.88 | 87.94 | 60.75 | 46.25 |
| LAC | 103.90 | 125.58 | 122.30 | 114.85 | 111.08 | 122.30 | 128.44 | 131.14 | 120.62 |
| MNA | 50.56 | 48.62 | 50.24 | 48.91 | 51.80 | 55.40 | 64.50 | 60.92 | 59.13 |
| SAS | 813.04 | 852.39 | 904.21 | 953.00 | 973.99 | 1031.48 | 1067.15 | 1115.54 | 1115.77 |
| India | 624.92 | 658.92 | 694.71 | 733.13 | 767.39 | 798.07 | 825.93 | 853.32 | 867.62 |
| SSA | 295.46 | 332.87 | 365.02 | 396.32 | 422.11 | 458.37 | 490.58 | 512.62 | 522.34 |
| Total | 2452.47 | 2492.81 | 2496.50 | 2646.09 | 2721.72 | 2665.66 | 2721.31 | 2647.22 | 2547.94 |
| Total excl. China | 1576.70 | 1673.70 | 1752.42 | 1826.98 | 1918.86 | 2016.19 | 2093.75 | 2122.98 | 2095.69 |

*Note*: For region identifiers see Table 24.2.

*Source*: Chen and Ravallion (2007).

rates, based on 2005 prices, are about to become available. While existing poverty and inequality measures have not yet been revised accordingly, we comment later on some of the likely implications.

Once the international poverty lines have been appropriately converted into local currency, and local CPI has been used to inflate the line to the nominal currency of the survey year, poverty measures are calculated for each survey year. Naturally, different countries do not all field their household surveys (which are rarely annual) in the same year. In Table 24.1, we report the year(s) in which the latest surveys available to us were conducted in each country, and report poverty measures for those years. In Tables 24.2 and 24.3, where we seek to describe regional and global poverty aggregates, the poverty measures are lined up in time for each of a set of 'reference years' using the interpolation method described in Chen and Ravallion (2004a).

We will focus on the most common poverty measure, namely the headcount index ($H$), which gives the proportion of the country's population that lives in households with per capita incomes below the poverty line. Other measures are the poverty gap index ($PG$), which gives the average shortfall of income from that line, where the average is taken over the entire population (with the gap set to zero for incomes higher than the poverty line); the squared poverty gap index (Foster et al., 1984); and the Watts (1968) index. The latter two measures penalize inequality amongst the poor, and so are better at picking up differences in the severity of poverty. *PovcalNet* provides all these measures. In some of the discussion, we also multiply $H$ by the country's population, to yield the absolute number of poor people.

Table 24.1 presents the two inequality measures (Gini and MLD) and $H$ for the two poverty lines for every country for which we have household-survey data.[13] Wherever possible, we present results for two periods: (i) the 1990s (centered on 1994), and (ii) the 2000s (centered on 2004). Since most surveys have less-than-annual frequency and since countries field their surveys on different schedules, for each country we use the survey nearest to the two period centers, and indicate the year in the table.

The range of inequality measures across the 130 countries in Table 24.1 is very large indeed. The Gini index ranges from 0.20 in the Slovak Republic, to 0.74 in Namibia. The MLD ranges from 0.12 in Hungary to 0.71 in Bolivia using data for the 2000s; using data for the 1990s, the range is from 0.07 in the Slovak Republic to 1.13 in Namibia. In terms of country groupings, the high-income economies (including the OECD) and Eastern Europe and Central Asia (ECA) record the lowest inequality measures, and Sub-Saharan Africa (SSA) and Latin America and the Caribbean (LAC) have the highest. The predominance of measures using income,

---

[13]  An extended version of Table 24.1 is available from the authors giving $PG$ for both poverty lines.

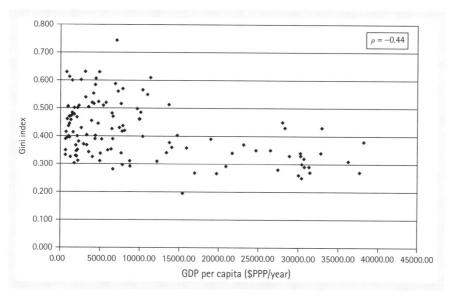

**Fig. 24.1. Income levels and inequality around the world**

rather than consumption, in LAC is a contributing factor to the high-inequality measures for that region. The high level of inequality in SSA thus deserves special mention, as many of the indices refer to distributions of consumption expenditures. The commonly held view that LAC is unambiguously the most unequal region in the world needs to be qualified accordingly.

Figure 24.1 plots inequality (measured by the latest available Gini coefficient) against GDP per capita for each country listed in Table 24.1. The figure reveals a negative correlation between inequality and mean incomes (measured by GDP per capita). The correlation coefficient is −0.44 (statistically significant at the 1% level). In addition, the variance of inequality is higher among poorer countries, but much smaller among richer ones. Above $20,000 per capita per annum, all Gini indices lie in the relatively narrow interval of (0.25, 0.45). The implication is that no country has successfully developed beyond middle-income status while retaining a very high level of inequality in income or consumption. High inequality (a Gini above 0.5, say) is a feature of underdevelopment. We do not explore the difficult issue of causality here: is it that high-inequality prevents growth, or is it that growth tends to reduce inequality? These issues are the subject of a large literature, which is summarized in Chapter 22. We simply note the significant negative correlation in levels, and that very high levels of inequality are not observed among rich countries in the present-day cross-section.

In terms of changes over time, there is no universal or common trend in in-equality between the 1990s and 2000s. Out of the 49 countries in Table 24.1 that have inequality measures for both periods, 30 (29) record an increase in the Gini

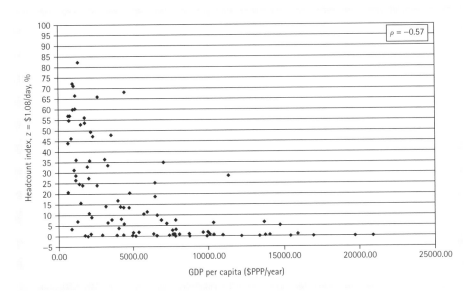

Fig. 24.2. Income levels and poverty around the world

(MLD[14]) index, 13 (16) record declines, and in 6 (3) countries there has been little or no change, which we (somewhat arbitrarily) define as being in the range (−2.5%, 2.5%). These numbers are consistent with the evidence of rising within-country inequality discussed in Chapter 23, but we caution against over-interpreting results in a selected sample of some 50 countries for which data were available on both periods.

The situation is somewhat different with regard to poverty: there is even greater variation in levels, the correlation with mean incomes is more pronounced, and there is a clearer pattern in the recent changes. Two important facts can be gleaned from Figure 24.2, which plots $H$ (for the $1-a-day threshold) against GDP per capita. The first is that absolute poverty incidence decreases markedly with mean income, as one would expect. The simple correlation coefficient is −0.57 and statistically significant at the 1% level. Above a GNP per capita of approximately $15,000 p.a., this extreme kind of absolute poverty essentially vanishes.[15] In fact, dollar-a-day poverty is not even estimated for the high-income countries listed in Table 24.1, and they are not included in Figure 24.2. The second fact is that this relationship between mean income and poverty is not statistically 'tight'. The points

---

[14]  Forty-nine countries report Gini coefficients in both periods. Forty-eight report MLDs in both periods.

[15]  Which may explain why researchers looking at developed countries tend to be more concerned with inequality than with poverty and, even when addressing the latter, usually rely on alternative concepts of poverty, such as relative poverty, social exclusion (see Chapter 13), or 'low pay' (see Chapter 11).

in Figure 24.2 do not lie neatly along a specific curve or line. Below a per capita GDP of around $12,000, there is considerable variation in the incidence of extreme poverty for each level of mean income. In fact, at around $2,000, one can find countries with the same per capita income levels reporting poverty rates in a range from zero to 65%. Latent country-level heterogeneity may well be confounding the ability to detect the true relationship; we will return to this point. However, as we will see in the next section, this heterogeneity in poverty levels conditional on mean incomes has a lot to do with between-country differences in the level of inequality.

To look at poverty trends over time, we resort to a longer time series than the one presented in Table 24.1. Chen and Ravallion (2007) compile poverty time-series indicators for 560 surveys from 100 countries (essentially the same sample of countries used by *PovcalNet*). Since poverty incidence at the $1-a-day threshold is effectively zero in high-income economies (which accounts for the main differences between the *PovcalNet* data set and that presented in Table 24.1) we restrict our attention to the Chen–Ravallion sample of countries.

Tables 24.2 and 24.3 present the world and regional average poverty levels, both as incidence ($H$) and in absolute numbers of the poor for selected reference years spanning 1981–2004. Table 24.2 uses the $1-a-day poverty line, while Table 24.3 uses the $2-a-day line. There is clear evidence of a decline in absolute poverty in the developing world over the last quarter-century. The incidence of $1-a-day poverty, as a proportion of the developing world's population, fell from 40% in 1981 to 18% in 2004. By 2004, the developing world as a whole was only four percentage points short of attaining MDG1 (a poverty rate of 14.3% by 2015). The corresponding proportions for the total population of the world are 34% and 15%, assuming that nobody lives below $1 a day in the high-income countries. Although the rapid reduction of poverty in China (from 63% to 10%) accounts for much of this global decline, there has clearly been progress elsewhere too: global poverty incidence excluding China falls from 31% to 21% over 1981–2004.

The rates of poverty reduction have been quite disparate in different countries. If one partitions the country sample into the broad regions defined by the World Bank, we see clear heterogeneity in poverty reduction across regions (Table 24.2). The most pronounced decline was registered in East Asia (from 58% to 9%). South Asia came second, with a fall from 50% to 31%. At the other end of the spectrum, poverty incidence actually rose in ECA during the period of transition from so-cialism to market economies, though showing encouraging signs of progress since the late 1990s. In Sub-Saharan Africa, poverty was essentially the same in 2004 and 1981, having first grown during the 1980s, and then declined slowly since the late 1990s. Such a small decline in poverty rates, combined with a growing population, translates into a rise in the absolute number of people living in households below the $1-a-day poverty line, as can be seen from panel (b) in Table 24.2. In fact, the

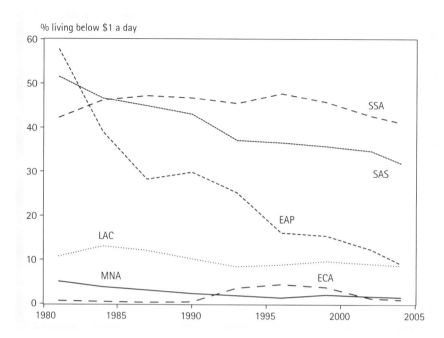

**Fig. 24.3. Trends in the incidence of absolute poverty in less developed countries, by region**

*Note*: For region identifiers see Table 24.2.
*Source*: Chen and Ravallion (2007).

number of poor people rose not only in Africa and Eastern Europe and Central Asia, but also in Latin America, where economic stagnation and persistent inequality in the last decades prevented substantial progress against poverty. These regional trends in poverty reduction are summarized in Figure 24.3, which is also taken from Chen and Ravallion (2007). The dominant role of poverty reduction in East Asia is immediately apparent.

Trends are somewhat more muted for the $2-a-day poverty line. Global incidence in the developing world fell from 67% to 48% (59% to 52% if China is excluded). Poverty also fell markedly in the Middle East and North Africa (MENA), and South Asia, but doubled in ECA. Because of population growth, the absolute number of poor people (under $2-a-day) rose in every region other than East Asia. Given a very substantial decline in East Asia, the world total grew only slightly, from 2.45 billion to 2.55 billion. This is in contrast to a decline in the absolute number of poor (under $1-a-day), from 1.47 billion to 0.97 billion in the same period. See Tables 24.2 and 24.3.[16]

---

[16] For a more detailed discussion, including their recent estimates when accounting for cost-of-living differences between rural and urban areas, see Chen and Ravallion (2007).

The 1993 PPP exchange rates on which these calculations were based are known to have a number of problems. In particular, the two most populous countries, China and India, did not participate in the 1993 price surveys, so their PPPs are subject to larger margins of error. This will be corrected in the 2005 PPPs, in which both countries participated. The preliminary release of the new estimates at the time of writing indicates higher price levels in both China and India than implied by the 1993 PPPs, so the poverty rates in these two countries will rise relative to the rest of the developing world. Aggregate poverty counts will then rise, although the rates of aggregate progress over time will actually be higher than implied by Tables 24.2 and 24.3, given that India and (especially) China had high rates of poverty reduction over time. (Note that, while the new PPPs change the level comparisons, the real growth rates in a given country are unaffected.)

## 2. GLOBAL INEQUALITY

If *constructing* internationally comparable poverty measures is harder than computing comparable inequality measures (because the latter are scale-, and thus exchange-rate-invariant), *aggregation* into a single global measure is more difficult for inequality than for poverty. Standard poverty measures are immediately decomposable by population subgroups and, therefore, easy to aggregate up from subgroups. The numbers of poor can simply be added across countries, while poverty incidences and poverty gaps are first weighted by the country's population share and then summed. This simple procedure underlies the global poverty incidence and the global absolute numbers of the poor that are reported in the previous section.

The analogous procedure for inequality indices is more involved for two reasons. First, it has to contend with the fact that global inequality is not merely an aggregation of within-country inequalities. It also contains a component that corresponds to inequality *between* countries. Second, once the world is treated as a single entity, with a well-defined distribution of living standards, then the scale in which each individual national distribution is expressed matters again. While PPP exchange rate calculations are not needed if one simply wants to compare national levels of inequality, they are crucial for the construction of a global inequality index.

By 'global inequality' we shall mean inequality amongst all people of the world, ignoring where they live. This is calculated by combining the surveys from all the different countries (at the appropriate PPP exchange rates) into a single world distribution of income, and then computing inequality indices for this distribution. As long as the inequality index is additively decomposable (such as MLD), it will be possible to separate this overall measure into a component corresponding to inequality between countries, and one that aggregates the inequality within all the different countries. Only recently have household surveys been available for a sufficient number of countries for this approach to be feasible. Since then, this approach has become dominant among researchers interested in global interpersonal inequality—for the simple reason that it does not ignore inequality within countries.

The earlier literature contains two (simpler) approaches to measuring overall inequality in the world. The first takes each country as the relevant unit of observation, and computes inequality between these 'country means'. This is what Milanovic (2005) calls Concept 1 inequality, and what World Bank (2005) calls inter-country inequality. Second, it is possible to take account of different population sizes by weighting each country mean by its share of world population—giving Milanovic's Concept 2 inequality, or what World Bank (2005) calls international inequality. Both of these approaches are unsatisfactory since they ignore inequality within countries, and capture only the between-country differences.

In the last few years, a number of studies have sought to quantify global inequality, and to investigate its dynamics. One of the most ambitious was a paper by Bourguignon and Morrisson (2002), who constructed a time series of world inequality estimates for the period from 1820 to 1992. For all but the last 10 to 20 years of that series, disaggregated household survey data are not available for many countries. The authors thus grouped countries into 33 'blocs', the composition of which changed over time, depending on data availability (see Bourguignon and Morrisson, 2002, for details). The distributions are constructed in such a manner that all the members of a 'bloc' are assumed to have the same distribution as a country for which data are actually available in the relevant time period. The authors construct a distribution based on decile (and some ventile) shares, and on GDP per capita figures. Individuals are assumed to have the same incomes within 10ths (or 20ths) of the distribution, where that income corresponds to the group's share of GDP per capita. This set of strong assumptions allowed the authors to construct a long time series covering most of the 19th and 20th centuries.[17]

The main finding of the study is that world inequality rose almost continuously from the onset of the industrial revolution until the First World War. During that period, the world's Gini index rose from 0.50 to 0.61. Although inequality was also rising within most countries for which data were available, the real driving force for this increase in global disparity was inequality *between* countries, that is, international inequality (see Figure 24.4).

---

[17] Given the long-run perspective of this exercise, however, it is likely that some of the problems associated with using means from the National Accounts had only limited importance. In particular, the estimated evolution of GDP per capita over such a long period is likely to be very strongly correlated with any measure of household welfare.

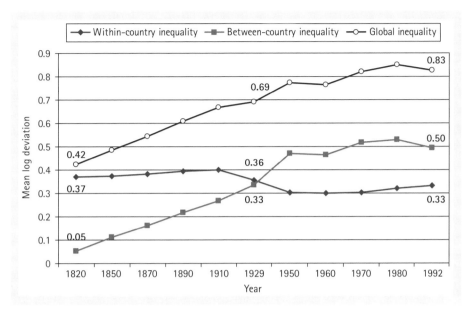

Fig. 24.4. **Global inequality and its components, 1820–1992**

*Sources*: Bourguignon and Morrisson (2002) and World Bank (2005).

Between the two world wars, and until around 1950, a decline in within-country inequality was observed, but the rise in inequality across countries continued apace and proved to be the dominant force.[18] The world Gini index rose further to 0.64. From the middle of the 20th century onwards, the rise of global inequality slowed, as Japan and parts of East Asia started growing faster than Europe and North America. This process became particularly pronounced after the take-off of China in the 1980s. Broadly speaking, global inequality changes in the second half of the last century are much less significant than in the 130 years that preceded it: there was certainly a reduction in the rate of growth of inequality and, towards the end of the period, the level actually started to decline.

When considering the last decades of the 20th century, however, better and more comprehensive data are available, enabling researchers to work with approximations to the world income distribution based on (and only on) fully disaggregated household surveys. Looking at the second half of the century with these new data, three interesting regularities emerge. First, even as (unweighted) inter-country inequality continued to grow between 1950 and 2000, international inequality (when population-weighted) began to fall. The disparate behavior in these two inequality

---

[18] The increase in inter-country inequality between 1914 and 1950 took place *during* each of the two world wars, and most markedly during the Second World War. The inter-war period properly defined (1919–39) actually saw a reduction in inter-country inequality. On the association between wars and rising international inequality, and between crises and its decline, both during this period and in 1890–5, see Milanovic (2006).

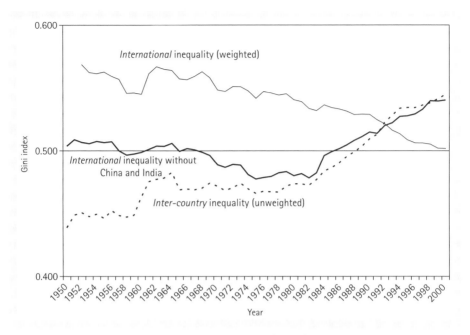

**Fig. 24.5. Inter–country inequality and international inequality, 1950–2000**

*Source*: World Bank (2005).

concepts has been one of the reasons behind the discordant discourse on globalization and inequality. The continuing rise in inter-country inequality (to which
Pritchett, 1997, refers as 'divergence, big time') was due largely to slow growth
in most poor (and small) countries, relative to some middle-income and richer
countries. The decline in international inequality, which refers to a population-
weighted distribution, was due fundamentally to rapid growth in two large nations
that started out very poor: China and, to a lesser extent, India. As Figure 24.5
suggests, once China and India are excluded from the international distribution,
the post-1980 trend in that inequality concept changes dramatically, and becomes
much closer to the rising trend in inter-country inequality.

The second regularity is that the last two decades in the 20th century saw resump-
tion in the upward trajectory of aggregate within-country inequality, defined as the
contribution of within-country inequality to total inequality. The rise in within-
country inequality prevented the decline in international inequality (which began,
slowly, around the 1960s) from translating immediately into a decline in global
inequality. Recall that global inequality is the sum of (appropriately aggregated)
within-country inequality and international inequality. Indeed, Milanovic (2002,
2005) finds that global income inequality between people was still rising between
1988 and 1993, but appears to have fallen between 1993 and 1998. This is confirmed
by World Bank (2005), which extends Milanovic's data set by a couple of years, and
is consistent with the findings reported in Chapter 23.

The third regularity is that there are signs of *inequality convergence* over time, whereby inequality has a tendency to rise in low-inequality countries, and fall in high-inequality ones. This was first noticed by Bénabou (1996), although his tests did not deal with the concern that the signs of convergence may stem solely from measurement error. Subsequent tests by Ravallion (2003) indicate that convergence is still evident when one uses better data and an econometric method that allows for classical measurement errors in the inequality data.

Bénabou interprets inequality convergence as an implication of a neoclassical growth model. Ravallion points instead to an explanation in terms of the policy and institutional convergence that has occurred in the world since about 1990. Low-inequality socialist economies have become more market-oriented, which has increased inequality. On the other hand, non-socialist economies have adopted market-friendly reforms. In some of these economies pre-reform controls benefited the rich, keeping inequality high (Brazil is an example), while in others the controls had the opposite effect, keeping inequality low (India is an example). Thus liberalizing economic policy reforms can entail sizeable redistribution between the poor and the rich, but in opposite directions in the two groups of countries. However, as Ravallion also notes, the process of convergence toward medium inequality implied by his finding is not particularly rapid, and it should not be forgotten that there are deviations from these trends, both over time and across countries.

The foregoing discussion has been about relative inequality. What about the competing concept of absolute inequality, which depends on the absolute gaps in levels of living between the 'rich' and the 'poor'?[19] As Figure 24.6 shows, the two concepts give rise to completely different trends for international inequality: whereas relative inequality measures (such as the Gini and the MLD) fall from around 1980 onwards, absolute measures record substantial increases.[20] This figure is drawn for (population-weighted) international inequality, but the difference is as important when considering global inequality.

Although this chapter (and the broader debate) has focused on income inequality and poverty trends, there should be no presumption that it is the only inequality that matters. Indeed, from some perspectives, international disparities in health status and educational achievement may matter inherently just as much (in addition to being instrumentally important in shaping income inequality and poverty). Since around 1930 there has been convergence in the inter-country and international distributions of life expectancy at birth (LEB). As (weighted) mean world LEB rose from 53.4 years in 1960 to 64.8 years in 2000, its distribution moved from bimodality to unimodality and the coefficient of variation fell from 0.233 to 0.194 (World Bank,

---

[19]   For further discussion of the role played by the concept of absolute inequality in debates about the distributional impacts of economic growth and trade openness see Ravallion (2004).

[20]   Although we include only two relative and one absolute measure, the opposing trends between relative and absolute measures over this period are robust to the choice of index. See Atkinson and Brandolini (2004).

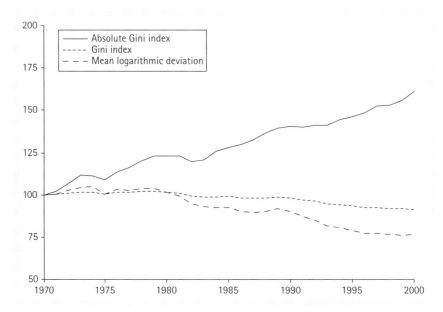

**Fig. 24.6. Absolute and relative inequality in the world, 1970–2000**

*Source:* Atkinson and Brandolini (2004).

2005). This heartening trend was partly reversed, however, during the 1990s, when LEB fell precipitously in some of the world's poorest countries, due largely to the spread of HIV/AIDS.[21]

Educational inequality, measured for the distribution of years of schooling, has also fallen substantially over the last four decades or so. As mean years of schooling in the world rose from 3.4 in 1960 to 6.3 in 2000, the coefficient of variation fell from 0.739 to 0.461. (Note that inequality measures for variables like life expectancy or years of education have to be interpreted with care, as both variables are effectively bounded from above.) This pattern of rising means and falling inequality in attainment was common to all regions of the world and, in addition, all regions also saw a reduction in gender disparities, as measured by the male to female schooling ratio (World Bank, 2005).[22]

Unfortunately, this reduction in *attainment* inequality has not always meant a reduction in the disparities in true educational *achievement*. Indeed, internationally comparable test score data suggest that these disparities remain strikingly large with, for example, the reading competence of the average Indonesian student in 2001 being equivalent to that of a student in the 7th percentile of the French distribution.

---

[21]  See Deaton (2003) on the relationship between health outcomes and inequality more broadly.
[22]  See also Castello and Domenech (2002) on international inequality in education.

These changes in the distribution of health and education should be taken into account when assessing global inequality in a broad sense. While this chapter provides only a very brief summary of the existing evidence along each dimension, a number of scholars have attempted to explore the correlations among the different dimensions. Because increases in longevity have been greater in poorer countries, for instance, Becker *et al.* (2005) argue that inequality in measures of well-being that account for the quantity, as well as quality, of life have been declining throughout the post-war period.

# 3. THE GROWTH–POVERTY–INEQUALITY TRIANGLE

Given the negative correlation between mean incomes and inequality levels across countries that is illustrated in Figure 24.1, it is not surprising that there is an even stronger correlation between mean incomes and poverty rates. Given the mathematical relationship that must always hold between mean income, poverty, and inequality, the first correlation more or less automatically implies the second. To see why, we can assume (without loss of generality) that the shape of the Lorenz curve can be fully captured by a vector of (functional form) parameters $\pi$, such that $L(p, \pi)$ is the share of consumption (or income) held by the poorest $p$ proportion of the population, ranked by household consumption per person. It is well known that the slope of the Lorenz curve $L(p, \pi)$ with respect to $p$ (denoted $L_p(p, \pi)$) is simply the ratio of the quantile function $(y(p))$ to the mean $\mu$.[23] By evaluating that derivative at $p = H$, we can write the following equation for the headcount index of poverty, given a poverty line $z$:

$$H = L_p^{-1}(z/\mu, \pi) \tag{1}$$

where $L_p[L_p^{-1}(.), \pi] = z/\mu$.

Equation (1) is an identity that relates the incidence of poverty at any given (real) poverty line to two aspects of the distribution: the mean $\mu$ and inequality or, more precisely, the Lorenz curve. From (1) it can be seen that the partial derivative of poverty with respect to the mean (holding the Lorenz curve parameters fixed) is always negative so that, if the poverty line is fixed and inequality is constant, poverty must fall as the mean rises.[24] In the scatter-plot of Figure 24.2, the poverty line is the same across all countries. If Lorenz curves did not differ systematically with

---

[23] The quantile function is the inverse of the cumulative distribution function, $p = F(y)$.
[24] This is a general result because the Lorenz curve is always (by construction) an increasing and convex function of the percentiles of the income distribution.

GDP per capita, poverty should be lower as GDP rises. This association is only strengthened by the negative correlation between GDP and inequality levels in the cross-section: higher income levels are associated with lower poverty both because of the direct effect of a higher mean at a given Lorenz curve, and because there exists an inverse empirical relationship between income levels and inequality.[25]

But the cross-country correlation between mean incomes and inequality need not be informative of the growth process of a particular country, since there may well be country-specific idiosyncrasies that cloud temporal patterns in the cross-section. So, what happens to inequality as a particular country grows over time? The first careful attempt to answer that question, by Simon Kuznets (1955), has become so influential that it still guides a great deal of thinking on the topic. Building on the Lewis (1954) model of development as a transfer of resources from a low-productivity, low-inequality sector (say, traditional agriculture) to a higher-productivity, higher-inequality sector (say, manufacturing or modern commercial agriculture), Kuznets hypothesized that inequality would rise during an initial phase of the process (as labor begins to move across sectors), and then eventually decline (as most workers are already in the modern sector, and the intersectoral gap loses significance). Kuznets found empirical support for this inverted-U inequality trajectory in the data he had available at the time, for the USA, England, and Germany. Some cross-sectional studies have found evidence consistent with an inverted-U relationship between inequality and mean income, and there is a hint of this relationship in Figure 24.1.[26]

As data on changes in inequality over time have accumulated for many more countries, however, it has become apparent that the inverted-U relationship hypothesized by Kuznets does not hold in general. It does not hold systematically for individual countries for which there are long time series of inequality measures. Bruno et al. (1998) compiled time-series data on inequality measures amongst growing developing countries and found almost no cases that conformed to the prediction of the Kuznets Hypothesis. And its 'dynamic version', which postulates a relationship between rates of GDP growth and changes in inequality, does not seem to hold on average either. Using all countries in the *PovcalNet* data set for which there are more than one survey, Ravallion (2007) plots proportional changes in the income Gini against proportional changes in mean income for 290 observations, representing 80 countries. (This can be thought of as a re-estimation of the relationship in Figure 24.1 in which we restrict the sample to developing countries and allow for the existence of country-level fixed effects, potentially correlated with

[25]  It is interesting to note that the negative correlation between GDP and inequality levels is much weaker if the sample is restricted to developing countries only.

[26]  Following the most common specification in the literature on testing the Kuznets Hypothesis, we regressed the Gini index on a quadratic function of log GDP per capita using the data in Figure 24.1. The coefficient on log GDP was positive and that on its squared value was negative, and both coefficients were significant at the 1% level. The turning point was within the range of the data.

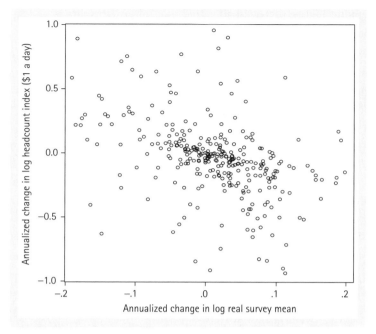

**Fig. 24.7.** Growth in poverty headcount against growth in survey mean consumption or income in less developed countries, 1981–2004

mean income.) A small negative correlation ($r = -0.15$) is found in the data, which is insignificant at the 10% level. Among growing economies, inequality tends to rise as often as it falls.[27] Thus we have:

*Stylized Fact 1: Economic growth tends to be distribution-neutral on average in developing countries, in that inequality increases about as often as it decreases in growing economies.*

It is not then surprising that there is a strong correlation between growth rates and changes in absolute poverty. This is evident in Figure 24.7, which plots the proportionate changes in the poverty rate (using the $1-a-day line) against the growth rates in the survey mean; the correlation coefficient is $-0.44$ and the regression coefficient is $-1.76$ with a White standard error of $0.24$; $n = 290$ after trimming likely outliers due to measurement error. Thus we have:[28]

*Stylized Fact 2: Measures of absolute poverty tend to fall with economic growth in developing countries.*

---

[27] Among economies experiencing contractions during the spells used by Ravallion (2007), inequality increases are somewhat more frequent than inequality reductions.

[28] This second stylized fact was noted by Ravallion (1995), Ravallion and Chen (1997), Fields (2001), Dollar and Kraay (2002) amongst others.

In discussing Figure 24.2 we had noted that, although there is a clear negative correlation between GDP per capita and poverty levels, there is also considerable heterogeneity around the average relationship. Figure 24.7 shows that a similar relationship holds after we take proportional differences: growth in GDP is strongly associated with poverty reduction, but there is considerable variation in the size of the effect. An illustration is provided by Ravallion (2001), who estimated a regression coefficient on a scatter-plot very much like that in Figure 24.7. The 95% confidence interval on that coefficient implies that a 2% rate of growth in mean income (which is about the average rate for developing countries in the 1980s and 1990s) will bring anything from a 1% to a 7% annual decline in poverty incidence.

Why are there such large differences across countries (and time periods) in the impact of growth on poverty? Given equation (1), it is unsurprising that the answer has to do with inequality. Interestingly, though, it has to do both with the initial level of inequality (i.e. how unequal a country is *before* a given growth spell) and with *changes* in that level (i.e. on the 'incidence' of economic growth). Taking the differential of equation (1) yields two terms,[29] one of which accounts for the impact of changes in the mean (i.e. growth), holding the initial distribution constant, while the other captures the change in the distribution (i.e. the Lorenz curve), holding the mean constant:

$$\frac{dH}{H} = -\frac{L_{pp}^{-1}z}{L_p^{-1}\mu}\cdot\frac{d\mu}{\mu} + \frac{L_{p\pi}^{-1}}{L_p^{-1}}d\pi \tag{2}$$

The first term is the *growth component* of poverty reduction, while the second term is the *distributional component* (the weighted sum of all changes in the distributional parameters).[30] Given the convexity of the Lorenz curve, equation (2) shows that the partial growth elasticity of poverty reduction ($\frac{\partial H}{H}\frac{\mu}{\partial\mu}$) is always negative. This result conforms to intuition: holding the poverty line and the Lorenz curve constant, poverty must fall when the mean rises. But the sign of the second term is ambiguous, since it depends on the marginal change in the Lorenz curve—in other words, it depends on the incidence of economic growth: on how the new income from growth is distributed.

The two ways in which inequality affects the impact of growth on poverty can be seen clearly in equation (2). First, initial inequality reduces the growth component of poverty reduction (in absolute value), because $L_p^{-1}$ tends to be higher in more unequal distributions. This stands to reason: the growth component captures how a given amount of growth would affect poverty if there were no change in the Lorenz curve. In other words: how it would affect poverty if the gains from growth

---

[29]  This is true if we hold the poverty line constant in real terms. If that is allowed to change over time (giving a relative poverty measure), there will be a third term for the change in the poverty line.

[30]  For further discussion of this decomposition see Datt and Ravallion (1992) and Kakwani (1993).

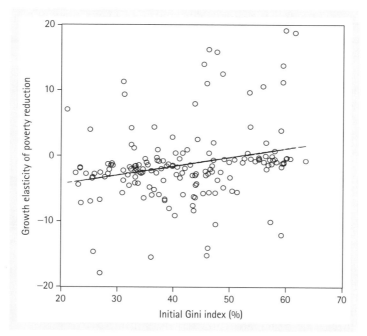

**Fig. 24.8. Empirical growth elasticities of poverty reduction against initial Gini index: less developed countries in 1981–2004**

*Source:* Ravallion (2007).

were distributed proportionately to existing household incomes. Clearly, the more unequal the original distribution, the smaller the share of the growth accruing to the poor, and the lower the poverty reduction arising from that given growth; this was first demonstrated empirically by Ravallion (1997b).[31]

Figure 24.8, which is also taken from Ravallion (2007), plots the total growth elasticity of poverty reduction against initial inequality, for a sample of countries during 1981–2005, when poverty is defined by the $1-a-day line.[32] It can be seen that the average empirical (total) elasticity is higher (in absolute value) the lower the initial inequality. The correlation coefficient of 0.26 is statistically significant at the 1% level. Whereas the elasticity averaged −4 for countries with Gini indices in the mid-20s, it was very close to zero for countries with a Gini index of about 0.60. To illustrate the important role played by initial inequality, Ravallion (2007) uses a parsimonious parametric model, based on essentially the same data, to simulate the rate of poverty reduction with a 2% rate of growth and a headcount index of 40%. In a low-inequality country—a Gini index of 0.30 (say)—the headcount index will

---

[31] For an update see Ravallion (2007).
[32] Period elasticities are smoothed by taking the simple average over two contiguous spells, and 15 extreme elasticities (lower than −20 or above +20) are excluded.

be halved in 11 years. In a high-inequality country—a Gini index of 0.60 (say)—it will take about 35 years to halve the initial poverty rate.[33]

A second mechanism through which inequality affects the impact of growth on poverty is through changes in inequality during the growth process. If the aggregate changes in the Lorenz curve in the second term on the right-hand side of equation (2) are poverty increasing then the effect of growth on poverty will be less than the partial effect, holding distribution constant. Figure 24.8 also suggests that changes in initial inequality have considerable empirical importance, since this (and measurement error) accounts for the spread around the regression line.

We can summarize these observations as:

*Stylized Fact 3: The higher the initial level of inequality in a country or the greater the increase in inequality during the growth spell, the higher the rate of growth that is needed to achieve any given (proportionate) rate of poverty reduction.*

We can thus sum up the analysis of the empirical inter-relationships between growth, poverty, and inequality as follows. Despite some evidence that this might be changing in the 1990s, the balance of the evidence for the last quarter-century suggests that there is no systematic empirical relationship between economic growth rates and changes in inequality (Stylized Fact 1). Given the relationship that must hold between poverty, inequality, and mean income in levels, Stylized Fact 1 implies that there must be a negative correlation between changes in poverty incidence and economic growth. This is indeed the case empirically: growth *is* good for the poor (Stylized Fact 2). But the relationship between mean income and poverty is mediated by the Lorenz curve, so that the power of growth to reduce poverty depends on inequality. In fact, that power tends to decline both with the initial level of inequality, and with increases in inequality during the growth process (Stylized Fact 3).

# 4. EXPLORING THE ECONOMICS BEHIND THESE STYLIZED FACTS

How can we go beyond the mathematical relationship between mean income, poverty, and inequality to gain a deeper understanding of the economic forces behind changes in inequality and poverty, and their relationship with aggregate

---

[33] The opposite also holds: high inequality protects the poor from the adverse impact of aggregate economic contraction. For example, high-inequality districts of Indonesia experienced less dramatic rates of increase in poverty during the 1998 financial crisis than did low-inequality districts (Ravallion and Lokshin, 2007).

growth? In this section, we review some of the insights from three branches of the literature that has tried to explore these determinants.

The first branch seeks to exploit spatial variation in the geographic and sectoral patterns of growth and in initial demographic and distributional conditions within countries to shed light on what makes growth more or less 'pro-poor', that is, to examine its incidence within a country. Datt and Ravallion (1998) and Ravallion and Datt (2002) for India, Ravallion and Chen (2007) and Montalvo and Ravallion (2008) for China, Ravallion and Lokshin (2007) for Indonesia and Ferreira *et al.* (2007) for Brazil all follow this approach. In essence, these studies compute a panel of poverty rates across states (or provinces) and over time, and regress the changes against sector-specific rates of growth in each spatial unit. Control variables typically include differences in initial conditions across states, including pre-sample differences in land or income inequality, literacy, and the like. There may also be time-varying state-level controls, such as changes in various types of public spending in each state.

These studies require relatively long series of repeated cross-section household surveys, and are easiest to conduct in large countries, where spatially disaggregated sub-samples retain statistical representativeness. Looking across the studies carried out so far, a few lessons emerge. First, the sectoral composition of growth does seem to matter for poverty reduction. In all four countries, the growth elasticities of poverty reduction varied substantially and significantly across sectors. But the relative sector ranking varied across countries: agricultural growth was by far the most effective in reducing poverty in China, while growth in the services sector had a higher impact on poverty in Brazil and India. In these three countries, the effect of manufacturing growth on poverty reduction seemed to vary significantly across states, suggesting that diverse geographic, distributional, or institutional conditions can affect the growth elasticity of poverty reduction, even within a single country.

It was generally found that less 'initial' (i.e. pre-sample) inequality was associated with a greater effectiveness of growth in reducing poverty (as the previous section would suggest). Greater literacy and better initial health conditions (often measured inversely by infant mortality rates) also help make growth more poverty-reducing. In India, about half of the range in long-term rates of poverty reduction across India's states (between the best performer, Kerala, and the worst one, Bihar) can be attributed to the difference in initial literacy rates (Datt and Ravallion, 1998). The elasticity of poverty to *non-farm* economic growth in India was particularly sensitive to differences in human resource development (Ravallion and Datt, 2002). In Brazil, one interesting finding was that a greater level of voice or 'empowerment'—proxied by the rate of unionization more than 10 years before the sample started—also raised the elasticity of poverty reduction with respect to growth (in manufacturing).

Other policies can also affect the pattern of distributional change (and thus of poverty reduction), even after one controls for differences in the pattern of growth. A repeated finding is that higher rates of inflation result in lower rates of poverty reduction (in Brazil, China, and India). The Brazilian case study revealed two important changes in the policy environment which contributed to greater success against poverty: a dramatic reduction in the country's previously massive rate of inflation (in 1994), and a substantial increase in the amount of social security and social assistance payments, accompanied by some improvements in targeting, during the period 1988–2004.

A second branch of literature is even more micro-oriented, and takes the individual household, rather than a state or province, as the unit of observation. This approach is exemplified by the various chapters in Bourguignon *et al.* (2005) and can be thought of as a set of statistical decompositions of the *growth incidence curve*, as given by $g(p) = d \ln y(p)$ (where it will be recalled that $y(p)$ is the quantile function).[34] $g(p)$ is the income growth rate at percentile $p$ of the distribution (for example, $g(0.5)$ is the growth rate of the median income). In these studies, a small set of models for key economic relationships—such as earnings regressions, participation equations, or education demand functions—is estimated for both the initial and terminal years of the period under study. Then various counterfactual income distributions can be simulated by importing sets of parameters from either date into the corresponding models for the other date. The spirit of the exercise follows that of Oaxaca (1973) and Blinder (1973) and the results, like the original Blinder–Oaxaca decomposition, are best interpreted as a statistical decomposition of changes in the distribution, rather than as measures of causal effects.

Nevertheless, some of the empirical regularities arising from the studies of Latin America and East Asia in Bourguignon *et al.* (2005) are quite interesting. First, the increase in the returns to schooling that accompanied rapid growth in countries like Taiwan (China) or Indonesia tended to contribute to increases in inequality. This effect was also present in countries that grew less rapidly, like Mexico, and is reminiscent of the so-called 'Tinbergen Race' between increases in the demand for schooling (arising from technological progress) and the rising supply of skilled workers (brought about by expansions in the educational system). In most countries in the sample, the demand side dominated, leading to increased earnings inequality; the only exceptions were Brazil and Colombia.

Greater earnings inequality often led to higher inequality in household incomes, but not always. An interesting example is provided by Taiwan, where a marked

---

[34]  On the properties of the growth incidence curve see Ravallion and Chen (2003). When making distributional comparisons over time, the growth incidence curve can be calculated from any two cross-sectional surveys (which do not need to be panel surveys, given the usual anonymity assumption). Alternatively, one of the two quantile functions can be a counterfactual distribution. It can also be shown that the changes in most commonly used poverty and inequality measures can also be written as functionals of the corresponding growth incidence curve, usually with weights that can be interpreted as the sensitivity of the particular measure to changes in the distribution at each percentile. This is particularly simple for the Watts index of poverty; it can be readily shown that the change in this index is given by the area under the growth incidence curve up to the headcount index of poverty (Ravallion and Chen, 2003).

increase in labor force participation by women led to a divergence between the earnings and income distributions. While the entry of relatively skilled women into the labor force reduced earnings inequality (as they entered roughly in the middle of the distribution), it contributed to an increase in the dispersion of household incomes: most of these new workers were married to skilled men, and lived in households that were already relatively well-off. The importance of changes in labor force participation and occupational structure is not an isolated characteristic of the Taiwanese experience. In Brazil, too, between 1976 and 1996, a substantial increase in extreme poverty was associated primarily with an increase in unemployment, informality, and underemployment. In Indonesia, a large share of the overall increase in inequality was associated with large movements of labor away from wage employment (in agriculture) towards (predominantly urban) self-employment.

This approach also illustrates the ambiguous effect of rising levels of education on inequality. In Colombia, Indonesia, and Mexico, substantial increases in the average level of schooling of the population did not lead to lower inequality. On the contrary, when one controls for the changes in returns, it seemed to be associated with higher inequality levels. This result was due to two effects: increases in the education stock that raised inequality in educational attainment itself (i.e. where most of the increase is accounted for by rises among the better-educated), but also the fact that when returns to education are convex, even a distribution-neutral increase in schooling can lead to higher earnings inequality. Of course, educational expansions can offset this effect if they lower returns to schooling, but this is less likely to happen in countries experiencing sharp increases in demand for skills.

By its very nature, this generalized Blinder–Oaxaca approach is, in isolation, incapable of attributing the causal origin of any of these changes to specific exogenous or policy shocks. This is particularly true when broad policy changes, such as a large-scale liberalization of trade, or a permanent change in the exchange rate, are expected to have substantial general equilibrium effects, affecting many variables at the same time. Wide-ranging changes in tariffs, for instance, can affect the distribution of income or consumption through changes in consumer prices, changes in relative wage rates, and changes in employment levels across industries. All of these variables will be changing in the micro-simulations that generate counterfactual growth incidence curves, but which share of the changes is due to the trade liberalization policy is anyone's guess.

To address this point, a third branch of the literature has sought to combine macroeconomic or general equilibrium models with micro-simulations on household survey data. Examples include Bourguignon *et al.* (2002) for the Indonesian crisis, Chen and Ravallion (2004b) for China's accession to the WTO, and Ferreira *et al.* (2004) for Brazil's devaluation in 1998–9. These models are still in their early, experimental phase, and are subject to the usual criticisms leveled against computable general equilibrium models (CGEs). Nevertheless, when the model is run on a single household survey, and its predictions are checked against a separate, ex-post survey (as in the case of Brazil), its distributional prediction performance is superior to those of the previous generation of representative-agent CGEs.[35]

A common finding in these exercises concerns the importance of worker and employment flows across sectors, in response to shocks or policy changes that affect relative prices. Developing country labor markets are often *de facto* very flexible (despite sometimes significant *de jure* rigidities), because of the existence of large informal sectors. When relative goods prices change in response to a change in the exchange rate (as in Brazil, in 1998) or policy change (as in China's accession to the WTO), different industries contract and expand in response, and workers move across these sectors.

# 5. CONCLUSIONS

Absolute poverty is clearly a bigger problem in developing countries—where over four-fifths of the world's population lives—than in developed ones. Virtually all of the one billion people subsisting on per capita incomes less than $1 per day live in developing countries. Perhaps more surprisingly, inequality is also a bigger problem in developing countries. Looking at the world as a whole, there is a clear negative correlation between average levels of inequality and the level of development, and all countries with really high income inequality—a Gini index of (say) 0.50 or higher—are developing economies.

However, the evidence from the available cross-section of developing countries suggests that there is little aggregate tendency for these inequality levels to fall with economic growth. Although there are no developed countries today with inequality levels above a Gini index of 0.50, growth rates among developing countries are virtually uncorrelated with changes in inequality levels. This is our first stylized fact.

The absence of a robust cross-country correlation between changes in inequality and growth necessarily implies that there must be a strong negative correlation between growth and changes in poverty. This is confirmed empirically: on average, economies that grow faster reduce absolute poverty much more rapidly—our second stylized fact.

But this does not mean that policymakers in developing countries can ignore inequality. There are a number of reasons why persistently high inequality is a

---

[35] An intermediate approach seeks to identify the causal effects of policy changes econometrically, and then estimate their share within the different components of a micro-simulation-based decomposition. Ferreira *et al.* (2007) regress changes in wages and employment levels disaggregated by sectors on (arguably exogenous) changes in tariffs and exchange rates. These trade-mandated changes are then used to generate counterfactual growth incidence curves which can be interpreted alongside other micro-simulation results.

concern. Two primary reasons were not discussed here, namely the fact that higher inequality may be ethically objectionable in its own right, and the possibility that greater inequality may generate certain inefficiencies that could actually reduce the future rate of economic growth. World Bank (2005) contains summary discussions of both points; on the second also see Chapter 22. In this chapter, we have focused on a third reason why persistent inequality may be undesirable in developing economies: the fact that, even for a given growth rate, inequality tends to reduce the growth elasticity of poverty reduction—our third stylized fact. Other things equal, one percentage point of growth leads to a smaller reduction in poverty in a very unequal country than in a less unequal one. And if inequality rises during the growth process, things are worse yet.

While these three stylized facts can be identified from a macro, cross-country perspective, an understanding of the economic factors behind changes in distribution (or behind the levels and incidence of growth) in developing countries requires a more microeconomic approach which exploits differences in conditions within countries. Changes in income distribution respond to so many different stimuli—in a general equilibrium environment—that no single method has yet been developed to fully identify the causes of all observed changes. Instead, researchers have relied on a variety of different approaches. Sub-national regression analysis (using geographical panel data) sheds light on the relative importance of sectoral growth patterns, and of initial differences in the distribution of land or human capital. Micro-simulation-based decompositions of growth incidence curves can help us understand the relative roles of changes in household endowments; changes in returns to those endowments; and changes in participation and occupational choices. Finally, combining such micro-simulations with models capable of capturing the general equilibrium transmission of initial shocks can help us understand the distributional impact of broad, economy-wide policy changes.

As we move forward, more research is needed on all of these fronts, and in their integration. It is only from such research that we can hope to learn what enables some countries (such as Vietnam) to grow rapidly with little or no rise in inequality, and thus to enjoy dramatic rates of poverty reduction. The diversity of country experience has established that equitable growth is possible, and that it is particularly pro-poor. But much remains to be learned about both the general economic conditions and the policy context within which it is achievable.

# REFERENCES

ACKLAND, R., DOWRICK, S., and FREYENS, B. 2006. 'Measuring Global Poverty: Why PPP Methods Matter'. Mimeo. Research School of Social Sciences, Australian National University.

ATKINSON, A., and BRANDOLINI, A. 2004. 'Global Income Inequality: Absolute, Relative or Intermediate?' Paper presented at the 28th General Conference of the International Association for Research on Income and Wealth. Aug. 22. Cork, Ireland.

BANERJEE, A., and PIKETTY, T. 2005. 'Top Indian Incomes, 1922–2000'. *The World Bank Economic Review*, 19: 1–20.

BECKER, G., PHILIPSON, T., and SOARES, R. 2005. 'The Quantity and Quality of Life and the Evolution of World Inequality'. *American Economic Review*, 95(1): 277–91.

BÉNABOU, R. 1996. 'Inequality and Growth', in B. Bernanke and J. Rotemberg (eds.), *National Bureau of Economic Research Macroeconomics Annual*. Cambridge, Mass.: MIT Press, 11–74.

BLINDER, A. 1973. 'Wage Discrimination: Reduced Form and Structural Estimates'. *Journal of Human Resources*, 8: 436–55.

BOURGUIGNON, F. 1979. 'Decomposable Income Inequality Measures'. *Econometrica*, 47: 901–20.

——Ferreira, F., and Lustig, N. 2005. *The Microeconomics of Income Distribution Dynamics in East Asia and Latin America*. Washington: The World Bank.

——and MORRISSON, C. 2002. 'Inequality Among World Citizens: 1820–1992'. *American Economic Review*, 92(4): 727–44.

——Robilliard, A.-S., and Robinson, S. 2002. 'Crisis and Income Distribution: A Macro–Micro Model for Indonesia'. Mimeo. IFPRI, Washington, Apr.

BRUNO, M., RAVALLION, M., and SQUIRE, L. 1998. 'Equity and Growth in Developing Countries: Old and New Perspectives on the Policy Issues', in V. Tanzi and K. Chu (eds.), *Income Distribution and High-Quality Growth*. Cambridge, Mass.: MIT Press.

CASTELLO, A., and DOMENECH, R.. 2002. 'Human Capital Inequality and Economic Growth: Some New Evidence'. *Economic Journal*, 112(478): C187–200.

CHEN, S., and RAVALLION, M. 2001. 'How Did the World's Poor Fare in the 1990s?' *Review of Income and Wealth*, 47(3): 283–300.

————2004a. 'How Have the World's Poorest Fared Since the Early 1980s?' *World Bank Research Observer*, 19(2): 141–70.

————2004b. 'Household Welfare Impacts of WTO Accession in China'. *World Bank Economic Review*, 18(1): 29–58.

————2007. 'Absolute Poverty Measures for the Developing World, 1981–2004'. *Proceedings of the National Academy of Sciences of the United States of America*, 104(43): 16757–62.

COULTER, F. A. E., COWELL, F. A., and JENKINS, S. P. 1992. 'Equivalence Scale Relativities and the Extent of Inequality and Poverty'. *Economic Journal*, 102: 1067–82.

DATT, G., and RAVALLION, M. 1992. 'Growth and Redistribution Components of Changes in Poverty Measures: A Decomposition with Applications to Brazil and India in the 1980s'. *Journal of Development Economics*, 38: 275–95.

————1998. 'Why Have Some Indian States Done Better than others at Reducing Rural Poverty?' *Economica*, 65: 17–38.

DEATON, A. 1997. *The Analysis of Household Surveys: Microeconometric Analysis for Development Policy*. Baltimore: The Johns Hopkins University Press.

——2003. 'Health, Inequality and Economic Development'. *Journal of Economic Literature*, 41(1): 113–58.

DOLLAR, D., and KRAAY, A. 2002. 'Growth is Good for the Poor'. *Journal of Economic Growth*, 7(3): 195–225.

FERREIRA, F., LEITE, P., PEREIRA DA SILVA, L., and PICCHETTI, P. 2004. 'Can the Distributional Impacts of Macroeconomic Shocks be Predicted? A Comparison of the Performance of Macro–Micro Models with Historical Data for Brazil'. Policy Working Paper 3303. World Bank.

——— and RAVALLION, M. 2007. 'Poverty Reduction without Economic Growth? Explaining Brazil's Poverty Dynamics 1985–2004'. Policy Research Working Paper 4431. The World Bank.

——— and WAI-POI, M. 2007. 'Trade Liberalization, Employment Flows, and Wage Inequality in Brazil'. Policy Research Working Paper 4108. The World Bank.

FIELDS, G. S. 2001. Distribution and Development. New York: Russell Sage Foundation.

FOSTER, J., GREER, J., and THORBECKE, E. 1984. 'A Class of Decomposable Poverty Measures'. Econometrica, 52: 761–5.

GRIMM, M., HARTTGEN, K., MISSELHORN, M., and KLASEN, S. 2006. 'A Human Development Index by Income Groups'. Ibero-American Institute for Economic Research Discussion Paper no. 155. Ibero-American Institute for Economic Research, University of Göttingen.

KAKWANI, N. 1993. 'Poverty and Economic Growth with Application to Côte D'Ivoire'. Review of Income and Wealth, 39: 121–39.

KORINEK, A., MISTIAEN, J., and RAVALLION, M. 2006. 'Survey Nonresponse and the Distribution of Income'. Journal of Economic Inequality, 4(2): 33–55.

KUZNETS, S. 1955. 'Economic Growth and Income Inequality'. American Economic Review, 45: 1–28.

LANJOUW, P., and RAVALLION, M. 1995. 'Poverty and Household Size'. Economic Journal, 105: 1415–35.

LEWIS, W. A. 1954. 'Economic Development with Unlimited Supplies of Labour'. Manchester School of Economic and Social Studies, 22(2): 139–91.

MILANOVIC, B. 2002. 'True World Income Distribution, 1988 and 1993: First Calculation Based on Household Surveys Alone'. Economic Journal, 112(476): 51–92.

—— 2005. Worlds Apart: Measuring International and Global Inequality. Princeton: Princeton University Press.

—— 2006. 'Economic Integration and Income Convergence: Not Such a Strong Link?' Review of Economic and Statistics, 88(4): 659–70.

MONTALVO, J., and RAVALLION, M. 2008. 'The Pattern of Growth and Poverty Reduction in China'. Mimeo. Development Research Group, The World Bank.

OAXACA, R. L. 1973. 'Male–Female Wage Differentials in Urban Labor Markets'. International Economic Review, 9: 693–709.

PRITCHETT, L. 1997. 'Divergence, Big Time'. Journal of Economic Perspectives, 11(3): 3–17.

RAVALLION, M. 1995. 'Growth and Poverty: Evidence for Developing Countries in the 1980s'. Economics Letters, 48: 411–17.

—— 1997a. 'Good and Bad Growth: The Human Development Reports'. World Development, 25(5): 631–8.

—— 1997b. 'Can High Inequality Developing Countries Escape Absolute Poverty?' Economics Letters, 56: 51–7.

—— 2003. 'Inequality Convergence'. Economics Letters, 80(3): 351–6.

—— 2004. 'Competing Concepts of Inequality in the Globalization Debate', in S. Collins and C. Graham (eds.), Brookings Trade Forum 2004. Washington: Brookings Institution, 1–38.

RAVALLION, M. 2007. 'Inequality is Bad for the Poor', in J. Micklewright and S. Jenkins (eds.), *Inequality and Poverty Re-Examined*. Oxford: Oxford University Press.

—— 2001. 'Growth, Inequality and Poverty: Looking beyond Averages'. *World Development*, 29(11): 1803–15.

—— and CHEN, S. 1997. 'What Can New Survey Data Tell Us about Recent Changes in Distribution and Poverty?' *World Bank Economic Review*, 11(20): 357–82.

—— —— 2003. 'Measuring Pro-poor Growth'. *Economics Letters*, 78: 93–9.

—— —— 2007. 'China's (Uneven) Progress Against Poverty'. *Journal of Development Economics*, 82(1): 1–42.

—— —— 2002. 'Why Has Economic Growth Been More Pro-Poor in Some States of India than Others?' *Journal of Development Economics*, 68: 381–400.

—— and LOKSHIN, M. 2007. 'Lasting Impacts of Indonesia's Financial Crisis'. *Economic Development and Cultural Change*, 56(1): 27–56.

SALA-I-MARTIN, X. 2006. 'The World Distribution of Income: Falling Poverty and ... Convergence Period'. *Quarterly Journal of Economics*, 121(2): 351–97.

SLESNICK, D. T. 1998. 'Empirical Approaches to the Measurement of Welfare'. *Journal of Economic Literature*, 36(4): 2108–65.

WATTS, H. W. 1968. 'An Economic Definition of Poverty', in D. P. Moynihan (ed.), *On Understanding Poverty*. New York: Basic Books.

WORLD BANK 2005. *World Development Report 2006: Equity and Development*. New York: Oxford University Press.

# PART VII

## CHANGING
## INEQUALITIES

CHAPTER 25

...................................................................

# ECONOMIC INEQUALITY AND THE WELFARE STATE

...................................................................

## GØSTA ESPING-ANDERSEN
## JOHN MYLES

# 1. INTRODUCTION

...................................................................

BECAUSE it taxes and spends, the welfare state is by definition redistributive, but the degree to which this is associated with more equality is an open empirical question. A quick historical glance at social reform will dispel any notion that the welfare state was pursued for purely egalitarian reasons. Its earliest foundations were mainly laid by conservative reformers who, like Bismarck, sought primarily to reproduce, rather than to alter, prevailing social hierarchies. When the opportunity arose, social reformist governments pushed for social policies that would better the conditions of workers, eliminate poverty, and equalize opportunities.[1]

Following Barr (2001), the welfare state combines the role of piggy bank and Robin Hood. The former implies collective insurance against social risks and

---

[1] See Rimlinger (1971), Baldwin (1990), and Esping-Andersen (1990) for general historical and comparative treatments of welfare state evolution.

cannot be expected to produce much equality; the latter, aiming to ameliorate need and poverty, is more explicitly egalitarian in terms of reducing welfare disparities. The balance between the two will in great measure dictate the equalizing impact of redistribution.

It is useful to distinguish between horizontal and vertical redistribution (Hills, 2004: 185). Social insurance is primarily designed for horizontal redistribution, seeking to reallocate income across the life course. Like commercial insurance plans, there is no attempt to redistribute between 'rich' and 'poor'. Instead, the aim is to smooth lifetime income and guarantee well-being in the face of bad luck (like illness) or foreseeable need (like old age). The Robin Hood dimension is exemplified by vertical redistribution and the degree of equalization will depend, in part, on the progressivity of the tax system and, in part, on the degree to which social benefits go disproportionately to the least well-off. Estimates of the relative weight of horizontal and vertical redistribution show substantial variation across welfare states. Measured on a lifetime income basis, the horizontal dimension accounts for about half of all redistribution in the Australian welfare state, two-thirds in the British, and as much as 82 percent in the Swedish (Hills, 2004: 197; Stahlberg, 2007). As Stahlberg emphasizes, welfare states that favor heavy targeting of benefits will generally boast a relatively stronger vertical redistribution. But then these kinds of welfare states tend to spend much less.

Measures of the redistributive effects of welfare states typically begin and end by comparing the difference in inequality levels before and after taxes and transfers. This can be quite problematic because the baseline of comparison, the pre-tax and pre-transfer distribution, is itself very much influenced by what the welfare state does.[2] Policies affect the market-based distribution in two major ways.

First, the welfare state artificially induces substantial inequality in market incomes because it produces large populations with low or even zero market incomes, such as pensioners or women on maternity leave. People who are well protected by government pensions are unlikely to save much for retirement and arrive therefore at old age with little market income. And if pensions are generous, they are unlikely to continue working. Social protection and tax systems also affect work incentives and, hence, earnings (Atkinson, 1995; Milanovic, 2000; Beramendi, 2001).

Secondly, welfare states provide resources to citizens that affect their earnings potential. These derive primarily from services such as education, health care, training programs, or support to working mothers. In this regard the welfare state plays an important social investment function and the design of such policies will dictate inequalities in people's lifetime earnings power. Policies that ensure a more equal opportunity structure will inevitably also diminish inequalities in the distribution of market income. Put differently, there are powerful countervailing welfare state effects that influence market inequalities.

---

[2]  For a discussion, see Atkinson and Stiglitz (1987: 286 ff).

To really estimate redistribution we would need to invent a counter-factual 'virgin' distribution that was unaffected by social policy altogether. No such distribution exists in the real world. The degree of distortion that ensues from a comparison of pre- and post-redistribution inequalities will vary very much across welfare states. Those that encourage mass early retirement or that suffer from high unemployment will create more zero earnings; so will those that provide generous maternity and parental leaves. In contrast, welfare states that maximize employment and narrow earnings differentials will help establish a more equal 'original', market-based income distribution (Kenworthy, 2004). There are additional reasons why a simple pre-post redistribution approach is ill-suited to capture what we really wish to identify. The provision of social services can have major effects on the distribution of well-being but such effects go unmeasured in income statistics. Since social insurance primarily serves to smooth incomes across the life cycle, its relevant redistributive effects must be related to income on a lifetime basis.

All this considered, we need to be especially attentive to three basic issues. First, welfare states embrace distinct redistributive principles, some of which may promote more equality of outcomes or of opportunities, while others may actually work in the opposite direction. Pension systems illustrate this well. Most rich nations combine three pension pillars: earnings-related insurance, tax-subsidized private pension plans, and a general revenue-financed basic pension guarantee. The latter is likely to be highly redistributive in favor of low income retirees whereas tax deductions for private schemes favor the rich. Insurance schemes are commonly financed via a proportional levy on the wage bill. This would suggest a relatively neutral distributional outcome were it not for the fact that high income earners typically live substantially longer and therefore end up receiving a disproportionate slice of the pension budget. Secondly, the income data that we routinely use pick up only a part of the overall welfare state effect. And, thirdly, the most interesting impact of welfare states may in fact be their influence on the 'virgin' primary distribution.

## 2. THEORIES OF WELFARE STATE REDISTRIBUTION

Most empirical research is guided by one of three theoretical perspectives. Economic theories see the welfare state as replacing insurance markets to compensate for market and information failures (Barr, 1998, 2001). Government may be a more efficient insurer of risks, in particular under conditions of strong information asymmetries, credit constraints, and adverse selection. A recent literature adds a global economy angle to this perspective, arguing that heightened economic vulnerability in global markets intensifies social risks and explains why welfare states are exceptionally large in very open economies (Rodrik, 1998; Iversen and Cusack, 2000; Garrett, 1998).

If the welfare state is primarily an insurer, its role in creating equality would appear irrelevant. But there are three kinds of social risks, each with its unique redistributive logic: *life course risks*, *inter-generational risks*, and *class risks* (Esping-Andersen, 1999: 40–3). Pooling life-cycle risks, like old-age infirmity, implies primarily horizontal redistribution across the life course—Barr's 'piggy bank'. Inter-generational risks are related to social inheritance in the sense that social origins influence life chances. The relevant policies here are related to equal opportunity measures. As examined in Chapter 22, the prevailing level of inequality in the parental generation helps dictate differences in parental investment in their children's life chances. If so, there is also a strong case for vertical redistribution. Class risks refer to those that concentrate in distinct social groups: miners are more prone to work injury than college professors; the unskilled are more vulnerable to low earnings and unemployment; lone mothers are over-represented among the poor. Class risks have given rise to a plethora of policy responses, including targeted support to the vulnerable, corporative risk pooling such as distinct insurance plans for high-risk clienteles (like miners' insurance), or universal pooling of the entire population regardless of its risk profile (like universal child benefits, or the Scandinavian tradition of a 'people's' pension). Risk pooling can produce a complex combination of redistributive logics and cannot, as economic theory often assumes, be equated with horizontal redistribution.

As discussed above, targeted welfare states are, relatively speaking, more biased in favor of vertical redistribution. This, however, may not imply that the overall net effect is more egalitarian. The 'paradox of redistribution' thesis argues that narrowly targeted policies are typically ungenerous and potentially stigmatizing due to lack of broad electoral support. In contrast, universal benefits marshal broad citizen support and will, hence, offer more generous benefits that additionally will reach all the needy with greater certainty (Korpi and Palme, 1998). In this perspective we should expect that pro-targeting welfare states, like the American or Australian, produce less income equalization than universalistic ones.

Political theories offer a further source of guidance.[3] One tradition links redistribution to the legislative power of left parties. The straightforward argument is that left parties represent the less well-off, and if they gain sufficient political power, they will redistribute in their favor. There is substantial, if not overwhelmingly strong, evidence to support this thesis (Korpi, 1983; Huber and Stephens, 2001). Another tradition applies median-voter models (Meltzer and Richard, 1981; Perotti, 1996; Milanovic, 2000; Moene and Wallerstein, 2001, 2003). In this framework, high levels of earnings inequality fuel demand for redistribution, in particular if median

---

[3] The political theories are examined in more detail in Chapter 24.

earnings fall far below the mean. Empirical analyses fail to provide clear support for the thesis. Some, like Milanovic (2000), conclude positively while most, like Moffitt *et al.* (1998), argue that the more unequal is the primary income distribution, the less support for the poor.

Moene and Wallerstein (2003) offer an explanation for these ambiguous findings. They show that the theory appears irrelevant for large items such as pensions and health care, while some, like unemployment insurance, do seem to respond to levels of pre-redistribution inequality—but not in the way predicted by theory. They find that spending is more generous in nations with more egalitarian distributions. Most interestingly, they show that more inequality generates a double, counteracting effect: on the one hand, increasing demand for redistribution and, on the other hand, raising demand for (non-redistributive) insurance.

Thirdly, much research has been influenced by derivatives of Wagner's Law, according to which public expenditure will grow disproportionately faster than GDP growth once we reach a certain stage of development. The upshot is that welfare state expansion—and thus more redistribution—is intrinsic to advanced economies. Wilensky (1975) is the classic example in this tradition.

The origins of welfare states can be dated back to the late 1800s, but social expenditure initially grew very slowly. This is understandable since, in most cases, population coverage was incomplete and entitlements were modest. And once introduced, the big spending items such as pensions required very long maturation periods. Accordingly, social expenditures in Europe rarely exceeded 3 percent of GDP before World War II. The concept of the welfare state, indeed, emerged only in the post-war decades. By 1960, the median level of social outlays in the affluent democracies had risen to 10 percent of GDP. The real take-off occurred in the 1970s, following a major social reform wave in terms of benefit generosity and population inclusion. By 1990, the median level of social expenditures had risen to 24 percent of GDP, but this hides substantial dispersion, ranging from 15 percent in the USA to more than 30 percent in Scandinavia. With the exception of laggard countries, particularly in Southern Europe, spending volumes have grown little since.[4]

Since income inequality declined in tandem with welfare state consolidation, and since there is a fairly strong cross-national correlation between welfare state size and equality, the 'size-redistribution thesis' appears credible. Early comparative research generally assumed direct causality (Curtright, 1967; Sawyer, 1976; Stark, 1977). In truth neither their data, nor their methodology, permitted such causal argumentation. As will be explained below, truly comparable data on income

---

[4] For an overview of historical trends, see Lindert (2004). By convention, social spending includes government income support to individuals (pensions, unemployment and sickness benefits, family allowances, social assistance, and the like) and social services such as health care and family services. Education is usually not regarded as social policy, and active labor market programs are typically classified as labor market spending. The concept of the welfare state, however, usually encompasses all such programs.

distributions (and on social spending) emerged only from the 1980s onwards. This does not mean that the thesis should be rejected. Smeeding (1997), using high quality data, finds a strong association between levels of spending and degrees of poverty reduction.

The size-redistribution thesis has been questioned on many grounds. First, the historical pattern appears very non-linear. Social spending trends combine periods of relative stagnation with sudden leaps and bounds. In the past decades, social spending has been stagnant notwithstanding sustained economic growth. Secondly, some argue that welfare state growth may actually imply diminished redistribution. If large welfare states imply increasingly universal coverage, the middle classes will become the principal beneficiaries (Le Grand, 1982; Tullock, 1983; Goodin and Le Grand, 1987; Pampel and Williamson, 1989). Le Grand (1982: 3) asserted boldly that 'almost all public expenditure on the social services benefits the better off to a greater extent than the poor'.

A major source of erroneous inference lies in the conventional use of *gross* spending volumes. This creates distortion because, first, gross figures do not adjust for the taxation of benefits that then flows back into the government treasury. Countries differ hugely in terms of how much they tax social transfer payments. Very large welfare states, as in the Nordic countries, tax back far more than the leaner spenders. The second distortion is related to tax expenditures, that is, using tax deductions to subsidize private welfare purchases. The leaner welfare states, such as the USA, score high on this count. To arrive at a more meaningful measure, the OECD has calculated *net* public social expenditure (Adema and Ladaique, 2005). With this measure, international differences in welfare state size appear far less dramatic. Sweden and the USA represent the two extreme ends. In gross terms, the spending ratio between the two is 2.2; in net terms, only 1.6.

Using the most recent data, Figure 25.1 presents the association between *net* social expenditure and the percentage reduction of income inequality (using the Gini coefficient) after taxes and income redistribution for 15 OECD countries. Some might interpret the graph as support for the size-redistribution thesis. Regression estimation suggests that a 10 percent increase in social spending would produce 1 percent more inequality reduction. Others, however, might stress the presence of many important outlier countries, both above and below the line, and the relatively modest explanatory power of spending (which accounts for only 25 percent of the variation). The USA, Spain, and Sweden are less redistributive than one would have expected and, vice versa, the Czech Republic, Denmark, and Finland are 'overshooters'.

We should therefore question any straightforward link between higher levels of social spending and more income redistribution. As Esping-Andersen (1990, 1999), Palme (2006), and Moene and Wallerstein (2001, 2003), suggest, the important effects may derive from the institutional design, rather than sheer size, of welfare states.

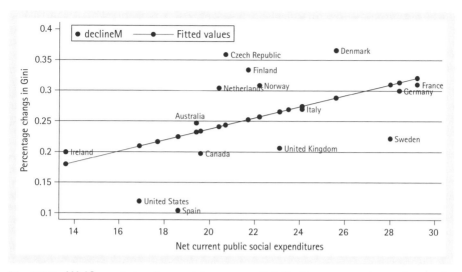

**Fig. 25.1. Welfare state size and income redistribution, percentage change in Gini, after taxes and transfers, c.2000**

*Note:* DeclineM shows the difference between market and disposable income Ginis as a percentage of market Gini.
*Source:* OECD SOCX database and LIS.

# 3. WELFARE STATE DESIGN AND WELFARE REGIMES

Citizens obtain welfare from three basic sources: markets, family, and government. The market provides income and sells commercial welfare inputs such as child-minding or medical insurance. For most people, during most of their lives, the market is undoubtedly the chief source of well-being. Families, too, play a pivotal role in welfare packaging, in part by providing services and care for kin, in part via income transfers. Income pooling in families is the norm and income transfers between the generations is substantial—in particular from the elderly to the young (Albertini *et al.*, 2007). To fully understand welfare *states* we need to situate them in the full context of welfare production and consumption. Esping-Andersen (1990) terms this the *welfare regime*.

With some simplification, we can distinguish three distinct regimes.[5] The Anglo-Saxon countries represent the 'liberal' regime, one that favors minimal public intervention under the assumption that the majority of citizens can obtain adequate welfare from the market. The role of government is, in part, to nurture rather than replace market transactions, and this explains why these countries favor subsidizing private welfare via tax deductions. The USA is the extreme case

[5] This section draws on Esping-Andersen (1990, 1999).

where tax expenditures for social purposes exceed 2 percent of GDP, and where private social spending represents 9 percent of GDP (Adema and Ladaique, 2005, table 6).

A second hallmark of the liberal regime is its preference for targeting public benefits at the neediest, traditionally via means-testing, but recent years have seen a shift towards work-conditional, negative income tax type policies. This, again, mirrors the principle that government's role should be restricted to a demonstrable inability to uphold one's own livelihood.

In line with its support for market solutions, this regime favors unregulated labor markets under the assumption that this bolsters employment growth. But it also promotes greater labor turnover, which heightens social insecurity, and greater wage inequality, which, in turn, increases the risks of poverty.

The combination of a pro-market bias and targeting should, in principle, lead to contradictory distributional outcomes. Private welfare reliance, bolstered by tax subsidies, should have a clear adverse effect on equality while we should expect that targeting in favor of the neediest sponsors equality. The latter may, however, be weakened by the 'paradox of redistribution' effect. Indeed, as the thesis would predict, social benefits to the poor are relatively ungenerous in the Anglo-Saxon countries, and this helps explain why poverty remains exceptionally high, in particular among the most vulnerable such as lone mothers.

The Nordic countries represent a second, 'social-democratic', regime that is, above all, characterized by its emphasis on universal inclusion and its comprehensive definition of social entitlements. It is also one that has been vocally committed to equalizing living conditions across the citizenry. For this reason, policy has deliberately sought to marginalize the role of private welfare markets and of targeted social assistance. The model is internationally unique also in its emphasis on 'defamilializing' welfare responsibilities, especially with regard to care for children and the elderly. Denmark and Sweden now boast *de facto* complete coverage both for child and elderly care. The upshot is, on one hand, a boost to the female labor supply and, on the other hand, an unusually service-intensive welfare state. Excluding health care, social services now account for more than 20 percent of all social expenditure in Denmark and Sweden (compared to a 4–5 percent average for the OECD countries). Since data on income distributions do not capture the monetary value of services, we may accordingly end up with a misleading picture of these welfare states' true redistributive effects.

Yet another hallmark of the Nordic model is its unique synchronization of social and labor market policies. While labor markets are fairly regulated, both in terms of hiring and firing (with the exception of Denmark) and in terms of wage setting, social policy has played a major role in promoting maximum employment. Female employment rates are now basically similar to men's and increasingly on a full-time basis. This has potentially huge consequences for income distribution. Female employment will promote more income equality the more it is embraced in bottom quintile households. Here is one clear example where social services and family policy have an essentially invisible, yet potentially decisive, effect on the distribution of income. Active labor market policies are a second crucial instrument for minimizing unemployment. By guaranteeing generous benefits to participants, the policy gives huge incentives to participate in training, retraining, and job relocation programs.

The net distributional impact of these features is difficult to predict—and measure. Since most benefits are universal, they may not have a major equalizing effect. But since they are all (except family allowances) taxed, the net outcome should be more vertical redistribution (high income retirees are taxed more heavily than their low income equivalents). And returning to the 'paradox of redistribution', minimal targeting should actually promote more equality of outcome.

But the Nordic regime's service-intensive nature means also that many egalitarian outcomes cannot be identified with standard income data. Take child-care services. Since standards and quality are identical for children of poor and rich parents, the marginal welfare improvement is surely much larger for low income families. Or take, again, the female employment dividend of 'mother-friendly' policy. Its real distributive effect is once-removed. Overall, to the extent that the model delivers maximum employment, perhaps the most decisive redistribution occurs via the equalization of primary, pre-redistribution incomes. The *de facto* universality of employment should translate into exceptionally low poverty risks.

The third, and somewhat more heterogeneous, regime embraces the majority of Continental European countries, Austria, Belgium, France, Germany, Italy, the Netherlands, and Spain.[6] These welfare states all have conservative origins. The foundations were built around mandatory social insurance but often along narrowly defined occupational distinctions. This implies that entitlements depend primarily on life-long employment which has, historically, helped cement the male-breadwinner logic of social protection. With the partial exception of Belgium and France, this regime is strongly familialistic, assuming that primary welfare responsibilities lie with family members. Policies that help reconcile motherhood and careers are relatively undeveloped. Hence, these welfare states are transfer-heavy and service-lean.

The role of private welfare is marginal, as in the Nordic countries, primarily because social insurance offers generous benefits and broad coverage of the employed population, but also due to high prices for private services—brought about by high fixed labor costs. Strong labor market regulation and high labor costs have

---

[6]  It has been argued that the Mediterranean countries constitute a special model. This is usually justified on the grounds that their social assistance schemes are unusually undeveloped and that they are characterized by very strong familialism. The Netherlands is an ambiguous case since it combines features, such as a large private sector role, that are similar to the Anglo-Saxon regime, but its welfare state design lies rather close to the other Continental countries. For a discussion, see Esping-Andersen (1999). I omit here Greece and Portugal.

influenced patterns of employment in several ways. First, while prime-age workers risk little unemployment, entry into first employment is made difficult. Youth unemployment is, except in Germany, extraordinarily high. Secondly, the lack of support for working mothers means that female employment has remained low, especially among less educated women. And thirdly, early retirement has been used intensely as a vehicle for clearing the labor market of older workers, thus lowering overall employment rates and raising pension expenditure.

Its redistributive profile is therefore likely to diverge from that of the other two. The dominance of insurance implies an accent on horizontal redistribution. Low employment rates, particularly among older workers, imply however that redistribution will appear strong, the reason being that extensive early retirement helps bloat the number of zero-earners whose main income derives from pensions. Low female participation, especially within the lower deciles of the income distribution, implies also greater household vulnerability—which, of course, is partially offset by strong employment protection. But low female employment means that groups like lone mothers are vulnerable.

There is no clear connection between these institutional features and welfare state size, as Table 25.1 shows. The liberal regime is, unsurprisingly, a low spender. But notwithstanding their institutional differences, the Nordic and Continental regimes basically converge in terms of spending. Regime distinctions are more accentuated when we examine the role of private welfare, social servicing intensity, and degree of targeting (here excluding transfers to the elderly). We can also capture differences by examining the generosity and distribution of transfer incomes to households— especially among non-retirees. In the Nordic countries, average transfer income (for active age households) equals 18 percent of median gross income, compared to 10 percent in Germany, and 14 percent in Britain. The targeted profile of Britain's welfare state emerges clearly when we compare the ratio of transfer income in the lowest and highest income quintile (4.6:1). The Swedish ratio, in comparison, is 2.5:1 (Fritzell, 2000).[7]

# 4. MEASURING WELFARE STATE REDISTRIBUTION

We cannot compare income distributions before and after the advent of the welfare state. One can examine how changes in policy (say, a pension reform) influenced

---

[7] Maitre *et al.* (2005, table 2), explicitly addressing welfare regime effects, conduct a similar analysis for all households, including the elderly, and find pretty much the same picture. The bottom:top transfer ratio is 5:1 in Denmark and 20:1 in the UK. But as also Fritzell's data show, there are no marked differences in terms of targeting between the Nordic and Continental European regimes—except that the average value of transfers is substantially higher in the former.

Table 25.1. Expenditure profiles in three welfare regimes

| Regime | Public social spending (% GDP)[1] | Private as % total social spending | Non–health services as % of total public spending | Targeting: % of transfers to bottom quintile[2] |
|---|---|---|---|---|
| Nordic | 25 | 5 | 18 | 34 |
| Anglo-Saxon | 19 | 19 | 4 | 43 |
| Continental Europe | 26 | 8 | 5 | 30 |

*Notes:* [1] Data refer to *net* social spending.
[2] Excluding retired households.
*Sources*: Calculations from Adema and Ladaique (2005, table 6) and from Forster and d'Ercole (2005).

the income distribution but then, of course, we are not measuring total welfare state effects. Almost all research seeks therefore recourse to year-specific cross-national comparisons. The measurement of welfare state redistribution faces severe obstacles, both in terms of getting the right data and in terms of methodology.

The early attempts to compare across countries, such as Sawyer (1976) and Stark (1977), were severely hampered by the incomparability of national income data. This all changed thanks to the efforts of the Luxembourg Income Study (LIS), and later also the OECD, to harmonize national income surveys (Mitchell, 1991; Atkinson *et al.*, 1995; Forster, 2000). The LIS data allowed, from the 1980s onward, researchers to obtain truly comparable estimates of income distributions (Atkinson *et al.*, 1995). The lion's share of comparative research over the past decades uses the LIS data.

But drawbacks remain. The data for any given country may represent an atypical year, due, for example, to external economic shocks. It also means that we cannot distinguish whether a household's reported income reflects a transitory or stable situation. The mix of transient and persistent poverty may differ across countries. A second major drawback is that we have generally no information on the distribution of public service consumption which, we know, varies hugely across welfare states.

The methodological obstacles are no less severe. A first consideration has to do with how we measure distributions.[8] Under the assumption that members of a household pool their income, the logical unit to study is the household.[9] In the literature we find three prevailing approaches: a summary measure, such as the Gini coefficient, a decile approach, where inequalities are captured via ratios (such as the top-to-bottom income decile), and a poverty-rate approach. It is broadly recognized that income alone may not give us an adequate picture of well-being and many argue therefore in favor of a more comprehensive, multidimensional measure of living conditions and household resources (Erikson and Aaberg, 1985; Nolan and

[8] For an overview, see Jesuit and Smeeding (2002).
[9] Assuming income pooling does not mean equal sharing among the members of the household. See Chapter 16 for a discussion.

Whelan, 2007). This, however, creates greater obstacles for obtaining internationally comparable data.

A huge amount of research has focused on welfare states' effectiveness in reducing poverty and this implies the need to define a meaningful poverty line. One hotly debated issue is whether to adopt a relative or 'absolute' measure. The reason that the vast majority prefer the former is to capture the meaning of being poor within the society one lives in. An American family with a $10,000 annual income might appear very rich to a Senegalese, but will have severe difficulties making ends meet in the USA.[10] A second issue is where to draw the line. The latter can have massive repercussions, all depending on where the poor are situated. A good example is Britain, where we frequently find very high poverty rates when the line is drawn at 50 percent of median income, but if we draw the line at 40 percent, poverty rates fall abruptly. The reason is that British public income support is typically pegged at a level of support that lies below the 50-percent line, but above the 40-percent line. Drawing the line will, in all cases, provoke some artificiality of assessment. There may, for example, be a large population that falls just immediately below the line. They would be classified as poor whereas those with just a few additional Euros would not. The standard approach that has been adopted in most studies is the 50-percent of median line, although the EU has officially chosen a 60-percent line. Studies that wish to capture the 'poverty gap', that is, how far below the line the poor find themselves, calculate either a gap measure or use several poverty lines (Mitchell, 1991; Kenworthy, 1999).

The prevailing consensus is that the income data must be weighted by the number of members in the household. See Chapters 3 and 4 in this Handbook. A single person and a family of four with identical incomes will obviously experience different welfare levels simply because of the number that needs to be fed and clothed. Following Atkinson et al. (1995), most studies adopt the square-root scale according to which the adjustment equals the square root of a household's size.[11]

A second methodological challenge lies in the difficulty of distinguishing between flux and stability. For a detailed examination, see Chapter 13. Cross-sectional data confound the two and this means that short-lived, transitory low (or high) income is given the same importance as persistent levels. This problem is most acute in studies that focus on poverty. We know that poverty is short-lived among a significant share of poor households (Duncan et al., 1993; Bradbury et al., 2001; Aaberge et al., 2002; Burkhauser and Poupore, 1997; Gangl, 2005; Jarvis and Jenkins, 1998). Studies that use permanent income, averaged over five or more years, find

---

[10]   There is surely a case to be made for an 'absolute' measure to the extent that someone below the poverty line in one country may be, consumption-wise, far better off than his/her equivalent in another country. To capture this possibility some researchers have made PPP adjustments to income data (Osberg et al., 2004).

[11]   Buhmann et al. (1988) present a detailed overview of alternative equivalence scales.

substantially less inequality than those that measure just one year. Those that are comparative find, additionally, that national differences are less accentuated than when we measure poverty rates in any given year (Duncan et al., 1993; Bradbury et al., 2001). Our ability to distinguish between transient as opposed to persistent or recurrent poverty is vital for understanding the effectiveness of welfare state guarantees. Although country differences are less marked, the evidence we have does suggest less persistence—especially among families with children—in strong welfare states, such as the Nordic. Whelan and Maitre (2007, table 6), using a more comprehensive measure of vulnerability, find that the share of the poor who are persistently vulnerable is substantially lower in Denmark than elsewhere. This they attribute mainly to the Danish active labor market policies that are explicitly designed to minimize long-term joblessness.

Few comparative studies have attempted to tackle the role of services. Most research includes only a sampling of services (typically education and health) and assign a per capita value (based on the cost to government of the service) across households (Smeeding et al., 1993; Smeeding and Rainwater, 2002; Osberg et al., 2004; Garfinkel et al., 2006). This approach may be unproblematic in the case of universally consumed services, such as elementary schools, but is obviously inadequate for services that have different take-up profiles across society. We know from research on inequalities in health care that the greater is the reliance on private financing, the more regressive is the effect. But even in countries with universal health care there exist strong social gradients in health-care consumption (Wagstaff and van Doorslaer, 2000). There are very few comparative studies that estimate the global service effect. Musgrave et al. (1974) were pioneers in attempting to assess the global redistributive impact of government programs, but their study was limited to the USA. The OECD provides what is probably the only existing comparative effort at estimating the impact of services (Marical et al., 2006).[12] A major advantage of the latter is that the distribution of services has been estimated via micro data on reported use by household members.

The final and surely most intractable methodological problem has to do with the inherent endogeneity between primary incomes and the welfare state. Some studies suggest that welfare state efforts to equalize opportunities, reconcile motherhood and careers, maximize employment, or homogenize early childhood development have decisive effects on equalizing lifetime earnings and career prospects and on reducing poverty (Kenworthy, 2004; Carneiro and Heckman, 2004; Esping-Andersen,

---

[12] Harding et al. (2006) offer a very comprehensive examination, but the study is limited to an Australian–UK comparison. They conclude that services are less redistributive than income transfers. But they are clearly redistributive (more so in Australia than in the UK). A study by the Economic Council of Denmark suggests that the overall effect of services is egalitarian. Taxation and cash transfers account for about two-thirds, and services for about one-third, of the total inequality reduction effect of government spending (Okonomisk Raad, 2001). See also Rele (2007) for the Netherlands.

1999, 2007). These may in fact overshadow the role of direct redistribution via taxes and income transfers. But, on this front, empirical research has made very little progress, basically because the counter-factual is virtually impossible to define.

The distortion is obviously greatest when we measure redistribution across the entire population. By focusing on particular population or age segments, we can control for some of the bias. To avoid the massive zero-earner retiree effect one might, for example, confine the study to households with heads in the active ages or even more narrowly defined population segments. An alternative, but rarely used, approach is to use micro-simulation techniques to test for the counter-factuals.[13] Rainwater and Smeeding (2003: 88 and 116), for example, simulate what child poverty rates would have been in other countries if their income support system (and demographic mix) were identical to the American.

# 5. WHAT DOES EMPIRICAL RESEARCH CONCLUDE?

There is, regardless of the many methodological problems, no doubt that welfare states redistribute in an egalitarian direction. Post-redistribution Gini coefficients, decile ratios, and poverty rates are systematically lower than for primary income distributions. What is also clear is that welfare states do it differently and vary substantially in their degree of equalization. A common characteristic, however, is that the lion's share of redistribution (typically around two-thirds) is accounted for by spending rather than taxation (Mitchell, 1991; Mahler and Jesuit, 2006; Immervoll *et al.*, 2005). As we would expect, the relative impact of taxation falls as the volume of spending rises. Moreover, social insurance contributions have almost no redistributive effect (Immervoll *et al.*, 2005)

A first step towards ascertaining welfare state effects would be to compare the level of nations' income inequality (measured, for example, by the Gini coefficient) between 'original' market incomes and post-redistribution disposable incomes. Few studies actually adopt this approach due primarily to the huge problem of zero-market-income populations among the elderly. Those that do find routinely that the large welfare states are more redistributive (Forster, 2000). Following the welfare regime approach, it is clear that the Anglo-Saxon group is systematically far

---

[13] See e.g. Immervoll *et al.* (2005) and Dang *et al.* (2006), both of which utilize the Euromod simulation model. Bergh (2005) attempts to identify the bias via theoretical simulation. Of particular interest is his attempt to identify distinctly different kinds of bias that are related to the design of countries' social protection system. He concludes that the bias is greater in countries with a prevalence of flat-rate benefits.

less redistributive than the other two, which, in turn, appear surprisingly similar within such aggregate comparisons. But when one excludes the elderly population, the convergence disappears and the Continental European welfare states begin to look more 'liberal'. This suggests an important difference in welfare state design. The Continental European countries' tax-transfer system is far more pensioner-biased, as is also clear in Dang *et al.* (2006). Such aggregate redistribution data confirm in another way the distinctiveness of welfare regimes, since intra-regime similarities in redistribution are overall surprisingly strong—the only real exception being Italy, which looks more similar to the Anglo-Saxon group.

A major shortcoming of cross-national comparisons of this type is that they provide only snapshots and fail, accordingly, to capture how welfare states respond to changes in economic inequality. Market incomes have, in the majority of OECD countries, experienced a strong inegalitarian trend over the past decades (Atkinson, 2003). In some countries, like the UK and the USA, the inegalitarian tide has been quite dramatic. This raises the question as to the welfare state's ability to stem, or even roll-back, the tide via an added redistributive effort. Research, so far, suggests that, in most OECD countries the jump in market inequalities has not been paralleled by a similar jump for disposable incomes (Esping-Andersen, 2007a). 'Stemming the tide' should provide a revealing indicator of a welfare state's commitment to equality. Kenworthy and Pontusson's (2005, figure 7) data suggest that the UK and the USA have done least to stem the tide, whereas Germany excels in the other direction. The Nordic countries have avoided any major surge in disposable income inequality by increased redistribution.

## The Impact of Welfare State Services

As noted, the OECD provides one of the very few attempts to assess the redistributive impact of social services across a broad number of countries.[14] Table 25.2 presents data on the level of public service expenditure (as a percentage of disposable income) in the first column. This provides an idea of the welfare state's servicing intensity. The second column shows the percentage reduction of *post-tax and transfer* income inequality attributable to services, measured with the Gini coefficient. The take-up of health and education services is, with very few exceptions, practically universal. What really distinguishes welfare regimes is the 'other' category, such as family services or elderly care. As noted, such services play a central role in the Nordic welfare states' pursuit of equality. The third column, as in the second, assesses their redistributive effect having already considered that of taxes and income transfers.

[14]  The reader should be warned that the OECD estimates are partly based on imputed recipiency (for details, see Marical *et al.*, 2006). The data refer to year 2000 and include health, education (all levels), social housing, and other services (such as old-age residencies).

Table 25.2. The impact of services on household inequality reduction

|  | Spending on services (% disposable income) | Percent inequality reduction of disposable income (all services) | Percent reduction excluding health and education |
|---|---|---|---|
| Denmark | 37 | 41 | 18 |
| Finland | 27 | 28 | 8 |
| Norway | 34 | 36 | 16 |
| Sweden | 40 | 42 | 21 |
| Regime mean | 35 | 37 | 16 |
| Australia | 28 | 30 | 7 |
| Canada | 26 | 21 | 3 |
| Ireland | 23 | 23 | 3 |
| N. Zealand | 25 | 24 | 3 |
| UK | 20 | 21 | 3 |
| USA | 22 | 22 | 2 |
| Regime mean | 24 | 24 | 4 |
| Austria | 26 | 24 | 0 |
| France | 33 | 30 | 7 |
| Germany | 28 | 26 | 4 |
| Italy | 25 | 24 | 0 |
| Netherlands | 20 | 20 | 4 |
| Spain | 23 | 22 | 0 |
| Regime mean | 26 | 24 | 3 |

Source: Recalculations from Marical et al. (2006, table A9).

To obtain an idea of how much they matter for total welfare state redistribution, non-health and education services account for 20 percent of the total monetary-plus-service effect in the Nordic regime, 15 percent in the Anglo-Saxon, and only 8 percent in the Continental European.[15]

Both in terms of spending and redistributive incidence, the Anglo-Saxon and Continental European regimes look very similar. Indeed, the latter is exceptionally service lean beyond the conventional health and education services and, unsurprisingly, the redistributive effect borders on zero. The Nordic regime (with Finland as an exception) clearly stands out, in terms of the redistributive impact of all services and especially of the 'other' category.[16] In fact, when we decompose the redistributive effect according to all the specific service categories, the 'other services' tends to be the single most redistributive (and education the least) in the Nordic countries.

All told, we must conclude that services are generally redistributive in an egalitarian direction, albeit less so than are cash transfers. This, once again, leads us to

[15]  The tax and transfer effect of redistribution, not shown, is based on the Luxembourg Income Study's Fiscal Redistribution data set.

[16]  Finland is in fact the only Nordic country that, like many Continental European countries, has pursued a cash-subsidy policy for caring for small children and dependent kin.

seriously question the thesis of Le Grand (1982). Since the redistributive effect of services also differs so strongly among countries, it should be evident that redistribution studies based exclusively on money incomes will provide a very incomplete and somewhat distorted picture of how much equality welfare states create.

Additional confirmation of the positive redistributive effect of services comes from Bergh's (2005) study of how much welfare states may be affecting the primary distribution of incomes. He concludes, on the basis of ordinary least squares (OLS) regressions, that spending on lower levels of education increases equality to the extent that it diminishes human capital differentials. Spending on higher education has the opposite effect. This is very consistent with research that focuses specifically on human capital policy (Carneiro and Heckman, 2003; Blanden *et al.*, 2004; Esping-Andersen, 2007b). What is particularly interesting in this regard is that such services undoubtedly yield a double egalitarian effect: they influence market-based incomes and government redistribution, both in a positive direction.

## Welfare States and Poverty

Poverty reduction is arguably the single most relevant measure of welfare state redistribution and, unsurprisingly, it has become the favored approach in empirical research. Theoretically, it provides a good test of the Rawlsean maximin principle of justice, namely that any redistribution should be to the greatest benefit of the worst off. It also speaks most directly to vertical, Robin Hood redistribution. For two reasons, research has especially centered on child poverty. One is that poverty in childhood is known to have seriously adverse consequences for later outcomes such as schooling, health, and social integration (Duncan and Brooks-Gunn, 1997; Vleminckx and Smeeding, 2001). Secondly, a welfare state's investment in children's well-being is potentially a very powerful tool for promoting greater equality of opportunities (Esping-Andersen, 2007b).

Virtually all studies conclude similarly that poverty reduction, in particular among families with children, is closely associated with levels of social expenditure. The Nordic countries are typically the most redistributive while the Anglo-Saxon (especially the USA) are the least (McFate *et al.*, 1995; Jäntti and Danziger, 2000; Bradbury and Jäntti, 2001; Smeeding, 2005a and 2005b). Smeeding (2005a: figure 1) shows a correlation of .6 between levels of cash social spending and poverty among non-elderly households. Corak (2005) shows, similarly, a strong correlation between welfare state spending on families and poverty reduction among children.

The country differences are in fact far more accentuated than when we use aggregate redistribution indicators like the Gini coefficient. At one extreme we find, once again, the USA, where government redistribution has only a very minor impact on child poverty and at the other extreme we find Sweden, where child poverty almost

Table 25.3. Poverty reduction in families with children, mid–1990s[1]

| | Market poverty | Post–redistribution of poverty | Percent reduction |
|---|---|---|---|
| Denmark | 30 | 6 | 80 |
| Finland | 18 | 3 | 83 |
| Norway | 29 | 5 | 83 |
| Sweden | 39 | 4 | 90 |
| Regime mean | 29 | 5 | 84 |
| Australia | 32 | 17 | 47 |
| Canada | 29 | 16 | 45 |
| Ireland | 28 | 15 | 46 |
| UK | 39 | 21 | 46 |
| USA | 31 | 26 | 16 |
| Regime mean | 32 | 19 | 40 |
| Belgium | 31 | 6 | 81 |
| France | 40 | 10 | 75 |
| Germany | 31 | 12 | 61 |
| Italy | 37 | 21 | 43 |
| Netherlands | 25 | 8 | 68 |
| Spain | 30 | 13 | 57 |
| Regime mean | 32 | 12 | 64 |

Note: [1] Poverty is less than 50% of median equivalent income.
Source: LIS-based estimates, from Bradbury and Jäntti (2001: 83).

disappears. In Sweden transfers account for almost 70 percent of income in poor households, compared to little more than 30 percent in the USA; in the USA, the primary policy vehicle is social assistance; in Sweden, targeted assistance plays a peripheral role (Rainwater and Smeeding, 2003; Smeeding, 2005b, table 8).

Maitre *et al.* (2005) adopt a welfare regime approach similar to ours and find a distinctly strong redistributive incidence in the Nordic regime and a weak incidence in the Southern European regime when examining poverty reduction across all households. Research that centers on child poverty suggests, however, that two Continental European welfare states (Belgium and France) perform more similarly to Scandinavia, while others, especially Italy, appear more similar to the US (Rainwater and Smeeding, 2003; Smeeding, 2005b). Table 25.3 presents data on poverty reduction in child families.

A remarkable feature is that pre-redistribution poverty rates vary little between countries. In terms of market incomes, there is, in fact, more child poverty in Sweden than in the USA. This reflects, of course, the artificiality of the 'original' income distribution. The universality of paid maternity leave in Sweden and the lack thereof in the USA implies a large number of zero-earner mothers in Sweden compared to the USA. The regime differences emerge when we shift attention to redistribution: a very homogeneous and strong redistributive effect is seen in the

Nordic countries. With the USA as an extreme case, the Anglo-Saxon group is only half as redistributive as is the Nordic. The Continental European countries are, once again, quite heterogeneous. Italy's performance lies closer to the Anglo-Saxon regime.

Research that focuses specifically on exceptionally vulnerable families, such as lone mothers, comes generally to similar conclusions. As we might expect, the differences in welfare state performance become even more accentuated (Bradbury and Jäntti, 2001; Smeeding, 2005a).

For different reasons, research on child and elderly poverty has been particularly concerned about the counter-factual problem. For child poverty, the main question is whether social transfers or support for mothers' employment constitutes the most effective means of poverty reduction. It is well-established that maternal employment reduces child poverty dramatically—typically by a factor of three or four. It is also evident that child poverty is especially acute in no-work households (Esping-Andersen, 1999; Rainwater and Smeeding, 2003; Whiteford and Adema, 2007). One reason why child poverty is especially low in the Nordic countries lies in the comparatively high maternal employment rates in vulnerable families, such as lone mother households.[17] But, of course, such high employment rates are attained in part via welfare state services, child care in particular, that we usually do not measure. Here we have additional support for Kenworthy's (2004) argument that welfare states' pursuit of maximum employment may be the really crucial strategy for equality.

Turning to elderly poverty, the counter-factual problem is multifaceted and only rarely examined in all its complexities in the comparative literature. The first and most basic problem is that welfare states typically compel the elderly to retire, thus forcing upon this population a prevalence of zero or very low market earnings. We must assume that this varies considerably across countries for a number of reasons, including normal age of retirement, rules regarding pension entitlements and continued earnings, and the prevalence of wives' incomes. In studies that focus on old-age poverty, the bias that is created by women's employment patterns is especially acute, since the large majority of poor elderly households are composed of widows with meager pension savings. A second major problem lies in the public–private mix of retirement savings and, in particular, in how welfare states' encourage private pension plans.

Lefebvre (2007) presents a rare attempt to disentangle all such effects cross-nationally, using both Gini coefficients and poverty rates. Unsurprisingly, he finds that poverty is the norm when we examine pre-transfer poverty, ranging from 90+ percent in Austria, Belgium, and France to a low of 54 percent in Finland. More to the point, he decomposes the marginal effect of earnings, property income,

---

[17]   As the US data suggest, high rates of lone mother employment may fail to stem poverty if lone mother earnings are low.

private pensions, and public transfers on final inequality. Earnings contribute very importantly to inequality, in particular because the highly skilled are more likely to continue working. This suggests that compulsory retirement reduces inequalities. Property income and private pensions are, likewise, a source of inequality. Their impact is minor in most European countries, but potentially large in the USA. Unfortunately, Lefebvre's (2007) study excludes the Anglo-Saxon countries but finds, interestingly, that private pensions reduce inequality in France and raise inequality in Sweden. Here, once more, the explanation lies in the interface of welfare state and markets: in France, private pension schemes are actually subject to government mandating and this results in near-universal inclusion among employees; in Sweden, the (small) private pension system is a negotiated supplement to government pensions which is strongly linked to earnings. All this considered, it nonetheless remains the case that government transfers account for most of the post-redistribution inequality among the elderly. Lefebvre finally concludes, like Korpi and Palme (1998), that welfare states that stress targeting the poor elderly are far less redistributive than are comprehensive (and therefore generous) pension programs (Lefebvre, 2007: 10). Nevertheless, contrary to Korpi and Palme, Canada's highly targeted old-age pensions achieve very low levels of old-age poverty.

## Welfare States and Income Dynamics

One-year-based snapshots of income inequality can be misleading if there are major cross-national differences in the relative salience of transitory and persistent low (or high) income. Research has approached the issue in two ways. One is to obtain measures of 'permanent income', that is, measured over several years so as to eliminate short-term (and possibly inconsequential) fluctuations. Ideally one might estimate inequality via lifetime incomes. Another is to focus on the persistency of poverty over several years, as do Whelan *et al.* (2003). Data limitations pose severe obstacles for international comparisons, however.

The few studies available on lifetime and permanent income inequality all suggest that, measured this way, overall inequality is significantly lower than when we examine one-year snapshots. We confront two problems in the study of persistency. The first, addressed by Whelan *et al.* (2003) and by Nolan and Marx (this volume, Chapter 13), is that there may be a large group of recidivists who exit and then re-enter poverty over a number of years. The second is that we need to avoid confounding 'real' and 'trivial' poverty exits. Table 25.4 addresses the second problem by stipulating that exit must imply moving above the 60-percent poverty line. As earlier, we focus on child families and trace poverty persistency over three or more years, beginning with the first year after measured poverty.

Table 25.4. The persistency of income poverty in families with children[1]

|  | One year | Two years | Three+ years |
|---|---|---|---|
| Denmark | 0.41 | 0.28 | 0.03 |
| France | 0.59 | 0.42 | 0.13 |
| Germany | 0.49 | 0.30 | 0.09 |
| Italy | 0.64 | 0.41 | 0.16 |
| Spain | 0.60 | 0.37 | 0.12 |
| UK | 0.49 | 0.29 | 0.11 |
| USA | 0.81 | 0.71 | 0.58 |

*Notes:* [1] Persistency has been estimated with Kaplan–Mayer survival functions. Income poverty is measured as <50% of adjusted median, and moving out of poverty is >60% of adjusted median income.

*Sources:* European Community Household Panel (ECHP), 1994–2001 for Europe and the Panel Study of Income Dynamics (PSID), 1993–7, for the USA.

In this case, the welfare regime distinction is not very helpful. Denmark performs particularly well in terms of avoiding long-term poverty (almost 60 percent have left poverty after the first year and by the third year there is basically no one left any more), but this is closely matched by Germany, and the UK is not far behind. Italy and especially the USA suffer from strong poverty persistency that, in both cases, can be linked to the welfare state. Their basic safety nets are comparatively very weak and ungenerous.

Such data do not, of course, identify the welfare state effect directly. Studies that attempt to do so conclude that demographic effects—in particular family structural change, such as lone motherhood—provide the main explanation for persistency in the USA, while employment-related factors and welfare state redistribution dominate in EU countries (Whelan *et al.*, 2003; Fourage and Layte, 2005).

# 6. CONCLUSIONS AND FURTHER RESEARCH

As discussed, we need a prohibitively comprehensive approach in order to adequately assess welfare state redistribution: at a minimum, such an approach needs to incorporate taxation, income transfers, and services, and also take care of the counter-factual problem. We must, additionally, recognize that income inequalities, poverty, and government responses are surely also a function of the society's underlying demography and social composition. Some countries are more aged than others and some have far higher rates of lone parenthood. The social composition of key groups can also be of major relevance. In the USA and UK, lone parenthood is far more slanted towards low-educated women than elsewhere. This implies that two welfare states with identical egalitarian commitments may produce different results, or that a welfare state with unfavorable demographics must make an additional redistributive effort to reach the same end-result.

We have, as yet, no single study that adequately incorporates all the above issues. Micro-data-based simulation (such as the EUROMOD) can help overcome some of these shortcomings to the extent that it permits us to control for differences in socio-demographic composition, and partially address the counter-factual— the latter by simulating what the effect would be if one country were to adopt a different country's welfare state. This kind of approach has been adopted by Sutherland (2001), Matsaganis *et al.* (2004), Immervoll *et al.* (2005), and Rainwater and Smeeding (2003). The latter, using LIS data, simulate what child poverty would have been in a number of countries *if* their demographic profile were similar to the USA and *if* their welfare states offered the kind of income support found in the American welfare state. US demography may be adverse in terms of child poverty but some other countries' (particularly Australia and the UK) poverty rates would actually diminish if saddled with a similar demography. In any case, the impact of demography pales in comparison with the welfare state effect. Rainwater and Smeeding find that child poverty in the Nordic countries would double and even triple if their welfare states performed like the American welfare state (2003). Pretty much the same picture obtains for Belgium, France, Germany, and the Netherlands. Only in Spain and Italy would the adoption of the US policy model actually contribute to a fall in child poverty.

Matsaganis *et al.* (2004) address an issue that is of special interest from a welfare regime perspective, namely what effects a Nordic-type child support policy would have on child poverty in Southern Europe—where, as we have seen, policy is unusually undeveloped (and child poverty substantial). They find that benefits targeted at the poor tend to be inefficient since take-up is very incomplete. Therefore, a Danish-style universal benefit model will have a far greater poverty-reduction effect, especially if pegged at Denmark's generosity level. A Danish benefit system would lower child poverty by almost 4 percentage points in Portugal and Spain but at a very high additional budgetary cost.[18]

So far we only have simulations that examine specific components of the welfare state, such as family benefit systems. A priority for future research is to address the counter-factual problem more comprehensively. To meet this challenge we need to develop a simulation methodology that allows us to obtain a more reliable and realistic picture of how market-based inequalities are patterned by the welfare state. Bergh's (2005) study shows that simulation based on artificially generated data can yield major insights into the influence of welfare states on the market-based distribution of income.

---

[18]   In Italy, surprisingly, a Danish policy would increase child poverty.

## References

AABERGE, R., BJÖRKLUND, A., JÄNTTI, M., PALME, M., PEDERSEN, P., SMITH, N., and WENNEMO, T. 2002. 'Income Inequality and Income Mobility in the Scandinavian Countries Compared to the United States'. *Review of Income and Wealth*, 48: 443–69.

ADEMA, W., and LADAIQUE, M. 2005. 'Net Social Expenditure'. OECD Social, Employment and Migration Working Paper 29.

ALBERTINI, M., KOHLI, M., and VOGEL, C. 2007. 'Intergenerational Transfers of Time and Money in European Families'. *Journal of European Social Policy*, 17: 319–34.

ATKINSON, A. B. 1995. 'The Welfare State and Economic Performance'. *National Tax Journal*, 48: 171–98.

—— 2003. 'Income Inequality in OECD Countries: Data and Explanations'. *CESifo Economic Studies*, 49: 479–513.

—— RAINWATER, L., and SMEEDING, T. 1995. *Income Distribution in OECD Countries*. Paris: OECD.

—— and STIGLITZ, J. 1987. *Lectures on Public Economics*. New York: McGraw-Hill.

BALDWIN, P. 1990. *The Politics of Social Solidarity*. Cambridge: Cambridge University Press.

BARR, N. 1998. *The Economics of the Welfare State*. Oxford: Oxford University Press.

—— 2001. *The Welfare State as Piggy Bank: Information, Risk, Uncertainty and the Role of the State*. Oxford: Oxford University Press.

BERAMENDI, P. 2001. 'The Politics of Income Inequality in the OECD: The Role of Second-Order Effects'. Luxembourg Income Study Working Paper 284.

BERGH, A. 2005. 'On the Counterfactual Problem of Welfare State Research: How Can we Measure Redistribution?' *European Sociological Review*, 21: 345–57.

BLANDEN, J., GOODMAN, A., GREGG, P., and MACHIN, S. 2004. 'Changes in Intergenerational Mobility in Britain', in M. Corak (ed.), *Generational Income Mobility*. Cambridge: Cambridge University Press, 122–46.

BRADBURY, B., and JÄNTTI, M. 2001. 'Child Poverty across Twenty-Nine Countries', in Bradbury *et al.* (2001), 62–91.

BRADBURY, B., JENKINS, S., and MICKLEWRIGHT, J. 2001. *The Dynamics of Child Poverty in Industrialized Countries*. Cambridge: Cambridge University Press.

BUHMANN, B., RAINWATER, L., SCHMAUS, G., and SMEEDING, T. 1988. 'Equivalence Scales, Well-Being, Inequality and Poverty: Sensitivity Estimates across Ten Countries'. *Review of Income and Wealth*, 34: 115–42

BURKHAUSER, R., and POUPORE, J. 1997. 'A Cross-National Comparison of Permanent Inequality in the United States and Germany'. *Review of Economics and Statistics*, 81: 251–68.

CARNEIRO, P., and HECKMAN, J. 2003. 'Human Capital Policy', in J. Heckman and A. Krueger (eds.), *Inequality in America*. Cambridge, Mass.: MIT Press, 77–240.

CORAK, M. 2005. 'Principles and Practicalities for Measuring Child Poverty in Rich Countries'. Luxembourg Income Study Working Paper 406.

CURTRIGHT, P. 1967 'Income Redistribution: A Cross-National Analysis'. *Social Forces*, 46: 180–90

DANG, T., IMMERVOLL, H., MANTOVANI, D., ORSINI, K., and SUTHERLAND, H. 2006. 'An Age Perspective on Economic Well-Being and Social Protection in Nine OECD Countries'. IZA Working Paper 2173.

DUNCAN, G., and BROOKS-GUNN, J. 1997. *Consequences of Growing up Poor*. New York: Russell Sage.

—— GUSTAFSSON, B., HAUSER, R., SCHMAUS, G., MUFFELS, R., NOLAN, B., and RAY, J. 1993. 'Poverty Dynamics in Eight Countries'. *Journal of Population Economics*, 6: 295–334.

ERIKSON, R., and AABERG, R. 1985. *Welfare in Transition*. Oxford: Clarendon.

ESPING-ANDERSEN, G. 1990. *The Three Worlds of Welfare Capitalism*. Cambridge: Polity Press.

—— 1999. *Social Foundations of Postindustrial Economies*. Oxford: Oxford University Press.

—— 2007a. 'More Inequality and Fewer Opportunities? Structural Determinants and Human agency in the Dynamics of Income Distribution', in D. Held and A. Kaya (eds.), *Global Inequality*. Cambridge: Polity Press, 216–51.

—— 2007b. 'Childhood Investments and Skill Formation'. *International Tax and Finance Journal*, 15: 14–49.

FORSTER, M. 2000. 'Trends and Driving Forces in Income Distribution and Poverty in the OECD Area'. OECD Labor Market and Social Policy Occasional Papers 42.

—— and D'ERCOLE, M. 2005. 'Income Distribution and Poverty in OECD Countries in the Second Half of the 1990s'. OECD Social, Employment and Migration Working Paper 22.

FOURAGE, D., and LAYTE, R. 2005. 'Welfare Regimes and Poverty Dynamics'. *Journal of Social Policy*, 34: 1–20.

FRITZELL, J. 2000. 'Still Different? Income Distribution in the Nordic Countries in a European Comparison'. Luxembourg Income Study Working Paper 238.

GANGL, M. 2005. 'Income Inequality, Permanent Incomes, and Income Dynamics: Comparing Europe to the United States'. *Work and Occupations*, 32: 140–62.

GARFINKEL, I., RAINWATER, L., and SMEEDING, T. 2006. 'A Re-examination of Welfare State and Inequality in Rich Nations'. *Journal of Policy Analysis and Management*, 25: 897–919.

GARRETT, G. 1998. *Partisan Politics in the Global Economy*. Cambridge: Cambridge University Press.

GOODIN, R., and LE GRAND, J. 1987. *Not Only For the Poor: The Middle Classes and the Welfare State*. London: Allen & Unwin.

HARDING, A, WARREN, N., and LLOYD, R. 2006. 'Moving beyond the Traditional Cash Measures of Economic Well-Being'. National Centre for Social and Economic Modelling (Canberra) Working Paper 61.

HILLS, J. 2004. *Inequality and the State*. Oxford: Oxford University Press.

HUBER, E., and STEPHENS, J. 2001. *Political Choice in Global Markets*. Chicago: University of Chicago Press.

IMMERVOLL, H., LEVY, H., LIETZ, C., MANTOVANI, D., O'DONOGHUE, C., SUTHERLAND, H., and VERBIST, G. 2005. 'Household Incomes and Redistribution in the European Union'. EUROMOD Working Paper no. EM9/05.

IVERSEN, T., and CUSACK, T. 2000. 'The Causes of Welfare State Expansion'. *World Politics*, 52: 313–49.

JÄNTTI, M., and DANZIGER, S. 2000. 'Income Poverty in Advanced Countries', in A. Atkinson and F. Bourguignon (eds.), *Handbook of Income Distribution*. Amsterdam: North-Holland.

JARVIS, S., and JENKINS, S. 1998 'How much Income Inequality is there in Britain?' *Economic Journal*, 108: 428–43.

JESUIT, D., and SMEEDING, T. 2002. 'Poverty and Income Distribution'. Luxembourg Income Study Working Paper 293.

KENWORTHY, L. 1999. 'Do Social Welfare Policies Reduce Poverty?' *Social Forces*, 77: 1119–39.
—— 2004. *Egalitarian Capitalism*. New York: Russell Sage.
—— and PONTUSSON, J. 2005. 'Rising Inequality and the Politics of Redistribution in Affluent Countries'. *Perspectives on Politics*, 3: 449–71.
KORPI, W. 1983. *The Democratic Class Struggle*. London: Routledge and Kegan Paul.
—— and PALME, J. 1998. 'The Paradox of Redistribution and Strategies of Equality'. *American Sociological Review*, 63: 661–87.
LEFEBVRE, M. 2007. 'The Redistributive Effects of Pension Systems in Europe: A Survey of the Evidence'. Luxembourg Income Study Working Paper 457.
LE GRAND, J. 1982. *The Strategy of Equality*. London: Allen & Unwin.
LINDERT, P. 2004. *Growing Public. Social Spending and Economic Growth since the Eighteenth Century*. Cambridge: Cambridge University Press.
McFATE, K., SMEEDING, T., and RAINWATER, L. 1995. 'Markets and States: Poverty Trends and Transfer System Effectiveness in the 1980s', in K. McFate, R. Lawson, and W. J. Wilson (eds.), *Poverty, Inequality and the Future of Social Policy*. New York: Russell Sage, 67–108.
MAHLER, V., and JESUIT, D. 2006. 'Fiscal Redistribution in the Developed Countries'. *Socio-Economic Review*, 4: 483–512.
MAITRE, B., NOLAN, B., and WHELAN, C. 2005. 'Welfare Regimes and Household Income Packaging in the European Union'. *Journal of European Social Policy*, 15: 157–71.
MARICAL, F., d'ERCOLE, M., VAALAVUO, M., and VERBIST, G. 2006. 'Publicly Provided Services and the Distribution of Resources'. OECD Social, Employment and Migration Working Paper 45.
MATSAGANIS, M., O'DONOGHUE, C., LEVY, H., COROMALDO, M., MERCADER-PRATS, M., RODRIGUES, C., TOSO, S., and TSAKLOGLOU, P. 2004. 'Child Poverty and Family Transfers in Southern Europe'. Euromod Working Paper no. EM2-04.
MELTZER, A., and RICHARD, S. 1981. 'A Rational Theory of the Size of Government'. *Journal of Political Economy*, 89: 914–27.
MILANOVIC, B. 2000. 'The Median-Voter Hypothesis, Income Inequality and Income Redistribution'. *European Journal of Political Economy*, 16(2–3): 367–410.
MITCHELL, D. 1991. *Income Transfers in Ten Welfare States*. Sydney: Avebury.
MOENE, K., and WALLERSTEIN, M. 2001. 'Inequality, Social Insurance and Redistribution'. *American Political Science Review*, 95: 859–914, 927–74.
—— —— 2003. 'Earnings Inequality and Welfare State Spending'. *World Politics*, 55: 485–516.
MOFFITT, R., RIBAR, D., and WILHELM, M. 1998. 'The Decline of Welfare Benefits in the US: The Role of Wage Inequality'. *Journal of Public Economics*, 68: 421–52.
MUSGRAVE, R., CASE, K., and LEONARD, H. 1974. 'The Distribution of Fiscal Burdens and Benefits'. *Public Finance Quarterly*, 2: 259–311.
NOLAN, B., and WHELAN, C. 2007. 'On the Multi-dimensionality of Poverty and Social Exclusion', in J. Micklewright and S. Jenkins (eds.), *Inequality and Poverty Re-examined*. Oxford: Oxford University Press.
OKONOMISK RAAD. 2001. *Dansk Okonomi*. Copenhagen: Det Okonomisk Raad.
OSBERG, L., SMEEDING, T., and SCHWABISH, J. 2004. 'Income Distribution and Public Social Expenditure', in K. Neckerman (ed.), *Social Inequality*. New York: Russell Sage, 821–60.
PALME, J. 2006. 'Welfare States and Inequality: Institutional Designs and Distributive Outcome'. *Research in Social Stratification and Mobility*, 24: 387–403
PAMPEL, F., and WILLIAMSON, J. 1989. *Age, Class, Politics and the Welfare State*. New York: Cambridge University Press.

PEROTTI, R. 1996. 'Growth, Income Distribution and Democracy'. *Journal of Economic Growth*, 1(2): 149–87.

RAINWATER, L., and SMEEDING, T. 2003. *Poor Kids in a Rich Country*. New York: Russell Sage.

RELE, H. 2007. 'Measuring the Lifetime Redistribution Achieved by Dutch Taxation, Cash Transfer and Non-Cash Benefit Programs'. *Review of Income and Wealth*, 53: 335–62.

RIMLINGER, G. 1971. *Welfare Policy and Industrialization in Europe, America and Russia*. New York: John Wiley.

RODRICK, D. 1998. 'Why do More Open Economies have Larger Governments?' *Journal of Political Economy*, 106: 997–1033.

ROEMER, J. 1998. 'Why the Poor do Not Expropriate the Rich'. *Journal of Public Economics*, 70: 399–424.

SAWYER, M. 1976. *Income Distribution in OECD Countries*. Paris: OECD.

SMEEDING, T. 1997. 'Financial Poverty in Developed Countries'. Luxembourg Income Study Working Paper 115.

—— 2005a. 'Government Programs and Social Outcomes: The United States in Comparative Perspective'. Luxembourg Income Study Working Paper 426.

—— 2005b. 'Poor People in Rich Nations: The United States in Comparative Perspective'. Luxembourg Income Study Working Paper 419.

—— and RAINWATER, L. 2002. 'Comparing Living Standards across Nations'. Luxembourg Income Study Working Paper 266.

—— SAUNDERS, S., CODERN, J., JENKINS, S., FRITZELL, J., HAGENAARS, A., HAUSER, R., and WOLFSON, M. 1993. 'Poverty, Inequality and Family Living Standards across Seven Nations: The Effect of Non-Cash Subsidies for Health, Education and Housing'. *Review of Income and Wealth*, 39(3): 229–56.

STAHLBERG, A. C. 2007. 'Redistribution across the Life Course in Social Protection Systems', in OECD, *Modernizing Social Policy for the New Life Course*. Paris: OECD, 201–17.

STARK, S. 1977. *The Distribution of Income in Eight Countries*. The Royal Commission on the Distribution of Income and Wealth. London: Her Majesty's Stationary Office.

SUTHERLAND, H. 2001. 'Reducing Child Poverty in Europe: What Can Static Microsimulation Tell Us?' Euromod Working Paper no. EM5-01.

TULLOCK, G. 1983. *Economics of Income Distribution*. Boston: Kluwer.

VLEMINCKX, K., and SMEEDING, T. 2001. *Child Well-Being, Child Poverty, and Child Policy in Modern Nations*. Bristol: Policy Press.

WAGSTAFF, A., and van DOERSLAER, E. 2000. 'Equity in Health Care Financing and Delivery', in A. Culyer and J. Nehouse (eds.), *Handbook of Health Economics*. New Holland: Elsevier, chapter 40.

WHELAN, C., LAYTE, R., and MAITRE, B. 2003. 'Persistent Income Poverty and Deprivation in the European Union'. *Journal of Social Policy*, 32: 1–18.

—— and MAITRE, B. 2007. 'The Dynamics of Economic Vulnerability: A Comparative European Analysis'. ESRI Working Paper no. 202.

WHITEFORD, P., and ADEMA, W. 2007. 'What Works Best in Reducing Child Poverty: A Benefit or Work Strategy?' OECD Social, Employment and Migration Working Paper 51.

WILENSKY, H. 1975. *The Welfare State and Inequality*. Berkeley: University of California Press.

# CHAPTER 26

# THE POLITICAL ECONOMY OF INEQUALITY AND REDISTRIBUTION

## NOLAN McCARTY

## JONAS PONTUSSON

## 1. INTRODUCTION

WITH economic inequality rising in many advanced industrial countries, the question of how economic and social inequalities affect politics and the extent to which the disadvantaged can influence government and policy has become a central concern of many political scientists. There is also renewed interest in the question of how political processes and institutions determine the distribution of resources in society. Because purely economic explanations are unlikely to account fully for cross-sectional variation in levels and trajectories of inequality, many economists have recognized the importance of politics and joined this conversation.

From Aristotle to Madison to modern political economists, many have long believed that democratic political processes and institutions have an equalizing effect. Ideally, popular participation would generate government reactions that ensured that both prosperity and hardship were widely shared. But a simple relationship between democracy and equality is elusive and incomplete. There are great disparities in indicators of economic inequality across the world's affluent countries despite the democratic nature of their political systems. In some advanced democracies, moreover, governments have retreated from efforts to ameliorate inequalities at the very time that economic forces have pushed toward a less equitable distribution of rewards.

The literature on the politics of inequality and redistribution in advanced democracies has become very large in recent years. In this chapter, we focus on several areas where we feel that important new arguments are being put forward. We review recent work on the interaction of unions and employers, the role of political parties and electoral institutions, and the effects of racial and religious diversity. We also discuss the implications of recent work in behavioral economics and political science that helps us to understand cross-national variation in political responses to inequality. We highlight the distinctive contributions of several 'schools' of research, but, most importantly, we try to identify linkages across different analytical approaches.

## 2. Outcomes of Interest

This section identifies and illustrates some of the cross-national variation that has animated comparative studies of the determinants of welfare-state development and redistributive policy. To begin with, there is a large literature that aspires to explain over-time as well as cross-national variation in the size of the welfare state. The dependent variable in this literature is typically some measure of social spending expressed as a percentage of GDP. Such measures have become increasingly refined, but 'gross' measures of social spending remain standard.

Table 26.1 presents recent figures for two alternative measures of social spending. Both measures encompass old-age and disability pensions, unemployment insurance, sick pay and parental leave insurance, family allowances, social assistance, housing subsidies, health care, child care, care for the elderly and disabled, as well as active labor market programs. While the figures in the first column of Table 26.1 refer to gross government spending on such programs, the figures in the second column refer to 'net government and government-mandated social spending'. The latter measure includes private social expenditures mandated by government as well as the value of tax credits that serve social policy purposes (treating foregone tax revenues as equivalent to government expenditures) and also takes account of direct and indirect taxation of cash benefits received from the government.

Table 26.1. Public and publicly mandated social spending as a percentage of GDP, 2003

|  | Gross | Adjusted net |
|---|---|---|
| Sweden | 31.3 (1) | 24.6 (3) |
| France | 28.7 (2) | 25.8 (2) |
| Denmark | 27.6 (3) | 20.4 (8) |
| Germany | 27.3 (4) | 26.4 (1) |
| Belgium | 26.5 (5) | 22.9 (4) |
| Austria | 26.1 (6) | 18.2 (12) |
| Norway | 25.1 (7) | 21.2 (5) |
| Italy | 24.2 (8) | 21.2 (5) |
| Portugal | 23.5 (9) | 21.2 (5) |
| Finland | 22.5 (10) | 19.9 (9) |
| Netherlands | 20.7 (11) | 18.3 (11) |
| UK | 20.6 (12) | 19.9 (9) |
| Switzerland | 20.5 (13) | n.a. |
| Spain | 20.3 (14) | 17.6 (15) |
| New Zealand | 18.0 (15) | 15.1 (18) |
| Australia | 17.9 (16) | 18.2 (12) |
| Japan | 17.7 (17) | 18.2 (12) |
| Canada | 17.3 (18) | 17.2 (17) |
| USA | 16.2 (19) | 17.6 (15) |
| Ireland | 15.9 (20) | 14.0 (19) |

*Notes*: Gross = direct social spending by government; Adjusted net = direct spending plus tax credits and government-mandated private spending minus direct and indirect taxes on benefits.

*Source*: OECD, 'The Social Expenditure Database: An Interpretive Guide' (2007: 20, 81).

Measuring public welfare provision in terms of net government and government-mandated spending, the range of variation among advanced democracies is more compressed than the conventional picture, based on gross spending data, would have it. The rank ordering of the countries is also quite different. In particular, the Scandinavian countries fall in the rank ordering while Germany and France rise to the top as we move from a gross to a net measure of social spending. At the same time, it should be noted that there is a strong correlation between the two measures of social spending presented in Table 26.1 ($r = 0.848$).

Although some scholars consider spending levels to be an outcome of intrinsic interest, many (e.g. Alesina and Glaeser, 2004) conceive the level of social spending as a proxy for the degree of redistribution. As better comparative data on income distribution have become available (in the first instance, from the Luxembourg Income Study(LIS)), comparativists interested in redistributive politics have begun to use measures of redistribution as their dependent variable (e.g. Bradley *et al.*,

2003; Iversen and Soskice, 2006). The standard measure of redistribution in this new literature is the percentage change in Gini coefficients that we observe as we move from market income (before taxes and transfers) to disposable income (after taxes and transfers), but some studies look at changes in relative poverty rates (e.g. Moller *et al.*, 2003). The range of variation among advanced democracies on such measures is even wider than the range of variation on measures of social spending. At the low end of the spectrum, taxes and transfers reduced the Gini coefficient for household income by 22% in Switzerland in 2000. At the other end of the spectrum, the corresponding figure for Denmark was 47% (see Chapter 4, Figure 4.7).

As Esping-Andersen and Myles stress in Chapter 25, measuring the redistributive effects of the welfare state as the difference between market-income and disposable-income inequality ignores the many ways that taxes and benefits affect the distribution of market income or, in other words, the 'second-order effects' of the welfare state (cf. Beramendi, 2001). Most obviously, generous public pension schemes reduce the incentives of individuals to save for their retirement. In Sweden, many retired people have no income at all before they receive their public pension, but this does not make them 'poor' in any conventional sense. To get around this problem, recent LIS-based studies restrict the analysis of the redistributive effects of taxes and transfers to working-age households (e.g. Milanovic, 2000; Bradley *et al.*, 2003; Kenworthy and Pontusson, 2005). Yet taxes and transfers are also likely to affect relative (gross) earnings within the working-age population. Suffice it to note here that second-order effects represent a difficult theoretical as well as empirical problem that the existing literature on the politics of redistribution has yet to tackle in a comprehensive way.

An important strand of comparative welfare-state research, building on Esping-Andersen's (1990) seminal work, downplays the significance of aggregate social spending and instead focuses attention on eligibility principles and the institutional configuration of welfare states (see also Chapter 25). As this literature demonstrates, welfare states can be distinguished in terms of the importance of cash benefits relative to services ('in-kind benefits'). The extent to which means-testing is used to determine benefits eligibility represents another important dimension of cross-national variation. Thirdly, social insurance schemes may be organized on a universalistic basis or on an occupational basis.[1]

For our purposes, the critical claim of this literature is that the way welfare states are organized mediates the relationship between levels of spending and redistributive effects (cf. Korpi and Palme, 1998). Generally speaking, overall levels of social spending provide a reasonably good predictor of the difference between market-income and disposable-income inequality measured by Gini coefficients or relative poverty rates (Smeeding, 2005). However, the more universalistic Nordic

---

[1]  A fourth dimension of cross-national variation concerns the implications of family support and other social policies for women's participation in the labor market.

welfare states clearly stand out as particularly redistributive by standard LIS-based measures (Chapter 4, Figure 4.7) even though they do not stand out relative to continental European welfare states in terms of net social spending.[2] It is also noteworthy that reliance on means testing is not associated with poverty reduction among OECD countries (see Pontusson, 2005: 156–60). The standard explanation of this puzzle is that means testing generates middle-class resistance to taxation. Simply put, targeting benefits to the poor produces more redistribution per dollar spent, but also reduces the total amount of social spending (cf. Korpi and Palme, 1998).

Finally, we must keep in mind that government policies that are not typically associated with the welfare state also affect the distribution of income. Most obviously, macroeconomic policy, trade policy, regulatory and industrial policies, and educational policy have important distributive consequences. On the other hand, modern welfare states serve many purposes and redistribution of (current) income represents but one outcome metric by which they might be compared. Put differently, the politics of redistribution and the politics of the welfare state should not be conflated. The literature that we review in this chapter pertains to the overlap between the two, but the models of redistributive politics generated by this literature ought to be relevant to other policy spheres as well and, by the same token, should not be read as providing a complete account of the development of modern welfare states.

# 3. INCOME AND PREFERENCES FOR REDISTRIBUTION

One way to approach the problem of explaining the cross-national patterns described above is to consider how voters form preferences for redistribution or social insurance and how political processes aggregate these preferences. We begin by considering two simple and influential models along these lines.

In the Meltzer and Richard (MR) (1981) model, the median voter seeks to maximize current income. If there are no deadweight costs to redistribution, all voters with incomes below the mean maximize their utility by imposing a 100% tax rate and receiving a lump-sum payment equal to the average income. Conversely, all voters with incomes above the mean prefer a tax rate of zero. When taxation is costly, that is, reduces average income, voters with incomes above the mean still prefer a tax rate of zero, but voters with below mean incomes no longer prefer a

---

[2]  Taking into account the redistribution of consumption through publicly provided services makes the Nordic welfare states stand out even more: see Garfinkel *et al.* (2006).

100% tax. Instead, their preferred tax rate is a decreasing function of their personal income and an increasing function of average income. The core implication of the MR model is that inequality increases the demand for redistribution by the median voter so long as the income distribution is right-skewed and the mean income remains constant.

Moene and Wallerstein (MW) (2001, 2003) present models where social spending not only redistributes income but also provides insurance. In the MW model, voters choose both the income transfer that citizens receive when unemployed and the taxes needed to pay for these benefits. Given standard assumptions about preferences for risk, an increase in the gap between the pre-benefit income of the unemployed and the income of an employed worker leads the employed worker to demand more insurance in the form of unemployment benefits. In the MW model, a mean-preserving spread of wages reduces the gap between the incomes of the unemployed and those with wages below the mean. This in turn leads to a decline in the demand for social insurance and consequently a lower preferred tax rate.

In the MR model, higher inequality implies that the median voter demands more redistribution while just the opposite holds for the MW model. It has become more or less conventional wisdom in the comparative political economy literature that the empirical association between inequality and redistribution in the OECD countries conforms to the predictions of the MW model rather than the MR model. If one plots social spending as a percentage of GDP or some measure of redistribution against wage inequality, one finds that more egalitarian countries consistently have larger, more redistributive welfare states than less egalitarian countries (see e.g. Iversen and Soskice, 2007). According to Lindert (2004: 15), 'history reveals a "Robin Hood paradox," in which redistribution from rich to poor is least present when and where it seems to be most needed'.

When one instead plots redistribution (or social spending in % of GDP) against Gini coefficients for market income (or gross earnings) among working-age households, however, there is no cross-national association at all between these variables (Kenworthy and Pontusson, 2005: 458). Milanovic (2000) estimates a series of fixed-effects models with redistribution as the dependent variable and different measures of household income inequality (before taxes and transfers) as the main regressor. With this specification, market income inequality turns out to be positively (and significantly) associated with redistribution. In other words, the pattern of within-country variation countries appears to be broadly consistent with the core prediction of the MR model and contrary to the MW model (see also Kenworthy and Pontusson, 2005). At the same time, Milanovic shows that taxes and transfers consistently tend to reduce the share of total income of households in the fifth and sixth deciles of the 'pre-fisc' distribution.[3] Assuming that the median voter falls

---

[3]  The fifth decile is a net taxpayer in 49 and the sixth decile is a net taxpayer in 54 of the 68 country-years included in Milanovic's analysis.

in this range, the causal mechanism posited by Meltzer and Richard (the median voter seeking to maximize current income) cannot explain the association between market inequality and redistribution. If the median voter determines government policy, she must be motivated by some form of altruism or affinity with people below the median income or, alternatively, by concerns about insuring herself against downward mobility.

As illustrated by the MR and MW models, the existing literature tends to juxtapose redistribution and insurance as alternative motivations behind the expansion of the welfare state. This strikes us as unfortunate. Not only are both motives in play, providing the basis for broad, cross-class support for welfare-state expansion (different voters/groups supporting social spending for different reasons), but public insurance against risks such as unemployment and illness is itself redistributive to the extent that risk exposure varies inversely with income. Demand for insurance may rise with income, as MW postulate, but income-differentiated risk exposure works in the opposite direction. Furthermore, higher-income individuals have many more private alternatives for insurance against income fluctuations, especially their own wealth, a factor that the MW model does not take into account. At the individual level, income is in fact inversely associated with support for social spending in most, perhaps all, advanced industrial democracies (see Iversen and Soskice, 2001).

It is commonplace to criticize the MR model for assuming that all income earners vote or, at least, that there is no income bias in voting. This line of criticism is in fact a red herring. The critical variable in the MR model is the distance between the income of the median voter and the mean income, *not* the distance between the median income and the mean income (cf. Nelson, 1999; McCarty et al., 2006). One of Meltzer and Richard's main points is that, with income inequality held constant, the extension of the franchise to include low-income earners reduces the relative income of the median voter and, as a result, generates more redistributive government. In testing the predictions of either the MR model or the MW model, it is essential to control for income bias in voting. Most of the quantitative studies reviewed here (including Moene and Wallerstein, 2001, 2003) attempt to do so by controlling for aggregate voter turnout.[4]

A more important limitation of the MR and MW models is that they rest on a majoritarian conception of the political process. Both models posit that the median voter determines the outcome of elections and that political parties cater to the preferences of the median voter not only in their election campaigns but also in government. A second commonality of these models is that voters are motivated (entirely) by maximizing the expected utility of consumption and, as

---

[4] Needless to say perhaps, income bias in voting is bound to diminish as aggregate turnout approaches 100%. Mahler (2008) demonstrates that there is a strong negative correlation between aggregate turnout and income bias across advanced democracies.

a result, their preferences can be inferred straightforwardly from their position in the income distribution. Either of these assumptions may account for the failure of the MR and MW models to provide robust accounts of observed cross-national patterns of social spending and redistributive outcomes. In what follows, we first discuss theoretical traditions and empirical research that question the universal applicability of the majoritarian conception of politics and explore the significance of political institutions for the aggregation of voter preferences. In due course, we will take up the question of how voter preferences might be conceptualized differently.

# 4. Government Partisanship and Organized Interests

The baseline models of redistributive politics discussed in the previous section neglect the role of political parties. Contemporary partisan theories posit that parties are not only office-seeking, as Downs (1957) proposed, but also policy-seeking and that they represent distinctly different segments of the electorate (core constituencies). According to such theories, parties are not oblivious to the policy preferences of the median voter, but uncertainty about the preferences of the median voter leads parties to choose divergent policy positions (see Wittman, 1977 and Calvert, 1985). Furthermore, the convergence predicted by Downs does not hold in models of multiparty competition, which is the typical state of affairs in European welfare states.

In the comparative welfare-state literature, the proposition that the partisan composition of government matters to policy outcomes is closely associated with the 'power resources theory' (PRT) developed by Korpi (1983, 2006) and adopted, with modifications, by Stephens (1979), Esping-Andersen (1990), and Huber and Stephens (2001) among others. As formulated by Korpi, PRT treats trade unions and left parties as representatives of working-class interests in the 'democratic class struggle'. The public provision of social welfare caters to the interests of workers, defined broadly as wage-earners with limited economic resources, by insuring their income stream against the vicissitudes of the market, reducing their dependence on particular employers if not their dependence on employment in general, and by redistributing income and consumption opportunities. PRT expects employers and other social groups that do not primarily depend on income from dependent employment to resist the expansion of public welfare systems, especially public welfare systems based on the principle of social citizenship. The extent to which governments provide for social protection and redistribution thus depends first and foremost on the ability of unions and left parties to mobilize workers politically.[5]

Several modifications of PRT since its initial formulation in the 1970s deserve to be noted. To begin with, the traditional partisanship argument, based on juxtaposing left parties representing labor to any and all other parties to their right, has been modified by recognizing that Christian Democratic parties have a long tradition of support for public provision of social welfare. Secondly, PRT proponents have sought to unpack social spending and to explore the effects of partisanship on dimensions of cross-national variation other than sheer size of the welfare state. Thirdly, they have incorporated the idea of a 'hegemony effect'. Simply put, strong left parties that are successful in enacting social reforms force center-right parties to embrace more redistributive policies in order to compete electorally (Korpi, 1983). From a Downsian perspective, we might say that hegemonic parties induce a shift in the preferences of the median voter.

To capture the long-term effects of partisanship, Huber and Stephens (2001) use cumulative cabinet shares held by left parties and Christian Democratic parties in their analysis of levels of government spending over the period 1960–85. Huber and Stephens find that government participation by left parties had a substantial positive effect and that government participation by Christian Democratic parties had an even larger effect on overall government spending in this period. While Christian Democratic participation in government is more strongly associated with spending on social security transfers, the share of cabinet seats held by left parties emerges as a much better predictor of civilian government consumption and especially the size of the public sector (cf. Iversen and Cusack, 2000).

PRT provides a ready explanation of the aforementioned 'Robin Hood paradox'. In this theoretical framework, strong unions and left parties promote both wage compression and redistributive government (Bradley *et al.*, 2003). Thus the inverse cross-sectional correlation between wage compression and redistribution can be considered spurious, caused by the omission of labor-movement strength. The finding that market inequality is positively associated with redistribution once we introduce country-specific fixed effects (Milanovic, 2000) poses something of a challenge to PRT, however.

The PRT-inspired literature seems to assume that employers (capital) are invariably opposed to any and all forms of social protection. In critical dialog with power resource theory, a new literature has recently emerged that explores cross-national variation in employer attitudes towards the welfare state and emphasizes

---

[5] Though the PRT literature typically relies on unionization as the principal measure of working-class mobilization, Korpi (1983) points to voter turnout as an alternative measure. As Kenworthy and Pontusson (2005) suggest, power resources and median-voter theories might be construed as complementary in the sense that the former addresses the question of who the median voter is while the latter addresses the question of how parties behave.

the role of 'cross-class alliances' in the development of the welfare state.[6] Closely associated with the idea of 'Varieties of Capitalism' (VofC), one strand of this literature focuses on the link between social policy and skill formation. In a pioneering essay, Estevez-Abe *et al.* (2001) proceed from the observation that the 'coordinated market economies' (CMEs) of continental Europe rely more heavily on firm- and industry-specific skills than do 'liberal market economies' (LMEs) such as the USA and UK and that continental Europe is also distinguished from the Anglo-Saxon countries by more extensive employment protection and more generous unemployment insurance (see also Iversen, 2005). The core argument here is that investment in specific skills entails greater risks than investment in general skills and that social policy arrangements shape individual decisions about investment in different kinds of skills. To invest in firm-specific skills, workers must feel reasonably sure than they will work for the same employer for an extended period of time. Similarly, to invest in industry-specific skills, they need assurance of good long-term employment prospects within the same industry and income support during possible unemployment spells.

Iversen and Soskice (2001) complement this argument by showing that, controlling for income, skill specificity is strongly associated with support for social spending in all OECD countries for which the requisite survey data are available. For our present purposes, however, the key point is that employers who have invested in production systems that rely on firm- or industry-specific skills benefit from the social policies characteristic of continental Europe. In CMEs, according to Estevez-Abe *et al.* (2001: 147), the welfare state is supported by 'a strong alliance between skilled workers and their employers'.

Estevez-Abe *et al.* assert that welfare-state retrenchments have been more extensive in LMES than in CMEs as exposure to global market forces has increased over the last 20 to 30 years. It is not altogether self-evident that this is indeed the case. On average, overall social spending growth was actually somewhat stronger in LMEs than in CMEs in the 1980s and 1990s. It is also noteworthy that unemployment benefits were cut in virtually all European CMEs from 1985 and 1999, often quite severely (see Pontusson, 2005). Leaving contemporary developments aside, the reinterpretation of the welfare state proposed by Estevez-Abe *et al.* is circular in the sense that social policy is invoked to explain investment in co-specific assets while investment in co-specific assets is simultaneously invoked to explain social policy. Put differently, these authors explain the existence of two separate welfare-skills equilibria, but do not provide any systematic account of why different countries ended up in one or the other equilibrium. Following Korpi (2006), one might plausibly argue that working-class mobilization and partisan politics gave

---

[6] The 'employer-centered' approach discussed here stands in marked contrast to the 'firm-centered' approach discussed in Chapter 9.

rise to different welfare-state arrangements, which in turn led workers to invest in different skills and firms to choose different production strategies.

Swenson's (2002) detailed account of social policy developments in Sweden and the USA over the twentieth century provides a different solution to the problem of 'historical origins'. The central puzzle motivating Swenson's inquiry is why Sweden, despite strong unions and Social Democratic control of the government, lagged behind the USA in terms of social legislation in the 1930s and 1940s. Swenson argues that employer strategies for regulating labor markets are the key to this puzzle. In brief, many large American companies adopted 'segmentalist strategies' in the early decades of the twentieth century, paying wages above market-clearing rates and providing social benefits as a way to recruit and retain workers. These firms were vulnerable to competition from low-cost producers during economic downturns and supported New Deal legislation, which effectively set a floor for competition among firms in the labor market. By contrast, export-oriented Swedish employers adopted a 'solidaristic' strategy, seeking to hold wages below market-clearing rates. Sustained by the depressed inter-war economic conditions, this strategy became problematic as members of the employers' confederation began to use employer-provided benefits to compete with each other when labor markets became tight in the aftermath of World War II. In the 1950s, according to Swenson, Swedish employers embraced comprehensive state-provided social insurance as a means to curtail this kind of competition.

Swenson's critics (Hacker and Pierson, 2002, 2004; Korpi, 2006) charge that he exaggerates the role of business in the USA as well as the Swedish case and, specifically, that he fails to distinguish between 'first-order' and 'strategic' business preferences (see also Swenson's (2004) reply). According to the critics, segments of the business community consented to social legislation in both cases, but this consent was conditioned by political conditions that were unfavorable to business and should not be interpreted to mean that business actively wanted the legislation to pass. Given that first-order preferences cannot be directly observed, distinguishing first-order preferences from strategic policy preferences is first and foremost a theoretical challenge.

Mares (2003) moves the employer-centered literature forward by articulating theoretical propositions about the kinds of social policy that different firms and sectors favor. Invoking considerations that do not depend on the consequences of social policy, such as firm size and the incidence of workplace hazards, Mares avoids the circularity of Estevez-Abe *et al.*'s discussion and effectively uses historical case studies from Germany and France as evidence in support of her predictions. Her approach directs our attention to variation in social policy preferences among employers in the same country.

As Mares clearly recognizes, the preferences of other actors and the politics of coalition-building must be taken into account in order to move from employer preferences to social policy outcomes. The employer-centered literature has generated important new insights, but it does not have much to say about the redistributive effects of modern welfare states. Indeed, redistribution appears to be simply a by-product of the regulation of labor markets in this literature. Equally striking, and related to the neglect of redistribution, electoral competition and government partisanship play hardly any role at all in the VofC approach to the politics of the welfare state.

Focusing on the role of employers, the debate between proponents of PRT and the VofC approach has directed attention away from another important limitation of the PRT literature, namely its conceptualization of 'labor' as a more or less homogeneous constituency with a common set of preferences for social insurance and/or redistribution. In the power resources framework, unionization is a key variable, yet none of the PRT-inspired literature reports significant effects of unionization on social spending or redistribution. PRT scholars typically argue that the influence of unions operates through left parties. There is surely something to this argument, but it sidesteps the crucial question of which segments of the labor force and the income distribution are represented by unions (cf. Chapter 10). As union density rises, unions may well become more powerful in the political as well as the industrial sphere, but the interests they represent also become more heterogeneous. Put differently, the preferences of the median union member converge on those of the median voter as density approaches 100%.

Recent literature on the politics of 'insider–outsider conflict' (Mares, 2006; Rueda, 2007) usefully problematizes the interests of labor. These authors argue that unions and left parties primarily represent labor-market insiders, and that they are not particularly supportive of economic and social policies that target the long-term unemployed and the precariously employed. Even among labor-market insiders, however, preferences for redistribution will diverge. The role of unions in the politics of social insurance and redistribution may also depend on the influence of public-sector unions relative to private-sector unions or, alternatively, the influence of unions in sheltered sectors relative to unions in sectors exposed to international trade. More comprehensive comparative data on the composition of union membership is needed to explore these issues empirically.

# 5. POLITICAL INSTITUTIONS

It is commonplace in comparative political economy to argue that more or less formalized institutional arrangements or, in other words, the 'rules of the game' influence policy outcomes. Though they are often combined, there are two distinct versions of the institutionalist argument. One version holds that institutions shape the preferences of individual voters or interest groups. The second version holds that institutions influence the strategic behavior of political actors, perhaps also the balance of power among political actors. Leaving preference formation aside for the time being, this section discusses specific examples of the latter version of the institutionalist argument.

Empirically, cross-national quantitative studies of social spending have identified two apparently robust institutional effects. First, federalism is associated with lower levels of social spending and, at least by implication, less redistributive government (e.g. Huber and Stephens, 2001). Secondly, it appears to be the case that countries in which parliamentary elections are contested under proportional representation (PR) typically have larger and more redistributive welfare states than countries in which such elections are contested in single-member districts (SMD) under plurality rules (Persson and Tabellini, 2003; Alesina and Glaeser, 2004; Verardi, 2004; Iversen and Soskice, 2006). The federalism effect can partly be explained in terms of competition for capital and skilled labor among sub-national governmental units (states or provinces). In addition, as political scientists are keen to point out, federalism increases the number of access points for 'special interests' or, in other words, the number of veto players in the political process (Immergut, 1992; Tsebelis, 1995). Through either mechanism, federalism arguably thwarts the policy preferences of the median voter and/or the majority party.

Although there is a broad consensus about implications of federalism in the existing literature, the implications of electoral rules have only recently begun to be explored by scholars interested in the politics of redistribution. As a first cut, Persson and Tabellini (2000, 2003) argue that plurality systems favor geographically targeted spending while PR (especially with large districts) favors more broad-based or 'universalistic' spending programs (cf. also Alesina and Glaeser, 2004). The incentive for politicians to target spending geographically derives from the fact that under plurality rules parties win elections by winning a majority of electoral districts rather than a majority of votes in the electorate as a whole. If universalistic spending is more redistributive than geographically targeted spending, as Persson and Tabellini assume, different electoral incentives might thus be invoked to explain why government tends to be more redistributive in PR systems.

An obvious limitation of Persson and Tabellini's original model is that it takes the party system as fixed: in effect, the model assumes a two-party system and then compares party strategies and policy outcomes under different electoral rules. This setup is problematic since countries with PR almost always have multiparty systems. Recognizing this problem, Persson et al. (2007) develop a model in which the effect of PR on government spending hinges on the greater probability of a multiparty coalition government under PR rules. In this model, competition among the parties in the governing coalition leads to greater spending. Empirically, Persson et al. show that PR has no direct effect on the level of spending once we control for the size of the governing coalition. Although the initial Persson–Tabellini model pertains to the allocation of government spending and does not explain why spending levels tend to be higher under PR, the model developed by Persson *et al.* does not provide any strong prediction about the extent to which greater government spending is redistributive.

The model presented by Iversen and Soskice (2006) is similar to that of Persson *et al.* in that the effects of PR on redistribution are indirect and have to do with the composition of governments. For Iversen and Soskice, however, the crucial feature that distinguishes PR systems from SMD systems is not the size of governing coalitions *per se*, but rather the fact that government participation by left parties is much more common under PR. Their model is premised on the electorate consisting of three groups of voters of equal size: low-, middle-, and high-income voters (L, M, and H). Under majoritarian rules, there will be two parties, a center-left and a center-right party. The former has its core base of support in L, whose first preference is a policy that redistributes from both H and M to L, while the latter has its core base of support in H, whose first preference is zero redistribution. Both parties must appeal to M voters in order to win elections. Though M prefers a policy that redistributes from H to both M and L over a policy of zero redistribution, it prefers zero redistribution over a policy that redistributes from both H and M to L. So long as there is some possibility that parties will revert to the policies preferred by their core constituency after the election, M voters will favor center-right government. Under PR, by contrast, there will be a third party, with M as its core base of support. With each of the three parties representing the policy preferences of its core constituency, the problem of parties making credible commitments to voters no longer exists. After the election, the M party chooses whether to form a coalition with the L party or the H party. Since M prefers an LM policy over an HM policy, center-left government is more likely than center-right government under PR. Under certain assumptions about the dynamics of coalition formation, the Iversen–Soskice model also predicts that center-left government will be more redistributive under PR than under majoritarian rules.

Empirically, Iversen and Soskice demonstrate that left participation in government is associated with more redistribution, yet there still remains a significant direct effect of PR. A fundamental problem for all empirical efforts to explore the effects of electoral rules is that PR tends be bundled with a number of other institutional factors, such as parliamentary government, multipartism, corporatist interest representation, and centralized wage bargaining (see Lijphart, 1999 and Lupu and Pontusson, 2008). For this reason alone, the question of how electoral rules matter for the politics of redistribution is likely to remain a topic of debate among comparative political economists.

# 6. INCOME INEQUALITY AND PARTISAN POLITICS

Like the PRT-inspired literature discussed earlier, Iversen and Soskice's model of the effects of electoral rules assumes that policy differences between parties of the left and the right are more or less constant across countries and over time. What varies in these models is the incidence of left government (or, more precisely, left participation in government). As suggested above, however, there are good reasons to believe that the extent to which parties diverge from the preferences of the median voter also varies across countries and over time. Space does not allow us to explore this problematic fully, but we wish to mention briefly some of our own work on the dynamic relationship between inequality and partisan politics.

In the median-voter framework, increases in inequality move all parties either to the left (Meltzer–Richard) or to the right (Moene–Wallerstein). In the partisan-politics framework, by contrast, rising inequality can be expected to be a source of polarization to the extent that some parties are more responsive to the preferences of low-income voters while other parties are more responsive to the preferences of high-income voters. The basic intuition here is that voters with incomes below the mean income stand to gain more from redistribution whereas voters with incomes above the mean lose more from redistribution as inequality rises. An important consideration in this context is whether rising income inequality is associated with rising inequality in political participation. If low-income voters drop out of the political process, the incentives for left parties to pursue more redistribution will diminish.[7] Under this scenario, we might expect rising income inequality to be associated with right-skewed polarization.

For the USA, McCarty et al. (2006) show that there is a very close association between trends in income inequality and trends in partisan polarization (measured by congressional voting) over the twentieth century. Their analysis shows that partisan polarization from the 1970s onwards has primarily been due to the Republican Party moving sharply to the right (cf. Hacker and Pierson, 2006). McCarty et al. also demonstrate that support for the Democratic and Republican parties has become more stratified by income over this period, so that someone's income is today a much better predictor of party identification than it was in the 1960s. These results are consistent with the theory sketched above. As McCarty et al. point out, however, polarization also has resulted from other developments in American politics that are not directly connected to rising income inequality (e.g. the partisan realignment of the South), and rising income inequality is at least partly the result of policies pursued by an increasing conservative Republican Party

---

[7] Immigration of low-wage workers has a similar effect: see McCarty et al. (2006).

(see also Bartels, 2007) and political stalemate caused by polarization. In our view, it is neither possible nor necessary to parse definitively between these alternative interpretations.

Does the association between inequality and polarization hold in other advanced industrial states as well? Based on Comparative Manifesto data, we do not observe any secular trend towards partisan polarization across OECD countries, but we also do not observe the same sharp increase of inequality as in the USA. Although inequality of market income among working-age households has increased in most countries, wage inequality and inequality of disposable income have held steady in many countries. Controlling for the center of political gravity, Pontusson and Rueda (2008) show that wage inequality is associated with more leftist left parties when voter turnout and union density are high and that household income inequality is associated with more rightist right parties when turnout and density are low. Consistent with power resources theory, comparative analysis suggests that the consequences of inequality for partisan politics are contingent on political mobilization of low-income groups.

# 7. Revisiting Individual Preferences

Whether they are the preferences of the median voter or core voters of left and right parties, the models and theories discussed so far conceive individual preferences as derived directly from personal income and risk exposure. Although such theories benefit from parsimony, they neglect cognitive, psychological, and social factors that might cause preferences to diverge from purely self-interested ones based on income or risk. In recent years, behavioralists in political science and economics have begun to develop richer theories of preference formation and, in some cases, to incorporate these theories into models of redistributive politics. In this section, we begin by identifying what we consider to be the most important insights of this new literature and then explore related issues.

## Information and Beliefs

There is considerable evidence that support for the welfare state is correlated with popular views of the relationship between effort and income (or 'bad luck' and poverty). Fong (2001) focuses on the support of high-income, upwardly mobile American voters who are unlikely to benefit from redistribution. She finds that variation in support for redistribution among such voters depends primarily on how they respond to questions about the importance of luck and effort in poverty or wealth, the extent of economic opportunity in the USA, and whether the USA is a society of 'haves and have-nots'. Similarly, Bartels (2007, chapter 5) finds that citizens who profess support for egalitarian values have higher support for redistributive policies after controlling for income, education, and other material factors. Beliefs about upward mobility, both subjective and objective, also appear to play an important role in determining preferences over redistribution. Alesina and La Ferrara (2005) find that, holding current income constant, voters who have higher expected incomes and greater likelihoods of reaching the 70% percentile of the income distribution are more likely to oppose redistributive taxation.

Whether such beliefs can account for the observed cross-sectional variation in redistribution depends on a couple of questions. First, is there evidence that citizens of countries that redistribute more have more egalitarian values? Secondly, what can account for persistent differences in beliefs about the fairness of economic outcomes? There is considerable support for an affirmative answer to the first question. Alesina and Glaeser show that there is striking cross-national correlation between welfare spending (as a percentage of GDP) and the percentage of adults who agree with the proposition that luck determines income or that poverty is society's fault. Osberg and Smeeding (2006), however, find that differences between Americans and Europeans are more subtle. Using data on perceptions of what various occupations 'should' earn versus what they 'actually' earn, they find that there is little *average* difference in the views of American and Europeans on inequality. In Osberg and Smeeding's analysis, the US case is first and foremost distinguished by the fact that American views on the legitimacy of income differentials are more polarized, with a significant group of Americans embracing anti-egalitarian values.

Two important recent works, Piketty (1995) and Benabou and Tirole (2006), consider how variation in beliefs about the link between effort and income are sustained in the absence of any 'objective' circumstances that clearly vindicate one set of beliefs over another. The common feature of both of these models is that levels of taxes and transfers affect the ability of voters to learn the true relationship between effort and income. High taxes and transfers weaken the link between individual effort and income, leading voters to believe that incomes are more random and therefore to exert less effort. This in turn leads them to support high levels of taxes and transfers as social insurance. The models differ, however, with respect to the exact mechanisms whereby beliefs are formed and propagated over generations. In the Piketty model, agents update their beliefs based solely on family experiences. This pattern is consistent with his empirical finding that voters who experience either upward or downward mobility vote for left-wing parties at intermediate rates compared to the immobile rich or poor. Benabou and Tirole, alternatively, argue that in a society characterized by low levels of redistribution, citizens may have an incentive to suppress memories of 'unlucky' economic outcomes. This helps sustain a belief in the fairness of economic rewards that enhances effort.[8]

The Piketty and Benabou–Tirole models provide important microfoundations for cultural differences with respect to distribution and point to the need to relax strong assumptions about voter sophistication. As Bartels (2007, chapters 6–7) has colorfully argued, 'unenlightened self-interest' may be the best empirical description of how voters think about redistribution. In his study of the public opinion surrounding the Bush tax cuts, Bartels finds that voters who believed that they would benefit materially from the tax cuts tended to strongly support them. Voters, however, wildly overestimated their personal tax reductions. This problem was especially acute with respect to the estate tax where (according to the 2002 National Election Study) 67.6% voters supported repeal even though only 2% of estates were taxed pre-repeal.

The question of whether the lack of information about the links between policy and voters' interests can explain cross-national and temporal variation in redistribution has yet to be explored in any systematic fashion. From the evidence presented by Osberg and Smeeding (2005), it would appear that Americans are less well-informed about actual income differentials than the citizens of other advanced democracies. One plausible explanation for this contrast might be that more centralized wage bargaining renders income differentials more transparent and perhaps more politically salient as well. In this context, it is also noteworthy that across advanced democracies union members tend to be more supportive of redistributive social spending than non-union workers even when we control for income, education, and ideological self-placement (see Kwon and Pontusson, 2006).

## Religion

One of the oldest arguments for why there is apparently so little redistribution in democracies focuses on the way that religion distracts poor people from voting their economic interests or inhibits the creation of class-wide coalitions. Scheve and Stasavage (2006) show that religiosity is associated with lower levels of social spending and that the religious are consistently less like to support social spending than the non-religious across advanced democracies. Their novel explanation for these findings holds that religiosity directly affects preferences for social insurance. Drawing on literature in psychology, Scheve and Stasavage argue that religiosity

---

[8]  An obvious limitation of these models is that they do not explain how the two equilibria exemplified by the USA and 'Europe' arose in the first place. Roemer (1994) incorporates different beliefs about how the economy works into a model of redistribution. Unlike the Piketty and Benabou–Tirole models, voters' beliefs are manipulated in a political campaign rather than updated based on personal economic outcomes.

reduces the 'psychic costs' that the experience of economic shocks such as un-employment or illness entails. Because religious belief serves as a substitute for social insurance, it reduces the demand for social spending. Similarly, Benabou and Tirole argue that religious beliefs tying rewards in the after-life to industriousness 'on Earth' induce lower support for redistribution. In their model, religious voters oppose redistribution because non-believers also benefit and because it dulls their own incentives to work hard. Both models suggest that causality may run from inequality to religious beliefs. In societies lacking social protections, citizens are more likely to 'invest' in religion for the psychic benefits that it provides or to motivate themselves to work hard.

Religious adherence may not only have a psychological or normative effect on redistributive preferences. Huber and Stanig (2007) argue that religious organi-zations provide direct material substitutes for state-provided redistribution and social insurance. This argument dovetails with Esping-Andersen's (1990) idea of 'welfare regimes', with public provision being one of several different forms of 'so-cial protection'. Access to family support or employer-provided benefits constitute other variables that might mediate between income/risk and preferences of social policy. Regarding Huber and Stanig's specific argument, the obvious question is whether the level of transfers provided within congregations is significant enough to dampen demand for government support.

The literature on the influence of religiosity on individual attitudes stands in marked contrast to the literature on the historical role of Christian Democracy as a force promoting the development of European welfare states. In part, this puzzle might be resolved by recognizing differences between Catholic and Protestant social doctrine.

## Race and Ethnicity

Alesina and Glaser's (2004) calculations suggest that racial and ethnic fractionaliza-tion accounts for about 50% of the cross-sectional variance in social spending for a sample of some 52 developed and developing countries. The causal mechanisms involved here remain a subject for debate. The standard argument is that racism and xenophobia lead to lower levels of social solidarity and consequently lower the willingness of a majority group to tax itself for the benefits of a minority. Roemer *et al.* (2007, chapter 4) calibrate an equilibrium electoral model in which racial preferences may lower levels of redistribution through an 'issue bundling effect' (see below) but also through incomplete altruism or, in other words, an 'anti-solidarity' effect. Formally, voters have a preference for income equalization that declines in their degree of racism. Roemer *et al.* find that across the four pairs of US elections they study, racial preferences reduce the expected marginal tax rate on income from

11% to 18%, roughly the difference between the US and European welfare states. They attribute about 60% of this difference to the anti-solidarity effect. They obtain similar effects of anti-solidarity, attributable to immigration, in Britain, Denmark, and France.

Micro studies of individual behavior and attitudes help to clarify possible mechanisms that generate this anti-solidarity effect. Gilens (1999) shows that white voters in the USA have developed negative stereotypes of African-Americans that lead them to conclude that African-Americans are undeserving of public assistance. Furthermore, white Americans incorrectly believe that most of the poor are black (as distinct from the correct observation that many blacks are poor). Because they see poverty in racial terms, white Americans are disinclined to support welfare and other forms of assistance. While Gilens focuses on the role of perceptions of the racial composition of welfare recipients, Luttmer (2001) finds evidence of a strong effect of the local racial composition of caseloads on public attitudes and voting on initiatives related to welfare policy. When the percentage of welfare recipients who are black rises in a census tract, metropolitan statistical area, or county, welfare support of whites falls relative to that of blacks.[9]

Another prominent strand of thought on this topic is that racial and ethnic divisions generate 'identity politics' that displaces the class-based politics of the welfare state. Fernandez and Levy (forthcoming) argue that in diverse societies ethnically based groups often seek targeted public goods rather than universalistic redistribution. Consequently, high-income groups can form coalitions with certain ethnic groups to pursue a policy of minimal redistribution and group-based transfers. Based on a similar logic, Austen-Smith and Wallerstein (2006) propose a model of redistribution and affirmative action. In their model, workers can be either high-skilled or low-skilled and belong to one of two racial groups, white or black. On average, blacks are less skilled than whites. A legislature must determine a combination of two distinct policy instruments: social insurance that pays a benefit to workers in low-wage jobs and affirmative action which guarantees blacks a certain proportion of high-wage jobs. The main result is that legislative bargaining across representatives of each group may produce a coalition between high-income whites and blacks. This coalition promotes lower levels of social insurance and higher levels of affirmative action than a low-skilled white and black coalition prefers. Austen-Smith and Wallerstein argue that this finding comports well with the history of affirmative action in the USA, especially the Nixon Administration's support for affirmative action with the goal of splitting the New Deal coalition.

From a comparative perspective, there are clearly limits to the explanatory power of racial politics. There is a lot of unexplained variation in social spending

---

[9] In addition to this 'group loyalty' effect, Luttmer identifies a negative 'exposure' effect (more opposition to welfare as local caseloads increase).

among relatively homogeneous affluent countries (Pontusson, 2005). As Alesina and Glaeser (2004) suggest, hostility or indifference to minorities only seems to come into play to the extent that minorities are poor and therefore the primary beneficiaries of redistribution (or perceived to be so). Even in the canonical case of the USA, levels of redistribution have stagnated or fallen during a period in which levels of explicit racism among whites have fallen. White behavior undoubtedly continues to be affected implicitly by racial stereotypes, but it remains a puzzle why this modern racism would have significantly greater policy effects that its precursor.

## Issue Bundling

As the preceding discussion of religion and race suggests, voters and political parties are often concerned with issues other than economic distribution. An influential strand of comparative political science has stressed the 'post-material' nature of political life in advanced democracies (e.g. Inglehart, 1990). To the extent that such concerns overshadow distributive issues, we should expect to see less redistributive effort from governments. However, it is precisely when distributional conflicts are low that post-material concerns come to the forefront. Thus the salience of non-economic issues cannot be a complete explanation of levels of inequality or government policies to reduce inequality.

The one-dimensional nature of many models of redistributive politics, notably the Meltzer–Richard and Moene–Wallerstein models, emerges as a serious limitation in this context. Austen-Smith and Wallerstein's (2006) model of redistribution and affirmative action represents a recent attempt to tackle this problem. In a similar vein, Roemer (1998) develops a general model of two-party electoral competition where voters care about both redistribution and a party's position on some other dimension. Under certain technical conditions, the salience of the non-economic issue is such that parties converge on the median of that dimension. If the income of the median voter on the non-economic dimension is higher than the overall average income, even the party representing low-income voters will then propose a zero tax rate. If, however, the median voter on the non-economic dimension is poorer than the overall median, redistribution is enhanced. Thus Roemer argues that the implications of the second dimension for redistributive policy depend on the correlation between income and preferences on that dimension.

A limitation of Roemer's two-party framework is that it is impossible for voters to unbundle the two issues. In multiparty systems, there may be parties representing many more combinations of economic and non-economic policy positions. In such cases, the issue bundling occurs in the process of forming coalition governments. Whether predictions similar to Roemer's continue to hold is an open question.

## Social Affinities

Kristov *et al.* (1992) develop a model of redistributive social spending that can be related to some of the preceding discussion of norms of solidarity and group identities. These authors postulate that the policy preferences of the median voter depend on the distance between her income and those of the poor and the rich. If the distance to the poor is small, the median voter sympathizes with the poor or, alternatively, includes the possibility of becoming poor in her cost–benefit calculus. (Kristov *et al.* deliberately equivocate on the extent to which 'social affinity' boils down to 'self-insurance'.) If the distance to the rich is small, she leans against redistribution for similar reasons. What matters, then, is not the overall level of inequality, as in the Meltzer–Richard and Moene–Wallerstein models, but rather the structure of inequality. Compression of the lower half of the income distribution combined with dispersion of the upper half provides the conditions most favorable to redistributive politics. Empirically, Kristov *et al.* operationalize 'social distance' in terms of income differentials, but race or ethnicity could easily be incorporated into their theoretical framework. From this perspective, racial and ethnic fractionalization is not necessarily relevant to redistributive politics: racial and ethnic fractionalization matters to the extent that it maps onto the income distribution.

## Preferences Embedded in Welfare-State Institutions

One of the standard questions in international surveys asks respondents whether they agree with the proposition that 'government should act to redistribute income'. This question taps into norms about how much inequality is appropriate, but also norms about the proper role of government. In a study of trust and policy preferences in the USA, Hetherington (2004) finds evidence that low levels of trust in the federal government are associated with more conservative positions on a number of redistributive policy questions. This finding is consistent with Osberg and Smeeding's (2006) finding that Americans are less likely to believe that it is the government's responsibility to reduce income inequality than are citizens of European countries even though they do not necessarily find existing income differentials more legitimate.

Related to the question of the legitimacy of political relative to market allocation of resources (cf. Lane, 1986), there is quite a large empirical literature that suggests that the way public welfare provision is organized affects preferences for public welfare provision and redistribution. For Sweden as well as the USA, individual-level studies show that personal experience with means-tested social assistance tends to be associated with low levels of trust in political institutions and less support for redistributive policies (Kumlin, 2004). More broadly, the institutionalist theory proposed by Korpi and Palme (1998) and the macro-level evidence that they present suggest that universalistic social-insurance schemes generate more broad-based support for redistributive measures than occupational social-insurance schemes. Articulated in the language of median-voter models, Korpi and Palme's core argument holds that the tax rate preferred by the median voter is endogenous to the institutional design of public welfare provision. In a somewhat different vein, Kumlin and Svallfors (2007) show that class differences in preferences for redistribution increase with the size of the welfare state and argue that by engaging in redistribution governments politicize distributive issues and, in effect, create demand for redistribution among low-income voters.

# 8. CONCLUSION

As John Roemer argues in Chapter 27, there are very real limits to the extent to which inequality can be eliminated or even ameliorated by democratic market societies. The proposition that inequality is self-correcting in democracies clearly turns out to be inadequate to explain persistent inequalities or governmental responses to rising inequality. This should not be taken to mean that inequality does not matter to the politics of redistribution. As the preceding discussion suggests, partisan politics mediate the consequences of inequality for government policy. In addition, it may be necessary to consider more disaggregated measures of inequality in order to appreciate its political consequences. For example, as suggested by Kristov *et al.* (1992), dispersion in the lower half of the distribution may have different political consequences than dispersion in the upper half.

The preceding discussion also points to other factors that shape demands for redistribution and help explain differences in redistributive policy over time and across countries. The first is the perceptions and realities of social risk. The salience of aggregate risks that cannot be privately insured clearly has been and remains an important factor in the politics of the welfare state. As Dryzek and Goodin (1986) argue, pervasive uncertainty about risks associated with World War II led citizens of many countries to accept the notion that state provision of social insurance was necessary and that private insurance schemes would not suffice. As memories of such collectivized risks have faded, citizens have arguably become more tolerant of the privatization of risk and the reliance on private insurance mechanisms. As Hacker (2006) points out, governments (especially the US government) have begun to adopt policies that subsidize the privatization of risk further. Although there may be economic arguments for private pensions and private health care over social insurance, the political effects on support for the welfare state are unmistakable.

The second factor that emerges in our review is the role of information and beliefs in sustaining high levels of inequality. Both theoretical and empirical work has stressed how different beliefs about the link between individual effort and economic outcomes and mobility temper individual preferences about the desirable scope of the welfare state. Bartels (2008) also makes a persuasive case that citizens' lack of information about how government policies affect inequality may also be to blame. Clearly, many citizens of the USA either fail to see a link between policy and inequality or do not trust government to improve upon market outcomes. The extent to which this is true of other countries and how it varies remains an open question. The relative strength of institutions such as labor unions that inform and mobilize low-income workers and the ways in which the media cover social policy and inequality may be important factors in explaining divergent political responses to rising inequality.

The third factor in explaining variations in levels of inequality is the emergence and the continuing importance of 'non-economic' cleavages in electoral politics. The evidence is quite strong that diverse societies tend to be more unequal and redistribute less. But there is little agreement as to the mechanisms that produce this correlation. The processes by which cultural issues and identities form, change, and become salient will continue to be an important area of research for those interested in the welfare state and redistributive politics more generally.

Finally, the importance of political institutions for social policy outcomes is clear. The design of electoral systems not only influences the ways that political coalitions form and whether politicians have incentives to distribute across classes or across regions. Electoral design also influences the extent to which low-income voters can be mobilized and whether leftist parties can succeed. The separation of powers, bicameralism, and federalism create veto points that may impede the expansion of the welfare state but also protect it from retrenchment. And the welfare state itself is an important institution that affects redistributive politics. Experiences with welfare-state institutions shape preferences both through beliefs about 'luck and effort' as well as trust in government's ability to solve social problems. These beliefs in turn generate new demands either for retrenchment or expansion of welfare states. Consequently, to explain the rich variation in policy outcomes, scholars will need to continue to develop and refine arguments about path dependencies and policy feedbacks (cf. Pierson, 2004).

# REFERENCES

ALESINA, ALBERTO, and GLAESER, EDWARD. 2004. *Fighting Poverty in the US and Europe.* Oxford: Oxford University Press.

——and LA FERRARA, ELIANA. 2005. 'Preferences for Redistribution in the Land of Opportunities'. *Journal of Public Economics,* 89: 897–931.

AUSTEN-SMITH, DAVID, and WALLERSTEIN, MICHAEL. 2006. 'Redistribution and Affirmative Action'. *Journal of Public Economics*, 90: 1789–823

BARTELS, LARRY. 2008. *Unequal Democracy: The Political Economy of the New Gilded Age.* Princeton: Princeton University Press.

BENABOU, ROLAND, and TIROLE, JEAN. 2006. 'Belief in a Just World and Redistributive Politics'. *Quarterly Journal of Economics*, 121(2): 699–746.

BERAMENDI, PABLO. 2001. 'The Politics of Income Inequality in the OECD: The Role of Second Order Effects'. Luxembourg Income Study Working Paper 284.

BRADLEY, DAVID, HUBER, EVELYNE, MOLLER, STEPHANIE, NIELSEN, FRANÇOIS, and STEPHENS, JOHN D. 2003. 'Distribution and Redistribution in Postindustrial Democracies'. *World Politics*, 55: 193–228.

CALVERT, RANDALL L. 1985. 'Robustness of the Multidimensional Voting Model: Candidate Motivations, Uncertainty, and Convergence'. *American Journal of Political Science*, 29(1): 69–95.

DOWNS, ANTHONY. 1957. *An Economic Theory of Democracy.* New York: Harper and Row.

DRYZEK, JOHN S., and GOODIN, ROBERT E. 1986. 'Risk-Sharing and Social Justice: The Motivational Foundations of the Post-War Welfare State'. *British Journal of Political Science*, 16(1): 1–34.

ESPING-ANDERSEN, GØSTA. 1990. *The Three Worlds of Welfare Capitalism.* Princeton: Princeton University Press.

ESTEVEZ-ABE, MARGARITA, IVERSEN, TORBEN, and SOSKICE, DAVID. 2001. 'Social Protection and the Formation of Skills', in Peter Hall and David Soskice (eds.), *Varieties of Capitalism.* Oxford: Oxford University Press, 1–70.

FERNANDEZ, RACHEL, and LEVY, GILAT. Forthcoming. 'Diversity and Redistribution'. *Journal of Public Economics.*

FONG, CHRISTINA. 2001. 'Social Preferences, Self-Interest, and the Demand for Redistribution'. *Journal of Public Economics*, 82(2), Nov.: 225–46.

GARFINKEL, IRWIN, RAINWATER, LEE, and SMEEDING, TIMOTHY M. 2006. 'A Re-examination of Welfare States and Inequality in Rich Nations: How In-Kind Transfers and Indirect Taxes Change the Story'. *Journal of Policy Analysis and Management*, 25(4): 987–19.

GILENS, MARTIN. 1999. *Why Americans Hate Welfare.* Chicago: University of Chicago Press.

HACKER, JACOB. 2006. *The Great Risk Shift.* New York: Oxford University Press.

—— and PIERSON, PAUL. 2002. 'Business Power and Social Policy'. *Politics and Society*, 30(2): 277–325.

—— —— 2004. 'Varieties of Capitalist Interests *and* Capitalist Power: A Response to Swenson'. *Studies in American Political Development*, 18, Fall: 186–95.

—— —— 2006. *Off Center.* New Haven: Yale University Press.

HETHERINGTON, MARC. 2004. *Why Trust Matters: Declining Political Trust and the Demise of American Liberalism.* Princeton: Princeton University Press.

HUBER, EVELYN, and STEPHENS, JOHN. 2001. *Development and Crisis of the Welfare State.* Chicago: University of Chicago Press.

HUBER, JOHN, and STANIG, PIERO. 2007. 'Redistribution through Taxes and Charity: The Cost of "Compassionate Conservatism" to the Secular Poor'. Unpublished paper.

IMMERGUT, ELLEN. 1992. 'The Rules of the Game', in Sven Steinmo, Kathleen Thelen and Frank Longstreth (eds.), *Structuring Politics.* New York: Cambridge University Press, 57–89.

INGLEHART, RONALD. 1990. *Culture Shift in Advanced Industrial Society*. Princeton: Princeton University Press.

IVERSEN, TORBEN. 2005. *Capitalism, Democracy and Welfare*. New York: Cambridge University Press.

——and CUSACK, THOMAS. 2000. 'The Causes of Welfare State Expansion'. *World Politics*, 52, Apr.: 313–49.

——and SOSKICE, DAVID. 2001. 'An Asset Theory of Social Policy Preferences'. *American Political Science Review*, 95: 875–93.

————2006. 'Electoral Institutions and the Politics of Coalitions'. *American Political Science Review*, 100: 165–81.

————2007. 'Distribution and Redistribution: The Shadow of the Nineteenth Century'. Typescript. Harvard University.

KENWORTHY, LANE, and PONTUSSON, JONAS. 2005. 'Rising Inequality and the Politics of Redistribution in Affluent Countries'. *Perspectives on Politics*, 3(3): 449–71.

KORPI, WALTER. 1983. *The Democratic Class Struggle*. London: Routledge and Kegan Paul.

——2006. 'Power Resources and Employer-Centered Approaches in Explanations of Welfare States and Varieties of Capitalism'. *World Politics*, 58(2): 167–206.

——and PALME, JOAKIM. 1998. 'The Paradox of Redistribution and Strategies of Equality'. *American Sociological Review*, 63: 661–87.

KRISTOV, LORENZO, LINDERT, PETER, and MCCLELLAND, ROBERT. 1992. 'Pressure Groups and Redistribution'. *Journal of Public Economics*, 48: 135–63.

KUMLIN, STAFFAN. 2004. *The Personal and the Political*. New York: Palgrave Macmillan.

——and SVALLFORS, STEFAN. 2007. 'Social Stratification and Political Articulation', in Steffen Mau and Benjamin Veghte (eds.), *Social Justice, Legitimacy and the Welfare State*. Aldershot: Ashgate.

KWON, HYEOK YONG, and PONTUSSON, JONAS. 2006. 'Power Resource Theory Revisited and Revised: Unions and Welfare Spending in OECD Countries'. Paper presented at the annual meeting of the American Political Science Association, Marriott, Loews Philadelphia, and the Pennsylvania Convention Center, Philadelphia. Aug. 31.

LANE, ROBERT E. 1986. 'Market Justice, Political Justice'. *American Political Science Review*, 80: 383–402.

LIJPHART, ARENDT. 1999. *Patterns of Democracy*. New Haven: Yale University Press.

LINDERT, PETER. 2004. *Growing Public*. Cambridge: Cambridge University Press.

LUPU, NOAM, and PONTUSSON, JONAS. 2008. 'Inequality, Electoral Rules and the Politics of Redistribution'. Paper presented to the Comparative Political Economy Workshop, Yale University, May 2.

LUTTMER, ERZO F. P. 2001. 'Group Loyalty and the Taste for Redistribution'. *Journal of Political Economy*, 109(3): 500–28.

MCCARTY, NOLAN, POOLE, KEITH, and ROSENTHAL, HOWARD. 2006. *Polarized America*. Cambridge, Mass.: MIT Press.

MAHLER, VINCENT. 2008. 'Electoral Turnout and Income Redistribution by the State'. Forthcoming. *European Journal Political Research*, 47(2), Mar: 161–83.

MARES, ISABELA. 2003. *The Politics of Social Risk*. New York: Cambridge University Press.

——2006. *Taxation, Wage Bargaining and Unemployment*. New York: Cambridge University Press.

MELTZER, ALLAN H., and RICHARD, SCOTT F. 1981. 'A Rational Theory of the Size of Government'. *The Journal of Political Economy*, 89(5), Oct.: 914–27.

MILANOVIC, BRANKO. 2000. 'The Median-Voter Hypothesis, Income Inequality and Income Redistribution'. *European Journal of Political Economy*, 16: 367–410.

MOENE, KARL-OVE, and WALLERSTEIN, MICHAEL. 2001. 'Inequality, Social Insurance and Redistribution'. *American Political Science Review*, 95(4): 859–74.

—————— 2003. 'Earnings Inequality and Welfare Spending'. *World Politics*, 55: 485–516.

MOLLER, STEPHANIE, HUBER, EVELYNE, STEPHENS, JOHN D., BRADLEY, DAVID, and NIELSON, FRANÇOIS. 2003. 'Determinants of Relative Poverty in Advanced Capitalist Democracies'. *American Sociological Review*, 68: 22–51.

NELSON, PHILLIP. 1999. 'Redistribution and the Income of the Median Voter'. *Public Choice*, 98(1–2): 187–94.

OSBERG, LARS, and SMEEDING, TIMOTHY. 2006. ' "Fair" Inequality? An International Comparison of Attitudes to Pay Differentials'. *American Sociological Review*, 71, June: 450–73.

PEROTTI, ROBERTO. 1996. 'Growth, Income Distribution and Democracy'. *Journal of Economic Growth*, 1: 149–87.

PERSSON, TORSTEN, ROLAND, GERARD, and TABELLINI, GUIDO. 2007. 'Electoral Rules and Government Spending in Parliamentary Democracies'. *Quarterly Journal of Political Science*, 2(2): 155–88.

—— and TABELLINI, GUIDO. 2000. *Political Economics: Explaining Economic Policy*. Cambridge, Mass.: MIT Press.

—————— 2003. *The Economic Effects of Constitutions*. Cambridge, Mass.: MIT Press.

PICKETTY, THOMAS. 1995. 'Social Mobility and Redistributive Politics'. *Quarterly Journal of Economics*, 110: 551–84.

PIERSON, PAUL. 2004. *Politics in Time: History, Institutions and Social Analysis*. Princeton: Princeton University Press.

PONTUSSON, JONAS. 2005. *Inequality and Prosperity*. Ithaca, NY: Cornell University Press.

—— and RUEDA, DAVID. 2008. 'Inequality as a Source of Political Polarization: A Comparative Analysis of Twelve OECD Countries', in Christopher Anderson and Pablo Beramendi (eds.), *Democracy, Inequality, and Representation: A Comparative Perspective*. New York: Russell Sage Foundation.

ROEMER, JOHN E. 1994. 'The Strategic Role of Party Ideology when Voters are Uncertain How the Economy Works'. *American Political Science Review*, 88(2): 327–35.

—— 1998. 'Why the Poor do not Expropriate the Rich: An Old Argument in New Garb'. *Journal of Public Economics*, 70: 399–422.

—— LEE, WOOJIN, and VAN DER STRAETEN, KARINE. 2007. *Racism, Xenophobia, and Distribution*. Cambridge, Mass.: Harvard University Press.

RUEDA, DAVID. 2007. *Social Democracy Inside Out*. Oxford: Oxford University Press.

SCHEVE, KENNETH, and STASAVAGE, DAVID. 2006. 'Religion and Preferences for Social Insurance'. *Quarterly Journal of Political Science*, 1: 255–86.

SMEEDING, TIMOTHY. 2005. 'Public Policy, Economic Inequality and Poverty'. *Social Science Quarterly*, 86, supplement: 955–83.

STEPHENS, JOHN. 1979. *The Transition from Capitalism to Socialism*. London: Macmillan.

SWENSON, PETER. 2002. *Capitalists Against Markets*. Oxford: Oxford University Press.

—— 2004. 'Varieties of Capitalist Interests'. *Studies in American Political Development*, 18: 1–29.

TSEBELIS, GEORGE. 1995. 'Decision-Making in Political Systems'. *British Journal of Political Science*, 25: 289–325.

VERARDI, VINCENZO. 2004. 'Electoral Systems and Income Inequality'. *Economic Letters*, 86: 7–12.

WITTMAN, DONALD. 1977. 'Candidates with Policy Preferences: A Dynamic Model'. *Journal of Economic Theory*, 14: 180–9.

CHAPTER 27

..............................................................................

# PROSPECTS FOR ACHIEVING EQUALITY IN MARKET ECONOMIES

..............................................................................

JOHN E. ROEMER

## 1. INTRODUCTION

..............................................................................

THE rich countries, which are the prime subject of this book, are all highly developed market economies and democracies at the same time. This combination has not eliminated economic inequality, as this Handbook demonstrates. Even in cases where political action can boast some success, the problems of reducing market-based inequality are manifold (Chapter 26). The more fundamental question addressed here is whether democracy can be expected to eliminate inequality of opportunity in the long run.

We begin by proposing the degree of equality that we can expect or hope to achieve in the foreseeable future. The two grand strategies for achieving equality in the last century have been socialism and social democracy, which we define. Markets are necessary in any complex society, and they perform both a coordination function and an incentive function. We argue that an understanding of the relative importance of these functions is necessary in order to assess the degree to which economic equality can be achieved. The two most important institutions for achieving equality are redistributive taxation and the reduction in the variation of human capital through public education (Chapter 17 treats education and inequality). We discuss whether democracy can be expected to implement the kind of educational finance policies which would be necessary to eliminate dynastic variation in the distribution of human capital.

## 2. How Much Equality Should We Hope For?

In Chapter 2, we presented arguments for (and against) equality. Here, we discuss the prospects for achieving equality, from both the economic and political viewpoints. If one agrees that equality is desirable, what degree of equality could one hope to achieve? It would be too speculative to attempt to answer this question for the long run. I prefer to propose what we should reasonably hope to aim for as the next step in the egalitarian program. This, I believe, is to achieve equality of opportunity, in the sense of eliminating the differences in income and wealth distribution among children from parents of different socio-economic status.

One can argue that economic development consists in equalizing opportunities, in this sense. This is true in the long sweep of history, as feudal privileges which were inherited are replaced with capitalist inequality based upon traits which are, at least *de jure*, not inherited. It is also true taking a cross-section of countries at a given date. Today, the link between family background and wealth is tighter in poor countries than in rich countries (see Chapters 6 and 24). In the Nordic countries, the difference in mean incomes between children born to families of differing socio-economic status is smaller than anywhere (see Chapter 20 on intergenerational transmission). Achieving this degree of equality of opportunity in all countries would be an admirable goal for the next few decades.

It is logically possible that one could achieve equality of opportunity, in this sense, without lowering income Gini coefficients a great deal: the remaining inequality among children of parents of given socio-economic status (of a given *type*) could be high. That is, equalizing the rows of the intergenerational income transition matrix may still leave a high variance in each row. Whether this would in fact occur is a question that I will not attempt to address here. In the Nordic countries, intra-type inequality is also quite small. I do not claim that intra-type inequality is desirable, just that eliminating it is not the main task for the present.

Achieving equality of opportunity, in the sense of inter-dynastic equality, is a reasonable goal because there is general support among the citizenries of advanced market economies for it. Surveys conducted in many countries have shown that people oppose inequality to the extent that it is due to bad luck, but less so (or not at all) if it is due to low effort (Osberg and Smeeding, 2006). To the extent that people come to understand that the family into which one is born is a matter of luck, they will therefore come to support policies that will eliminate inter-dynastic inequality.

# 3. Efficiency, Socialism, and Social Democracy: Some Definitions

In thinking about the economic constraints against achieving an egalitarian distribution of income, it is useful to factor the economic mechanism into two parts: first, the process by which the endowments of citizens—of human and non-human capital—are produced and realized, and second, the manner in which the flows from these assets are distributed. Looking at the matter slightly differently, we are interested in whether there is a degree of freedom in the distribution of income for a society with a given amount of aggregate capital and a given distribution of human capital, subject to the constraint that that income distribution be dynamically efficient. For present purposes, define two income distributions, arising from given social endowments, in the sense just stipulated, as being equally efficient in the *static* sense if their average incomes are the same, and as equally efficient in the *dynamic* sense if their rates of average income growth are the same. The neo-liberal claim is that there is a unique dynamically efficient income distribution, the one achieved from private ownership of all assets, unfettered markets, and as little redistribution of flows through taxation as society will tolerate. The socialist and social-democratic claims are that there exist several degrees of freedom subject to the dynamic-efficiency constraint. Socialists claim there are two degrees of freedom: one in how capital assets, and/or the property rights to flows from those assets, are allocated to citizens, and a second in how taxation might reallocate those flows; social democrats believe that only the second degree of freedom exists.[1]

[1] This is somewhat inaccurate. Besides redistribution, the Nordic economies have used the solidaristic wage to reduce inequality. This is a second dimension of freedom, apparently, although it contravenes standard economic theory in which wage ratios must reflect skill endowments to achieve allocative efficiency.

Scandinavian social democracy, that is to say, is characterized by almost ubiquitous private and very unequal ownership of firms, but dramatic redistribution of
flows.

A parenthetical remark is in order on why I require only *dynamic* efficiency as a
stipulated constraint. First, society might wish to subsidize disadvantaged members
with extra resources, for instance in education, and that might reduce total output
for a period; if so, one cannot insist upon static efficiency. Second, societies may
choose different combinations of labor and leisure. A society that chooses a high
level of leisure would, by my definition, not be statically efficient, but it could be
dynamically efficient. I insist upon dynamic efficiency because I do not believe that
a democratic government is sustainable if it consistently has a lower rate of income
growth than neighboring countries.[2]

One might say that it suffices to show that the second degree of freedom with
respect to redistribution exists—the Nordic experience would seem to indicate that
with only redistribution through taxation, a quite egalitarian income distribution
can be implemented. I am, however, interested in whether both degrees of freedom
just alluded to exist, because it is possible that there are societies where it is easier to
redistribute asset ownership than to redistribute income flows, and so the question
is not entirely academic. In addition, the redistribution of asset ownership has a
long intellectual pedigree in the theory of socialism, and to understand the failures
of twentieth century socialism, the problems in attempting to redistribute asset
ownership must be understood.

Many believe that the failure of the centrally planned economies (CPEs) in
the late twentieth century proves that asset ownership cannot be socialized. Such
a proof has not been produced. What we can conclude from the failure of the
CPEs is that the conjunction of three institutions does not work: state ownership
of the capital stock, non-market allocation of resources and commodities, and
political dictatorship. Logically, no more can be deduced without a finer analysis
of the history. Consider, as a thought experiment, a system in which there are
many firms, shares in these firms are owned equally by the citizenry, markets
are competitive, and there is democracy, and therefore political accountability.[3]
For this system to be stable over time, there would have to be a mechanism for
maintaining relatively equal share ownership. It may be possible to design such
a system, and it might be efficient. The key issue involves the relationship between ownership and monitoring of firm management; theory in this area is very
much in flux. I would call such a system market socialist, to be distinguished
from social-democratic, in which there are no particular constraints on asset
ownership.

---

[2]    And this may also hold for some dictatorships. Many have noted that this was a cause of the fall
of East Germany in 1989.
[3]    This is roughly the institutional proposal of Meade (1965).

# 4. THE MARKET'S MAJOR FUNCTIONS

Why might such a system be economically feasible and efficient? To answer this we must ask what the principal beneficial characteristics of the market institution are. Markets serve at least two purposes: they *coordinate* economic activity and they provide *incentives* for people to train themselves and to innovate. I cannot here provide a precise definition that distinguishes between the coordination and incentive functions. A first stab at what I mean would be to say that coordination is involved in allocating resources and goods which exist or we know how to produce, while incentives are involved when resources (such as skills) have not yet been produced, or goods (which do not yet exist) may be invented. This distinction between the coordination and incentive functions of markets focuses upon the present and the known versus the future and the unknown. The distinction is imperfect, but it will provide an indication of at what I am aiming.[4]

Which is the more important attribute of markets—their incentive-engendering function or their coordinating function? We have a natural experiment whose examination could shed light on this question: the Soviet economy. With respect to Soviet history, one hears stories of massive failures of coordination: factory managers had to search for inputs, complex barter arrangements were made between firms, and there were long queues for consumer goods. One also hears stories of incentive failures, encapsulated in the joke, 'They pretend to pay us, we pretend to work'. Some writers question the view that incentive failures were as important as they are currently thought to be by economists; Burawoy (1985) claims that factory workers in the centrally planned economies were ingenious in their ability to produce useful commodities from scrap. The simplest observation, with regard to the non-failure of incentives, is that the level of education of the populace in the USSR did not seem to suffer from the absence of markets, despite there being much less of a premium to educated labor than is typical of market economies. Nor has education suffered, for that matter, in Cuba, which has the highest literacy rate in Latin America. Thus, low rates of return to education did not cause young people, generally speaking, to drop out of school.[5]

Robert Allen's (2003) recently published economic history of the Soviet Union argues that planners did indeed fulfill the plans—he claims there was no (important) incentive failure at the level of the firm. The problem, beginning around 1970, was that planners made mistakes. Assuming the planners were well motivated, a plausible claim, this must be viewed as an error in coordination: lacking prices,

---

[4] Perhaps the most important work that distinguishes between the coordination and incentive functions of the market is Makowski and Ostroy (1995). They, however, conceive of incentives and coordination differently.

[5] The fact that there are non-material returns to education, which motivate people to become educated, is precisely the salient point for what follows.

planners could not guess the right way to develop the Soviet economy. Allen argues that this only became a problem after the completion of post-war reconstruction, and after the migration of essentially unemployed labor from the farms to the factories had ended. As long as a large semi-employed agricultural population existed, the development strategy was simple: move those workers from the farms, where they were unproductive, into the factories, where they would be. By 1970, the transition had been completed: the low hanging fruit of economic development had been picked. At that point, when development became a more subtle project, a fairly small planning bureau made bad guesses that had important negative effects on economic growth. Here, Hayek's (1945) important point, about the decentralization of economic knowledge in the heads of millions of people, comes into its own. In 1970, the Soviet Union could have used a million entrepreneurial ideas, instead of just the few in the heads of the planners.

Indeed, it is interesting to note that Hayek's insightful discussions of market socialism and central planning, written in the 1930s and 1940s, rarely mention the incentive problem. Hayek assumed that firm managers in the Soviet Union were 'loyal and capable'. The problem, he said, is that they do not know the true costs of production, because there are no prices to guide them, and so they cannot economize. This is an issue of coordination. And if one reads the anti-Soviet propaganda of the west in the immediate post-war period, the attack is not based on the bad incentive properties of the system, but rather on its lack of democracy and freedom.

I do not want to present a one-sided picture. Hayek also discusses, importantly, how markets provide entrepreneurial opportunities, which work in part because people want to get rich. But even here, one must distinguish between the coordination property, of how markets aggregate decentralized information, and the incentive property, that people innovate in order to make money. For Joseph Schumpeter, champion of the entrepreneur, entrepreneurs are motivated more by the love of the game than the desire to get rich. It is not clear that *material* incentives are terribly important in Schumpeter's view (see McCraw, 2007). Investors want to get rich, but according to Schumpeter, the entrepreneur is rarely an investor himself.

It was not until 1973 that the term 'principal–agent problem' entered the economic lexicon (see Ross, 1973), and I believe that, until then, the centrally planned economies were viewed in the west as suffering equally from lack of coordination and from poor incentives,[6] to the extent that they were viewed at all as deficient.

---

[6] In 1960, Conservative British Prime Minister Harold Macmillan concluded, 'They [the USSR] are no longer frightened of aggression. They have at least as powerful nuclear forces as the West. They have interior lines [of communication]. They have a buoyant economy and will soon outmatch capitalist society in the race for material wealth' (Judt, 2005: 248). Given this view held by many sophisticated observers in 1960, it is perhaps more reasonable to conjecture that the ensuing downward slide in Soviet economic performance was due more to problems in coordinating an increasingly complex economy without prices, than to a massive failure of incentives.

Within the Soviet Union, the debate around the ideas of Evsey Liberman (see Treml, 1968), concerning the introduction of prices, was entirely about the problem of rational calculation of costs, not about incentives.[7] Leonid Kantorovich received the Nobel Prize for solving the transportation problem—purely a problem of coordination. He did not invent contract theory. The view, at least in the west, changed quite rapidly after 1970, and the deleterious incentive effects of central planning emerged as the key culprit. I think we still need an economic history of the Soviet period that attempts to assess the relative importance of poor coordination and poor incentives in the failure of that model—Allen's surely is a start. Of course, the principal–agent terminology may have emerged because it summarized an important economic problem: but on the other hand, once one invents the hammer, every problem looks like a nail.[8]

I close this section with an example that will illustrate the relationship of the 'incentives versus coordination' question to achieving equality. Imagine an economy in which commodities are produced by profit-maximizing firms that hire workers in a competitive labor market. Workers maximize utility in the usual fashion, with two amendments to the usual specification: there is no leisure–income trade-off (that is, everyone works a standard work year independent of post-tax wages), and each worker has a strong preference for a given occupation, so that changes in relative wages of occupations have only a small or null effect on the occupational composition of labor supply. Then one can impose an arbitrary redistributive income-tax schedule without reducing efficiency. In the limit, if occupational choice is completely inelastic, then under any income-tax regime, the competitive equilibrium allocation of this economy is Pareto efficient.

This is an example where prices have a purely allocative function, and no incentive function. What changes as the tax regime changes is the composition and distribution of output: but prices have no influence on the formation of skills (occupational choice). To the extent that real economic agents have preferences of this sort, redistributive taxation has no efficiency costs. I am suggesting that a study of this question is worthwhile. The evolution of economic theory in the last thirty years, from studying general equilibrium to studying contracts under conditions of asymmetric information, is associated with an increasing emphasis on incentive questions and a decreasing emphasis on the allocative role of prices. Is this new perception of the relative importance of prices in these two functions correct? I have suggested that it may not be: but surely the possibilities for redistribution in market economies depends upon the answer.

---

[7] In 1962, the Soviet economist Liberman published an article in Pravda entitled 'The Plan, Profits, and Bonuses', which began a debate upon introduction of markets in the USSR.

[8] My views have changed somewhat since writing on market socialism (Roemer, 1994). In that book, I blamed the Soviet economic failure on the conjunction of three principal–agent problems.

# 5. MARKET SOCIALISM

If markets are needed primarily for coordination, and not primarily for (material) incentives, then it should be possible to alter the flows of profits without harming output, while continuing to use markets. The first explanation of capitalism's vitality was that it encourages entrepreneurial ideas: the hero, if you will, is the entrepreneur. This is Hayek's view. Eventually, however, entrepreneurial firms were largely replaced by large corporations, run by paid managers. Innovation was largely carried out by salaried researchers either in corporate or academic settings.[9] The problem by the 1970s was seen as the monitoring of management; the capitalist hero now becomes not the entrepreneur but the large stockholder or the corporate raider, who has the incentive to monitor management, who can purchase a controlling share in a weak firm, fire the management, and reorganize the firm. Attention shifts away from the market's role in discovering entrepreneurs, to its role in monitoring management, through the market for corporate control.

Recent scandals have underscored the point that the market does an imperfect job of monitoring management. In many advanced countries, excepting the USA and the UK, firms are monitored not by large private shareholders, but by institutions of various kinds. In these countries, it is not the principal recipients of corporate income who are directly involved in monitoring. There has been, at least in Germany and Japan, a separation of ownership from control. But if this is possible, modulo the efficiency constraint, then it is only a matter of degree to further separate the distribution of a firm's income from the mechanism of managerial oversight. Thus, the possibility is opened for what I have called market socialism—of diffuse distribution of profit flows without sacrificing competent managerial monitoring.

Suppose, then, that shares in the profits of a nation's firms were distributed relatively equally to citizens, and that mechanisms were put in place to prevent vastly unequal shareholdings from evolving. How to accomplish this feat is a large topic; I have written something about it (Roemer, 1994); I am not sure it can be done, but I think it may well be possible. Nevertheless, the income distribution thereby produced would not be the one prized by socialists and egalitarians. Profits, interest, and rents comprise 25–35% of the total income of a typical advanced market economy: the remainder is labor earnings. In the USA, mean household per capita income is approximately $50,000 today. About 65–70% of GNP comprises labor earnings. Thus, every household would receive, in the hypothetical market-socialist reorganization that I have been discussing, at most, let us say, $15,000 as capital income. That would do a great deal towards the elimination of poverty. But

[9] This is a bold and contentious claim. Its evaluation requires understanding the role of venture capital, the importance of new firms in the creation of new commodities, issues which are beyond my scope here.

household incomes would still be vastly unequal because of the inequality of human capital and consequent labor earnings.

Indeed, recent work by Piketty and Saez (2003) has shown that an important change has occurred over the past century in the USA: the top 0.1% of the income distribution is now populated by individuals who earn their income from salaries, not from capital. Most of the richest people in the USA are movie stars, super athletes, and CEOs, not rentiers and capitalists, as they were a century ago. If the incomes of these high fliers are competitively determined—and they may well be—then the standard Marxian indictment of capitalism loses some of its bite.

Even without these very high fliers, it is clear that an egalitarian distribution of share ownership in firms would not bring about the kind of income distribution that many egalitarians desire. Roemer (2008) calculates that were capital to be publicly owned and the entire product distributed in proportion to the value of labor performed by workers, then the Gini coefficient of income would actually be *higher* then the present post-fisc Gini coefficient of income. In other words, American 'social democracy' is more egalitarian than would be a pure 'socialist' system in which the national product were distributed entirely in proportion to the value of labor performed, and there were no welfare state. This result dramatizes the extent to which inequality today, at least in the USA, is due to differential skills, not differential ownership of capital.[10]

I have thus far not discussed the political feasibility of alternative systems to capitalism—whether it is politically feasible to move to the market-socialist pattern of capital endowments. My concern has been simply to argue for its economic feasibility, and to point out that, even if feasible, it would not engender the kind of income distribution that egalitarians desire, because of the large differences in labor earnings that exist, and presumably would continue to exist, if the only reform were an egalitarian redistribution of capital ownership.[11]

# 6. SOCIAL DEMOCRACY

We do know, however, that systems of extensive redistribution of *income flows* are economically feasible: we have the example of Europe, and especially northern

---

[10]  The calculation referred to conventionally assumes that the present distribution of labor earnings, market determined as it is, reflects the distribution of skills—that is, that labor markets are competitive.

[11]  Some may question my not discussing worker control as a market-socialist variant. I believe worker control, even if implementable on a large scale, would not do much to alter income distribution. For the most sophisticated recent discussion, see Dow (2003).

Europe, and especially the five Nordic countries. Despite the predictions of some conservatives that the welfare state is dying, that is not the case. The welfare states of these countries are changing at their fringes, largely because of changing demographics and immigration, but they are not disappearing (see Chapters 25 and 26). Indeed, Lindert (2004) has recently argued that the efficiency cost of redistributive taxation is essentially nil. The secret, according to Lindert, is that the welfare states tax cleverly. There is just no evidence that growth rates have been lower in the large welfare states than in other countries. The *level* of income per capita is lower in many European countries than in the USA, but that is because Europeans choose more leisure time: labor productivity per hour is not lower.

Alternatively, I have suggested in Section 3, that efficient redistribution could be the consequence not only of clever taxation, but of inelasticity in occupational choice.

My conjecture is that citizen homogeneity has been the key of northern Europe's successful redistributive systems. This is not a new idea, although my argument is different from the usual one—that homogeneity engenders citizen solidarity. I conjecture that in the initial historical stage, it is homogeneity of *risks* across citizens that is key. Homogeneity of risks is induced by educational and cultural homogeneity. By risk homogeneity I do not mean risks are correlated, but rather that the probability of a bad state's occurring (such as unemployment or illness) is approximately the same for everyone. Because risk profiles are similar, it is *selfishly* rational for workers to insure each other. To be more precise, with risk homogeneity it is a relatively simple problem to design social insurance: optimal insurance requires that everyone pay the same premium (or tax), even if they have different preferences regarding risk, so long as all are risk averse to some degree. To the contrary, it is not (selfishly) rational for a group with low risk to enter into insurance with a group with high risk, if all pay the same premium. More subtle social insurance is required—hence insurance which is more politically difficult to organize. So, I conjecture that worker homogeneity may have facilitated the first social insurance schemes in northern Europe, following which people developed a *taste* for equality. Insurance against sickness and old-age pensions produced a pleasant society, and people came to value that—there was endogenous preference change. And so citizens extended the welfare state further. I believe that now the welfare states of the Nordic countries go farther than rational self-interested insurance requires: they have reached their present levels because of the taste for equality that the consequences of earlier insurance schemes engendered. For direct evidence on these preferences, see Osberg and Smeeding (2006).

There are several pieces of evidence that this two-step path to social democracy was the actual one—not the path that says homogeneity engenders solidarity *directly*. The first is that the US Social Security Act was passed in 1934. The Great Depression had destroyed the wealth of many Americans—in particular, it had homogenized risk to a great extent. The second is that the European welfare states took off after World War II—and the war, destroying wealth, was also a homogenizing historical episode.[12] A third is that, as Cameron (1978) has argued, the welfare states became large in open economies because of the risks associated with foreign trade. This, too, is a factor which homogenizes risks for the citizens of a country.

There is a second process in the Nordic countries that must be mentioned, the so-called solidaristic wage policy. In the 1950s, unions and employers conspired to equalize wages of workers across firms in an industry, following the views of Rudolf Meidner and Gosta Rehn. This policy was justified not with ethical reasons, but primarily because it provided a way of weeding out uncompetitive firms, an act that was seen as necessary to maintain international competitiveness. Recall that these countries were heavily dependent on the export market. Firms that could not pay the relatively high wages to unskilled labor that were part of the policy disappeared. Eventually, wage solidarity also extended to narrowing within-firm differentials. The consequence is that the Nordic countries have the most equal pre-fisc distributions of income, not just equal post-fisc distributions. See Moene and Wallerstein (2003) and Wallerstein and Moene (2003) for a discussion of the logic of wage solidarity and the large Nordic welfare states.

The Nordic states, then, are a valuable example, although they may not be widely replicable. They are valuable because they disprove the central contention of the political right, that massive redistribution will destroy incentives and hence reduce the rate of economic growth. They may not be replicable, however, if citizen homogeneity is necessary to begin the process of social insurance, which leads, so I have argued, to a taste for equality. And as I have said, an additional factor in Scandinavia, besides citizen homogeneity, was dependence on the export market, which made the solidaristic wage an efficiency-inducing policy.

# 7. Will Democracy Engender Opportunity-Equalizing Educational Policies?

Equality of opportunity is a quite ubiquitous ethic in western democracies, and many believe that the main inequality of opportunity is manifested in the unequal rows of the intergenerational income (or educational) transition matrix. For example, in 1990, young American men whose parents were college educated had a 70% chance of attending college, while young men of parents who were high school drop-outs had a 15% chance. This fact would seem to be inconsistent with a social

---

[12] I am grateful to Tony Atkinson for these observations.

ethic of equal opportunity, especially if that concept is interpreted as it is defined in Chapter 2.

Increasing the level of educational attainment of children from disadvantaged families may require a variety of policies, only one of which is educational finance. Indeed, some question whether educational finance has any significant role to play. In this section, I wish to focus on another question. Given that educational finance *can* be effective in improving the attainments of disadvantaged children, what is the *political* feasibility of eliminating differences in wage-earning capacities among children from different socio-economic circumstances through such policies? Here, I summarize some results of Roemer (2006) on this question.

In the long run, can we expect competitive democratic politics, in which political parties represent different economic classes, to bring about an educational finance policy that eliminates the imprint of family culture on the wage-earning capacity of children?

Consider a model of a society consisting of families, where each family comprises a parent and a child, and the parents are characterized by a distribution of wage-earning capacity. The educational production function is of the following form:

$$w' = a w^b r^c$$

where $w$ is the wage or human capital of the parent, $r$ is the investment in the child by the school system, and $w'$ is the future wage or human capital of the child. This is a deterministic relation. In particular, any differences in talent or capacity among children from parents of a given economic status (wage) are assumed away—not because these do not exist, but because the aim is to study socially, rather than genetically, determined inequalities. Interpret the educational production function as saying that there are two factors that determine the future human capital of the child—the 'culture of the household', for which the parent's wage, or human capital, is the proxy, and the investment by the school system in the child. Because $c$ is positive, educational finance can in principle improve the wage-earning capacities of children from poor (low $w$) families.

The cohort of parents now engages in political competition over redistribution of income and the educational budget. Political parties form and equilibrium policies ensue, where a *policy* stipulates a system of taxation which redistributes income, collects an educational budget, and allocates the budget to schools, in such a way that educational finance can be targeted precisely according to the socio-economic status of the child—that is, according to his parent's wage. In other words, part of an equilibrium policy for each party is a function which specifies the amount of educational investment to be made in a child from a $w$-family. We stylize reality by saying there is one election per generation. The victorious party implements its educational finance policy, thereby determining, through the educational technology, the distribution of wages of the next generation.

Then the next generation engages in the same kind of political competition. Parties form, propose policies, and one party wins the election. It implements its educational finance policy, which determines the distribution of wages of the third generation.

Imagine now that this process continues forever. What happens to the distribution of human capital? More precisely, does the coefficient of variation of this distribution converge to zero? That would be a situation where, at least in the long run, equality of opportunity is achieved, in the sense that the wage of distant descendants becomes independent of the wage of the initial Eve of the dynasty.

It is assumed that parents care only about the consumption of the family and the amount invested by the state in the child's education. Parties represent different constituencies of parents (one the relatively poor, the other the relatively rich). They compete on a large space of possible policies, which specify redistribution and educational financing. Parties may also vary in the extent to which they are *vote seeking* (opportunist) or *representative of* (partisan) their constituencies.

In brief, the results are the following:

(1) If politics are sufficiently opportunist in every period, then the coefficient of variation of the wage distribution approaches in the limit a positive number, never zero;

(2) If politics are sufficiently partisan in every period *and* the initial wage distribution is sufficiently left-skewed, then there is a *positive probability*, less than one, that the limit coefficient of variation of wages is zero;

(3) If politics are partisan in every period and the initial wage distribution is insufficiently left-skewed, then the limit coefficient of variation of wages is surely positive.

The upshot is that democracy never *guarantees* the elimination of familial influences on human capital: at best, it eliminates these influences with a *positive probability*, and that only under certain conditions.

This seems to be a quite pessimistic conclusion. There are, however, important caveats. The model makes two important assumptions: that the returns to educational investment are *purely private*, and that each parent (voter) cares only about her own family. Suppose we relax the first assumption, and replace the educational production function with the following one:

$$w' = aw^b r^{1-b} \bar{r}^d,$$

where $\bar{r}$ is the average investment in all children. Now, there is a positive externality to investment: my child's future wage will increase if more is invested in other children. There are a number of reasons why this technology might be more realistic than the earlier one: a more highly educated workforce increases the speed of technical progress, more highly educated children provide good neighborhood effects on other children, and so on. The upshot is that if the ratio $\frac{d}{1-b}$ is sufficiently large, then even with completely opportunist politics, the coefficient of variation of the distribution of human capital will converge to zero in the long run. If we relax the second assumption, and assume that parents care about other parents' children, then there is a similar effect. It is not surprising that solidarity, in this sense, will improve the tendency towards equality.

The summary of this investigation, then, is that *if* voters care only about their own dynasty, and *if* there are no or small positive externalities in educational investment, then democratic competition will only have a positive probability of eliminating economic classes, in the sense of a pattern of dynasties which are associated with low and high incomes, if the original distribution of wages is highly skewed and politics are sufficiently partisan.

This result shows the egalitarian limits of democracy. The premise that dynasties are self-interested is, however, contentious, because in many countries, solidarity across dynasties is a real and important phenomenon. Solidarity across dynasties, however, is less likely to develop when populations are racially, ethnically, or religiously heterogeneous. When this is the case, then it is incorrect to model political competition as taking place only over economic issues. In the USA, for example, the race issue itself has been an important dimension of politics for at least 150 years, as struggles over slavery, voting rights, school desegregation, civil rights, and affirmative action have shown.

# 8. SUMMARY AND CONCLUSION

Economists often say that their task is to propose institutions that will implement desirable outcomes, given the preferences of individuals. I find this approach somewhat limited: in democracies, citizens choose their institutions, and (we economists say) they choose them by implementing the outcomes the majority desires (assuming knowledge and rationality and a well-functioning political system). Egalitarians must then ask what are the conditions that will induce citizens to choose institutions that will produce relative equality of incomes.[13] I have argued here that traditional market-socialist institutions are insufficient, even if feasible, and that the social-democratic solution may only be achievable in heterogeneous societies which experience a risk-homogenizing episode (such as a depression or a war, or massive export dependency). Section 7 argued that a democracy in which voters are

---

[13]  Levy and Temin (2007) provide a history of the post-war American experience, in which they argue that the rapid increase in inequality in recent years is largely due to the disintegration of equality-inducing institutions, such as unions, and progressive taxation.

interested only in their own dynasties is unlikely to produce equality through its chosen pattern of educational finance.

One must not underestimate the importance of ideas. Egalitarians must undertake an educational campaign to teach people what constitutes justice, and that fraternity is its vital component. As I argued, there is a basis for doing so, in societies where most people support the concept of equal opportunity. The Reagan and Thatcher years ushered in anti-egalitarian ideas that were accompanied with an economic ideology that Levy and Temin (2007) call the 'Washington Consensus', and which replaced the post-war ideology, which they call the 'Treaty of Detroit'. American trade unions, formerly the schools that to some extent taught solidarity, atrophied. Progressive taxation was sharply reduced. Think tanks propounding very conservative economic ideology prospered, with very few propounding solidaristic ideology to counter them.[14]

My proposed emphasis on the importance of *ideas* and *ethos* for improving egalitarian prospects is decidedly different from what is normally emphasized by economists—either exogenous events, or institutions. As I wrote above, institutions must be formed by people, often in their capacity as voters, and hence the importance of ideas and ethos. Narrowly self-interested behavior and greed are not inscribed in our genes. Argument and persuasion have an important role to play in bringing about more solidaristic societies. And in tandem with 'external' events such as globalization and climate change, which may homogenize risk profiles for citizens in the advanced democracies, they can induce preference changes among citizens that could induce the choice of a more egalitarian path.

## REFERENCES

ALLEN, R. 2003. *Farm to Factory: A Reinterpretation of the Soviet Industrial Revolution.* Princeton: Princeton University Press.

BURAWOY, M. 1985. *The Politics of Production: Factory Regimes under Capitalism and Socialism.* London: Verso.

CAMERON, D. 1978. 'The Expansion of the Public Economy: A Comparative Analysis'. *American Political Science Review*, 72: 1243–61.

DOW, G. 2003. *Governing the Firm: Workers' Control in Theory and Practice.* Cambridge: Cambridge University Press.

HAYEK, F. A. 1945. 'The Use of Knowledge in Society'. *American Economic Review*, 35: 519–30

—— 1988. *The Fatal Conceit: The Errors of Socialism.* Chicago: University of Chicago Press.

JUDT, T. 2005. *Postwar: A History of Europe since 1945.* New York: Penguin Press.

LEE, W., and ROEMER, J. 2006. 'Racism and Redistribution in the US: A Solution to the Problem of American Exceptionalism'. *Journal of Public Economics*, 90: 1027–52.

---

[14]  See Rich (2005) for an analysis of the ineffectiveness of liberal think tanks in the USA in the war of ideas.

LEVY, F., and TEMIN, P. 2007. 'Inequality and Institutions in 20th Century America'. MIT Department of Economics Discussion Paper.

LINDERT, P. 2004. *Growing Public: Social Spending and Economic Growth since the Eighteenth Century.* New York: Cambridge University Press.

McCRAW, T. 2007. *Prophet of Innovation: Joseph Schumpeter and Creative Destruction.* Cambridge, Mass.: Harvard University Press.

MAKOWSKI, L., and OSTROY, J. 1995. 'Appropriation and Efficiency: A Revision of the First Theorem of Welfare Economics'. *American Economic Review*, 85: 808–27.

MEADE, J. E. 1965. *Efficiency, Equality, and Ownership of Property.* Cambridge, Mass.: Harvard University Press.

MOENE, K., and WALLERSTEIN, M. 2003. 'Earnings Inequality and Welfare Spending: A Disaggregated Analysis'. *World Politics*, 55: 485–516.

OSBERG, L., and SMEEDING, T. 2006. ' "Fair" Inequality? Attitudes toward Pay Differentials: The United States in Comparative Perspective'. *American Sociological Review*, 71: 450–73.

PIKETTY, T., and SAEZ, E. 2003. 'Income Inequality in the United States, 1913–1998'. *Quarterly Journal of Economics*, 118: 1–39.

RICH, A. 2005. 'War of Ideas: Why Mainstream Liberal Foundations and the Think Tanks they Support are Losing in the War of Ideas in American Politics'. *Stanford Social Innovation Review*, <http://www.ssireview.com/pdf/2005SP_feature_rich.pdf>.

ROEMER, J. 1994. *A Future for Socialism.* Cambrige, Mass.: Harvard University Press.

—— 2006. *Democracy, Education, and Equality.* New York: Cambridge University Press.

—— 2008. 'Socialism vs. Social Democracy as Income-Equalizing Institutions'. *Eastern Economic Journal*, 34: 14–26.

ROSS, S. 1973. 'The Economic Theory of Agency: The Principal's Problems'. *American Economic Review*, 63: 134–9.

TREML, V. 1968. 'The Politics of "Libermanism" '. *Soviet Studies*, 19: 567–72.

WALLERSTEIN, M., and MOENE, K. 2003. 'Does the Logic of Collective Action Explain the Logic of Corporatism?' *Journal of Theoretical Politics*, 15: 271–97.

# Index

Note: page numbers in *italics* refer to Figures and Tables.

# DATE DUE

BRODART, CO.

Cat. No. 23-221-003